Lecture Notes in Computer Science 9218

Commenced Publication in 1973
Founding and Former Series Editors:
Gerhard Goos, Juris Hartmanis, and Jan van Leeuwen

More information about this series at http://www.springer.com/series/7412

Yu-Jin Zhang (Ed.)

Image
and Graphics

8th International Conference, ICIG 2015
Tianjin, China, August 13–16, 2015
Proceedings, Part II

 Springer

Editor
Yu-Jin Zhang
Department of Electronic Engineering
Tsinghua University
Beijing
China

ISSN 0302-9743   ISSN 1611-3349 (electronic)
Lecture Notes in Computer Science
ISBN 978-3-319-21962-2   ISBN 978-3-319-21963-9 (eBook)
DOI 10.1007/978-3-319-21963-9

Library of Congress Control Number: 2015944504

LNCS Sublibrary: SL6 – Image Processing, Computer Vision, Pattern Recognition, and Graphics

Springer Cham Heidelberg New York Dordrecht London

Printed on acid-free paper

Springer International Publishing AG Switzerland is part of Springer Science+Business Media
(www.springer.com)

Preface

These are the proceedings of the 8th International Conference on Image and Graphics (ICIG 2015), held in Tianjin, China, during August 13–16, 2015.

The China Society of Image and Graphics (CSIG) have organized this series of ICIG conferences since 2000. This time, Microsoft Research Asia was the co-organizer, and the Tianjin Society of Image and Graphics was again the host. Some information about the past seven conferences, as well as the current one, can be found in the following table:

Conference	Place	Date	Sub.	Proc.
First (ICIG 2000)	Tianjin, China	August 16–18	220	156
Second (ICIG 2002)	Hefei, China	August 15–18	280	166
Third (ICIG 2004)	Hong Kong, China	December 17–19	460	140
Fourth (ICIG 2007)	Chengdu, China	August 22–24	525	184
Fifth (ICIG 2009)	Xi'an, China	September 20–23	362	179
Sixth (ICIG 2011)	Hefei, China	August 12–15	329	183
Seventh (ICIG 2013)	Qingdao, China	July 26–28	346	181
Eighth (ICIG 2015)	Tianjin, China	August 13–16	345	170

This time, the proceedings are published by Springer in their LNCS series. The titles, abstracts, and biographies of the five invited speakers of plenary talks are presented first. To ease in the search of a required paper in these proceedings, the 164 regular papers have been arranged in alphabetical order according to their titles. Another six papers forming a special topic are included at the end.

Sincere thanks go to all the contributors (around 1,000), who came from around the world to present their advanced works at this event. Special thanks go to the members of Technical Program Committee (more than 100 with half from outside of mainland China) who carefully reviewed every single submission and made their valuable comments for improving the accepted papers.

The proceedings could not have been produced without the invaluable efforts of the publication chairs, the web chairs, and a number of active members of CSIG.

June 2015   Yu-Jin Zhang

Organizing Committee

(Alphabetical Listing)

Honorary Chairs

Thomas Huang	University of Illinois at Urbana-Champaign, USA
Yunhe Pan	Chinese Academy of Engineering, China
Guanhua Xu	Ministry of Science and Technology, China

General Chairs

Chang Wen Chen	State University of New York at Buffalo, USA
Wen Gao	Peking University, China
Yong Rui	Microsoft Research Asia, China

Program Committee Chairs

Ioannis Pitas	Aristotle University of Thessaloniki, Greece
Yu-Jin Zhang	Tsinghua University, China
Ce Zhu	University of Electronic Science and Technology, China

Publicity Chairs

Shuo Li	GE Healthcare, Canada
Hanzi Wang	Xiamen University, China

Publication Chairs

Yanwei Pang	Tianjin University, China
Lei Wang	University of Wollongong, Australia

Organizing Committee Chairs

Gang Cheng	Tianjin Jinhang Computing Technology Research Institute, China
Guohui Ding	Tianjin Jinhang Computing Technology Research Institute, China
Kailong Liu	China Society of Image and Graphics, China
Tao Mei	Microsoft Research Asia, China
Nenghai Yu	University of Science and Technology of China, China

Overseas Liaisons

Guobin Wu   Microsoft Research Asia, China
Lun Yu   Fuzhou University, China
David Zhang   Hong Kong Polytechnic University, Hong Kong, SAR China

Finance Chair

Boxia Xu   Tianjin Jinhang Computing Technology Research Institute,
                   China

Exhibition Liaison

Xiaojuan Yu   China Society of Image and Graphics

Web Chairs

Yang Xu   Tianjin Society of Image and Graphics, China
Mandun Zhang   Hebei University of Technology, China

Local Arrangements Chair

Dianguo Zhang   Tianjin Jinhang Computing Technology Research Institute,
                   China

Technical Program Committee

Ru An   Hohai University, China
Huihui Bai   Beijing Jiaotong University, China
Xiao Bai   Beihang University, China
Josep Blat   Universitat Pompeu Fabra, Spain
Zhanchuan Cai   Macau University of Science and Technology, Macau,
                   SAR China
Huibin Chang   Tianjin Normal University, China
Chao Chen   Rutgers University, USA
Fuhua Chen   West Liberty University, USA
Jiansheng Chen   Tsinghua University, China
Jyh-Cheng Chen   National Yang Ming University, Taiwan, China
Wei Chen   UIUC, ECE, USA
Mingming Cheng   Nankai University, China
Wen-Huang Cheng   Academia Sinica, Taiwan, China
Casey Chow   University of Wollongong, Australia
Shen-Yang Dai   Google Inc., USA
Xiang Deng   GE Healthcare, China
Fuqing Duan   Beijing Normal University, China
Thomas Fevens   Concordia University, Canada

Pascal Frossard	École Polytechnique Fédérale de Lausanne, Switzerland
Shujun Fu	Shandong University, China
Fei Gao	Siemens, USA
Junbin Gao	Charles Sturt University, Australia
Yongying Gao	Beijing Huaxingvision Technologies Co., Ltd., China
Zexun Geng	Information and Engineering University, PLA, China
Guodong Guo	West Virginia University, USA
Zhiqiang Hou	Air Force Engineering University, China
Dong Hu	Nanjing University of Posts and Telecommunications, China
Xuelong Hu	Yangzhou University, China
Fan Jiang	Facebook Inc., USA
Xiangwei Kong	Dalian University of Technology, China
Adam Krzyzak	Concordia University, Canada
Dengfeng Kuang	Nankai University, Tianjin, China
Chaofeng Li	Jiangnan University, China
Peihua Li	Dalian University of Technology, China
Shuai Li	University of Electronic Science and Technology, China
Xuelong Li	Chinese Academy of Science, China
Zhu Li	Samsung Telecomm America, USA
Haixia Liang	Xi'an Jiaotong-Liverpool University, China
Jianming Liang	University of Arizona, USA
Yawei Liang	Royal Military College of Canada, Canada
Shu Liao	Siemens Medical Solutions, USA
Baodi Liu	China University of Petroleum, China
Jun Liu	Beijing Normal University, China
Lingqia Liu	University of Adelaide, Australia
Wenyu Liu	Huazhong University of Science and Technology, China
Xiaofeng Liu	GE Global Research, USA
Xiao Min Liu	Hologic Inc., USA
Huimin Lu	Kyushu Institute of Technology, Japan
Le Lu	NIH, USA
Bin Luo	Anhui University, China
Xiongbiao Luo	University of Western Ontario, Canada
Jianhua Ma	Southern Medical University, China
Tao Mei	Microsoft Research Asia, China
Yanwei Pang	Tianjin University, China
Charley Paulus	Canal+ (French TV channel), France
Mingtao Pei	Beijing Institute of Technology, China
Son Lam Phung	University of Wollongong, Australia
Qiuqi Ruan	Beijing Jiaotong University, China
Bing Shen	Purdue University, USA
Shengli Sheng	University of Central Arkansas, USA
Yuying Shi	North China Electric Power University, China
Weidong Sun	Tsinghua University, China
Xue-Cheng Tai	University of Bergen, Norway
Huachun Tan	Beijing Institute of Technology, China

Plenary Talks

From Shape-from-Shading Through e-Heritage

Katsushi Ikeuchi

The University of Tokyo
http://www.cvl.iis.u-tokyo.ac.jp/~ki/katsu-index-j3.html

Abstract. This talk overviews my research activities from the shape-from-shading through the current e-Heritage project, which digitizes tangible and intangible heritage, analyzes such data for archaeological research and displays in the cloud computer for preservation and promotion.

I began my post-doctoral career at MIT working on shape-from-shading under BKP Horn. Later, I began a project at CMU, with Raj Reddy and Takeo Kanade, to obtain not only shape but also reflectance. This attempt later grew into image-based modeling. After returning to Japan, I applied these modeling and analyzing techniques for the preservation, analysis, and promotion of cultural heritage.

In this talk, I will not only cover current results but also overview the flow of research conducted along this line with emphasis on what were the motivations and how each research step moved into the next level of research; I will also try to extract key lessons learned through these activities.

This is an extended version of my distinguished researcher award talk at Barcelona ICCV with the addition of new archaeological findings obtained from the analysis of the e-Heritage data.

References

1. Ikeuchi, K., Horn, B.K.P: Numerical shape from shading with occluding boundaries. AIJ **17**, 141–184
2. Ikeuchi, K., Miyazaki, D.: Digitally Archiving Cultural Objects. Springer

Biography

Dr. Katsushi Ikeuchi is Professor at the University of Tokyo. He received a PhD degree in Information Engineering from the University of Tokyo in 1978. After working at the Massachusetts Institute of Technology's AI Lab for 2 years, at the Electro-technical Lab, Japan, for 5 years, and Carnegie Mellon University for 10 years, he joined Tokyo University in 1996. His research interest spans computer vision, robotics, and computer graphics. He was general/program chair of more than a dozen international conferences, including IROS 1995, CVPR 1996, ICCV 2003, ICRA 2009, and ICPR

2012. He is an EIC of International Journal of Computer Vision. He has received several awards, including the IEEE Marr Award, the IEEE RAS "most active distinguished lecturer" award, and the IEEE PAMI-TC Distinguished Researcher Award as well as ShijuHoushou (the Medal of Honor with purple ribbon) from the Emperor of Japan. He is a fellow of the IEEE, IEICE, IPSJ, and RSJ.

Tasking on the Natural Statistics of Pictures and Videos

Alan Conrad Bovik

Laboratory for Image and Video Engineering (LIVE)
The University of Texas at Austin

Abstract. I will discuss a variety of topics related to the statistics of pictures and videos of the real world, how they relate to visual perception, and most importantly how they can be used to accomplish perceptually relevant picture-processing and video-processing tasks. Underlying my talk is the thesis that pictures and videos of the real world obey lawful statistical behavior that can be modeled. These models supply useful statistical priors that can be used to define or regularize the solutions to a variety of visual problems. I will address the application of these models to such visual tasks as visual quality assessment, efficient video data delivery in rate-adaptive network environments, face detection in difficult environments, and depth estimation from a single image. I will describe the ongoing work in LIVE in these areas and pose some general problems to be solved in the future.

Biography

Al Bovik is the Curry/Cullen Trust Endowed Chair Professor at The University of Texas at Austin. He has received a number of major awards from the IEEE Signal Processing Society, including: the Society Award (2013); the Technical Achievement Award (2005); the Best Paper Award (2009); the Education Award (2007); the Magazine Best Paper Award (2013); the Distinguished Lecturer Award (2000); the Young Author Best Paper Award (2013); and the Meritorious Service Award (1998). He has also received the SPIE Technology Achievement Award in 2012, the IS&T Honorary Membership in 2014, and was named Imaging Scientist of the Year by IS&T/SPIE in 2011. He is the author/co-author of *The Handbook of Image and Video Processing*, *Modern Image Quality Assessment*, and two recent books, *The Essential Guides to Image and Video Processing*.

Al co-founded and was the longest-serving Editor-in-Chief of the *IEEE Transactions on Image Processing* (1996–2002), and created and served as the first General Chairman of the IEEE International Conference on Image Processing, held in Austin, Texas, in November, 1994.

Region of Interest Coding for Monitoring the Ground with an Unmanned Aerial Vehicle

Jörn Ostermann

Electrical Engineering and Communications Engineering
The University of Hannover and Imperial College London

Abstract. For the transmission of aerial surveillance videos taken from unmanned aerial vehicles, region-of-interest-based coding systems are of growing interest in order to cope with the limited channel capacities available. We present a fully automatic detection and coding system that is capable of transmitting HD-resolution aerial videos at bit rates below 1 Mbit/s. In order to achieve this goal, we extend the video coder HEVC by affine global motion compensation. Results of the computer vision algorithms control the extended HEVC encoder.

For detection of moving objects, we analyze the video and compare a motion-compensated previous image with the current image. Image segmentation based on superpixels helps to select entire moving objects. In order to achieve low false-positive rates and low data rates, we use different motion-compensation algorithms for video analysis and video coding. Depending on the size of the moving objects on the ground, we can save up to 90 % of the data rate of regular HEVC without loss of image quality and the additional benefit of providing a mosaic of the video with moving objects.

Biography

Jörn Ostermann studied Electrical Engineering and Communications Engineering at the University of Hannover and Imperial College London, respectively. He received Dipl.-Ing. and Dr.-Ing. degrees from the University of Hannover in 1988 and 1994, respectively. From 1988 to 1994, he worked as Research Assistant at the Institut für Theoretische Nachrichtentechnik conducting research in low bit-rate and object-based analysis-synthesis video coding. In 1994 and 1995 he worked in the Visual Communications Research Department at AT&T Bell Labs on video coding. He was a member of Image Processing and Technology Research within AT&T Labs–Research from 1996 to 2003. Since 2003 he is Full Professor and Head of the Institut für Informationsverarbeitung at the Leibniz Universität Hannover (LUH), Germany. From 2007 to 2011, he served as head of the Laboratory for Information Technology.

From 1993 to 1994, he chaired the European COST 211 sim group coordinating research in low bit-rate video coding. Within MPEG-4, he organized the evaluation of video tools to start defining the standard. He chaired the Ad Hoc Group on Coding of Arbitrarily Shaped Objects in MPEG-4 Video. Since 2008, he has been the Chair of the Requirements Group of MPEG (ISO/IEC JTC1 SC29 WG11). From 2011 to 2013, he served as Dean of the Faculty of Electrical Engineering and Computer Science at LUH.

Jörn was a scholar of the German National Foundation. In 1998, he received the AT&T Standards Recognition Award and the ISO award. He is a Fellow of the IEEE (class of 2005) and member of the IEEE Technical Committee on Multimedia Signal Processing and past chair of the IEEE CAS Visual Signal Processing and Communications (VSPC) Technical Committee. Jörn served as a Distinguished Lecturer of the IEEE CAS Society (2002/2003). He has published more than 100 research papers and book chapters. He is coauthor of a graduate-level textbook on video communications. He holds more than 30 patents.

His current research interests are video coding and streaming, computer vision, 3D modeling, face animation, and computer–human interfaces.

Big Data in Smart City

Deren Li

State Key Laboratory of Information Engineering in Surveying, Mapping,
and Remote Sensing,
Wuhan University, Wuhan 430079, China

Abstract. In this lecture, I will introduce the concept of smart city and summarize its development process. Then, I will describe the key technologies of smart cities and the proposed smart city infrastructure. Smart city is based on digital city, Internet of Things (IOT), and cloud computing, which will integrate the real world with the digital world. In order to achieve a comprehensive awareness and control of people and things, with intelligent service followed, smart city with mass sensors will continue to collect vast amounts of data, called big data. Typical types of big data such as geospatial image, graph and video data, are analyzed in my talk. The big data of smart city are not only a frontier, but also the driving force to promote the development of smart city, which will bring new opportunities and challenges. I will also propose a strategy for dealing with big data and will define the basic framework for a smart city big data operation center, which will eventually lead to a bright future for smart cities.

Keywords: Smart city; Big data; Digital city; IOT; Cloud computing; Intelligence service; Data mining; smart city big data operation center

Biography

Prof. Dr.-Ing Li Deren is a researcher in photogrammetry and remote sensing, and is a member of both the Chinese Academy of Sciences and the Chinese Academy of Engineering as well as the Euro-Asia International Academy of Science. He is a professor and PhD supervisor at Wuhan University, and is Vice-President of the Chinese Society of Geodesy, Photogrammetry and Cartography, and Chairman of the Academic Commission of Wuhan University and the National Laboratory for Information Engineering in Surveying, Mapping and Remote Sensing (LIESMARS). He has concentrated on research and education in spatial information science and technology represented by remote sensing (RS), global navigation satellite systems (GNSSs), and geographic information systems (GISs). His majors are analytic and digital photogrammetry, remote sensing, mathematical morphology and its application in spatial databases, theories of object-oriented GIS and spatial data mining in GIS, as well as mobile mapping systems, etc.

Professor Deren Li served as Comm. III and Comm. VI President of ISPRS in the periods 1988–1992 and 1992–1996, worked for CEOS during 2002–2004, and was president of the Asia GIS Association during 2003–2006. He received the title Dr.h.c. from ETH in 2008. In 2010 and 2012 he was elected ISPRS fellow and honorary member.

Computing Paradigms: Transformation and Opportunities

Thinking on Data Science and Machine Intelligence

Jinpeng Huai

President, Beihang University, China

Abstract. The arrival of the big data era is changing our traditional understanding and methodologies of computing. This includes, for example, the possibility of accessing enormous and statistically diversified data in their entirety, the shift from exactitude to inexactitude and from the pursuit of accuracy to quick forecasts of macro trends, and the possibility of extracting correlations across domains.

On the verge of this paradigm shift, we advocate three important features desirable in big data computation: inexactness, incrementalness, and inductiveness (3 *I*s). Firstly, finding inexact solutions with bounds shall substitute seeking exact solutions in the traditional regime. Secondly, incremental models and algorithms are desired to accommodate data that are being continuously and rapidly produced and updated.

Finally, correlations hidden among multiple data sources present greater demands for induction and pattern generalization. We will discuss relevant scientific problems exemplifying these three computing features.

Biography

Dr. Huai Jinpeng, born in December 1962, is Fellow of the Chinese Academy of Sciences and President of Beihang University (BUAA) in Beijing, China. He received his PhD in Computer Science from Beihang University.

Dr. Huai's research focus has been on computer science and software. His work has effectively broken through the limitations and difficulties of network resource sharing and utilization. He has established algebraic theories and algorithms for cryptographic protocol analyses, which greatly improved the security of critical information systems. He has also proposed a "zero-programming" model for process-oriented software developments, which significantly enhanced the automatic development of large-scale distributed applications. These works have benefited China's economic and social development.

Dr. Huai has won many prominent awards, including second prize in the National Award of Scientific and Technological Advancement (twice), second prize in the National Award of Technological Invention, the Scientific and Technological Advancement Award from the Ho Leung Ho Lee Fund, the 4th IET-Founder

University President Award, and the insignia of Knight of French National Order of the Legion of Honor. He has published more than 120 papers, owns more than 30 Chinese patents, has been invited to 14 international conferences as a keynote speaker, and has chaired conferences of considerable importance, such as WWW 2008 and SRDS 2007.

Dr. Huai has been Chief Scientist on the Steering Committees on the IT domain and advanced computing technology subject, both of the National High-Tech R&D Program (863 Program), since 2001. He is also Chair of the Steering Committee on Foundational Software for National Science and Technology Major Project and Deputy Chair of the China Computer Federation. He has made significant contributions to national strategic R&D planning and the industrialization of information technology, especially computing in China.

Contents – Part II

Blind Motion Deblurring Based on Fused ℓ_0-ℓ_1 Regularization   1
Kai Wang, Yu Shen, Liang Xiao, Zhihui Wei, and Linxue Sheng

Blood Vessel Segmentation of Retinal Images Based on Neural Network. . . .   11
Jingdan Zhang, Yingjie Cui, Wuhan Jiang, and Le Wang

Compressed Binary Discriminative Feature for Fast UAV Image
Registration   18
Li-Chuan Geng, Ze-xun Geng, and Guo-xi Wu

Context-Aware Based Mobile Augmented Reality Browser
and its Optimization Design   34
Yi Lin, Yue Liu, and Yong-tian Wang

Contour-Based Plant Leaf Image Segmentation Using Visual Saliency.   48
Zhou Qiangqiang, Wang Zhicheng, Zhao Weidong, and Chen Yufei

Cooperative Target Tracking in Dual-Camera System with Bidirectional
Information Fusion   60
Jingjing Wang and Nenghai Yu

Cute Balloons with Thickness.   75
Qingyun Wang, Xuehui Liu, Xin Lu, Jianwen Cao, and Wen Tang

Decision-Tree Based Hybrid Filter-Wrapping Method for the Fusion
of Multiple Feature Sets.   90
Cuicui Zhang, Xuefeng Liang, and Naixue Xiong

Depth Map Coding Method for Scalable Video Plus Depth   103
Panpan Li, Ran Ma, Yu Hou, and Ping An

Depth Map Upsampling Using Segmentation and Edge Information   116
Shuai Zheng, Ping An, Yifan Zuo, Xuemei Zou, and Jianxin Wang

Design of a Simulated Michelson Interferometer for Education Based on
Virtual Reality   127
Hongling Sun, Xiaodong Wei, and Yue Liu

Detecting Deterministic Targets by Combination of Polarimetric Fork
and Cloude-Pottier Decomposition for Polarimetric Synthetic
Aperture Radar Imagery.   138
Sheng Sun, Zhijia Xu, and Taizhe Tan

Detection of Secondary Structures from 3D Protein Images of Medium
Resolutions and its Challenges   147
   Jing He, Dong Si, and Maryam Arab

Determination of Focal Length for Targets Positioning with Binocular
Stereo Vision   156
   Wang Jian, Wang Yu-sheng, Liu Feng, Li Qing-jia, and Wang
   Guang-chao

Dimensionality Reduction for Hyperspectral Image Based on Manifold
Learning   164
   Yiting Wang, Shiqi Huang, Hongxia Wang, Daizhi Liu, and Zhigang Liu

Discriminative Feature Learning with Constraints of Category
and Temporal for Action Recognition   173
   Zhize Wu, Shouhong Wan, Peiquan Jin, and Lihua Yue

Discriminative Neighborhood Preserving Dictionary Learning
for Image Classification   185
   Shiye Zhang, Zhen Dong, Yuwei Wu, and Mingtao Pei

Distribution of FRFT Coefficients of Natural Images   197
   Li Jiang, Guichi Liu, and Lin Qi

Dual-Projection Based High-Precision Integral Imaging Pickup System   208
   Zhao-Long Xiong, Qiong-Hua Wang, Huan Deng, and Yan Xing

Eave Tile Reconstruction and Duplication by Image-Based Modeling   219
   Li Ji Jun Nan, Geng Guo Hua, and Jia Chao

Edge Directed Single Image Super Resolution Through the Learning
Based Gradient Regression Estimation   226
   Dandan Si, Yuanyuan Hu, Zongliang Gan, Ziguan Cui, and Feng Liu

Evacuation Simulation Incorporating Safety Signs and Information Sharing   240
   Yu Niu, Hongyu Yang, Jianbo Fu, Xiaodong Che, Bin Shui,
   and Yanci Zhang

Facial Stereo Processing by Pyramidal Block Matching   252
   Jing Wang, Qiwen Zha, Yubo Yang, Yang Liu, Bo Yang, Dengbiao Tu,
   and Guangda Su

Fast Algorithm for Finding Maximum Distance with Space Subdivision
in E^2   261
   Vaclav Skala and Zuzana Majdisova

Fast Unconstrained Vehicle Type Recognition with Dual-Layer
Classification 275
    Xiao-Jun Hu, Bin Hu, Chun-Chao Guo, and Jian-Huang Lai

Feature Matching Method for Aircraft Positioning on Airdrome 284
    Jian Wang and Yubo Ni

Flow Feature Extraction Based on Entropy and Clifford Algebra. 292
    Xiaofan Liu, Wenyao Zhang, and Ning Zheng

Frame Rate Up-Conversion Using Motion Vector Angular
for Occlusion Detection 301
    Yue Zhao, Ju Liu, Guoxia Sun, Jing Ge, and Wenbo Wan

Fusion of Skeletal and STIP-Based Features for Action Recognition
with RGB-D Devices. 312
    Ting Liu and Mingtao Pei

GA Based Optimal Design for Megawatt-Class Wind Turbine Gear Train . . . 323
    Jianxin Zhang and Zhange Zhang

Generalized Contributing Vertices-Based Method for Minkowski Sum
Outer-Face of Two Polygons 333
    Peng Zhang and Hong Zheng

Handwritten Character Recognition Based on Weighted Integral Image
and Probability Model 347
    Jia Wu, Feipeng Da, Chenxing Wang, and Shaoyan Gai

Hard Exudates Detection Method Based on Background-Estimation 361
    Zhitao Xiao, Feng Li, Lei Geng, Fang Zhang, Jun Wu, Xinpeng Zhang,
    Long Su, Chunyan Shan, Zhenjie Yang, Yuling Sun, Yu Xiao,
    and Weiqiang Du

Hierarchical Convolutional Neural Network for Face Detection. 373
    Dong Wang, Jing Yang, Jiankang Deng, and Qingshan Liu

Human-Object Interaction Recognition by Modeling Context 385
    Qun Zhang, Wei Liang, Xiabing Liu, and Yumeng Wang

Image Annotation Based on Multi-view Learning 396
    Zhe Shi, Songhao Zhu, and Chengjian Sun

Image Denoising with Higher Order Total Variation and Fast Algorithms . . . 407
    Wenchao Zeng, Xueying Zeng, and Zhen Yue

Improve Neural Network Using Saliency 417
    Yunong Wang, Nenghai Yu, Taifeng Wang, and Qing Wang

Improved Spread Transform Dither Modulation Using Luminance-Based
JND Model   430
   Wenhua Tang, Wenbo Wan, Ju Liu, and Jiande Sun

Incorporation of 3D Model and Panoramic View for Gastroscopic
Lesion Surveillance   438
   *Yun Zong, Weiling Hu, Jiquan Liu, Xu Zhang, Bin Wang, Huilong Duan,
and Jianmin Si*

Interactive Browsing System of 3D Lunar Model with Texture
and Labels on Mobile Device   446
   Yankui Sun, Kan Zhang, and Ye Feng

Interactive Head 3D Reconstruction Based Combine of Key Points
and Voxel   453
   Yanwei Pang, Kun Li, Jing Pan, Yuqing He, and Changshu Liu

Lighting Alignment for Image Sequences   462
   Xiaoyue Jiang, Xiaoyi Feng, Jun Wu, and Jinye Peng

Modelling and Tracking of Deformable Structures in Medical Images   475
   Saïd Ettaïeb, Kamel Hamrouni, and Su Ruan

Moving Object Extraction in Infrared Video Sequences   491
   Jinli Zhang, Min Li, and Yujie He

Moving Object Segmentation by Length-Unconstrained Trajectory
Analysis   500
   Qiyu Liao, BingBing Zhuang, Jingjing Wang, and Nenghai Yu

Multidimensional Adaptive Sampling and Reconstruction for Realistic
Image Based on BP Neural Network   510
   Yu Liu, Changwen Zheng, and Fukun Wu

Modeling and Simulation of Multi-frictional Interaction Between
Guidewire and Vasculature   524
   *Dongjin Huang, Yin Wang, Pengbin Tang, Zhifeng Xie, Wen Tang,
and Youdong Ding*

Multi-modal Brain Image Registration Based on Subset Definition
and Manifold-to-Manifold Distance   538
   Weiwei Liu, Yuru Pei, and Hongbin Zha

Multimodal Speaker Diarization Utilizing Face Clustering Information   547
   *Ioannis Kapsouras, Anastasios Tefas, Nikos Nikolaidis,
and Ioannis Pitas*

Multi-object Template Matching Using Radial Ring Code Histograms   555
  Shijiao Zheng, Buyang Zhang, and Hua Yang

Novel DCT Features for Detecting Spatial Embedding Algorithms   565
  Hao Zhang, Tao Zhang, Xiaodan Hou, and Xijian Ping

Novel Software-Based Method to Widen Dynamic Range
of CCD Sensor Images   572
  Wei Wen and Siamak Khatibi

Object Contour Extraction Based on Merging Photometric Information with
Graph Cuts.   584
  Rongguo Zhang, Meimei Ren, Jing Hu, Xiaojun Liu, and Kun Liu

Object-Based Multi-mode SAR Image Matching.   600
  Jie Rui, Chao Wang, Hong Zhang, Bo Zhang, Fan Wang, and Fei Jin

OCR with Adaptive Dictionary.   611
  Chenyang Wang, Yanhong Xie, Kai Wang, and Tao Li

One Simple Virtual Avatar System Based on Single Image   621
  Lanfang Dong, Jianfu Wang, Kui Ni, Yatao Wang, Xian Wu,
  and Mingxue Xu

Optimized Laplacian Sparse Coding for Image Classification   636
  Lei Chen, Sheng Gao, Baofeng Yuan, Zhe Qi, Yafang Liu, and Fei Wang

Author Index   647

Blind Motion Deblurring Based on Fused ℓ_0-ℓ_1 Regularization

Kai Wang[1(✉)], Yu Shen[1], Liang Xiao[1,2], Zhihui Wei[1], and Linxue Sheng[3]

[1] School of Computer Science and Engineering, Nanjing University of Science
and Technology, Xiaolingwei 200, Nanjing 210094, Jiangsu, China
mfranciswong@163.com, shenyu0305@126.com, gswei@mail.njust.edu.cn
[2] Key Lab of Intelligent Perception and Systems for High-Dimensional Information
of Ministry of Education, Xiaolingwei 200, Jiangsu 210094, Nanjing, China
xiaoliang@mail.njust.edu.cn
[3] School of Science, Nanjing University of Science and Technology,
Xiaolingwei 200, Jiangsu 210094, Nanjing, China
njustslx@outlook.com

Abstract. In blind motion deblurring, various regularization models
using different priors of either the image or the blur kernel are proposed
to estimate the blur kernel, with tendency towards naive ℓ_0 norm or its
approximations. In this paper, we propose a novel fused ℓ_0-ℓ_1 regularization approach to estimate the motion blur kernel by imposing sparsity
and continuation properties on natural images. A fast numerical scheme
is then deduced by coupling operator splitting and the Augmented
Lagrangian method to solve the proposed model efficiently. Experimental results on both synthetic and real data demonstrate the effectiveness
of the proposed method and the superiority over the state-of-the-art
methods.

Keywords: Blind motion deblurring · Blur kernel estimation · Split
agumented lagrangian

1 Introduction

Blind motion deblurring, also known as blind deconvolution, has been extensively studied since the pioneering work of [1]. Although it achieves significant
success with a few encouraging solutions, the results are still far from perfect.
In the current literature, most blind deconvolution approaches share a common
Bayesian framework, which fall into two camps, Max a Posterior (MAP) [2–8]
and Variational Bayesian (VB) [1, 9–12]. An invigorating work [9] primarily analyzes the failure of natural image statistics that would lead to no-blur solutions.
Recently, an insightful theoretical analysis [12] further demonstrates that the VB
methodology can be recast as an unconventional MAP problem with a particular
prior. Although VB methods have theoretical and empirical superiority to conventional MAP algorithms, the posterior inference of VB methods remains less
tractable [9, 11, 12]. Both of these methods mentioned above will be discussed as
follows, particularly in aspect of prior choice.

© Springer International Publishing Switzerland 2015
Y.-J. Zhang (Ed.): ICIG 2015, Part II, LNCS 9218, pp. 1–10, 2015.
DOI: 10.1007/978-3-319-21963-9_1

1.1   Related Works

Prior blind deconvolution approaches are basically with regard to exploiting techniques to utilize salient edges, either explicitly or implicitly. For instance, Cho et al. [2], and Xu et al. [3] have utilized bilateral filtering or Gaussian filtering together with shock filtering to predict sharp edges, which involve explicit filtering and edge selection. Shan et al. [4] have adopted a sparse image prior and used a weighting scheme to remove harmful subtle image structures. Krishnan et al. [5] have imposed a scale-invariant sparsity measure to better discriminate sharp images from blurry ones. It is obviously to see that the new sparsity prior is a good approximation of ℓ_0 norm, the natural interpretation of sparsity. Another alternative approximation is the unnatural ℓ_0 regularizer which is proposed by Xu et al. [6]. Coinstantaneously, Pan et al. [7] have directly imposed ℓ_0 norm on image gradients. On the VB camp, Babacan et al. [11] have developed a general sparsity-inspired prior on the image which has been practically demonstrated more powerful than others [1,9]. It is highly consistent with the theoretical presentation in Wipf et al.'s work [12]. More recently, Krishnan et al. [8] shows that all these successful approaches rely on a key principle, that is, sparsity promotion in the image gradient domain.

Summarizing above discussions, the top-performing methods have placed a great deal of effort on the choice of proper priors both on the image and the blur kernel. Essentially, the most effective unnatural image priors may not reflect the true statistics of natural images in blind deconvolution. There is a common feature that all these sparsity-inducing priors can be regarded as some approximations of the ℓ_0 norm via different techniques or naive ℓ_0 norm prior.

1.2   Our Contributions

In this paper, we propose a novel sparsity-inducing model fused with ℓ_0 norm and a difference penalty term, which is found to be akin to the fused LASSO [13]. It is worth noting that we use ℓ_0 norm and not ℓ_1 norm based on the theory [9] that an ℓ_1 norm based image prior naturally leads to a trivial no-blur solution. By introducing this prior, namely the fused ℓ_0-ℓ_1 prior, the proposed method is fairly different from previous works in the following aspects:

(1) The fused ℓ_0-ℓ_1 regularization, as a new sparsity-inducing model on the sharp image, is specifically proposed for the kernel estimation. Benefit from enforcing continuation in the new model, it helps to produce higher quality sharp image which has continuous salient edges. Since salient edges serves as an important clue for blur kernel estimation, the model further generate accurate blur kernel with nearly true support of a desired blur kernel.

(2) The new model for motion blur kernel estimation is then practically formulated as a compound regularized problem with respect to alternatively estimating sharp image and blur kernel, and can be transformed into two subproblems using variable splitting technique. Furthermore, by coupling operator splitting and the Augmented Lagrangian method as well as exploiting fast Fourier transform (FFT), we deduce a fast numerical algorithm to efficiently solve the bilinear optimization problem.

By comparing our results with some of the leading motion deblurring methods, both in synthetic experiments and real-world motion blurred images, we demonstrate that our approach outperforms most of the current methods.

2 Fused ℓ_0-ℓ_1-Regularized Kernel Estimation

2.1 The Proposed Method

Generally, the formation process of motion blur can be modeled as

$$B = I \otimes k + n, \tag{1}$$

where B, I, k and n represent the blurred image, latent image, blur kernel and the additive Gaussian noise, respectively. $\otimes$ denotes the convolution operator. Currently, most of the previous methods [1,5,7–9] have demonstrated that the sharp edges are the vital clue of the kernel estimation. Therefore, instead of recovering latent images, we estimate the blur kernel in the derivative space. Specifically, the kernel estimation model is written as

$$\min_{x,k} \|x \otimes k - y\|_2^2 + \lambda\Phi(x) + \eta\Psi(k), \tag{2}$$

where x denotes $\nabla I = [\nabla_h I, \nabla_v I]$, y denotes $\nabla B = [\nabla_h B, \nabla_v B]$, and λ, η are regularization weights.

Model (2) consists of three terms. The first term is the data fitting term, the second term $\Phi(x)$ is the regularization term on x, and the third term $\Psi(k)$ is the regularization term on blur kernel k.

Since the unnatural ℓ_0 norm or its approximating priors, no matter explicitly or implicitly [5–8,12], have shown their effectiveness. It roughly reveals that the desired sharp image compromising of salient edges performs better than original image in motion blur kernel estimation. A good candidate of sharp image should have two essential factors: (1) preserving as many continuous salient edges as possible; (2) reducing the staircase and ringing artifacts along the salient edges, while eliminating ringing artifacts inside the homogeneous regions as much as possible. In order to impose the continuation on latent image, as well as enforce unnatural sparsity, we propose a new prior to produce a better intermediate image results as far as possible to fulfill aforementioned factors.

Similar to Eq. (2), a cost function with the new sparsity-inducing prior is given as follows

$$\min_{x,k} \|x \otimes k - y\|_2^2 + \lambda_1\|x\|_0 + \lambda_2\|Dx\|_1 + \eta\|k\|_2^2, \tag{3}$$

where λ_1, λ_2 and η are regularization weights. The new image prior combines ℓ_0 norm and a continuation constraint to suppress isolated points along the generated salient edges, and to prevent the unpleasant staircase and ringing artifacts at the same time. The so called fused ℓ_0-ℓ_1 regularization term inherit the effectiveness of recovering salient edges from ℓ_0 norm and the ability of preserving continuation from the difference penalty term.

2.2   Numerical Algorithm

By now, we come to the issue of alternatively estimating motion blur kernel and sharp edges. Therefore, the proposed method addresses the motion kernel estimation by solving the following two splitting optimization problems with respect to x and k.

Sharp Edges Restoration. In the first step, i.e., the sharp edges restoration, the problem can be formulated as

$$\min_{x} \|x \otimes k - y\|_2^2 + \lambda_1 \|x\|_0 + \lambda_2 \|Dx\|_1. \tag{4}$$

Here, we formulate the difference penalty term by introducing the difference operator $D = (D_1, D_2)$ for computation simplicity, where $D_1 = [1, -1]$, $D_2 = [1, -1]^T$. It is difficult to directly solve the discrete optimization problem (4) because of its non-convexity. It should be noted that a similar numerical scheme is considered in [14, 15] by coupling variable splitting and augmented Lagrangian. Borrowing the idea of the so called Split Augmented Lagrangian (SAL) method, we first convert model (4) to the following equivalent constrained problem,

$$\min_{u,v,x} \quad \|x \otimes k - y\|_2^2 + \lambda_1 \|u\|_0 + \lambda_2 \|v\|_1,$$

$$s.t. \quad u = x, v = Dx. \tag{5}$$

Then, we have the following associated Lagrangian function,

$$L(u, v, x, J_1, J_2) = \|x \otimes k - y\|_2^2 + \lambda_1 \|u\|_0 + \lambda_2 \|v\|_1 + < J_1, x - u >$$
$$+ < J_2, Dx - v > + \tfrac{\xi_1}{2} \|x - u\|_2^2 + \tfrac{\xi_2}{2} \|Dx - v\|_2^2, \tag{6}$$

where J_1, J_2 are the vectors of Lagrange multipliers, and ξ_1, ξ_2 are positive constants. Hence, the corresponding iterative scheme of the SAL method is given as follows,

$$\begin{cases} u^{t+1} = \arg\min_{u} L(u, v^t, x^t, J_1^t, J_2^t), \\ v^{t+1} = \arg\min_{v} L(u^{t+1}, v, x^t, J_1^t, J_2^t), \\ x^{t+1} = \arg\min_{x} L(u^{t+1}, v^{t+1}, x, J_1^t, J_2^t), \\ J_1^{t+1} = J_1^t + \xi_1(x^{t+1} - u^{t+1}), \\ J_2^{t+1} = J_2^t + \xi_2(Dx^{t+1} - v^{t+1}), \end{cases} \tag{7}$$

where $0 \leq t \leq T - 1$ denotes the t-th iteration and T represents the maximum iterations.

For the two sub-problems of updating auxiliary variables u and v, the solutions u^{t+1} and v^{t+1} can be easily computed through some straightforward manipulations and given as

$$u^{t+1} = \arg\min_{u} \tfrac{\xi_1}{2} \|x^t + \tfrac{1}{\xi_1} J_1^t - u\|_2^2 + \lambda_1 \|u\|_0$$

$$= \Theta_{\text{Hard}}(x^t + \tfrac{1}{\xi_1} J_1^t, (\tfrac{2\lambda_1}{\xi_1})^{\frac{1}{2}}), \tag{8}$$

$$v^{t+1} = \arg\min_{v} \tfrac{\xi_2}{2}\|Dx^t + \tfrac{1}{\xi_2}J_2^t - v\|_2^2 + \lambda_2\|v\|_1$$
$$= \Theta_{\text{Soft}}(Dx^t + \tfrac{1}{\xi_2}J_2^t, \tfrac{\lambda_2}{\xi_2}), \tag{9}$$

where $\Theta_{\text{Hard}}(\cdot)$ and $\Theta_{\text{Soft}}(\cdot)$ are the hard-thresholding operator and soft-thresholding operator respectively.

Since the x sub-problem is a least square problem, the closed form solution can be given by

$$x^{t+1} = \arg\min_{x} \|x \otimes k - y\|_2^2 + \tfrac{\xi_1}{2}\|x + \tfrac{1}{\xi_1}J_1^t - u^{t+1}\|_2^2 + \tfrac{\xi_2}{2}\|Dx + \tfrac{1}{\xi_2}J_2^t - v^{t+1}\|_2^2$$
$$= \left(K^T K + \tfrac{\xi_1}{2} + \tfrac{\xi_2}{2}D^T D\right)^{-1} \cdot$$
$$\left(K^T y + \tfrac{\xi_1}{2}u^{t+1} - \tfrac{1}{2}J_1^t + \tfrac{\xi_2}{2}D^T(v^{t+1} - \tfrac{1}{\xi_2}J_2^t)\right). \tag{10}$$

In fact, a circular convolution is assumed for the observation model (1), and hence (10) can be computed efficiently using the FFT instead of the gradient descent based methods.

To summarize, the numerical algorithm of the sharp edges restoration is presented in Algorithm 1. Note that the Augmented Lagrangian method has been proved to be equivalent to the Split Bregman method [16], thus the convergence property can be guaranteed in theory.

Algorithm 1. SAL method for Sharp Edge Restoration

Input: blurred image B; blur kernel k; Lagrangian multipliers $J_1^0 = J_2^0 = 0$; regularization parameters λ_1, λ_2; Augmented Lagrangian penalty parameters ξ_1, ξ_2; index of iterations $t = 0$.
  while $\xi_1 \leq 2^8$ **and** $\xi_2 \leq 2^8$ **do**
    Step 1: Update u^{t+1} by computing (8);
    Step 2: Update v^{t+1} by computing (9);
    Step 3: Update x^{t+1} by computing (10) based on FFT;
    Step 4: Update $J_1^{t+1} = J_1^t + \xi_1(x^{t+1} - u^{t+1})$ and $J_2^{t+1} = J_2^t + \xi_2(Dx^{t+1} - v^{t+1})$;
    $t \leftarrow t + 1$;
  end while
Output: sharp edges x^t.

Motion Kernel Estimation. In the kernel estimation step, the latent blur kernel is obtained by minimizing the following optimization functional

$$\min_{k} \|x \otimes k - y\|_2^2 + \eta\|k\|_2^2. \tag{11}$$

Evidently, it is a least square problem whose solution can be also computed by using the FFT, i.e.,

$$k = \mathcal{F}^{-1}\left(\frac{\overline{\mathcal{F}(x)}\mathcal{F}(y)}{\overline{\mathcal{F}(x)}\mathcal{F}(x) + \eta}\right), \tag{12}$$

where $\mathcal{F}(\cdot)$ and $\mathcal{F}^{-1}(\cdot)$ denote the FFT and inverse FFT, respectively, and $\overline{\mathcal{F}(\cdot)}$ is the complex conjugate operator.

Finally, we summarize the proposed method in Algorithm 2.

Algorithm 2. Algorithm for fused ℓ_0-ℓ_1 regularized kernel estimation

---

Input: blurred image B; kernel size S; regularization parameters λ_1, λ_2, η; parameter
  decreasing factor ρ_1, ρ_2; maximum iteration number L.
  for $l = 1 \to L$ **do**
    Step 1: Update sharp edges x_l by Algorithm 1;
    Step 2: Update blur kernel k_l by computing (12);
    Step 3: Compute $\lambda_1 \leftarrow \rho_1 \lambda_1$, $\lambda_2 \leftarrow \rho_2 \lambda_2$;
  end for
Output: Ultimate blur kernel k.

In order to further reduce the risk of trapping into local extrema, a widely used technique is the multi-scale (S scales) mechanism which is similar to all top-performing [1–8] methods. This efficient mechanism progressively estimates the motion blur kernel from coarse to fine. At the coarsest scale $s = 1$, we use the down-sampled version of the blurred image as an initialization of latent image, and delta function as the initialization of the blur kernel. At each scale s, the input of the motion kernel estimation can be up-sampled by bilinear interpolation from the final restored sharp edges obtained at the coarser scale $s - 1$. After all, once the kernel k has been estimated, a non-blind deconvolution approach [17] is exploited to restore the final sharp image I.

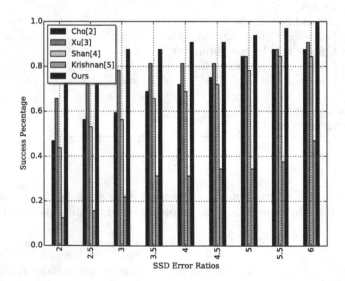

Fig. 1. Cumulative histograms of the SSD error ratio across test examples from benchmark [9].

Fig. 2. Blind motion deblurring with the real-world example (image size: 640 × 480, kernel size: 21 × 21). From left to right, top to bottom: blurred image, deblurred images with estimated blur kernel by Cho *et al.* [2], Xu and Jia [3], Krishnan *et al.* [5], Xu *et al.* [6] and the proposed approach.

3 Experimental Results

In this section, we present some experimental results of our approach which requires a few parameters given below. As the kernel size is an important requirement for most algorithms, it also should be specified by users in our approach and does not have much influence on kernel estimation if its support area can accommodate the blur kernel. As for the initial parameters, the maximum iteration number is set to 10, and the regularization parameters $\lambda_1, \lambda_2, \eta, \xi_1, \xi_2$ are uniformly provided as $\lambda_1 = 0.03, \lambda_2 = 0.01, \eta = 0.001, \xi_1 = 0.03, \xi_2 = 0.01$ across most of the experiments. In order to achieve faster convergence, the decreasing factor ρ_1, ρ_2 are fixed as $\rho_1 = 0.55, \rho_2 = 0.8$ to progressively reduce the image regularization weights, leading to accommodating more edges into x.

3.1 Synthetic Data

In this subsection, we first test the proposed method on the benchmark image dataset of [9], which consists of 32 examples generated with 4 natural images and 8 different motion blur kernels. To quantitatively measure the quality of restored images, we use the Sum of Square Difference (SSD) ratio defined in [9] which quantifies the error between the estimated and the original images. The formula is given as

$$\text{SSD ratio} = \frac{\|x_{est} - x_{sharp}\|_2^2}{\|x_{gt} - x_{sharp}\|_2^2}, \tag{13}$$

where x_{est} and x_{gt} are respectively the restored image of estimated and ground-truth blur kernel adopting the same settings.

Fig. 3. Blind motion deblurring with the real-world example (image size: 800 × 800, kernel size: 51 × 51). From left to right, top to bottom: blurred image, deblurred images with estimated blur kernel by Cho *et al.* [2], Xu and Jia [3], Krishnan *et al.* [5], Xu *et al.* [6] and the proposed approach.

For fair comparison, we use the non-blind deconvolution approach [17] to perform all the methods [2–5] to be compared. The cumulative histograms of the SSD error ratio are shown for different methods in Fig. 1. The r-th bin in the figure counts the percentage of the motion blurred images in the dataset achieving error ratio below r. For instance, the bar in Fig. 1 corresponding to bin 5 indicates the percentage of test images with SSD error ratios below 4. For each bin, the higher the bar the better the deblurring performance. As pointed out by Levin *et al.* [9], deblurred images are visually plausible in general as their SSD error ratios are below 3, and in this case the blind motion deblurring is considered to be successful. As can be seen from Fig. 1, the performance of the proposed method is better than the other methods quantitatively.

3.2   Real Data

To further demonstrate the effectiveness, we apply the proposed method to the real-world motion blur images and compare it with four state-of-the-art MAP methods [2,3,5,6]. As reviewed in the introduction section, two of them [2,3] are based on explicit filtering and edge selection, the rest two methods [5,6] involve implicit regularization. The point to be noted is that our approach estimate the blur kernel using the gray version of the color image.

As shown in Figs. 2 and 3, two real-world examples with different image sizes and blurring levels are utilized to compare the performance of these methods. It is observed that our approach achieves visually more accurate motion blur kernels with stronger continuity and less singular points, as well as produces visually plausible restored images. Specifically, in Fig. 2, our approach generates reasonable blur kernels and visually clear deblurred image but the other four methods fail in kernel estimation in some sense and the restored images are accounted to be unnatural. In Fig. 3, our approach also perform well on the moderate blurring level. The corresponding estimated blur kernels of [3,6] seem still less accurate. By comparison, our approach can successfully recover the true support of the blur kernel in the case of medium size blur kernel. And the visual quality is also comparable with the top-ranking method [6] which has even incorporated with some post-processing procedures.

4   Conclusion

We have presented an effective and efficient method for blind motion deblurring, providing a novel fused ℓ_0-ℓ_1 prior on sharp images. A fast numerical scheme based on split Augmented Lagrangian has also been developed to solve the deduced compound regularized problem. Extensive experiments both on a synthetic benchmark image dataset and two real-world motion blurred images have intensively validated the performance of the proposed method and testified the superiority over the state-of-the-art methods.

Acknowledgements. This work was supported in part by the Fundamental Research Funds for the Central Universities under Grant No. 30915012204, the Natural Science Foundation of China under Grant No. 61171165 and 11431015 and also sponsored by The Six Top Talents of Jiangsu Province under Grant No. 2012DZXX-036.

References

1. Fergus, R., Singh, B., Hertzmann, A., Roweis, S.T., Freeman, W.T.: Removing camera shake from a single photograph. ACM Trans. Graph. **25**(3), 787–794 (2006)
2. Cho, S., Lee, S.: Fast motion deblurring. ACM Trans. Graph. **145**(8), 145:1–145:8 (2009)
3. Xu, L., Jia, J.: Two-phase kernel estimation for robust motion deblurring. In: Daniilidis, K., Maragos, P., Paragios, N. (eds.) ECCV 2010, Part I. LNCS, vol. 6311, pp. 157–170. Springer, Heidelberg (2010)
4. Shan, Q., Jia, J., Agarwala, A.: High-quality motion deblurring from a single image. ACM Trans. Graph. **27**(3), 73:1–73:10 (2008)
5. Krishnan, D., Tay, T., Fergus, R.: Blind deconvolution using a normalized sparsity measure. In: CVPR, pp. 233–240 (2011)
6. Xu, L., Zheng, S., Jia, J.: Unnatural L0 sparse representation for natural image deblurring. In: CVPR, pp. 1107–1114 (2013)
7. Pan, J., Su, Z.: Fast L0-regularized kernel estimation for robust motion deblurring. IEEE Sig. Process. Lett. **20**(9), 841–844 (2013)
8. Krishnan, D., Bruna, J., Fergus, R.: Blind deconvolution with re-weighted sparsity promotion (2013). arXiv:1311.4029
9. Levin, A., Weiss, Y., Durand, F., Freeman, W. T.: Efficient marginal likelihood optimization in blind deconvolution. In: CVPR, pp. 2657–2664 (2011)
10. Levin, A., Weiss, Y., Durand, F., Freeman, W.T.: Understanding blind deconvolution algorithms. IEEE Trans. Pattern Anal. Mach. Intell. **33**(12), 2354–2367 (2011)
11. Babacan, S.D., Molina, R., Do, M.N., Katsaggelos, A.K.: Bayesian blind deconvolution with general sparse image priors. In: Fitzgibbon, A., Lazebnik, S., Perona, P., Sato, Y., Schmid, C. (eds.) ECCV 2012, Part VI. LNCS, vol. 7577, pp. 341–355. Springer, Heidelberg (2012)
12. Wipf, D., Zhang, H.: Revisiting Bayesian blind deconvolution (2013). arXiv: 1305.2362
13. Tibshirani, R., Saunders, M., Rosset, S., Zhu, J., Knight, K.: Sparsity and smoothness via the fused lasso. J. Royal Stat. Soc. Ser. B **67**(1), 91–108 (2005)
14. Wenze, S., Haisong, D., Zhihui, W.: The magic of split augmented Lagrangians applied to K-frame-based ℓ_0-ℓ_2 minimization image restoration. Sig. Image Video Process. **8**, 975–983 (2014)
15. Afonso, M., Bioucas-Dias, J., Figueiredo, M.: Fast image recovery using variable splitting and constrained optimization. IEEE Trans. Image Process. **19**(19), 2345–2356 (2010)
16. Yin, W., Osher, S., Goldfarb, D., Darbon, J.: Bregman iterative algorithms for L1 minimization with applications to compressed sensing. SIAM J. Imag. Sci. **1**, 143–168 (2008)
17. Krishnan, D., Fergus, R.: Fast image deconvolution using Hyper-Laplacian priors. In: NIPS, pp. 1033–1041 (2009)

Blood Vessel Segmentation of Retinal Images Based on Neural Network

Jingdan Zhang[1(✉)], Yingjie Cui[1], Wuhan Jiang[2], and Le Wang[1]

[1] Department of Electronics and Communication, Shenzhen Institute of Information Technology,
Shenzhen 518172, China
zhangjd358@163.com, {cuiyj,wangle}@sziit.com.cn
[2] Fada Road, Longgang District, Shenzhen 518129, China
whjiang_1114@163.com

Abstract. Blood vessel segmentation of retinal images plays an important role in the diagnosis of eye diseases. In this paper, we propose an automatic unsupervised blood vessel segmentation method for retinal images. Firstly, a multi-dimensional feature vector is constructed with the green channel intensity and the vessel enhanced intensity feature by the morphological operation. Secondly, self-organizing map (SOM) is exploited for pixel clustering, which is an unsupervised neural network. Finally, we classify each neuron in the output layer of SOM as retinal neuron or non-vessel neuron with Otsu's method, and get the final segmentation result. Our proposed method is validated on the publicly available DRIVE database, and compared with the state-of-the-art algorithms.

Keywords: Medical image segmentation · Retinal images · Self-organizing map · Otsu's method

1 Introduction

Several pathologies affecting the retinal vascular structures due to diabetic retinopathy can be found in retinal images. Blood vessel segmentation from retinal images plays a crucial role for diagnosing complications due to hypertension, diabetes, arteriosclerosis, cardiovascular disease and stroke [1]. Automatic and accurate blood vessel segmentation system could provide several useful features for diagnosis of various retinal diseases, and reduce the doctors' workload. However, the retinal images have low contrast, and large variability is presented in the image acquisition process [2], which deteriorates automatic blood vessel segmentation results.

Many studies for retinal vessel segmentation have been reported, including rule-based method [3], model-based method [4–7], matched filtering [8–10], and supervised method [2, 11–14].

In this paper, we propose an automatic unsupervised segmentation method to partition the retinal images into two types: vessel and non-vessel. For improving the segmentation results, we construct a multi-dimensional feature vector with the green channel intensity and the enhanced intensity feature by the morphological operation. Then, an unsupervised neural network – self-organizing map (SOM) is exploited as the classifier

© Springer International Publishing Switzerland 2015
Y.-J. Zhang (Ed.): ICIG 2015, Part II, LNCS 9218, pp. 11–17, 2015.
DOI: 10.1007/978-3-319-21963-9_2

for pixel clustering. Finally, we classify each neuron in the output layer of SOM as retinal neuron or non-vessel neuron with Otsu's method, and get the final segmentation results.

The rest of this paper is organized as follow. Section 2 presents our proposed vessel segmentation method for retinal images. In Sect. 3, experimental results are presented, followed by the conclusion in Sect. 4.

2   Our Proposed Retinal Vessel Segmentation Method

In this section, a detailed description about our proposed segmentation method is presented. Firstly, a multi-dimensional feature vector is extracted for each pixel. Then, the algorithm based on neural network is proposed for automatic blood vessel segmentation.

2.1   Feature Extraction

Retinal images often show important lighting variations, poor contrast and noise [2]. In this paper, we expand each pixel of retinal image into a multi-dimensional feature vector, characterizing the image data beyond simple pixel intensities.

The Green Channel Intensity Feature. In original RGB retinal images, the green channel shows the best vessel-background contrast, while the red and blue channels show low contrast and are noisy [2, 11]. So, we select the green channel from the RGB retinal image, and the green channel intensity of each pixel is taken as the intensity feature. Figure 1(a) is the original RGB retinal image from DRIVE database, and the green channel image is shown in Fig. 1(b).

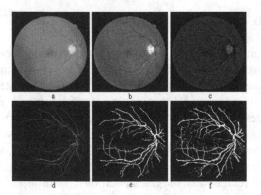

Fig. 1. Illustration of the feature extraction process. (a) Original RGB retinal image. (b) The green channel of the original image. (c) Shade-corrected image. (d) Vessel enhanced image. (e) The segmentation result with our proposed method. (f) The manual segmentation result by the first specialist (Color figure online).

Vessel Enhanced Intensity Feature. Retinal images often contain background intensity variation because of uniform illumination, which deteriorates the segmentation results.

In the present work, the shade-correction method mentioned in [15] is used to remove the background lightening variations. The shade-correction image of Fig. 1(b) is presented in Fig. 1(c).

After background homogenization, the contrast between the blood vessels and the background is generally poor in the retinal images. Vessel enhancement is utilized for estimating the complementary image of the homogenized image, and subsequently applying the morphological top-hat transformation with a disc of eight pixels in radius. Figure 1(d) is the vessel enhancement image of Fig. 1(c).

In order to generate the features which could overcome the lighting variation, we integrate the enhanced intensity feature with the green channel intensity as the pixel feature vector.

2.2 Segmentation System

Self-Organizing Map. In present, neural-network-based method is often used in retinal image segmentation [11]. As an unsupervised clustering method, Kohonen's self-organizing map (SOM) [16] is a two-layer feedforward competitive learning neural network that can discover the topological structure hidden in the data and display it in one or two dimensional space. Therefore, we exploit SOM method for blood vessel segmentation.

SOM consists of an input layer and a single output layer of M neurons which usually form a two-dimensional array. In the output layer, each neuron i has a d-dimensional weight vector $w_i = [w_{i1}, \dots, w_{id}]$. At each training step t, the input vector x_p of pixel p in the retinal image I is randomly chosen. Distance $d_{x_p,i}(t)$ between $x_p(t)$ and each neuron i in the output layer is computed. The winning neuron c is the neuron with the weight vector closest to x_p, $c = \arg\min_i d_{x_p,i}(t)$, $i \in \{1, \dots, M\}$.

A set of neighboring neurons of the winning node c is denoted as N_c, which decreases its neighboring radius of the winning neuron with time. $N_t(c, i)$ is the neighborhood kernel function around the winning neuron c at time t. The neighborhood kernel function is a non-increasing function of time t and of the distance of neuron i from the winning neuron c in the 2-D output layer. The kernel function can be taken as a Gaussian function

$$N_t(c, i) = \exp(-\frac{\|r_i - r_c\|^2}{2N_c^2(t)})$$

where r_i is the coordinate of neuron i on the output layer and $N_c(t)$ is the kernel width. The weight-updating rule in the sequential SOM algorithm can be written as $w_i(t + 1) = w_i(t) + \alpha(t)N_t(c, i)(x_p(t) - w_i)$ $\forall i \in N_c$, $p \in I$. The parameter $\alpha(t)$ is the learning rate of the algorithm. Generally, the learning rate $\alpha(t)$ and the kernel width $N_c(t)$ are monotonically decreasing functions of time [16].

SOM possesses some very useful properties. Kohonen [17] has argued that the density of the weight vectors assigned to an input region approximates the density of the inputs occupying this region. Second, the weight vectors tend to be ordered according to their mutual similarity.

In our work, we exploit self-organizing map [16] to cluster pixels in the retinal image. Vessels of the retinal image belong to the detail information. To reserve the thin and small vessels in the segmentation result, we set the size of output layer with 4×4. So, there are multiple neurons in the output layer (vessel neurons or non-vessel neurons) after SOM clustering.

Labeling the Output Neurons' Class. After clustering with SOM algorithm, there are multiple output neurons including vessel neurons and non-vessel neurons. We use Otsu's method to estimate the neuron class.

Otsu's method is used to automatically perform clustering-based image thresholding [18]. The algorithm assumes that the image contains two classes of pixels following bi-modal histogram (foreground pixels and background pixels), and then calculates the optimum threshold separating the two classes so that their combined spread (intra-class variance) is minimal [19].

Postprocessing. Finally, in the visual inspection, small isolated regions misclassified as blood vessels are also observed. If the vessel region is connected with no more than 30 pixels, it will be reclassified as non-vessel. The segmentation result of our proposed method is shown in Fig. 1(e).

3   Experimental Results

3.1   Database and Similarity Indices

The DRIVE database [13] is used in our experiments. This dataset is a public retinal image database, and is widely used by other researchers to test their blood vessel segmentation methods. Moreover, the DRIVE database provides two sets of manual segmentations made by two different observers for performance validation. In our experiments, performance is computed with the segmentation of the first observer as ground truth.

To quantify the overlap between the segmentation results and the ground truth for vessel pixels and non-vessel pixels, accuracy (Acc) are adopted in our experiments. The accuracy of our segmentation method.

For visual inspection, Fig. 2 depicts the blood vessel segmentation results on different retinal images from DRIVE database. Figure 2(a), (d) and (g) are original retinal images with different illumination conditions, and their segmentation results using our proposed method are shown in Fig. 2(b), (e) and (h) respectively. The manual segmentation results by the first specialist are presents in Fig. 2(c), (f) and (i) for visual comparison. It is evident that our method is robust to the low contrast and large variability in the retinal images, and gets accurate segmentation results.

In addition, we give a quantitative validation of our method on the DRIVE database with available gold standard images. Since the images dark background outside the field-of-view (FOV) is provided, accuracy (Acc) values are computed for each image considering FOV pixels only. The results are listed in Table 1, and the last row of the table shows average Acc value for 20 images in the database.

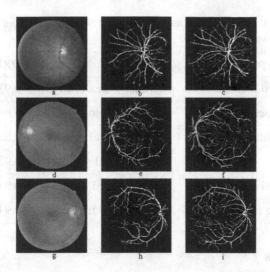

Fig. 2. Examples of application of our segmentation method on three images with different illumination conditions. (a), (d), (g) Original RGB retinal images. (b), (e), (h) Segmentation results with our method. (c), (f), (i) The manual segmentation results by the first specialist (Color figure online).

Table 1. Performance results on DRIVE database images, according to Acc value.

Image	1	2	3	4	5
Acc	0.946	0.946	0.932	0.943	0.938
Image	6	7	8	9	10
Acc	0.936	0.938	0.937	0.945	0.944
Image	11	12	13	14	15
Acc	0.924	0.946	0.937	0.943	0.944
Image	16	17	18	19	20
Acc	0.940	0.942	0.947	0.955	0.921
Average	**0.940**				

3.2 Comparing the Performance of Our Algorithm with Other Methods

In order to compare our approach with other retinal vessel segmentation algorithms, the average Acc value is used as measures of method performance. We compare our method with the following published methods: Martinez-Parez et al. [3], Jiang and Mojon [4], Chaudhuri et al. [8], Cinsdikici and Aydin [10], and Niemeijer et al. [12]. The comparison results are summarized in Table 2, which indicate our proposed method outperforms most of the other methods.

Table 2. Comparing the segmentation results of different algorithms with our method on DRIVE database in terms of average Acc value.

Method type	Method	DRIVE
Rule-based method	Martinez-Perez et al. [3]	0.934
Model-based method	Jiang and Mojon [4]	0.891
Matched filter	Chaudhuri et al. [8]	0.877
	Cinsdikici and Aydin [10]	0.929
Supervised methed	Niemeijer et al. [12]	0.941
Clustering method	Our proposed method	0.940

4   Conclusions

This study proposes a retinal vessel segmentation method based on neural network algorithm. To overcome the problem of low contrast and large variability in retinal images, we construct the feature vector with the intensity from green channel and the vessel enhanced intensity feature. Then, we classify the pixels in retinal image with SOM algorithm. Finally, we label each neuron in the output layer of SOM as retinal neuron or non-vessel neuron with Otsu's method, and get the final segmentation results.

Our method is validated on the DRIVE database with available gold standard images. From the visual inspection and quantitative validation of our method in the experiments, it is evident that our method is robust to the low contrast and large variability in the retinal images, and gets accurate segmentation results. In addition, we compare our method with the state-of-art methods, and the experimental results indicate that out method outperforms most of the other methods.

Acknowledgements. This project is supported in part by Shenzhen Science and Technology plan Project (JCYJ20120615101059717), and Project of Shenzhen Institute of Information Technology (SYS201004).

References

1. Kanski, J.J.: Clinical Ophthalmology: A Systematic Approach. Butterworth-Heinemann, London (1989)
2. Roychowdhury, S., Koozekanani, D.D., Parhi, K.K.: Blood vessel segmentation of fundus images by major vessel extraction and sub-image classification. IEEE J. Biomed. Health Inform. **99** (2014). doi:10.1109/JBHI.2014.2335617
3. Marinez-Perez, M.E., Hughes, A.D., Thom, S.A., Bharath, A.A., Parker, K.H.: Segmentation of blood vessels from red-free and fluorescein retinal images. Med. Imaging Anaysis **11**, 47–61 (2007)

4. Jiang, X., Mojon, D.: Adaptive local thresholding by verification-based multithreshold probing with application to vessel detection in retinal images. IEEE Trans. Pattern Anal. Mach. Intell. **25**(1), 131–137 (2003)
5. Vermeer, K.A., Vos, F.M., Lemij, H.G., Vossepoel, A.M.: A model based method for retinal blood vessel detection. Comput. Biol. Med. **34**, 209–219 (2004)
6. Lam, B., Yan, H.: A novel vessel segmentation algorithm for pathological retina images based on the divergence of vector fields. IEEE Trans. Med. Imaging **27**(2), 237–246 (2008)
7. Al-Diri, B., Hunter, A., Steel, D.: An active contour model for segmenting and measuring retinal vessels. IEEE Trans. Med. Imaging **28**, 1488–1497 (2009)
8. Chaudhuri, S., Chatterjee, S., Katz, N., Nelson, M., Goldbaum, M.: Detection of blood vessels in retinal images using two-dimensional matched filters. IEEE Trans. Med. Imaging **8**(3), 263–269 (1989)
9. Odstrcilikb, J., Kolar, R., Budai, A., et al.: Retinal vessel segmentation by improved matched filtering: evaluation on a new high-resolution fundus image database. IET Image Proc. **7**, 373–383 (2013)
10. Cinsdikici, M.G., Aydin, D.: Detection of blood vessels in ophthalmoscope images using MF/ant (matched filter/ant colony) algorithm. Comput. Methods Programs Biomed. **96**, 85–95 (2009)
11. Marin, D., Aquino, A., Gegundez-Arias, M.E., Bravo, J.M.: A new supervised method for blood vessel segmentation in retinal images by using gray-level and moment invariants-based features. IEEE Trans. Med. Imaging **30**, 146–158 (2011)
12. Niemeijer, M., Staal, J., Ginneken, B.V., Loog, M., Abramoff, M.D.: Comparative study of retinal vessel segmentation methods on a new publicly available database. SPIE Med. Imag. **5370**, 648–656 (2004)
13. Staal, J., Abramoff, M.D., Niemeijer, M., Viergever, M.A., Ginneken, B.: Ridge-based vessel segmentation in color images of the retina. IEEE Trans. Med. Imaging **23**, 501–509 (2004)
14. Kande, G.B., Savithri, T.S., Subbaiah, P.V.: Segmentation of vessels in fundus images using spatially weighted fuzzy C-means clustering algorithm. Int. J. Comput. Sci. Netw. Secur. **7**, 102–109 (2007)
15. Niemeijer, M., van Ginneken, B., Staal, J.J., Suttorp-Schulten, M.S.A., Abramoff, M.D.: Automatic detection of red lesions in digital color fundus photographs. IEEE Trans. Med. Imaging **24**, 584–592 (2005)
16. Kohonen, T.: The self-organizing maps. Proc. IEEE **78**, 1464–1480 (1990)
17. Kohonen, T.: Self-organizing Maps. Springer, New York (1995)
18. Sezgin, M., Sankur, B.: Survey over image thresholding techniques and quantitative performance evaluation. J. Electron. Imaging **13**, 146–165 (2004)
19. Otsu, N.: A threshold selection method from gray-level histograms. IEEE Trans. Sys. Man. Cyber. **9**, 62–66 (1979)

Compressed Binary Discriminative Feature for Fast UAV Image Registration

Li-Chuan Geng[1,2(✉)], Ze-xun Geng[1,2,3], and Guo-xi Wu[1,2]

[1] School of Urban Planning and Landscaping,
Xuchang University, Xuchang, China
glchl982@163.com
[2] The UAVLRS Collaborative Innovation Center,
Xuchang University, Xuchang, China
[3] The PLA Information Engineering University, Zhengzhou, China

Abstract. Efficiently UAV images mosaicking is of critical importance for the application of disaster management, in which fast image registration plays an important role. Towards fast and accurate image registration, the key design lies in the keypoint description, to which end SIFT and SURF are widely leveraged in the related literature. However, the expensive computation and memory costs restrict their potential in disaster management. In this paper, we proposed a novel keypoint descriptor termed CBDF (Compressed Binary Discriminative Feature). A cascade of binary strings is computed by efficiently comparing image gradients static information over a log-polar location grid pattern. Extensive evaluations on benchmark datasets and real-world UAV images show that CBDF yields a similar performance with SIFT and SURF, and it is much more efficient in terms of both computation time and memory.

Keywords: Image mosaic · Image registration · Unmanned aerial vehicles (UAV) · CBDF

1 Introduction

Unmanned Aerial Vehicles (UAV) is widely used in civilian applications. Comparing to standard airborne aerial, UAV system is more flexible, efficient, especially for small area coverage [1], which is especially suitable for time critical events where rapidly acquiring current and accurate spatial information is critically important. In such a case, a large number of UAV images should be processed, e.g. building an image mosaic, in a short time, with moderate accuracy, a near-orthophoto accuracy. However, the traditional photogrammetry and automatic aerial triangulation (AAT) cannot efficiently create such mosaic due to the high variation of UAV images.

One of the approaches is to decompose an image into local regions of interest, or so-called 'features' to alleviate the time complexity. To this end, the past decades have seen considerable advances in feature descriptors and matching strategy. Representative approaches include SIFT [2, 3] and its variants, which are distinctive and invariant to various image transformations. However, since SIFT is computationally expensive,

Y.-J. Zhang (Ed.): ICIG 2015, Part II, LNCS 9218, pp. 18–33, 2015.
DOI: 10.1007/978-3-319-21963-9_3

alternative methods such as SURF [4], PCA-SIFT [5] have been proposed to speed up. These methods have similar matching rates with SIFT while much faster performance.

Unfortunately, these gradient based methods still hard to meet the requirement of real-time image mosaic, especially on mobile devices with low computing power and memory capacity. As a result, algorithms with fixed-point operations and low memory load are preferred, such as Binary Robust Independent Elementary Feature (BRIEF) [7], Oriented Fast and Rotated BRIEF (ORB) [8], Binary Robust Invariant Scalable Keypoints (BRISK) [9], and Fast Retina Keypoint (FREAK) [10]. Such hand-crafted and heavily-engineered features are difficult to generalize to new domains. Other works [14, 20] learn short binary codes by minimizing the distances between positive training feature descriptors, while maximizing the negative pairs. Binarization is usually performed by multiplying the descriptors by a projection matrix, subtracting a threshold vector, and retaining only the sign of the result. Although low memory load, these new descriptors tend to perform worse than the floating point descriptors.

Aiming to bridge this performance gap between floating descriptors and binary descriptors without increasing the computation cost, a Compressed Binary Discriminative Feature (CBDF) is proposed for fast image registration. First, a Gaussian smoothing is applied to the image patch around the keypoint, and then local image gradients are computed. Second, the image patch is split up into smaller sub-regions, similar to GLOH [6], and a vector of the gradient statistic information is calculated for each sub-region, our binary descriptor is computed by a comparison of these vectors. Since low bit-rate feature descriptor means fast to match and low memory footprint, our goal is to produce low bit-rate descriptors which maintain the highest possible fidelity. We optimize our descriptor by a supervised learning method to find the dimensions in the descriptor which are informative to the descriptor. The advantage of our feature descriptor is that the gradient information is contained in our binary keypoint descriptor, which makes our binary descriptor much more discriminative than the simple pixel intensity comparison descriptors, in the meantime, a learning process is performed to realize dimension reduction, and this process makes our descriptor more compact.

The rest of this paper is organized as follows: The related work is presented in Sect. 2. The method to construct our CBDF descriptor is described in details in Sect. 3. In Sect. 4, we compare the performances of our CBDF descriptor with the state-of-the-art methods. Finally, we conclude our work in Sect. 5.

2 Related Work

Due to the fast development of UAV system, low altitude remote sensing is becoming more and more attractive for commercial and military applications. Such technique, if applicable, can be widely used in earthquake relief work, forest fire surveillance and flood disaster.

In such a scenario, one important step is to mosaic the UAV image in real-time. Here, one key technique is image registration. Different from the state-of-the-art image registration algorithms like SIFT matching [11], where the registration accuracy is of fundamental importance, under the UAV circumstance the efficiency is more important. To speed up, several approaches are proposed in the literature like PCA-SIFT [5], SURF [4], CHOG [21], DAISY [23], etc. For instance, PCA-SIFT reduces the description vector from 128 to 36 dimension using principal component analysis. The matching time is reduced, but the time to build the descriptor is increased leading to a small gain in speed and a loss of distinctiveness. The SURF descriptor sums responses of Haar wavelets, which is fast by using integral image. SURF addresses the issue of speed. However, since the descriptor is a 64-vector of floating point, its representation still requires 256 bytes, which becomes crucial when millions of descriptors must be stored. Chandrasekhar et al. [21] applies tree-coding method for lossy compression of probability distributions to SIFT-like descriptors to obtain compressed histogram of gradients (CHOG). Brown et al. [22] use a training method to optimize the filtering and normalization steps that produce a SIFT-like vector. However, the dimensionality of the feature vector is still too high for large-scale applications, such as image retrieval or 3D reconstruction.

Much research has been done recently focusing on designing binary descriptor to reduce both the matching time and storage cost [12, 13]. For example, Calonder et al. [7] show that it is possible to shortcut the dimensionality reduction step by directly building a short binary descriptor in which each bits are independent, called BRIEF. The descriptor vector is obtained by comparing the intensity of 512 pairs of pixels or even 256 pairs after applying a Gaussian smoothing. The smoothing step is to reduce the noise sensitivity. The positions of the pixels are pre-selected randomly according to a Gaussian distribution or Uniform distribution around the patch center. However, this descriptor is not invariant to scale and rotation changes. Rublee et al. [8] propose the Oriented Fast and Rotated BRIEF (ORB) descriptor. This binary descriptor is invariant to rotation, which is robust to noise but not invariant to scale change while relying on a greedy optimization. Leutenegger et al. [9] propose a binary descriptor called BRISK, which is invariant to scale and rotation. Its key design lies in the application of a novel scale-space. To build the descriptor bit-stream, a limited number of points in a polar sampling pattern are used. Each point contributes many pairs. The pairs are divided into short-distance and long-distance subsets. The long-distance subset is used to calculate the direction of the keypoint, while the short-distance subset is used to build the binary descriptor. Alahi et al. [10] propose a keypoint descriptor termed Fast Retina Keypoint (FREAK), which is inspired by the human retina topology. A cascade of binary strings are computed by comparing image intensities efficiently over a retinal sampling pattern. Strecha et al. [20] map the SIFT descriptor vectors into the Hamming space by a LDA method. Although these binary feature descriptors are fast to compute and match, they tend to be less robust than their floating point equivalents.

3   The Method

Most of the local image descriptors are extracted based on the keypoints returned by interest point detectors, such as Harris [17], DoG [2], MSER [18], Hessian-Affine [19] or FAST [15]. Our proposed CBDF descriptor can be combined with any of these local

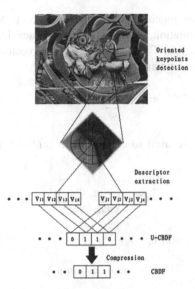

Fig. 1. Overview of the computation of CBDF descriptor

feature detectors. As finding a rotation-invariant and efficient detector is important to image registration, especially in the aerial images. So here we take the FAST as our keypoint detector. Unfortunately, FAST does not consider the orientation of the keypoint, so we proposed an enhanced-version of FAST, called orientation FAST. After oriented keypoints extraction, we build our CBDF descriptor by dividing the image patch surrounding the keypoints into subregions, and then we static the gradient information for each subregion, a four dimension vector is acquired. CBDF descriptor is constructed by comparing and threshholding these vectors. At last a dimension reduction scheme is applied on the descriptor to make our descriptor more compact.

The computation of CBDF includes the following three steps (as illustrated in Fig. 1): (1) Oriented FAST feature point extraction; (2) Oriented binary discriminative feature descriptors; (3) Descriptor compression.

3.1 Oriented FAST Keypoint Extraction

FAST keypoint detector is extensively used in computer vision applications for its efficiency and rotation invariance. There is only one parameter in FAST, which is the intensity threshold between the center pixel and those in a circular ring around the center. Typically 9–16 mask is usually used, it require at least 9 consecutive pixels in the 16-pixel circle which are sufficiently brighter or darker than the central pixel. In such a way, FAST detector has large responses along edges. We defined s as the maximum threshold considering an image point as a corner. The currently testing point needs to fulfill the maximum condition with respect to its 8 neighboring FAST scores. We do not employ a scale pyramid of the image, as for consecutive UAV frames the image scales are almost all the same. Without scale pyramid transformation of input image, we can also save much time on feature point detection and matching. To measure the corner orientation, we assume that the intensity of corner is offset from its center, as intensity centroid **C** named in [16], this vector is used to calculate an orientation. The patch moments are defined as:

$$m_{pq} = \sum_{x,y} x^p y^q I(x,y) \tag{1}$$

Then these moments are used to compute the centroid of a patch as defined in Eq. (2).

$$\mathbf{C} = \left(\frac{m_{10}}{m_{00}}, \frac{m_{01}}{m_{00}} \right) \tag{2}$$

The orientation of the patch is:

$$\theta = \text{atan2}(m_{01}, m_{10}) \tag{3}$$

where atan2 is the quadrant-aware version of arctan. To guarantee the rotation invariance, we choose the pixels with positions within a circular area of radius r to calculate the moments.

3.2   Oriented Binary Discriminative Feature Descriptor

Most recent local feature descriptors are based on the statistics of the gradients of pixel intensity in a patch. e.g. SIFT, SURF, GLOH This is because gradients is highly distinctive yet as invariant as possible to remaining variations, such as change in illumination or 3D viewpoint [3]. We follow this trend to build our binary descriptor, yet in a much simplified way. After normalizing the rotation, the proposed CBDF descriptor applies the sampling pattern rotated by θ around the detected keypoints with patch size 32 × 32. Then, the intensities of the rotated patch is calculated by nearest neighbor interpolation.

After rotation, gradients of each pixels are computed by a discrete derivative masks. There are several derivative masks can be used to calculate the gradients, such as 1-D point derivatives uncentred $[-1, 1]$, centred $[-1, 0, 1]$, as well as 2 × 2 diagonal ones $\begin{bmatrix} 0 & 1 \\ -1 & 0 \end{bmatrix}, \begin{bmatrix} -1 & 0 \\ 0 & 1 \end{bmatrix}$, 3 × 3 Sobel mask and Prewitt mask, we tested these masks in our experiments to chose the best one. And then, gradients are smoothed by Gaussian smoothing. The size of the smoothing template is also tested including $\sigma = 0$ (none). From the experiment results, we find that Sobel mask at $\sigma = 4$ with a size of 5 × 5 gaussian kernel window works best, and the 1-D point derivative uncentred mask performs almost the same with Sobel, since it's much time saving than Sobel mask, we choose it for our final descriptor. Experiment results are given in Sect. 4. The image patch is then split up regularly into 16 smaller sub-regions in two styles as shown in Fig. 3, and a accumulated gradient magnitude vector **v** is calculated for each sub-region:

$$\mathbf{v} = \left(\sum d_x, \sum d_y, \sum |d_x|, \sum |d_y| \right) \tag{4}$$

After this step, each sub region has a four-parameter vector, from which our bit-vector descriptor $\mathbf{x}$ is assembled by a comparison of these parameters between each vector, such that each bit b corresponds to:

$$\forall i = 1, \ldots, S, j = 1, \ldots, S, k = 1, \ldots, 4, i \neq j \quad b = \begin{cases} 1, & v_{ik} > v_{jk} \\ 0, & otherwise \end{cases} \tag{5}$$

where S is the number of the sub regions, k denotes which parameter of the vector to be compared.

For the sake of generating a low bit-rate binary descriptor, we do not compare all sub-regions. Because if we do so, the descriptor length will be $C_{16}^{15} \times 4 = 480$, it is a little too long. Instead, we compare the vector of sub regions linked by the arrow in different and sparse styles as shown in Fig. 2. The radius of the three circles in GV, GVI, GVII, GVIII are set to be 2, 10, 15 pixels. The performance of the different test strategies are given in Sect. 4, experiment results show that even be a 224 bits descriptor, our method out performs several longer descriptors, e.g. BRIEF, ORB, BRISK.

3.3 Descriptor Compression

Fewer dimensions mean low memory footprint and fast to match, although our descriptor is much shorter than several state-of-art binary descriptors, we apply a dimension reduction process to our descriptor. However, it is important that we do not adversely affect the performance of the descriptor.

Our keypoint descriptor $\mathbf{x}$ is represented as n-dimensional binary vector in hamming space $\mathbf{H}^n$. We attempt to find a $m \times n$ matrix $\mathbf{P}$ which takes its value in $\{0, 1\}$ to map our descriptor to an m-dimensional hamming space $\mathbf{H}^m$. Our goal in finding such a matrix is in two-fold. First, $\mathbf{H}^m$ should be a more efficient representation. This implies that m must be smaller than n. Secondly, through this mapping, the performance should not degrade too much. To better take advantage of training data, we present a supervised optimization scheme that is inspired by [20, 24]. In [24], they use AdaBoost to compute the projection matrix, but there is no guarantee the solution it finds is optimal. We compute a projection matrix that is designed to minimize the in-class covariance of the descriptors and maximize the covariance across classes. In essence, we perform Linear Discriminant Analysis (LDA) on the descriptor.

Here, we limit our attention to dimension reduction of the form:

$$\mathbf{y} = \mathbf{P}\mathbf{x} \tag{6}$$

$\mathbf{y}$ is constructed to minimize the expectation of the Hamming distance on the set of positive pairs, while maximizing it on the set of negative pairs. This can be expressed as minimization of the loss function:

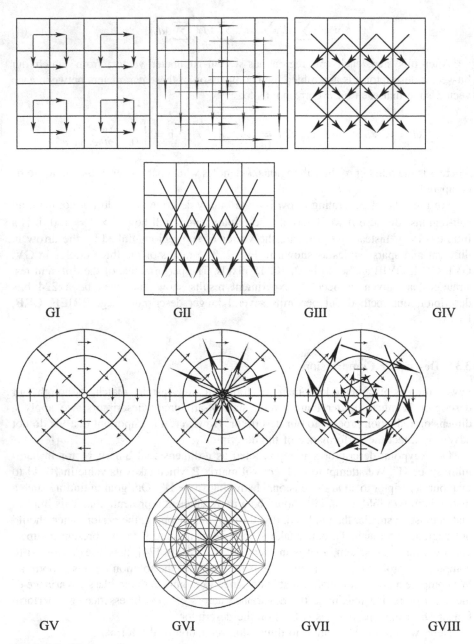

Fig. 2. The binary test strategies, note that we compare the vector parameters of the sub regions linked by the arrows

$$L = \mathrm{E}\{d_{\mathbf{H}^m}(\mathbf{y}, \mathbf{y}')|P\} - \mathrm{E}\{d_{\mathbf{H}^m}(\mathbf{y}, \mathbf{y}')|N\} \tag{7}$$

Equation (7) is equivalent to the minimization of:

$$L = \mathrm{E}\{\|\mathbf{y} - \mathbf{y}'\|^2 | P\} - \mathrm{E}\{\|\mathbf{y} - \mathbf{y}'\|^2 | N\} \tag{8}$$

The direct minimization of Eq. (8) is difficult since the solution of the resulting non-convex problem in $m \times n$ variables is challenging. It can be found that:

$$\mathrm{E}\{\|\mathbf{P}\mathbf{x} - \mathbf{P}\mathbf{x}'\|^2 | P\} = \mathrm{tr}(\mathbf{P}\Sigma_P\mathbf{P}^{\mathrm{T}}) \tag{9}$$

where $\Sigma_P = \mathrm{E}\{(\mathbf{x} - \mathbf{x}')(\mathbf{x} - \mathbf{x}')^T | P\}$ is the covariance matrix of the positive descriptor vector differences, Eq. (9) turns to be:

$$L = \mathrm{tr}\{\mathbf{P}\Sigma_P\mathbf{P}^T\} - \mathrm{tr}\{\mathbf{P}\Sigma_N\mathbf{P}^T\} \tag{10}$$

Pre-multiplying $\mathbf{x}$ by Σ_N^{-1} turns the second term of Eq. (10) into a constant, leaving:

$$L \propto \mathrm{tr}\{\mathbf{P}\Sigma_P\Sigma_N^{-1}\mathbf{P}\} = \mathrm{tr}\{\mathbf{P}\Sigma_R\mathbf{P}^T\} \tag{11}$$

where $\Sigma_R = \Sigma_P\Sigma_N^{-1}$ is the ratio of the positive and negative covariance matrices. Since Σ_R is a symmetric positive semi-definite matrix, it admits the eigendecomposition $\Sigma_R = \mathbf{U}\mathbf{S}\mathbf{U}^{\mathrm{T}}$, where $\mathbf{S}$ is a non-negative diagonal matrix. An orthogonal $m \times n$ matrix $\mathbf{P}$ minimizing $\mathrm{tr}\{\mathbf{P}\Sigma_R\mathbf{P}^{\mathrm{T}}\}$ is a projection onto the space spanned by the m smallest eigenvectors of Σ_R, this yields:

$$\mathbf{P} = \tilde{\mathbf{U}}_m \tag{12}$$

where $\tilde{\mathbf{U}}_m$ is the $m \times n$ matrix with the corresponding eigenvectors. Note that we aim to find a $m \times n$ projection matrix $\mathbf{P}$ which takes its value in $\{0, 1\}$, the result in Eq. (12) does not conform this. The index of the m smallest elements of the principal diagonal elements of Σ_R is denoted as $\mathbf{S}$. We approximate $\mathbf{P}$ by setting the elements of $\mathbf{P}(ind, \mathbf{S}_{ind}) = 1, ind = 1, \ldots, m$ and others to be 0. m is set to be 196 and 128, the original 224 bits U-CBDF descriptor is compressed to 196 bits and 128 bits, denote as CBDF_{196}, CBDF_{128}.

4 Experimental Results

In this section, we first describe our evaluation framework, and then present a set of initial experiments. These experiments validate our approach and allow us to select the appropriate parameters for the descriptor. Finally, we compare our method to other descriptors including BRIEF, ORB, BRISK, SIFT and SURF. Finally, we apply our proposed CBDF descriptor in a real UAV image registration application.

4.1   Performance Evaluation Protocol

We evaluate the performance of our method using two datasets. The first dataset is proposed by Mikolajczyk and Schmid [6, 11]. This dataset contains several sub datasets. Each of the sub datasets contains a sequence of six images exhibiting an increasing amount of transformation. This dataset is used to detect the appropriate parameters for our descriptor. We use precision rate as a quality criterion, we show the Nb best matches and count the number of correct matches n_c. The precision rate is calculated by $r = n_c/ Nb$. We set $Nb = 300$ in our experiment, we tune the threshold of each method to get 300 best matches. However, it's usually hard to get exactly 300 matches, we get an approximate number, and the deviation is constrained no more than 2.

The second dataset contains two sub datasets: *Notre Dame* and *Liberty* [14]. Each of them contains over 400 k scale- and rotation-normalized 64×64 patches. These patches are sampled around interest points which detected using Difference of Gaussian, and the correspondences between patches are found using a multi-view stereo algorithm. The resulting datasets exhibit substantial perspective distortion and light changing conditions. The ground truth available for each of these datasets describes 100k, 200k and 500k pairs of patches. We train matrix $\mathbf{P}$ with these datasets. The performance of our CBDF descriptor is compared against U-CBDF and the state-of-the-art descriptors. The test set contains 100,000 pairs in which 50 % match pairs, and 50 % non-match pairs.

4.2   Initial Experiments

There are several parameters that influence the performance of our descriptor as been mentioned in Sect. 3: the smoothing scales σ, the size of the smoothing template, the mask to compute the gradient, and the test strategy to generate our descriptor. We use the *Wall* dataset proposed in [6, 11] to test these parameters. It contains five image pairs, with the first image being the same in all pairs and the second image shot from a monotonically growing baseline, which makes matching increasingly more difficult. Figure 4(a) shows the first image of the *Wall* sequence. All the initial experiments are tested on the U-CBDF descriptor. When we test the influence of one of the parameters, other parameters are set to be the correct value which we finally use. Figure 3(a) shows the results obtained for different values of σ. For most of the values of σ, the performance are optimal for $\sigma = 2$, so we keep $\sigma = 2$ in the remaining experiments. Figure 3 (b) shows the precision rates for different smoothing templates. The 5×5 mask outperforms other masks, so we keep 5×5 Gaussian smoothing template for our final descriptor. Figure 3(c) shows the influence of different gradient masks, we find that the Sobel mask performs slightly better that the 1-D point derivative uncentred mask, since 1-D point derivative uncentred mask is much time saving than Sobel mask, we choose it for our final descriptor. The influence of different test strategies is shown in Fig. 3(d). We also calculate the precision rate of $BRIEF_{512}$ which has a length of 512 bits. Clearly, the symmetrical and regular GV, GVI, GVII, GVII strategies enjoy a big advantage over the other four in most cases. GVIII performs the best and it has a length of 224 bits. For this reason, in all further experiments presented in this paper, it is the

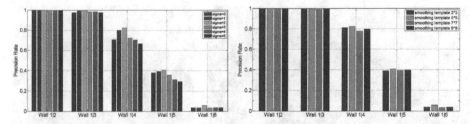

(a) Precision rate comparison for different sigma (b) Precision rate comparison for different smoothing templates

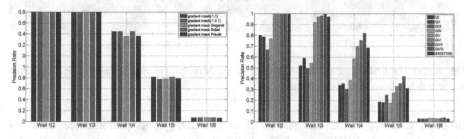

(c) Precision rate comparison for different gradient masks   (d) Precision rate comparison for different test strategies and BRIEF$_{256}$

Fig. 3. Precision rate comparison for different parameters and BRIEF256

one we will use. We also find that GVII and GVIII strategies perform better than BRIEF$_{256}$ in all cases, in which GVII has a length of only 128 bits.

Using the above-mentioned parameters for our U-CBDF descriptor, we train the matrix **P** with both the *Notre Dame* and *Liberty* datasets. **P** is used to compress U-CBDF descriptor.

4.3 Descriptor Comparison

In this section, we use the *Notre Dame* and *Liberty* datasets as our training and test datasets. Figure 4(b) shows some image patches from the *Liberty* dataset. We compare our binary descriptors both uncompressed and compressed to the very recent BRIEF, ORB, BRISK binary descriptors, results obtained with SIFT and SURF are also presented. All the experiments are performed on a desktop computer with an Intel core2 2.80 Hz CPU. For SIFT, BRIEF, ORB, and BRISK, we use the publicly available library OpenCV2.4.3. For SURF, we use the implementation available from their authors. During testing, we compute the distances of all match/non-match descriptors, and sweep a threshold on the descriptor distance to generate a ROC curve. We also report 85 % error rate in Table 2, 85 % error rate is the percent of incorrect matches obtained when 85 % of the true matches are found.

Figure 5 provides the ROC curves for U-CBDF, CBDF and the state-of-the-art methods on different training and test datasets. Both Fig. 5(a) and (b) show that

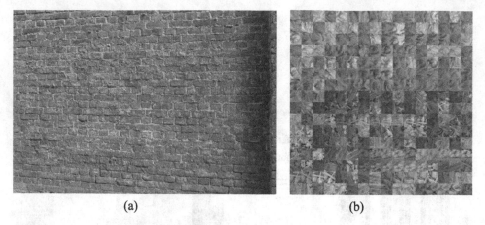

(a)   (b)

Fig. 4. (a) The first image of *Wall* sequence of the Mikolajczyk and Schmid dataset (b) some image patches from the *Liberty* dataset.

although $CBDF_{192}$ is 32 bits shorter than $U\text{-}CBDF_{224}$, its performance does not degrade too much. $CBDF_{192}$ performs better than its binary competitors at all error rates. $CBDF_{192}$ remains competitive to SURF, even though it has a much shorter representation. SIFT performs the best of all tested descriptors, though its complexity is prohibitive for real-time application. BRISK performs the worst at high false positive rate although it is much longer.

The first row of Table 1 clearly shows that $CBDF_{192}$ provides up to 28 % improvement over BRISK and up to 11 % improvement over BRIEF and ORB in terms of 85 % error rate, $CBDF_{128}$ provides up to 24 % improvement over BRISK and up to 7 % improvement over BRIEF and ORB. While $CBDF_{128}$ requiring only 16 bytes instead of 64 bytes for BRISK and 32 bytes for BRIEF. It also shows that $CBDF_{128}$ remains competitive to the much longer and much more computationally expensive floating-point SURF. The second row of Table 2 shows the similar results with the first row.

4.4   Timings

The timings of our method and its competitors are extensively tested with the boat image sequence by Mikolajczyk and Schmid dataset which are shown in Table 2. We use the first image and the second image of this sequence (size: 850 × 680). We also use FAST corner detector for BRIEF just like ORB, because there is no special key-point extractor for BRIEF, so the timings of detection are almost the same. Their differences are in feature descriptor. By tuning the threshold of each method, we extract 1000 keypoints on each image. The matching of each method is based on a brute-force descriptor distance computation. We ran each method for 100 times and calculate the average time cost.

The timings show an advantage of $CBDF_{192}$. Its descriptor computation time is typically two times faster than the one of SURF, and three times faster than the one of

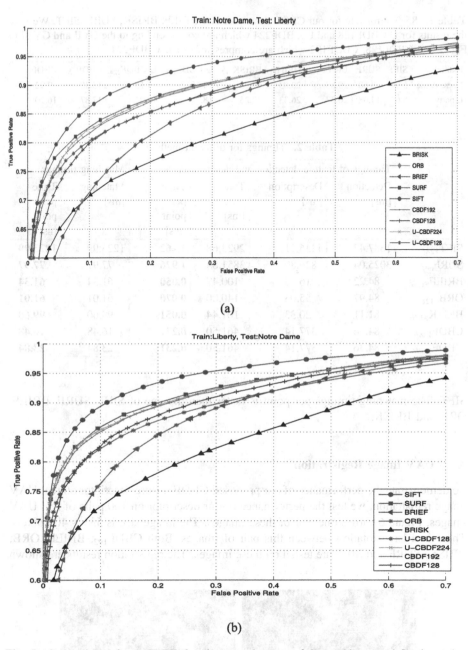

Fig. 5. Comparison of our CBDF descriptor to the state-of-the-art binary and floating-point descriptors

Table 1. 85 % error rate for our CBDF descriptor and BRIEF, BRISK, SURF, SIFT. We give the results for U-CBDF128 and U-CBDF224 which are corresponding to the GVII and GVIII in Fig. 1 and CBDF128, CBDF192 which are compressions of U-CBDF224.

Dataset	SIFT	SURF	BRIEF$_{512}$	ORB$_{512}$	BRISK$_{512}$	U-CBDF$_{128}$	U-CBDF$_{224}$	CBDF$_{128}$	CBDF$_{192}$
Notre dame	5.04	8.60	20.83	20.83	37.93	14.68	9.15	13.30	9.92
Liberty	8.67	14.08	26.33	26.33	42.25	18.75	15.04	17.87	16.10

Table 2. Timings for different methods

	Timings of feature detection and description				Matching timings	
	Detection [ms]	Description [ms]	Total time [ms]	Time per point [ms]	Matching [ms]	Time per point [ns]
SIFT$_{128f}$	1687.47	1236.21	2923.68	**1.462**	1223.99	**1223.99**
SURF$_{64f}$	3025.04	826.80	3851.84	**1.926**	77.97	**77.97**
BRIEF$_{512b}$	84.22	16.25	100.47	**0.050**	61.34	**61.34**
ORB$_{512b}$	84.97	55.03	140.00	**0.070**	61.01	**61.01**
BRISK$_{512b}$	81.11	20.33	101.44	**0.051**	99.60	**99.60**
CBDF$_{128b}$	84.36	377.14	461.50	**0.231**	16.48	**16.48**
CBDF$_{192b}$	84.36	377.14	461.50	**0.231**	23.84	**23.84**

SIFT. The matching timings per point is faster than the one of SIFT, SURF, BRIEF, ORB and BRISK.

4.5   UAV Image Registration

To demonstrate the performance of our proposed CBDF feature descriptor on real UAV image registration, we test the performance of our descriptor on 100 pairs of real UAV images. Figure 6 shows one pair of these images. The image size is 533 × 400 pixels. There is a large rotation between this pair of images. Both CBDF$_{192}$, BRIEF, ORB, BRISK, SURF and SIFT are tested on these images. The registration results are shown

Fig. 6. UAV images to be registration

(a)CBDF192 registration results (300 pair points, 100% precision rate)

(b)SURF registration results (297 pair points, 100% precision rate)

(c) SIFT registration results (295 pair points, 100% precision rate)

(d)BRIEF registration results (304 pair points, 14.47% precision rate)

(e)ORB registration results (312 pair points, 100% precision rate)

(f)BRISK registration results (302 pair points, 62.91% precision rate)

Fig. 7. UAV image registration results

Table 3. Timings for different methods with UAV images

	Points in the two images	Match points	Detection time [ms]	Description time [ms]	Matching time [ms]	Total time [ms]	Inliers rate [%]
CBDF$_{192}$	1011, 1031	300	34.33	268.70	23.21	**326.2**	100
SURF	1004, 1001	297	2693.31	660.33	73.20	**3426.8**	100
SIFT	1000, 1000	295	515.72	734.31	122.58	**1372.6**	100
BRIEF	1000, 1000	304	35.67	11.53	58.33	**105.5**	14.47
ORB	1000, 1000	312	34.44	27.22	57.80	**119.5**	100
BRISK	993, 996	302	121.70	14.97	99.70	**236.4**	62.91

in Fig. 7. The timings are listed in Table 3. One shall note that all our method is almost 10 times faster than SURF and 4 times faster than SIFT.

5 Conclusions

In this paper, we have defined a new oriented binary discriminative feature for UAV image registration. With only 192 bits or even 128 bits per descriptor, CBDF out-performs its binary state-of-the-art competitors in terms of accuracy while significantly reducing the memory footprint, and comparing to SIFT and SURF, the method offers faster alternative at comparable matching performance. Experiments with real UAV images justify that this framework can fulfill the near real-time image registration application requirement.

Acknowledgments. This work is supported by the Nature Science Foundation of China (No.11373043), the National 863 Project of China (No.2014****), and the Collaborative Innovation Special Foundation of Xuchang University.

References

1. Zhou, G.: Geo-referencing of video flow from small low-cost civilian UAV. IEEE Trans. Autom. Sci. Eng. **7**(1), 156–166 (2010)
2. Lowe, D.G.: Object recognition from local scale-invariant features. In: Proceedings of the Seventh IEEE International Conference on Computer Vision, vol. 2, pp. 1150–1157 (1999)
3. Lowe, D.G.: Distinctive image features from scale-invariant keypoints. Int. J. Comput. Vis. **60**(2), 91–110 (2004)
4. Bay, H., Tuytelaars, T., Van Gool, L.: SURF: speeded up robust features. In: Leonardis, A., Bischof, H., Pinz, A. (eds.) ECCV 2006, Part I. LNCS, vol. 3951, pp. 404–417. Springer, Heidelberg (2006)
5. Ke, Y., Sukthankar, R.: PCA-SIFT: a more distinctive representation for local image descriptors. In: The 2004 IEEE Computer Society Conference on Computer Vision and Pattern Recognition, vol. 2, p. II-506 (2004)

6. Mikolajczyk, K., Schmid, C.: A performance evaluation of local descriptors. IEEE Trans. Pattern Anal. Mach. Intell. **27**, 1615–1630 (2005)

7. Calonder, M., Lepetit, V., Strecha, C., Fua, P.: BRIEF: binary robust independent elementary features. In: Daniilidis, K., Maragos, P., Paragios, N. (eds.) ECCV 2010, Part IV. LNCS, vol. 6314, pp. 778–792. Springer, Heidelberg (2010)

8. Rublee, E., Rabaud, V., Konolige, K., Bradski, G.: ORB: an efficient alternative to SIFT or SURF. In: 2011 IEEE International Conference on Computer Vision (ICCV), pp. 2564–2571 (2011)

9. Leutenegger, S., Chli, M., Siegwart, R.Y.: BRISK: binary robust invariant scalable keypoints. In: 2011 IEEE International Conference on Computer Vision (ICCV), pp. 2548–2555 (2011)

10. Alahi, A., Ortiz, R., Vandergheynst, P.: Freak: fast retina keypoint. In: The 2012 IEEE Conference on Computer Vision and Pattern Recognition (CVPR), pp. 510–517 (2012)

11. Mikolajczyk, K., Tuytelaars, T., Schmid, C., Zisserman, A., Matas, J., Schaffalitzky, F., Van Gool, L.: A comparison of affine region detectors. Int. J. Comput. Vis. **65**(1–2), 43–72 (2005)

12. Gionis, A., Indyk, P., Motwani, R.: Similarity search in high dimensions via hashing. In: Proceedings of The International Conference on Very Large Data Bases, pp. 518–529 (1999)

13. Weiss, Y., Torralba, A., Fergus, R.: Spectral hashing. In: NIPS (2008)

14. Gong, Y., Lazebnik, S.: Iterative quantization: a procrustean approach to learning binary codes. In: 2011 IEEE Conference on Computer Vision and Pattern Recognition (CVPR), pp. 817–824 (2011)

15. Rosten, E., Drummond, T.W.: Machine learning for high-speed corner detection. In: Leonardis, A., Bischof, H., Pinz, A. (eds.) ECCV 2006, Part I. LNCS, vol. 3951, pp. 430–443. Springer, Heidelberg (2006)

16. Rosin, P.L.: Measuring corner properties. Comput. Vis. Image Underst. **73**(2), 291–307 (1999)

17. Harris, C., Stephens, M.: A combined corner and edge detector. In: Alvey Vision Conference, vol. 15, pp. 50 (1988)

18. Matas, J., Chum, O., Urban, M., Pajdla, T.: Robust wide-baseline stereo from maximally stable extremal regions. Image Vis. Comput. **22**(10), 761–767 (2004)

19. Mikolajczyk, K., Schmid, C.: Scale & affine invariant interest point detectors. Int. J. Comput. Vis. **60**(1), 63–86 (2004)

20. Strecha, C., Bronstein, A.M., Bronstein, M.M., Fua, P.: LDAHash: improved matching with smaller descriptors. IEEE Trans. Pattern Anal. Mach. Intell. **34**(1), 66–78 (2012)

21. Chandrasekhar, V., Takacs, G., Chen, D., Tsai, S., Grzeszczuk, R., Girod, B.: CHoG: compressed histogram of gradients a low bit-rate feature descriptor. In: 2009 IEEE Conference on Computer Vision and Pattern Recognition, pp. 2504–2511 (2009)

22. Brown, M., Hua, G., Winder, S.: Discriminative learning of local image descriptors. IEEE Trans. Pattern Anal. Mach. Intell. **33**(1), 43–57 (2011)

23. Tola, E., Lepetit, V., Fua, P.: Daisy: An efficient dense descriptor applied to wide-baseline stereo. IEEE Trans. Pattern Anal. Mach. Intell. **32**(5), 815–830 (2010)

24. Shakhnarovich, G.: Learning task-specific similarity. Ph.D. dissertation, MIT (2005)

Context-Aware Based Mobile Augmented Reality Browser and its Optimization Design

Yi Lin, Yue Liu$^{(\boxtimes)}$, and Yong-tian Wang

Beijing Engineering Research Center of Mixed Reality and Advanced Display,
Beijing Institute of Technology, Beijing China
`linyi_bit@163.com, {liuyue,wyt}@bit.edu.cn`

Abstract. The latest research shows that despite user's increasing interests in the Augmented Reality service, its usage frequency is low and the usage time is short. The intrinsic reason lies in its ignorance of human factors, which causes the design defect in the design stage of Augmented Reality browsers. In order to improve the quality of user experience, this paper introduces the design and optimization of a mobile Augmented Reality browser system by adopting the concept of context-aware service pushing based on scene classification, and proposes a novel interactive mode which combines Virtual Reality and Augmented Reality (AR/VR) on the basis of mental model theory. The whole design flow is verified by the design of the AR/VR hybrid interface. Experimental result shows that the proposed system of adopting hybrid interactive mode based on context-aware frameworks can not only increase the user acceptance of Augmented Reality browser, but also significantly improve quality of experiences of human-computer interaction.

Keywords: Context-aware · Mobile augmented reality browser · Mental model · User experience

1 Introduction

Grubert et al. [1] at the University of Graz, Austria, carries on analysis and research on the status of the use of Augmented Reality service based on the data collected in LimeSurvey [2] in 2011 and the survey results are shown in Fig. 1. It can be seen from Fig. 1(a) and (b) that people have more understandings and interests in the Augmented Reality technology. However, it can be seen from Fig. 1(c) that about a third of the participants (34 %) tried out the browsers only a few times and on the other hand 42 % used the browsers at most once a week. In addition, it can be seen from Fig. 1(d) that the average session time with an Augmented Reality browser was between 1–5 min. Such results indicate that despite user's increasing interests in the Augmented Reality services, there is a contradictory phenomenon of high installation rate and low usage

---

Y. Lin—No academic titles or descriptions of academic positions should be included in the addresses. The affiliations should consist of the author's institution, town, and country.

© Springer International Publishing Switzerland 2015
Y.-J. Zhang (Ed.): ICIG 2015, Part II, LNCS 9218, pp. 34–47, 2015.
DOI: 10.1007/978-3-319-21963-9_4

rate. Inherent reason for such discrepancy lies in the browser's own design. How to improve the Augmented Reality browser design, and how to mobilize the enthusiasm of users are all worthy of study.

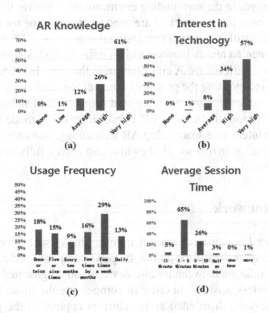

Fig. 1. User survey data of using augmented reality services (Source: Augmented reality browser survey, pp. 1–11)

At present, the following problems restrict the development of Augmented Reality browser, which includes poor cross-platform operation, hardware limitation of work mode and insufficient attention to the cognitive research. In order to improve the user experiences of mobile Augmented Reality browser, by analyzing the original require-ments of users and finding the user's cognitive rules, this paper aims to create a new Augmented Reality browser system and optimize the design of new systems. With the development of software and optimization of interface design, the user experience of Augmented Reality browser can be significantly improved.

Lee et al. [3] of Chonnam National University in South Korea proposed a new method to deploy context-aware framework for augmented reality browser in 2008, the virtual models is embedded into physical environment by using augmented reality. It provides an immersive visual and interactive experience, realizes the bidirectional enhancement between the physical and virtual space. However, augmented reality visu-alization and interaction is established on the basis of tracking and registration based on markers. This system without markers will stop working in complex outdoor environ-ment. Woensel et al. [4] proposed a new method which describes the context data and the relationships between each other by adopting semantic network technology in 2008. The context-aware framework constructed by employing their new method improves the efficiency of pushing personalized services. However, visualization of augmented reality required by application layer still is luck of in-depth research in this paper.

Coppola et al. [5] redefined the composition of context-aware browser in 2010. The search engine, Webpage content and automatically download module are integrated into the MoBe system they proposed. MoBe can provide detailed retrieval for web content according to the changes in the surrounding environment, however the user interface is still relatively drab, only images and text are used to organize the user interface, user's interactive experience still stay in two-dimensional space.

The mobile augmented reality browser and its optimization design proposed by this dissertation has two contributions. A contribution is that the classification accuracy of the system constructed by using the proposed scene classification method is improved, furthermore it deepen user's cognition of the operation object in an interactive environment. Another contribution is that AR/VR hybrid interactive mode based on Mental Model broadens the interactive space using AR technology. Not only can the consumer access virtual information in real world, they also can enter a fully virtualized environment for more information.

2   System Framework

Due to the hardware limitations of current mobile phone, such processing as image recognition which requires real-time and high-speed computing must be processed on PC side. The data exchange between mobile devices and Augmented Reality server is performed via a wireless network. In order to compensate the limited data processing ability of mobile devices, distributed architecture is applied in the proposed mobile Augmented Reality browser system. Different computing tasks are respectively performed in client and server. Both offline scene learning and online recognition are processed on the back-end cloud AR servers. Besides target tracking, user positioning and annotation rendering are also carried on the Mobile phone. With the exchange and processing of data across two side, AR/VR hybrid human-computer interaction experience can be provided to the customers on the mobile phone platform. First the camera is launched to capture image sequences of real world and feature points are extracted from the captured images. Then the data of feature points and user's position are sent to cloud server through wireless network. The target information is quickly recognized in cloud server and sent to mobile phone after the sample training is completed. Finally the virtual items are rendered around the real objects for augmented display. With the help of the attitude data from compass sensor, mobile client can achieve precise tracking, which means that the virtual tags always move with the real objects. Figure 2 shows the frameworks of MARB system.

2.1   Large Scale Scene Recognition

The application of Augmented Reality technology in mobile devices means that the mobile devices should have real-time image acquisition, 3D scene display and orientation tracking. Higher requirements for the calculation of equipment capacity and speed is made. Automatic target recognition which has the largest amount of calculation is processed by high-performance computing server.

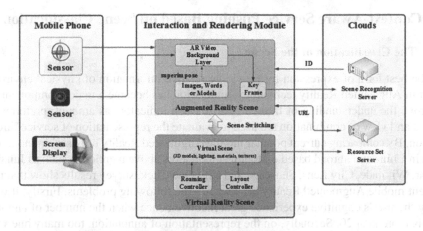

Fig. 2. Framework of MARB system

There are two stages for the large scale scene recognition by Mobile Augmented Reality Browser (MARB) proposed in this paper. Rough positioning of the point of interest (POI) is first achieved through the location data collected by GPS, then the sensing data and information of the target are transmitted to the cloud after the feature information is captured by a mobile phone camera. Finally, using the visual information retrieval method carries on building accurate recognition by the server.

Speeded up robust features [6] (SURF) has been widely used in image recognition and description. In order to achieve the accurate identification of large scale outdoor scene, local features (SURF key points) is adopted as the feature of object description [7] by MARB. The image information of the object is mapped into a set of keywords by using statistical analysis algorithm based on dictionary [8] proposed by Nister in 2006. By comparing the set of keywords constructed by training sample and set of keywords for image querying in online stage, the image that is the most close to the training sample is chosen as the final recognition result.

2.2 Tracking and Registration

The MARB system uses Keyframe-based real-time camera tracking [9]. In order to realize parallel tracking and matching for natural feature [10], parallel registration strategy based on double thread was firstly adopted in the system design. Then KLT (Kanade-Lucas-Tomasi) algorithm [11] is employed to tracking and registration in one thread and BRISK feature matching algorithm is used for wide baseline correction and the corresponding relations between 2D and 3D in another thread in another thread. Finally, by fusing the matching information based on the model and information of front and rear frame, the Objective optimization function is constructed. Finally, the iterative optimization algorithm is utilized to improve the tracking accuracy of the positioning.

3   Context-Aware Service Pushing Based on Scene Classification

3.1   The Classification of the Scene

As the best form of expression for providing relative information of physical environment in Augmented Reality technology, annotation has become a major component to improve the understanding of the real world. Such indicators as amount, preference, layout and view of combination are used to evaluate the representation of service information. By comparing current popular mobile Augmented Reality browser's annotation both in China and abroad based on four test indicators above mentioned such as Junaio, Layar, Wikitude, City Lens, Senscape and City One Click, survey results show that the current mobile Augmented Reality browser has the following problems. Firstly, it will bring the user's cognitive experience great inconvenience when the number of annotation is more than 20. Secondly, on the representation of annotation, too many hue will increase the cost of user's perception to the POI and reduce the efficiency of target retrieval. Thirdly, there are still such unsolved difficulties with the marker less recognition based on computer vision in the outdoor environment as lighting change, occlusion and transmission efficiency.

In order to solve the above-mentioned problems, this paper proposed a new concept of scene. The user must perform multiple steps of the task to achieve a goal. The environment (context) will change during the time of performing such steps of task. Multiple sets of tasks to be achieved by user in a context is defined as a scene. User will experience the process of performing multiple sets of tasks when planning to achieve a goal. Therefore, the system can provide services to assist the user to complete different tasks based on the perception and reasoning to the current context. Grouping tasks by using scene can not only easy to push perceived service for the user by the system, but also deepen the cognition of the operation object in an interactive environment. Take real estate information query as an example, a number of tasks are divided into three scenario of POI's positioning and selection, path finding navigation and POI's recognition and browsing in this paper.

3.2   The Structure of the Module and Context-Aware Services

(1) POI's Positioning and Selection Scenario. The structure of the module in POI's positioning and selection scenario is shown in Fig. 3. There are location and tracking module, the image capture module, context adapter and rendering module in the mobile client. Location service database and context reasoning in context service layer are distributed in cloud.

User firstly enters the POI's positioning and selection scenario after MARB is launched. User's goal is to identify and select the POI in this scenario. Therefore the first task to Figure out their location. Then, built on location search center, all POI are scanned within the specified radius. Finally, user should make the selection decision after the profile information of POI is checked through. In this scenario, according to the tasks the user needs to perform, MARB provide context-aware

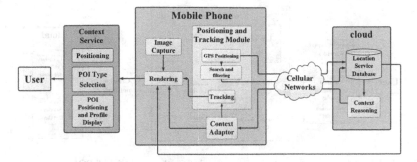

Fig. 3. Module structure and context-aware service in the scenario of POI's positioning and selection

    services such as user positioning, POI type selection and POI positioning and profile display.

(2) Path Finding Navigation Scenario. The structure of the module in the path finding navigation scenario is shown in Fig. 4. There is context adapter, map calls, navigation mode selection, path generation and rendering in mobile client. Location service database and context reasoning is distributed in cloud.

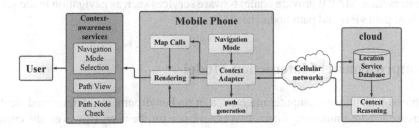

Fig. 4. Module structure and context-aware service in the scenario of path finding navigation

    The navigation request is sent after the label of POI is selected in the first scenario, then MARB change into the path finding navigation scenario. By drawing a shortest path from the current position to the appointed place on a flat map, path navigation service is provided by MARB for users. In order to taking convenience for users to get the information of arriving at destination location by using different modes of transport, there are not only many navigation mode such as walking, by bus, by car, etc. available to select, but also draw a path for every navigation mode in this scenario. User can check node information such as bus stations, subway station or intersections, etc. through the path.

(3) POI's Recognition and Browsing Scenario. The structure of the module in POI's recognition and browsing scenario is shown in Fig. 5. There is image capture, listener, context reasoning, context adapter and rendering module in the mobile client. Location service database and resource services database is distributed in cloud.

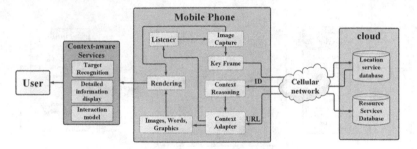

Fig. 5. Module structure and context-aware service in the scenario of POI's recognition and browsing

The user is firstly find a building wanted to know after reaching the real estate scene of POI. Then look at building details and deepen understanding through the interaction with the 3D model. Details of building such as building structure, type area, sales price and property information, etc. is present in two-dimensional images or text labels. In order to bring a more intuitive browsing experience, user can rotate or scaling a three-dimensional model of the building by touch control during the interaction. MARB provide context-aware services such as navigation mode selection, path view and path node check.

4   Improvement of Interaction Model

Compared with human-computer interaction in real environments, Augmented Reality can create a more immersing interactive experience for the user. However, the current interactive mode of Augmented Reality browsers only improves interactive experience in the horizontal dimension of user perception. It still lacks a novel interactive mode to guide the user obtain an in-depth understanding to POI from vertical aspect. Therefore, being aimed at the goal of improving interactive mode, this paper proposed an Augmented Reality and Virtual Reality (AR-VR) hybrid interactive mode based on the theory of mental mode. This type of interactive mode based on user's requirement has both types of Augmented Reality and Virtual Reality technology features.

In the outdoor part of the proposed system, augmented information which usually is concerned about is actively pushed to customer when preview housing such as the sales prices, residential area, surrounding environment, traffic conditions, and way of contact. The customers always have the demand of taking a closer look of inside structure of housing when some set of apartments is chosen. Clicking on the corresponding housing units preview image, interactive space can be smoothly switched to the VR environment. In pure virtual space, the user can not only roam in the house, but also replace the furniture or adjust the layout of items according to their own wishes. Touching AR button at the lower right corner, it can be returned again from VR indoor space back to outdoor AR scene. It is shown in Fig. 6.

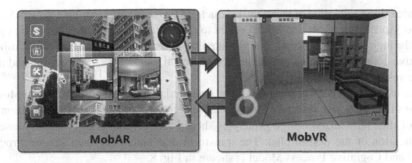

Fig. 6. AR and VR scene switch

Mental Model concept was first proposed by the Scottish psychologist Kenneth Craik in 1943, Johnson-Laird and others [12] give a clearer representation of this conception in the book <Mental Model>, He thinks Mental Model is the structural analogy in physical world, it generated after the information is offered and filtered by perception (visual, auditory, tactile, olfactory). Young suggested that Mental Models consist of several components, each part is divided into several groups, and the entire model can be described by series of affinity diagram of behavior [13].

Take the example of AR-VR hybrid mobile browsing system, the affinity diagram of behaviors is shown in Fig. 7. Such parts as check structure preview image and switch to indoor separated by the longitudinal axis above the horizontal axis are called mental space. Each mental space is cut into several parts. Below horizontal axis, interaction module is corresponding to each mental module. By contrast, weak point can be found from the interactive function. By interactive operation of click on image, AR space in the right side can be switched into VR environment from left side.

The Metal Model can be classified as two types of models. One type is Macro Mental Model. Its recognition must satisfy the user's original psychological needs of the product

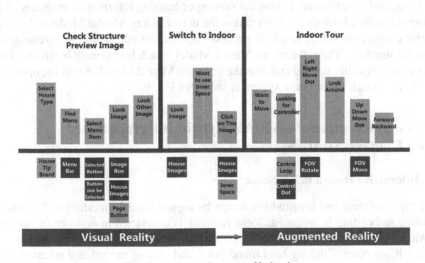

Fig. 7. Affinity diagram of behaviors

or service during the time of using the product or service by user. Another type is Micro Mental Model. Micro Mental Model refers to the Mental Model when a specific operation through the whole system is completed by user. After iterative usability testing, cognitive conflict point between the aspects of visual, interactive, copywriting and user can be solved.

The user experience interface should be designed to match the user's Mental Model. It means the interactive interface must correspond to user's habits and life cognition. In view of this, humanized design principles should reflects the ease of use and ease of identification of the design plan. The transform and match between Design Process Model and Cognitive Process Model is shown in Fig. 8.

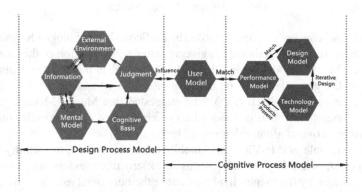

Fig. 8. Structural model of the user cognitive processes and product design

Macro Mental Model is a description of user's needs and demand structure. The purpose is to help designers to construct the experience process from the overall perspective. Micro Mental Model describe the interactive process between the user and interface just from the operation level. It can validate whether this interface is available, easy to use and easy to learn. During the process of housing information exchange, AR-VR hybrid mobile browsing system makes the use of macro Mental Model to build up the entire structure which interface process required based on user's psychological cognitive structure. Then, the macro Mental Model which has already horizontal built is taken into a specific vertical task to make up micro Mental Model. A specific operation workflow of a task in the entire system is shown in Fig. 9.

5 Design Example of a VR/AR Hybrid Interface Based on Context-Aware Service

5.1 Interactive Design in VR Scene

After the transverse and longitudinal design by mental model, interface of VR Indoor browsing and editing is produced. Scene roaming is conducted in first-person perspective view. As shown in Fig. 10, the direction controller is placed on the lower left side of the VR interface. Clicking-hold round point and sliding toward any orientation by

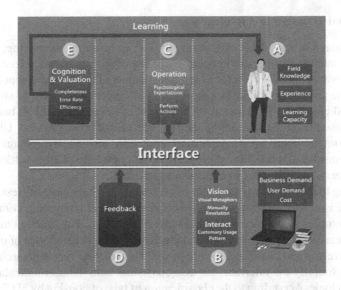

Fig. 9. Single-tasking operating process of micro mental model

Fig. 10. Indoor selecting and editing effects

touch input, user can move in relative direction in virtual space according to the controller. Two buttons are placed on upper left side of interface. The left button is item selecting, while item editing button at the right. Items in this circumstance are highly customizable. It means that objects can be replaced and rearranged to satisfy the needs of users. After the item is selected, clicking on item editing button, user can operate commands such as move, rotation or scaling which is appear in the pop-up menu. Only requires simple touches, by the editing operation to the objects, user can have immersive experience using different decoration scheme. A richer interactive experience for mobile housing preview is realized in this way. Scene can be switched back to AR scene when clicking on the AR button on the lower right corner of the VR interface.

5.2   Interactive Design in AR Scene

For the UI design in AR scene, considering the use environment is moving, limited to the space of interactive operation is narrow caused of mobile phone screen size, user cannot keep watching the screen for a long time compared to desktop computer screen. Therefore, the principles of interface design should reflect the concept of simple, easy to understand efficiency and clear at the first sight. UI design should be based on the following principles. First, due to the interference of video background, UI elements should be simple, intuitive, metaphorical and easy to identify. Second, gesture commands must be supported for slide, scale or other gestures. Last, switching design between scenes should be easy to understand and operate.

According to the preliminary analysis of user needs and later usability testing, visual design of UI is consist of icon, menu, description box and navigation compass. The navigation compass provides users with a sense of direction. The function menu offers information classified by different option item. There are two categories of description box, respectively is text boxes and picture boxes. This "drawer type" hierarchical menu can not only simplify the interface, but also consistent with the user's mental mode in the operation logic. According to the classification of type of housing by 3D Tips Board, there are different menu items corresponding to different types of housing. It simplifies the user's operation process and avoids interactive barriers caused by the confusion of concepts. Visual metaphors are used by two kind of next page button to guild the user to query for more hidden information. User interface design is shown in Fig. 11.

5.3   Transformation Between Virtual Reality Space
and Augmented Reality Space

By calling the checkpoints script of Unity engine, MARB system can switch scenes between Virtual Reality and Augmented Reality. Every scene obtains an identity number of corresponding checkpoints after the Virtual Reality and Augmented Reality scene

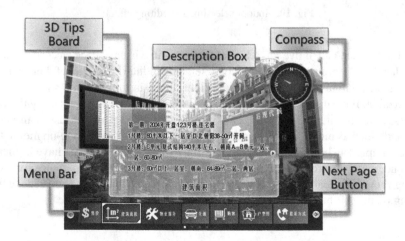

Fig. 11. Indoor selecting and editing effects

files which have been completely designed are added into "building settings". Scene switching command "Application.LoadLevel(index)" is triggered by button events "GUI.Button" in a script when users are required to switch scenes. Index parameters in this command corresponding to the previous identity number of checkpoints in "building settings". In accordance with the above steps, scene switch can be made.

6 Evaluation Experiment and Conclusion

By randomly selecting 30 participants, the preliminary evaluation of AR interface as shown in Fig. 11 is conducted. The evaluation team consists of 18 males aged 20–30 and 12 females aged 22–31. Two male participants have been involved in the testing of Augmented Reality application. Questionnaire survey is designed to measure four aspects which are most important in human-computer interaction design: Aesthetic, Navigation, Recognition and Efficiency. Aesthetic is the measuring element of slinky of UI. Rationalization of interact can be inspected through Navigation aspect. Recognition is an important indicator of the visual design. Efficiency factor show the logic of interaction design.

The results of evaluation experiment are shown in Fig. 12 by radar chart, aesthetic is the measuring element of slinky of UI. Rationalization of interact can be inspected through Navigation aspect. Recognition is an important indicator of the visual design. Efficiency factor show the logic of interaction design. Predilection is the comprehensive evaluation of the scheme. According to the statistical report of feedback from evaluators, three kinds of software are basically the same in aesthetic and recognition aspects. It means that user is able to correctly identify the operating indicator during operating period. The aesthetic design of the interface can be separated from the complex video background. In navigation aspect, MARB and Layar are both better than Wikitude. Due to the hierarchical menu design, the former is lightly better than the latter. This is attributed to the iterative design based on micro Mental Model. Affected by the navigation factors, MARB and Layar have better efficiency than Wikitude. During the period of single task, the average response time for button interaction is less than 0.3 s.

Taking the logic order of operation for retrieving and browsing POI, numerous operating behaviors are divided into three scenarios which include "POI's positioning and selection", "Path finding navigation" and "POI's recognition and browsing". The system module of MARB providing context-aware services is built in each scene based on context-aware services framework. The efficiency of pushing Augmented Reality services is improved for each module in the scene. In addition, Virtual Reality and Augmented Reality hybrid interaction mode widen the interactive way for human-computer interaction, increase the user acceptance of browser and significantly improve human-computer interactive experience.

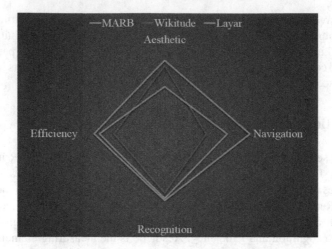

Fig. 12. Radar chart of evaluation experiment

References

1. Grubert, J., Langlotz, T., Grasset, R.: Augmented reality browser survey, Institute for Computer Graphics and Vision, University of Technology Graz, Technical report, 1101, pp. 1–11 (2011)
2. May, P.: Limesurvey. www.limesurvey.org
3. Lee, J.Y., Seo, D.W., Rhee, G.: Visualization and interaction of pervasive services using context-aware augmented reality. Expert Syst. Appl. 35(4), 1873–1882 (2008)
4. Van Woensel, W., Casteleyn, S., De Troyer, O.: A framework for decentralized, context-aware mobile applications using semantic web technology. In: Meersman, R., Herrero, P., Dillon, T. (eds.) OTM 2009 Workshops. LNCS, vol. 5872, pp. 88–97. Springer, Heidelberg (2009)
5. Coppola, M., Della, M.V., Gaspero, D.L.: The context-aware browser. Intell. Syst. 25(1), 38–47 (2010)
6. Bay, H., Ess, A., Tuytelaars, T., Van Gool, L.: Speeded-up robust features (SURF). Comput. Vis. Image Underst. 110(3), 346–359 (2008)
7. Bay, H., Tuytelaars, T., Van Gool, L.: SURF: speeded up robust features. In: Leonardis, A., Bischof, H., Pinz, A. (eds.) ECCV 2006, Part I. LNCS, vol. 3951, pp. 404–417. Springer, Heidelberg (2006)
8. Nister, D., Stewenius, H.: Scalable recognition with a vocabulary tree, Scalable recognition with a vocabulary tree, pp. 2161–2168 (2006)
9. Dong, Z., Zhang, G., Jia, J., Bao, H.: Keyframe-based real-time camera tracking, pp. 1538–1545 (2009)
10. Yang, L., Chao, S., Mingmin, Z., Wenjie, Z., Zhigeng, P.: Parallel tracking and matching for natural feature based AR registration. J. Image Graph. 16(4), 680–685 (2011)
11. Birchfield, S.: Derivation of Kanade-Lucas-Tomasi Tracking Equation, Department of Electrical and Computer Engineering, Clemson University (1997)

12. Johnson-Laird, P.N.: Mental Models: Towards a Cognitive Science of Language, Inference, and Consciousness. Harvard University Press, Cambridge (1983)
13. Young, I.: Mental Models: Aligning Design Strategy with Human Behavior. Rosenfeld Media, Brooklyn (2008)

Contour-Based Plant Leaf Image Segmentation Using Visual Saliency

Zhou Qiangqiang[1,2], Wang Zhicheng[1(✉)], Zhao Weidong[1],
and Chen Yufei[1]

[1] College of Electronics and Information, Tongji University, Shanghai, China
2012zqq@tongji.edu.cn
[2] College of Computer and Information, Jiangxi Agriculture University,
Nanchang, China

Abstract. Segmentation based on active contour has been received widespread concerns recently for its good flexible performance. However, most available active contour models lack adaptive initial contour and priori information of target region. In this paper, we presented a new method that is based on active contours combined with saliency map for plant leaf segmentation. Firstly, priori shape information of target objects in input leaf image which is used to describe the initial curve adaptively is extracted with the visual saliency detection method in order to reduce the influence of initial contour position. Furthermore, the proposed active model can segment images adaptively and automatically. Experiments on two applications demonstrate that the proposed model can achieve a better segmentation result.

Keywords: Active contour model · Image segmentation · Saliency detection · Plant leaf

1 Introduction

Currently, precision agriculture has become one of the frontier researches in the field of agriculture. Promote the use of precision agriculture could make use of resources reasonably, increasing crop yields, cut production costs and improve agricultural competitiveness. But the most relevant studies are based on the basic data of crop growth, which related with the shape features computation of plant leaf.

In agriculture, numerous image-processing based computerized tools have been developed to help farmers to monitor the proper growth of their crops. Special attention has been put towards the latest stages when crop is near harvesting. For example, at the time of harvesting, some computer tools are used to discriminate between plants and other objects present in the field. In the case of machines that uproot weeds, they have to discriminate between plants and weeds, whilst in the case of machines that harvest; they have to differentiate one crop from the other.

Previous studies have identified the challenges and have successfully produced systems that address them. The requirements for reduced production costs, the needs of

© Springer International Publishing Switzerland 2015
Y.-J. Zhang (Ed.): ICIG 2015, Part II, LNCS 9218, pp. 48–59, 2015.
DOI: 10.1007/978-3-319-21963-9_5

organic agriculture and the proliferation of diseases have been the driving forces for improving the quality and quantity of food production. In fact, the main source of plant diseases comes from leaves, such as leaf spot, rice blast, leaf blight, etc. When plants become diseased, they can display a range of symptoms such as colored spots, or streaks that can occur on the leaves, stems, and seeds of the plant. These visual symptoms continuously change their color, shape and size as the disease progresses.

Thus, in the area of disease control, most researches have been focused on the treatment and control of weeds, but few studies focused on the automatic identification of diseases. Automatic plant disease identification by visual inspection can be of great benefit to those users who have little or no information about the crop they are growing. Such users include farmers, in underdeveloped countries, who cannot afford the services of an expert agronomist, and also those living in remotes areas where access to assistance via an internet connection can become a significant factor.

During the past few decades,there has been substantial progress in the field of image segmentation and its application, that's a prerequisite for computer vision and field management automation. Camargo [1] study an image-processing based algorithm to automatically identify plant disease visual symptoms, the processing algorithm developed starts by converting the RGB image of the diseased plant or leaf, into the H, I3a and I3b color transformations, then segmented by analyzing the distribution of intensities in a histogram. Minervini [2] proposed an image-based plant phenotyping with incremental learning and active contours for accurate plant segmentation. This method is a vector valued level set formulation that incorporates features of color intensity, local texture, and prior knowledge. Sonal [3] presented a classification algorithm of cotton leaf spot disease using support vector machine. Prasad [4] explores a new dimension of pattern recognition to detect crop diseases based on Gabor Wavelet Transform. But there are many difficulties during leaf image process such as complex color components, irregular texture distribution, light shadow, and other random noises, even with some of complex and heterogeneity background, so leaf segmentation is still a nut for image analysis.

Recently, segmentation algorithms based on active contours has been received widespread concerns by many researchers due to their variable forms, flexible structure and excellent performance. However, most available active contour models suffer from lacking adaptive initial contour and priori information of target region. In this paper, we presented a new object segmentation method that is based on active contours with combined saliency map. Firstly, priori shape information of target objects in input images which is used to describe the initial curve adaptively is extracted with the visual saliency detection method in order to reduce the influence of initial contour position. Furthermore, the proposed active model can segment images adaptively and automatically, and the segmented results accord with the property of human visual perception. Experimental results demonstrate that the proposed model can achieve better segmentation results than some traditional active contour models. Meanwhile our model requires less iteration and with better computation efficiency than traditional active contours methods although the background of the image is clutter.

2 Saliency Detect Model

When it comes to the concept of saliency, another term visual attention is often referred. While the terms attention, saliency are often used interchangeably, each has a more subtle definition that allows their delineation. Attention is a general concept covering all factors that influence selection mechanisms, whether they are scene-driven bottom-up or expectation-driven top-down. Saliency intuitively characterizes some parts of a scene-which could be objects or regions-that appear to an observer to stand out relative to their neighboring parts. The term "salient" is often considered in the context of bottom-up computations [5]. Modeling visual attention—particularly stimulus-driven, saliency-based attention—has been a very active research area over the past 25 years. Many different models of attention are now available, which aside from lending theoretical contributions to other fields, have demonstrated successful applications in computer vision, mobile robotics, and cognitive systems.

Our saliency detect algorithm consists of three parts (Fig. 1):

Firstly, color-complexity features extraction. Decomposes a given image into a color histogram after quantizing each color channel to have 12 different values to speed up our algorithm, which once proposed by Cheng et al. [6]. And then compute color contrast differences between colors over a global image to construct a saliency map.

Secondly, color-spatial features extraction. In order to establish the color distributions of pixels in an image, k-means is exploited to find k centers of masses for each color. And a relative minimum method was proposed to calculate spatial distances between different colors to obtain the spatial weightings. Then saliency map was adjusted by spatial weightings.

Lastly, a smoothing procedure (see also [6]) is used to reduce the noise disturbance due to quantization.

Overall, our method integrated the contrast map with colors spatial distribution to derive a saliency measure that produces a pixel-accurate saliency map which uniformly covers the region of interest and consistently separates foreground and background. Specifically details can refer to our paper in [7].

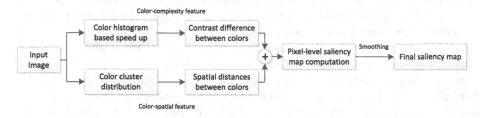

Fig. 1. Saliency detect algorithm

2.1 Color-Complexity Feature

A saliency value of a pixel is definition by its differences with all other pixels in image. Formula (1) is the pixel I_i saliency value in an image I,

$$S(I_i) = \sum_{\forall I_j \in I} CD(I_i, I_j) \tag{1}$$

where $CD(I_i, I_j)$ is the color distance metric between pixels I_i and I_j in the $L*a*b*$ color space [6, 8]. The following formula (2) is obtained by expanding this equation,

$$S(I_i) = CD(I_i, I_1) + CD(I_i, I_2) + \ldots + CD(I_i, I_N) \tag{2}$$

where N is the number of pixels in image I. Its means that pixel with the same color value would be have a same saliency value according to (2). Thus (2) need further restructured, such that the terms with the same color c_q are rearranged to be together,

$$S(I_i) = S(c_p) = CD(c_p - c_1) + CD(c_p - c_2) + \ldots + CD(c_p - c_n)$$
$$S(I_i) = S(c_p) = \sum_{q=1}^{n} f_q \cdot CD(c_p, c_q) \tag{3}$$

where c_p represents the color of pixel I_i, f_q is the occurrence frequency of color c_q in image I and n is the total number of colors Color category. The histogram was exploited to make a statistics of color distribution for its simple and rapid process.

The computational complexity of Eq. (3) is $O(N) + O(n^2)$, which means that reducing the number of colors n is a key for computation speed up. The color has 256^3 possible values, where the value of each color channel locates in the range of [0, 255]. Zhai and Shah [8] reduce the number of colors to $n^2 = 256^2$ only adopted luminance, because of its only employs two color channels, whereas the information of the third color channel was ignored. In this paper, full color space instead of luminance was used by dividing each color channel into 12 values for reduce the number of colors to $n^3 = 12^3$ rapidly, which once proposed by Cheng et al. [6] At the same time, considering that some colors just appears rarely and the resulting saliency map almost suffered from no affect if without them, so we can further reduce n by ignoring those colors that with less occurring frequencies. Thus by this means, the number of colors n was reduced greatly which made computation more efficiently.

2.2   Color-Spatial Feature

Performance comparison of HC and RC [6] implies that taking spatial information into account could improve the results substantially. To the same contrast difference extent, those surrounding regions have more contribution for a region saliency than those far-away regions. So naturally we integrate spatial weighting to increase the effects of closer regions and decrease the effects of farther regions.

According to the foregoing discussion, the number of colors n was reduced to a considerable small number around by choosing more frequently occurring colors and ensuring these colors cover the colors of more than 95 % of the image pixels, we typically are left with around $n = 85$ colors. Then calculate the spatial distance between colors after finding k mass centers exploiting k-means for each color. The initial value

k for k-means algorithm should be decided by taking both accuracy and efficiency of saliency computation into consideration.

Figure 2 shows details of how spatial distance computed between colors c_p and c_q. For illustrates convenience here $k = 3$. In Fig. 2, color c_p has three mass centers, represented by yellow points, from top to bottom in turn is $c_{p,1}$, $c_{p,2}$, $c_{p,3}$. Likewise, green points (i.e. $c_{q,1}$, $c_{q,2}$, $c_{q,3}$) are the mass centers of color c_q. We use set_p and set_q to represent the mass centers of colors c_p and c_q respectively for illustrate clearly. Then the algorithm of compute the **relative minimum distance** between these two sets as follow:

(1) For $c_{p,1}$ in set_p, find the closest point to it in set_q, in this example below is $c_{q,1}$. Then they form pairwise naturally.
(2) Accordingly, $c_{p,1}$ and $c_{q,1}$ are removed from its set respectively.
(3) Continually for the remaining points in set_p likes step 1 and 2, until set_p is empty.

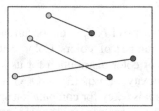

Fig. 2. Spatial distance compute (Color figure online)

The spatial distance of the two colors is defined in (4).

$$SD(c_p, c_q) = \frac{1}{k}\sum_{l=1}^{k}\sum_{r=1}^{k} min\|c_{p,l} - c_{q,r}\| \quad satisfy \text{ (2) in the algorithm above;} \quad (4)$$

where k is the number of cluster centers, $\|\,.\,\|$ represent the point distance metric. Then the saliency value for each color is defined as,

$$S(I_i) = S(c_p) = \sum_{q=1}^{n} f_q CD(c_p, c_q) SDW(c_p, c_q) \quad (5)$$

where c_p is the color of pixel I_i, n denotes the number of colors, $CD(c_p, c_q)$ is the color distance metric between c_p and c_q in L^*a^*b color space. And

$$SDW(c_p, c_q) = exp\{-SD(c_p, c_q)/2\sigma_s^2\} \quad (6)$$

is the spatial weighting between colors c_p and c_q, where σ_s controls the strength of spatial weighting.

Finally, a smoothing procedure will be taken to refine the saliency value for each color. The saliency value of each color is adjusted to the weighted average of the saliency values of similar colors,

$$S'(c) = \frac{1}{(m-1)M} \sum_{i=1}^{m} (M - CD(c,c_i))S(c_i) \tag{7}$$

where m is the number of nearest colors to c, and we choose $m = n/4$, $M = \sum_{i=1}^{m} CD(c,c_i)$ is the sum of distances between color c and its m nearest neighbors c_i.

3 Salient Region-Based Active Contour Model

While the above steps provide a collection of regions of saliency and an initial rough segmentation, the goal of this section is to obtain a highly accurate segmentation of each plant. Operating on a smaller portion of the image allows us to use more complex algorithms, which likely would not have been efficient and effective in the full image. The motivation for using an active contour method for object segmentation is its ability to model arbitrarily complex shapes and handle implicitly topological changes. Thus, the level set based segmentation method can be effectively used for extracting a foreground layer with fragmented appearance, such as leaves of the same plant.

Let $\Omega \subset \Re^2$ is the 2D image space, and $I: \Omega \to \Re$ be a given gray level image. In [9], Mumford and Shah formulated the image segmentation problem as follows: given an image I, finding a contour C which segments the image into non-overlapping regions. The energy functional was proposed as following:

$$F^{MS}(u,C) = \int_{\Omega} (u-I)^2 dx + \mu \int_{\Omega \setminus C} |\nabla u|^2 dx + v|C| \tag{8}$$

Where $|C|$ is the contour length, $\mu, v > 0$ are constants to balance the terms. The minimization of Mumford–Shah functional results in an optimal contour C that segments the given image I, u is an image to approximate the original image I, which is smooth within each region inside or outside the contour C. In practice, it is difficult to minimize the functional (8) due to the unknown contour C of lower dimension and the non-convexity of the functional.

To overcome the difficulties in solving Eq. (8), Chan and Vese [10] presented an active contour model to the Mumford–Shah problem for a special case where the image u in the functional (8) is a piecewise constant function. They proposed to minimize the following energy functional:

$$F^{CV}(C,c_1,c_2) = \lambda_1 \int_{outside(C)} |I(x) - c_1|^2 dx + \lambda_2 \int_{inside(C)} |I(x) - c_2|^2 dx + v|C| \tag{9}$$

Where outside (C) and inside (C) represent the regions outside and inside the contour C, respectively, and c_1 and c_2 are two constants that approximate the image intensity in outside (C) and inside (C).

But this Chan-Vese model does not suitable for our plant leaf processing, because the model has some difficulties for vector-valued color image with intensity inhomogeneity. Then Chan-Sandberg-Vese proposed a new algorithm in [11] for object detection in vector-valued images (such as RGB or multispectral). In this paper, since we want to take advantage of the existence of multiple image features (in the following we refer to them as channels) we build our salient region-based active contour model F^{SRAC} for vector valued images. Suppose we obtained an initial contour C that is a shape approximation of the object boundary through the saliency detection method mentioned above, and the image I divided into two parts-salient region Ω_S and non salient region Ω_{NS} by the contour C. Then add this prior shape knowledge into F^{SRAC}, and the overall energy functional for F^{SRAC} following the formulation in [11] is defined as:

$$F^{SRAC}(C, \vec{c}^+, \vec{m}^+, \vec{c}^-) = \int_{\Omega_S} \frac{1}{N} \sum_{i=1}^{N} \lambda_i^+ \theta_i^+(z) dz + \int_{\Omega_{NS}} \frac{2}{N} \sum_{i=1}^{N} \lambda_i^- \theta_i^-(z) dz$$
$$\theta_i^+(z) = |I_i - c_i^+|^2 + |I_i - m_i^+|^2$$
$$\theta_i^-(z) = |I_i - c_i^-|^2$$

$$(10)$$

where z denotes a pixel location in an image channel $I_i, i = 1 \ldots N, \lambda_i^+$ and λ_i^- define the weight of each term (inside and outside the contour), $\vec{c}^-$ is the vector valued representation of the mean for each channel outside the contour, and $\vec{c}^+$ and $\vec{m}^+$ are the vector valued representations of the mean and median respectively for each channel inside the contour. The way we estimate these statistical quantities will be described shortly.

Following standard level set formulations [11], we replace the contour curve C with the level set function ϕ [12]: $F^{SRAC}(\phi, \vec{c}^+, \vec{m}^+, \vec{c}^-)$.

The vectors $\vec{c}^+$, $\vec{m}^+$ and $\vec{c}^-$ are defined in similar fashion to other intensity driven active contour models as statistical averages and medians:

$$\begin{cases} \vec{c}^+(\phi) = average(I_i \in \phi(z) \geq 0), \\ \vec{m}^+(\phi) = median(I_i \in \phi(z) \geq 0), \\ \vec{c}^-(\phi) = average(I_i \in \phi(z) < 0), \end{cases}$$

$$(11)$$

for each channel I_i, $i = 1 \ldots N$, inside or outside the contour.

Using the level set function ϕ to represent the contour C in the image domain Ω, the energy functional can be written as follows:

$$F^{SRAC}(\phi, \overrightarrow{c}^+, \overrightarrow{m}^+, \overrightarrow{c}^-) = \int_{\Omega} \frac{1}{N} \sum_{i=1}^{N} \lambda_i^+ \theta_i^+(z) H(\phi(z)) dz$$

$$+ \int_{\Omega} \frac{2}{N} \sum_{i=1}^{N} \lambda_i^- \theta_i^-(z)(1 - H(\phi(z))) dz, \quad (12)$$

where H is the Heaviside function.

By keeping $\overrightarrow{c}^+$, $\overrightarrow{m}^+$ and $\overrightarrow{c}^-$ are fixed, we minimize the energy function $F^{SRAC}(\phi, \overrightarrow{c}^+, \overrightarrow{m}^+, \overrightarrow{c}^-)$ with respect to ϕ to obtain the gradient descent flow as:

$$\frac{\partial \phi}{\partial t} = \zeta^{SRAC} = \delta(\phi)[-\frac{1}{N} \sum_{i=1}^{N} \lambda_i^+ \theta_i^+(z) + \frac{2}{N} \sum_{i=1}^{N} \lambda_i^- \theta_i^-(z)] \quad (13)$$

where δ is the Dirac delta function.

4 Application and Experimental

4.1 Image-Based Plant Phenotyping Detect

Understanding biological function and the complex processes involved in the development of plants relies on understanding the interaction between genetic information and the environment, and how they affect the phenotype (the appearance or behavior) of the organism and consequently desirable traits. Model plant systems, such as Arabidopsis thaliana, have been used extensively for this purpose. However, as of today, inexpensive and automated phenotyping (phenomics) remains a bottleneck. Until recently most phenotypes (e.g., related to plant growth) were acquired in destructive ways (e.g., weigh the plant, or cut out and measure a leaf) or involved human survey (e.g., measuring leaf size or plant radius) in situ without destructing the plant. Naturally these methods are faced with low throughput and high productivity cost. Consequently, there has been a growing interest towards developing solutions for the automated analysis of visually observable traits of the plants [2].

In this section we propose a method adopt model mentioned above for the automated segmentation and analysis of plant images from phenotyping experiments of Arabidopsis rosettes. We use the image dataset in [13] which acquired in a general laboratory setting with a static camera that captures many plants at the same time for this plant segmentation test.

Prior Knowledge Map: From a computer vision perspective, a laboratory setup for plant phenotyping experiments presents several challenges such as neon light illumination, water reflection, shadows, and moss, contributing to noise and scene complexity. To eliminate issues of non uniform illumination (due to lighting distortion from neon lights and shadowing), when utilizing color information we convert the *RGB* color space to *ExG = 2G-R-B*, where *R, G, B* are the three components of *RGB* space, because the most colors of plant leaf in this test are green.

Map Fusion: After got the saliency map and the prior knowledge map, then we fusing them again through the following formula get the final map:

$$\text{Map}_f = 0.5 * \text{Map}_s + 0.5 * \text{Map}_p \tag{14}$$

where Map_f is fusing map, Map_s and Map_p denotes saliency map and prior map respectively, but Map_p must be tuned with same format as Map_s and normalized.

Finally, after the fusion map is generated by the formula (14), it is then binarized segmented by an adaptive threshold T_a proposed in [14], defined as twice the mean saliency of the Map_f image:

$$T_a = \frac{2}{W \times H} \sum_{x=1}^{W} \sum_{y=1}^{H} \text{Map}_f \tag{15}$$

where W and H are the width and the height of the saliency map respectively.

And the contour of the thresholded response forms the initial curve for the active contour model. The maximum number of iterations for contour evolution is set to 300, and we used $\lambda_i^+ = \lambda_i^- = 1$, for all i.

Post-processing: After the segmentation is performed based on the active contour model, small blobs containing foreground pixels are removed in a way similar to the procedure used in [15]. To be specific, all holes within each blob are filled by morphological operations and small blobs are removed based on the number of pixels in each filled blob. Empirically, a small blob is determined by the following criterion, that is, one smaller than the half of the largest blob: $0.5 \times max_{b \in B} |b|$ where b is an individual blob, B is the set of blobs and $|\cdot|$ the number of pixels in the blob.

To compare the segmentation performance between the "reference segmentation" marked by specialists in [13] and an outline from our model. We employed the following metrics:

$$Precision(\%) = \frac{TP}{TP + FP} \quad Recall(\%) = \frac{TP}{TP + FN} \quad Dice(\%) = \frac{2 \cdot TP}{2 \cdot TP + FP + FN}$$

where TP, FP, and FN represent the number of true positive, false positive, and false negative pixels, respectively, calculated by comparing algorithmic result and ground-truth segmentation masks. Precision is the fraction of pixels in the segmentation mask that matches the ground truth, whereas recall is the fraction of ground-truth pixels contained in the segmentation mask. The Dice similarity coefficients are used to measure the spatial overlap between algorithmic result and ground truth. All of these metrics are expressed in percentages, with larger values representing higher agreement between ground truth and algorithmic result.

This level of accuracy is observed across in [13] dataset. Table 1 reports averaged results of segmentation accuracy over the whole dataset. The Reference method is an approach based on K-means, due to its widespread adoption in plant segmentation which shows poor accuracy in terms of precision and Dice, and a very high recall value due to the constant over-segmentation (i.e., the plant is fully contained in the

Table 1. Accuracy comparison

System	Accuracy %		
	Precision	Recall	Dice
[11]	97.08	95.86	96.44
Reference	60.82	99.87	74.65
Ours	87.68	89.13	88.40

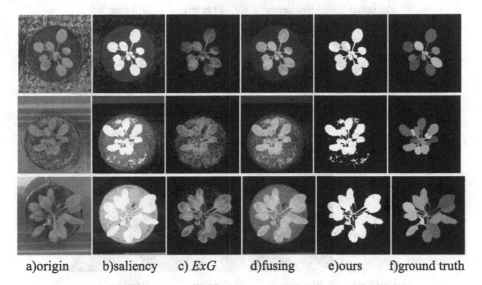

a)origin   b)saliency   c) *ExG*   d)fusing   e)ours   f)ground truth

Fig. 3. Image-based plant phenotyping detect (Color figure online)

segmentation mask, along with large portions of earth and moss from the background). The method in [2] appears the best in results for its balance in all influence factors. Our proposed system also achieves a good accuracy in this test as show in Table 1 and Fig. 3.

4.2   Diseased Plant Leaf Detect

This section describes an image processing based our method for identifies the visual symptoms of plant diseases, from an analysis of colored images. The plant diseases model is basically the same as the 4.1 above. Whereas the prior knowledge map in here is not the *ExG* but an *R*-channel in *RGB* map because the most color of plant diseases location is a deep color such as yellow-red. The adaptive threshold T_a defined as 1.5 times of the mean saliency Map$_f$ here. The test image dataset we used was referred to [1], which include 20 diseased leaves images. The experimental comparison illustrated as follow examples in Fig. 4 and Table 2 demonstrates that our model has a nearly good segmentation effect as [1], but we provided a novelty approach.

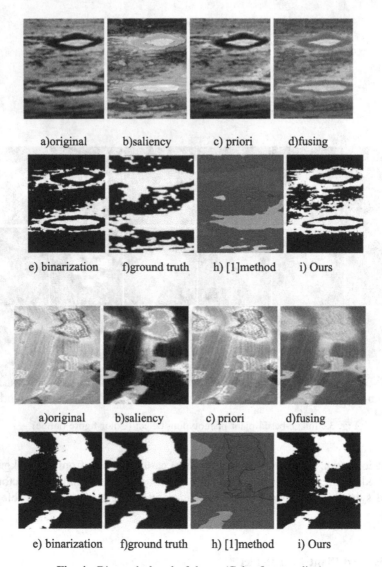

Fig. 4. Diseased plant leaf detect (Color figure online)

Table 2. Average matching and misclassified rate on 20 images

System	Matching %	Misclassified %
[1]	76.55	11.90
Ours	72.78	18.37

5 Conclusions

In this paper, we present a new plant leaf image segmentation method that is based on active contours combined with saliency map. It is known that saliency region detect can easily attain the approximate contour of the desirable object in image, and then set it as the initial position of evolution curve for active contour model to construct a new level set energy functional with a more faster evolution speed and more accurate object segmentation. Finally, experiments comparison on two applications demonstrates that our proposed model has a good effect on plant leaf image segmentation.

References

1. Camargo, A., Smith, J.S.: An image-processing based algorithm to automatically identify plant disease visual symptoms. Biosyst. Eng. **102**(1), 9–21 (2009)
2. Minervini, M., Abdelsamea, M.M., Tsaftaris, S.A.: Image-based plant phenotyping with incremental learning and active contours. Ecol. Inform. **23**, 35–48 (2014)
3. Patil, S.P.: Classification of cotton leaf spot disease using support vector machine. J. Eng. Res. Appl. **4**, 92–97 (2014)
4. Prasad, S., Kumar, P., Hazra, R., Kumar, A.: Plant leaf disease detection using Gabor wavelet transform. In: Panigrahi, B.K., Das, S., Suganthan, P.N., Nanda, P.K. (eds.) SEMCCO 2012. LNCS, vol. 7677, pp. 372–379. Springer, Heidelberg (2012)
5. Borji, A., Itti, L.: State-of-the-art in visual attention modeling. IEEE Trans. Pattern Anal. Mach. Intell. **35**(1), 185–207 (2013)
6. Cheng, M.M., Zhang, G.X., Mitra, N.J., Huang, X.L., Hu, S.M.: Global contrast based salient region detection. In: CVPR, pp. 409–416 (2011)
7. Wang, Z., Li, L., Chen, Y., et al.: Salient region detection based on color-complexity and color-spatial features. In: 2013 Fourth International Conference on Intelligent Control and Information Processing (ICICIP), pp. 699–704. IEEE (2013)
8. Zhai, Y., Shah, M.: Visual attention detection in video sequences using spatiotemporal cues. In: ACM Multimedia, pp. 815–824 (2006)
9. Mumford, D., Shah, J.: Optimal approximations by piecewise smooth functions and associated variational problems. Commun. Pure Appl. Math. **42**(5), 577–685 (1989)
10. Chan, T.F., Vese, L.A.: Active contours without edges. IEEE Trans. Image Process. **10**(2), 266–277 (2001)
11. Chan, T.F., Sandberg, B.Y., Vese, L.A.: Active contours without edges for vector-valued images. J. Vis. Commun. Image Represent. **11**(2), 130–141 (2000)
12. Zhao, H.K., Chan, T., Merriman, B., et al.: A variational level set approach to multiphase motion. J. Comput. Phys. **127**(1), 179–195 (1996)
13. http://www.plant-phenotyping.org/CVPPP2014-dataset
14. Achanta, R., Hemami, S., Estrada, F., Süsstrunk, S.: Frequency-tuned salient region detection. In: CVPR, pp. 1597–1604 (2009)
15. Koh, J., Kim, T., Chaudhary, V., Dhillon, G.: Segmentation of the spinal cord and the dural sac in lumbar mr images using gradient vector flow field. In: EMBC, pp. 3117–3120 (2010)

Cooperative Target Tracking in Dual-Camera System with Bidirectional Information Fusion

Jingjing Wang[✉] and Nenghai Yu

CAS Key Laboratory of Electromagnetic Space Information,
University of Science and Technology of China, Hefei, China
kkwang@mail.ustc.edu.cn, ynh@ustc.edu.cn

Abstract. The Dual-Camera system which consists of a static camera and a pan-tilt-zoom (PTZ) camera, plays an importance role in public area monitoring. The superiority of this system lies in that it can offer wide area coverage and highly detailed images of the interesting target simultaneously. Most existing works in Dual-Camera systems only consider simplistic scenarios, which are not robust in real situations, and no quantitative comparison between different tracking algorithms is provided. In this paper, we propose a cooperative target tracking algorithm with bidirectional information fusion which is robust even in moderately crowded scenes. Moreover, we propose a method to compare the algorithms quantitatively by generating a virtue PTZ camera. The experimental results on realistic simulations and the implementation on a real surveillance system validate the effectiveness of the proposed algorithm.

Keywords: Cooperative tracking · PTZ camera · Information fusion

1 Introduction

With rapidly growing demands of security in public area monitoring, multiple-camera surveillance system has become a hot subject in the field of computer vision. Among them, one popular example is the Dual-Camera system, which consists of a static camera and a PTZ camera. A static camera can cover a large public area. However, it cannot provide high resolution images of the interesting target which are useful for abnormal behaviour detection, gesture recognition, face identification, etc. This is where PTZ cameras compensate for the deficiencies of static cameras. A PTZ camera can pan and tilt to center the target in its view and zoom in to obtain desirable high-resolution images. The Dual-Camera system which combines these two types of cameras can monitor the large surveillance area and obtain close-up observation of the interesting target simultaneously. Figure 1 shows an example of images obtained from the static camera and the PTZ camera.

Dual-camera systems have been widely studied in surveillance [1–8]. References [2–5] use tracking results from the static camera to guide the movement of the PTZ camera. They use background subtraction algorithms to detect targets

© Springer International Publishing Switzerland 2015
Y.-J. Zhang (Ed.): ICIG 2015, Part II, LNCS 9218, pp. 60–74, 2015.
DOI: 10.1007/978-3-319-21963-9_6

Fig. 1. The left is the image obtained from the static camera, and heights of targets in the image are about 50 pixels. The right is the image obtained from the PTZ camera, and heights of tragets in the image are about 250 pixels.

and track targets by associating the detection responses with the corresponding targets. They pay more attention to the calibration between the static and PTZ cameras. However, it requires a level of pointing accuracy to keep a highly zoomed camera pointing at a moving target, that is not achievable from calibration alone [6]. Instead, [6–8] use control signals from the static camera only initially, to make the target within the view of the PTZ camera, and then perform real-time tracking in the PTZ camera to keep the camera centered on the target with desirable resolution. Considering the requirement of real time processing, most existing tracking systems which use PTZ cameras adopt simple and efficient algorithms to perform tracking in PTZ cameras. Reference [6] uses Mean-Shift algorithm [13] to track the target. References [7,8] use color-based particle filter algorithm to keep following the target. In [14], Mean-Shift tracker and KLT [15] tracker are combined for target tracking. Although these methods can guarantee real-time performance, they are not robust enough in practice. Mean-shift and color-based particle filter trackers may fail to differentiate between the interesting target and the background with similar color, by using color histogram. KLT tracker is not robust to background clutters and occlusion. Moreover, all these methods consider situations where only a few of targets appear without frequent occlusion. However, in real pubic surveillance areas, occlusion may frequently occur especially in crowded scenes. No information is fused between the cameras in these methods, which is very helpful for resolving occlusion.

In video tracking using PTZ cameras, comparing different methods directly is very difficult. It is not possible to work offline with recorded videos, since each frame in the PTZ camera depends on the pan, tilt and zoom parameters, and such parameters are differently set by the different tracking algorithms. To deal with this problem, [11] proposes an experimental framework which allows to compare different algorithms in repeatable scenarios. The key idea consists in projecting a video containing the target on a screen in front of the camera. However, it is difficult to use this framework in a cooperative tracking setting, since this framework cannot generate different image sequences for different cameras which have different view points. In [16], a synthetic camera network is placed in a virtual scene which is created through computer graphics. However, modelling realistic human behavior within a virtual environment is difficult. It is still different from real situations.

To overcome the drawbacks of previous methods, we propose a cooperative target tracking algorithm with bidirectional information fusion. Specifically, an efficient multi-target tracking algorithm is introduced for online tracking in the static camera, a robust single-target tracking algorithm is proposed in the PTZ camera and a bidirectional information fusion strategy is proposed to enhance the algorithm. The single-target tracking algorithm combines a state-of-the-art category detector and an online trained classifier. The category detector is offline trained and robust against the challenges in PTZ cameras, such as background clutters, abrupt motion and motion blur. The online trained classifier can differentiate the interesting target from the other detected targets and adapt to the appearance changes of the interesting target through online updating. The bidirectional information fusion method makes the algorithm robust even in moderately crowded scenes with frequent interactions and occlusions. Moreover, unlike the existing works in Dual-Camera systems which provide no quantitative comparison of different tracking algorithms, we propose a method to quantitatively compare different algorithms by generating a virtue PTZ camera. The experimental results on realistic simulations and the implementation on a real surveillance system show the effectiveness of our proposed algorithm.

2   System Overview

In our Dual-Camera system, the static camera detects and tracks multiple targets in a wide scene. When an interesting target is detected by an anomaly detection algorithm or specified by the user, the PTZ camera is directed to gaze at the target according to camera-to-camera calibration. Then a cooperative tracking algorithm is used to track the target. The camera control module adjusts parameters of the PTZ camera according to the tracking results in the PTZ camera to follow the target at high resolution. The purpose of the Dual-Camera system is to continuously keep the interesting target in the PTZ camera view to obtain high resolution images of the target.

The rest of the paper is organized as follows. The camera calibration and control strategy are introduced in Sect. 3. Section 4 describes the proposed cooperate tracking algorithm. Section 5 presents the experimental results. Section 6 summarises this paper.

3   Camera Calibration and Control

In this paper, we focus on the cooperative tracking algorithm, but camera calibration and camera control strategy are indispensable parts. So we first briefly introduce the camera calibration and control strategy. We denote the parameters of the PTZ camera at time t as (P_a^t, T_a^t, Z_a^t), where P_a^t and T_a^t represent the pan-tilt angles, and Z_a^t means the optical zoom of the PTZ camera. (P_a^t, T_a^t, Z_a^t) can be read from the interface of the PTZ camera, or estimated using the method proposed by [18]. In order to perform cooperative tracking, calibration between the static camera and the PTZ camera is needed. We use the method proposed by [5] to calibrate the two cameras for its simpleness. In [5], ground plane homography is exploited to realise camera collaboration, assuming that the two cameras share a common ground plane which is reasonable in typical surveillance scenes. The ground plane homography H_{gd} between the static camera and the PTZ camera at parameter (P_a^0, T_a^0, Z_a^0) is estimated offline using people correspondence. In online stage, the bottom center of the bounding box which contains the tracked target in the static camera image is mapped to the corresponding point in the image plane of the PTZ camera at parameter (P_a^0, T_a^0, Z_a^0). The pan and tilt angles which are needed to bring the interesting target to the center of the PTZ camera image can be computed. Please refer to [5] for more details. Once the same target is found in the PTZ camera, the cooperative tracking module is activated to track the target. During tracking, the projective transformation $H_{s \to a}^t$ which maps the bottom center of the target in the static camera image to the position in the PTZ camera image at frame t is computed as:

$$H_{s \to a}^t = K^t R^t (R^0)^{-1} (K^0)^{-1} H_{gd} \tag{1}$$

where R^t is the rotation matrix corresponding to the pan and tilt angles (P_a^t, T_a^t) at frame t, and K^t is the intrinsic matrix corresponding to the zoom Z_a^t. The intrinsic matrix K^t is estimated using the method proposed by [17]. For the camera control strategy during tracking, the current and previous distances between the position of the target and the center of the PTZ camera image are used to deal with the camera speed. If the distance becomes larger, we give a higher speed, and vice versa. This strategy can give a smoother tracking than absolute positioning.

4   Proposed Cooperative Tracking Algorithm

The overview of the proposed cooperative tracking algorithm is shown in Fig. 2. It consists of multi-target tracking in the static camera, single-target tracking in the PTZ camera, and information fusing through transferred positions from the previous tracking result. Details are described in subsections.

4.1   Multi-target Tracking in Static Camera

The multi-target tracking algorithm in the static camera follows the tracking-by-association framework [21]. At each frame, pairwise association is performed to associate detection responses with tracklets. In Dual-Camera systems, most existing methods use background subtraction algorithms to detect objects. However, they can only detect moving objects and it is difficult to model the background in PTZ cameras. Hence, we use a fast state-of-the-art object detector [19] to detect objects. For each tracklet, a Kalman Filter is applied to refine the positions and sizes of its detection responses and estimate its velocity. The affinity measure $A_{i,j}$ to determine how well a detection D_i and a tracklet T_j are matched is defined as:

$$A_{i,j} = A_{appr}(D_i|T_j) A_{pos}(D_i|T_j) A_{pos}(D_i|T_j) \tag{2}$$

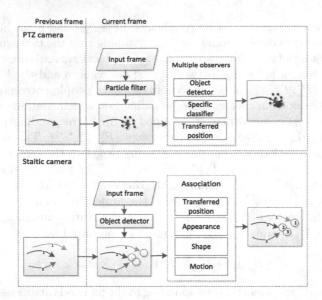

Fig. 2. The overview of the proposed cooperative target tracking algorithm.

The affinity is the product of affinities of appearance, shape and motion models, which are computed as follows:

$$
\begin{aligned}
A_{appr}(D_i|T_j) &= \textstyle\sum_{u=1}^m \sqrt{h_u(D_i)h_u(T_j)} \\
A_{size}(D_i|T_j) &= \exp\left(-\left\{\left|\frac{h_{D_i}-h_{T_j}}{h_{D_i}+h_{T_j}}\right| + \left|\frac{w_{D_i}-w_{T_j}}{w_{D_i}+w_{T_j}}\right|\right\}\right) \\
A_{pos}(D_i|T_j) &= \mathcal{N}(P_{T_j} + v_{T_j}\Delta t; P_{D_i}, \Sigma_s)
\end{aligned}
\tag{3}
$$

Color histograms of the detection responses of T_j are computed and averaged as the appearance model of T_j. The appearance affinity $A_{appr}(D_i|T_j)$ is the Bhattacharyya coefficient between the color histogram $h_u(D_i)$ of D_i and $h_u(T_j)$ of T_j. The bin number of the histogram is m. The shape affinity $A_{size}(D_i|T_j)$ is computed with the height h and width w of targets. $A_{pos}(D_i|T_j)$ is the motion affinity between P_{T_j} the last refined position of T_j and the position P_{D_i} of D_i with the frame gap Δt and velocity v_{T_j}. v_{T_j} is estimated by the Kalman Filter. The difference between the predicted position and the observed position is assumed to follow a Gaussian distribution $\mathcal{N}$.

Once the affinity matrix is computed, the optimal association pairs, which maximize the global association affinity in A, are determined using the Hungarian algorithm [20]. Detection responses which are not associated with any tracklet are used to generate new tracklets. To avoid false alarms, new tracklets are generated from detection responses with overlap bigger than 90 % in five consecutive frames.

4.2   Single-Target Tracking in PTZ Camera

For single-target tracking in the PTZ camera, we propose a robust algorithm within the particle filter framework. The particle filter approach is popularly used for visual tracking. It can approximate multi-modal probability density function, so it is suitable for tracking in clutter [9]. Let Z_t and Y_t denote the latent state and observation, respectively, at time t. A particle filter approximates the true posterior state distribution $p(Z_t|Y_{1:t})$ by a set of samples $\{Z_t^i\}_{i=1}^N$ with corresponding weights $\{w_t^i\}_{i=1}^N$ which sum to 1. This can be done by the well-known two-step recursion. One is the Prediction, which uses a motion model to propagate the particles; the other is the Update, which uses observation models to compute the weight of each particle. In our implementation, we define the state at time t as $Z_t = \{x_t, y_t, u_t, v_t, s_t\}$, where (x_t, y_t) is the 2D image position, (u_t, v_t) is the velocity, and s_t is the scale of the bounding box.

Motion Model. We use a constant velocity motion model, which is defined as:

$$
\begin{aligned}
(x_t, y_t) &= (x_{t-1}, y_{t-1}) + (u_{t-1}, v_{t-1}) + \varepsilon_1 \\
(u_t, v_t, s_t) &= (u_{t-1}, v_{t-1}, s_{t-1}) + \varepsilon_2
\end{aligned}
\tag{4}
$$

where ε_1 and ε_2 are drawn from zero-mean Gaussian distributions.

Observation Model. The observation model is a critical issue in the particle filter framework. The observation model should be robust against the main challenges in the PTZ camera tracking: abrupt motion, background clutters and appearance changes which are caused by occlusion, illumination variations and motion blur. To overcome these challenges, we propose a robust observation model. Firstly we use the category detector [19] to detect all the targets which belong to the same category. The category detector is trained offline, so it is more robust against background clutters, illumination variations and motion blur. Then an online classifier is trained to distinguish the interesting target from the other detections. If a detection is near the particles and is classified as positive by the classifier, we call this detection a strong observation. For each detection D_i in the PTZ camera, the matching score between a detection D_i and the interesting target T_a is measured as follows:

$$
S(D_i, T_a) = c(D_i)(\frac{1}{N} \sum_{k=1}^N \mathcal{N}(P_{D_i}; P_k, \Sigma_a))
\tag{5}
$$

where $c(D_i)$ is the classifier score; P_{D_i} and P_k are the positions of the detection D_i and the particle p_k; N is the number of particles. The detection with the maximum matching score among all the detections and the score of which is above a threshold θ, is considered as a strong observation D_*. The weight w_k for each particle p_k is computed as:

$$
w_k = c(P_k) + \alpha \cdot \mathcal{I}(D_*) \cdot \mathcal{N}(P_k; P_{D_*}, \Sigma_a))
\tag{6}
$$

where $c(P_k)$ is the classifier score of p_k, α is the parameter which controls the weight of the distance between the the particle p_k and the strong observation D_*, and $\mathcal{I}(D_*)$ is an indicator function that returns 1 if the strong observation is observed and 0 otherwise. If the strong observation is observed, it robustly guides the particles.

Classifier. In our implementation, we use online linear SVM as our classifier. The classifier score is measured as:

$$c(P) = \frac{1}{1 + \exp(-W \cdot F(I_P))} \tag{7}$$

where I_P is the image patch at the particle or detection location P with the corresponding size; $F(I_P)$ is the feature vector and W is the weights on features learned by linear SVM.

For efficiency, the same features (normalized gradient magnitude, histogram of oriented gradients, and LUV color) as the detector [19] are used by the classifier. When the same target is detected in the PTZ camera, positive samples are sampled near the detection, and negative samples are sampled from the other detections and background. In order to make the classifier robust against the detection noise, six image patches are sampled around the detection as positive samples with translations $\pm 0.05w$ in horizontal, translations $\pm 0.05h$ in vertical and scale changes $\pm 1/2^{\frac{1}{8}}$. w and h are the width and height of the detection bounding box. A linear SVM is trained using these samples. During tracking, to adapt to the appearance changes of the target, W is online updated using a passive-aggressive algorithm [10]. We only update the classifier when the strong observation is observed to prevent the tracking noise from being introduced into the classifier. The same sampling strategy is adopted to generate positive and negative samples for online updating.

4.3   Information Fusion

In situations with moderate crowd, in order to make the tracker robust against occlusions and target interactions, we use information fusion to improve the tracking accuracy.

We first define the tracking confidences in two cameras which are useful for information fusion. We denote the interesting target in the static camera as T_s, and in the PTZ camera as T_a. The multi-target tracking confidence for T_s at frame t is defined as:

$$conf_s^t = \frac{1}{M} \sum_{k=t-M+1}^{t} A_s(k) \tag{8}$$

where M is the length of the time window to compute the confidence, and $A_s(k)$ is the affinity score between T_s and the associated detection at frame k. $A_s(k)$ equals 0, if no detection is associated with T_s at that time. $conf_s^t$ is the average affinity score within the time window. The tracking confidence in the PTZ camera at frame t is defined as:

$$conf_a^t = \begin{cases} c^t(P_{D_*}) & \text{if strong observation is observed} \\ 0 & \text{otherwise} \end{cases} \tag{9}$$

where $c^t(P_{D_*})$ is the classifier score of the strong observation D_* at frame t.

In the association stage of multi-target tracking in the static camera, the affinity $A_{i,s}^f$ between T_s and the detection D_i with information fusion at frame t is measured as:

$$A_{i,s}^f = A_{pos}^f(D_i|T_s)A_{size}(D_i|T_s)A_{appr}(D_i|T_s) \qquad (10)$$

The only difference between Eqs. (2) and (10) is the motion affinity $A_{pos}^f(D_i|T_s)$ for the interesting target T_s. For other targets, the affinities are computed by Eq. (2). Let P_{T_s} and P_{T_a} represent the bottom centers of the target bounding boxes of T_s and T_a in corresponding camera images respectively, and P_{D_i} denotes the bottom center of the detection D_i. $A_{pos}^f(D_i|T_s)$ is calculated as:

$$A_{pos}^f(D_i|T_s) = \mathcal{N}(P_{T_s} + V_{T_s}\Delta t; P_{D_i}, \Sigma_s) + \beta \cdot conf_a^{t-1} \cdot \mathcal{N}(P_{a\rightarrow s}; P_{D_i}, \Sigma_s) \quad (11)$$

where $P_{a\rightarrow s} = (H_{s\rightarrow a}^{t-1})^{-1} P_{T_a}^{t-1}$ is the target position in the static camera image which is projected from the position of the target in the PTZ camera image at frame $t-1$, using the homography $H_{s\rightarrow a}^{t-1}$ computed by Eq. (1), and β controls the importance of the transferred position $P_{a\rightarrow s}$. Compared with the motion affinity defined in Eq. (3), $A_{pos}^f(D_i|T_s)$ incorporates the target position in the PTZ camera image. After long occlusion, the predicted position $P_{T_s} + V_{T_s}\Delta t$ is unreliable, and may cause the association to fail. At this time, the tracking result in the PTZ camera can help the target find the correct association.

In the PTZ camera, incorporating the tracking result in the static camera as an extra cue, the matching score between a detection D_i and the target T_a is measured as:

$$S^f(D_i, T_a) = c(D_i)\left(\frac{1}{N}\sum_{k=1}^{N}\mathcal{N}(P_{D_i}; P_k, \Sigma_a) + \gamma \cdot conf_s^{t-1} \cdot \mathcal{N}(P_{D_i}; P_{s\rightarrow a}, \Sigma_a)\right) \quad (12)$$

where P_k is the bottom center of particle p_k. Since the PTZ camera has changed its parameters at frame t, we use $H_{s\rightarrow a}^t$ rather than $H_{s\rightarrow a}^{t-1}$ to map the target position $P_{T_s}^{t-1}$ in the static camera image to the position $P_{s\rightarrow a}$ in the PTZ camera image, i.e. $P_{s\rightarrow a} = H_{s\rightarrow a}^t P_{T_s}^{t-1}$. The weight of the transferred position $P_{s\rightarrow a}$ is controlled by γ. The difference between Eqs. (5) and (12) is that the transferred position $P_{s\rightarrow a}$ is added into Eq. (12) as a motion cue. Since the particles may deviate from the true target position after long occlusion, the transferred position can help the target to be matched with the correct detection.

The weight of each particle k with information fusion is computed as:

$$w_k = c(P_k) + \eta \cdot \mathcal{I}(D_*) \cdot \mathcal{N}(P_k; P_{D_*}, \Sigma_a) + \zeta \cdot conf_s^{t-1} \cdot \mathcal{N}(P_k; P_{s\rightarrow a}, \Sigma_a) \quad (13)$$

where the parameters η and ζ balance the weights of the corresponding items. Compared with Eq. (6), the transferred position $P_{s\rightarrow a}$ is fused into Eq. (13) which can help to guide the particles and make them surround the true position when occlusion occurs.

5 Experiments

Due to the difficulty in repeating the experiments with PTZ cameras, so far now, there is no unique real video benchmark which allows a genuine global testing. Most existing works only provide qualitative experiments in real scenarios. In the experiments, we firstly compare our algorithm with some popular tracking algorithms which are popularly used in the PTZ camera tracking, on a realistic data set quantitatively. Then, our algorithm is implemented on a real Dual-Camera system to show its effectiveness qualitatively, as in the other literatures.

5.1 Parameter Setting

All the parameters are set experimentally and kept fixed for all experiments. The covariance matrix Σ_s in Eqs. (3) and (11) is set to $\text{diag}[10^2, 20^2]$. The variances of the ε_1 in Eq. (4) are set proportionally to the width w of the tracking target, i.e. $(0.01w^2, 0.01w^2)$. The variances of the ε_2 in Eq. (4) are set to $(2^2, 4^2, 0.01^2)$. The covariance Σ_a in Eqs. (5, 6, 12 and 13) is set to $\text{diag}[0.04w^2, 0.04w^2]$. The parameter α in Eq. (6), β in Eq. (11), γ in Eq. (12), η and ζ in Eq. (13) are set to 10, 2, 0.5, 10, 1 respectively. The number of particles N in Eq. (5) is set to 100. The threshold θ which is used to determinate the strong observation is set to 0.4. The length of the time window M in Eq. (8) is set to 10. For all the algorithms which use color histogram, the histogram is calculated in the HSV color space using $10 \times 10 \times 5$ bins.

5.2 Realistic Experiments

Data Set. We captured two synchronized videos at a shopping plaza using two cameras from different view points. The resolution of both videos is 1920×1080. One is served as the static camera video, and the other is served as the PTZ camera panorama video. For the static camera video, the resolution is reduced to 480×270 to simulate the static camera which monitors a large area. The static camera video is further cropped to 480×221 to ensure that all the pedestrians can be seen in the PTZ camera panorama video. For the PTZ camera panorama video, we generate the virtual PTZ camera view according to pan, tilt and zoom parameters using the method similar to [12]. The virtual view resolution of PTZ camera is set to 640×480. Some frames are shown in Fig. 3. The tracking results in the PTZ camera panorama video are labeled by us as ground truth (GT).

Evaluation Metrics. GT is projected to the PTZ camera view according to the camera pose and compared with the tracking result of the tracker in the PTZ camera image at the same time. The metrics proposed by [11] are used to compare different tracking algorithms:

- r_A^T: the mean overlap ratio between the bounding boxes of tracking results B_{tck} and the GT B_{GT}. The overlap ratio is computed as: $r_o = \frac{\|B_{GT} \cap B_{trk}\|}{\|B_{GT} \cup B_{trk}\|}$, where $\| \cdot \|$ is the area of the bounding box.

Fig. 3. (a) is the frame from the PTZ camera panorama view; (b) is the frame from the static camera view; (c) is the view generated from (a) with the virtual PTZ camera at parameters (pan:7.62, tilt:−2.17, focal length:4500); (d) is the view generated from (a) with the virtual PTZ camera at parameters (pan:−1.68, tilt:−4.37, focal length:5000)

- d_{ct}: the mean distance between the centers of B_{trk} and B_{GT}
- r_c: the percentage of correctly tracked frames (if $r_o \geq 0.5$)
- r_A^i: the mean overlap ratio between B_{GT} and the image bounding box B_i
- d_{ci}: the mean distance between the GT and the image center.

The first three criteria evaluate the accuracy of the algorithms, while the last two evaluate the ability of the system to keep the target in the center of the field of view and at the desirable resolution.

Compared Algorithms. According to which camera's tracking results are used to guide the PTZ camera, the tracking algorithms in Dual-Camera systems can be divided into two classes, static camera guided (SG) and PTZ camera guided (AG). Based on the information fusion strategy, the tracking algorithms can be categorized into four categories: with bidirectional fusion (BF), only with fusion from the static camera to the PTZ camera (AF), only with fusion from the PTZ camera to the static camera (SF), and without fusion (NF). Four popular tracking algorithms are compared: color-based particle filter(PF), KLT, Meanshift (MS) and TLD [22] which is a real time and effective tracker shown by [23]. In addition to these algorithms, we also compare our cooperative tracking algorithm (TD) with different fusion and camera guiding strategies: TD-NF-SG, TD-NF-AG, TD-SF-SG, TD-AF-AG and TD-BF-AG, where NF, SF, AF and

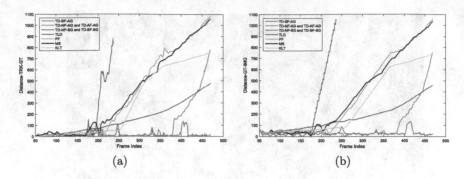

(a)   (b)

Fig. 4. (a) and (b) are the frame-by-frame tracking results in terms of the distance (in pixels) between the tracking result and the GT, and the distance (in pixels) between the GT and the image center, respectively. **Best viewed in color** (Color figure online).

Table 1. Comparison of different trackers. Bold font indicates best performance.

Methods	r_A^T	d_{ct}	r_c	r_A^i	d_{ci}
KLT	0.215	264.412	0.191	0.023	254.231
MS	0.163	337.003	0.170	0.021	326.09
PF	0.184	335.261	0.189	0.022	323.581
TLD	0.172	139.861	0.191	0.023	151.084
TD-SF-SG	0.415	104.334	0.299	0.035	152.855
TD-NF-SG	0.415	104.334	0.299	0.035	152.855
TD-AF-AG	0.508	76.725	0.756	0.041	80.662
TD-NF-AG	0.508	76.725	0.756	0.041	80.662
TD-BF-AG	**0.618**	**14.243**	**0.883**	**0.051**	**27.882**

BF indicate the information fusion strategies; SG and AG represent the camera guiding strategies. For example, TD-BF-AG represent our cooperative tracking algorithm with bidirectional information fusion, and using the tracking results in the PTZ camera to guide the movement of the PTZ camera. If not otherwise specified, in the tracking algorithms, the tracking result in the PTZ camera is used to guide the movement of the PTZ camera, due to its accuracy, and no information fusion is used as in the other literatures.

Results. Figure 4 illustrates the tracking results frame by frame in terms of the distance between the tracking result and the GT, and the distance between the GT and the image center. Table 1 shows the quantitative comparison results. From the tracking results, we can see that: due to the robust tracking algorithm in the PTZ camera, without information fusion, our method TD-NF-AG outperforms the other tracking algorithms; the tracking performance of the algorithm with one-directional information fusion is the same as the algorithm without information fusion; with bidirectional information fusion, our method TD-BF-AG achieves the best performance. Since the tracking results of TD-NF-SG and

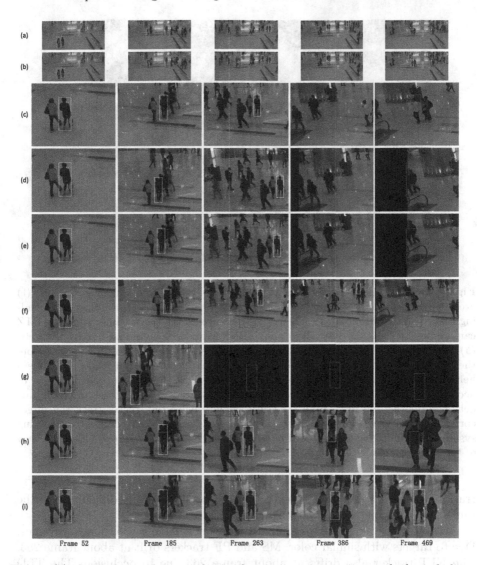

Frame 52   Frame 185   Frame 263   Frame 386   Frame 469

Fig. 5. (a) shows the tracking results in the static camera using methods excluding TD-BF-AG. (b) shows the tracking results in the static camera using TD-BF-AG. The interesting target in the static camera is indicated by the yellow bounding box. (c)∼(i) show tracking results in the PTZ camera, where (c)∼(f) use KLT, MS, PF and TLD trackers respectively; (g) shows the tracking results of TD-SF-SG and TD-NF-SG; (h) shows the results of TD-AF-AG and TD-NF-AG; (i) shows results using TD-BF-AG. Tracking results of the interesting target are represented by the red bounding boxes in the PTZ camera, and the ground truth is shown by white bounding boxes.

TD-SF-SG exceed the view of the PTZ camera panorama video after frame 263, their tracking results in Table 1 only consider frames from 52 to 263. This shows that static camera guided tracking is less accurate than PTZ camera guided

Fig. 6. An illustration of our cooperative tracking system. The left images in (a)∼(f) are the images in the static camera, and the right images in (a)∼(f) are the corresponding images in the PTZ camera. The tracking results in the static camera and the PTZ camera are indicated by the yellow bounding box and red bounding box respectively. (a) shows the interesting target is tracked by our algorithm. In (b), due to occlusion, the tracker fails in the static camera. The information fused from the PTZ camera helps the static camera find the correct association as shown in (c). In (d), due to occlusion in the PTZ camera, the tracker deviates from the true position of the target. The information fused from the static camera helps the tracker track the target correctly again when the target reappears, as shown in (e). Our cooperative tracking system keeps following the target at high resolution until the target exits from the view of the static camera as shown in (f).

tracking. The reason is that tracking in the static camera is difficult since the targets are small in the static camera images.

We try to give a qualitative comparison by showing in Fig. 5 some key frames. Due to targets with similar color, MS and PF trackers drift at about frame 263. The KLT tracker also drifts at about frame 263 due to occlusion. The TLD tracker fails at about frame 263, because the scale change is not estimated by the TLD tracker accurately, and makes the TLD detector fail. TD-SF-SG and TD-NF-SG fail at about frame 185, due to the target interactions. Although TD-SF-SG fuses information from the PTZ camera, it uses the results in the static camera to guide the PTZ camera which makes the target exit from the view of the PTZ camera before the information fusion helps it find the correct association. TD-AF-AG and TD-NF-AG fail at about frame 386 due to long occlusion. Although TD-AF-AG fuses information from the static camera, but the tracker has already failed in the static camera at about frame 185. The TD-BF-AG tracker can follow the target correctly through the whole sequence. The tracker fails in the static camera at about frame 185, but due to bidirectional information fusion, the tracker correctly tracks the target again. At frame 386, due to long occlusion, the online classifier fails in the PTZ camera, but the particles are guided by the transferred position from the static camera. The target is correctly tracked again when the target reappears.

5.3 Real Trials

We apply the proposed robust cooperative tracking algorithm with bidirectional information fusion in a Dual-Camera system. Our Dual-Camera system is consist of two off-the-shelf AXIS PTZ Network Cameras Q6032-E. One is fixed to serve as the static camera to monitor a wide area, and the other is used as the PTZ camera. Our algorithm is implemented in C++ using OpenCV on an Intel Core I7-4700MQ 2.40 GHz with 8 GB RAM. Duo to the multithreaded implementation, our algorithm can run in real time at 20 fps. Some key frames are shown in Fig. 6 with a detailed description.

6 Conclusion

In this paper, we have proposed a robust tracking algorithm within the particle filter framework in the PTZ camera, which combines a category detector and an online classifier to make the algorithm robust against background clutters. Furthermore a bidirectional information fusion method is proposed to enhance the performance of cooperative tracking in crowded scenes. Finally, we compare different tracking algorithms which are frequently used by other researchers in realistic experiments, and also show the efficiency of our method in real trials. To the best of our knowledge, this is the first time different tracking algorithms in Dual-Camera systems are evaluated, and the results show our method outperform the others.

Acknowledgement. This work is supported by National Natural Science Foundation of China (NO. 61371192).

References

1. Wang, X.: Intelligent multi-camera video surveillance: a review. Pattern Recogn. Lett. **34**(1), 3–19 (2013)
2. Scotti, G., Marcenaro, L., Coelho, C., Selvaggi, F., Regazzoni, C.: Dual camera intelligent sensor for high definition 360 degrees surveillance. IEE Proc.-Vis. Image Sig. Process. **152**(2), 250–257 (2005)
3. Chen, C., Yao, Y., Page, D., Abidi, B., Koschan, A., Abidi, M.: Heterogeneous fusion of omnidirectional and PTZ cameras for multiple object tracking. IEEE Trans. Circ. Syst. Video Technol. **18**(8), 1052–1063 (2008)
4. Ghidoni, S., Pretto, A., Menegatti, E.: Cooperative tracking of moving objects and face detection with a dual camera sensor. In: 2010 IEEE International Conference on Robotics and Automation, pp. 2568–2573 (2010)

5. Cui, Z., Li, A., Feng, G., Jiang, K.: Cooperative object tracking using dual-pan-tilt-zoom cameras based on planar ground assumption. In: IET Computer Vision (2014)
6. Zhou, X., Collins, R.T., Kanade, T., Metes, P.: A master-slave system to acquire biometric imagery of humans at distance. In: First ACM SIGMM International Workshop on Video Surveillance, pp. 113–120 (2003)
7. Lu, Y., Payandeh, S.: Cooperative hybrid multi-camera tracking for people surveillance. Can. J. Elect. Comput. Eng. **33**(3/4), 145–152 (2008)
8. Fahn, C., Lo, C.: A high-definition human face tracking system using the fusion of omni-directional and PTZ cameras mounted on a mobile robot. In: The 5th IEEE Conference on Industrial Electronics and Applications, pp. 6–11 (2010)
9. Nummiaroa, K., Koller-Meierb, E., Van Gool, L.: An adaptive color-based particle filter. Image Vis. Comput. **21**(1), 99–110 (2003)
10. Crammer, K., Dekel, O., Keshet, J., Shalev-Shwartz, S., Singer, Y.: Online passive-aggressive algorithms. J. Mach. Learn. Res. **7**, 551–585 (2006)
11. Salvagnini, P., Cristani, M., Del Bue, A., Murino, V.: An experimental framework for evaluating PTZ tracking algorithms. In: Crowley, J.L., Draper, B.A., Thonnat, M. (eds.) ICVS 2011. LNCS, vol. 6962, pp. 81–90. Springer, Heidelberg (2011)
12. Possegger, H., Rüther, M., Sternig, S., Mauthner, T., Klopschitz, M., Roth, P.M., Bischof, H.: Unsupervised calibration of camera networks and virtual PTZ cameras. In: 17th Computer Vision Winter Workshop (2012)
13. Comaniciu, D., Ramesh, V., Meer, P.: Kernel-based object tracking. IEEE Trans. Pattern Anal. Mach. Intell. **25**(5), 564–577 (2003)
14. Bernardin, K., Van De Camp, F., Stiefelhagen, R.: Automatic person detection and tracking using fuzzy controlled active cameras. In: IEEE Conference on Computer Vision and Pattern Recognition, pp. 1–8 (2007)
15. Shi, J., Tomasi, C.: Good features to track. In: IEEE Computer Society Conference on Computer Vision and Pattern Recognition, pp. 593–600 (1994)
16. Qureshi, F.Z., Terzopoulos, D.: Surveillance in virtual reality: system design and multi-camera control. In: IEEE Conference on Computer Vision and Pattern Recognition, pp. 1–8 (2007)
17. Wu, Z., Radke, R.J.: Keeping a pan-tilt-zoom camera calibrated. IEEE Trans. Pattern Anal. Mach. Intell. **35**(8), 1994–2007 (2013)
18. Del Bimbo, A., Lisanti, G., Masi, I., Pernici, F.: Continuous recovery for real time pan tilt zoom localization and mapping. In: 8th IEEE International Conference on Advanced Video and Signal-Based Surveillance, pp. 160–165 (2011)
19. Dollár, P., Appel, R., Belongie, S., Perona, P.: Fast feature pyramids for object detection. IEEE Trans. Pattern Anal. Mach. Intell. **36**(8), 1532–1545 (2014)
20. Ahuja, R.K., Magnanti, T.L., Orlin, J.B.: Network flows (1988)
21. Bae, S., Yoon, K.: Robust online multi-object tracking based on tracklet confidence and online discriminative appearance learning. In: IEEE Conference on Computer Vision and Pattern Recognition, pp. 1218–1225 (2014)
22. Kalal, Z., Mikolajczyk, K., Matas, J.: Tracking-learning-detection. IEEE Trans. Pattern Anal. Mach. Intell. **34**(7), 1409–1422 (2012)
23. Wu, Y., Lim, J., Yang, M.: Online object tracking: a benchmark. In: IEEE Conference on Computer Vision and Pattern Recognition, pp. 2411–2418 (2013)

Cute Balloons with Thickness

Qingyun Wang[1], Xuehui Liu[1(✉)], Xin Lu[1], Jianwen Cao[1], and Wen Tang[2]

[1] State Key Laboratory of Computer Science, Institute of Software,
China Academy of Sciences, Beijing, China
{wangqy,lxh,lxin}@ios.ac.cn, jianwen@iscas.ac.cn
[2] The Faculty of Science and Technology, Bournemouth University, Poole, UK
wtang@bournemouth.ac.uk

Abstract. Based on the finite element method, we present a simple volume-preserved thin shell deformation algorithm to simulate the process of inflating a balloon. Different other thin shells, the material of balloons has special features: large stretch, small bend and shear, and incompressibility. Previous deformation methods often focus on typical three-dimensional models or thin plate models such as cloth. The rest thin shell methods are complex or ignore the special features of thin shells especially balloons. We modify the triangle element to simple three-prism element, ignore bending and shearing deformation, and use volume preservation algorithm to match the incompressibility of balloons. Simple gas model is used, which interacts with shells to make the balloons inflated. Different balloon examples have been tested in our experiments and the results are compared with those of other methods. The experiments show that our algorithm is simple and effective.

Keywords: Finite element method · Physically based simulation · Thin shell · Volume preservation · Deformation animation of balloons

1 Introduction

Physically based deformation simulation has emerged in the late 1980s to make animations more physically plausible and to make the simulation of complex passively moving object easier. The simulation of thin shells is one of the difficult issues among the physically based deformation animation field. Rubber balloons belong to thin shells with large deformation.

Similar to thin plates, thin shells are thin flexible structures with a thickness much more smaller than other dimensions. The difference between them is that thin shells have a curved undeformed configuration (e.g., leaves, hats, balloons) while thin plates have a flat one (e.g., clothes). Thin shells are difficult to simulate because of the degeneracy of one dimension. They should not be treated as three-dimensional solids, otherwise the numerics become ill-conditioned. Due to the similarity of thin shells and thin plates, thin shells are treated as curved surface in many works [1,18] just like the approximation made for thin plates. Unfortunately, the thickness, which is very important for some materials such as rubber,

© Springer International Publishing Switzerland 2015
Y.-J. Zhang (Ed.): ICIG 2015, Part II, LNCS 9218, pp. 75–89, 2015.
DOI: 10.1007/978-3-319-21963-9_7

is discarded in such methods. Different thickness will lead to different elastic force. Ignoring the thickness will cause artifacts. Additionally, for some complex object, the material points demanded by these works [1, 18] are hard to get.

Compared to typical thin shells, the material of balloons has special features [1]. First, the main force leading to deformation is stretching force, while bending force is tiny. Second, significant transverse shearing should not exist. Last, the deformation of balloons is volume-preserving. A balloon becomes thinner when inflated. By adding gas, the expansion of the balloon under gas pressure will be stretched with the elastic force increasing. Meanwhile, the volume of gas is increasing and the pressure is dropping. In the end, gas pressure and elastic force balance.

Considering the characteristics of thin shells and balloons, we propose a simple volume-preserved thin shell algorithm to simulate the process of inflating a balloon, based on finite element method.

Our algorithms are mainly divided into two phases. In the first phase, finite element method is applied to solve the temporary shape of the object in the next time step. In the second phase, volume-preservation constraint is used to get the final shape. In contrast to other system, we adopt three-prism element instead of triangle element in order to involve thickness. The three-prism element is modified from triangle element by adding a thickness property. Despite there are six vertices in a three-prism, we need not to use all of them as there are not significant transverse shearing in rubber material. In the first phase, our method is similar to the finite element method based on triangle element. The thickness is treated as a parameter. The force caused by thickness is counted as the force of vertices. Thus, it is necessary to update the thickness and vertices in volume-preservation algorithm. A position based method [28] is applied in our volume-preservation algorithm, which is simple and effective. The gas pressure of every point inside the balloon is equal and the coupling of gas and balloon is simplified.

Our contributions:

– A simple thin shell finite element method with modification from finite element method based on triangle element.
– A volume constraint for thin shells.
– A method simulating the process of inflating a balloon with a simple gas model and capturing thickness effect.

2   Related Work

Physically based deformation simulation has emerged in the late 1980s. One of the first studies was the pioneering work of Terzopoulos et al. [2], which presented a simulation method about deformable objects based on finite differences. After that, many different approaches were proposed, such as mass-spring system [3,4], the boundary element method [5], the finite element method [6]. More approaches can be found in surveys of this field [7,8].

Due to the limitation of the calculation speed of computers, most of early methods were based on linear elasticity, which will lead to artifact in large deformation. Non-linear finite element methods were introduced to improve the accuracy of simulation [9,10], which cost too much computation time. Considering the fact that large deformation is caused by rotation in many deformable objects, corotated finite element method [11, 12] was presented to simulation such objects with acceptable speed and accuracy. However, such methods are not suitable for objects with large stretching deformation. McAdams et al. [13] overcame the shortcomings of corotated method to simulate the deformation of skin based on hexahedral element. But the improvement could not be extended to other types of element such as triangle element.

Thin Shells. Due to the degeneracy of one dimension (the high radio of width to thickness), thin shells are difficult to simulate. Robust finite element based thin shell simulation is an active and challenging research area in physics, CAD and computer graphics. Arnold [14] analyzed thin shells and pointed out the issues in simulation. Based on Kirchhoff-Love thin shell theory, Cirak et al. [15] adopted subdivision basis as the shape function in finite element method. The accuracy of simulation was improved, neglecting the low speed. Green et al. [16] applied the method of Cirak et al. [15] in computer graphics and improved the speed with multi-level method. Grinspun et al. [17] also proposed an accelerated framework, which was simpler and more adaptable. Grinspun et al. [18] presented the simplest discrete shells model to simulate thin shells with large bending deformation such as hats and papers. Bonet et al. [1] simulated thin shells under gas pressure with the approach for clothes. 2D material points are demanded in this method, which are difficult to calculate in some complex thin shells. Inspired by the work of Bonet et al. [1], Skouras et al. [19] modified the form of deformation gradient to make every element volume-preserved during deformation and got rid of the demand of material points. Nevertheless, the new deformation gradient will lead to a complex system, which may be ill-conditioned. Most of the works above use triangle element, ignoring the thickness when simulating thin shells. But for materials like rubber, thickness is a very important property, which should be considered. On the other hand, thin shells should not be simulated based on tetrahedral element, as the degeneracy of one dimension. In this paper, we present a compromise method by using three-prism elements, which is simple and keep the thickness information meanwhile.

Gas Model. Gas is a type of fluid, which is a active research area in recent years. Guendelman et al. [20] and Robinson et al. [21] coupled fluid with thin shells and thin plates. The coupling process is very complex as thin structures and fluid belong to two different system. Batty et al. [22] accelerated the coupling of fluid and rigid bodies. However, the coupling of fluid and soft bodies is still a difficult problem. It is not necessary to use such complex system, when there is not significant movement of gas. Chen et al. [23] proposed a three-layer model to simulate the air effect between clothes and soft bodies. The air flow was calculated by simple diffusion equation. In the deformation of balloons, the equilibrium of gas pressure force and elastic force is achieved quickly so we can just ignore the movement and treat the gas uniform [19].

Volume-Preservation. Volume loss can be an obvious artifact when simulating large deformation. With meshless method, Müller et al. [24] adjusted material parameters such as Poisson's radio to make the deformation volume-preserved. Bargteil et al. [25] proposed a plasticity model to preserve volume, which could only be used in offline simulation. Local volume-preserving method was presented by Irving et al. [26], which preserve the local volume around every vertex. Position based method could also be used to preserve volume by adding volume constraint [28]. Müller et al. [29] then improved this method with multi-grid to accelerate the solving of constraints. Similar to Müller [28], Diziol et al. [30] also use position based method, but they solve constraints of not only positions but also velocities.

3   Overview

The balloon model is expressed by a triangles mesh, with gas inside. The mesh is represented by three-prism elements with a set of N vertices. A vertex $i \in [1, \ldots, N]$ has a mass m_i, a initial position $\mathbf{x}_i^0$, a current position $\mathbf{x}_i^n$ and a current velocity $\mathbf{v}_i^n$. With a time step Δt, the whole volume-preserved deformation algorithm for thin shells is as follows:

ALGORITHM 1. BALLOON INFLATED DEFORMATION.
1   Set parameters: gas pressure p, balloon density ρ, initial thickness h^e.
2   **for** all vertices i
3   **do** initialize $\mathbf{x}_i^0, \mathbf{v}_i^0$, compute mass m_i
4   **while** system dose not converge
5   **do for** all elements e
6   **do** compute $\mathbf{f}_i^{elastic}, \mathbf{f}_i^p$ of the three vertices
7   compute $\delta\mathbf{f}^{elastic} = -\mathbf{K}^{elastic}\delta\mathbf{x}$, $\delta\mathbf{f}^p = -\mathbf{K}^p\delta\mathbf{x}$
8   compute the time integration by implicit method
9   solve the equation to get all $\mathbf{v}_i^{n+1}, \mathbf{x}_i^{n+1}$
10   Volume preserving, update all $\mathbf{x}_i^{n+1}, h^e$
11   **for** all vertices i
12   **do** $\mathbf{v}_i^{n+1} = \left(\mathbf{x}_i^{n+1} - \mathbf{x}_i^n\right)/\Delta t$

Lines 1–3 set the parameters and initialize the positions and velocities of vertices. The core of the algorithm are two parts, the finite element method part (lines 5–9) and volume preserving part (line 10). Lines 11–12 update the positions and velocities at last.

In the finite element method part, the elasticity forces and the pressure forces of vertices are computed according to current positions $\mathbf{x}_i^n$ and initial positions $\mathbf{x}_i^0$ in every element in line 6. In line 7, the variations related to stiffness matrix and gas tangent matrix of every element are computed, which will be assembled in the variations related to stiffness matrix and gas tangent matrix of the system. After these computed for all elements, the implicit time integration is used to construct system equation in line 8 by combining the matrixes above. At last, the new velocities are solved by Newton-Raphson method and Conjugate Gradient method in line 9.

In volume preserving part, current positions $\mathbf{x}_i^{n+1}$ and thicknesses h^e are used to compute the change of volume, and the positions and thicknesses are updated in order to preserve the volume.

4   Balloon Model

In most of previous works, thin shells are simulated by triangle elements, which ignore the thickness information, or tetrahedral elements, which may be ill-conditioned. We present a three-prism element to keep the thickness. As there is no significant shear in rubber material, we just add a thickness property on the typical triangle element to get a three-prism element (see Fig. 1).

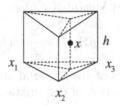

Fig. 1. Interpolating method of three-prism element.

The deformation of objects is represented by the deformation function ϕ : $\Omega \to \mathbf{R}^3$, which maps a material point $\bar{\mathbf{x}}$ to its deformed point $\mathbf{x} = \phi(\bar{\mathbf{x}})$. Inside the three-prism element, the location of a point $\mathbf{x}(\alpha)$ can be interpolated by three vertices and the thickness property (see Fig. 1) and α is the interpolating parameter.

In element e, let $\bar{\mathbf{x}}_1^e, \bar{\mathbf{x}}_2^e, \bar{\mathbf{x}}_3^e \in \mathbf{R}^3$ denote the vertices positions in undeformed configuration, $\bar{h}^e \in \mathbf{R}$ denote the thickness, and $\bar{\mathbf{e}}_{ij} = \bar{\mathbf{x}}_j^e - \bar{\mathbf{x}}_i^e$ denote the edges. Let $\mathbf{x}_1^e, \mathbf{x}_2^e, \mathbf{x}_3^e \in \mathbf{R}^3$ denote the respective deformed vertices positions, $h^e \in \mathbf{R}$ denote the deformed thickness and $\mathbf{e}_{ij} = \mathbf{x}_j^e - \mathbf{x}_i^e$ denote the deformed edges. Using linear interpolating method, a point within element e in undeformed configuration $\bar{\mathbf{x}}^e(\alpha)$ and its respective deformed position $\mathbf{x}^e(\alpha)$ can be represented as the same form

$$\bar{\mathbf{x}}^e(\alpha) = (1 - \alpha_1 - \alpha_2)\bar{\mathbf{x}}_1^e + \alpha_1\bar{\mathbf{x}}_2^e + \alpha_2\bar{\mathbf{x}}_3^e + \alpha_3\bar{h}^e\bar{\mathbf{d}}, \bar{\mathbf{d}} = \frac{\bar{\mathbf{e}}_{12} \times \bar{\mathbf{e}}_{13}}{|\bar{\mathbf{e}}_{12} \times \bar{\mathbf{e}}_{13}|} \quad (1)$$

Within every element, the deformation is assumed to be constant, and can be described by the deformation gradient $\mathbf{F}^e \in \mathbf{R}^{3\times3}$

$$\mathbf{F}^e = \frac{\partial \mathbf{x}^e(\alpha)}{\partial \bar{\mathbf{x}}^e(\alpha)} = \frac{\partial \mathbf{x}^e(\alpha)}{\partial \alpha} \cdot \left(\frac{\partial \bar{\mathbf{x}}^e(\alpha)}{\partial \alpha}\right)^{-1} \quad (2)$$

From Eq. (1), the partial derivative of $\bar{\mathbf{x}}^e(\alpha)$ to α is

$$\frac{\partial \mathbf{x}^e(\alpha)}{\partial \alpha} = \begin{bmatrix} \mathbf{e}_{12} & \mathbf{e}_{13} & \mathbf{d}h^e \end{bmatrix}, \frac{\partial \bar{\mathbf{x}}^e(\alpha)}{\partial \alpha} = \begin{bmatrix} \bar{\mathbf{e}}_{12} & \bar{\mathbf{e}}_{13} & \bar{\mathbf{d}}\bar{h}^e \end{bmatrix} \tag{3}$$

At last, the deformation gradient $\mathbf{F}^e$ can be represented as

$$\mathbf{F}^e = \begin{bmatrix} \mathbf{e}_{12} & \mathbf{e}_{13} & \mathbf{d}h^e \end{bmatrix} \cdot \begin{bmatrix} \bar{\mathbf{e}}_{12} & \bar{\mathbf{e}}_{13} & \bar{\mathbf{d}}\bar{h}^e \end{bmatrix}^{-1} \tag{4}$$

Deformation could cause strain energy, which is defined by deformation gradient

$$E = \int_{\Omega} \psi(\mathbf{F}) d\bar{\mathbf{x}} \tag{5}$$

where ψ is the energy density function as a function of deformation gradient to measure the strain energy per unit undeformed volume. Different material has different energy density. Take St. Venant-Kirchhoff material for example

$$\psi(\mathbf{F}) = \mu \mathbf{E} : \mathbf{E} + \frac{\lambda}{2} tr^2(\mathbf{E}) \tag{6}$$

where μ, λ are Lamé coefficients of the material and $\mathbf{E} \in \mathbf{R}^{3 \times 3}$ is Green strain tensor, which is a nonlinear function of deformation gradient

$$\mathbf{E} = \frac{1}{2}(\mathbf{F}^T\mathbf{F} - \mathbf{I}) \tag{7}$$

With strain energy, the elastic forces are defined as

$$\begin{aligned}
\mathbf{f}_i^{elastic} &= -\frac{\partial E}{\partial \mathbf{x}_i} = \sum_e \left(-\frac{\partial E^e}{\partial \mathbf{x}_i} \right) = \sum_e \mathbf{f}_i^e \\
&= \sum_e -V^e \frac{\partial \psi(\mathbf{F}^e)}{\partial \mathbf{x}_i} = \sum_e -V^e \frac{\partial \psi(\mathbf{F}^e)}{\partial \mathbf{F}^e} \frac{\partial \mathbf{F}^e}{\partial \mathbf{x}_i} \\
&= \sum_e -V^e \mathbf{P}(\mathbf{F}^e) \frac{\partial \mathbf{F}^e}{\partial \mathbf{x}_i}
\end{aligned} \tag{8}$$

where V^e is the volume of element e, $\mathbf{P}(\mathbf{F}) = \frac{\partial \psi}{\partial \mathbf{F}}$ is 1st Piola-kirchhoff stress tensor, which of St. Venant-Kirchhoff material is

$$\mathbf{P}(\mathbf{F}) = \mathbf{F}[2\mu\mathbf{E} + \lambda tr(\mathbf{E})\mathbf{I}] \tag{9}$$

If we use explicit time integration, we can compute the accelerations of all vertices and then update the positions and velocities. However, the explicit time integration is not stable in large time step. In order to apply implicit time integration, the stiffness matrix need to be computed

$$\mathbf{K}^{elastic} = -\frac{\partial \mathbf{f}^{elastic}}{\partial \mathbf{x}} \tag{10}$$

From Eqs. (4) and (8), we can see that deformation gradient and stress tensor are complex functions of $\mathbf{x}$. Thus solving $\mathbf{K}^{elastic}$ directly is difficult. However,

$\mathbf{K}^{elastic}$ always multiply a vector like $\mathbf{K}^{elastic}\mathbf{w}$, so we just compte the variation of elastic forces $\delta\mathbf{f}^{elastic} = -\mathbf{K}^{elastic}\delta\mathbf{x}$

$$\delta f_i{}^{elastic} = \sum_e -V^e \mathbf{P}(\mathbf{F}^e; \delta\mathbf{F}^e)\frac{\partial\delta\mathbf{F}^e}{\partial\delta\mathbf{x}_i} \tag{11}$$

Now we can use implicit time integration to solve positions and velocities.

5   Gas Model

As the equilibrium of gas pressure force and elastic force is achieved quickly when inflating the balloon, we assume that the gas pressure is uniform and the gas pressure of every point inside the balloon is the same. The pressure p and the volume of gas V have a relationship as

$$pV = nRT \tag{12}$$

where n is the amount of gas contained in volume V, T is the temperature and R is the gas constant. In an enclosed balloon, the amount of gas, the temperature and the gas constant do not change, so the product of pressure and volume remains invariant. Increasing the volume will decrease the pressure.

In our model, when the mesh is very fine, the volume of the gas can be approximately formed from tetrahedrons made up of triangles and the origin point (see Fig. 2)

$$V = \sum_e \frac{1}{3}\cdot\frac{1}{3}(\mathbf{x}_1^e + \mathbf{x}_2^e + \mathbf{x}_3^e)\cdot\mathbf{n}^e\cdot A^e \tag{13}$$

where $\mathbf{n}^e$ is the normal vector of element e and A^e is the area.

With the initial pressure p_0, initial volume V_0 and current volume V, current pressure is defined as

$$p = \frac{p_0 V_0}{V} \tag{14}$$

The value of the pressure force of element e is the product of the pressure p and the triangle area A^e of element e. The direction of the pressure force of element e is the normal vector of the triangle $\mathbf{n}^e$. The the discrete nodal pressure forces can be derived as

$$\mathbf{f}_i^p = \sum_{e\in T^i}\frac{1}{3}pA^e\mathbf{n}^e = \sum_{e\in T^i}\frac{1}{3}p\cdot\frac{1}{2}(\mathbf{e}_{12}^e \times \mathbf{e}_{13}^e) \tag{15}$$

where T^i is the set of elements incident to vertex i, $\frac{1}{3}$ are weights.

The tangent matrix of pressure force is calculated and we neglect the derivative of area and normal vector to vertex position in order to make tangent matrix positive definite. The tangent matrix between vertex i, j is derived as

$$[\mathbf{K}^p]_{ij} = \sum_{e\in T^i} -\frac{\partial[\mathbf{f}^p]_i^e}{\partial\mathbf{x}_j{}^T}$$

$$\approx -\sum_{e\in T^i}\frac{1}{3}\left(\frac{\partial p}{\partial\mathbf{x}_j{}^T}A^e\mathbf{n}^e\right) \tag{16}$$

$$\approx \frac{1}{27}\frac{p_0 V_0}{V^2}\left(\sum_{e\in T^i}A^e\mathbf{n}^e\right)\left(\sum_{e\in T^j}A^e\mathbf{n}^e\right)^T$$

Fig. 2. Volume of the gas.

The tangent matrix is dense while the stiffness matrix is sparse. So the time complexity of the tangent matrix is $O(N^2)$. In order to speed up, just like the stiffness matrix, we compute the variation of pressure forces $\delta \mathbf{f}^p = -\mathbf{K}^p \delta \mathbf{x}$ directly. Let $\mathbf{An}_i = \sum\limits_{e \in T^i} A^e \mathbf{n}^e$, the variation of pressure forces is derived as

$$\delta \mathbf{f}_i^p = -\sum_j [\mathbf{K}^p]_{ij} \delta \mathbf{x}_j = -\frac{1}{27} \frac{p_0 V_0}{V^2} \mathbf{An}_i \left(\sum_j (\mathbf{An}_j)^T \delta \mathbf{x}_j \right) \tag{17}$$

The time complexity of above is $O(N)$.

6   Time Integration

Implicit time integration is used as in [31] and we get

$$\mathbf{M}\mathbf{a} = \mathbf{f}^{elastic}(\mathbf{x}^{n+1}) + \mathbf{f}^p(\mathbf{x}^{n+1}) - \mathbf{C}\mathbf{v}^{n+1} + \mathbf{f}^{ext} \tag{18}$$

where $\mathbf{a} = \frac{\mathbf{v}^{n+1} - \mathbf{v}^n}{\Delta t}$ is the acceleration of vertices, $\mathbf{v}^n$ is the velocity matrix at time n, $\mathbf{C}$ is the damping matrix, $\mathbf{f}^{ext}$ is the external forces such as gravity and $\mathbf{M}$ is the mass matrix. The discrete nodal mass is derived as

$$m_i = \sum_{e \in T^i} w_i \rho \cdot V^e \tag{19}$$

where w_i are weights and ρ is the density of material.

As Eq. 18 is nonlinear, we use Newton-Raphson method to solve it. We will construct sequences of approximations $\mathbf{x}_{(k)}^{n+1} : \mathbf{x}_{(0)}^{n+1}, \mathbf{x}_{(1)}^{n+1}, \mathbf{x}_{(2)}^{n+1}, \dots$ and $\mathbf{v}_{(k)}^{n+1} :$ $\mathbf{v}_{(0)}^{n+1}, \mathbf{v}_{(1)}^{n+1}, \mathbf{v}_{(2)}^{n+1}, \dots$ such that $\lim\limits_{k \to \infty} \mathbf{x}_{(k)}^{n+1} = \mathbf{x}^{n+1}$ $\lim\limits_{k \to \infty} \mathbf{v}_{(k)}^{n+1} = \mathbf{v}^{n+1}$. Initialize $\mathbf{x}_{(0)}^{n+1}$ $= \mathbf{x}^n, \mathbf{v}_{(0)}^{n+1} = \mathbf{v}^n$ and define the correction variables

$$\Delta \mathbf{x}_{(k)} = \mathbf{x}_{(k+1)}^{n+1} - \mathbf{x}_{(k)}^{n+1}, \Delta \mathbf{v}_{(k)} = \mathbf{v}_{(k+1)}^{n+1} - \mathbf{v}_{(k)}^{n+1} \tag{20}$$

Linearize the elastic force and pressure force as

$$\mathbf{f}(\mathbf{x}^{n+1}) \approx \mathbf{f}(\mathbf{x}^n) + \frac{\partial \mathbf{f}}{\partial \mathbf{x}} \Delta \mathbf{x} \tag{21}$$

Then we use Eqs. 18, 20 and 21 to derive system linear equation

$$
\begin{aligned}
\frac{\mathbf{M}\left(\mathbf{v}_{(k+1)}^{n+1}-\mathbf{v}^{n}\right)}{\Delta t} &= \mathbf{f}^{elastic}\left(\mathbf{x}_{(k)}^{n+1}\right) + \mathbf{f}^{p}\left(\mathbf{x}_{(k)}^{n+1}\right) + \mathbf{f}^{ext} \\
&-\mathbf{K}^{elastic}\left(\mathbf{x}_{(k)}^{n+1}\right)\Delta\mathbf{x}_{(k)} - \mathbf{K}^{p}\left(\mathbf{x}_{(k)}^{n+1}\right)\Delta\mathbf{x}_{(k)} - \mathbf{C}\mathbf{v}_{(k+1)}^{n+1}
\end{aligned}
\tag{22}
$$

With $\Delta\mathbf{x}_{(k)} = \Delta\mathbf{v}_{(k)}\Delta t$, we get

$$
\begin{aligned}
\mathbf{A}\Delta\mathbf{v}_{(k)} &= \mathbf{b} \\
\mathbf{A} &= \mathbf{M} + \Delta t\mathbf{C} + \Delta t^{2}\left(\mathbf{K}^{elastic}\left(\mathbf{x}_{(k)}^{n+1}\right) + \mathbf{K}^{p}\left(\mathbf{x}_{(k)}^{n+1}\right)\right) \\
\mathbf{b} &= \mathbf{M}\left(\mathbf{v}^{n} - \mathbf{v}_{(k)}^{n+1}\right) + \Delta t\left(\mathbf{f}^{elastic}\left(\mathbf{x}_{(k)}^{n+1}\right) + \mathbf{f}^{ext} + \mathbf{f}^{p}\left(\mathbf{x}_{(k)}^{n+1}\right) - \mathbf{C}\mathbf{v}_{(k)}^{n+1}\right)
\end{aligned}
\tag{23}
$$

$\Delta\mathbf{v}$ is solved by Conjugate Gradient method and $\mathbf{v}^{n+1} = \mathbf{v}^{n}+\Delta\mathbf{v}$ is the velocities in time $n + 1$. In conclusion, The detailed process in lines 5–9 of Algorithm 1 is

1. Compute the deformation gradient of each element using Eq. 4.
2. Compute discrete nodal elastic forces and pressure forces using Eqs. 8 and 15.
3. Construct system linear equation using Eq. 23.
4. Solve sequences of approximations $\mathbf{x}_{(k)}^{n+1}$: $\mathbf{x}_{(0)}^{n+1}, \mathbf{x}_{(1)}^{n+1}, \mathbf{x}_{(2)}^{n+1}, \ldots$ and $\mathbf{v}_{(k)}^{n+1}$: $\mathbf{v}_{(0)}^{n+1}, \mathbf{v}_{(1)}^{n+1}, \mathbf{v}_{(2)}^{n+1}, \ldots$ and compute the variations $\delta\mathbf{f}_{i}^{elastic}$, $\delta\mathbf{f}_{i}^{p}$ during the process using Eqs. 11 and 17.
5. $\mathbf{v}^{n+1} = \mathbf{v}_{(k+1)}^{n+1}, \mathbf{x}^{n+1} = \mathbf{x}_{(k+1)}^{n+1}$.

7   Volume Preservation

Volume preservation is an important feature of balloons. During deformation, the volume of gas is changing while the volume of balloon remains the same(see Fig. 3).

There are three vertices and one thickness property in an element. For the convenience of calculation, we convert the thickness property to a virtual vertex, which is located in the center of the upper triangle of three-prism (see Fig. 3). After volume preservation, we will convert the virtual vertex to thickness property.

The volume constraint is defined as the equality of initial volume and current volume of the balloon

$$
C(\mathbf{x} + \Delta\mathbf{x}) = V^{b}(\mathbf{x} + \Delta\mathbf{x}) - V_{0}^{b} = 0
\tag{24}
$$

where $\mathbf{x}$ are current positions of $N + N_1$ vertices(N_1 are the virtual vertices). We need to solve the correction $\Delta\mathbf{x}$, which meet the constraint. Linearize C

$$
C(\mathbf{x} + \Delta\mathbf{x}) \approx C(\mathbf{x}) + \frac{\partial C(\mathbf{x})}{\partial\mathbf{x}}\Delta\mathbf{x}
\tag{25}
$$

And compute the volume of the balloon from the volume of all three-prisms

$$
V^{b}(\mathbf{x}) = \sum_{e}\frac{1}{2}\mathbf{e}_{14}\cdot(\mathbf{e}_{12}\times\mathbf{e}_{13})
\tag{26}
$$

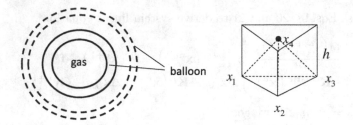

Fig. 3. Volume preservation of balloon. Left: The solid line represents the balloon before stretching, and the dot line represents the balloon after stretching, which is thinner than before. Right: The virtual vertex in volume preserving algorithm.

The correction is solved by position based method [28]

$$\Delta \mathbf{x}_i = -\frac{(N + N_1)\, w_i}{\sum_j w_j}\, \frac{w_i C(\mathbf{x})}{\sum_j \left\| \frac{\partial C(\mathbf{x})}{\partial \mathbf{x}_j} \right\|^2} \cdot \frac{\partial C(\mathbf{x})}{\partial \mathbf{x}_i} \tag{27}$$

where w_i are weights $w_i = 1/m_i'$. The new masses are computed using Eq. 19 with weight $1/6$ for original three vertices and $1/2$ for the virtual vertex. The derivation of C to vertex is easy to derive

$$\frac{\partial C(\mathbf{x})}{\partial \mathbf{x}_i} = \sum_e \frac{\partial C^e(\mathbf{x})}{\partial \mathbf{x}_i}$$
$$= \sum_{e:t_1^e=i} \tfrac{1}{2}\mathbf{e}_{24} \times \mathbf{e}_{23} + \sum_{e:t_2^e=i} \tfrac{1}{2}\mathbf{e}_{13} \times \mathbf{e}_{14} + \sum_{e:t_3^e=i} \tfrac{1}{2}\mathbf{e}_{14} \times \mathbf{e}_{12} + \sum_{e:t_4^e=i} \tfrac{1}{2}\mathbf{e}_{12} \times \mathbf{e}_{13}$$
$$\tag{28}$$

where $t_1^e, t_2^e, t_3^e, t_4^e$ are the four indices of the vertices belonging to element e.

The volume of balloon is preserved as follows

ALGORITHM 2. VOLUME PRESERVATION.

1 **for** all elements e
2   **do** Compute the virtual vertex $\mathbf{x}_4^e$ and add it to vertices matrix $\mathbf{x}$
3   Compute new masses m_i' using Eq. 19
4   Using Eq. 28 to compute $\frac{\partial C^e(\mathbf{x})}{\partial \mathbf{x}_i}$ and add it to $\frac{\partial C(\mathbf{x})}{\partial \mathbf{x}_i}$
5 **for** all vertices i
6   **do** Using Eq. 27 to compute $\Delta \mathbf{x}_i$
7          $\mathbf{x}_i = \mathbf{x}_i + \Delta \mathbf{x}_i$
8 **for** all elements e
9   **do** Compute thickness h^e from virtual vertices

8 Results

All of our examples are tested on an Intel Core i7 3.4 Ghz CPU with 16 GB memory. In order to explore the capabilities of our method, we make tests with

Fig. 4. Inflating result of the teddy. Left top is the undeformed shape, left bottom is the deformed shape and right are detail images.

a variety of different shapes from The Princeton Shape Benchmark as the undeformed balloons and the results are rendered by POV-Ray. For each shape, an inflating animation is made and we choose some frames to analysis.

Figure 4 shows the inflating result of teddy. The shape of teddy's head is some of a big sphere, on which the ear is some of a small hemisphere. During the animation, the big parts such as the head and the body are inflated fast, while the small ones are inflated slowly like the ears. The reason is that the big parts have equable curvature while the small ones have steep curvature. The steeper the nodal's curvature is, the smaller pressure force it gets (see Fig. 5). Additionally, as the head is inflated faster than the ears, the vertices connecting the two parts will have larger elastic forces than those belong to ears and so the base area of the ears will enlarged while the height is shorten correspondingly. As a result, the ears seem like shrinking and merged into the head just like the balloons in reality do.

More results are given in Fig. 6. From the results, we can see that the big parts are inflated faster than the small ones and they are merged gradually. However, parts with the similar size will keep their shapes and be inflated separately. Additionally, the regions between different parts become flat gradually. The rough regions in the Vase model get smooth while the plates in the Cube & Cylinder model get curved. The balloons simulated by our algorithm act just like the real balloons.

Thickness Analysis and Comparison. The balloons in same shape are deformed in different ways with different thicknesses. With larger thickness, the balloons are more difficult to stretch due to larger elastic forces. We experiment with different thicknesses of 0.3 mm, 0.2 mm and 0.1 mm in Fig. 7.

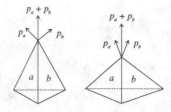

Fig. 5. The relationship with curvature and pressure force.

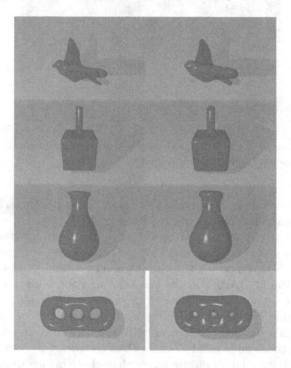

Fig. 6. Results of more shapes. Left column are undeformed shapes and right column are deformed shapes.

From the results, we can see that the balloon is deformed more slowly with larger thickness but the effect of emerging is more obvious. With thickness 0.3 mm, the ears are barely inflated and the deformation is mainly from the stretch of the connecting part with the head. At last, the two parts get merged quickly. With thickness 0.1 mm, the deformation of the ears is mainly from the inflating of itself and the ears never be merged with the head. With thickness 0.2 mm, the deformation of the ears is the combination of the two effects.

The results show that thickness is an important property of balloons. Different thicknesses will cause different effects, which is ignored in other methods. The last figure in Fig. 7 is the result of Skouras et al. [19]. In their method, the deformation gradient is complex and the volume is preserved by brutely setting

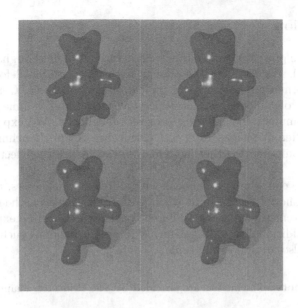

Fig. 7. Results of different thicknesses and comparison with the result of Skouras et al. [19]. Left top is the result of thickness 0.3, right top is the result of thickness 0.2, left bottom is the result of thickness 0.1, right bottom is the result of Skouras et al. [19].

the thickness to balance the changing of the area of triangles. Thus the method can not realize the different effects of different thicknesses.

Performance. We provide computation times and volume radios for all examples shown in this paper in Table 1. The volume radio is the radio of current volume and the initial volume of the balloon. The thickness of all models is 0.3 mm and the the number of iterations of Newton-Raphson method is 3. We calculate the average computation time and volume radio of 300 frames.

It can be seen that the computation times are acceptable and the volume radios of all models are almost 1, which means that our volume preservation algorithm works well. Due to the rough surface, there are too much details in the Vase model, thus the volume preservation performance is not as good as other models.

Table 1. Computation times and volume radio.

Model	#vertices	#faces	Time [ms]	Volume radio
Teddy	11090	22176	278.0	1.0000026
Bird	7849	15694	187.2	1.0000028
Holes	5884	11776	207.6	1.0000065
Vase	14599	29194	522.6	0.9924975
Cube & Cylinder	15505	31006	484.2	1.0000036

9 Conclusion

In this paper, we present a simple thin shell deformation method, based on finite element method. We focus on the objects with large stretch deformation and little bend deformation, balloons are typical objects of which. Considering the special features of balloons, we introduce gas model and volume preservation algorithm to simulate the inflating process of balloons. We experiment with a variety of different shapes from The Princeton Shape Benchmark and get good results. Compared to other methods, we can realize the effects of different thicknesses.

Although we can simulate balloons with different thicknesses, the thickness of all elements should be the same when initialized. However, the real balloons often have different thicknesses in different parts, which will be explored in our future work. Additionally, adding external forces on balloons such as grabbing or pinching is also an interesting topic.

Acknowledgments. The models are provided by The Princeton Shape Benchmark.

References

1. Bonet, J., Wood, R.D., Mahaney, J., et al.: Finite element analysis of air supported membrane structures. Comput. Methods Appl. Mech. Eng. **190**(5–7), 579–595 (2000)
2. Platt, J., Fleischer, K., Terzopoulos, D., et al.: Elastically deformable models. Comput. Graph. **21**(4), 205–214 (1987)
3. Provot, X.: Deformation constraints in a mass-spring model to describe rigid cloth behavior. In: Graphics Interface, pp. 147–154 (1995)
4. Desbrun, M., Schröder, P., Barr, A.: Interactive animation of structured deformable objects. Graph. Interface **99**(5), 10 (1999)
5. James, D.L., Pai, D.K.: ArtDefo: accurate real time deformable objects. In: Proceedings of the 26th Annual Conference on Computer Graphics and Interactive Techniques. ACM Press/Addison-Wesley Publishing Co., pp. 65–72 (1999)
6. O'brien, J.F., Hodgins, J.K.: Graphical modeling and animation of brittle fracture. In: Proceedings of the 26th Annual Conference on Computer Graphics and Interactive Techniques. ACM Press/Addison-Wesley Publishing Co., pp. 137–146 (1999)
7. Gibson, S.F.F., Mirtich, B.: A survey of deformable modeling in computer graphics. Technical report, Mitsubishi Electric Research Laboratories (1997)
8. Nealen, A., Müller, M., Keiser, R., et al.: Physically based deformable models in computer graphics. Comput. Graph. Forum **25**(4), 809–836 (2006). Blackwell Publishing Ltd.,
9. Eischen, J.W., Deng, S., Clapp, T.G.: Finite-element modeling and control of flexible fabric parts. IEEE Comput. Graph. Appl. **16**(5), 71–80 (1996)
10. Jannski, L., Ulbricht, V.: Numerical simulation of mechanical behaviour of textile surfaces. ZAMM J. Appl. Math. Mechanics/Zeitschrift fr Angewandte Mathematik und Mechanik **80**(S2), 525–526 (2000)

11. Müller, M., Dorsey, J., McMillan, L., et al.: Stable real-time deformations. In: Proceedings of the 2002 ACM SIGGRAPH/Eurographics Symposium on Computer Animation, pp. 49–54. ACM (2002)

12. Etzmuß, O., Keckeisen, M., Straßer, W.: A fast finite element solution for cloth modelling. In: Proceedings of the 11th Pacific Conference on Computer Graphics and Applications, 2003, pp. 244–251. IEEE (2003)

13. McAdams, A., Zhu, Y., Selle, A., et al.: Efficient elasticity for character skinning with contact and collisions. ACM Trans. Graph. (TOG) **30**(4), 37 (2011). ACM

14. Arnold, D.: Questions on shell theory. In: Workshop on Elastic Shells: Modeling, Analysis, and Computation (2000)

15. Cirak, F., Scott, M.J., Antonsson, E.K., et al.: Integrated modeling, finite-element analysis, and engineering design for thin-shell structures using subdivision. Comput. Aided Des. **34**(2), 137–148 (2002)

16. Green, S., Turkiyyah, G., Storti, D.: Subdivision-based multilevel methods for large scale engineering simulation of thin shells. In: Proceedings of the Seventh ACM Symposium on Solid Modeling and Applications, pp. 265–272. ACM (2002)

17. Grinspun, E., Krysl, P., Schröder, P.: CHARMS: a simple framework for adaptive simulation. ACM Trans. Graph. (TOG) **21**(3), 281–290 (2002). ACM

18. Grinspun, E., Hirani, A.N., Desbrun, M., et al.: Discrete shells. In: Proceedings of the 2003 ACM SIGGRAPH/Eurographics Symposium on Computer Animation, pp. 62–67. Eurographics Association (2003)

19. Skouras, M., Thomaszewski, B., Bickel, B., et al.: Computational design of rubber balloons. Comput. Graph. Forum **31**(2pt4), 835–844 (2012). Blackwell Publishing Ltd.,

20. Guendelman, E., Selle, A., Losasso, F., et al.: Coupling water and smoke to thin deformable and rigid shells. ACM Trans. Graph. (TOG) **24**(3), 973–981 (2005)

21. Robinson-Mosher, A., Shinar, T., Gretarsson, J., et al.: Two-way coupling of fluids to rigid and deformable solids and shells. ACM Trans. Graph. (TOG) **27**(3), 46 (2008). ACM

22. Batty, C., Bertails, F., Bridson, R.: A fast variational framework for accurate solid-fluid coupling. ACM Trans. Graph. (TOG) **26**(3), 100 (2007)

23. Chen, Z., Feng, R., Wang, H.: Modeling friction and air effects between cloth and deformable bodies. ACM Trans. Graph. **32**(4), 96–96 (2013)

24. Müller, M., Keiser, R., Nealen, A., et al.: Point based animation of elastic, plastic and melting objects. In: Proceedings of the 2004 ACM SIGGRAPH/Eurographics Symposium on Computer animation, pp. 141–151. Eurographics Association (2004)

25. Bargteil, A.W., Wojtan, C., Hodgins, J.K., et al.: A finite element method for animating large viscoplastic flow. ACM Trans. Graph. (TOG) **26**(3), 16 (2007)

26. Irving, G., Schroeder, C., Fedkiw, R.: Volume conserving finite element simulations of deformable models. ACM Trans. Graph. **26**(3) (2007)

27. Hong, M., Jung, S., Choi, M.H., et al.: Fast volume preservation for a mass-spring system. IEEE Comput. Graph. Appl. **26**(5), 83–91 (2006)

28. Müller, M., Heidelberger, B., Hennix, M., et al.: Position based dynamics. J. Vis. Commun. Image Representation **18**(2), 109–118 (2007)

29. Müller, M.: Hierarchical position based dynamics (2008)

30. Diziol, R., Bender, J., Bayer, D.: Robust real-time deformation of incompressible surface meshes. In: Proceedings of the 2011 ACM SIGGRAPH/Eurographics Symposium on Computer Animation, pp. 237–246. ACM (2011)

31. Baraff, D., Witkin, A.: Large steps in cloth simulation. In: Proceedings of the 25th Annual Conference on Computer Graphics and Interactive Techniques, pp. 43–54. ACM (1998)

Decision-Tree Based Hybrid Filter-Wrapping Method for the Fusion of Multiple Feature Sets

Cuicui Zhang[1], Xuefeng Liang[1(✉)], and Naixue Xiong[2]

[1] IST, Graduate School of Informatics, Kyoto University, Kyoto 606-8501, Japan
zhang@vision.kuee.kyoto-u.ac.jp, xliang@i.kyoto-u.ac.jp
[2] School of Computer Science, Colorado Technical University, Colorado Spring, USA
nxiong@coloradotech.edu

Abstract. This paper proposes a decision-tree based hybrid filter-wrapping method to solve multiple-feature recognition problems. The decision tree is constructed by various feature sets. Each tree node comprises all possibilities of individual feature combinations: the original features, the serial fusion of original features, and the parallel fusion of original features. In order to generate the best discriminate feature set, a two-stage feature searching algorithm is developed. The first stage is a kind of feature filtering method to find out the local optimal individual features in each level of the tree using a LDA-motivated discrimination criterion. The second stage is a global optimal feature vector generation based on a kind of forward wrapping method. In contrast to literature feature fusion methods which considered filter and wrapping separately, our method combines them together. Furthermore, since our method takes all possibilities of feature combinations into consideration, it is more likely to generate the best discriminate feature set than other feature fusion methods. In addition, our method also compensates discrimination if some portions of original features are missing. The effectiveness of our method is evaluated on a 3D dataset. Comparative experimental results show that our method can impressively improve the recognition accuracy and has better performance than existing methods.

Keywords: Decision-tree · Hybrid filter-wrapping · Feature fusion · Face recognition

1 Introduction

Information fusion is promising for a large extent of applications in modern image/video retrieval or pattern recognition systems. The multimodality fusion strategies are often categorized by feature fusion, match score fusion, and decision fusion [13]. Compared with match score fusion and decision fusion, feature fusion shows obvious advantages [4]. Wisely integrating multiple feature vectors extracted from the same pattern or from different patterns will not only enhance the discrimination of the features, but also eliminate redundancies.

© Springer International Publishing Switzerland 2015
Y.-J. Zhang (Ed.): ICIG 2015, Part II, LNCS 9218, pp. 90–102, 2015.
DOI: 10.1007/978-3-319-21963-9_8

Existing feature fusion methods can be divided into two categories: serial feature fusion and parallel feature fusion [13]. Serial fusion groups multiple feature vectors into a new vector, and is doomed to deal with high dimensional feature vectors. Recently, several methods of this kind were proposed. For example, Canonical Correlation Analysis (CCA) in [6,12] was used to fuse audio-visual features in which the representations of projected audio and visual features in their own subspaces were able to preserve the correlation conveyed by the original audio and visual feature spaces. However, the applications of CCA are merely limited to the situation that the covariance matrix of the feature space is nonsingular. Another method presented in [1] used Partial Least Squares (PLS) regression for feature pair fusion. Although the fused feature set using this method may have better discrimination, its (the feature vector) dimension is also multiplied. This obviously leads to more difficulties in afterward processing. Parallel feature fusion is achieved by combining multiple feature vectors into a new vector in parallel. The popular parallel feature fusion methods include Probabilistic fusion methods [10], Adaptive Neuro-Fuzzy Inference System (ANFIS), Support Vector Machine (SVM) [3], sum rule [7], Fisher Linear Discriminate Analysis (FLDA) [5,8,9], Radial Basis Function Neural Network (RBFNN) [18], and so on. These feature fusion methods simply concatenate or integrate several heterogeneous features together [4]. Nevertheless, systems adopting such feature fusion may not always have a better performance due to unbalanced combination of multiple feature sets. Considering the limitations of current feature fusioin methods, we are trying to develop a new approach to overcome aforementioned drawbacks.

In supervised learning, feature selection algorithms are usually grouped into two categories: filtering and wrapping. Filters use an evaluation function that relies solely on properties of the data, thus are independent on any particular algorithm. Wrappers use the inductive algorithm to estimate the value of a given subset. Wrapper methods are widely recognized as a superior alternative in supervised learning. However, even for algorithms that exhibit a moderate complexity, the number of executions that the search process requires results in a high computational cost. This paper proposes a hybrid filter-wrapping method based on a decision tree to combine the advantages of filter and wrapper together while avoiding their shortcomings meanwhile. The decision tree is constructed by hybrid feature combinations of original feature sets. For a modality system with n feature sets of the same length N, the i-th $(i = 1, 2, \ldots N)$ level of the decision tree has $[n + 2(C_n^2 + C_n^3 + \cdots + C_n^n)]^{i-1}$ tree nodes, and each node at the same level possesses the same children including n sub-features in the i-th dimension of the original feature sets, $C_n^2 + C_n^3 + \cdots + C_n^n$ serial fusion of these sub-features, and $C_n^2 + C_n^3 + \cdots + C_n^n$ parallel fusion of these sub-features. An example consisting of three feature sets is shown in Fig. 1. The advantage of using decision-tree is that all possibilities of feature combinations can be taken into consideration. However, if the best feature set searching exhausts all possibilities, it requires extremely high computational cost. In order to do it efficiently and effectively, a two-stage feature searching algorithm is proposed. The first stage is

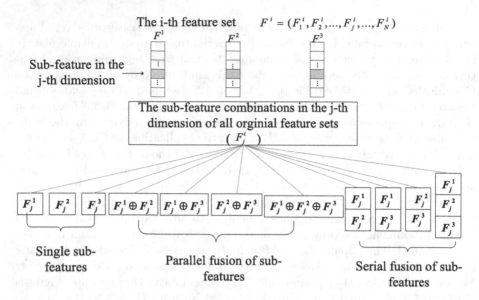

Fig. 1. An example of individual feature combinations: the combination of the j-th features of multiple features sets

a filter seeming method to find out the local optimal individual features in each level of the tree based on a LDA-motivated discrimination criterion. The second stage is a forward wrapping method to generate the global optimal feature set. However, our method differs from the classical wrappers that usually combine and visit all features. Through doing experiments, we find that some features are redundant or even downgrading the performance. Here, PCA + LDA is used to generate features in much lower dimensional feature space. This scheme does not only guarantee the accuracy improvement, also reduces the computational cost significantly.

The advantages of our method are as follows: 1. The two-stage feature searching algorithm, which combines filter and wrapping together, not only finds out the local best individual features, but also generates a global optimal feature set; 2. Our method takes all possibilities of feature combinations into account: the original features, the serial fusion of original features, and the parallel fusion of original features. This characteristic makes our method more likely to generate the best feature vector than literature feature fusion methods; 3. Once some portions of original features are missing, the proposed algorithm can self-adjust the weights among original features so that it can compensate feature missing problem.

The remaining of this paper is organized as follows: Sect. 2 presents the construction of the decision tree, and the two-stage feature searching algorithm in details. In Sect. 3, comparative experiments are reported and the performance of our method is analyzed. Finally, Sect. 4 concludes this paper.

2   Decision-Tree Based Hybrid Filter-Wrapping Method for Feature Fusion

The method can be roughly divided into four steps: 1. the construction of the decision-tree; 2. the local optimal feature selection based on a proposed Maximal Classifiable Criterion (MCC); 3. the sorting of the feature vector according to the MCC score; and 4. the forward global optimal feature selection.

2.1   Construction of the Decision Tree

Feature fusion is performed after feature extraction using PCA [15] and LDA [2]. Here, PCA is used for dimension reduction and LDA is used to generate feature vectors in the lower dimensional space. LDA is implemented via scatter matrix analysis. For an n-class problem, the within-class and between-class scatter matrices S_w, S_b are calculated as follows:

$$S_w = \sum_{i=1}^{n} Pr(C_i)\Sigma_i. \tag{1}$$

$$S_b = \sum_{i=1}^{n} Pr(C_i)(\mathbf{m}_i - \mathbf{m}_0)(\mathbf{m}_i - \mathbf{m}_0)^T, \tag{2}$$

where $Pr(C_i)$ is the prior class probability and usually replaced by $1/n$ with the assumption of equal priors. Please refer to [2] for more details.

The decision tree is constructed by the sub-features in the same dimension of the original feature sets. The node at the j-th level comprises the sub-features in the j-th dimension of original feature sets and the new serial and parallel fused sub-features. Thus, the height of the tree equals to the number of dimensions N of the original feature sets. For a modality system of n different feature sets, each tree node at j-th level has $n + 2(C_n^2 + C_n^3 + \cdots + C_n^n)$ children nodes including the n original sub-features in the $(j+1)$-th dimension, the $C_n^2 + C_n^3 + \cdots + C_n^n$ serial fusion of these sub-features, and the $C_n^2 + C_n^3 + \cdots + C_n^n$ parallel fusion of these sub-features. All the tree nodes at the same level have the same children. Figure 1 shows an example. There are three heterogeneous feature sets: F^1, F^2, and F^3. Each tree node at j-th level has 11 children, including 3 original sub-features in the $(j + 1)$-th dimension, 4 parallel fused sub-features and 4 serial fused sub-features. The decision tree is shown in Fig. 2.

The serial fusion sequentially connects all original sub-features in the same dimension to generate a new feature. The parallel fusion often linearly combines all sub-features by a weighted sum rule defined in Eq. (3).

$$V = w_1 X_1 + w_2 X_2 \cdots + w_i X_i \cdots + w_n X_n, \tag{3}$$

where X_i denotes the i-th original feature set. In [11,14,16], the weights are determined by the recognition accuracy of each original feature set. In [9], the weights are defined by $trace(S_b./S_w)$, where S_b and S_w are defined in Eqs. (1) and (2), respectively. Through conducting these two weight calculation methods, we find that the latter is not always proportional to the former one. For example, the $trace(S_b./S_w)$ of three feature images: maximum principal curvature image

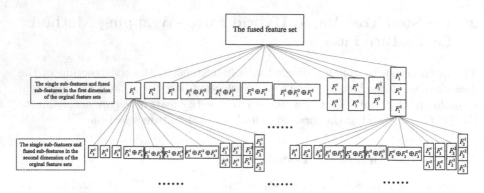

Fig. 2. An example decision-tree for a modality system of 3 feature sets. The nodes at the j-th level represent the combinations of the individual sub-features in the j-th dimension: the original sub-features, the parallel fusion of these sub-features, and the serial fusion of these sub-features. Each node at the same level has the same children. The height of the tree equals to the dimensions of the original feature sets.

(MPCI), average edge image (AEI), and range image (RI) have a order as RI > AEI > MPCI, however the recognition accuracy of them are RI > MPCI > AEI. Therefore, we can say that either the $trace(S_b./S_w)$ or the recognition accuracy alone is not adequately robust to determine weights for fusion. In this paper, a new weight calculation method which combines the two weight calculation method together is proposed as follows:

$$w_{(i,j)} = \tfrac{1}{2} \times (nTrace_{(i,j)}(S_b./S_w) + dA_{(i,j)}), \tag{4}$$

where $w_{(i,j)}$ is the weight of the sub-features in the j-th dimension of the i-th feature set, $Trace_{(i,j)}$ is the trace of the $S_b./S_w$, calculated from these sub-features, and the $dA_{(i,j)}$ (short for $dimensional Accuracy_{(i,j)}$) is the recognition accuracy of these sub-features. As $trace_{(i,j)}$ and $dA_{(i,j)}$ are of different data ranges, we, therefore, normalize the trace to the range of [0,1] by

$$nTrace_{(i,j)}(S_b./S_w) = \frac{trace_{(i,j)}}{max(trace_{(1,j)},trace_{(2,j)},...,trace_{(n,j)})}. \tag{5}$$

And $w_{(i,j)}$ is normalized by

$$w_{(i,j)} = \frac{w_{(i,j)}}{w_{(1,j)}+w_{(2,j)}+\cdots+w_{(n,j)}}. \tag{6}$$

In [11], feature fusion is performed on the whole feature sets using Eq. (3), and w_i is given by the recognition accuracy of each original feature set. In [9], the trace of $S_b./S_w$ is also generated from the whole feature set. In our work, feature fusion is performed on the sub-features in the same dimension of the original feature sets sequentially. Thus, we calculate the weight for each dimensional sub-features rather than on the whole original feature set. This weight determination at microlevel lets the fused feature more fit to the data.

2.2 Local Optimal Feature Selection

The local optimal feature selection is to find out the best sub-features at each level of the decision tree from the original sub-features and the fused sub-features. Selection is performed based on a classification criterion defined in Eq. (4). The feature with the maximal classifiable criterion score (MCC) is considered as the best feature in this level. Since the mechanism of parallel fusion differs from that of serial fusion, MCC is defined under two conditions:

(1) for original sub-features in the j-th dimension of the i-th feature set, and the parallel fusion of these original sub-features, MCC is defined by

$$max(nTrace_{(i,j)}(S_b./S_w) \times dA_{(i,j)}); \tag{7}$$

(2) for the serial fusion of these original sub-features, MCC is defined by

$$\frac{\sum_{i=1}^{n} nTrace_{(i,j)}(S_b./S_w) \times dA_{(i,j)}}{\sum_{i=1}^{n} dA_{(i,j)}}. \tag{8}$$

The reason we define a different MCC for serial fusion is that a new serial fused feature is created by linking original sub-features sequentially. Then, the trace of the serial fused feature is the integration of traces of those original sub-features. As each original sub-feature performs with its own accuracy that is varied from others, weighting these traces with respect to their accuracies will more fit to the new feature.

2.3 Sorting of the Feature Vector

The local optimal sub-feature at each tree level form a feature vector going through the tree from root to leaves. Elements in this feature vector are then sorted in a descending order according to the MCC score to form the feature set F'.

2.4 Global Optimal Feature Selection

The global optimal feature selection aims at eliminating the feature redundancy and removing noisy features from the feature set F' generated in Sect. 2.3. It is a wrapper seeming method which selects features forward from the top to the bottom. The selected sub-feature at j-th dimension of F' will be inserted into the final discriminate feature set $\hat{F}$ sequentially. If this feature does not improve the recognition accuracy of $\hat{F}$, then it will be eliminated from $\hat{F}$. Since the sub-features in each dimension is independent with each other, feature elimination here will not affect the discriminative power of the subsequent feature integration. Please see Fig. 3 for demonstration. After this procedure, the best discriminate feature set $\hat{F}$ is obtained for recognition.

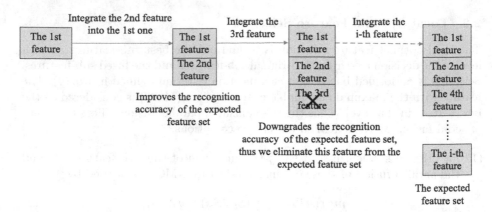

Fig. 3. The forward global feature selection

2.5 Handing with Feature Missing

Apart from intralmodal fusion where multiple features from a single modality are integrated, our method can also be applied to intermodal fusion (multimodal fusion), where complementary features from multiple patterns are integrated. Such a case is Audio Visual Automatic Speech Recognition, where fusing visual and audio cues can lead to improved performance. One motivation of multimodal fusion is to solve missing feature problems. If some portion of a feature vector is missing, other feature vectors should compensate to guarantee the recognition accuracy. This can be done in the first stage of our feature searching algorithm. Local feature selection assigns specific weights to different sub-features according to their discriminative powers, higher discriminative power larger weight. There usually exits a key feature in the system, such as the RI feature in our experimental system. However, when it is missing in some tree levels, our method will take other kinds of features into consideration, such as MPCI. Therefore, our algorithm can still maintain the performance in case of feature missing.

3   Experimental Results and Analysis

3.1   3D Dataset and Feature Extraction

The experiment is performed on the 3D dataset consisting of 38 face classes. Each face class possesses 10 samples, 9 of which are of various head poses and 1 of different lighting conditions. For each person, 6 samples are selected randomly and put into the training subset while the other 4 samples are put into the test subset. Here, 3D face models are represented by triangular meshes. In order to reduce data size, mesh simplification [19] is used here. The goal of mesh simplification is to use fewer vertices and fewer triangles to reconstruct the 3D face model while preserving the shape and feature points as much as possible. Data ratio is defined by the percent of the data after mesh simplification to

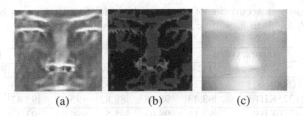

Fig. 4. Three kinds of facial feature images (a) MPCI, (b) AEI, (c) RI

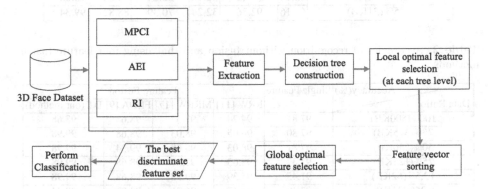

Fig. 5. Our feature fusion method for 3D face recognition

that before mesh simplification. For each 3D face data, mesh simplification is performed at 6 levels to get 6 kinds of data files: the file with 100 % data (the original data file), 50 % data, 25 % data, 12.5 % data, and 6.25 % data.

After data normalization, three kinds of facial feature images are generated using the method in [17]: the maximal principal curvature image (MPCI), the average edge image (AEI), and the range image (RI) (see Fig. 4). Feature extraction based on PCA [17] and LDA [2] is performed to generate three feature sets to build up the decision tree. The procedure is shown in Fig. 5.

3.2   Performance Analysis

In this section, two experiments are performed to evaluate the efficiency of our method. In the first experiment, our method is compared with recognition without fusion (using single feature sets) and recognition using several existing feature fusion methods. The recognition accuracy of three single feature sets are calculated first, which are shown in Table 1. The average recognition accuracy of these feature sets is used to compare with our method in order to preserve the diversity of features' performances (see the second column of Table 2). In [11, 14, 16], a parallel fusion based on a weighted sum rule defined by Eq. (3) was developed. We call these recognition rate based weight calculation method as RRW (see the third column of Table 2). In [17], a modified weight calculation

Table 1. Recognition accuracies of three single facial feature images based on PCA and PCA + LDA for data files of six levels, respectively

Accuracy(%) Data Ratio	MPCI		AEI		RI	
	PCA	PCA+LDA	PCA	PCA+LDA	PCA	PCA+LDA
100%(500KB)	92.76	98.03	85.53	96.71	92.76	**98.68**
75%(375KB)	93.43	98.68	88.82	95.39	93.42	**99.34**
50%(250KB)	92.11	98.03	85.53	96.05	93.42	**99.34**
25%(125KB)	92.76	97.37	71.71	95.39	94.08	**99.34**
12.5%(62KB)	82.24	93.42	50.00	82.24	94.08	**98.68**
6.25%(31KB)	63.16	92.76	32.24	70.39	88.82	**99.34**

Table 2. Accuracies of recognition without fusion and that using four feature fusion methods

Accuracy(%) Data Ratio	Single Feature	Feature Fusion			
		RRW [11]	MRRW [17]	FLDA [9]	DT (our method)
100%(500KB)	97.81	94.74	97.37	**98.68**	**98.68**
75%(375KB)	97.80	96.05	98.03	98.68	**99.98**
50%(250KB)	97.81	98.03	98.68	99.34	**99.98**
25%(125KB)	97.37	98.03	97.37	98.68	**99.98**
12.5%(62KB)	91.45	95.39	**99.98**	98.68	**99.98**
6.25%(31KB)	87.49	89.47	96.71	98.03	**99.34**

method was proposed. It was defined as follows:

$$w_i' = (10w_i - min(\lfloor 10w_1 \rfloor, \lfloor 10w_2 \rfloor, \dots \lfloor 10w_n \rfloor))^2, \qquad (9)$$

where w_i is the recognition accuracy of the i-th original feature set ($i = 1, 2, \dots n$). w_i' is its new weight. We call this method as MRRW (the modified RRW, see the third column of Table 2). Another feature fusion method gained wide popularity is the one based on fisher linear discriminate analysis (FLDA) [9]. It uses the discriminate criterion defined by S_b and S_w. The recognition results of this method are shown in the fourth column of Table 2. The last column represents the recognition results using our method. We call our method 'DT' for short. Table 2 reveals that our method has a better performance than recognition using single features and that using the aforementioned feature fusion methods. It achieves at a remarkable recognition accuracy even when the data file is small. In addition, comparing the performance of RRW and that without fusion, we can see that in some cases, recognition using feature fusion even performs worse than ones without fusion. The reason is that the weights of different features are not balanced well. Compared to the existing feature fusion methods based on simple fusion strategies, our method is more likely to find the best discriminate feature set thanks to its characteristic of taking all the feature combination possibilities into account and its efficient two-stage feature selection algorithm.

Another three important parameters to evaluate the performance of pattern recognition algorithms are also investigated: the false rejection rate (FRR),

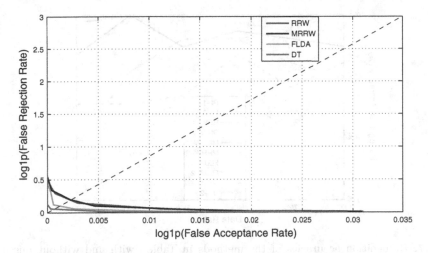

Fig. 6. ROC curves of four feature fusion methods

Table 3. Recognition accuracies of recognition using single features and feature fusion methods while portions of RI are missing.

Accuracy(%) Data Ratio	Single Feature		Feature Fusion			
	RI	MPCI	RRW [11]	MRRW [17]	FLDA [9]	DT (our method)
100%(500KB)	94.08	**98.03**	94.08	96.05	96.71	**98.03**
75%(375KB)	94.74	**98.68**	90.13	94.08	95.39	**98.68**
50%(250KB)	95.39	**98.03**	94.08	96.71	96.05	**98.03**
25%(125KB)	94.74	97.37	94.08	93.42	93.42	**98.68**
12.5%(62KB)	94.08	93.42	87.49	92.76	90.13	**95.39**
6.25%(31KB)	94.74	92.76	85.53	92.76	86.84	**96.05**

the false acceptance rate (FAR), and the equal error rate (EER). The ROC curves plot log (FAR) against log (FRR) of those aforementioned four feature fusion methods in Fig. 6. ROC curves are plotted by log(FAR) against log(FRR) because it makes the relationship of FAR and FRR clearer than conventional ROC diagrams. We can see that EER of our method approximately equals to 0. It is smaller than that of other feature fusion methods. This suggests that our method obtains a very satisfactory performance not only in recognition accuracy but also in FAR, FRR.

The second experiment is performed to verify that our method can deal with missing feature problems. RI is the key feature in the first experiment since it achieves a higher recognition accuracy than MPCI and AEI (see Table 1). In this experiment, we randomly remove portions (20 %) of RI features of some samples (10 % samples). Table 3 shows the comparative result. In the first three rows, the performance of our method keeps the same as using MPCI alone. The reason is that the missed portions have seriously downgraded the discrimination of RI, and affected results of other three feature fusion methods. Comparatively, MPCI

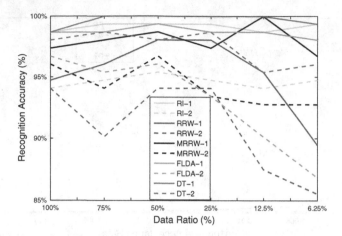

Fig. 7. Recognition accuracies of the methods in Table 3 with and without missing features, where solid curves represent recognition accuracy without missing features and dot lines represent that method with missing features (Color figure online).

rises to the first priority comparing with other fused features in each dimension. Thus, our method assigns larger weight to MPCI and selects it alone to perform recognition. That is why our method has the same performance as MPCI. In the next three rows, our method performs better than other all. Because the mesh simplification in MPCI is significant (the data ratio is no greater than 25 %), and also seriously downgrades the discrimination of MPCI. Then, our method uses the generated new features under this case. In Table 3, as other feature fusion methods are not capable of rebalancing the weights after feature missing, their performances downgrade significantly. Figure 7 plots the recognition accuracy curves of all methods before and after feature missing. It clearly shows that the degeneration affected by feature missing of our method (red line) is the least.

4   Conclusion

In this paper, a hybrid filter-wrapping method is proposed based on decision-tree for the fusion of multiple feature sets. This work has four contributions: 1. It combines two kinds of feature selection methods: filter and wrapper together using a two-stage feature searching algorithm to ensure efficiency and effectiveness of finding the best discriminate feature set. This strategy develops the advantages of filters and wrappers while avoiding their shortcomings meanwhile; 2. Our method takes all possibilities of feature combinations into account including the original features, the serial fusion of original features, and the parallel fusion of original features. This characteristic makes our method more likely to find out the optimal feature vector than literature feature fusion methods which treat serial fusion and parallel fusion separately; 3. To ensure the performance of parallel fusion, we designed a new weight calculation method which takes both the trace and the dimensional recognition accuracy into consideration; 4. The two-stage algorithm has an ability to solve missing feature problems.

Our feature fusion method has been evaluated by 3D face recognition. Experimental results show that our method outperforms methods using single features and other feature fusion approaches in [9,11,17], respectively. The EER of our method approximately equals zero, which shows that our method achieves at a very satisfactory performance.

Acknowledgement. This work is supported by: JSPS Grants-in-Aid for Scientific Research C (No.15K00236).

References

1. Barker, M., Rayens, W.: Partial least squares for discrimination. J. Chemometr. **17**(3), 166–173 (2003)
2. Belhumeur, P., Hespanha, J., Kriegman, D.: Eigenfaces vs. fisherfaces: recognition using class specific linear projection. IEEE Trans. Pattern Anal. Mach. Intell. **20**(7), 711–720 (1997)
3. Fang, Y., Tan, T., Wang, Y.: Fusion of global and local features for face verification. IEEE Confernce on ICPR, pp. 382–385 (2002)
4. Fu, Y., Cao, L., Guo, G., Huang, T.: Multiple feature fusion by subspace learning. In: Proceedings of ACM International Conference on Image and Video Retrieval, pp. 127–134 (2008)
5. Gan, J., Liang, Y.: A method for face and iris feature fusion in identity authentication. IJCSNS **6**(2), 135–138 (2006)
6. Kim, T., Wong, S., Cipolla, R.: Tensor canonical correlation analysis for action classification. In: IEEE Conference on CVPR (2007)
7. Lee, C., Wang, S.: A gabor filter-based approach to finngerprint recognition. In: IEEE Workshop on Signal Processing Systems, pp. 371–378 (1999)
8. Liu, Z., Liu, C.: Fusion of color, local spatial and global frequency information for face recognition. Patterns Recogn. **43**, 2882–2890 (2010)
9. Patra, A., S. Das, B.: Dual space based face recognition using feature fusion. In: International Conference on Visual Information Engineering, pp. 155–160 (2006)
10. Rao, K., Rajagopalan, A.: A probabilistic fusion methodology for face recognition. J. Appl. Sig. Process. **17**, 2772–2787 (2005)
11. Ross, A., Govindarajan, R.: Feature level fusion using hand and face biometrics. In: Proceedings of SPIE Conference on Biometric Technology for Human Identification, pp. 196–204 (2004)
12. Sargin, M., Yemez, Y., Erzin, E., Tekalp, A.: Audiovisual synchronization and fusion using canonical correlation analysis. IEEE Trans. Multimedia **9**(7), 1396–1403 (2007)
13. Sun, Q., Zeng, S., Liu, Y., Heng, P., Xia, D.: A new method of feature fusion and its application in image recognition. Pattern Recogn. **38**, 2437–2448 (2005)
14. Sun, Y., Tang, H., Yin, B.: The 3d face recognition algorithm fusing multi-geometry features. J. Acta Autom. Sinica **34**(12), 1483–1489 (2008)
15. Turk, M., Pentland, A.: Eigenfaces for recognition. J. Cogn. Neurosci. **3**(1), 71–86 (1991)

16. Xiang, Y., Su, G.: Multi-parts and multi-feature fusion in face recognition. In: IEEE Computer Society Conference on Computer Vision and Pattern Recognition Workshops, CVPRW 2008, pp. 1–6 (2008)
17. Zhang, C., Uchimura, K., Zhang, C., koutaki, G.: 3d face recognition using multi-level multi-feature fusion. In: The 4th Pacific Symposium on Image and Video Technology, pp. 21–26 (2010)
18. Zhang, H., Sun, X., Zhao, L., Liu, L.: Image fusion algorithm using RBF neural networks. In: Corchado, E., Abraham, A., Pedrycz, W. (eds.) HAIS 2008. LNCS (LNAI), vol. 5271, pp. 417–424. Springer, Heidelberg (2008)
19. Zhou, Y., Zhang, C., He, P.: Feature preserving mesh simplification algorithm based on square volume measure. Chin. J. Comput. **32**(2), 203–212 (2009)

Depth Map Coding Method for Scalable Video Plus Depth

Panpan Li[1], Ran Ma[1,2(✉)], Yu Hou[1], and Ping An[1,2]

[1] School of Communication and Information Engineering, Shanghai University,
Shanghai 200072, China
maran@shu.edu.cn
[2] Key Laboratory of Advanced Display and System Application of the Ministry
of Education, Shanghai 200072, China

Abstract. Depth map coding along with its associated texture video plays an
important role in the display of 3D scene by Depth Image Based Rendering
technique. In this paper, the inter-layer motion prediction in Scalable Video
Coding is applied in order to utilize the similarity of the motion data between
texture video and its associated depth map. Additionally, in order to preserve the
edge in depth map, the edge detection algorithm is proposed in depth map
coding, which combines the conventional Sobel edge detection and the
block-based coding scheme of SVC. And the dynamic quantization algorithm is
proposed to preserve the information of boundary regions of the depth
map. Simulation results show that the proposed method achieves the BDPSNR
gains from 0.463 dB to 0.941 dB for the depth map, and the Bjøntegaard bitrates
savings range from 9.72 % to 19.36 % for the video plus depth.

Keywords: 3D video · Video plus depth · Scalable Video Coding · Boundary
region · Inter-layer prediction · Edge detection

1 Introduction

With the rapid development of the Internet and video display devices, the video
multimedia services have attracted great interest of people. Compared with the traditional 2D video, 3D video can provide more realistic scene. Hence, the research of 3D
video is regarded as a hot area and lots of progresses have been made. As one of the 3D
video formats [1, 2], texture video plus depth map (V + D) is able to provide 3D scene
by Depth Image Based Rendering (DIBR) technique [3], which can synthesis a virtual
view based on a texture video and its associated depth map. Accordingly, it is quite
necessary to transmit the depth map in addition to the texture video.

As an extension of the H.264/AVC standard [4], Scalable Video Coding (SVC) can
provide some significant functionalities by dividing the bit stream into one base layer
(BL) bit stream and several enhancement layers (ELs) bit streams [5]. In the process of
transmission, the decoder can get an optimal bit stream through selectively discarding
enhancement layer bit streams. In order to provide scalable 3D scene in the display
side, the texture video and its associated depth map should be transmitted to the display
device simultaneously. One simplest way is to encode them separately in the SVC

© Springer International Publishing Switzerland 2015
Y.-J. Zhang (Ed.): ICIG 2015, Part II, LNCS 9218, pp. 103–115, 2015.
DOI: 10.1007/978-3-319-21963-9_9

encoder and then synthesis the 3D video in the display side. However, this method doesn't exploit the correlation between texture video and its associated depth map. More redundant information could be removed and the compression efficiency could be further improved when they are jointly encoded.

In the process of 3D video coding, it can effectively improve the coding efficiency of the multi-view video transmission by adding the depth map. So, there were many studies about depth map coding. In [6], Tao et al. proposed a novel method of compressing the texture video and depth map jointly by using the correlation of the motion field and brought significant coding gain for the associated depth map. In [7], Lei et al. proposed a new depth map coding scheme based on the structure and motion similarities between the texture video and its associated depth map, a new type of block named OD-Block and a DTCC based prediction method are presented for the depth map coding, which can improve the coding efficiency and the rendering quality. The similarity of motion vectors between texture video and depth map were also used for the depth map coding in [8, 9].

Besides, some new edge-preserving algorithms were proposed for the reason that boundary regions play an important role in view rendering [10–13]. In [10], Zamarin et al. proposed a new edge-preserving intra mode for depth macroblocks (MBs) to improve the compression efficiency and the rendering quality. Kao and Tu proposed a novel compression method which includes an edge detection module, a homogenizing module and a compression encoding module for depth map in [11].

However, those methods mentioned above didn't combine the importance of the depth map edge and the correlation between texture video and its associated depth map when encoding the texture video and depth map in a scalable way. In this paper, a depth map coding method in the SVC is studied. A new depth map edge detection algorithm and a dynamic quantization algorithm based on the edge regions are proposed.

The rest of this paper is organized as follows. First, in Sect. 2, the proposed single-view video plus depth map coding method is described in detail. Then, the simulation results are shown in Sect. 3. Finally, Sect. 4 concludes the paper with a summary.

2   The Proposed Method

The depth map corresponding to the texture video, as shown in Fig. 1, can be regarded as a special color image whose pixel value represents the distance between the camera and the object. Besides, the depth map consists of two parts, namely boundary region (BR) and homogeneous region(HR). Specifically, the depth map is used for view rendering, rather than being displayed in the display devices.

Compared with the SVC scheme of the 2D texture video, there's no doubt that it's very worthy of studying the depth map coding method in the SVC scheme of video plus depth. So in this section, the SVC scheme of video plus depth, which is compatible with quality scalable and stereoscopic display, is firstly presented and the inter-layer prediction is also discussed. Then, the quantization algorithm based on edge detection for depth map coding is analyzed and studied to improve the quality of the depth map.

(a)   (b)

Fig. 1. The video plus depth format of 3D video: (a) the texture video; (b) the depth map.

2.1 SVC Scheme of Video Plus Depth

Tao et al. in [6] encoded the single-view video plus depth map into two layers, one is the BL whose input is the texture video, and the other is the EL whose input is the depth map. Based on Tao's scheme, the improved encoding scheme proposed in this paper is illustrated in Fig. 2. Here, the three-layer coding structure is used.

In the BL, the hybrid temporal and spatial prediction mode is used to encode the texture video to get the basic video quality in Fig. 2. EL1, the newly added layer in our structure, is a texture quality enhancement layer. The data in EL1 is the refinement of texture information. When the decoder gets BL or/and EL1 bit stream, 2D video with different qualities can be displayed. In EL2, the depth map is input. When the decoder gets the whole bit stream that includes the BL, EL1 and EL2, 3D scenes are available by using the DIBR technique. Therefore, compared with Tao's scheme, our encoding scheme can realize not only the quality scalable but also stereoscopic display.

In the SVC scheme, inter-layer prediction is used, which is a prediction tool added to spatial SVC [5]. Specifically, inter-layer prediction can be divided into three types: inter-layer motion prediction, inter-layer residual prediction and inter-layer intra prediction. When encoding the enhancement layer, if the co-located MB in the reference

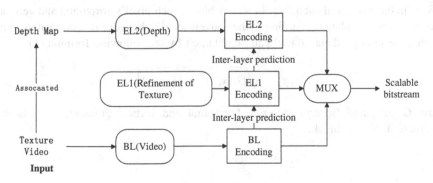

Fig. 2. The encoding scheme.

layer is inter-coded, then the current MB is also inter-coded, and its motion vectors and reference indexes can be derived from the co-located MB in the reference layer by inter-layer motion prediction. Besides, quality SVC can be considered as a special case of spatial SVC with the same video sizes for BL and ELs, so the inter-layer prediction can also be applied for it.

When encoding the EL1, the above three inter-layer prediction tools are all applied to improve the coding efficiency. In fact, it is the 2D quality SVC with BL and EL1, and the coding scheme is the same as the H.264/SVC, so it isn't discussed in this paper. When encoding the EL2, only the inter-layer motion prediction is applied to improve the coding efficiency of the depth map. There are several reasons for this. Firstly, it is easy to see that the structure between the texture video and the depth map is very similar from Fig. 1. Secondly, because the texture video and its associated depth map are shot in the same place and at the same time, they may have similar motion vectors. Actually, lots of researchers have already verify the motion similarity between them and the coding efficiency is improved a lot by using the similarity, such as the papers mentioned above [6–9]. Thirdly, the inter-layer residual prediction and inter-layer intra prediction are not applied because the residual information and pixel value of the depth MB is quite different from the texture MB.

2.2   Depth Map Edge Detection

Due to the effect of BR of the depth map on the quality of the synthesized view, the boundary data should be preserved as exactly as possible in the process of encoding. Therefore, for the depth map encoding, we should first extract the boundary area from the depth map. The edge preserving methods mentioned above are all based on the pixel. However, in the H.264/SVC standard, the basic encoding unit is MB and in the process of mode decision, the sizes of the blocks that compose of the MB partition modes can be divided into 16×16, 8×8, and 4×4. Therefore, designing an edge detection algorithm based on blocks of different sizes is more suitable for block based coding scheme than the pixel based edge detection algorithm. So in this paper, a block-based Sobel (BBS) edge detection algorithm is proposed to extract the boundary region. The basic idea of the proposed BBS algorithm is as follows:

The current MB has multiple prediction modes with the block size of $N \times N$ ($N = 16, 8, 4$) in the process of encoding. In $N \times N$ block, each pixel's horizontal and vertical gradient can be calculated according to the conventional Sobel edge detection algorithm and then the joint gradient $G(x, y)$ can be obtained by the following formula (1):

$$G(x, y) = \sqrt{G_x(x, y)^2 + G_y(x, y)^2} \tag{1}$$

where, $G_x(x, y)$ and $G_y(x, y)$ represent horizontal and vertical gradient, (x, y) is the coordinate in $N \times N$ block.

For $N \times N$ block, the average gradient value of $(x, y)(x, y \in [1, N - 2])$ is set as the block-gradient of current $N \times N$ block. So, the block-gradient of $N \times N$ block can be expressed by formula (2):

$$G_N = \frac{\sum_{x=1}^{N-2} \sum_{y=1}^{N-2} G(x, y)}{(N - 2)^2} \tag{2}$$

After obtaining the block-gradient of $N \times N$ block, it is compared with a threshold (*Thr*), which is set to 15 based on the empirical value. If $G_N > Thr$, then the current $N \times N$ block is in the BR, otherwise it's in the HR. *Breakdancers* sequence and *Ballet* sequence are experimented with the proposed BBS edge detection algorithm, and the results are shown in Figs. 3 and 4.

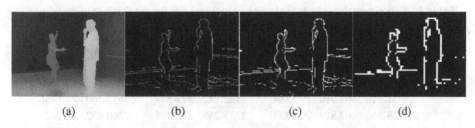

(a)   (b)   (c)   (d)

Fig. 3. Results of *Ballet* sequence: (a) the original depth map; (b) BR with 4 × 4 block size; (c) BR with 8 × 8 block size; (d) BR with 16 × 16 block size.

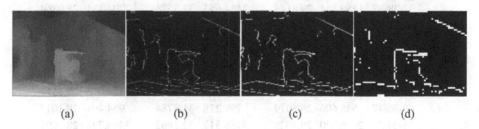

(a)   (b)   (c)   (d)

Fig. 4. Results of *Breakdancers* sequence: (a) the original depth map; (b) BR with 4 × 4 block size; (c) BR with 8 × 8 block size; (d) BR with 16 × 16 block size.

As we can see from Figs. 3 and 4, the proposed BBS edge detection algorithm can extract the BR of the depth map in a relatively accurate manner, and the smaller of the block size is, the more accurate the BR will be.

2.3 Dynamic Quantization

In the process of quantization, if the QP of the texture video has been decided, it's quite important to choose a suitable QP for the depth map to get a good quality of the synthetic view. When the bit rate of the depth map accounts for 10 %–20 % of the bit rate of the texture video, a good quality of the depth map can be gotten [14]. So some experiments are carried out to choose a better QP for the depth map based on the distribution of quantitative parameters for texture and depth. In our experiments, four groups of QP are selected for texture videos, (28,24), (32,28), (36,32) and (40,36) respectively. And in each group, the first parameter is for the BL and the second parameter is for the quality EL1. Three representative sequences are tested in our experiments, including *Ballet*, *Breakdancers* and *Newspaper*. The first two sequences have violent motion and the last one has slow motion. For the QP of the depth map, it is obtained by adding the QP Difference to the QP for the texture video of BL. In our experiments, we take the quality of the synthetic view as an evaluation criterion for the reason that the purpose of getting a high quality depth map is to get a high quality synthetic view. The experimental results can be seen in Table 1.

Table 1. Experimental results for selecting an optimal QP for the depth map encoding.

QP difference	QP	Sequences					
		Ballet		Breakdancers		Newspaper	
		Bitrates (kbps)	SynView PSNR (dB)	Bitrates (kbps)	SynView PSNR (dB)	Bitrates (kbps)	SynView PSNR (dB)
3	28-24-31	2469.010	29.8384	4422.182	32.4539	3615.360	28.1486
	32-28-35	1462.819	29.8333	2233.258	32.3399	2260.032	28.1421
	36-32-39	938.856	29.8198	1334.515	32.2544	1486.594	28.0958
	40-36-43	604.757	29.8057	855.922	32.0188	987.014	28.0607
5	28-24-33	2320.637	29.8322	4239.907	32.4227	3526.046	28.1025
	32-28-37	1359.854	29.8148	2124.653	32.3578	2202.134	28.0864
	36-32-41	874.402	29.8056	1274.107	32.1264	1453.238	28.0778
	40-36-45	572.472	29.7925	824.108	31.9590	968.962	28.0730
7	28-24-35	2189.789	29.8317	4095.979	32.3846	3451.411	28.1734
	32-28-39	1283.890	29.8269	2045.563	32.3513	2161.589	28.1710
	36-32-43	828.576	29.8154	1227.907	32.1184	1429.018	28.1512
	40-36-47	548.606	29.8079	798.278	31.8784	954.494	28.1013
9	28-24-37	2086.070	29.8029	3988.517	32.2862	3393.797	28.1091
	32-28-41	1221.288	29.8012	1986.101	32.2351	2128.368	28.0993
	36-32-45	797.275	29.8002	1197.254	32.0283	1410.744	28.0569
	40-36-49	530.952	29.7974	781.234	31.8232	944.894	27.9828

In Table 1, the *QP Difference* (*may be* 3, 5, 7, 9) means the difference of the QP between the BL and EL2. *Bitrates* is the summation of the bit rate of the texture video and the depth map when encoding them together. *SynView PSNR* is the PSNR of the synthetic view. According to the experimental results in Table 1, the RD curves can be drawn, as shown in Fig. 5.

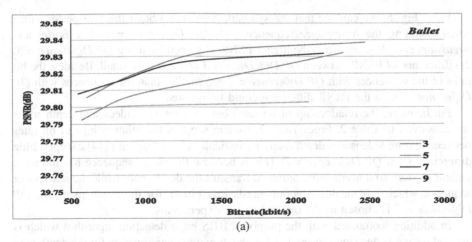

(a)

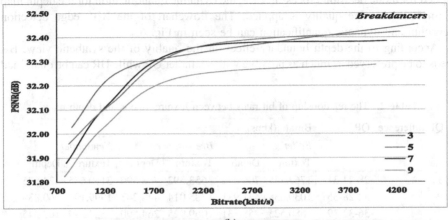

(b)

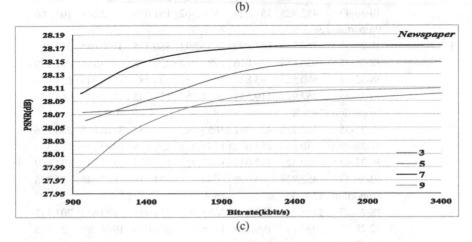

(c)

Fig. 5. RD curves of different sequences with *QP Difference = n:* (a) *Ballet;* (b) *Breakdancers;*
(c) *Newspaper.*

From Fig. 5, we can see that the synthetic view can obtain the best performance when encoding the *Newspaper* sequence with *QP Difference* = 7. For *Ballet* and *Breakdancers*, although when the higher PSNR is gained by using *QP Difference* = 3, the difference of PSNR between *QP Difference* = 3 and 7 is very small. Besides, the bit rates of the sequences with *QP Difference* = 7 are smaller than the sequences with *QP Difference* = 3, so the PSNR difference could be ignored.

Furthermore, the relationship of bit rates between texture videos and depth maps are illustrated in Table 2. From Table 2, we can see that the relationships of bit rates between texture videos and depth maps are basically consistent with [14] except a little difference when *QP Difference* = 7. This is because the *Ballet* sequence has the most violent motion, so it needs more bitrate to transmit the depth map, while the newspaper sequence which has the least motion needs less bitrate for the depth map. So, *QP Difference* = 7 is chosen as the optimal in our experiments.

In addition, combined with the proposed BBS edge detection algorithm which is applied for mode decision process in EL2, the dynamic quantification for the depth map to improve its edge quality is applied. The flowchart of the BBS edge detection algorithm and dynamic quantification can be seen in Fig. 6.

According to the depth boundary effect on the quality of the synthetic view, BR needs to be preserved as much as possible with a smaller QP while HR can be quantified

Table 2. The relationship of bit rates between texture videos and depth maps

QP difference	QP	Bitrate (kbps)					
		Ballet		*Breakdancer*		*Newspaper*	
		Texture	Depth	Texture	Depth	Texture	Depth
3	28-24-31	1762.738	706.272	3653.592	768.590	3190.685	424.675
	32-28-35	1030.838	431.981	1785.014	448.243	1999.195	260.839
	36-32-39	680.525	258.331	1069.925	264.590	1324.349	162.245
	40-36-43	452.928	151.829	694.862	161.059	882.648	104.366
	Proportion	38.3 %		23.5 %		12.5 %	
5	28-24-33	1762.738	557.899	3653.592	586.315	3190.685	335.362
	32-28-37	1030.838	329.016	1785.014	339.638	1999.195	202.939
	36-32-41	680.525	193.877	1069.925	204.182	1324.349	128.890
	40-36-45	452.928	119.544	694.862	129.245	882.648	86.314
	Proportion	29.5 %		18.2 %		10.0 %	
7	28-24-35	1762.738	427.051	3653.592	442.387	3190.685	260.726
	32-28-39	1030.838	253.052	1785.014	339.638	1999.195	162.394
	36-32-43	680.525	148.046	1069.925	157.977	1324.349	104.669
	40-36-47	452.928	95.678	694.862	103.416	882.648	71.846
	Proportion	22.8 %		15.3 %		8.0 %	
9	28-24-37	1762.738	323.339	3653.592	334.925	3190.685	203.112
	32-28-41	1030.838	190.450	1785.014	201.086	1999.195	129.173
	36-32-45	680.525	116.750	1069.925	127.330	1324.349	86.395
	40-36-49	452.928	78.024	694.862	86.371	882.648	62.246
	Proportion	17.5 %		11.0 %		6.6 %	

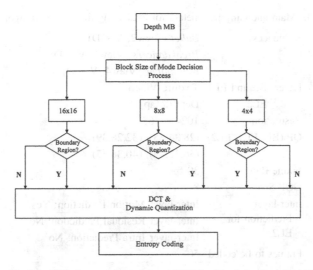

Fig. 6. The flowchart of the proposed BBS edge detection algorithm.

with a larger QP than the initial QP set in the configuration file. So a dynamic quanti-zation based on the depth BR is proposed, and the final QP can be expressed as:

$$QP = QP_{init} + \Delta QP_{H/B} \tag{3}$$

where QP_{init} is the initial QP set in the configuration file and $\Delta QP_{H/B}$ is a variable value that can be adjusted based on block sizes and the region. When the current block belongs to BR, $\Delta QP_{H/B}$ is a negative value, otherwise it is a positive value. And the smaller the block size is, the more important the block will be. So it should be quantified with a small QP. In our experiments, $\Delta QP_{H/B}$ is set as:

$$\Delta QP_{H/B} = \begin{cases} -2, CurrentBlock \in BR \ and \ 16 \times 16 \\ -3, CurrentBlock \in BR \ and \ 8 \times 8 \\ -5, CurrentBlock \in BR \ and \ 4 \times 4 \\ 4, CurrentBlock \in HR \end{cases} \tag{4}$$

Since different QP are set for the boundary regions and homogeneous regions, the average changes of the amount of the bit stream will be small.

3   Simulation Results

Some experiments are carried out for evaluating the proposed method in SVC reference software JSVM 9–19. Three different video sequences: *Ballet*, *Breakdancers*, and *News-paper*, are tested in this paper. The main encoding parameters are presented in Table 3.

The same inter-layer prediction is applied both in our coding scheme and the standard JSVM model. In addition, the initial QP for the depth map is selected by

Table 3. Main encoding parameters for evaluating the proposed algorithm.

Sequences		*Ballet* (View2, V + D)
		Breakdancers (View4, V + D)
		Newspaper (View4, V + D)
Layer	BL and EL1	Texture Video
	EL2	Depth Map
Resolution		1024 × 768
QP (BL, EL1, EL2)		(28,24,35), (32,28,39)
		(36,32,43), (40,36,47)
Frame Rate		30 fps
GOP Size		8
Inter-layer Prediction for EL2		Inter-layer Motion Prediction: Yes
		Inter-layer Residual Prediction: No
		Inter-layer Intra Prediction: No
Frames to be coded		50

adding 7 to the QP for the texture video, which has been verified in the previous section. The bitrate and PSNR values of the proposed method and the standard three-layer JSVM model without edge detection are shown in Table 4.

Since the texture video inputted to the BL and EL1 is processed in the same way with the texture video in JSVM standard model, the reconstructed quality of BL and EL1 in our coding method are substantially unchanged comparing with the JSVM standard model. So the bitrates and PSNR in Table 4 represent overall bitrates of all layers and the PSNR of the depth map respectively. The Bjøntegaard bitrates (BDBR, %) and the Bjøntegaard PSNR (BDPSNR, dB) [15] between the proposed method and the original JSVM method are calculated. From Table 4, the proposed method can

Table 4. Comparison of the proposed method and the original JSVM method.

Sequences	QP	Proposed		JSVM			
		Bitrates (kbps)	PSNR (dB)	Bitrates (kbps)	PSNR (dB)	BDBR (%)	BDPSNR (dB)
Ballet	28-24-35	2275.070	41.097	2189.788	40.460	−11.52	0.616
	32-28-39	1348.286	38.783	1283.890	38.058		
	36-32-43	877.502	36.732	828.576	35.733		
	40-36-47	581.222	34.767	548.606	33.383		
Breakdancers	28-24-35	4120.349	40.311	4095.979	39.845	−9.72	0.463
	32-28-39	2185.906	39.020	2124.653	38.487		
	36-32-43	1246.968	35.591	1227.907	34.995		
	40-36-47	808.464	33.506	798.278	32.755		
Newspaper	28-24-35	3644.016	42.284	3545.774	41.366	−19.36	0.941
	32-28-39	2246.458	40.477	2186.299	39.502		
	36-32-43	1464.269	38.609	1421.616	37.461		
	40-36-47	972.624	36.852	945.667	35.563		

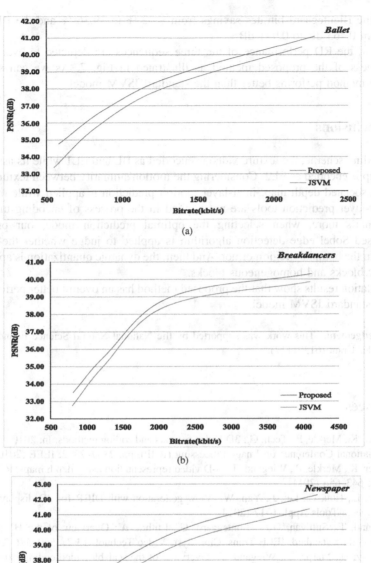

(a)

(b)

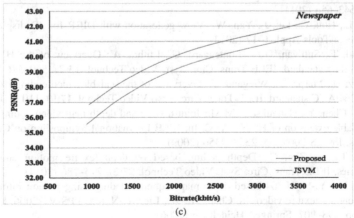

(c)

Fig. 7. RD performance comparisons: (a) *Ballet*; (b) *Breakdancers*; (c) *Newspaper*.

achieve the Bjøntegaard bitrates savings from 9.72 % to 19.36 % and the BDPSNR gains from 0.463 dB to 0.941 dB.

At last, the RD performance of the three sequences are depicted to evaluate the effectiveness of the proposed method as illustrated in Fig. 7. As we can see, our proposed method performs better than the standard JSVM model.

4   Conclusions

In our coding scheme, the texture video is encoded as BL and EL1 while its associated depth map is encoded as EL2. Considering the motion similarity between texture video and its associated depth map, inter-layer motion prediction is applied while the other two inter-layer prediction tools are not applied in the process of encoding the depth map. What's more, when selecting the optimal prediction mode, our proposed block-based Sobel edge detection algorithm is applied to judge whether the current block is in the boundary region or not. And then, the dynamic quantization is applied in boundary blocks and homogeneous blocks.

Simulation results show that the proposed method has an overall better performance than the standard JSVM model.

Acknowledgement. This work was supported by the National Natural Science Foundation of China under Grant (61301112).

References

1. Muller, K., Merkle, P., Tech, G.: 3D Video formats and coding methods. In: 2010 17th IEEE International Conference on Image Processing (ICIP), pp. 2389–2392. IEEE (2010)
2. Muller, K., Merkle, P., Wiegand, T.: 3-D video representation using depth maps. Proc. IEEE **99**(4), 643–656 (2011)
3. Wang, L., Hou, C., Lei, J., Yan, W.: View generation with DIBR for 3D display system. Multimedia Tools Appl. 1–17 (2014)
4. Wiegand, T., Sullivan, G.J., Bjontegaard, G., Luthra, A.: Overview of the H. 264/AVC video coding standard. IEEE Trans. Circ. Syst. Video Technol. **13**(7), 560–576 (2003)
5. Schwarz, H., Marpe, D., Wiegand, T.: Overview of the scalable video coding extension of the H. 264/AVC standard. IEEE Trans. Circ. Syst. Video Technol. **17**(9), 1103–1120 (2007)
6. Tao, S., Chen, Y., Hannuksela, M.M.: Joint texture and depth map video coding based on the scalable extension of H. 264/AVC. In: IEEE International Symposium on Circuits and Systems, ISCAS 2009, pp. 2353–2356 (2009)
7. Lei, J., Li, S., Zhu, C.: Depth coding based on depth-texture motion and structure similarities. IEEE Trans. Circ. Syst. Video Technol. **25**(2), 275–286 (2014)
8. Oh, H., Ho, Y.-S.: H.264-based depth map sequence coding using motion information of corresponding texture video. In: Chang, L.-W., Lie, W.-N. (eds.) PSIVT 2006. LNCS, vol. 4319, pp. 898–907. Springer, Heidelberg (2006)
9. Daribo, I., Tillier, C., Pesquet-Popescu, B.: Motion vector sharing and bitrate allocation for 3D video plus depth coding. EURASIP J. Appl. Sig. Process. (3), 3 (2009)

10. Zamarin, M., Salmistraro, M., Forchhammer, S.: Edge-preserving intra depth coding based on context-coding and H. 264/AVC. In: 2013 IEEE International Conference on Multimedia and Expo (ICME), pp. 1–6. IEEE (2013)
11. Kao, J., Tu, J.: The compression method of depth map in 3D video. In: 5th IET International Conference on Wireless, Mobile and Multimedia Networks (ICWMMN 2013), pp. 189–192. IET (2013)
12. Zhang, X., Xiong, H.: Multiscale edge coding and adaptive lifting for depth maps coding in 3-D video. In: Data Compression Conference (DCC), p. 439. IEEE (2014)
13. Liu, S., Lai, P., Tian, D., Chen, C.W.: New depth coding techniques with utilization of corresponding video. IEEE Trans. Broadcast. 57(2), 551–561 (2011)
14. Smolic, A., Mueller, K., Stefanoski, N., Ostermann, J., Gotchev, A., Akar, G.B., Koz, A.: Coding algorithms for 3DTV—a survey. IEEE Trans. Circ. Syst. Video Technol. 17(11), 1606–1621 (2007)
15. Bjøntegaard, G.: Calculation of average PSNR differences between RD-curves. Document VCEG-M33 ITU-T Q6/16, TX, USA, pp. 2–4. Austin (2001)

Depth Map Upsampling Using Segmentation and Edge Information

Shuai Zheng[1,2], Ping An[1,2(✉)], Yifan Zuo[1,2], Xuemei Zou[1], and Jianxin Wang[1,2]

[1] School of Communication and Information Engineering, Shanghai University,
Shanghai 200072, China
[2] Key Laboratory of Advanced Display and System Application of the Ministry of Education,
Shanghai 200072, China
zs_thinking@126.com, anping@shu.edu.cn

Abstract. A depth upsampling method based on Markov Random Field is proposed, considering the depth and color information. First, the initial interpolated depth map is inaccurate and oversmooth, we use a rectangle window centered on every pixel to search the maximum and minimum depth value of the depth map to find out the edge pixels. Then, we use the depth information to guide the segmentation of the color image and build different data terms and smoothness terms for the edge and non-edge pixels. The result depth map is piecewise smooth and the edge is sharp. In the meanwhile, the result is good where the color information is consistent while the depth is not or where the depth information is consistent while the color is not. Experiments show that the proposed method performs better than other upsampling methods in terms of mean absolute difference (MAD).

Keywords: Depth map · Upsampling · Segmentation · Edge

1 Introduction

Recently, three-dimension television (3DTV) has been attractive and more applications such as human pose recognition, interactive free-viewpoint video, and 3D games have been put into use, the fundamental problem is the acquisition of the depth information and color information of the same scene. The fully-developed color camera makes the acquisition of the color information easy. However, the high complexity and low robustness of the passive methods, like stereo algorithms, limit the acquisition of the depth image. In recent years, with the advent of the low-cost depth sensors, such as Time-of-Flight (TOF) range sensors [1] and Kinect [2], the active sensor-based methods to gain the depth information become more popular. The TOF sensor measures the traveling time for a reflected light beam from the sender to an object to the receivers [1]. The tiny camera can overcome the shortcomings of the traditional passive methods and generate real-time depth map and intensity image. However, the current TOF sensors can only deliver limited spatial resolution depth image with noise and radial distortion. The Swiss Ranger 4000 [3] from company Swissranger, for example, can only produce 176×144 depth map,

Y.-J. Zhang (Ed.): ICIG 2015, Part II, LNCS 9218, pp. 116–126, 2015.
DOI: 10.1007/978-3-319-21963-9_10

which is rather low compared to the color image of conventional color camera, the resolution is usually 1280×960 or 1920×1080. Therefore, in order to acquire high-quality depth maps in 3DTV and other applications, the upsampling and distortion correction are necessary, this paper focuses on the upsampling of the depth image.

As for depth upsampling problem, the traditional method such as: nearest neighbor, bilinear and bicubic interpolation always generate oversmooth image especially at the depth discontinuities, the blurry boundaries make it hard to use. Hence, the upsampling method considering the low-resolution depth map and high-resolution color image gains much attention.

Depth map upsampling based on low-resolution depth map and high-resolution color image can be classified into two categories: filter-based upsampling approaches and Markov random field (MRF) based methods. As for filter-based upsampling method, Kopf et al. [4] propose a joint bilateral upsampling strategy when a high resolution prior is available to guide the interpolation from low to high resolution, but when the depth discontinuity is not consistent with the color edge, the texture transfer artifact is inevitable. To avoid the texture transfer artifacts, Chan et al. [5] propose noise aware filter for depth upsampling (NAFDU), which enables us to fuse the data from a low-resolution depth camera and a high-resolution color camera while preserving features and eliminating texture transfer artifact, but the image edge structure is easy to be broken using this method, thus the over-smoothing problem at the depth discontinuity is obvious. Yang et al. [6] quantize the depth values, build a cost volume of depth probability. They iteratively apply a bilateral filter on the cost volume, and take the winner-takes-all approach to update the HR depth values. However, the result is oversmooth at the depth discontinuity. He et al. [7] propose a guide filter to preserve the edge. Lu et al. [8] present a cross-based framework of performing local multipoint filtering to preserve the edge and the structure. David et al. [9] propose an anisotropic diffusion tensor, calculated from a high resolution intensity image to guide the upsampling of the depth map. Min et al. [10] propose a joint bilateral filter combined with the time information to ensure the temporal correlation. The filter-based method is fast, but it will cause over-smoothing problem somehow. For MRF method, Diebel and Thrun [11] propose a 4-node MRF model based on the fact that depth discontinuities and color difference tend to co-align, but the result is not that good. Lu et al. [12] presents a new data term to better describe the depth map and make the depth map more accurate, but the result at the depth discontinuities is still not good. Park et al. [13] use non-local means regularization to improve the smoothness term. Most of these algorithms are solved by Graph Cuts (GC) [14–16] or Belief Propagation (BP) [17]. Yin and Collins [18] use a 6-node MRF model combined the temporal information, which make the depth map more reliable. In addition, more and more weighting energy equations are proposed, papers [19, 20] combine the intensity map from the TOF camera as confidence map and the last frame image as time confidence to gain the depth map.

These methods are based on the assumption that the depth discontinuities and the boundaries of the color map are consistent. But when the depth value is the same while the color information is not or otherwise, the result is bad, as shown in Fig. 1.

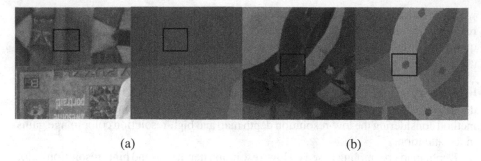

Fig. 1. Inconsistency in the color image and depth map: (a) the depth value is the same while the color information is different; (b) the color information is the same while the depth value is different (Color figure online)

The paper proposes a method that can ensure the accuracy of the smooth region, the depth discontinuities and solve the problems shown in Fig. 1. The remainder of the paper is organized as follows: In Sect. 2, we review the MRF-based depth map upsampling method. The proposed method is presented in Sect. 3, followed by the experimental results and comparisons between the former work with our method in Sect. 4. Finally, we conclude our work in Sect. 5.

2 Depth Map Upsampling Method Based on MRF

An image analysis problem can be defined as a modeling problem, to solve the image problem is to find a solution to the model. The depth map upsampling problem can be transformed to seeking a solution to the MRF problem. The depth value of the image is related to the initial depth value and the depth value around. In MRF model, each node represents a variable including the initial depth value, the corresponding color information and the depth value around. The edge between the two nodes represents the connection between the two variables. Let the low-resolution depth map be D_0, and the high-resolution color image be $I = \{z\}$. $p = (i, j)$ is the pixel in the result high-resolution depth map $D = \{d_p\}$. Using a MRF model to describe the problem, then it transforms to a maximum posterior probability of $P(d, z)$. The maximum posterior probability is:

$$P(d|z) = \frac{P(d, z)}{P(z)} \tag{1}$$

According to the theory of Hammersley-Clifford, solving the maximum posterior probability can be transformed to solving the minimum of the energy equation of (2) [21], $N(i)$ represents the neighboring nodes of the node i, λ_s is smoothness coefficient.

$$E = \sum_i D(i) + \sum_{\substack{i,j \\ j \in N(i)}} \lambda_s V(i, j) \tag{2}$$

The data term is used to ensure the result depth getting close to the initial depth value, σ is a threshold of the truncated absolute difference function:

$$D(i) = \min(|d_i - d_i^0|, \sigma) \tag{3}$$

The smoothness term is used to ensure the depth of the pixel getting close to the depth of the neighboring pixels and the depth map is piecewise smooth:

$$V(i,j) = W_{ij} \times \min(|d_i - d_j|, \sigma) \tag{4}$$

Thus, the minimum energy equation problem turns to label assigning problem, a high-probability depth label is given to every pixel according to the maximum posterior probability acquired from the initial depth map and the color map, the high-resolution depth map is acquired.

But there is blurring at the depth discontinuities of the interpolated initial depth map, which results in the depth value which the data term relies on is incorrect. The paper builds a rectangle window to search the maximum depth value and the minimum to get the difference value. If the difference is bigger than some threshold, it is regarded as an edge pixel, such that the accurate pixel of the initial depth map is acquired. The modified graph-based image segmentation method is used to get the segmentation information. Different smoothness weights of the edge pixel and non-edge pixels are built based on the edge and segmentation information to ensure the depth map is piecewise smooth and the edge is sharp. In the meanwhile, the area where the color information is consistent while the depth is not or otherwise is well dealt with.

3   Proposed Method

First, the bicubic interpolation method is used to the low-resolution depth map to get the initial depth map, then get the edge pixels and use the initial depth map to guide the segmentation of the color image, and build new data term and smoothness term based on the edge and segmentation information to get the high-resolution depth map. The section is described according to the above.

3.1   Acquisition of the Edge Pixels of the Depth Map

The interpolated initial depth map is blurry at the depth discontinuities, and the depth value is inaccurate, as show in Fig. 2. The depth changes instantly at the discontinuities in the ground truth while in the interpolated depth map the depth changes gradually. We find out that when the upscale factor is n, the neighboring $(2n + 1)$ pixels changes gradually.

So we build a $n \times n$ rectangle window centered on every pixel to find out the maximum and minimum depth value to get the difference:

$$Dis(i) = \max_{i \in W(i)} D(i) - \min_{i \in W(i)} D(i) \tag{5}$$

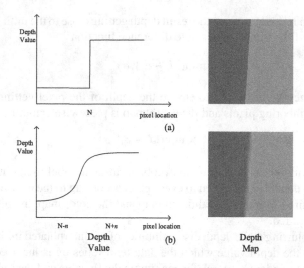

Fig. 2. Depth transformation at depth discontinuities: (a) depth map of ground truth and the depth value changes instantly at depth discontinuities; (b) depth map of the bicubic interpolated depth map and the depth value changes in the range of (N − n, N + n)

If $Dis(i)$ is bigger than the threshold, then the pixel is edge or the pixel is non-edge.

$$D_{edge}(i) = \begin{cases} 1 & if\ Dis(i) > th_{edge} \\ 0 & else \end{cases} \quad (6)$$

We use the depth image and the corresponding color image of the dataset Middle-bury, take the "*Art*" image as example, as shown in Fig. 3(a). Downscale the depth image with factor 8 as shown in Fig. 3(b), and then the bicubic interpolation method is used to enlarge the low-resolution depth image as shown in Fig. 3(c). It can be seen there is blurring at the depth discontinuities after the bicubic interpolation. If the traditional canny, sobel edge extracting method is used to get the edge, there are some mistakes. While using the above method to get the edge range, we can ensure the depth value of the non-edge area is the same as the ground truth, as shown in Fig. 3(d).

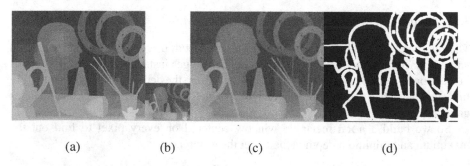

(a)   (b)   (c)   (d)

Fig. 3. Acquisition of edge map: (a) ground truth; (b) low-resolution depth map; (c) bicubic interpolation depth map; (d) edge map acquired by formula (6)

3.2 Depth-Guided Color Image Segmentation

The graph-based segmentation [22] uses the adaptive threshold to segment the image. First compute the dissimilarity between every pixel and its neighboring 4 pixels, and sort the edge between two pixels increasingly, if the dissimilarity is no bigger than the inner dissimilarity, merge the two pixels and then go to the next edge. The inner difference of a district $Int(C)$ is the biggest intensity difference and the difference between the districts $Diff(C_1, C_2)$ is the smallest dissimilarity among all the edges between the two districts. If the dissimilarity between the districts is no bigger than the two inner difference:

$$Diff(C_i, C_j) \leq \min(Int(C_i) + r(C_i), Int(C_j) + r(C_j)) \qquad (7)$$

Merge the two districts. In this paper, the condition of merging two districts is changed to use the segmentation image to guide the depth upsampling. As shown in Fig. 4, when the depth difference between the two districts is less than α ($7 < \alpha < 11$) and the difference of the two districts is no bigger than the inner difference of the two

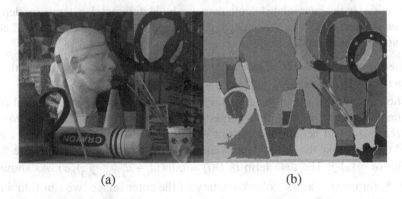

(a)   (b)

Fig. 4. Segmentation result: (a) color image; (b) segmentation image (Color figure online)

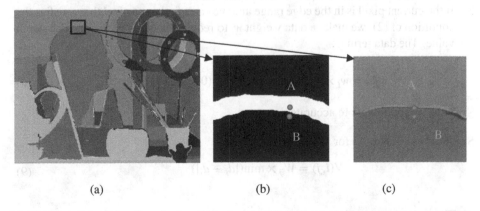

(a)   (b)   (c)

Fig. 5. Close-ups of the edge pixels and pixels around the edge: (a) segmentation image; (b), (c) close-ups of the edge map and the segmentation image of highlighted rectangle region in (a)

districts, merge the two districts, or merge the two districts only when the depth difference is less than β $(0 < \beta < 3)$. In other words, the segmentation takes the color information and depth map into account, but if the depth difference is very little which tends to 0, it is regarded as an area where the depth is the same while the color information is not, merge the two districts directly, the result is shown in Fig. 4(b).

3.3   The New Data Term and Smoothness Term

In the paper, we use an 8-node MRF model to deal with the depth map upsampling problem. The initial depth map is the interpolated depth map, and the color image is mean shift filtered [23] which can join the area with similar color, wipe some details and preserve the edge in the meantime. The MRF energy equation consists of two terms, the following describes the improvement of the data term and smoothness term respectively.

Data Term. In MRF model, the data term is used to ensure the depth value getting closed to the initial depth value, but because of the inaccuracy of the depth value at depth discontinuities in the interpolated depth map, we build different data terms for depth in edge area and non-edge area. The edge area acquired in 3.1 includes almost all edges pixels, and the data term is as follows:

1. If the current pixel i is not edge pixel, then the initial depth value is trustworthy, the data term is $D(i) = \min(|d_i - d_i^0|, \sigma)$.
2. If the current pixel i is in the edge range, then we can't rely on the initial depth value completely, we find out a non-edge pixel j which is $(n + 3)$ pixels from the current pixel and belong to a district with the current pixel. If the pixel can be find out, we make the initial depth value of the current pixel i equal to the depth value of pixel j. The data term is $D(i) = \min(|d_i - d_{j,|j-i|=n+3}^0|, \sigma)$. As shown in Fig. 5, for point A at the color boundary of the color image, we can find a non-edge pixel point B which is $(n + 3)$ pixels from the point A, so we make the initial depth value of A equal to the depth value of B.
3. If the current pixel is in the edge range and we can't find out a pixel that satisfies the condition of (2), we make a data weight w_i to reduce the effect of the original depth value. The data term is:

$$D(i) = w_i \times \min(|d_i - d_i^0|, \sigma) \quad (0 < w_i < 1) \tag{8}$$

Thus, we build a more accurate data term.

Smoothness Term. As for smoothness term:

$$V(i,j) = W_{ij} \times \min(|d_i - d_j|) \tag{9}$$

The smoothness weight W_{ij} consists of two sub-weight: $W_{seg,ij}$ and $W_{lab,ij}$, $W_{seg,ij}$

represents the segmentation information of the two neighboring pixels and $W_{lab,ij}$ describes the color difference between the two pixels, the two weights are used to control the influence of the neighboring pixels.

1. If the pixel i and its neighboring pixel j are non-edge pixels: $D_{edge}(i) = 0$ and $D_{edge}(j) = 0$, the segmentation information is ignored, because the depth value of the two pixels must be the same, we set $W_{seg,ij} = 1, W_{lab,ij} = 1$.

2. For the pixel i and its neighboring pixel j, if one is edge pixel and the other is non-edge pixel: $D_{edge}(i) = 0, D_{edge}(j) = 1$ or otherwise. Then the two pixels are around the edge range, because we expand the edge range in the search of edge points, the depth value should be the same: $W_{seg,ij} = 1, W_{lab,ij} = \gamma (\gamma \geq 1)$.

3. If the pixel i and its neighboring pixel j are in the edge range, we can't define whether the pixel i and j is edge pixel or not. We combine the color information and the segmentation information to define the smoothness weight. The similarity in color image is defined in LAB color space:

$$W_{lab} = e^{-\frac{\sqrt{(l_i-l_j)^2+(a_i-a_j)^2+(b_i-b_j)^2}}{\delta}} \tag{10}$$

The more similar the color image is, the possibility of the depth value being the same is larger. But if it is an area where the color information is consistent while the depth is not, the result depth map is wrong. So we make a segmentation weight in addition:

$$W_{seg} = \begin{cases} 1 & if\ seg(i) = seg(j) \\ \tau(0 < \tau < 1) & else \end{cases} \tag{11}$$

If the two neighboring pixels belong to one district, we just consider the color information of the two pixels. While if the two pixels don't belong to one district, then weaken the dependency relation of the two pixels, so the result is more accurate where the color information is consistent while the depth is not.

4   Experiment Results

The experiments are performed on an Intel Core i7-4790 CPU, 3.60 GHz with 8 GB memory system using Microsoft visual C++ platform. We use 4 test image sets including the color image and the corresponding depth map provided by Middlebury dataset [24]: "Art", "Books", "Moebius" and "Dolls". First, the ground truth maps are downscaled by factors 2, 4 and 8 to get the low-resolution depth map, and then use bicubic interpolation to upsample the depth map, thus, we can get the initial depth map. Then the energy equation is built considering the segmentation and edge information described above, and solved by Graph Cut (GC). We set the parameters as follow: $\lambda_s = 1.5, \sigma = 35, th_{edge} = 10, \gamma = 5, \tau, w_i$ are set 0.7. For "Art", "Books", "Moebius", the parameters α and β are set as: $\alpha = 10, \beta = 3$. For "Dolls", the parameters α and β are set as: $\alpha = 7, \beta = 2$. This is because the depth difference between depth areas in "Dolls" is small, to reduce the two parameters is to get better segmentation result. To evaluate the method, we compare our method with the former work [6–11] about depth up sampling, the result for TGV and Edge are quoted from paper [9, 10]. From Table 1, it can be seen: as for Mean Absolute Difference (MAD), most of our method is improved. And the result is good where the color is consistent but the depth is not, as shown in Fig. 6. The results in Fig. 7 show that texture copying and edge blurring problems have been reduced with our method.

Table 1. Quantitative comparison on Middlebury dataset (in MAD)

magnitude	*Art*			*Book*			*Moebius*			*Dolls*		
	2	4	8	2	4	8	2	4	8	2	4	8
MRF[11]	0.59	0.96	1.89	0.21	0.33	0.61	0.24	0.36	0.65	0.19	0.34	0.68
JBFcv[6]	0.55	0.68	1.44	0.29	0.44	0.62	0.38	0.46	0.67	0.29	0.38	0.72
Guided[7]	0.63	1.01	1.70	0.22	0.35	0.58	0.23	0.37	0.59	0.28	0.35	0.56
CLMF0[8]	0.43	0.74	1.37	**0.14**	0.28	0.51	**0.15**	0.29	0.52	0.24	0.34	0.66
CLMF1[8]	0.44	0.76	1.44	**0.14**	0.28	0.51	**0.15**	0.29	0.51	0.23	0.34	0.60
TGV[9]	0.45	0.65	1.17	0.18	**0.27**	0.42	0.18	0.29	0.49	0.21	0.33	0.70
Edge[10]	0.41	0.65	1.03	0.17	0.30	0.56	0.18	0.29	0.51	**0.16**	**0.31**	0.56
our method	**0.41**	**0.58**	**1.01**	0.17	**0.27**	**0.41**	0.18	**0.27**	**0.44**	0.23	**0.31**	**0.53**

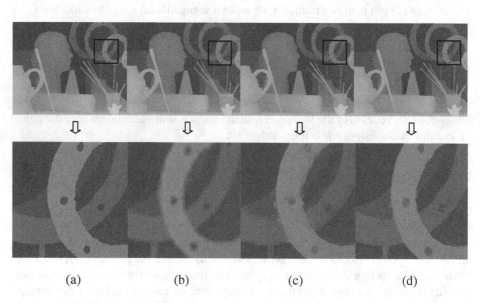

(a)   (b)   (c)   (d)

Fig. 6. Close-ups of the depth map *"Art"*: (a) ground truth; (b) depth map acquired by MRF [11]; (c) depth map acquired by JBFcv [6]; (d) depth map of our method

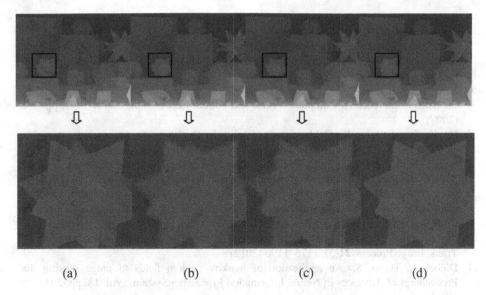

(a)   (b)   (c)   (d)

Fig. 7. Close-ups of the depth map *"Moebius"*: (a) ground truth; (b) depth map acquired by MRF [11]; (c) depth map acquired by JBFcv [6]; (d) depth map of our method

5   Conclusion

In the paper, a depth upsampling method based on MRF model is proposed. Usually, there is blurring at the depth discontinuities of the interpolated initial depth map, and the depth value is not accurate. This results in the depth value which the data term relies on is incorrect. The paper builds a rectangle window to search the maximum and the minimum depth value to get the difference value. If it is bigger than some threshold, it is regarded as an edge pixel. The accurate pixel of the initial depth map is acquired through the method. The graph-based image segmentation method is used. Different smoothness weights of the edge pixel and non-edge pixel are built to ensure the depth map is piecewise smooth and the edge is sharp. In the meanwhile, the depth evaluation of the area where the color information is consistent while the depth is not or otherwise is well dealt with.

Acknowledgement.   This work was supported in part by the National Natural Science Foundation of China, under Grants U1301257, 61172096, 61422111, and 61301112.

References

1. Remondino, F., Stoppa, D.: TOF Range-Imaging Cameras, vol. 68121. Springer, Heidelberg (2013)
2. Microsoft Kinect for Windows. http://kinectforwindows.org/
3. SwissRanger™ SR4000 Data Sheet. http://www.mesaimaing.ch/prodview4k.php

4. Kopf, J., Cohen, M.F., Lischinski, D., Uyttendaele, M.: Joint bilateral upsampling. J. ACM Trans. Graph. **26**(3), 96:1–96:5 (2007)
5. Chan, D., Buisman, H., Theobalt, C., Thrun, S.: A noise-aware filter for real-time depth upsampling. In: ECCV Workshop on Multicamera and Multimodal Sensor Fusion Algorithms and Applications, pp. 1–12 (2008)
6. Xiong, Q., Yang, R., Davis, J., Nister, D.: Spatial-depths super resolution for range images. In: IEEE Conference on Computer Vision and Pattern Recognition, CVPR 2007, pp. 1–8 (2007)
7. He, K., Sun, J., Tang, X.: Guided image filtering. In: Daniilidis, K., Maragos, P., Paragios, N. (eds.) ECCV 2010, Part I. LNCS, vol. 6311, pp. 1–14. Springer, Heidelberg (2010)
8. Lu, J., Shi, K., Min, D., Lin, L., Do, M.N.: Cross-based local multipoint filtering. In: 2012 IEEE Conference on Computer Vision and Pattern Recognition (CVPR), pp. 430–437 (2012)
9. Ferstl, D., Reinbacher, C., Ranftl, R., Rüther, M., Bischof, H.: Image guided depth upsampling using anisotropic total generalized variation. In: 2013 IEEE International Conference on Computer Vision (ICCV), pp. 993–1000 (2013)
10. Min, D., Lu, J., Do, M.N.: Depth video enhancement based on weighted mode filtering. IEEE Trans. Image Process. **21**(3), 1176–1190 (2012)
11. Diebel, J., Thrun, S.: An application of markov random fields to range sensing. In: Proceedings of Advances in Neural Information Processing Systems, vol. 18, pp. 291–298 (2006)
12. Lu, J., Min, D., Pahwa, R.S., Do, M.N.: A revisit to MRF-based depth map super-resolution and enhancement. In: 2011 IEEE International Conference on Acoustics, Speech and Signal Processing (ICASSP), pp. 985–988 (2011)
13. Park, J., Kim, H., Tai, Y.W., Brown, M.S., Kweon, I.S.: High quality depth map upsampling for 3D-TOF cameras. In: 2011 IEEE International Conference on Computer Vision (ICCV), pp. 1623–1630 (2011)
14. Kolmogorov, V., Zabih, R.: What energy functions can be minimized via graph cuts. IEEE Trans. Pattern Anal. Mach. Intell. **26**(2), 147–159 (2004)
15. Boykov, Y., Veksler, O., Zabih, R.: Fast approximate energy minimization via graph cuts. IEEE Trans. Pattern Anal. Mach. Intell. **23**(11), 1222–1239 (2001)
16. Boykov, Y., Kolmogorov, V.: An experimental comparison of min-cut/max-flow algorithms for energy minimization in vision. IEEE Trans. Pattern Anal. Mach. Intell. **26**(9), 1124–1137 (2004)
17. Ihler, A.T., Lii, J., Willsky, A.S.: Loopy belief propagation: convergence and effects of message errors. J. Mach. Learn. Res. **6**, 905–936 (2005)
18. Yin, Z.Z., Collins, R.: Belief propagation in a 3D spatio-temporal MRF for moving object. In: IEEE Conference on Computer Vision and Pattern Recognition, pp. 1–8 (2007)
19. Choi, O., Jung, S.-W.: A consensus-driven approach for structure and texture aware depth map upsampling. IEEE Trans. Image Process. **23**(8), 3321–3335 (2014)
20. Schwarz, S., Sjostrom, M., Olsson, R.: A weighted optimization approach to time-of-flight sensor fusion. IEEE Trans. Image Process. **23**(1), 214–225 (2014)
21. Zhu, J., Wang, L., Gao, J.: Spatial-temporal fusion for high accuracy depth maps using dynamic MRFs. IEEE Trans. Pattern Anal. Mach. Intell. **32**(5), 899–909 (2010)
22. Felzenszwalb, P.F., Huttenlocher, D.P.: Efficient graph-based image segmentation. Int. J. Comput. Vis. **58**(2), 167–181 (2004)
23. Comaniciu, D., Meer, P.: Mean shift: a robust approach toward feature space analysis. IEEE Trans. Pattern Anal. Mach. Intell. **24**(5), 603–619 (2002)
24. Middlebury Stereo Datasets. http://vision.middlebury.edu/stereo/data/

Design of a Simulated Michelson Interferometer for Education Based on Virtual Reality

Hongling Sun, Xiaodong Wei, and Yue Liu[✉]

Beijing Engineering Research Center of Mixed Reality and Advanced Display,
School of Optoelectronics, Beijing Institute of Technology,
Beijing 100081, China
liuyue@bit.edu.cn

Abstract. The physical experiment based on science inquiry learning shows its advantages compared with traditional class demonstration. However, the participation in physical experiments is often stylized and there are still many limitations when promoting the laboratory learning. This paper presents the construction of a Virtual Optics Laboratory which is applied to the experiment of the Michelson interferometer. On the current platform, the phenomena of interference and background theories are visualized for the purpose of efficiently promoting conceptual understanding. Factors of the experimental environment such as wavelengths, properties of optical elements and perspectives can be altered with interactive tools, enabling students to set up the system, observe the phenomena of interference as well as measure wavelengths and small displacements. The simulated laboratories can be of great assistance in the development of inquiry skills to enhance school education.

Keywords: Simulated Michelson interferometer · Visualization · Interaction · Virtual reality

1 Introduction

Research shows advantages for science inquiry learning where students conduct investigations compared with typical instruction featuring lectures or teacher demonstrations and the value of physical laboratories for science learning is generally recognized [1]. However, there are many limitations and problems when promoting the laboratory learning. Firstly, schools located in remote areas may not be equipped with advanced facilities which are essential to physical hands-on experiments. Secondly, even for students who can get access to the facilities, the participation in laboratory experiments is often stylized in which the students just follow the instructions to manipulate devices, collect data and draft experimental reports which function as the main reference for teachers' evaluation. What's more, since students usually work in groups in the physical laboratory, those diligent and capable members may undertake most work while others just take a free ride.

© Springer International Publishing Switzerland 2015
Y.-J. Zhang (Ed.): ICIG 2015, Part II, LNCS 9218, pp. 127–137, 2015.
DOI: 10.1007/978-3-319-21963-9_11

As for the optics laboratory as shown in Fig. 1(a), students often possess some misconceptions about the electromagnetic wave, interference, diffraction and polarization etc. when taking part in the experiments although the comprehension of such qualitative concepts is a basic prerequisite for many higher-order concepts [2]. When performing the experiments, it is hard for students to feel confident since they are unfamiliar with optical elements along with the experimental environment. Students tend to neglect the experimental principles as they just follow the operation steps described on the textbook. In addition, optical elements are easy to be soiled or broken and the alignment of rays calls for extremely high accuracy. To save cost as well as time, teachers tend to set up the equipment, calibrate the devices in advance and just let students complete the following work in real optics laboratories.

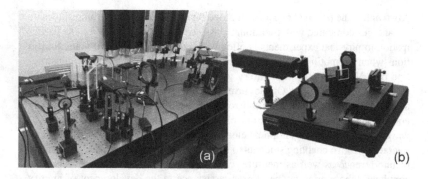

Fig. 1. (a) The optics laboratory in reality (b) the Michelson interferometer

The virtual reality technology [2] can help to address the mentioned problems with the visualization of the laboratory environment and the simulation of experimental procedures with a relatively low requirement for equipment. Participants are immersed in the virtual laboratory and the interaction methods for altering the relative factors are flexible to arouse interests as well as develop their inquiry skills. This paper presents the construction of a Virtual Optics Laboratory and the system of the Michelson interferometer experiment which allows students to set up and calibrate the apparatus, observe the phenomena of interference, measure wavelengths and small displacements in the immersive environment. Section 2 presents the virtual reality technology and its applications in education. The construction of the Virtual Optics Laboratory and the simulated experiment of the Michelson interferometer are described in Sect. 3 and follow by the conclusion in Sect. 4.

2   Virtual Reality Technology and its Applications in Education

Virtual reality is an emerging technology that was first proposed in 1960s [2] and can be defined as a synthetic environment which gives its user a feeling of "being there" [3]. It develops rapidly with the continuing improvements of high-performance graphical processing unit and the display technology, allowing the creation of increasingly convincing virtual environments [4]. So far there have been extensive applications of virtual reality in the areas such as remote operation [5], task assistance [6], manufacturing planning [7], preservation of culture [8] and the enabling technology has reached a sufficient level of maturity for it to be seriously applied to education [9], training [10], and research in higher education [11].

Virtual reality augments learning with experience [10], offering an unprecedented avenue for the delivery of experiential education to students of all ages and in all disciplines [2]. It is certain that the flexibility provided by a system of virtual reality will be a major attraction to the educational community [11] and the high level of interactivity and immersion makes the learner an active participant. Researches show that the experience of immersion can enhance education in at least three ways: by allowing multiple perspectives, situated learning, and transfer [12]. The world of virtual reality can also be used to circumvent the physical, safety, and cost constraints that limit schools in the types of environments they can provide for learning-by-doing [11]. Besides, virtual laboratories add value to physical experiments by allowing students to explore unobservable phenomena [1]. For example, it would be very helpful to allow students to study the transmission of invisible light such as infrared or ultraviolet rays which could be visualized by adding some special effects in the virtual environment.

3   The Virtual Optics Laboratory and the Michelson Interferometer Experiment

A Virtual Optics Laboratory was constructed, offering an immersive environment for the conduction of various optical experiments. The configuration of the Michelson interferometer which was invented by Albert Michelson aiming at measuring the relative speed between the earth and the ether is shown in Fig. 1(b). The Michelson-Morley experiment denied the ether hypothesis and proved the constancy of the light speed, which is of great meaning in the history of physics. Since the Michelson interferometer is the basis of many other interferometers and learning about its principles assists students to develop a better understanding of the wave theory as well as the interference theory, the Michelson interferometer experiment, as one of the most classical optical experiments, is designed and conducted in the Virtual Optics Laboratory.

3.1   Software and Hardware Environments

Because computer technologies now offer virtual laboratories where investigations involve simulated material and apparatus [1], it is a feasible idea to promote virtual laboratories in the schools that are not so well-equipped, with all the resources being shared on the Internet. The models of optical elements as well as the laboratory furniture can be downloaded from 3D warehouse and modified with SketchUp. The optical elements used in the experiment include a laser, two mirrors, a collimating lens, a beam splitter, a compensating plate, a reference mirror, a measuring mirror, an imaging lens and a screen.

The virtual scene for the experimental platform is rendered in Unity. With a powerful engine and integrated development environments, Unity helps to realize the real-time performance of 3D scenes. Interfaces used in the experiments are drawn with NGUI, a plug-in compiled with C# that provides event notification frameworks and many animation effects.

Compared with laboratory experiments, it is more convenient for students to perform virtual experiments because only a personal computer is required to operate this Virtual Optics Laboratory with the mouse and the keyboard to input instructions. The experimental system also offers alternative display techniques so users can choose to view the experimental scenes on the desktop screens or utilize head mounted displays (HMDs) to achieve better sensory immersion, as shown in Fig. 2(a) and (b).

Fig. 2. (a) Viewing the virtual laboratory on the desktop screen (b) viewing the virtual laboratory through the HMD

3.2 Visualization

Teaching Videos. In general, it is not enough for students to gain a thorough comprehension of quite abstract optical conceptions in class but they have to enter the real laboratories with these misconceptions, which is obviously not beneficial to accelerate their learning process. So the experimental system of the Michelson interferometer that is presented here in the Virtual Optics Laboratory covers the teaching content of basic knowledge which is demonstrated by videos so that some conceptions and theories such as the wave theory of light can be visualized and interpreted by animations, making a vivid impression on students and helping with their comprehension. Besides, some background information which is useful to arouse the learner's interest on optics may not be mentioned in real classes, e.g. the history of the Michelson interferometer and its relationship with the ether hypothesis. The teaching videos can involve all the meaningful information.

The teaching process will take a period of time and participants tend to feel impatient watching the complex demonstrations without a break. So the videos are divided into four parts which cover "the nature of light", "the ether hypothesis and Michelson-Morley experiment", "the interference theory" and "the principle of the Michelson interferometer" as shown in Fig. 3, to help the participants to concentrate better and learn efficiently.

For the purpose of improving the level of interaction, there are interaction pages after each video which contains either questions or small games. Only when students answer the question correctly or succeed in the game can they have access to the next part, otherwise they have to watch the video again.

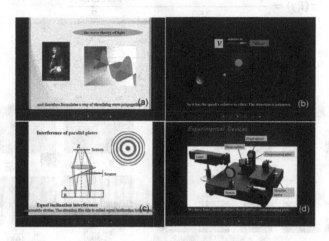

Fig. 3. Teaching videos (a) the nature of light (b) ether hypothesis and Michelson-Morley experiment (c) interference theory (d) the principles of the Michelson interferometer

Interference Fringes. One of the limitations of traditional optical experiments is that they are not so helpful when it comes to the investigation of unobservable or unobvious phenomena. The Virtual Optics Laboratory can fix this problem by visualizing the light rays and the interference fringes without environmental disturbances. Virtual rays can demonstrate the traveling path of light but they cannot interfere with each other and generate interference patterns. The system is for educational use so it is significant to display the interference patterns according to the theoretical calculations. Since it is extremely convenient to conduct matrix calculations with MATLAB, the interference patterns drawn with MATLAB are imported into Unity and displayed on the virtual screen.

According to the interference theory, if two light waves interfere with each other, the resultant light intensity I is described as follows, where I_1 and I_2 are respectively the intensity of two initial light waves while $\Delta\varphi$ is the phase difference.

$$I = I_1 + I_2 + 2\sqrt{I_1 I_2} \cos(\Delta\varphi) \qquad (1)$$

With MATLAB, the intensity of each point in the picture is derived from several parameters in the experimental setup. For the equal inclination interference, the interference pattern is drawn in the size of $721 \times 721 \times 3$ pixels. To get the intensity value of each pixel in the picture, some transforms need to be conducted from the size of screen in millimeters to the size of picture in pixels. The intensity value of each pixel is shown in Eqs. (2) and (3), where $r(i,j)$ is the theoretical distance between the point (i,j) and the center of the picture while *screensize* is the size of the screen. f is the focal length of the imaging lens and d is the relative position between the measuring mirror and the reference mirror. The sample equal inclination interference patterns are shown in Fig. 4(a).

$$r(i,j) = \frac{\sqrt{(i-361)^2 + (j-361)^2}}{360} \cdot \frac{screensize}{2} \tag{2}$$

$$I(i,j,1) = 1 + \cos\left(\frac{2\pi}{\lambda} \cdot 2d \frac{f}{\sqrt{f^2 + r^2}}\right) \tag{3}$$

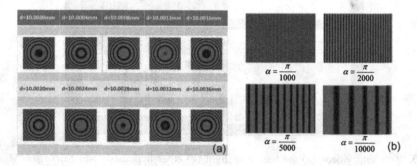

Fig. 4. (a) Equal inclination interference patterns (b) equal thickness interference patterns ($\lambda = 632.8$ nm, $f = 100$ mm, $screensize = 3$ mm)

For the equal thickness interference, the interference pattern is drawn in the size of $721 \times 500 \times 3$ pixels. The calculation of the intensity value of each pixel is shown as follows, where α is the angle of the measuring mirror. The sample equal thickness interference patterns are shown in Fig. 4(b).

$$d(i,j) = 1 + (j-361) \times \tan(\alpha) \tag{4}$$

$$I(i,j,1) = 1 - \cos\left(\frac{2\pi}{\lambda} \cdot 2d\sqrt{1 - \frac{r^2}{f^2 + r^2}}\right) \tag{5}$$

3.3 Interactions

Perspectives of Users. After entering the Virtual Optics Laboratory, it is significant for users to observe the experimental platform from different perspectives in order to get acquainted with the experimental environment. As the immersion degree increases, the controls and feedback need to be appropriately correlated in a step-by-step manner so that users can successfully manage the main controls and feel confident to continue [8]. The instructions are given to teach users to zoom in or out as well as to rotate the viewing angle with the mouse. In this way, users can get familiar with the controls and concentrate on the experimental environment.

Position Adjustments of the Optical Elements. Optical elements such as the measuring mirror need to be adjusted with high accuracy in the experiment. In the real experiment, the micrometer screw is used to control the movement of the measuring mirror but it is of great complexity for an inexperienced student to use. In the virtual experiments, a slider is set on the control panel for the fine adjustment of the measuring mirror as shown in Fig. 5(a). The control panel is a sprite placed on the corner of the screen and integrated with the commands necessary for the experiments. The shift of the sliding box is correlated with the translation of the measuring mirror and the value of the mirror's displacement will be displayed in a textbox.

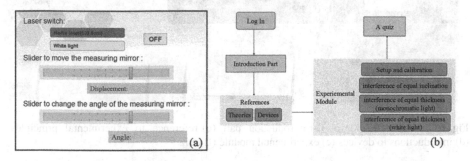

Fig. 5. (a) The control panel (b) the flowchart of the virtual Michelson Interferometer experiment system

Angle Adjustments of the Optical Elements. For the observation of equal thickness interference, the angular adjustment of the measuring mirror also requires high accuracy. One solution is that a textbox for inputting the value of angle can be created on the control panel. But in this way, the angle won't change continuously and neither will the interference pattern. In addition, only when the angle of the measuring mirror changes within the specific range could the interference fringes be observed on the screen. But the students are not aware of the range and don't know how to input the proper value. Another approach is similar to the fine adjustment of the position. A slider is used to control the angle whose value will be displayed in a textbox. The range of the slider is mainly occupied by the angular range in which the interference fringes of equal thickness are obvious enough to be seen.

The experiment also needs the switch for the laser which is also set on the control panel. Users can click on the button to turn on/off the laser as well as to decide whether the light is monochromatic or polychromatic.

3.4 The Flowchart and Interfaces

The flowchart of the experimental system is described in Fig. 5(b). In the Virtual Optics Laboratory, students no longer work in groups and everyone has to complete the experiments on their own. The system is quite customized and can log each student's performance, which allows the students to review their manipulation and helps the teacher to identify the ones who need specialized tutoring [1]. As shown in Fig. 6(a), the login interface is arranged at the entrance of the Virtual Optics Laboratory system. Students may be unfamiliar with the experimental environment and procedures at the very beginning so the introduction page along with the teaching videos covering basic knowledge necessary for the following experiments comes after the login interface, as shown in Fig. 6(b).

Fig. 6. Interfaces (a) log in (b) introduction part (c) reference to experimental principles (d) introductions to devices (e) experimental module (f) quiz

Since not everyone can remember all the information mentioned in the teaching videos, two reference pages are arranged in the experimental system in case they need to look up some detailed information about the experimental principles and devices, as shown in Fig. 6(c) and (d). If a student wants more detailed information about the interference theory, he/she can click on the corresponding button and then a sprite will appear explaining relevant knowledge in the forms of words, formulas and diagrams.

As shown in Fig. 6(e), four experimental parts are linked to four buttons on the experimental module page, including "setup and calibration", "interference of equal inclination", "interference of equal thickness (monochromatic light)" and "interference of equal thickness (polychromatic light)". In order to evaluate the learning outcomes of the participants, there is a small quiz at the end of the system as shown in Fig. 6(f).

3.5   Experimental Procedures

Setup and Calibration. In reality, students seldom have chances to set up and calibrate apparatus in optics experiments due to the complexity of optical systems but the Virtual Optics Laboratory system can make up for it by allowing students to manipulate models of devices on the virtual experimental platform without worrying about smudging or breaking any optical elements. During the experiment, students need some instructions to guide their manipulation so a small sprite is set beside the 3D experimental scene as a guidebook to be referred to in each step. The experimental schematic (Fig. 7) and instructions are shown on the sprite. Following the instructions, students place devices on the corresponding positions, turn on the laser and observe how the light transmits.

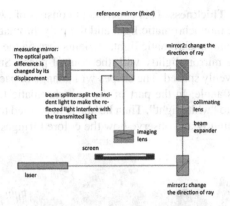

reference mirror (fixed)

measuring mirror:
The optical path
difference is
changed by its
displacement

mirror2: change the
direction of ray

beam splitter:split the incident light to make the reflected light interfere with
the transmitted light

collimating
lens

beam
expander

imaging
lens

screen

laser

mirror1: change
the direction of ray

Fig. 7. Experimental schematic

In the Virtual Optics Laboratory, the calibration work is simplified and students only need to guarantee that the light goes through or gets reflected on the center of devices. For a device in the light path, if the position is still biased, the emergent ray will be set darker compared with the incident ray. Once the devices are calibrated well one by one, all the sections of light rays will share the same brightness and interference patterns would appear on the screen.

Interference of Equal Inclination. Students are encouraged to measure small displacements of the movable mirror in the experiment of equal inclination interference. If the relative position between the reference mirror and the measuring mirror changes, the difference between the two split optical paths will change and so will the interference pattern.

Students are instructed by the guidebook to move the measuring mirror slowly along the light path, observing the screen and counting the number of the fringes that have poured out or in, as shown in Fig. 8. After that they are required to input the number and calculate to get the value of the displacement.

Fig. 8. The experiment of the equal inclination interference

Interference of Equal Thickness. This experiment consists of two parts, equal thickness interference of the monochromatic light and the polychromatic light, as shown in Fig. 9. In the part of the monochromatic light, students turn on the laser and change the angle of the measuring mirror slightly with the control panel. Straight stripes would appear on the screen, evenly spaced. The stripes will change in pace with the change of the measuring mirror's angle. In the part of the polychromatic light, the student can switch the light source to "white light". Then he/she is instructed to change the angle of the measuring mirror slightly and observe how the colored fringes form on the screen.

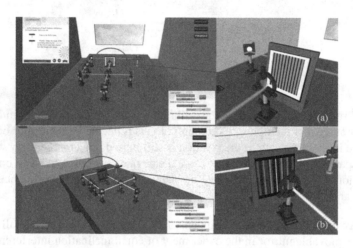

Fig. 9. The experiment of the equal thickness interference (a) equal thickness interference of the monochromatic light (b) equal thickness interference of the polychromatic light (Color figure online)

4   Conclusion and Future Work

Experimental experiences are significant for students to investigate scientific phenomena and develop inquiry skills. Virtual reality technologies could contribute to the learning process in school education by enabling each student to get access to the virtual customized experiments, making up for the lack of equipment in some areas. The immersive learning experiences inspire the participants to explore the unfamiliar events and solve problems independently. The Virtual Optics Laboratory presented in this paper adds value to traditional optics experiments by the high efficiency as well as the visualization of some unobservable phenomena and confusing conceptions, enabling students to get a better understanding of basic knowledge and enhance their experimental skills.

However, it is clear that the virtual experiments cannot replace the physical hands-on experiments totally although both of them can achieve similar goals. After all, the scientific research should be based on authentic materials and students ought to experience challenges in reality and learn to take all the factors into consideration to solve problems. Combinations of physical and virtual experiments can capitalize on the features of each approach [1]. So the Virtual Optics Laboratory system can function as a tool which assists students to preview or review the realistic hands-on experimentation.

For the virtual laboratory system, further work is needed to improve the level of interaction and immersion. Traditional input methods like the mouse and the keyboard can be replaced by gesture recognition technologies. Besides, the augmented reality technology could also be applied to the virtual experiments. For example, different markers can be utilized and when users shift the markers on the table, the camera will capture the markers and overlay the corresponding virtual devices on them in the screen. In this way, students would feel that they are moving the real devices on the table. It is also important to extend the applications of the Virtual Optics Laboratory to other optical experiments and the system can be also made web-based to support the remote teaching.

Acknowledgments. This work has been supported by the National Natural Science Foundation of China (Grant No. 61370134) and the National High Technology Research and Development Program (Grant No. 2013AA013904).

References

1. De Jong, T., Linn, M.C., Zacharia, Z.C.: Physical and virtual laboratories in science and engineering education. Science **340**(6130), 305–308 (2013)
2. Bowen Loftin, R., Engleberg, M., Benedetti, R.: Applying virtual reality in education: a prototypical virtual physics laboratory. In: Proceedings of IEEE 1993 Symposium on Research Frontiers in Virtual Reality, 1993, pp. 67–74. IEEE (1993)
3. Jayaram, S., Connacher, H.I., Lyons, K.W.: Virtual assembly using virtual reality techniques. Comput. Aided Des. **29**(8), 575–584 (1997)
4. van Veen, H.A.H.C., Distler, H.K., Braun, S.J., et al.: Navigating through a virtual city: using virtual reality technology to study human action and perception. Future Gener. Comput. Syst. **14**(3), 231–242 (1998)
5. Ding, G., Zhang, J., He, Y., et al.: VR-based simulation on material handling remote operation for engineering machine. In: Fourth International Conference on Image and Graphics, 2007, ICIG 2007, pp. 984–989. IEEE (2007)
6. Oda, O., Sukan, M., Feiner, S., et al.: Poster: 3D referencing for remote task assistance in augmented reality. In: IEEE Symposium on 2013 3D User Interfaces (3DUI), 2013, pp. 179–180. IEEE (2013)
7. Doil, F., Schreiber, W., Alt, T., et al.: Augmented reality for manufacturing planning. In: Proceedings of the Workshop on Virtual Environments 2003, pp. 71–76. ACM (2003)
8. Chen, S., Pan, Z., Zhang, M., et al.: A case study of user immersion-based systematic design for serious heritage games. Multimedia Tools Appl. **62**(3), 633–658 (2013)
9. Valdez, M.T., Ferreira, C.M., Maciel Barbosa, F.P.: Distance education using a desktop virtual reality (VR) system. In: Proceedings of the 24th EAEEIE Annual Conference (EAEEIE), 2013, pp. 145–150. IEEE (2013)
10. Psotka, J.: Immersive training systems: virtual reality and education and training. Instr. Sci. **23**(5–6), 405–431 (1995)
11. Kim, J.H., Park, S., Lee, H., et al.: Virtual reality simulations in physics education. Interact. Multimedia Electron. J. Comput. Enhanced Learn. **3**(2) 2001
12. Dede, C.: Immersive interfaces for engagement and learning. Science **323**(5910), 66–69 (2009)

Detecting Deterministic Targets by Combination of Polarimetric Fork and Cloude-Pottier Decomposition for Polarimetric Synthetic Aperture Radar Imagery

Sheng Sun[1(✉)], Zhijia Xu[2], and Taizhe Tan[1]

[1] School of Computer Science, Guangdong University of Technology, Guangzhou, China
shengsun@189.cn, taizhetan@gdut.edu.cn
[2] School of Mechanical Engineering, Guiyang University, Guiyang, China
xzjbelinda@163.com

Abstract. For detecting the deterministic targets in polarimetric synthetic aperture imagery, an improved method is suggested in this paper. A concise introduction is put forward about the principle of detecting single targets using polarimetric fork at first. The first drawback of the classic method is that the threshold of coherence can not be automatically obtained. The rest of drawback of the classic method is that diverse scattering mechanisms share a same threshold. A revised schema using Cloude-Pottier decomposition is suggested. The distribution of entropy value of Cloude-Pottier decomposition is used to calculate threshold. While a coarse classification is done on the image data and this procedure can be employed to obtain the threshold of various scattering mechanisms. An experiment is put into practice for measuring the validity of detection. The new proposed method outperforms the classic method via the experiment.

Keywords: Deterministic target · Polarimetric fork · Cloude-Pottier decomposition · Entropy · Averaged alpha angle

1 Introduction

The remote-sensing technology via synthetic aperture radar is experiencing a period of fast development, owing to its ability to cut through clouds and work without the solar illumination. Compared with the single polarimetric system, the polarimetric synthetic aperture radar systems, shorted for PolSAR, can gather much more features of ground object. Thereupon great attention has been given to the data processing of polarimetric synthetic aperture radar systems over the last two decades. The detecting and classifying methods for observed object are developing rapidly in recently years. Among these methods the category which exploited the polarimetric information of the targets is in a period of rapid rise [1, 2].

This paper is mainly focused on detecting deterministic targets in the scene to be observed. Deterministic targets usually correspond to some important objects, such as artificial buildings and metal objects, in a scene [3, 4]. Single detecting procedure is

© Springer International Publishing Switzerland 2015
Y.-J. Zhang (Ed.): ICIG 2015, Part II, LNCS 9218, pp. 138–146, 2015.
DOI: 10.1007/978-3-319-21963-9_12

indispensable to SAR image interpretation and other applications. Existing detecting methods are divided into two categories: statistical approaches with a priori information and physical approaches without a priori information. Traditional single target detecting methods generally utilize the statistical properties of the target. The representative algorithm of the first category is ILR, which makes a substitution of covariance matrix with a scaled identity matrix. However, this algorithm requires a priori knowledge of the targets [5]. Another typical method of the first category is OPD, which exploits the full statistical information of the target component and clutter component [6, 7]. As for the physical approaches, the first representative one is called single channel detector. This detector considers only the power of a sole channel, such as co-polarization or cross-polarization channel. The single target detecting can be accomplished by calculating the power of the selected channel [8]. The main shortcoming is that it performs less well in respect of miss detections and false alarms. The second representative one is called PWF, which is based on the principle of statistical signal processing and does not require a priori statistical information. It has been demonstrated that it owns the best performance among existing methods without a priori information. However this detector is also more likely to yield miss detection due to weak targets and partially developed speckle [9]. In recent times, a new detector appears which exploits a special attribute of polarimetric target response. This detector is a pure physical approach based on the response sensitivity to polarimetric changes. Based on polarimetric fork and perturbation analysis, this detector can pick out the single target by their coherence value [10, 11]. However, there exist two main drawbacks about this detector. At first, the threshold of the coherence value can not be captured automatically. Secondly, a sole threshold is shared by all the scattering mechanisms. Such scheme can be further revised. In this paper, amelioration will be put forward for the single targets detection. The Cloude-Pottier decomposition is combined with polarimetric fork to achieve the ends of detection. The rest of this paper is organized as follows. In Sect. 1, we introduce the basic principle of detecting single targets. The improvement to for classical method is presented in Sect. 2. A series of experiments using some classic methods and new proposed method have been performed in Sect. 3. Brief conclusions are drawn in Sect. 4.

2 Basic Principle of the Detector

2.1 Representation of the Scattering Mechanism

In general, the incident and scattered waves by imaging radar are respectively denoted by $\underline{E}_I$ and $\underline{E}_S$. As for the scattering process occurring at the target of interest, a matrix, called scattering matrix, is commonly employed to express the relationship of the above two waves. All the elements of the scattering matrix are called complex scattering coefficients. The diagonal elements of this matrix are commonly known as co-polar terms. Furthermore the off-diagonal elements are often called cross-polar terms. The former relate in fact the incident waves and scattered waves of the identical polarization state. The latter relate the incident waves and scattered waves of orthogonal polarization state. This procedure is listed in formula (1).

$$E_S = \frac{e^{-jkr}}{r} \begin{bmatrix} S_{11} & S_{12} \\ S_{21} & S_{22} \end{bmatrix} \underline{E}_I \tag{1}$$

Furthermore, it is needed to assign a specific coordinate system because the values of the scattering elements depend on the chosen coordinate system and polarization basis. For simplicity our discussion will be limited in monostatic backscattering case, in which the transmitting and receiving antennas are fixed at the same location. In general case, the horizontal-vertical basis is most widely-used for describing the coordinate system. The scattering matrix can be denoted as formula (2) in such cases. The terms S_{HH} correspond to the power return when the incident wave is in horizontal polarization state and the scattered wave is also in horizontal polarization state. The denotation is similar for the other three items. According to the reciprocity theorem, the scattering matrix is symmetric with $S_{HV} = S_{VH}$. For the convenience of calculation, the scattering matrix is often presented as a vector, which is denoted by the symbol Ω. This vector is commonly called target vector, listed in formula (3).

$$S = \begin{bmatrix} S_{11} & S_{12} \\ S_{21} & S_{22} \end{bmatrix} = \begin{bmatrix} S_{HH} & S_{HV} \\ S_{VH} & S_{VV} \end{bmatrix} \tag{2}$$

$$\Omega = \begin{bmatrix} S_{HH} \\ \sqrt{2}S_{HV} \\ S_{VV} \end{bmatrix} \tag{3}$$

It is very important to note that not all the target in natural scene can be simply characterized by a scattering matrix. In fact, not all radar targets are stationary or fixed, but instead changing in time. Most natural targets vary with time so that the wave no longer has the coherent, monochromatic, completely polarized shape. Then the scattering procedure can be viewed as a stochastic process. In such cases, a new matrix, called covariance matrix, is needed to denote this scattering process of targets, which is called distributed targets. This matrix C_3, demonstrated in formula (4) employs the operator of assembly average to characterize the distributed targets.

$$C_3 = <\Omega\Omega^{*T}> = <\begin{bmatrix} C_{11} & C_{12} & C_{13} \\ C_{12}^* & C_{22} & C_{23} \\ C_{13}^* & C_{23}^* & C_{33} \end{bmatrix}> = <\begin{bmatrix} |S_{HH}|^2 & \sqrt{2}S_{HH}S_{HV}^* & S_{HH}S_{VV}^* \\ \sqrt{2}S_{HV}S_{VV}^* & 2|S_{HV}|^2 & \sqrt{2}S_{HV}S_{VV}^* \\ S_{VV}S_{HH}^* & \sqrt{2}S_{VV}S_{HV}^* & |S_{VV}|^2 \end{bmatrix}> \tag{4}$$

2.2 Inner Mechanisms Using GPF

The primary principle of geometrical perturbation filter is based on calculation of polarimetric coherence. Polarimetric coherence is used to characterize the similarity of two different scattering mechanisms, which is presented in formula (5). The variable $i(\Sigma_k)$ is the projection of scattering vector on a specific scattering mechanism. For acquiring a perturbed scattering mechanism, it is needed to import a transformation named Huynen transformation. After adopting such kind of transformation, nine parameters can be obtained. Then a new set of parameters can be gotten by a minor adjustment of one of the nine parameters. This new set of parameters corresponds to a new vector which has been perturbed. This new vector is very close to the original scattering mechanism in physical property.

The detection procedure for single target is realized as follows. Firstly, the pixel to be detected is selected and a neighboring windows of $N * N$ pixels is determined. Secondly, one scattering mechanism is picked out for detecting. A minor perturbation is carried out for this scattering mechanism. Thirdly, the coherence value can be calculated within the window in the first step. If the coherence value is higher than the threshold T, then this pixel can be divided into the corresponding scattering mechanism.

$$\gamma = \frac{< i(\Sigma_1)i^*(\Sigma_2) >}{\sqrt{< i(\Sigma_1)i^*(\Sigma 1) >< i(\Sigma_2)i^*(\Sigma_2) >}} \qquad (5)$$

$$i(\Sigma_k) = \Sigma_k^{*T} \Sigma \qquad (6)$$

3 Improvement of the Detector

3.1 Analysis for the Classic Method

Classic detecting method using geometrical perturbation filter and polarization fork has been expounded in the last section. However the main drawback is that the hard threshold value $T = 0.98$ is set for determining whether the target is single target or not. It is known that the observed scene is variable, so that a hard threshold is irrational for these diverse observed scenes. A simple example will be put forward here to demonstrate this problem. Suppose that there is polarimetric SAR image I. Slight noise is added to this image I. Then the coherence value calculated based on the noised image is different from the original one. Then the hard threshold will bring some bias on the final result. Obviously it is needed to design a dynamic threshold according to the specific scene. And the dynamic threshold should not be calculated with the involvement of human factor.

3.2 Improved Detecting Schema for Single Targets

Based on the above analysis an improvement based on Cloude-Pottier decomposition will be put forward for the purpose of capturing dynamic threshold.

Firstly, the entropy value, denoted by for each pixel of a specific PolSAR image will be gotten after adopting Cloude-Pottier decomposition [12–14]. The entropy H characterizes the degree of statistical disorder of each individual scattering type within the ensemble window. Besides, this parameter is defined on eigenvalues such that it is independent of the specific matrix basis. A large number of experiments have proved that if the entropy value of one pixel is relatively low then it can be viewed as a single target. A coarse threshold for this can be set to 0.3. Because the entropy value is obtained by a weighted average within a neighboring window, it is less affected by the noise.

Secondly, the sole threshold is shared by diverse scattering mechanisms in the classic method. Such schema is also not reasonable for these actual cases. Another parameter, named average alpha angle, can be employed to achieve a coarse classifying for diverse scattering mechanisms. The average alpha angle can be used to classify roughly all the pixels to one scattering mechanism. This tip can shrink the scope of the specific scattering mechanism. According the above coarse classification results the threshold for each distinct scattering mechanism can be obtained. More specifically, a detailed step for this revised algorithm will be listed as follows.

Step 1:   Applying Cloude-Pottier decomposition on the selected PolSAR image I. calculating the averaged alpha angle H and entropy value α for each pixel.

Step 2:   Making a coarse classification for all the pixels in image I. For each classic scattering mechanism, calculate the ratio factor $R\%$ after traversing all the pixels within one specific scattering mechanism if the $H < 0.3$.

Step 3:   For a specific scattering mechanism, calculating all the coherence value, denoted by γ, and sorting all the pixels for this scattering mechanism according to the ratio factor $R\%$ obtained in last step. The pixel located on top $R\%$ coherence is the tipping point. The corresponding coherence value can be used as threshold for this scattering mechanism.

The flow chart of this algorithm is listed in Fig. 1.

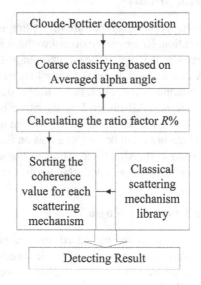

Fig. 1.   Flow chart of detecting single targets.

4   Experiments

4.1   The Experimental Data and Schema

The dataset provided by Airborne Synthetic Aperture Radar (shorted for AIRSAR) system from Jet Propulsion Laboratory (shorted for JPL) is selected to validate the effectiveness of the above proposed method. A quantitative measurement will be performed on the sample data named DTH_VALLEY with its key parameters listed in Table 1.

Table 1. Parameters for sample data DTH_VALLEY

Polarization	Full
Slant range pixel spacing	6.6621 m
Azimuth pixel spacing	12.1569 m

In the first step of this experiment, it needs to build a library for classic scattering mechanisms which includes six type of scattering targets. These are the odd bounce scatters, horizontal dipole scatters, oriented dipole scatters, dihedral scatters, right helix scatters and left helix scatters. The representing color for these six scattering mechanisms is listed in Fig. 2. The black one represents distributed scattering mechanism and the green one represents odd bounce scattering, and so on.

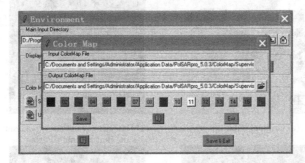

Fig. 2. The color allocation for six scattering mechanisms (Color figure online).

In the second step, speckle filter is performed before detection. The Lee Refined filter is selected to accomplish this task. Then Cloude-Pottier decomposition is carried out with the yield of averaged alpha angle and entropy. The coarse classification based on averaged alpha angle is done thereafter. The ratio factor R % can be calculated from the statistical distribution of entropy value. The scattering model is selected from the library successively and the corresponding coherence value is calculated from the covariance data. The final threshold can be determined by sort the coherence value.

4.2 Experimental Results and Analysis

According to the experimental schema in the last section, the detecting experiment is completed on the data of DTH_VALLEY. The detecting results in exhibited in Fig. 3. The original Pauli image, the results using classic method without filtering, the results using classic method with filtering and the results using new proposed method with filtering are presented in the subplot of Fig. 3. It can be seen from the second subplot that the speckle noise can interfere the detecting results. It can also be seen from the third subplot that the disturbance imported by speckle noise is alleviated after adopting speckle filter. However some scatters can not be detected due to the hard threshold value held by the classic method. The improvement can be viewed from the last subplot after adopting our new proposed method. For quantitative measuring the detecting validity, several entropy profiles of pixels selected are listed in Fig. 4. The first and second subplots represent two single targets which are located in the top-left corner of the scene. The entropy value is lower than 0.3 that can verify the detecting validity. In addition, the last two subplots demonstrate that the target scatters is distributed targets due to the vegetation interspersed in the hollow area of the scene.

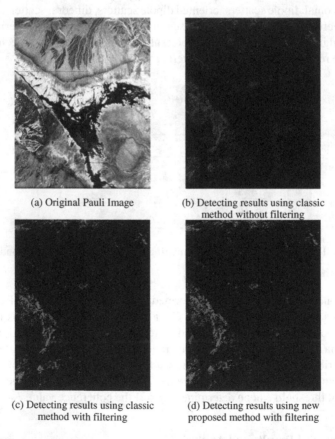

(a) Original Pauli Image

(b) Detecting results using classic method without filtering

(c) Detecting results using classic method with filtering

(d) Detecting results using new proposed method with filtering

Fig. 3. The comparison for detecting results on DTH_VALLEY image.

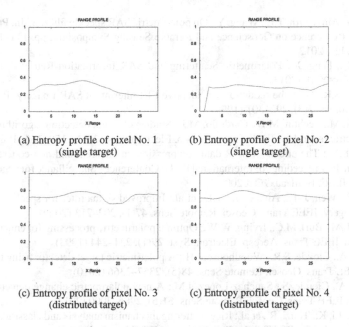

(a) Entropy profile of pixel No. 1   (b) Entropy profile of pixel No. 2
        (single target)   (single target)

(c) Entropy profile of pixel No. 3   (c) Entropy profile of pixel No. 4
     (distributed target)   (distributed target)

Fig. 4. The entropy profile of four pixels.

5 Conclusions

The improvement program for detecting single targets in certain PolSAR imagery is thoroughly explored in this paper. The main drawbacks of the classic detecting method using geometric perturbation filter are investigated. One of the incoherent decomposition operators, named Cloude-Pottier decomposition, is chosen to accomplish a coarse classification. The parameters yield by adopting decomposition operators is employed for determining threshold of the coherence. The new proposed schema for determining threshold is validated in an experiment of sample data.

Acknowledgments. The paper is supported in part by the innovative talents projects of Education Bureau of Guangdong Province under Grant No. 15zk0117, the cooperation project in industry, education and research of Shunde district under Grant No. 2013CXY09 and Guizhou science and technique fund with Grant No. LH [2014]7206.

References

1. Lee, J.-S., Pottier, E.: Polarimetric Radar Imaging: From Basics to Applications, pp. 160–161. CRC Press, Boca Raton (2009)
2. Ma, J., Zhao, J., Tian, J., Yuille, A., Zhuowen, Tu: Robust point matching via vector field consensus. IEEE Trans. Image Process. **23**(4), 1706–1721 (2014)

3. Lee, J.-S., Ainsworth, T.L., Wang, Y.: On polarimetric SAR speckle filtering. In: Proceedings of IEEE Conference on Geoscience and Remote Sensing Symposium, pp. 111–114. IEEE, Munich, July 2012
4. Jin, Y.-Q., Feng, X.: Polarimetric Scattering and SAR Information Retrieval, pp. 20–22. Wiley, New York (2013)
5. DeGraaf, S.R.: Sidelobe reduction via adaptive FIR filtering in SAR imagery. IEEE Trans. Image Process. 3(3), 292–301 (1994)
6. Novak, L.M., Sechtin, M.B., Cardullo, M.J.: Studies of target detection algorithms that use polarimetric radar data. IEEE Trans. Aerosp. Electron. Syst. 25(2), 150–165 (1989)
7. Novak, L.M.: The effects of SAR data compression on coherent and non-coherent change detection. In: Proceedings of International Radar Conference - Surveillance for a Safer World, pp. 1–6. IEEE, Bordeaux, Oct 2009
8. Lee, J.-S., Wen, J.-H., Ainsworth, T.L., et al.: Improved sigma filter for speckle filtering of SAR imagery. IEEE Trans. Geosci. Remote Sens. 47(1), 202–213 (2009)
9. Novak, L.M., Burl, M.C., Irving, W.W.: Optimal polarimetric processing for enhanced target detection. IEEE Trans. Aerosp. Electron. Syst. 29(1), 234–244 (1993)
10. Marino, A., Cloude, S.R., Woodhouse, I.H.: A polarimetric target detector using the huynen fork. IEEE Trans. Geosci. Remote Sens. 48(5), 2357–2366 (2010)
11. Marino, A., Cloude, S., Sanchez-Lopez, J.M.: A new polarimetric change detector in radar imagery. IEEE Trans. Geosci. Remote Sens. 51(5), 2986–3000 (2013)
12. Shao, Y., Li, K., Touzi, R., et al.: Rice scattering mechanism analysis and classification using polarimetric RADARSAT-2. In: Proceedings of IEEE International Geoscience and Remote Sensing Symposium, pp. 1445–1448. IEEE, Munich, July 2012
13. Ma, J., Qiu, W., Zhao, J., Ma, Y., Yuille, A.L., Tu, Z.: Robust L_2E estimation of transformation for non-rigid registration. IEEE Trans. Sig. Process. 63(5), 1115–1129 (2015)
14. Ponnurangam, G.G., Rao, Y.S., Bhattacharya, A.: Evaluation of various polarimetric parameters for soil moisture inversion using polarimetric SAR data. In: Proceedings of 10th European Conference on Synthetic Aperture Radar, pp. 1–4. VDE, Berlin, June 2014

Detection of Secondary Structures from 3D Protein Images of Medium Resolutions and its Challenges

Jing He$^{(\boxtimes)}$, Dong Si, and Maryam Arab

Department of Computer Science, Old Dominion University,
Norfolk, VA 23529, USA
{jhe,dsi,marab}@cs.odu.edu

Abstract. Protein secondary structures such as α-helices and β-strands are major structural components in most proteins. The position of secondary structures provides important constraints in computing the tertiary structure of a protein. Electron cryomicroscopy is a biophysical technique that produces 3-dimensional images of large molecular complexes. For images at medium resolutions, such as 5–10 Å, major secondary structures may be computationally detected. This paper summarizes our recent work in detection of secondary structures using *SSETracer*, *SSELearner*, *StrandTwister* and *StrandRoller*. The detection of helices and β-strands is illustrated using *SSETracer* and *StrandTwister* with a small dataset.

Keywords: Image · Protein · Secondary structure · Electron cryo-microscopy · Pattern recognition · Geometrical modeling

1 Introduction

Proteins are essential in all biological processes. A protein is a polymer of amino acids folded in 3-dimensional space. The sequence of a protein refers to the linear order of amino acids. In nature, there are only twenty different kinds of amino acids, and therefore a protein can be considered as a string of twenty alphabets. Certain segments of the protein sequence tend to fold into helices and other segments tend to fold into β-strands (Fig. 1A). Multiple β-strands are stabilized by hydrogen bonds between them to form a β-sheet (Fig. 1). For example, the protein in Fig. 1 has five helices and one β-sheet containing four β-strands. Helices and β-sheets are major secondary structures of a protein. Almost all proteins contain helices and/or β-sheets. Therefore, secondary structures provide essential information about the tertiary structure of the protein.

Although proteins are small objects with typical sizes in the nanometer scale, experimental techniques are available to obtain 3D images of proteins. One of such techniques is called electron cryo-microscopy (cryo-EM), a biophysical technique to produce 3D images of large assembly of proteins [1–4]. Depending on the nature of biological specimen and accuracy of experimental procedures, the resulting images may reveal different level of details and have different resolutions. With a high-resolution image, structural details are resolved well enough to derive the atomic structure. At medium

Y.-J. Zhang (Ed.): ICIG 2015, Part II, LNCS 9218, pp. 147–155, 2015.
DOI: 10.1007/978-3-319-21963-9_13

resolutions, such as 5–10 Å, structural details are not well resolved. However, major secondary structures such as helices and β-sheets are visible. In principle, a helix with more than two turns appears as a cylinder, and a β-sheet appear as a thin layer of density. However, due to noise or incomplete data in the image, automatic detection of secondary structures is still challenging in certain situations. Various methods and tools have been developed to detect secondary structures from such images [5–12]. In this paper, we summarize the methods and tools we have developed recently and the challenges encountered.

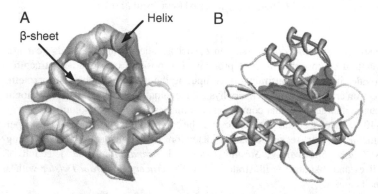

Fig. 1. Detection of helices and β-sheets from protein density images using *SSETracer*. (A) The backbone of a protein structure (PDB ID 2ITG) is shown as a ribbon (cyan). The surface view of its corresponding density image (gray) is superimposed. A helix and a β-sheet of the backbone are labeled. (B) Helices (colored lines) and a β-sheet (blue voxels) detected from density image using *SSETracer* are overlaid with the true structure of the protein (ribbon) (Color figure online).

2   Protein Secondary Structure Detection from 3D Images

2.1   Protein Density Images and the Pattern of Secondary Structures

The protein density map obtained using cryo-EM experimental technique is a 3D volumetric image, in principle, representing electron density of the protein. Those voxels with high values of density generally correspond to the locations where more atoms are located. Due to the nature of a helix, many atoms are positioned along the protein chain in a helical manner. At medium resolution such as 5–10 Å resolution, a helix generally appears as a cylinder, and a β-sheet may appear as a thin layer of density (Fig. 1A). Although such patterns are generally observed, they are affected by their closely located neighbors. The problem of secondary structure detection is to detect the location of helices, β-sheets and β-strands from a 3D image of the protein. In order to detect β-strands, β-sheets need to be detected first for images of medium resolutions. We have developed four methods for the detection of secondary structures *SSETracer*, *SSELearner*, *StrandTwister* and *StrandRoller*. Their relationship is illustrated in Fig. 2.

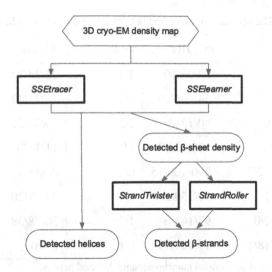

Fig. 2. Tools we developed for detection of protein secondary structures.

2.2 *SSETracer* and *SSELearner* for Detection of Helices and β-Sheets

SSETracer is a method for automatic identification of helices and β-sheets from 3D cryo-EM images at medium resolutions [9]. The methodology of the method was published in [9]. We here provide additional test cases using the most updated version. *SSETracer* characterizes three main local features: local structure tensor, distribution of skeleton voxels and local thickness. A simple voting procedure was used to determine if a particular point belongs to a helix or a β-sheet. We show the results of *SSETracer* using eight cases randomly selected from the Protein Data Bank (PDB). For each protein, the true structure downloaded from PDB was used to simulate a density image to 10 Å resolution using Chimera [13]. *SSETracer* was applied to such density maps and the results are summarized in Table 1. As an example for 2ITG, *SSETracer* correctly detected five of the six helices in this protein. The detected position of a helix is represented as a line that corresponds to the central axis of the helix. It missed a small 3_{10} helix with five amino acids in length (row 2 column 2 of Table 1). It wrongly detected a small helix (at the back of the protein, not clearly visible in Fig. 1B) that is supposed to be a turn. A turn of a protein chain may appear as a short cylinder in the image and therefore it can be confused with a short helix. Alternatively, we may estimate the accuracy in terms of the number of Cα atoms that are located along the helices. There are sixty-six Cα atoms in the six helices of the protein, and fifty-four were correctly detected. Seven Cα atoms were wrongly detected due to the wrongly detected short helix and the longer detected length than expected for some helices. There is one β-sheet in this protein and eighteen Cα atoms on the β-sheet were correctly detected. A correctly detected Cα atom refers to a Cα atom that has a detected helix/β-sheet voxel within 2.5 Å radius of the atom.

Table 1. The accuracy of identified helixes and β-Sheets using SSETracer.

PDB ID	#Hlx[a]	#C$_\alpha$ Hlx[b]	#Sht[c]	#C$_\alpha$ Sht[d]	Time[e]
1WAB	6/8/1	67/96/10	1/1	22/24/14	0:32
2ITG	5/6/1	54/66/7	1/1	18/21/17	0:23
4CSV	8/10/0	80/121/0	2/2	30/37/25	0:40
1CV1	8/9/0	108/123/4	1/1	11/14/0	0:23
4P1T	19/22/2	290/400/15	0/1	0/4/0	1:26
4D44	7/11/1	90/150/2	1/1	33/37/20	0:40
4XDA	8/12/0	97/143/6	1/2	50/78/38	0:39
4OZW	13/18/1	198/257/4	0/1	0/4/0	0:32

[a]The number of correctly detected/total number/wrongly detected helices.
[b]The number of correctly detected/total number/wrongly detected Cα atoms of helices.
[c]The number of correctly detected/total number of β-sheets.
[d]The number of correctly detected/total number/wrongly detected Cα atoms in β-sheets.
[e]Time (in minutes) of the detection.

Table 2. The accuracy of identified helices and β-sheets using SSELearner.

PDB ID	#Hlx[a]	#C$_\alpha$ Hlx[b]	# Sht[c]	#C$_\alpha$ Sht[d]	Time[e]
1WAB	7/8/0	88/96/7	1/1	23/24/9	1:29
2ITG	6/6/1	62/66/6	1/1	19/21/7	1:23
4CSV	9/10/2	103/121/15	1/2	28/37/14	1:48
1CV1	8/9/0	107/123/9	1/1	10/14/13	1:01
4P1T	19/22/0	369/400/3	1/1	2/4/4	2:27
4D44	8/11/1	105/150/6	1/1	23/37/23	1:52
4XDA	11/12/2	112/143/36	2/2	59/78/30	2:01
4OZW	16/18/0	224/257/5	1/1	2/4/2	1:22

See Table 1 for caption a–d.
[e]Time (in minutes) of the detection without the time of model generation.

We previously developed a machine learning approach, *SSELearner*, to automatically identify helices and β-sheets by using the knowledge from existing volumetric images [10]. The first component of the method develops features using local structure tensor and local thickness. The second component performs multi-task classification using Support Vector Machine (SVM). The post-processing step performs additional voxel clustering and filtering. *SSELearner* shows that it is possible to use one cryo-EM map for learning in order to detect helices or β-sheet in another cryo-EM map of similar quality. With careful training, it is possible to improve detection accuracy using machine learning in the secondary structure detection problem [10].

We applied *SSETracer* and *SSELearner* on the same set of data containing eight protein images. The accuracy appears to be generally comparable between the two methods (Tables 1 and 2), although *SSELearner* is slightly more sensitive detecting more Cα atoms. In certain cases such as 4XDA, it is less specific than *SSETracer* by detecting more wrong Cα atoms. The main difference between the two methods is two-fold. *SSETracer* uses skeleton and *SSELearner* does not. *SSELearner* is a machine learning method that needs to generate models in the training process. *SSETracer* runs faster than *SSELearner* (Column 6 of Tables 1 and 2). For example, it takes about 1 min 26 s to run *SSETracer* and 2 min 27 s to run *SSELearner*. Note that the time does not include the time to generate a model for *SSELearner*. It may take many hours to produce a model. Libsvm library that was used in *SSELearner* needs to be tuned according to the actual problem for optimal performance. Our current version uses the default parameters of Libsvm in model generation, and that is a bottle neck of the method.

Table 3. Accuracy of β-strands detected using *StrandTwister*.

PDB ID	#Strands[a]	#Cα[b]	Time[c]
1WAB	5/5	22/24	2:33
2ITG	4/4	16/21	2:38
4CSV	4/5	18/31	2:31
4D44	6/7	12/37	10:55
4XDA	8/9	29/45	17:25

[a]The correctly detected/total number of β-strands in the β-sheet.
[b]The correctly detected/total number of Cα atoms of the β-sheet.
[c]Execution time (in minute) to derive top ten possible sets of β-strands using *StrandTwister*.

2.3 *StrandTwister* to Predict β-Strands for Single Sheets

SSETracer is a tool to detect helices and β-sheets from 3D images, but it does not detect β-strands. Each β-sheet is composed of multiple β-strands. The spacing between two β-stands is 4.5–5 Å that makes it almost impossible to be visualized in a density image with 5–10 Å resolution. We proposed a new method, *StrandTwister* [8], to predict the traces of β-strands from a chunk of isolated β-sheet density. It does not rely on the existence of separation of β-strands and can be applied to images at lower resolutions. We showed that it is possible to predict the orientation of β-strands through the analysis of twist of a β-sheet. *StrandTwister* has two major components. The first one simplifies the voxels of a β-sheet into a polynomial surface. The second, also the major step, identifies right-handed β-twist from the polynomial surface model. *StrandTwister* appears to detect the traces of β-strands on major β-sheets quite accurately, particularly at the central area of a β-sheet. The requirement of the program is to provide an image of an isolated single sheet. The current version of the program does not handle an image with multiple β-sheets. We report the result of β-strand prediction for five new cases in Table 3. As an example in 2ITG, the isolated density of β-sheet (gray in Fig. 3) was generated from *SSETracer*. *StrandTwister* produces ten possible sets of β-strands. The best detection (red lines in Fig. 3) refers to the set of detected lines that are closest to the true β-strands. In this case, the best detection contains all four β-strands of the β-sheet or sixteen of the twenty-one Cα atoms of the β-sheet (Table 3 row 2). We observe in the five test cases and also previously that if the estimation of a β-sheet has good accuracy, *StrandTwister* often produces accurate results [8].

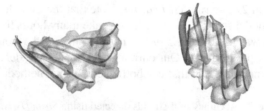

Fig. 3. Detection of β-strands from isolated β-sheet density using *StrandTwister*. β-sheet density (gray, same as the β-sheet in Fig. 1) is detected using *SSETracer* for sheet A of protein 2ITG (PDB ID). It is superimposed with the β-traces (red lines) best predicted using *StrandTwister* and the true structure (ribbon). The side view (left) and the top view (right) are shown (Color figure online).

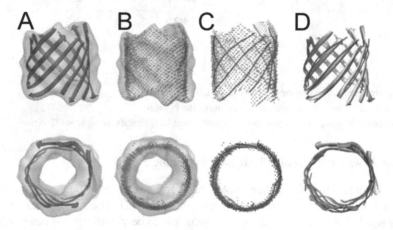

Fig. 4. Detection of β-strands from isolated β-barrel image using *StrandRoller*. (A) β-barrel image (gray) was simulated to 10 Å resolution using β-barrel structure (ribbon, PDB ID: 1RRX sheet A12). (B) The model surface (yellow) fit in the image. (C) The best predicted β-traces (red lines) were generated using *StrandRoller*. (D) The predicted β-traces superimposed with the true structure (ribbon) (Color figure online).

2.4 *StrandRoller* to Predict β-Strands for a β-Barrel Image

Various shapes of β-sheets have been observed in nature, particularly for β-sheets with long β-strands and/or more number of β-strands. A β-barrel is a β-sheet with an overall shape of a barrel (Fig. 4A). Many β-barrels are large β-sheets forming channels for trans-membrane activities. We proposed a method called *StrandRoller* to predict possible sets of β-traces from a β-barrel image at medium resolutions [14]. A β-barrel surface model (yellow in Fig. 4B) is first fit in the image and then possible sets of β-strands are modeled by strand-walking. The results of *StrandRoller* suggest that it is possible to derive a small set of possible β-traces (red lines in Fig. 4D) from a β-barrel image even when it is not possible to visualize the separation of β-strands [8].

3 Challenges in Secondary Structure Detection

The first method in automatic detection of secondary structures from 3D cryo-EM images is *Helixhunter*, developed in 2001 [5]. It was able to detect helices but not β-sheets. Although many methods have been developed to detect secondary structures, it is still challenging to detect them accurately. In this paper we showed four methods developed in our group to address this problem. We showed that the combination of image processing and geometrical modeling is capable of deriving new information that is not possible to derive using image processing alone. Deriving the position of β-strands from 3D images that do not, in principle, resolve β-strands has been a challenging problem in the last ten years. We showed that using image processing techniques, β-sheets can be first identified using *SSETracer* or other methods. The isolated β-sheet density image can be modeled geometrically using *StrandTwister* through the analysis of twist to derive the position of β-strands. Alternatively, the isolated β-barrel can be modeled using tilt angle knowledge to derive β-strands for β-barrels.

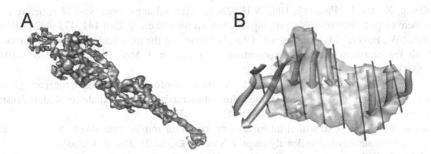

Fig. 5. Challenges in Secondary Structure Detection. (A) E2 monomer image (gray) from Encephalitis Virus (EMD_5276) at 4.4 Å resolution. The upper left region has much weaker density than the main part of the density map. (B) β-sheet image (gray) detected from simulated image of protein 4XDA (PDB ID) using *SSETracer*. The best predicted β-traces (red lines) are superimposed with the true structure (ribbon) of β-sheet AA1 (Color figure online).

In spite of improvement in methodology, cryo-EM data present great challenges for understanding 3D images. The 3D images obtained from cryo-EM technique are noisy and incomplete in many places. Even in the same image, it is often observed that certain regions have much better quality than others. As an example, the upper left region of the 3D image in Fig. 5A appears weaker than other regions. In this case, the resolution of the map is 4.4 Å. It is harder to interpret this region than others. A good secondary structure detection method needs to be aware of the local quality of the image. Although *StrandTwister* is able to predict β-strands from many β-sheet images, it is not very accurate for large and complicated β-sheets. For example, the β-sheet in Fig. 5B contains eight β-strands. Unlike a typical β-sheet, the β-strand near the middle of the sheet is very short in this case. As a result, there is over-estimation of the β-sheet at the middle and the β-strands predicted are not accurate for some strands. The nature of cryo-EM data and the biological diversity of molecules present interesting and challenging future for the understanding of 3D images.

Acknowledgements. The work in this paper is partially supported by NSF DBI-1356621, M&S fellowship and FP3 fund of the Old Dominion University. Authors' contribution: MA conducted the tests with the help of DS. DS prepared the figures. JH guided the project and wrote the manuscript.

References

1. Hryc, C.F., Chen, D.H., Chiu, W.: Near-atomic-resolution cryo-EM for molecular virology. Curr. Opin. Virol. **1**(2), 110–117 (2011)
2. Zhou, Z.H.: Towards atomic resolution structural determination by single-particle cryo-electron microscopy. Curr. Opin. Struct. Biol. **18**(2), 218–228 (2008)
3. Zhou, Z.H., Dougherty, M., Jakana, J., He, J., Rixon, F.J., Chiu, W.: Seeing the herpesvirus capsid at 8.5 A. Science **288**(5467), 877–880 (2000)
4. Zhang, X., Jin, L., Fang, Q., Hui, W.H., Zhou, Z.H.: 3.3 angstrom cryo-EM structure of a nonenveloped virus reveals a priming mechanism for cell entry. Cell **141**, 472–482 (2010)
5. Jiang, W., Baker, M.L., Ludtke, S.J., Chiu, W.: Bridging the information gap: computational tools for intermediate resolution structure interpretation. J. Mol. Biol. **308**(5), 1033–1044 (2001)
6. Kong, Y., Zhang, X., Baker, T.S., Ma, J.: A structural-informatics approach for tracing beta-sheets: building pseudo-C(alpha) traces for beta-strands in intermediate-resolution density maps. J. Mol. Biol. **339**(1), 117–130 (2004)
7. Kong, Y., Ma, J.: A structural-informatics approach for mining beta-sheets: locating sheets in intermediate-resolution density maps. J. Mol. Biol. **332**(2), 399–413 (2003)
8. Si, D., He, J.: Tracing beta-strands using strandtwister from cryo-EM density maps at medium resolutions. Structure **22**(11), 1665–1676 (2014)
9. Si, D., He, J.: Beta-sheet detection and representation from medium resolution cryo-EM density maps. In: BCB 2013: Proceedings of ACM Conference on Bioinformatics, Computational Biology and Biomedical Informatics, Washington, D.C., pp. 764–770, 22–25 Sept 2013
10. Si, D., Ji, S., Nasr, K.A., He, J.: A machine learning approach for the identification of protein secondary structure elements from electron cryo-microscopy density maps. Biopolymers **97**(9), 698–708 (2012)

11. Dal Palu, A., He, J., Pontelli, E., Lu, Y.: Identification of alpha-helices from low resolution protein density maps. In: Proceeding of Computational Systems Bioinformatics Conference (CSB), pp. 89–98 (2006)
12. Rusu, M., Wriggers, W.: Evolutionary bidirectional expansion for the tracing of alpha helices in cryo-electron microscopy reconstructions. J. Struct. Biol. **177**(2), 410–419 (2012)
13. Pettersen, E.F., Goddard, T.D., Huang, C.C., Couch, G.S., Greenblatt, D.M., Meng, E.C., Ferrin, T.E.: UCSF chimera—a visualization system for exploratory research and analysis. J. Comput. Chem. **25**(13), 1605–1612 (2004)
14. Si, D., He, J.: Combining image processing and modeling to generate traces of beta-strands from cryo-EM density images of beta-barrels. In: Proceeding of EMBC, Chicago, 26–30 Aug 2014

Determination of Focal Length for Targets Positioning with Binocular Stereo Vision

Wang Jian[1], Wang Yu-sheng[1(✉)], Liu Feng[2], Li Qing-jia[3],
and Wang Guang-chao[1]

[1] School of Electronic Information Engineering,
Civil Aviation University of China, Tianjin 300300, China
307327200@qq.com
[2] MOEMS Education Ministry Key Laboratory,
Tianjin University, Tianjin 300072, China
[3] Sino-European Institute of Aviation Engineering,
Civil Aviation University of China, Tianjin 300300, China

Abstract. Targets positioning with binocular stereo vision has the potential of usage for surveillance on airdrome surface. This paper analyses the impact of focal length of a camera on the accuracy of positioning targets on the ground and proposes a way of determining the value of the focal length, with which measuring errors on the edges of the surveillance area could be mitigated. With profound analysis of the impact of many system parameters on the coordinates of targets, it is found that the focal length predominates. In order to establish the basis for calibration, a set of non-linear equations are solved for relevant system parameters, thus yielding their explicit expressions. An on-site experiment is implemented for calibration for parameters, as well as measuring the positions of targets. A test environment is established and data are obtained for calculating curves of coordinates versus the focal length, which gives us a clearer indication of determining the focal length of the camera. In a similar way, the curve gives also an implication of selecting the appropriate points where to place calibration objects, thus **reducing errors of** *targets positioning*.

Keywords: Binocular stereo vision · Positioning targets · System parameters · Calibration · Focal length

1 Introduction

With an ever increasing traffic volume of surface movement on airdromes, the situation is complex and maneuvering is becoming more difficult for air traffic controllers. Although there have been already several means of surveillance quipped on the airdromes, most of them are just for cooperative targets, which is not sufficient in the next generation of air traffic control management. Therefore, finding a new method of

This work is supported by the joint funded project of National Natural Science Fund Committee and the Civil Aviation Administration of China (No. 61179043).

© Springer International Publishing Switzerland 2015
Y.-J. Zhang (Ed.): ICIG 2015, Part II, LNCS 9218, pp. 156–163, 2015.
DOI: 10.1007/978-3-319-21963-9_14

surveillance for non cooperative targets on a surface is of great importance. A method of positioning these sorts of targets based on binocular stereo vision has the potential for this purpose.

Having finished modeling binocular stereo vision for remote coordinate measurement in our previous work, reasonable calibration is critical for on-site positioning targets with improved accuracy. In three-dimensional machine vision systems, the position, size and other information of objects are calculated from the information of acquired images from cameras [1]. In order to obtain the correspondence of spatial points to camera image pixels accurately, the cameras are supposed to calibrated [2]. There are several ways of obtaining parameters from camera calibration, but most of them just calibrate parameters of the camera lens based on pinhole imaging [3, 4].

Analysis of the impact of system and camera parameters on the measurement accuracy of targets shows that the focal length contributes the most to the accuracy. Therefore, finding a reasonable focal length is meaningful, although its nominal value is usually provided. This paper proposes a method of determining the focal length for targets positioning with binocular stereo vision. An explicit formulation of expressing the focal length is derived from a well established calibration equation, a non linear one in which iteration is needed for solution before. Simulation is made showing the relationship between the coordinates and the focal length and other parameters. It is necessary to establish an appropriate mathematical model of the camera to solve for the relation between the two-dimensional image coordinates and the three-dimensional world coordinates [5]. Papers [4, 6] have made several experiments to calculate system parameters, *positions of objects, and* analyzed *the accuracy concerned under the prerequisite of β equaling 0. In this paper, β is calibrated and the focal length is probed as an internal parameter mainly for the final goal of finding a reasonable value of the focal length.*

2   Derivation of Explicit Expressions for Calculation

Considering a positioning system applied in a wide area based on binocular stereo vision, it is preferable to begin with the pinhole imaging model to get an expression of solving for coordinates of targets. In the same way, the model of calibrating system and camera parameters is also from the same principle based on perspective projection matrix, with which a mapping equation is established, expressing the relation among a world coordinate, a camera coordinate and an image coordinate system. When the origin of world coordinate is a point where two optical axes of binocular cameras meet, the equation could be well simplified and written as follows [5, 6]:

$$
\begin{aligned}
(X_w + S_x)(X \sin \alpha - Y \cos \alpha \sin \beta - f \cos \alpha \cos \beta) \\
+ (Z_w + S_z)(X \cos \alpha + Y \sin \alpha \sin \beta + f \sin \alpha \cos \beta) = 0
\end{aligned}
\tag{1}
$$

where, (X,Y) is a point expressed in pixel of a target on an image, (α,β) and f are the rotation angles of and the focal length of the camera, (S_x, S_z) is the coordinate of a camera in the world plane coordinate system. Suppose system and camera parameters can be made known, and the pixel value can be determined with image processing, there remain only two unknowns X_w and Z_w, representing the surface position of a target in the world coordinate system.

In the typical configuration of using a binocular stereo vision, two cameras are separated apart, focusing the same area for obtaining an image, denoted as pixel numbers (X_1, Y_1) and (X_2, Y_2) for the same target. When two cameras are installed, two equations, with the form of Eq. (1) but a pair of different parameters denoted as (α_1, β_1), f_1, (S_{x1}, S_{z1}) and (α_2, β_2), f_2, (S_{x2}, S_{z2}), are combined to solve for X_w and Z_w, yielding the coordinate of the target.

For calibration, parameters (α, β) and f are supposed to be unknown. In this case, solving for these three parameters, three equations as (1) with different (X_w, Z_w) and (X, Y) are needed and combined. For this purpose, targets should be placed in the field, with known positions in the world and image coordinate systems. Suppose the coordinates are denoted as $P(X_{w1}, Z_{w1})$, $P(X_{w2}, Z_{w2})$ in the world coordinate system, (X_1, Y_1) and (X_2, Y_2) in the image coordinate system, equations can be obtained by taking them into the Eq. (1). With α being less than $90°$, it can be solved from each equation for one camera as follows:

$$\tan\alpha = \frac{(X_{w1} + S_x)(Y_1 \sin\beta + f \cos\beta) - (Z_{w1} + S_z)X_1}{(X_{w1} + S_x)X_1 + (Z_{w1} + S_z)(Y_1 \sin\beta + f \cos\beta)} \tag{2}$$

$$\tan\alpha = \frac{(X_{w2} + S_x)(Y_2 \sin\beta + f \cos\beta) - (Z_{w2} + S_z)X_2}{(X_{w2} + S_x)X_2 + (Z_{w2} + S_z)(Y_2 \sin\beta + f \cos\beta)}. \tag{3}$$

When combining expressions (2) and (3), rotation angle β can be found to be one of four roots from a quartic equation of β by eliminating the parameter f.

After parameters (α, β) have been solved for, the **focal length** can be written as an expression **as follows:**

$$f = \frac{((X_{w1} + S_x)\sin\alpha\cos\beta - (Y_{w1} + S_y)\sin\beta + (Z_{w1} + S_z)\cos\alpha\cos\beta)X_1}{(X_{w1} + S_x)\cos\alpha - (Z_{w1} + S_z)\sin\alpha} \tag{4}$$

Calibration of both α and β requires that at least two targets should be used. The focal length can be calculated under the premise that some values remain unchanged.

To show the impact of focal length on the coordinates (X_w, Z_w) of a target, expressions for both X_w and Z_w can be solved for from equations similar to Eq. (1) and calculation will yield the following relation, fixing all other parameters, except the focal

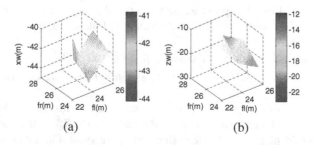

(a)   (b)

Fig. 1. Relation between world coordinate and f

length on the left and right camera. From this figure, it is obvious that focal length has great impact on X_w and Z_w (Fig. 1).

3   Determination of Focal Length

Although the nominal value of the focal length of a camera is usually provided, finding a reasonable value of the focal length is meaningful for targets positioning with binocular stereo vision.

3.1   Setup of Experiment

An experimental schematic diagram is shown in Fig. 2, with an overall arrangement for positioning and calibration system parameters are as follows, the distance from the coordinate origin to the left station and to the right station are 345.2046 m and 328.58 m, respectively. Angles between a line from the origin to the station and the north direction from the station are 160.3395° and 129.7745°. These parameters are obtained by using differential GPS with accuracy of 20 ml.

Components of one station for this experiment are shown in Fig. 3. The two stations transmit images with microwave, and the left and right computers transmit images to a host computer, which processes the data from the experiment and output results on site.

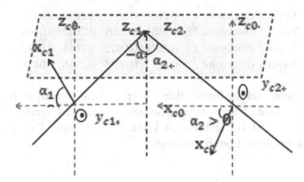

Fig. 2. Experimental schematic diagram

Fig. 3. Components of a station

3.2   Experimental Data and Results

With the data ($f_l = 24.7859$ mm, $f_r = 25.2338$ mm) above and the data in the Table 1 below.

Table 1. Data from experiment

Test points	Left station pixels		Right station pixels		Longitude	Latitude	Ellipsoidal heights
	u	v	u	v			
Central point	799	200	800	199	117.2450202654	39.0831836498	−5.958
Target 1	414	197	317	188	117.2449162872	39.0830587517	−6.14
Checkpoint 1	614	197	523	192	117.2449777350	39.0831002492	−5.926
Target 2	1254	203	1201	208	117.2452115604	39.0832082246	−5.833
Checkpoint 2	1389	204	917	99	117.2453054454	39.0830347370	−5.784

We can get the parameters α and β, the results are shown below in the Table 2.

Table 2. Calibration of α and β (Unit: rad)

	Left station		Right station	
	α	β	α	β
Target 1 checkpoint 1	−0.2680	0.007	0.2652	0.012
Target 1 checkpoint 2	−0.2681	0.0201	0.2652	0.0195
Target 2 checkpoint 1	−0.2678	0.0072	0.2655	0.0092
Target 1 checkpoint 2	−0.2677	0.0235	0.2656	0.0478

In the experiment, and the image planes keep vertical ($\beta = 0$) or β can be a fixed small value for the sake of convenience. So here α and f are recalculated again and $\alpha_l = -14.6514$, $\alpha_r = 16.0415$ and $f_l = 24.8$ mm, $f_r = 25.3$ mm. The subscripts l and r denote the left and right station, respectively.

3.3   Reasonable Value of the Focal Length

Though values of α and β have been known, it's essential to find suitable (X_w, Z_w) to find a more reasonable value of the focal length in the experimental scene. When a target or a checkpoint is in one place, it constitutes a straight line with a station on the plane of the world coordinate system. In order to obtain a more accurate value of f to calculate object coordinates, it's indispensable to find some proper points to calculate it in the line. This requires us to find corresponding relation between X_w and the focal length according to the expression (4) above once an equation is determined. Additionally, left station and target 1, checkpoint 1 and checkpoint 2 constitute three lines as $Z_w = -7X_w + 278$, $Z_w = -5X_w + 98$ and $Z_w = -2X_w - 137$ respectively according to their coordinates in the world coordinate system. The relation between X_w and the focal length is in Fig. 4 below.

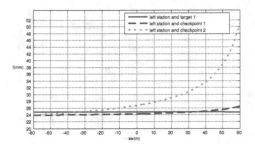

Fig. 4. The relation between X_w and f (left)

There are many values between 0.0247 m and 0.0249 m if the range of these values and step length can be smaller than above. It's instructive to select suitable locations to calculate f of cameras based on the relation in Fig. 4 if target 1, checkpoint 1 or checkpoint 2 and the left station constitute a straight line on the plane of the world coordinate system. From the Fig. 4, it can be seen that the relation between left station and the check point 2 changes obviously while the other two lines are steady relatively. It is more easier to calibrate the cameras if the target 1 is selected compared with the checkpoint 1 and 2. In the experimental scene it is hard to select the proper points directly though the lines are determined here. So quick selecting the points according to the grid generated by the linear equation $Z_w = -7X_w + 278$ above seems be advisable in Fig. 5 below.

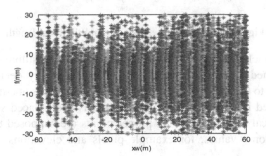

Fig. 5. The relation between X_w and the focal length

Analogously, when the right station and target 1, checkpoint 1 and checkpoint 2 constitute three lines as $Z_w = -2.25X_w - 112$, $Z_w = -2.639X_w - 71.1732$ and $Z_w = 3.9325X_w + 41.2750$ respectively according to their coordinates in the world coordinate system, the relation between X_w and the focal length is in Fig. 6 below.

Similarly, from the Fig. 6, it can be seen that the relation between right station and the target 1 changes obviously while the other two lines are steady relatively. It seems that calibration of the two cameras should choose the target 1 as the proper point to calculate the focal length. In the experimental scene it is also hard to select the proper

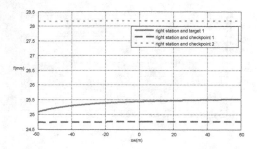

Fig. 6. The relation between X_w and f (right)

points directly though the lines are determined for right station. So quick selecting the points according to the grid generated by the linear equation $Z_w = 2.25X_w - 112$ above seems be advisable in Fig. 7 below.

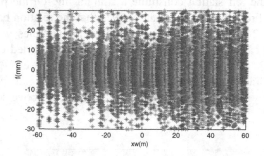

Fig. 7. The relation between X_w and the focal length

So, it can be included that the focal length and X_w constitute a non-linear relationship in a defined area or the focal length remains steady decline or rise as X_w changes according to the Figs. 4 and 6. Additionally, the points about the calibration of f should be selected in a line once the first point has been placed somewhere for the accuracy of the focal length, and some proper points are supposed to be found under the premise that some values, for example pixels and elevations of targets, remain unchanged.

4 Conclusion

The experiment shows the correctness and reliability of the calibrated model with the calibration of α and β showing its correctness. The relation between f and (X_w, Z_w) has been investigated, and it's important to calculate (X_w, Z_w) if we can narrow the difference between the reference value and f calibrated. It can be concluded that selecting suitable locations can improve the accuracy of objects on the plane of the world coordinate system. Therefore, the method related can be instructive for calibration based on binocular vision measurement in the paper, and the cameras will have a fast calibration about its parameters.

Acknowledgments. This work is supported by the National Natural Science Foundation of China (No. 61179043).

References

1. Sundareswara, R., Schater, P.R.: Bayesian modeling of camera calibration and reconstruction. In: Proceedings of the Fifth International Conference on 3-D Digital Imaging and Modeling, pp. 394–401. IEEE (2005)
2. Peng, T., Yingming, X.: Improved calibration method technology based on radial constraint. Sci. Technol. Vis. **12**, 11–12 (2014)
3. Liying, Z., Fengjuan, M., Lei, Z.: Research on camera calibration technology based on binocular vision system. Technol. Forum **5**, 124–125 (2013)
4. Jian, W., Xiangjun, W., Feng, L.: A scheme for parameter calibration in super-size two-dimensional scale events sensing and positioning system using binocular stereo vision. In: The International Society for Optical Engineering, vol. 8908 (2013)
5. Wei, Z.: Research on camera calibration method based on machine vision. Electron. Compon. Device Appl. **1011**, 70–72 (2008)
6. Huan-huan, W., Jian, W., Feng, L.: A verification and errors analysis of the model for object positioning based on binocular stereo vision for airport surface surveillance. In: Proceedings of SPIE – The International Society for Optical Engineering, vol. 9297 (2014)

Dimensionality Reduction for Hyperspectral Image Based on Manifold Learning

Yiting Wang$^{(\boxtimes)}$, Shiqi Huang, Hongxia Wang, Daizhi Liu,
and Zhigang Liu

Department Xi'an Research Institute of Hi-Tech,
Xi'an, People's Republic of China
appie5744@sina.com

Abstract. A novel dimensionality reduction method named spectral angle and geodesic distance-based locality preserving projection (SAGD-LPP) was proposed in this paper. Considering the physical characters of hyperspectral imagery, the proposed method primarily select neighbor pixels in the image based on spectral angle distance. Then, using the geodesic distance matrix construct a weighted matrix between pixels. Finally, based on this weighted matrix, the idea of locality preserving projection algorithm is applied to reduce the dimensions of hyperspectral image data. The use of spectral angle to measure the distance between pixels can effectively overcome the spectral amplitude error caused by the uncertainty. At the same time, the use of geodesic distance to construct weight matrix can better reflect the internal structure of the data manifold than the use of Euclidean distance. Therefore, the proposed methods can reserve effectively the original characters of dataset with less loss in the useful information and less distortion on the data structure. Experimental results on real hyperspectral data demonstrate that the proposed methods have higher detection accuracy than the other methods when applied to the target detection of hyperspectral imagery after dimensionality reduction.

Keywords: Hyperspectral · Manifold learning · Target detection

1 Introduction

Hyperspectral sensors measure the radiance of the materials within each pixel area at a very large number of contiguous spectral bands and provide image data containing both spatial and spectral information. The resulting "image cube" is a stack of images in which each pixel has an associated spectral signature or fingerprint that uniquely characterizes the underlying objects. And due to its "one map" and high spectral resolution, hyperspectral remote sensing has opened up new opportunities for analyzing a variety of land cover materials [1].

Although this spectral feature provides sufficient discriminative information of the objects, hyperspectral target detection is always a great challenge due to its high dimensionality. Meanwhile, due to the nonlinear changes of solar radiation and nonlinear propagation of electromagnetic waves in the atmosphere, hyperspectral data has a typical non-linear characteristic. This further increases the difficulty of the

© Springer International Publishing Switzerland 2015
Y.-J. Zhang (Ed.): ICIG 2015, Part II, LNCS 9218, pp. 164–172, 2015.
DOI: 10.1007/978-3-319-21963-9_15

hyperspectral data processing. So how to effectively learn and discover nonlinear structure of hyperspectral data and reasonably reduce the dimensionality of data has important implications for hyperspectral image processing and application [2].

Manifold learning is a kind of common nonlinear dimensionality reduction algorithm. Among them, the typical manifold learning algorithms are isometric feature mapping (ISOMAP) [3], locally linear embedding (LLE) [4], Laplacian eigenmaps (LE) [5], etc. Manifold learning pursuits the goal to embed data that originally lies in a high dimensional space into a lower dimensional space, while preserving characteristic properties. Generally, it is difficult to know the geometry of the data manifold. ISOMAP is a technique that attempts to preserve pairwise geodesic distances between data points to keep the geometry of the data. In LLE, the local properties of the data manifold are constructed by writing the high-dimensional data points as a linear combination of their nearest neighbors. In the low-dimensional representation of the data, LLE attempts to retain the reconstruction weights in the linear combinations as good as possible. Similar to LLE, LE find a low-dimensional data representation by preserving local properties of the manifold. In LE, the local properties are based on the pairwise distances between near neighbors. The dimensionality reduction data obtained from the above manifold learning methods are all able to maintain a good global or local geometry of the original data.

While, an important requirement for dimensionality reduction techniques is the ability to embed new high-dimensional data points into an existing low-dimensional data representation, that is so-called out-of-sample extension. For the above nonlinear dimensionality reduction techniques, they yield mappings that are defined only on the training data points and it remains unclear how to naturally evaluate the maps on novel testing points. Therefore, some approximate out-of-sample extensions have been proposed that is based on computing a linear transformation from a set of landmark points to the complete dataset, in which neighborhood preserving embedding (NPE) algorithm is a linear approximation to the LLE [6], and locality preserving projection (LPP) algorithm is a linear approximation to the LE [7]. At present, these dimensionality reduction techniques are most conducted in the field of hyperspectral image classification but few in the field of target detection. So in this paper, we propose a new linear dimensionality reduction algorithm, called spectral angle and geodesic distance-based locality preserving projection (SAGD-LPP), so as to achieve the purpose of dimensionality reduction and improving target detection performance.

2 LPP Algorithm

LPP is designed for preserving local structure of high-dimensional data. It is likely that a nearest neighbor search in the low dimensional space will yield similar results to that in the high dimensional space. As a linear approximation of the LE, LPP suppose there exist a linear transformation between the high dimensional data point $\mathbf{x}_i$ and low dimensional data point $\mathbf{y}_i$, i.e. $\mathbf{y}_i = \mathbf{a}^T \mathbf{x}_i$, where $\mathbf{a}$ is a transformation vector. Then the algorithmic procedure of LPP is formally stated below:

1. Select neighbor pixels and construct the adjacency graph G: in graph G every data point $\mathbf{x}_i$ is connected to its k nearest neighbors.
2. Construct the weight matrix: the weight of the edge in the graph G is computed using the Gaussian kernel function. If nodes i and j are connected, put

$$w_{ij} = e^{-\|\mathbf{x}_i - \mathbf{x}_j\|/\sigma^2} \tag{1}$$

and, $w_{ij} = 0$ if there is no such edge.
3. Compute the low-dimensional representations $\mathbf{Y}$: a reasonable criterion for choosing a "good" map $\mathbf{Y} = [\mathbf{y}_1, \mathbf{y}_1, \ldots, \mathbf{y}_m]$ is to minimize the following objective function

$$\sum_{i,j} \|\mathbf{y}_i - \mathbf{y}_j\|^2 w_{ij} \tag{2}$$

Because $\mathbf{y}_i = \mathbf{a}^T \mathbf{x}_i$, the objective function can be reduced to

$$\sum_{i,j} (\mathbf{y}_i - \mathbf{y}_j)^2 w_{ij} = \sum_{i,j} (\mathbf{a}^T \mathbf{x}_i - \mathbf{a}^T \mathbf{x}_j)^2 w_{ij} = 2\mathbf{a}^T \mathbf{X} \mathbf{D} \mathbf{X}^T \mathbf{a} - 2\mathbf{a}^T \mathbf{X} \mathbf{W} \mathbf{X}^T \mathbf{a} = 2\mathbf{a}^T \mathbf{X} \mathbf{L} \mathbf{X}^T \mathbf{a} \tag{3}$$

where $\mathbf{X} = [\mathbf{x}_1, \mathbf{x}_2, \ldots, \mathbf{x}_m]$, and $\mathbf{D}$ is a diagonal matrix, $d_{ii} = \sum_j w_{ij}$. $\mathbf{L} = \mathbf{D} - \mathbf{W}$ is the Laplacian matrix of graph G. And a constraint is imposed as follows:

$$\mathbf{a}^T \mathbf{X} \mathbf{D} \mathbf{X}^T \mathbf{a} = 1 \tag{4}$$

Finally, the minimization problem reduces to finding:

$$\underset{\mathbf{a}^T \mathbf{X} \mathbf{D} \mathbf{X}^T \mathbf{a}=1}{\arg\min} \ \mathbf{a}^T \mathbf{X} \mathbf{L} \mathbf{X}^T \mathbf{a} \tag{5}$$

It is a generalized eigenvector problem:

$$\mathbf{X} \mathbf{L} \mathbf{X}^T \mathbf{a} = \lambda \mathbf{X} \mathbf{D} \mathbf{X}^T \mathbf{a} \tag{6}$$

Suppose the eigenvectors $\mathbf{a}_0, \mathbf{a}_1, \ldots, \mathbf{a}_d$ are the solutions of Eq. (6), and their corresponding eigenvalues $\lambda_0 < \lambda_1 < \ldots < \lambda_d$, Thus, the embedding is

$$\mathbf{y}_i = \mathbf{a}^T \mathbf{x}_i, \mathbf{a} = [\mathbf{a}_0, \ldots, \mathbf{a}_d] \tag{7}$$

When the transformation vector $\mathbf{a}$ is computed out based on the training data, an explicit expression of linear maps can be obtained, so the new testing data could be embedded into the existing low-dimensional data representation.

3 SAGD-LPP Algorithm

In hyperspectral image, due to the widespread of the uncertainty, the spectral radiant intensity of the same class feature show large changes. At the same time, the spectral radiation of the object in shaded areas is greatly different from that of the same object in non-shaded areas. However, regardless of how changes in the amplitude of the spectral curve, the spectral shape of the same class feature is substantially similar. According to this physical characteristic of hyperspectral image, we can know that if we select the neighbor pixels based on the Euclidean distance, there will be a large errors in constructing the adjacency graph G. And this may lead to the physical neighbor pixels in the hyperspectral image extend away from each other in the low-dimensional data, reducing the accuracy of target identification.

Therefore, in the first step of our proposed algorithm SAGD-LPP, we select the neighbor pixels based on the spectral angle distance to construct the adjacency graph G. Spectral angle distance can overcome errors caused by changes in the spectrum amplitude, making the physical neighbor pixels similar with each other. The spectral angular distance between two pixels can be expressed as:

$$d(\mathbf{x}_i, \mathbf{x}_j) = arc \cos \left[\frac{\sum\limits_{k=1}^{p} x_{ik} x_{jk}}{\left(\sum\limits_{k=1}^{p} x_{ik}^2 \right)^{\frac{1}{2}} \left(\sum\limits_{k=1}^{p} x_{jk}^2 \right)^{\frac{1}{2}}} \right] \tag{8}$$

where, P is the number of bands.

Moreover, compared to the Euclidean distance, geodesic distance can better reflect the internal structure of the high dimensional manifold. Therefore, in the second step of the algorithm, we use the geodesic distance to construct the weight matrix $\tilde{\mathbf{W}}$. And it can be expressed as:

$$\tilde{w}_{ij} = e^{-d_G(\mathbf{x}_i, \mathbf{x}_j)\sigma^2} \tag{9}$$

where, $d_G(\mathbf{x}_i, \mathbf{x}_j)$ is the geodesic distance between pixel $\mathbf{x}_i$ and $\mathbf{x}_j$.

Then, the objective function in the third step of proposed algorithm is translated to

$$\arg \min \sum\nolimits_{i,j} \left\| \mathbf{y}_i - \mathbf{y}_j \right\|^2 \tilde{w}_{ij} \tag{10}$$

i.e.

$$\underset{\mathbf{a}^{\mathrm{T}}\mathbf{X}\tilde{\mathbf{D}}\mathbf{X}^{\mathrm{T}}\mathbf{a}=1}{\arg \min} \ \mathbf{a}^{\mathrm{T}}\mathbf{X}\tilde{\mathbf{L}}\mathbf{X}^{\mathrm{T}}\mathbf{a} \tag{11}$$

where $\mathbf{D}$ is a diagonal matrix, $\tilde{d}_{ii} = \sum\limits_{j} \tilde{w}_{ij}$. $\tilde{\mathbf{L}} = \tilde{\mathbf{D}} - \tilde{\mathbf{W}}$ is the Laplacian matrix.

4   Experimental Validation

In this section, we first use the proposed method to obtain a dimension reduction data based on the real hyperspectral image data. Then, based on the obtained low-dimensional data, two detection methods constrained energy minimization (CEM) [8] algorithm and adaptive coherence estimator (ACE) [9] will be applied to target detection. Finally, the detection results are used to validate the effectiveness of the proposed method. In this experiment, the proposed method is compared with three classical dimensionality reduction methods that are PCA, NPE, LPP. The ROC curve is adopted to quantitatively measure the effect of target detection [10]. If the target is more similar to the background and it is hard to be detected, the ROC curve will become straighter, and the area under the curve (AUC) will be smaller. While, if the target is less similar to the background, that is, the target is more easily detected, the curve will bend to the left, and the AUC will be larger.

4.1   Experimental Data

The experimental data is obtained from AVIRIS hyperspectral image of the United States Santiago North Island Naval airport. The original image size is 400 × 400 with a total of 224 bands, and its spatial resolution is 3.5 m. Remove the invalid bands and left 189 effective bands. The image data used in this experiment are two interceptions from the original image; the size of the two images respectively is 100 × 100. Figure 1 shows a diagram of the experimental data. The image is an airport tarmac. The aircraft is the goal of detection. Figure 1(a) is the gray image of sub image I on band 10. Figure 1(b) is the gray image of sub image II on band 10.

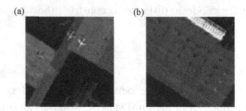

(a)   (b)

Fig. 1.   Experimental image of AVIRIS data (a) Sub image I (b) Sub image II

4.2   Experimental Results

Because of the variation of spectral characteristics between different objects, it is difficult to know the optimal dimensionality of the data. So we choose the optimal detection result that can be achieved by each of the algorithm for the comparison. Figure 2 show the detection results based on sub image I by using CEM detector. Figure 2(a) shows the detection result based on the original image data and Fig. 2(b)–(e) respectively show the detection result based on the new obtained low dimensionality data by using the NPE, PCA, LPP and SAGD-LPP. Similarly, Fig. 3(a)–(e) show the corresponding results of sub image I obtained by ACE detector. Figure 4(a)–(b) show the corresponding ROC comparison figure under the two detection methods. Table 1 lists the corresponding AUC value of ROC curve and the optimal dimensionality of each method.

It can be found from Figs. 2 and 3, the detection results are unsatisfactory, when apply the both detection method to the original data and the low dimensionality data obtained by NPE. And based on the low dimensionality data obtained by PCA and LPP, all of three planes are detected, but the background information is not suppressed enough having a high false alarm rate. Based on the data obtained by SAGD-LPP algorithm not only all of the three planes are detected, but also good background suppression is get which having a low false alarm rate. It can be seen from Fig. 4 and Table 1, the SAGD-LPP performs outperforms other three algorithms, followed by LPP and PCA. The NPE performs poorly.

Fig. 2. Detection result based on sub image I by using CEM detector (a) Original data (b) NPE (c) PCA (d) LPP (e) SAGD-LPP

Fig. 3. Detection result based on sub image I by using ACE detector (a) Orignal data (b) NPE (c) PCA (d) LPP (e) SAGD-LPP

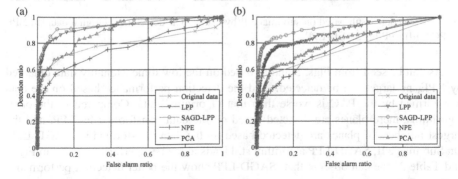

Fig. 4. ROC comparison figure obtained from sub image I (a) CEM detector (b) ACE detector

Table 1. Target detection results obtained from sub image I via different dimensionality reduction methods

Dimensionality reduction method	CEM detector		ACE detector	
	AUC	Dimensionality	AUC	Dimensionality
Original image	0.7914	198	0.7600	198
NPE	0.7666	30	0.7366	32
PCA	0.8019	4	0.8903	2
LPP	0.9314	8	0.9100	8
SAGD-LPP	0.9361	12	0.9275	12

Figures 5(a)–(e) and 6(a)–(e) respectively show the detection results of sub image II by using CEM and ACE detector based on the original image data and the new obtained low dimensionality data by NPE, PCA, LPP and SAGD-LPP. Figure 7(a)–(b) show the corresponding ROC comparison figure of sub image II. Table 2 lists the AUC value of ROC curve and the optimal dimensionality of each method corresponding to Fig. 7.

Fig. 5. Detection result based on sub image II by using CEM detector (a) Orignal data (b) NPE (c) PCA (d) LPP (e) SAGD-LPP

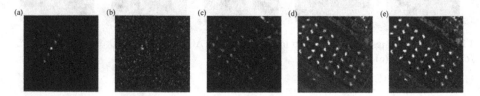

Fig. 6. Detection result based on sub image II by using ACE detector (a) Orignal data (b) NPE (c) PCA (d) LPP (e) SAGD-LPP

As can be seen from Figs. 5 and 6, based on the low dimensionality data obtained by NPE, no target can be detected. And the detection performance based on the data transformed by the PAC is worse than that of original data. Compared to the other algorithms, more planes are detected based on the data transformed by LPP, and the largest numbers of planes are detected based on the data transformed by SAGD-LPP. On Sub image II, SAGD-LPP algorithm still leads to the best performance. From Fig. 7 and Table 2, one can observe that, SAGD-LPP show the better detection performance

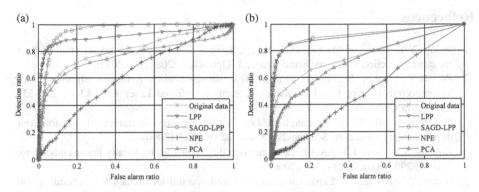

Fig. 7. ROC comparison figure obtained from sub image II (a) CEM detector (b) ACE detector

Table 2. Target detection results obtained from sub image II via different dimensionality reduction methods

Dimensionality reduction method	CEM detector		ACE detector	
	AUC	Dimensionality	AUC	Dimensionality
Original image	0.8115	198	0.7638	198
NPE	0.6813	39	0.4973	39
PCA	0.7610	30	0.7255	33
LPP	0.9112	13	0.9062	11
SAGD-LPP	0.9502	9	0.9151	10

than other algorithms in terms of AUC. And the AUC of SAGD-LPP increased by approximately 3 % compared with the LPP, and increased by approximately 18 % compared with other algorithm.

5   Conclusion

This paper presents a novel dimensionality reduction algorithm called spectral angle and geodesic distance-based locality preserving projection (SAGD-LPP). The proposed algorithm is based on the physical characteristics of hyperspectral data, so the structure of low-dimensional manifold can be better identified and the redundant information of hyperspectral data can be effectively removed during the dimensionality reduction. Real hyperspectral data experimental results show that the proposed SAGD-LPP method significantly outperformed the other methods dimensionality reduction applying to the target detection area.

Acknowledgment. This work was supported by the National Natural Science Foundation of China under project No. 41174093.

References

1. Wang, Y.T., Huang, S.Q., Liu, D.Z., Wang, B.H.: A new band removed selection method for target detection in hyperspectral image. J. Opt. **42**(3), 208–213 (2013)
2. Pu, H.Y., Wang, B., Zhang, L.M.: New dimensionality reduction algorithms for hyperspectral imagery based on manifold learning. Infrared Laser Eng. **43**(1), 232–237 (2014). (in Chinese)
3. Tenenbaum, J.B., Silva, V., Langford, J.C.: A global geometric framework for nonlinear dimensionality reduction. Science **290**(5500), 2319–2323 (2000)
4. Roweis, S.T., Saul, L.K.: Nonlinear dimensionality reduction by locally linear embedding. Science **290**(5500), 2323–2326 (2000)
5. Belkin, M., Niyogi, P.: Laplacian eigenmaps and spectral techniques for embedding and clustering. Adv. Neural Inf. Process. Syst. **14**, 585–591 (2001)
6. He, X.F., Cai, D., Yan, S.C., et al.: Neighborhood preserving embedding. In: Proceedings of the 10th IEEE International Conference on Computer Vision (ICCV 2005), pp. 1208–1213. Beijing (2005)
7. He, X.F., Niyogi, P.: Locality preserving projections. In: Proceedings of Neural Information Processing System. MIT, Vancouver (2003)
8. Gholizadeh, H., et al.: A decision fusion framework for hyperspectral subpixel target detection. Photogrammetrie Fernerkundung Geoinformation **3**, 267–280 (2012)
9. Kraut, S., Scharf, L.L.: The CFAR adaptive subspace detector is a scale-invariant GLRT. IEEE Trans. Signal Process. **47**(9), 2538–2541 (1999)
10. Manolakis, D., Marden, D., Shaw, G.A.: Hyperspectral image processing for automatic target detection applications. Lincoln Lab. J. **14**(1), 79–116 (2003)

Discriminative Feature Learning
with Constraints of Category and Temporal
for Action Recognition

Zhize Wu[✉], Shouhong Wan, Peiquan Jin, and Lihua Yue

Key Laboratory of Electromagnetic Space Information,
School of Computer Science and Technology, Chinese Academy of Sciences,
University of Science and Technology of China, Hefei, Anhui, China
wuzhize@mail.ustc.edu.cn, {wansh,jpq,llyue}@ustc.edu.cn

Abstract. Recently, with the availability of the depth cameras, a lot of studies of human action recognition have been conducted on the depth sequences. Motivated by the observations that each pose has its relative location during a complete action sequence, and similar actions have the fine spatio-temporal differences. We propose a novel method to recognize human actions based on the depth information in this paper. Representations of depth maps are learned and reconstructed using a stacked denoising autoencoder. By adding the category and temporal constraints, the learned features are more discriminative, able to capture the subtle but significant differences between actions, and mitigate the nuisance variability of temporal misalignment. Greedy layer-wise training strategy is used to train the deep neural network. Then we employ temporal pyramid matching on the feature representation to generate temporal representation. Finally a linear SVM is trained to classify each sequence into actions. We compare our proposal on MSR Action3D dataset with the previous methods, and the results shown that the proposed method significantly outperforms traditional model, and comparable to, state-of-art action recognition performance. Experimental results also indicate the great power of our model to restore highly noisy input data.

Keywords: Action recognition · Category · Temporal · Feature learning · Stacked denoising autoencoders

1 Introduction

Human action recognition has been an active field of research in computer vision. The goal of action recognition is to recognize people's behavior from videos in a given scenario automatically. It has many potential applications including content-based video search, human computer interaction, video surveillance, sports video [22,28]. Most of these applications require high level understanding of spatial and temporal information from videos that are usually composed of multiple simple actions of persons.

© Springer International Publishing Switzerland 2015
Y.-J. Zhang (Ed.): ICIG 2015, Part II, LNCS 9218, pp. 173–184, 2015.
DOI: 10.1007/978-3-319-21963-9_16

Inferring high-level knowledge from a color video especially in a complex and unconstrained scene is very difficult and costful. However, the recent availability of depth cameras such as Kinect [18] has tremendously improved the abilities to understand human activities. Depth maps have several advantages over traditional intensity sensors. First, depth sensors can obtain the holistic 3D structure of the human body, which is invariant to color and texture. Second, color and texture methods perform worse in the dim lighter and the shadows may bring ambiguity. But depth images are insensitive to changes in lighting conditions. Third, depth sensors greatly simplify the process of foreground extraction, removing plenty of noise and disturbance in the background [12, 14].

Furthermore, the 3D skeleton joint positions can be estimated from the depth map accurately following the work of Shotton *et al.* [18]. The extracted skeleton joints have strong representation power, which is more discerning and compact than depth or color sequences. Although with these benefits, two significant aspects arise when one employe joint features for depth-based action recognition. First, existing skeleton joints are not complete, some of the estimated joints are not reliable when the human body is partly in view, moreover, the overlapping of human limbs in some interactive actions can lead to the missing of some joints as well. Second, the action can be performed at difference paces and thus spanning different time durations, which largely influence the performance of action recognition, but it is very difficult to specify effective temporal alignment on action sequences.

To address these two challenging problems, we focus on learning feature, which is robust to the incomplete skeleton, and is mitigatory to the nuisance variability of temporal misalignment. Inspired by the satisfactory performance of previous work on exploring relative 3D joint features [4, 7, 22], we propose a novel method to learn discriminative features from joint 3D features to recognize human actions. We build a deep neural network and employ denoising autoencoders, which has proved their strong abilities to reconstruct and denoise data, as the basic unit of our architecture. This work is also motivated by the observations that each pose has its relative location during a complete action sequence, similar actions have the subtle spatio-temporal differences, we simply add the category and temporal constraints on denoising autoencoders to fuse time-series, intra- and inter-class information into features. We stack the denoising autoencoders with category constraint and greedy layer-wise training strategy is used to train the model. Then we use temporal pyramid matching on the feature representation to generate temporal representation. Finally a linear SVM is trained to classify each sequence into actions. Experiments show that this algorithm achieves superior results.

The contributions of this paper are manifold. First, a new discriminative feature learning algorithm is proposed to recognize depth-based videos. Second, a novel category and temporal constraints are added into denoising autoencoders to preserve temporal, intra-and inter class information. Third, the experiments show that our model has a strong capacity to reconstruct and denoise corrupted data. The remainder of this paper is organized as follows. Section 2 reviews the related work. Section 3 describes the entire flow of our methodology to recognize actions. Section 4 discusses the experimental results. Section 5 concludes the paper.

2   Related Work

Since human motion can be considered as a continuous evolution of the spatial configuration of the segments or body posture. Therefore, effective representation of the body configuration and its dynamics over time has been the central to the research of human activity recognition.

Recently, low-level hand-crafted features have been designed to recognize human actions. Spatio-temporal salient points like STIP [7] or some local features, like Cuboids [4], HOG/HOF [8] and SIFT [24] have been widely used. However, directly employ these original methods for color sequences on depth data is infeasible, mainly because of contamination of undefined depth points. In [14] Omar and Zicheng conducted an experiment using MSR-Daily Activity Dataset [22] and found that 60 % of the detected Dollar [4] interest points were fired on locations irrelevant to the action of interest and the corresponding classification accuracy is very low (52 %). Therefore, recent methods for action recognition in depth sequences explore alternative features particularly for depth-based videos. Li *et al.* [11] projected the depth map into three orthogonal planes and sampled representative 3D points to obtain a bag of 3D points. An action graph was deployed to model the dynamics of the salient postures. Lu *et al.* [25] extracted spatio-temporal interest points from depth videos and built a cuboid similarity feature. Similarly, in [14], Omar and Zicheng quantized the 4D space and represented the possible directions for the 4D normal in order to build a histogram in the 4D space. Due to the temporal misalignment, Su *et al.* [19] introduced a metric to analyze the rate-invariant of trajectories on Riemannian Manifolds with application in visual speech recognition, Jiang Wang [23] proposed a learning-based temporal alignment method, called maximum margin temporal warping (MMTW), to align two action sequences and measure their matching score.

As mentioned before, skeletal information has strong representation power. Lu *et al.* [26] computed histograms of 3D joint locations, reprojected the extracted features using LDA [17], and clustered them into visual words. The temporal evolutions of these words were modeled by HMMs [15]. Jiang *et al.* [22] combined skeleton and depth information to obtain Local Occupancy Patterns (LOP) at each joint and built a Fourier Temporal Pyramid, an actionlet ensemble was learn to represent the actions. Jiajia [12] proposed a dictionary learning algorithm adding the group sparsity and geometry constrains, obtain an over complete set of the input skeletal features. The Temporal Pyramid Matching was used for keeping the temporal information.

In a view of research of unsupervised feature learning [1,13,20], which is a set of algorithms that attempt to learn a hierarchy of features by building high-level features from low-level ones. Some models such as CNN [10], DBN [5] and Autoencoders [6] have been shown to yield excellent results in several tasks, e.g. object recognition, natural language processing, and audio classification. One reason for the success of deep learning methods is that they usually learn to capture the posterior distribution of the underlying explanatory factors for the data [2]. However, their extension to the depth maps case is still an open issue. Therefore, rather than elaborately designing the hand-crafted features as in [14,16], we choose to learn high level features from data, during the process of learning, we simply add the category and temporal constraints, in order to capture the small but significant differences between actions, and mitigate the nuisance variability of temporal misalignment. The experimental results further prove the feasibility and validity of this feature learning architecture.

3   Proposed Method

In this section, we will first describe the basic Denoising Autoencoders. Next, we will extend the model by adding the category and temporal constraints, to make the learned features more discriminative and obtain better accuracies for recognizing actions. Then we introduce the stacking techniques to build a deep architecture. Finally, we employ TPM (temporal pyramid matching) to generate the representation and do classification.

3.1   Denoising Autoencoders

Autoencoders were proposed by Hinton [6] to recognize handwritten digits, which achieved the state of the art at that time. An autoencoder is a special kind of neural networks whose target values are equal to the input ones. A single-layer Autoencoder comprises two parts: **encoder** and **decoder**.

Encoder: The transformation function maps an input vector x into a hidden layer feature vector h. Its typical form is a non-linearity function. For each example $x^{(i)}$ from a data set $\{x^{(1)}, x^{(2)}, \ldots, x^{(n)}\}$, we define:

$$f_\theta(x^{(i)}) = s(Wx^{(i)} + b) \tag{1}$$

Decoder : The parameterized function maps the hidden layer feature vector h back to the input space, producing a reconstruction vector:

$$g_\theta(h^{(i)}) = s(W' h^{(i)} + c) \tag{2}$$

The set of parameters of this model is $\theta = \{W, W', b, c\}$, where W and W' are the encoder and decoder weight matrices and b and c are the encoder and decoder bias vectors. It is worth mentioning the input vector $x^{(i)}$ and the reconstruction vector $r^{(i)}$ have the same dimension d_x, the hidden layer $h^{(i)}$ has the dimension d_h, thus the size of W is the same as the size of transpose of W', which is $d_h * d_x$.

The basic autoencoders aim to minimize the reconstruction error of all samples:

$$L_{AE}(\theta) = \sum_i L(x^{(i)}, g_\theta(f_\theta(x^{(i)}))) \tag{3}$$

In practice, the choice of function s is usually a sigmoid function $s(x) = \frac{1}{1+e^{-x}}$ or a tanh function $s(x) = \frac{e^x - e^{-x}}{e^x + e^{-x}}$ and the loss function L is usually a square loss function $L(x, r) = \|x - r\|^2$.

Vincent [20] proposed Stacked Denoising Autoencoders (SDA), exploring a strategy to denoise corrupted version of input data. The input x is first corrupted into $\tilde{x}$ using stochastic mapping $\tilde{x} \sim q(\tilde{x}|x)$. This is like randomly selecting some nodes of the input and blinding them, that is, every node in the input layer has a possibility q to be switched to zero. The stochastic corrupted data is regarded as the input of next layer, see Fig. 1. This yields the following objective function:

$$L_{DAE}(\theta) = \sum_i \mathbb{E}_{q(\tilde{x}|x)} \left[L(x^{(i)}, g_\theta(f_\theta(x^{(i)}))) \right] \tag{4}$$

where $\mathbb{E}_{q(\tilde{x}|x)}[\cdot]$ is the expectation over corrupted examples $\tilde{x}$ drawn from the corruption process $q(\tilde{x}|x)$.

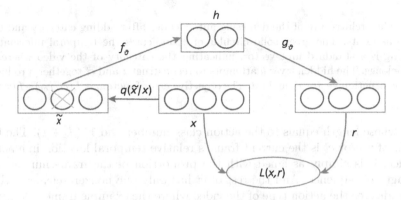

Fig. 1. The architecture of the denoising autoencoder. The input data x is stochastic corrupted into $\tilde{x}$ by mapping function. The autoencoder then maps $\tilde{x}$ to h and maps back h to r, the reconstruction result. $L(x, r)$ is the reconstruction error measurement function.

The reason why DAE can denoise corrupted data is that the training data usually concentrate near a lower-dimensional manifold, yet most of the time the corruption vector is orthogonal to the manifold. The model learns to project the corrupted data back onto the manifold, thus denoising the input.

3.2   Adding the Category and Temporal Constraints

Though the features learned by the denoised autoencoders can be highly expressive, as we use the frame-level joint features as the input, all the temporal and category information are discarded. Merely using the model mentioned above, the unsupervised learned features cannot distinguish the significant small differences between similar actions. We modify the denoising autoencoders, adding the category and temporal constraints, to make the model capable of emphasizing the imparities in different actions.

Figure 2 demonstrates our modified autoencoder. Based on the structure of denoising autoencoders, we add an extra target ct to the network where ct is a

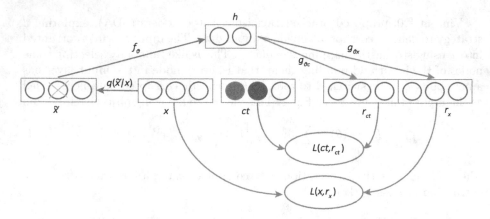

Fig. 2. The architecture of the denoising autoencoder after adding category and temporal constraints. The green solid circular of ct indicates the temporal information, remaining is a standard unit vector, indicating the category of the video where the frame belongs. The hidden layer h attempts to reconstruct x and ct together, producing the reconstruction vector r_x and r_{ct}. The objective error function is $L(ct, r_{ct}) + L(x, r_x)$.

vector whose length equals to the action class number and 1, $(d_c + 1)$. The first element of vector ct is the current frame's relative temporal location in a action sequence, it is simply assigned with the proportion of the frame number and the length of sequence. And the rest of ct has only one nonzero element whose index indicates the action type of the video where the example frame belongs. In consequence, a category vector r_{ct} has to be reconstructed by the hidden layer h using a new mapping function $g_{\theta ct}$. Similarly, r_x is the reconstruction vector of x by the mapping function $g_{\theta x}$. The new training objective of the denoised autoencoder with category and temporal constraints (DAE_CCT) is:

$$L_{DAE\_CCT}(\theta) = \sum_i \mathbb{E}_{q(\tilde{x}|x)} \left[L(x^{(i)}, g_{\theta x}(f_\theta(x^{(i)}))) + \lambda L(ct^{(i)}, g_{\theta ct}(f_\theta(x^{(i)}))) \right]$$

(5)

where λ is a hyper-parameter controlling the strength of the category and temporal regularization. It can be optimized by stochastic gradient descent, analogous to the process of optimizing traditional autoencoders.

The reason why we use a regularization term rather than directly learn the class labels as targets is that the input is the joint vector for one frame, yet the class labels are for the whole video. Apparently there are some similar postures among actions. For example, the *stand and put the hands down* posture appears at the beginning of almost all actions. Training the same posture for different labels will lead to trivial results. The regularization term establishes a trade-off between preserving category and temporal information and reconstructing the input data.

3.3   Stacked Architecture

By stacking several layers of denoising autoencoders with the category constraint,we build a deep neural network with great expressive power. Greedy
layer-wise training is employed: we first train the first layer to get the encoding
function f_1, then apply it on the clean input to compute the output value, which
is used to train the second layer autoencoder to learn f_2. The process is iteratively conducted. At last we fine-tune the deep neural network as in Fig. 3. We
use the output of the last autoencoder as the output for the stacked architecture.

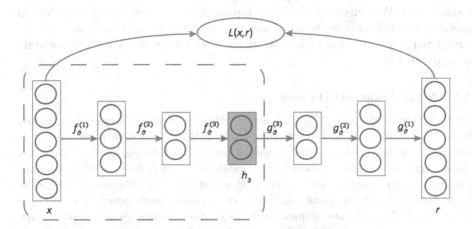

Fig. 3. Fine tuning of the stacking architecture. Each layer autoencoder is trained
successively to obtain the encoding and decoding functions, which are used to initialize the parameters of the stacking architecture. All parameters are fine tuning to
minimize the reconstruction error $L(x, r)$, by performing gradient descent. The structure inside the dotted box is the model to extract features and the deepest hidden layer
h_3 is the final representation we seek.

3.4   Feature Representation and Classification

To represent dynamic feature of a whole action sequence, a temporal pyramid
matching (TPM) [12] is employed. Motivated by Spatial Pyramid Matching
(SPM) [9], a max pooling function is used to generate the multiscale structure.
We recursively partition the video sequence into increasingly finer segments along
the temporal direction and use max pooling to generate histograms from each
sub-region. Typically, 4 levels with each containing 1, 2, 4 and 8 segments are
used. The final feature is the concatenation of histograms from all segments.
After the final representation for each video is obtained, a multi-class linear
SVM [3] is used to speed up the training and testing, results will be discussed
in the next section.

4   Experimental Results

We evaluate our proposal on a depth-based action recognition dataset, MSR Action3D dataset [11]. We compare our algorithm with the previous methods, and the emperimental results shown that the proposed method significantly outperforms traditional model, and attain better than, or comparable to, state-of-art action recognition performance. We also reveal the strong denoising capability of our method to reconstruct noisy 3D joint sequences. In all experiments, we train a deep architecture stacked by two autoencoders, where the first one contains 200 nodes in the hidden layer and the second one contains 400 nodes in the hidden layer. We penalize the average output $\bar{h}_j$ of the second autoencoder and pushing it to 0.1, in order to add some sparsity to the model and learn an overcompleted representation of joint features. The parameter λ is experimentally assigned to 1.3.

4.1   MSR Action3D Dataset

MSR Action3D dataset [11] is an action dataset of depth sequences captured by a depth camera. The dataset contains 20 actions: *high arm wave, horizontal arm wave, hammer, hand catch, forward punch, high throw, draw x, draw tick, draw circle, hand clap, two hand wave, sideboxing, bend, forward kick, side kick, jogging, tennis swing, tennis serve, golf swing, pick up & throw.* Each action is performed by 10 subjects, each subject performs each action 2 or 3 times. There are 567 depth map sequences in total. Some examples of the depth map sequences are shown in Fig. 4. The provided skeleton data is used to train and test our model.

Fig. 4. Sample frames of the MSR-Action3D dataset

We use the same experimental setting as in [22], half of the subjects are used for training and the rest half for testing. We compare with several recent methods and summarize the results in Table. 1. The recognition accuracy is computed by running the experiments 10 times and taking the average of each experiments accuracy. We obtain a recognition accuracy of 88.6 %, which is slightly lower than the state-of-the-art result (88.9 % [14]) by 0.3 %.

The confusion matrix is shown in Fig. 5. The proposed method performs very well on most of the actions. Some actions, such as catch and wave, are too similar to each other for the proposed method to capture the difference.

We also compare the recognition accuracy for each action of our stacked denosing autoencoders with and without the category and temporal constraints, correspondingly named DAE_CCT, DAE, in Fig. 6, and superiority is apparent for the most of the actions. The recognition accuracy rate is significantly improved 7 % from 81.6 % after adding the category and temporal constraints.

Table 1. Comparison of recognition rate on MSR Action3D Dataset

Method	Accuracy
Recurrent Neural Network [13]	0.425
STIP [7] + BOW	0.696
Action Graph on Bag of 3D Points [11]	0.747
Eigenjoints [27]	0.823
Random Occupy Pattern [21]	0.865
Actionlet Ensemble [22]	0.882
HON4D [14] + D_{desc}	0.889
Hidden Markov Model	0.63
Dynamic Temporal Warping	0.54
Proposed Method (without constraints)	**0.820**
Proposed Method (DAE_CCT)	**0.886**

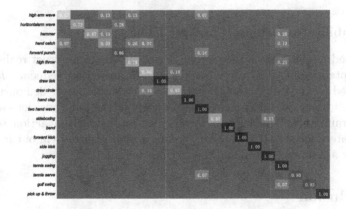

Fig. 5. Confusion matrix of the **DAE_CCT** on MSR Action3D dataset.

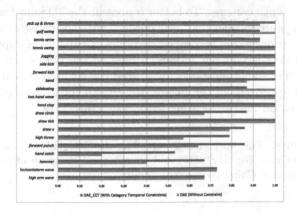

Fig. 6. Comparison of the recognition accuracy for each action before and after adding the category and temporal constraints, named **DAE**, **DAE_CCT** correspondingly.

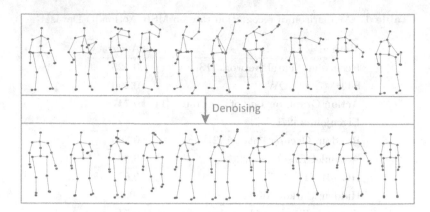

Fig. 7. Examples showing the capability of our model to denoise corrupted data. Top: the corrupted input 3D joint sequence *high arm wave* from MSR Action3D dataset. Bottom: the reconstructed 3D joint sequence

4.2 Capability to Denoise Corrupted Data

The proposed model also has the strong capability to reconstruct realistic data from corrupted input. The top row of Fig. 7 is an action sequence *high arm wave* selected from MSR Action3D dataset. In order to better demonstrate our algorithm efficiency, we add some Gaussian noise to the joint positions and leave out joints randomly. The bottom row is the reconstruction action sequence, where we can observe that the missing joints are all restored via our model and the motions are more natural and fluent than before.

5   Conclusion

This paper presented a novel feature learning methodology for human action recognition with depth cameras. To better represent the 3D joint features, a deep stacked denoising autoencoder that incorporated with the category and temporal constraints were proposed. The proposed model is capable of capturing subtle spatio-temporal details between actions, robust to the noises and errors in the joints positions. The experiments demonstrated the effectiveness and robustness of the proposed approach. In the future, we aim to integrate the more precise temporal information into our feature learning architecture.

Acknowledgments. This work was supported by the National Natural Science Foundation of China (Grant No. 61272317) and the General Program of Natural Science Foundation of Anhui of China (Grant No. 1208085MF90).

References

1. Bengio, Y.: Learning deep architectures for AI. Found. Trends® Mach. Learn. **2**(1), 1–127 (2009)
2. Bengio, Y., Courville, A., Vincent, P.: Representation learning: a review and new perspectives. IEEE Trans. Pattern Anal. Mach. Intell. **35**(8), 1798–1828 (2013)
3. Chang, C.-C., Lin, C.-J.: Libsvm: a library for support vector machines. ACM Trans. Intell. Syst. Technol. (TIST) **2**(3), 27 (2011)
4. Dollár, P., Rabaud, V., Cottrell, G., Belongie, S.: Behavior recognition via sparse spatio-temporal features. In: 2nd Joint IEEE International Workshop on Visual Surveillance and Performance Evaluation of Tracking and Surveillance, 2005, pp. 65–72. IEEE (2005)
5. Hinton, G., Osindero, S., Teh, Y.-W.: A fast learning algorithm for deep belief nets. Neural Comput. **18**(7), 1527–1554 (2006)
6. Hinton, G.E., Salakhutdinov, R.R.: Reducing the dimensionality of data with neural networks. Science **313**(5786), 504–507 (2006)
7. Laptev, I.: On space-time interest points. Int. J. Comput. Vis. **64**(2–3), 107–123 (2005)
8. Laptev, I., Marszalek, M., Schmid, C., Rozenfeld, B.: Learning realistic human actions from movies. In: IEEE Conference on Computer Vision and Pattern Recognition, CVPR 2008, pp. 1–8. IEEE (2008)
9. Lazebnik, S., Schmid, C., Ponce, J.: Beyond bags of features: spatial pyramid matching for recognizing natural scene categories. In: 2006 IEEE Computer Society Conference on Computer Vision and Pattern Recognition, vol. 2, pp. 2169–2178. IEEE (2006)
10. LeCun, Y., Bottou, L., Bengio, Y., Haffner, P.: Gradient-based learning applied to document recognition. Proc. IEEE **86**(11), 2278–2324 (1998)
11. Li, W., Zhang, Z., Liu, Z.: Action recognition based on a bag of 3d points. In: 2010 IEEE Computer Society Conference on Computer Vision and Pattern Recognition Workshops (CVPRW), pp. 9–14. IEEE (2010)
12. Luo, J., Wang, W., Qi, H.: Group sparsity and geometry constrained dictionary learning for action recognition from depth maps. In: 2013 IEEE International Conference on Computer Vision (ICCV), pp. 1809–1816. IEEE (2013)
13. Martens, J., Sutskever, I.: Learning recurrent neural networks with hessian-free optimization. In: Proceedings of the 28th International Conference on Machine Learning (ICML-11), pp. 1033–1040 (2011)
14. Oreifej, O., Liu, Z.: Hon4d: histogram of oriented 4d normals for activity recognition from depth sequences. In: 2013 IEEE Conference on Computer Vision and Pattern Recognition (CVPR), pp. 716–723. IEEE (2013)
15. Rabiner, L.: A tutorial on hidden markov models and selected applications in speech recognition. Proc. IEEE **77**(2), 257–286 (1989)
16. Sang, R., Jin, P., Wan, S.: Discriminative feature learning for action recognition using a stacked denoising autoencoder. In: Pan, J.-S., Snasel, V., Corchado, E.S., Abraham, A., Wang, S.-L. (eds.) Intelligent Data Analysis and Its Applications, Volume I. AISC, vol. 297, pp. 521–531. Springer, Heidelberg (2014)
17. Scholkopft, B., Mullert, K.-R.: Fisher discriminant analysis with kernels. In: Proceedings of the 1999 IEEE Signal Processing Society Workshop Neural Networks for Signal Processing IX, Madison, WI, USA, pp. 23–25 (1999)
18. Shotton, J., Sharp, T., Kipman, A., Fitzgibbon, A., Finocchio, M., Blake, A., Cook, M., Moore, R.: Real-time human pose recognition in parts from single depth images. Commun. ACM **56**(1), 116–124 (2013)

19. Su, J., Srivastava, A., de Souza, F.D.M., Sarkar, S.: Rate-invariant analysis of trajectories on riemannian manifolds with application in visual speech recognition. In: 2014 IEEE Conference on Computer Vision and Pattern Recognition (CVPR), pp. 620–627. IEEE (2014)
20. Vincent, P., Larochelle, H., Lajoie, I., Bengio, Y., Manzagol, P.-A.: Stacked denoising autoencoders: learning useful representations in a deep network with a local denoising criterion. J. Mach. Learn. Res. **11**, 3371–3408 (2010)
21. Wang, J., Liu, Z., Chorowski, J., Chen, Z., Wu, Y.: Robust 3D action recognition with random occupancy patterns. In: Fitzgibbon, A., Lazebnik, S., Perona, P., Sato, Y., Schmid, C. (eds.) ECCV 2012, Part II. LNCS, vol. 7573, pp. 872–885. Springer, Heidelberg (2012)
22. Wang, J., Liu, Z., Wu, Y., Yuan, J.: Mining actionlet ensemble for action recognition with depth cameras. In: 2012 IEEE Conference on Computer Vision and Pattern Recognition (CVPR), pp. 1290–1297. IEEE (2012)
23. Wang, J., Wu, Y.: Learning maximum margin temporal warping for action recognition. In: 2013 IEEE International Conference on Computer Vision (ICCV), pp. 2688–2695. IEEE (2013)
24. Wu, Z., Wan, S., Yue, L., Sang, R.: Discriminative image representation for classification. In: Pan, J.-S., Snasel, V., Corchado, E.S., Abraham, A., Wang, S.-L. (eds.) Intelligent Data Analysis and Its Applications, Volume II. AISC, vol. 298, pp. 331–341. Springer, Heidelberg (2014)
25. Xia, L., Aggarwal, J.K.: Spatio-temporal depth cuboid similarity feature for activity recognition using depth camera. In: 2013 IEEE Conference on Computer Vision and Pattern Recognition (CVPR), pp. 2834–2841. IEEE (2013)
26. Xia, L., Chen, C.-C., Aggarwal, J.K.: View invariant human action recognition using histograms of 3d joints. In: 2012 IEEE Computer Society Conference on Computer Vision and Pattern Recognition Workshops (CVPRW), pp. 20–27. IEEE (2012)
27. Yang, X., Tian, Y.: Eigenjoints-based action recognition using naive-bayes-nearest-neighbor. In: 2012 IEEE Computer Society Conference on Computer Vision and Pattern Recognition Workshops (CVPRW), pp. 14–19. IEEE (2012)
28. Yang, X., Zhang, C., Tian, Y.: Recognizing actions using depth motion maps-based histograms of oriented gradients. In: Proceedings of the 20th ACM international conference on Multimedia, pp. 1057–1060. ACM (2012)

Discriminative Neighborhood Preserving Dictionary Learning for Image Classification

Shiye Zhang[✉], Zhen Dong, Yuwei Wu, and Mingtao Pei

Beijing Laboratory of Intelligent Information Technology,
School of Computer Science, Beijing Institute of Technology, Beijing 100081, China
{zhangshiye,dongzhen,wuyuwei,peimt}@bit.edu.cn

Abstract. In this paper, a discriminative neighborhood preserving dictionary learning method is proposed. The geometrical structure of the feature space is used to preserve the similarity information of the features, and the features' class information is employed to enhance the discriminative power of the learned dictionary. The Laplacian matrix which expresses the similarity information and the class information of the features is constructed and used in the objective function. Experimental results on four public datasets demonstrate the effectiveness of the proposed method.

Keywords: Dictionary learning · Image classification · Similarity · Discriminative

1 Introduction

Sparse representation has been widely studied due to its promising performance [1–4]. It can be used in image classification [5–10], face recognition [11–14], image retrieval [15], and image restoration [16]. The basic idea is to represent an input signal as a sparse linear combination of the atoms in the dictionary. Since the dictionary quality is a critical factor for the performance of the sparse presentation, lots of approaches focus on learning a good dictionary. Aharon et al. [17] presented the K-SVD algorithm, which iteratively updated the sparse codes of samples based on the current dictionary, and optimized the dictionary atoms to better fit the data. The discriminative information resided in the training samples might be ignored in this method. To solve this problem, some approaches [18–24] aim to learn more discriminative dictionaries. Mairal et al. [22] added a discriminative reconstruction constraint in the dictionary learning model to gain discrimination ability. Pham et al. [23] proposed a joint learning and dictionary construction method with consideration of the linear classifier performance. Yang et al. [24] employed the Fisher discrimination criterion to learn a structured dictionary.

However, in these methods, features are used separately while learning the dictionary, which results that the similarity information between the features is lost. Similar features in the same class thus may be encoded as dissimilar codes,

© Springer International Publishing Switzerland 2015
Y.-J. Zhang (Ed.): ICIG 2015, Part II, LNCS 9218, pp. 185–196, 2015.
DOI: 10.1007/978-3-319-21963-9_17

while features in different classes may be encoded as similar codes with the
learned dictionary. In order to alleviate this problem, we propose a discriminative
neighborhood preserving dictionary learning method that explicitly takes the
similarity and class information of features into account. Figure 1 shows the idea
of our method. The circle represents the feature x_i's neighborhood which is
composed of features close to the x_i. Some of the neighbors are with the same
label as x_i, and others are not. Our method encourages the distance between
the codes of x_i and its neighbors in the same class as small as possible, at the
same time maintains the distance between the codes of x_i and its neighbors in
different classes. The learned dictionary can ensure that similar features in the
same class could be encoded as similar codes and the features in different classes
could be encoded as dissimilar codes.

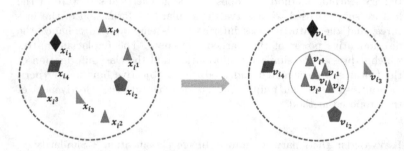

Fig. 1. The basic idea of our method. The left is the neighborhood of feature x_i which
contains the features close to x_i. The different colors represent the neighbors of different
classes. The blue features in the neighborhood are the neighbors of x_i with the same
label. The neighbors with the same label are expected to be encoded close to the code
of x_i, while other neighbors are expected to be encoded distant. Therefore, our method
is more discriminative for classification.

Inspired by [25,26], we construct a Laplacian matrix which expresses the
relationship between the features. The dictionary learned with this Laplacian
matrix can well characterize the similarity of the similar features and preserve
the consistence in sparse codes of the similar features. Different from [25,26],
the class information is taken into account to further enhance the discriminative
power of the dictionary in our method. Through introducing the class information, the Laplacian matrix is not only with the similarity information of the
features in the same class but also can distinguish features in different classes.
By adding the Laplacian term into the dictionary learning objective function,
our method is able to learn a more discriminative dictionary. The experimental
results demonstrate the encoding step is efficient with the learned discriminative
dictionary and the classification performance of our method is improved with
the dictionary.

The rest of this paper is organized as follows. In Sect. 2, we provide a brief
description of the sparse presentation problem and introduce our discriminative
neighborhood preserving dictionary learning method. In Sect. 3, the optimization

scheme of our method is presented, including learning sparse codes and learning the dictionary. The experimental results and discussions are displayed in Sect. 4. Finally, we conclude the paper in Sect. 5.

2 Discriminative Neighborhood Preserving Dictionary Learning Method

2.1 Sparse Representation Problem

We briefly review sparse representation. Given a data matrix $X = [x_1, \cdots, x_n] \in R^{d \times n}$, dictionary matrix $D = [d_1, \cdots, d_k] \in R^{d \times k}$, where each d_i represents a basis vector in the dictionary, coefficient matrix $V = [v_1, \cdots, v_n] \in R^{k \times n}$, where each column is a sparse representation for a data point. Each data point x_i can be represented as a sparse linear combination of those basis vectors in the dictionary. The objective function of sparse presentation can be formulated as follows:

$$\min \sum_{j=1}^{n} \|v_i\|_0 \quad s.t. X = DV \tag{1}$$

$\|v_i\|_0$ is the number of nonzero entries of v_i, representing the sparseness of v_i. However, the minimization problem for this sparse representation with l_0 norm is shown to be an NP-hard problem [27]. The most widely used approach is to replace the l_0 norm with its l_1 norm. With the loss function, the objective function then becomes

$$\min_{D,V} \|X - DV\|_F^2 + \lambda \sum_{i=1}^{n} \|v_i\|_1 \quad s.t. \|d_i\|^2 \leq c, \quad i = 1, \ldots, k \tag{2}$$

The first term in Eq. (2) represents the reconstruction error, λ is the parameter used to balance the sparsity and the reconstruction error.

2.2 Formulation of Discriminative Neighborhood Preserving Dictionary Learning

In most current methods, the features are used separately while learning the dictionary. The similarity information among the features is lost which lead to the similar features can be encoded as totally different codes. In order to alleviate this problem, we propose a discriminative neighborhood preserving dictionary learning method. The dictionary learned by our method can well represent the intrinsic geometrical structure of the features to better characterize the relationship between the features and get more discriminative power through the features' class information.

Given the training features set $X = \{x_1, x_2, \ldots, x_n\}$ and the label of the training features. For each feature x_i, we choose l-nearest neighbors of x_i in the same class to form $\{x_{i^1}, x_{i^2}, \ldots, x_{i^l}\}$ and choose m-nearest neighbors of x_i in different classes to form $\{x_{i_1}, x_{i_2}, \ldots, x_{i_m}\}$. All of these neighbors make up a local neighborhood of x_i which can be represented as $X_i = \{x_{i^1}, x_{i^2}, \ldots, x_{i^l}, x_{i_1}, x_{i_2}, \ldots, x_{i_m}\}$. $V_i = \{v_{i^1}, v_{i^2}, \ldots, v_{i^l}, v_{i_1}, v_{i_2}, \ldots, v_{i_m}\}$ is the codes of X_i about the dictionary. As shown in Fig. 1, the purpose of our method is to learn a discriminative dictionary which make the distance between v_i and its neighbors in the same class as small as possible and the distance between v_i and its neighbors in different classes as large as possible

$$\min \sum_{i=1}^{n} (\sum_{j=1}^{l} \|v_i - v_{ij}\|^2 - \beta \sum_{p=1}^{m} \|v_i - v_{i_p}\|^2) \qquad (3)$$

β is the metric factor. We define W as the similarity matrix corresponding to the features, whose entry W_{ij} measures the similarity between x_i and x_j. If x_i is among   the
l-nearest neighbors in the same class of x_j or x_j is among the l-nearest neighbors in the same class of x_i, $W_{ij} = 1$. If x_i is among the m-nearest neighbors in different classes of x_j or x_j is among the m-nearest neighbors in different classes of x_i, $W_{ij} = -\beta$, otherwise, $W_{ij} = 0$. Through the similarity matrix, the Eq. (3) can be represented as

$$\min \sum_{i=1}^{n} (\sum_{j=1}^{l} \|v_i - v_{ij}\|^2 - \beta \sum_{p=1}^{m} \|v_i - v_{i_p}\|^2) = \min \sum_{i=1}^{n} \sum_{j=1}^{l} \|v_i - v_j\|^2 W_{ij} \qquad (4)$$

We define the degree of x_i as $d_i = \sum_{j=1}^{n} W_{ij}$, and $D = diag(d_1, \ldots, d_n)$. The Eq. (4) can be converted as [28]

$$\frac{1}{2} \min \sum_{i=1}^{n} \sum_{j=1}^{l} \|v_i - v_j\|^2 W_{ij} = \min Tr(VLV^T) \qquad (5)$$

where $L = D - W$ is the Laplacian matrix. By adding this Laplacian term into the sparse presentation, we get the objective function of our method:

$$\min_{D,V} \|X - DV\|_F^2 + \lambda \sum_{i=1}^{n} \|v_i\|_1 + \alpha Tr(VLV^T) \qquad s.t. \|d_i\|^2 \le c, \quad i = 1, \ldots, k \qquad (6)$$

Due to the Laplacian term, both the similarity among the features and the class information are considered during the process of dictionary learning and the similarity of codes among the similar features can be maximally preserved.

The Eq. (6) is not convex for D and V simultaneously, but it is convex for D when V is fixed and it is also convex for V when D is fixed. Motivated by the work in [29], we propose the following two-stage strategy to solve the Eq. (6): learning the codes V while fixing the dictionary D, and learning dictionary D while fixing the codes V.

3 Optimization

3.1 Learning Codes V

When fixing the dictionary D, Eq. (6) becomes the following optimization problem:

$$\min_V \|X - DV\|_F^2 + \lambda \sum_{i=1}^{n} \|v_i\|_1 + \alpha Tr(VLV^T) \tag{7}$$

Equation (7) is an L1-regularized least squares problem. This problem can be solved by several approaches [30,31]. Instead of optimizing the whole codes matrix V, we optimize each v_i one by one until the whole V converges following [26,32]. The vector form of Eq. (7) can be written as

$$\min \sum_{i=1}^{n} \|x_i - Dv_i\|^2 + \lambda \sum_{i=1}^{n} \|v_i\|_1 + \alpha \sum_{i,j=1}^{n} L_{ij} v_i^T v_j \tag{8}$$

When updating v_i, the other codes $v_j (j \neq i)$ are fixed. We rewrite the optimization with respect to v_i as follow:

$$\min_{v_i} f(v_i) \|x_i - Dv_i\|^2 + \lambda \sum_{j=1}^{k} |v_i^{(j)}| + \alpha L_{ii} v_i^T h_i \tag{9}$$

where $h_i = 2\alpha(\sum_{j \neq i} L_{ij} v_j)$, $v_i^{(j)}$ is the j-th coefficient of v_i. We use the feature-sign search algorithm in [29] to solve this problem. Define $h(v_i) = \|x_i - Dv_i\|^2 + \alpha L_{ii} v_i^T v_i + v_i^T h_i$, then $f(v_i) = h(v_i) + \lambda \sum_{j=1}^{k} |v_i^{(j)}|$. If we know the signs (positive, zero, or negative) of the $v_i^{(j)}$ at the optimal value, we can use either $v_i^{(j)}$ (if $v_i^{(j)} > 0$), $-v_i^{(j)}$ (if $v_i^{(j)} < 0$), or 0 (if $v_i^{(j)} = 0$) to replace each of the terms $|v_i^{(j)}|$. Considering only nonzero coefficients, the Eq. (9) is reduced to a standard, unconstrained quadratic optimization problem, which can be solved analytically and efficiently. When we update each v_i in the algorithm, maintaining an active set of potentially nonzero coefficients and their corresponding signs (all other coefficients must be zero). Our purpose is to search for the optimal active set and coefficient signs which minimize the objective function. The algorithm proceeds in a series of feature-sign steps: on each step, it is given the active set and the signs of current target, then it computes the analytical solution about the Eq. (9) and updates the solution, the active set and the signs using an efficient discrete line search between the current solution and the analytical solution. The detailed steps of the algorithm are stated in Algorithm 1.

3.2 Learning Dictionary D

In this section, we present a method for learning the dictionary D while fixing the coefficients matrix V. Equation (6) reduces to the following problem:

$$\min_D \|X - DV\|_F^2 \qquad s.t. \|d_i\|^2 \leq c, i = 1, ..., k \tag{12}$$

Algorithm 1. Feature-sign Search Algorithm for Solving Eq. (9)

Input: the training data set X, the dictionary D, the Laplacian matrix L, the
            parameters α, λ, the initial codes V.
Output: the optimal codes matrix V.
For $1 \leq n \leq n$ do
Step 1. Initialization
If not exist(V)
$v_i = \overrightarrow{0}, \theta = \overrightarrow{0}$, active set is empty.
else
$\theta_j \in \{-1, 0, 1\}$ denotes sign $(v_i^{(j)})$, add $j(v_i^{(j)} \neq 0)$ to the active set.
Step 2. Activate
We define $\nabla_i^{(j)} h(v_i)$ as the subgradient value of the $h(v_i)$. From zero coefficients
of v_i, select $j = argmax_j |\nabla_i^{(j)} h(v_i)|$, active $v_i^{(j)}$ only if it locally improves the
equation (9), namely:
if $\nabla_i^{(j)} h(v_i) > \lambda$, then set $\theta_i = -1$, active set = $\{j\} \bigcup$ active set.
if $\nabla_i^{(j)} h(v_i) < -\lambda$, then set $\theta_i = 1$, active set = $\{j\} \bigcup$ active set.
Step 3. Feature-sign
Let $\widehat{D}$ be a submatrix of D that contains only the columns corresponding to the
active set. Let $\widehat{v_i}, \widehat{h_i}, \widehat{\theta}$ be the subvectors of v_i, h_i, θ corresponding to the active
set. Compute the analytical solution to the resulting unconstrained QP:

$$\min g(\widehat{v_i}) = \|x_i - \widehat{D}\widehat{v_i}\|^2 + \alpha L_{ii} \widehat{v_i}^T \widehat{v_i} + \widehat{v_i}^T \widehat{h_i} + \lambda \widehat{\theta}^T \widehat{v_i} \qquad (10)$$

Let $(\partial g(\widehat{v_i})/\partial \widehat{v_i}) = 0$,we can get the optimal value of v_i under the current
active set:

$$\widehat{v_i}^{new} = (\widehat{D}^T D + \alpha L_{ii} I)^{-1} (\widehat{D}^T x_i - (\lambda \widehat{\theta} + \widehat{h_i})/2) \qquad (11)$$

Perform a discrete line search on the closed line segment from $\widehat{v_i}$ to $\widehat{v_i}^{new}$, check
the objective value at $\widehat{v_i}^{new}$ and all points where any coefficient changes value,
update $\widehat{v_i}$ (and the corresponding entries in v_i) to the point with the lowest
objective value, remove zero coefficients from the active set and update
$\theta = sign(v_i)$.
Step 4. Check the optimality conditions
Condition (a): Optimality condition for nonzero coefficients:
$\nabla_i^{(j)} h(v_i) + \lambda sign(v_i^{(j)}) = 0, \forall v_i^{(j)} \neq 0$. If condition (a) is not satisfied, go to
Step 3(without any new activation); Else check condition(b).
Condition (b): Optimality condition for zero coefficients:
$\nabla_i^{(j)} h(v_i) \leq \lambda, \forall v_i^{(j)} = 0$. If condition (b) is not satisfied, go to Step 3; otherwise
return v_i as the solution, and update the V with current v_i.
End for

Equation (12) is a least squares problem with quadratic constraints. It can be
efficiently solved by a Lagrange dual method [29].

Let $\lambda = [\lambda_1, ..., \lambda_k]$, and λ_i is the Lagrange multiplier associated with the
i-th inequality constraint $\|d_i\|^2 - c \leq 0$, we obtain the Lagrange dual function:

$$\min_{D} L(D, \lambda) = Tr((X - DV)^T(X - DV)) + \sum_{j=1}^{n} \lambda_j (\sum_{i=1}^{k} d_{ij}^2 - c) \qquad (13)$$

Define $\Lambda = diag(\lambda)$, Eq. (13) can be written as

$$\min_{D} L(D, \lambda) = Tr(X^T X - XV^T(VV^T + \Lambda)^{-1}(XV^T)^T - c\Lambda) \qquad (14)$$

The optimal solution is obtained by letting the first-order derivative of Eq. (14) equal to zero

$$D^* = XV^T(VV^T + \Lambda)^{-1} \qquad (15)$$

Substituting Eqs. (15) into (14), the Lagrange dual function becomes:

$$\min_{\Lambda} Tr(XV^T(VV^T + \Lambda)^{-1}VX^T) + cTr(\Lambda) \qquad (16)$$

We optimize the Lagrange dual Eq. (16) using the conjugate gradient. After obtaining the optimal solution Λ^*, the optimal dictionary D can be represented by $D^* = XV^T(VV^T + \Lambda^*)^{-1}$.

4 Experiments

In this section, we evaluate our method on four public datasets for image classification: Scene 15, UIUC-Sport, Caltech-101, and Caltech-256. For each experiment, we describe the information of datasets and detailed settings. The effectiveness of our method is validated by comparisons with popular methods.

4.1 Parameters Setting

In the experiment, we first extract SIFT descriptors from 16×16 patches which are densely sampled using a grid with a step size of 8 pixels to fairly compare with others. Then we extract the spatial pyramid feature based on the extracted SIFT features with three grids of size 1×1, 2×2 and 4×4. In each spatial sub-region of the spatial pyramid, the codes are pooled together by max pooling method to form a pooled feature. These pooled features from each sub-region are concatenated and normalized by L2 normalization as the final spatial pyramid features of the images. The dictionary in the experiment is learned by these spatial pyramid features.

In our method, the weight of the Laplacian term α, the sparsity of the coding λ, and the constraints of the neighborhood in different classes β play more important roles in dictionary learning. According to our observation, the performance is good when β is fixed at 0.2 for Scene 15 and UIUC-Sport. For Caltech-101 and Caltech-256, 0.1 is much better for β. For Scene 15, the value of α is 0.2 and the value of λ is 0.4. For UIUC-Sport, Caltech-101, and Caltech-256, the value of α is 0.1 and the value of λ is 0.3.

4.2   Scene 15 Dataset

Scene 15 dataset contains 15 categories. Each category contains 200 to 400 images and the total image number is 4485. In order to compare with other work, we use the same setting to choose the training images. We randomly choose 100 images per category and test on the rest. This process is repeated for ten times to obtain reliable results.

Table 1 gives the performance comparison of our method and several other methods on the Scene 15 dataset. We can see that our method can achieve high performance on scene classification. It outperforms ScSPM by nearly 11 % by considering the geometrical structure of the feature space based on sparse representation and outperforms LScSPM by nearly 2 % by adding the class information. Both of them demonstrate the effectiveness of our method. Our discriminative neighborhood preserving dictionary learning method can not only make use of the geometrical structure of the feature space to preserve more similarity information, but also make the final dictionary more discriminative by considering the class information which can improve the image classification performance.

Table 1. Performance comparison on the Scene-15 dataset

Methods	Accuracy (%)
KSPM [33]	81.40 ± 0.5
KCSPM [35]	76.70 ± 0.40
ScSPM [6]	80.28 ± 0.93
HIK+OCSVM [34]	84.00 ± 0.46
LScSPM [25]	89.75 ± 0.50
LR-Sc^+SPM [7]	90.03 ± 0.70
DSC [9]	84.21 ± 0.44
DLMM [10]	83.67 ± 0.49
Our method	91.23 ± 0.84

4.3   UIUC-Sport Dataset

UIUC-Sport dataset contains 8 categories for image-based event classification and 1792 images in all. These 8 categories are badminton, bocce, croquet, polo, rock climbing, rowing, sailing and snow boarding. The size of each category ranges from 137 to 250. Following the standard setting for this dataset, we randomly choose 70 images from each class for training and test on the rest images. We repeat this process for ten times for fair comparison.

Table 2 gives the performance comparison of our method and several other methods on the UIUC-Sport dataset. We can see that our method outperforms ScSPM by nearly 5 % and outperforms LScSPM by nearly 2 %. This demonstrates the effectiveness of our proposed method.

Table 2. Performance comparison on the UIUC-Sport dataset

Methods	Accuracy (%)
ScSPM [6]	82.74 ± 1.46
HIK+OCSVM [34]	83.54 ± 1.13
LR-Sc$^+$SPM [7]	86.69 ± 1.66
LScSPM [25]	85.31 ± 0.51
DSC [9]	83.72 ± 1.68
DLMM [10]	86.93 ± 0.99
Our method	87.13 ± 1.02

4.4 Caltech-101 Dataset

The Caltech-101 dataset contains 9144 images in 101 classes with high intra-class appearance shape variability. The number of images per category varies from 31 to 800. We follow the common experimental setup and randomly choose 30 images per category for training and the rest for testing. This process is repeated for ten times.

The average classification rates of our method and several other methods on Caltech-101 dataset are reported in Table 3. From these results, we see that our method performs better than most existing methods. As compared to the LLC, our method makes a 2.4 % improvement. It demonstrates the effectiveness of our proposed method.

Table 3. Performance comparison on the Caltech-101 dataset

Methods	Accuracy (%)
KSPM [33]	64.40 ± 0.80
KCSPM [35]	64.14 ± 1.18
ScSPM [6]	73.20 ± 0.54
LLC [36]	73.44
LR-Sc$^+$SPM [7]	75.68 ± 0.89
DSC [9]	71.96 ± 0.83
DLMM [10]	74.87 ± 0.67
Our method	75.86 ± 0.78

4.5 Caltech-256 Dataset

Caltech-256 dataset contains 256 categories and a background class in which none of the image belongs to those 256 categories. The number of images is 29780 with much higher intra-class variability and higher object location variability as compared to Caltech-101. Therefore Caltech-256 is a very challenging dataset so far for object recognition and classification. The number of images per category is no less than 80. We randomly choose 30 images per category for training and repeat this process for ten times.

Table 4. Performance comparison on the Caltech-256 dataset

Methods	Accuracy (%)
KSPM [33]	34.10
KCSPM [35]	27.17 ± 0.46
ScSPM [6]	34.02 ± 0.35
LScSPM [25]	35.74 ± 0.10
DLMM [10]	36.22 ± 0.33
Our method	37.81 ± 0.21

The average classification rates of our method and several other methods on Caltech-256 dataset are reported in Table 4. We can see that our method can achieve the state-of-the-art performances on this dataset.

5   Conclusion

In this paper, we propose a discriminative neighborhood preserving dictionary learning method for image classification. We consider the geometrical structure of the feature space in the process of dictionary learning to preserve the similarity information of the features. By introducing the class information, the discriminative power of the learned dictionary is enhanced. The learned dictionary can ensure that the similar features in the same class are encoded as similar codes and the features in different classes are encoded as dissimilar codes. Experimental results on four public datasets demonstrate the effectiveness of our method.

Acknowledgments. This work was supported in part by the 973 Program of China under grant No. 2012CB720000, the Specialized Research Fund for the Doctoral Program of Higher Education of China (20121101120029), and the Specialized Fund for Joint Building Program of Beijing Municipal Education Commission.

References

1. Chen, X., Zou, D., Li, J., Cao, X., Zhao, Q., Zhang, H.: Sparse dictionary learning for edit propagation of high-resolution images. In: 27th IEEE Computer Society Conference on Computer Vision and Pattern Recognition, pp. 2854–2861. IEEE Press, Columbus (2014)
2. Lan, X., Ma, A.J., Yuen, P.C.: Multi-cue visual tracking using robust feature-level fusion based on joint sparse representation. In: 27th IEEE Computer Society Conference on Computer Vision and Pattern Recognition, pp. 1194–1201. IEEE Press, Columbus (2014)
3. Cherian, A.: Nearest neighbors using compact sparse codes. In: 31st International Conference on Machine Learning, pp. 1053–1061. ACM Press, Beijing (2014)
4. Eldar, Y.C., Mishali, M.: Robust recovery of signals from a structured union of subspaces. IEEE Trans. Inf. Theory **55**(11), 5302–5316 (2009)

5. Liu, B.-D., Wang, Y.-X., Shen, B., Zhang, Y.-J., Hebert, M.: Self-explanatory sparse representation for image classification. In: Fleet, D., Pajdla, T., Schiele, B., Tuytelaars, T. (eds.) ECCV 2014, Part II. LNCS, vol. 8690, pp. 600–616. Springer, Heidelberg (2014)

6. Yang, J., Yu, K., Gong, Y., Huang, T.: Linear spatial pyramid matching using sparse coding for image classification. In: 22th IEEE Computer Society Conference on Computer Vision and Pattern Recognition, pp. 1794–1801. IEEE Press, Miami (2009)

7. Zhang, C., Liu, J., Tian, Q., Xu, C., Lu, H., Ma, S.: Image classification by non-negative sparse coding, low-rank and sparse decomposition. In: 24th IEEE Computer Society Conference on Computer Vision and Pattern Recognition, pp. 1673–1680. IEEE Press, Colorado (2011)

8. Yuan, X.T., Liu, X., Yan, S.: Visual classification with multitask joint sparse representation. IEEE Trans. Image Process. $21(10)$, 4349–4360 (2012)

9. Liu, B.D., Wang, Y.X., Zhang, Y.J., Zheng, Y.: Discriminant sparse coding for image classification. In: 37th IEEE International Conference on Acoustics, Speech and Signal Processing, pp. 2193–2196. IEEE Press, Kyoto (2012)

10. Liu, B.D., Wang, Y.X., Zhang, Y.J., Shen, B.: Learning dictionary on manifolds for image classification. Pattern Recogn. $46(7)$, 1879–1890 (2013)

11. Yang, M., Dai, D., Shen, L., Gool, L.V.: Latent dictionary learning for sparse representation based classification. In: 27th IEEE Computer Society Conference on Computer Vision and Pattern Recognition, pp. 4138–4145. IEEE Press, Columbus (2014)

12. Yang, M., Zhang, L., Yang, J., Zhang, D.: Metaface learning for sparse representation based face recognition. In: 17th International Conference on Image Processing, pp. 1601–1604. IEEE Press, Hong Kong (2010)

13. Wagner, A., Wright, J., Ganesh, A., Zhou, Z., Mobahi, H., Ma, Y.: Toward a practical face recognition system: robust alignment and illumination by sparse representation. IEEE Trans. Pattern Anal. Mach. Intell. $34(2)$, 372–386 (2012)

14. Yang, M., Zhang, D., Yang, J.: Robust sparse coding for face recognition. In: 24th IEEE Computer Society Conference on Computer Vision and Pattern Recognition, pp. 625–632. IEEE Press, Colorado (2011)

15. Philbin, J., Chum, O., Isard, M., Sivic, J., Zisserman, A.: Object retrieval with large vocabularies and fast spatial matching. In: 20th IEEE Computer Society Conference on Computer Vision and Pattern Recognition, pp. 1–8. IEEE Press, Minneapolis (2007)

16. Mairal, J., Elad, M., Sapiro, G.: Sparse representation for color image restoration. IEEE Trans. Image Process. $17(1)$, 53–69 (2008)

17. Aharon, M., Elad, M., Bruckstein, A.: K-SVD: an algorithm for designing overcomplete dictionaries for sparse representation. IEEE Trans. Sig. Process. $54(11)$, 4311–4322 (2006)

18. Cao, X., Ren, W., Zuo, W., Guo, X., Foroosh, H.: Scene text deblurring using text-specific multiscale dictionaries. IEEE Trans. Image Process. $24(4)$, 1302–1314 (2015)

19. Zhou, N., Fan, J.: Jointly learning visually correlated dictionaries for large-scale visual recognition applications. IEEE Trans. Pattern Anal. Mach. Intell. $36(4)$, 715–730 (2014)

20. Gao, S., Tsang, I.H., Ma, Y.: Learning category-specific dictionary and shared dictionary for fine-grained image categorization. IEEE Trans. Image Process. $23(2)$, 623–634 (2014)

21. Bao, C., Quan, Y., Ji, H.: A convergent incoherent dictionary learning algorithm for sparse coding. In: Fleet, D., Pajdla, T., Schiele, B., Tuytelaars, T. (eds.) ECCV 2014, Part VI. LNCS, vol. 8694, pp. 302–316. Springer, Heidelberg (2014)
22. Mairal, J., Bach, F., Ponce, J., Sapiro, G., Zisserman, A.: Discriminative learned dictionaries for local image analysis. In: 21th IEEE Computer Society Conference on Computer Vision and Pattern Recognition, pp. 1–8. IEEE Press, Anchorage (2008)
23. Pham, D.S., Venkatesh, S.: Joint learning and dictionary construction for pattern recognition. In: 21th IEEE Computer Society Conference on Computer Vision and Pattern Recognition, pp. 1–8. IEEE Press, Anchorage (2008)
24. Yang, M., Zhang, D., Feng, X.: Fisher discrimination dictionary learning for sparse representation. In: 13th IEEE International Conference on Computer Vision, pp. 543–550. IEEE Press, Barcelona (2011)
25. Gao, S., Tsang, I.W., Chia, L.T., Zhao, P.: Local features are not lonely Laplacian sparse coding for image classification. In: 23th IEEE Computer Society Conference on Computer Vision and Pattern Recognition, pp. 3555–3561. IEEE Press, San Francisco (2010)
26. Zheng, M., Bu, J., Chen, C., Wang, C., Zhang, L., Qiu, G., Cai, D.: Graph regularized sparse coding for image representation. IEEE Trans. Image Process. 20(5), 1327–1336 (2011)
27. Donoho, D.L.: For most large underdetermined systems of linear equations the minimal L1-norm solution is also the sparsest solution. Commun. Pure Appl. Math. 59(6), 797–829 (2006)
28. Belkin, M., Niyogi, P.: Laplacian eigenmaps and spectral techniques for embedding and clustering. In: 15th Annual Conference on Neural Information Processing Systems, vol. 14, pp. 585–591. MIT Press, Vancouver (2001)
29. Lee, H., Battle, A., Raina, R., Ng, A.Y.: Efficient sparse coding algorithms. In: 20th Annual Conference on Neural Information Processing Systems, pp. 801–808. MIT Press, Vancouver (2006)
30. Koh, K., Kim, S.J., Boyd, S.P.: An interior-point method for large-scale L1-regularized logistic regression. J. Mach. Learn. Res. 8(8), 1519–1555 (2007)
31. Andrew, G., Gao, J.: Scalable training of L1-regularized log-linear models. In: 24st International Conference on Machine Learning, pp. 33–40. ACM Press, Oregon (2007)
32. Gao, S., Tsang, I.H., Chia, L.T.: Laplacian sparse coding, hypergraph laplacian sparse coding, and applications. IEEE Trans. Pattern Anal. Mach. Intell. 35(1), 92–104 (2013)
33. Lazebnik, S., Schmid, C., Ponce, J.: Beyond bags of features: spatial pyramid matching for recognizing natural scene categories. In: 19th IEEE Computer Society Conference on Computer Vision and Pattern Recognition, vol. 2, pp. 2169–2178. IEEE Press, New York (2006)
34. Wu, J., Rehg, J.M.: Beyond the euclidean distance: creating effective visual codebooks using the histogram intersection kernel. In: 12th IEEE International Conference on Computer Vision, pp. 630–637. IEEE Press, Kyoto (2009)
35. Boiman, O., Shechtman, E., Irani, M.: In defense of nearest-neighbor based image classification. In: 21th IEEE Computer Society Conference on Computer Vision and Pattern Recognition, pp. 1–8. IEEE Press, Anchorage (2008)
36. Wang, J., Yang, J., Yu, K., Lv, F., Huang, T., Gong, Y.: Locality-constrained linear coding for image classification. In: 23th IEEE Computer Society Conference on Computer Vision and Pattern Recognition, pp. 3360–3367. IEEE Press, San Francisco (2010)

Distribution of FRFT Coefficients
of Natural Images

Li Jiang, Guichi Liu[✉], and Lin Qi

Information School of Engineering,
Zhengzhou University, Zhengzhou 450001, China
{ieljiang, iegcliu, ielqi}@zzu.edu.cn

Abstract. For the convenience of providing temporal and spectral information by a single variable, fractional Fourier transformation (FRFT) is more and more applied to image processing recently. This paper focuses on the statistical regularity of FRFT coefficients of natural images and proposes that the real and imaginary parts of FRFT coefficients of natural images take on the generalized Gaussian distribution, the coefficient modulus follow the gamma distribution and the coefficient phase angles tend to the uniform distribution, moreover, the real and imaginary parts of coefficient phases similar to the extended beta distribution. These underlying statistics can provide theoretical basis for image processing in FRFT, such as dimensionality reduction, feature extraction, smooth denoising, digital forensics, watermarking, etc.

Keywords: Fractional Fourier transformation · Distribution of FRFT coefficients · Generalized Gaussian distribution · Gamma distribution · Uniform distribution · Beta distribution

Fractional Fourier transformation (FRFT), as a kind of generalized Fourier transformation (FT), can be interpreted as a rotation of the signal in the time-frequency plane. Different from wavelet transformation, short-time Fourier transformation, Gabor transformation and other common two-parameters time frequency distributions, FRFT can provide the related local information of the signal in the time domain and the frequency domain simultaneously by a single variable, thus it has a wide application prospect in the field of signal processing [1]. FRFT is also introduced into the image processing, which is a significant branch of signal processing, such as the data compression [2], the image registration [3], the facial expression recognition [4], the image encryption [5], the digital watermarking [6] and so on. For the image processing based on FRFT, it is necessary to learn the related prior knowledge of FRFT coefficients of natural images. However, to the author's knowledge, there has not been relevant research report currently. Thus, this paper will focus on the statistical probability distribution of FRFT coefficients of natural images. As the FRFT phase gaining more and more attention for carrying the important image texture information [4], this paper will explore the statistical distribution of the amplitude and phase parts also with the real and imaginary parts of FRFT coefficients of natural images.

L. Jiang—This work is supported in part by "the National Natural Science Foundation of China under Grant, 61402421, 61331021".

Y.-J. Zhang (Ed.): ICIG 2015, Part II, LNCS 9218, pp. 197–207, 2015.
DOI: 10.1007/978-3-319-21963-9_18

The following paper is organized as follows: firstly, introduces the FRFT briefly; and then discusses the probability distribution of the FRFT coefficients of natural images, including the real part, the imaginary part, the amplitude part and the phase part; finally, makes conclusions and points out the future research directions.

1 Fractional Fourier Transformation

The fractional Fourier transformation (FRFT) of the one-dimensional function $x(t)$ is defined as the follows:

$$X_p(u) = \int_{-\infty}^{\infty} x(t) \cdot K_p(t, u) dt \tag{1}$$

where the kernel function of FRFT is given as:

$$K_p(t, u) = \begin{cases} \sqrt{\frac{1 - j \cot \alpha}{2\pi}} e^{\frac{j(t^2 + u^2)}{2} \cot \alpha - jtu \csc \alpha} & \alpha \neq n\pi \\ \delta(t - u) & \alpha = 2n\pi \\ \delta(t + u) & \alpha = (2n + 1)\pi \end{cases} \tag{2}$$

where $\alpha = p\pi/2$ is the order of FRFT and p is a real number. For p only existing in the trigonometric function of the definition of FRFT, as (1) shows, the FRFT follows a period of $p = 4$. Furthermore, $k_p(t, u)$ shows symmetry properties in the range of $p \in (-2, 2]$, and so, only FRFT with $p \in [0, 1]$ is generally taken into account [7]. It must be pointed out that the FRFT of signal with $p = 0$ is just the original signal, while the FRFT of signal with $p = 1$ is the ordinary FT of signal. Therefore, when p changes from 0 to 1, the result of FRFT changes from the original signal to the ordinary FT signal smoothly, and the corresponding data domain changes from the time domain to the frequency domain.

The FRFT of two-dimensional function $x(s, t)$ is defined as the follows:

$$X_{p_1, p_2}(u, v) = \int_{-\infty}^{\infty} \int_{-\infty}^{\infty} x(s, t) K_{p_1, p_2}(s, t, u, v) ds dt \tag{3}$$

where the kernel function, $K_{p_1, p_2}(s, t, u, v)$, is given as:

$$K_{p_1, p_2}(s, t, u, v) = \frac{1}{2\pi} \sqrt{1 - j \cot \alpha} \sqrt{1 - j \cot \beta}$$
$$\cdot e^{\frac{j(s^2 + u^2)}{2} \cot \alpha - jsu \csc \alpha} \cdot e^{\frac{j(t^2 + v^2)}{2} \cot \beta - jsu \csc \beta} \tag{4}$$

where $\alpha = p_1\pi/2$, $\beta = p_2\pi/2$ are the orders of 2D-FRFT and p_1, p_2 are real numbers. According to the commutative and associative of multiplication, $K_{p_1, p_2}(s, t, u, v)$ can be decomposed as:

$$K_{p_1,p_2}(s,t,u,v) = \left[\sqrt{\frac{1-j\cot\alpha}{2\pi}} \cdot e^{\frac{j(s^2+u^2)}{2}\cot\alpha - jsu\csc\alpha}\right]$$
$$\cdot \left[\sqrt{\frac{1-j\cot\beta}{2\pi}} \cdot e^{\frac{j(t^2+v^2)}{2}\cot\beta - jsu\csc\beta}\right] = K_{p_1}(s,u) \cdot K_{p_2}(t,v) \tag{5}$$

Namely, the kernel of 2D-FRFT can be decomposed as the multiplication of two kernels of 1-D FRFT. Substituting (4) into (3), there are:

$$X_{p_1,p_2}(u,v) = \int_{-\infty}^{\infty}\int_{-\infty}^{\infty} x(s,t)K_{p_1,p_2}(s,t,u,v)dsdt$$
$$= \int_{-\infty}^{\infty}\left[\int_{-\infty}^{\infty} x(s,t)K_{p_1}(s,u)ds\right]K_{p_2}(t,v)dt \tag{6}$$

Comparing (5) with (1), it can be known that 2D-FRFT can be decomposed into column 1-D FRFT of original data matrix and then row 1-D FRFT of column transformed data matrix.

2 Statistic Distribution Modeling of the FRFT Coefficients of Natural Images

Through FRFT, the natural image data will become complex number, thus, the statistical analysis of the real and imaginary parts of FRFT coefficients of natural images will all be made in this paper. Furthermore, considering that more and more image processing algorithms pay attention to the FRFT phase for its carrying the importance image texture information [4], we also focus on the statistical analysis of the amplitude and phase parts of FRFT coefficients of natural images.

According to the analysis of the previous section, two FRFT orders $p_1, p_2 \in [0, 1]$ with the interval $\Delta = 0.1$ are adopted when analyzing the statistical probability distribution of FRFT coefficients of natural images. The experimental database $\{I_i\}$ consists of 96 commonly used 128×128 gray images, including Lena, Baboon etc. All images in $\{I_i\}$ are sequentially transformed with FRFT for different orders and the FRFT coefficients with the same orders (p_1^i, p_2^i), although from the different images, are stored together forming a data set for the statistical analysis.

2.1 Statistical Distribution of the Real and Imaginary Parts

Figure 1 shows the histograms for the real part $R = real(X_{p_1,p_2}(u,v))$ and the imaginary part $R = imag(X_{p_1,p_2}(u,v))$ of the FRFT coefficients of natural images along with the fitted generalized Gaussian distribution (GGD).

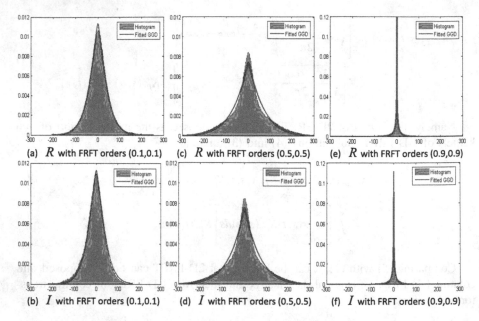

Fig. 1. Statistical histograms for the FRFT coefficients of natural images and the fitted GGD curves

The probability density function (pdf) of GGD can be defined as the follows:

$$f_{GGD}(x|\alpha, \beta) = \frac{\beta}{2\alpha\Gamma(1/\beta)} e^{-(|x|/\alpha)^{\beta}} \tag{7}$$

where $|\cdot|$ is the modulo operation, $\Gamma(\cdot)$ is the Gamma function, and the real parameter α is proportional to the peak width of pdf, while the real parameter β is inversely proportional to the peak rate of decline. Generally, α is called scale parameter and β is called shape parameter. Moreover, when $\beta = 2$, GGD becomes the Gaussian distribution; when $\beta = 1$, GGD is the Laplace distribution. Sharifi and Leon-Garcia [8] had given the moment estimation of the two parameters in GGD:

$$\alpha = \frac{\sigma}{\sqrt{\Gamma(3/\beta)/\Gamma(1/\beta)}} \tag{8}$$

$$\beta = F^{-1}(m/\sigma) \tag{9}$$

where $m = \frac{1}{N}\sum_{i=1}^{N}|x_i|$ is the mean of the sample modulus, $\sigma = \sqrt{\frac{1}{N}\sum_{i=1}^{N}x_i^2}$ is the standard deviation of samples, and $F^{-1}(\cdot)$ is the inverse function of $F(x) = \Gamma(2/x)/\sqrt{\Gamma(1/x) \cdot \Gamma(3/x)}$.

Although Fig. 1 seems clear that the GGD can accurately models the statistical distribution of R and I, this paper will further provide the quantitative analysis of fitting by the Kullback-Leibler divergence (KLD). KLD is a measure of the asymmetry between two discrete distributions with probabilities P and Q:

$$\text{KLD}(P,Q) = \sum_{i=1}^{M} P_i \ln \frac{P_i}{Q_i} \qquad (10)$$

where M is the number of the sample subspaces, P_i and Q_i represent the probabilities of the sample subspace i of P and Q, $\ln(\cdot)$ is the natural logarithm. Equation (9) makes sense only if $P_i > 0$ and $Q_i > 0$, else $P_i \ln(P_i/Q_i) = 0$. If $P = Q$, then $KLD(P,Q) = 0$. Namely, the smaller the KLD, the higher of the similarity between P and Q.

The α, β and KLD of the GGD fitting curve of the real and imaginary parts of FRFT coefficients with different orders of natural images are shown as the Fig. 2, from which it can be seen that:

- The real and imaginary parts of the FRFT coefficients of natural images are all similar to the GGD distribution. As the FRFT orders increase, the parameter α increases, while the shape parameter β decreases. Moreover, α and β are symmetric about the diagonal of FRFT orders, that is, the real and imaginary parts of FRFT coefficients with the orders (i,j) and (j,i) are similar to the same GGD distribution.
- The GGD shape parameters β of the real and imaginary parts of coefficients with different FRFT orders are all less than 2, namely, the statistical probability distributions of the real and imaginary parts of FRFT coefficients of natural images neither the Gaussian nor fixing on the Laplace.
- According to the KLD, when the FRFT order tends to 1, the fitting degree of the GGD curve, which is obtained by Sharifi and Leon-Garcia [8], decreases. This is mainly because the FRFT gradually transforms into the FT when its orders tend to 1. Due to the prominent energy aggregation property of FT, more transform coefficients turn to zeros, all the energy focuses on fewer singular values, and the peak of the statistical probability density curve becomes sharper, which is reflected in the GGD parameters α reduces to 0, while β increases to infinity, as is shown in Fig. 2. At this time, any slight error of the GGD parameters' moment estimation may greatly influence on the curve fitness. However, according to Fig. 1, a remarkable similarity can be found between the statistical distribution of the real and imaginary parts of FRFT coefficients and the GGDs, even when the FRFT orders tend to 1.

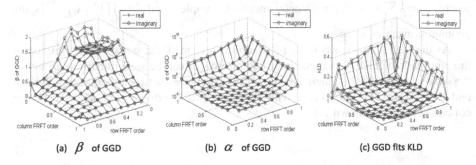

(a) β of GGD   (b) α of GGD   (c) GGD fits KLD

Fig. 2. The parameters of the fitted GGD curve with different FRFT orders

2.2 Statistical Distribution of the Coefficient Amplitudes

Taking the amplitude of FRFT coefficients of natural images as $V = \left| X_{p_1,p_2}(u,v) \right|$, it can be discovered that the statistical distribution of V is similar to the Gamma distribution (ΓD), as is shown in Fig. 3.

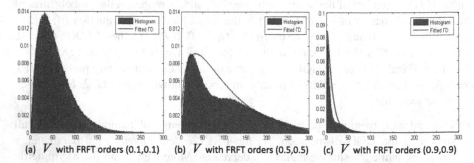

(a) V with FRFT orders (0.1,0.1)   (b) V with FRFT orders (0.5,0.5)   (c) V with FRFT orders (0.9,0.9)

Fig. 3. Statistical histograms for the FRFT amplitude of natural images and the fitted ΓD curves

The pdf of ΓD is defined as the follows:

$$f_{\Gamma D}(x|\alpha,\beta) = \frac{\alpha^\beta}{\Gamma(\beta)} x^{\beta-1} e^{-\alpha x} \tag{11}$$

where $x \geq 0$, the positive real parameter α is proportional to the peak width while the positive real parameter β is inversely proportional to the peak rate of decline. Thus, α is usually called the scale parameter and β is usually called the shape parameter. It is noted that ΓD becomes exponential distribution when $\beta = 1$. The maximum likelihood estimation of two parameters ΓD is given by Dang and Weerakkody [10]:

$$\alpha = \beta/\bar{x} \tag{12}$$

$$\beta = \frac{1 + \sqrt{1 + 4\log(\bar{x}/\hat{x})/3}}{4\ln(\bar{x}/\hat{x})} \tag{13}$$

where, $\bar{x} = \frac{1}{N}\sum_{i=1}^{N} x_i$ is the arithmetic mean of samples, and $\hat{x} = \left(\prod_{i=1}^{N} x_i\right)^{1/N}$ is the geometric mean of samples.

As the Fig. 3 shows, when the FRFT orders are small, the statistical distribution of the amplitude of FRFT coefficients of natural images can be well fitted by ΓD, but as the orders become higher, there are significant differences between them. From the α, β and KLD of the ΓD fitting curve with difference FRFT orders in Fig. 4, some further conclusions can be drawn as:

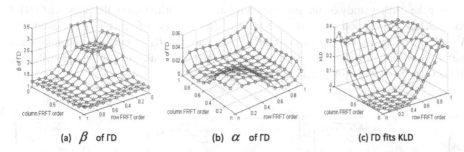

(a) β of ΓD   (b) α of ΓD   (c) ΓD fits KLD

Fig. 4. The parameters of the fitted ΓD curve with different FRFT orders

- The probability density of the amplitudes of the FRFT coefficients of natural images is similar to the ΓD and $\beta > 1$, which means the amplitudes of the FRFT coefficients of natural images do not follow the exponential distribution.
- With the FRFT orders becoming higher, the β obtained by the maximum likelihood estimation method in Dang and Weerakkody [10] decreases gradually. However, when FRFT orders higher than 0.5, $\beta < 2$, and there are significant differences between the statistical probability distribution of the amplitudes of FRFT coefficients of natural images and the ΓD fitting curve, just as Fig. 4(c) shows. Therefore, it's necessary to carry out further research on getting the fitting curve of the FRFT amplitudes with high orders of natural images.

2.3 Statistical Distribution of the Coefficient Phase

Taking the phase angles of the FRFT coefficients of natural images as $A = \arg tg(R/I)$, the statistical probability distribution of A gradually tends to the uniform distribution (UD) with the rising of the FRFT orders (Fig. 5).

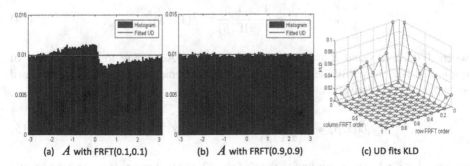

(a) A with FRFT(0.1,0.1)   (b) A with FRFT(0.9,0.9)   (c) UD fits KLD

Fig. 5. Statistical histograms for the FRFT phase angles of natural images and its fitted UD curves

For the further study on the statistical probability distribution of the phases of FRFT coefficients of natural images, we takes the phases of FRFT coefficients as $A' = X_{p_1,p_2}(u,v)/V$. Then we can find that, the real part $R_A = real(A')$ and imaginary part $I_A = imag(A')$ of the complex number A' are all similar to the beta distribution (BD) with the domain of $(-1,1)$, as is shown in Fig. 6.

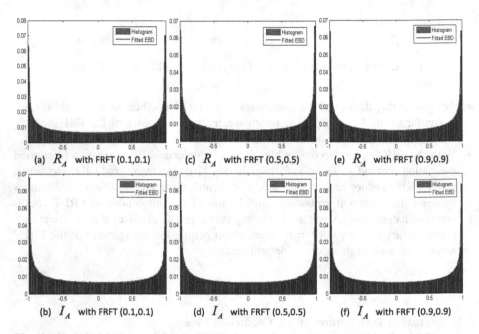

Fig. 6. Statistical histograms for the FRFT phases of natural images and its fitted BD curve.

The traditional BD is a two- parameters probability distribution with the domain of $(0,1)$, and its pdf is:

$$f_{\mathrm{BD}}(x|\alpha,\beta) = \frac{\Gamma(\alpha+\beta)}{\Gamma(\alpha)\Gamma(\beta)} x^{\alpha-1}(1-x)^{\beta-1} \tag{14}$$

where $0 < x < 1$, α and β are positive real numbers. According to the definition of traditional BD, the pdf of the extended BD with the domain of $(-1,1)$ can be obtained as *appendix for derivation:

$$f'_{\mathrm{BD}}(x|\alpha,\beta) = \frac{\Gamma(\alpha+\beta)}{\Gamma(\alpha)\Gamma(\beta)} \cdot 2^{1-(\alpha+\beta)}(1+x)^{\alpha-1}(1-x)^{\beta-1} \tag{15}$$

where $-1 < x < 1$. And according to the $f'_{BD}(x|\alpha,\beta)$, the first moment m_1 and the second moment m_2 of the extended BD can be obtained respectively as:

$$m_1 = E(x) = \int_{-1}^{1} x \cdot f_{BD}(x|\alpha, \beta)dx = \frac{\alpha - \beta}{\alpha + \beta} \tag{16}$$

$$m_2 = E(x^2) = \int_{-1}^{1} x^2 \cdot f_{BD}(x|\alpha, \beta)dx$$
$$= 1 - \frac{4\alpha\beta}{(\alpha + \beta)(\alpha + \beta + 1)} \tag{17}$$

And we can derive the two parameters α and β of the extended BD from (15) and (16) as:

$$\alpha = \frac{1 + m_1}{1 - m_1}\beta \tag{18}$$

$$\beta = \frac{1 - m_1 - m_2}{2(m_1^2 + m_2)} \tag{19}$$

The $\alpha\beta$ and KLD of the extended BD fitting curve of the real and imaginary parts of FRFT phases with different orders of natural images are listed in Fig. 7, and some further conclusions can be drawn as:

- The real and imaginary parts of the FRFT phases of natural images are all similar to the extended BD distribution. If the FRFT orders are non-zero, the α and β have no significant differences as the transformation order changing.
- The parameters α and β of the extended BD of the real and imaginary parts of FRFT phases of natural images are approximately equal to 0.5, and furthermore, they are symmetrical about 0.5 in a certain sense: the extended BD parameters of the real part (α_r, β_r) and the extended BD parameters of the imaginary part (α_i, β_i) with the same FRFT orders satisfy $\alpha_r - 0.5 \approx 0.5 - \alpha_i$ and $\beta_r - 0.5 \approx 0.5 - \beta_i$.
- According to the KLD, if there is zero in the FRFT orders, the fitting degree between the extended BD and the statistical distribution of the real and imaginary parts of FRFT phases of natural images may decrease. This is mainly because the natural images data remains unchanged when the FRFT orders are zero, which means the data is still the original real data and the phase equals zero.

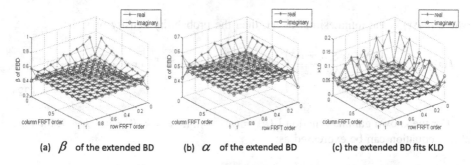

(a) β of the extended BD   (b) α of the extended BD   (c) the extended BD fits KLD

Fig. 7. The parameters of the fitted BD curve with different FRFT orders.

3 Conclusion

In this paper, we have studied the statistical distribution of FRFT coefficients of natural images and proposed that the real and imaginary parts of FRFT coefficients take on the generalized Gaussian distribution, the FRFT modulus follow the gamma distribution and the FRFT phase angles tend to the uniform distribution, moreover, the real and imaginary parts of FRFT phases meet the extended beta distribution with the definition domain of $(-1,1)$. These underlying statistics rules are expected to provide theoretical basis for the image processing in FRFT, such as dimensionality reduction, feature extraction, smooth de-noising, digital forensics and watermarking etc. These will be the key of our future work.

Appendix

The extended beta distribution with the definition domain of $(-1,1)$.

The traditional beta distribution (BD) originated from such a question: sampling n times for the random variable X uniformly distributed on $(0,1)$, then the distribution of the kth largest x_k is BD and its probability density function is as the follows:

$$f_{BD}(x|\alpha, \beta) = \frac{\Gamma(\alpha + \beta)}{\Gamma(\alpha)\Gamma(\beta)} x^{\alpha-1}(1-x)^{\beta-1}, \quad 0 < x < 1 \tag{20}$$

where $\alpha = k$ and $\beta = n - k + 1$. And then, we can extended the definition domain of BD to $(-1,1)$, which is to find the distribution of the kth largest x_k in the n times sampling of the random variable X uniformly distributed on $(-1,1)$.

Let $x_k \in (x, x + \Delta x)$, then its probability is:

$$P(x < x_k \le x + \Delta x) = C_n^1 \cdot C_n^{k-1} \cdot \left[\frac{x - (-1)}{2}\right]^{k-1} \cdot \frac{x + \Delta x - x}{2} \cdot \left[\frac{1 - (x + \Delta x)}{2}\right]^{n-k}$$

$$= \frac{n!}{(k-1)!(n-k)!} \cdot 2^{-n} \cdot (x+1)^{k-1} \cdot (1-x)^{n-k} \Delta x + o(\Delta x) \tag{21}$$

where $o(\Delta x)$ is the infinitesimal of Δx, then the probability density of x_k is:

$$f(x_k) = \lim_{\Delta x \to 0} \frac{P(x < x_k \le x + \Delta x)}{\Delta x} = \frac{n!}{(k-1)!(n-k)!} \cdot 2^{-n} \cdot (x+1)^{k-1} \cdot (1-x)^{n-k} \tag{22}$$

For the known gamma function $\Gamma(n) = (n-1)!$, let $\alpha = k$, $\beta = n - k + 1$, then the above equation can be expressed as:

$$f(x_k) = \frac{\Gamma(\alpha+\beta)}{\Gamma(\alpha)\Gamma(\beta)} \cdot 2^{1-(\alpha+\beta)}(1+x)^{\alpha-1}(1-x)^{\beta-1} \tag{23}$$

That is, the pdf of the extended BD defined on $(-1,1)$ is as the follows:

$$f'_{BD}(x|\alpha,\beta) = \frac{\Gamma(\alpha+\beta)}{\Gamma(\alpha)\Gamma(\beta)} \cdot 2^{1-(\alpha+\beta)}(1+x)^{\alpha-1}(1-x)^{\beta-1} \tag{24}$$

References

1. Sejdić, E., Djurović, I., Stanković, L.J.: Fractional Fourier transform as a signal processing tool: an overview of recent developments. Sig. Process. **91**, 1351–1369 (2011)
2. Vijaya, C., Bhat, J.S.: Signal compression using discrete fractional Fourier transform and set partitioning in hierarchical tree. Sig. Process. **86**(8), 1976–1983 (2006)
3. Pan, W., Qin, K., Chen, Y.: An adaptable-multilayer fractional Fourier transform approach for image registration. IEEE Trans. Pattern Anal. Mach. Intell. **31**, 400–414 (2009)
4. Gao, L., Qi, L., Chen, E., Mu, X., Guan, L.: Recognizing human emotional state based on the phase information of the two dimensional fractional Fourier transform. In: Qiu, G., Lam, K.M., Kiya, H., Xue, X.-Y., Kuo, C.-C., Lew, M.S. (eds.) PCM 2010, Part II. LNCS, vol. 6298, pp. 694–704. Springer, Heidelberg (2010)
5. Tao, R., Meng, X.Y., Wang, Y.: Image encryption with multiorders of fractional Fourier transforms. IEEE Trans. Inf. Forensics Secur. **5**, 734–738 (2010)
6. Savalonas, M.A., Chountasis, S.: Noise-resistant watermarking in the fractional Fourier domain utilizing moment-based image representation. Sig. Process. **90**(8), 2521–2528 (2010)
7. Tao, R., Deng, B., Wang, Y.: Fractional Fourier Transform and its Application, pp. 12–15. Tsinghua University Press, Beijing (2009)
8. Sharifi, K., Leon-Garcia, A.: Estimation of shape parameter for generalized gaussian distributions in subband decompositions of video. IEEE Trans. Circ. Syst. Video Technol. **5**(1), 52–56 (1995)
9. Kullback, S., Leibler, R.A.: On information and sufficiency. Ann. Math. Stat. **22**(1), 79–86 (1951)
10. Dang, H., Weerakkody, G.: Bounds for the maximum likelihood estimates in two-parameter gamma distribution. J. Math. Anal. Appl. **245**, 1–6 (2000)

Dual-Projection Based High-Precision Integral Imaging Pickup System

Zhao-Long Xiong, Qiong-Hua Wang$^{(\boxtimes)}$, Huan Deng, and Yan Xing

School of Electronics and Information Engineering, Sichuan University, Chengdu 610065, China
qhwang@scu.edu.cn

Abstract. In this paper, a high-precision integral imaging (II) pickup system for the real scene is proposed. The dual-projection optical pickup method is utilized to obtain the elemental image array for the II display. The proposed method is robust to the position deviations of the projectors and camera. The calibration of the camera is simplified. Furthermore, the pickup of the II is not limited by the complex optical and mechanical structures. Experimental results show that the proposed system can generate the continuous and tunable parallaxes. With the proposed II pickup and display system, the high-quality 3D images for the real scene can be reconstructed efficiently.

Keywords: Image processing · Electro-optical devices · Image reconstruction techniques

1 Introduction

Integral imaging (II) as an attractive three-dimensional (3D) technology can reconstruct the autostereoscopic 3D images without glasses and provide both horizontal and vertical parallaxes with continuous views [1–3]. Basically, the conventional II system consists of the pickup and display sections. In the pickup section, however, there are still some problems such as the limitations of 3D resolution, parallax range, and scene size, which delay the practical application of the II. In the past decades, many researchers have focused on solving these problems, and many technologies have been proposed, including optical pickup method, computer graphic technology, and depth camera based technology.

The conventional optical pickup method using a micro-lens array (MLA) is limited by the scene size, unnecessary beams, and aberrations [4–7]. It is difficult to capture the 3D information on a real and large-sized 3D scene in practice. The quality of the reconstructed 3D image is reduced because of the limitations imposed by the manufacturing technique used for the MLA. Some researchers replace the MLA with a certain camera array in the pickup part to collect the full-color and high-resolution 3D information of a large-sized real 3D scene [8–11]. Then the elemental image array (EIA) is generated with the 3D information by pixel mapping algorithms [11, 12]. Although, those methods can be applied for the large-sized real scene, they require some complex optical and mechanical structures. Furthermore, the calibration of the camera array is a difficulty when the camera array contains a large number of cameras [9, 11].

© Springer International Publishing Switzerland 2015
Y.-J. Zhang (Ed.): ICIG 2015, Part II, LNCS 9218, pp. 208–218, 2015.
DOI: 10.1007/978-3-319-21963-9_19

In recent years, with the development of the computer graphic technology, computer-generated integral imaging (CGII) has been proposed [12–16]. In the CGII, however, the limitations of computer graphic technology itself make the capturing of 3D information on real scenes difficult. For the simplification of the II pickup, a great contribution has been made by Chungbuk National University to collect the EIA of the real scene with a depth camera [17]. This method simplifies the pickup process, but it is limited by the accuracy and resolution of the depth camera. The occlusion and the holes in the depth map degrade the quality of the EIA seriously. Some researches combined the optical and computer-generated methods. The dual-camera enabled II pickup system has been proposed [18]. Obviously, the generated parallaxes are limited by the two-view stereoscopic camera and stereo matching algorithms [19].

In this paper, we propose a system to achieve a high-precision II pickup for the real scene. The dual-projection optical pickup (DPOP) method is used to capture the 3D information with no need of complex calibration. This method obtains the more complete reconstructed 3D shape. Then sub-images are generated based on the color texture and depth data of the real scene. The EIA for the II display are generated by interleaving the obtained sub-images. Experimental results verify the usefulness of the proposed system.

2 Principle of the Proposed II Pickup System

We achieve the high-precision II pickup system for real scene based on the DPOP method. In the proposed system, a more complete 3D shape of the real scene can be obtained. The continuous and tunable parallaxes, the sub-images, are extracted from the color texture and depth data. Interleaving the sub-images, the high-precision EIA can be obtained for the II display.

The architecture of the proposed system is composed of four parts: the input part including the parameters of the DPOP method and the II display input, the reconstruction part including the reconstruction of the more complete 3D shape and the capture of the corresponding color texture, the EIA generation part including the generation of the sub-images and the pixel mapping for the EIA, and the 3D display part showing the EIA through the MLA for the viewers.

2.1 Comparison of the Conventional and Proposed II Pickup System

In the conventional II pickup system, as shown in Fig. 1(a) and (b), the EIA is generated by the MLA or the camera array. In Fig. 1(a), the real scene is captured as elemental images through each micro-lens in the MLA. The size of the scene and the accuracy of the EIA are limited by the parameters of the MLA. The cross-talk effect between neighboring micro-lenses also reduces the quality of reconstructed 3D images [20]. In Fig. 1(b), the camera array is arranged to pick up the real scene. But the camera array needs accurate calibration, operation, and synchronism. Besides, the latency and bandwidth are both the limitations.

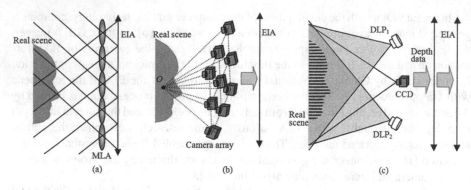

Fig. 1. Comparison of EIA generation in the II system (a) by the MLA, (b) by the camera array, and (c) by the proposed DPOP method.

In our proposed system, as shown in Fig. 1(c), we utilize two digital light processing projectors (DLPs) to project the structured light [21–24]. The utilization of the dual-projection, DLP_1 and DLP_2, avoids the error accumulation with the occlusion of a single DLP [25]. In the proposed DPOP method, DLP_1 and DLP_2 are used for projecting the grating patterns on the real scene, and the deformed patterns are captured by the charge coupled device (CCD). The 3D shape of the real scene is modulated in the deformed patterns. With the phase unwrapping algorithms and the mapping algorithms, the 3D shape can be extracted from the deformed patterns [26–29]. But the phase unwrapping algorithms are not suitable for the blind areas, which can cause the error accumulation in the reconstructed 3D shape. So the reconstructed 3D shape may be not complete based on single DLP projection [25]. In the proposed DPOP method, two DLPs project grating patterns from different directions, and the 3D shape is reconstructed with each of the DLPs, respectively. These 3D shapes have some imperfection, and we introduce the fusion and stitching algorithm to obtain the more complete 3D shape.

2.2   Reconstruction of 3D Shape for Real Scene by DPOP Method

In this paper, the DPOP method is proposed to obtain the complete 3D shape of the real scene. Two DLPs are utilized to project grating patterns to avoid the blind areas of single DLP. The reconstructed 3D shapes can be fused together completely.

As shown in Fig. 2, the DLP_1 and DLP_2 are arranged in the front of the real scene and project N grating patterns. N grating patterns are arranged by a sinusoidal rule. There is an equal $2\pi/N$ phase-shifting between the adjacent grating patterns. The CCD captures the j-th deformed patterns from the DLP_i ($i = 1, 2$), and the intensity of the captured deformed pattern is denoted as $I_i(x, y, j)$:

$$I_i(x,y,j) = R_i(x,y)\left\{A_i(x,y) + B_i(x,y)\cos[\varphi_i(x,y) + \sigma_j]\right\} \tag{1}$$

where $j = 1, 2,\ldots$, and N, and x, y are the pixel coordinates in the captured deformed patterns, $R_i(x, y)$ is the surface reflectance of the real scene, $A_i(x, y)$ represents the background light intensity, $B_i(x, y)$ is the fringe contrast, $\varphi_i(x, y)$ indicates the deformed phase modified by the real scene, and σ_j is the phase-shifting of the j-th deformed pattern.

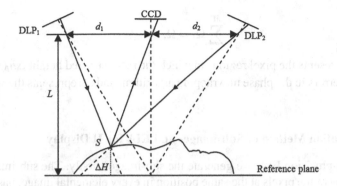

Fig. 2. Principle of the reconstruction of the 3D shape by the proposed DPOP method.

As the structured light illumination by single DLP [22, 29], the truncated phase $\varphi'_i(x, y)$ of the deformed phase $\varphi_i(x, y)$ can be deduced as:

$$\varphi'_i(x, y) = \arctan \frac{\sum\limits_{n=1}^{N} I_i(x, y, n) \sin(\sigma_n)}{\sum\limits_{n=1}^{N} I_i(x, y, n) \sin(\sigma_n)}. \tag{2}$$

According to the inverse trigonometric functions, $\varphi'_i(x, y)$ has a value in $[-\pi, \pi)$. For the continuous phase distributions, the truncated phase $\varphi'_i(x, y)$ needs to be unwrapped by the phase unwrapping algorithm [22, 28], and the unwrapped phase is denoted as $\Psi_i(x, y)$. Then the phase-changing $\Delta\Psi_i(x, y)$ between the real scene and the reference plane can be calculated. And according to the phase-to-height mapping algorithm, the height $\Delta h_i(x, y)$ of the captured real scene can be calculated as follows:

$$\frac{1}{\Delta h_i(x, y)} = a_i(x, y) + \frac{b_i(x, y)}{\Delta\varphi_i(x, y)} + \frac{c_i(x, y)}{\Delta\varphi_i^2(x, y)}, \tag{3}$$

where $a_i(x, y)$, $b_i(x, y)$ and $c_i(x, y)$ are the mapping parameters, which can be acquired by plane calibrations. After dealing with the deformed patterns information, we can get the height and contour information of the real scene. The height $\Delta h_i(x, y)$ obtained by the single DLP_i maybe not complete because of the blind areas. However, the obtained height $\Delta h_i(x, y)$ is simply determined by the real scene, not the measurement system. In other words, the height $\Delta h_i(x, y)$ is independent of the parameters in DPOP method. So the different height $\Delta h_i(x, y)$ can be fused and stitched together to obtain the more complete 3D shape. The fused height $\Delta H(x, y)$ can be obtained as:

$$\Delta H(x, y) = \sum_{i=1}^{M} \Delta h_i(x_i, y_i), \quad (x_i, y_i) \in \Omega_i, \tag{4}$$

$$\sum_{i=1}^{M} \Omega_i = \Omega, \tag{5}$$

where Ω_i represents the pixel regions in which the reconstructed height $\Delta h_i(x, y)$ has no accumulate errors in the phase unwrapping algorithm, and Ω represents the whole pixel region.

2.3 Generation Method of Sub-images and EIA for II Display

For the high-precision EIA, we generate the sub-images firstly. The sub-image, which is a collection of the pixels at the same position in every elemental image, has the orthographic projection geometry. In the II display, the sub-images represent a series of directional images. As shown in Fig. 3, the real scene imaged on the EIA plane by the MLA. The parallel rays with the same directional angle θ can be extracted to form an orthographic sub-image [16, 30]. The Fig. 3(a) and (b) show the generation geometries of the sub-images and EIAs with the different central depth planes. The pixel information of the sub-images is extracted from the color texture. And the pixel coordinates are decided by the central depth plane and the depth data. The depth data $\Delta D(x, y)$ can be transformed from the fused height $\Delta H(x, y)$:

$$\Delta D(x, y) = \Delta H(x, y) \frac{W}{R_w} = \Delta H(x, y) \frac{H}{R_h}, \tag{6}$$

where the W and H are the real width and height of the real scene, and the $R_w \times R_h$ is the resolution of captured deformed pattern. The Eq. 6 converts the height $\Delta H(x, y)$ from the true height to the pixel coordinates, as the depth data $\Delta D(x, y)$. In the sub-image, as shown in Fig. 3, the pixel information K is mapping to the pixel coordinate G, and the pixel shifting between K and G is denoted as Δq. According to the geometry shown in Fig. 3, the sub-image $I_\theta(x, y)$ for the projecting angle θ can be deduced as:

$$I_\theta(x, y) = T(x + \Delta q_x, y + \Delta q_y), \tag{7}$$

where $T(x, y)$ is the pixel information of the color texture, and Δq_x and Δq_y are the components along the x and y axes of the pixel shifting Δq, respectively. The pixel shifting Δq is depend on the depth data and central depth plane, and can be calculated as:

$$\Delta q = \left(\Delta D(x, y) - d_c \right) \tan \theta, \tag{8}$$

where d_c, described by pixel coordinate, is the distance between the zero plane of the depth data ($z = 0$) and the central depth plane.

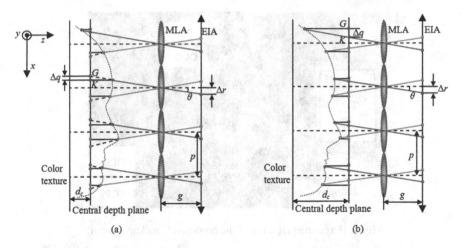

Fig. 3. Geometry of generations for the sub-images and EIAs in the proposed system: (a) and (b) with the different central depth plane.

In the proposed system, the projecting angle θ can be deduced by the parameters of the II display. As shown in Fig. 3, the gap between the MLA and the EIA is g and the interval between the elemental image's pixel and the centre is Δr. The projecting angle θ can be decided by:

$$\theta = \arctan \frac{\Delta r}{g}. \tag{9}$$

For the different intervals, the projecting angle θ is different. So the parallaxes are continuous and tunable.

With the sub-images obtained for all projecting angle, the EIA can be generated by interleaving the sub-images based on the viewpoint vector rendering method efficiently [30].

3   Experiments and Results

In our experiments, we use two projectors (CB-X24) as the DLP1 and the DLP2 to project N grating patterns. In our experiments, $N = 4$, so the phase-shifting $\sigma_j = 2\pi/4$. The CCD (GM501-H) captures the deformed patterns in 640×480 pixels. The generated EIA is displayed on the II pad [15]. The experimental setup is shown in Fig. 4.

The proposed II pickup system is configured with the specification in Table 1. The distance between the CCD and the DLPs is 0.331 m, and the center depth plane is located at the $d_c = 0$ pixel plane and $d_c = 130$ pixel plane.

In our experiments, a "man head" is used as the real scene. We reconstruct the 3D shapes of the head with the deformed patterns (Fig. 5(a) and (c)) by each of DLPs, respectively. As shown in Fig. 5(d) and (e), the 3D shapes are not complete by single DLP. The Fig. 5(e) shows the fused 3D shape in our proposed system. From the profile

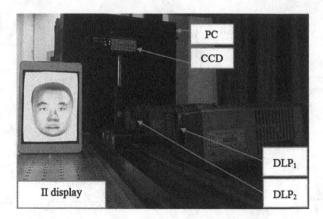

Fig. 4. Experimental setup of the proposed II pickup system.

shown in Fig. 5(d), we can see that the fused 3D shape is complete and no error accumulation.

We generate the sub-images by the proposed method from the depth data and color texture of the head as shown in Fig. 6(a)–(c). The projecting angle θ is continuous and tunable. The EIAs generated with the different central depth planes are shown in Figs. 6(d) and (e).

When the viewer moves in the front of the II display, the reconstructed images from different positions are captured, as shown in Fig. 7.

Table 1. Configuration parameters and experiment environment of the proposed II system

DPOP parameter	DLPs' resolution	1024×768 pixels
	CCD's resolution	640×480 pixels
	Distance	$d_1 = 0.331$ m
		$d_2 = 0.331$ m
		$L = 1.750$ m
II display parameter	EIA resolution	2048×1536 pixels
	Elemental image size	16×16 pixels
	Gap	3.38 mm
	Micro-lens pitch	1.25 mm
Central depth plane	d_c	0 pixel or 130 pixels

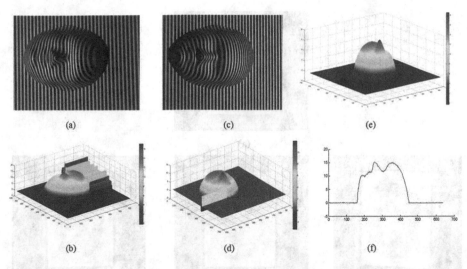

Fig. 5. Captured deformed patterns and reconstructed 3D shapes in experiments (a) and (c) the deformed patterns by DLP1 and DLP2, (b) and (d) the 3D shapes reconstructed with (a) and (c), (e) the fused 3D shape in the proposed system, and (f) the profile of the fused 3D shape (y = 230).

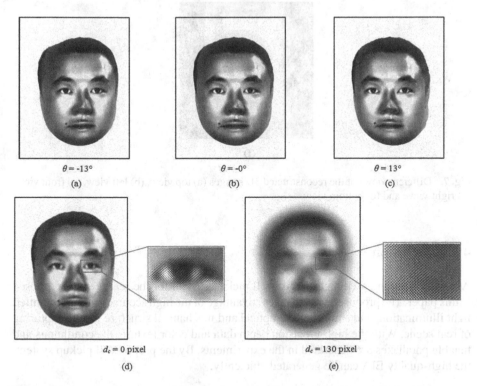

Fig. 6. Sub-images and generated EIAs by the proposed method (a), (b), and (c) the sub-images, (d) and (e) the EIAs with the different central depth planes.

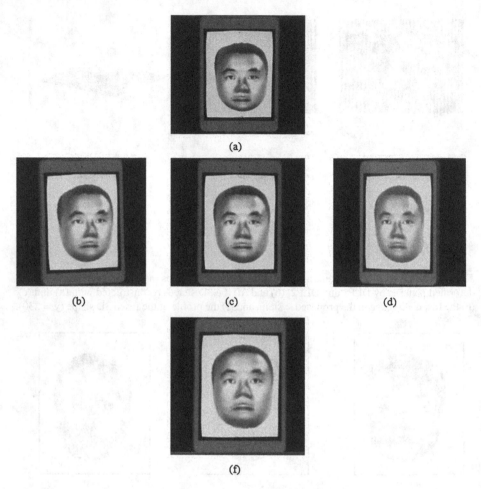

Fig. 7. Different views of the reconstructed 3D images (a) top view, (b) left view, (c) front view, (d) right view, and (e) bottom view.

4   Conclusion

A dual-projection based high-precision II pickup system for the real scene is proposed in this paper. The proposed system takes advantage of the high accuracy of the structured light illumination, and simplifies the optical and mechanical structure for the capturing of real scene. With the high-precision depth data and color texture, the continuous and tunable parallaxes are generated in the experiments. By the proposed II pickup system, the high-quality EIA can be generated efficiently.

Acknowledgment. The work is supported by the NSFC under Grant Nos. 61225022 and 61320106015, the "973" Program under Grant No. 2013CB328802, and the "863" Program under Grant No. 2015AA015902.

References

1. Lippmann, G.: La photographie integrale. C. R. Acad. Sci. **146**, 446–451 (1908)
2. Hong, J., Kim, Y., Choi, H.J., Hahn, J., Park, J.H., Kim, H., Min, S.W., Chen, N., Lee, B.: Three-dimensional display technologies of recent interest: principles, status, and issues. Appl. Opt. **50**(34), H87–H115 (2011)
3. Xiao, X., Javidi, B., Martinez-Corral, M., Stern, A.: Advances in three-dimensional integral imaging: sensing, display, and applications [Invited]. Appl. Opt. **52**(4), 546–560 (2013)
4. Okano, F., Hoshino, H., Arai, J., Yuyama, I.: Real-time pickup method for a three-dimensional image based on Integral Photography. Appl. Opt. **36**(7), 1598–1603 (1997)
5. Jang, J.S., Javidi, B.: Improved viewing resolution of three-dimensional integral imaging by use of nonstationary micro-optics. Opt. Lett. **27**(5), 324–326 (2002)
6. Yoo, H.: Axially moving a lenslet array for high-resolution 3D images in computational integral imaging. Opt. Express **21**(7), 8873–8878 (2013)
7. Arai, J., Okui, M., Yamashita, T., Okano, F.: Integral three-dimensional television using a 2000-scanning-line video system. Appl. Opt. **45**(8), 1704–1712 (2006)
8. Xu, Y., Wang, X.R., Sun, Y., Zhang, J.Q.: Homogeneous light field model for interactive control of viewing parameters of integral imaging displays. Opt. Express **20**(13), 14137–14151 (2012)
9. Sang, X.Z., Fan, F.C., Jiang, C.C., Choi, S., Dou, W.H., Yu, C., Xu, D.: Demonstration of a large-size realtime full-color three-dimensional display. Opt. Lett. **34**(24), 3803–3805 (2009)
10. Moon, I., Javidi, B.: Three-dimensional recognition of photon-starved events using computational integral imaging and statistical sampling. Opt. Lett. **34**(6), 731–733 (2009)
11. Navarro, H., Dorado, A., Saavedra, G., Llavador, A., Martínez-Corral, M., Javidi, B.: Is it worth using an array of cameras to capture the spatio-angular information of a 3D scene or is it enough with just two? In: Proceedings of SPIE vol. 8384, pp. 838406–838406-7 (2012)
12. Liao, H., Iwahara, M., Hata, N., Dohi, T.: High-quality integral videography using a multiprojector. Opt. Express **12**(6), 1067–1076 (2004)
13. Igarashi, Y., Murata, H., Ueda, M.: 3D display system using a computer generated integral photography. Jpn. J. Appl. Phys. **17**(9), 1683–1684 (1978)
14. Jang, Y.H., Park, C., Jung, J.S., Park, J.H., Kim, N., Ha, J.S., Yoo, K.H.: Integral imaging pickup method of bio-medical data using GPU and Octree. J. Korea Contents Assoc. **10**(6), 1–9 (2010)
15. Ji, C.C., Luo, C.G., Deng, H., Li, D.H., Wang, Q.H.: Tilted elemental image array generation method for moiré-reduced computer generated integral imaging display. Opt. Express **21**(17), 19816–19824 (2013)
16. Kwon, K.C., Park, C., Erdenebat, M.U., Jeong, J.S., Choi, J.H., Kim, N., Park, J.H., Lim, Y.T., Yoo, K.H.: High speed image space parallel processing for computer-generated integral imaging system. Opt. Express **20**(2), 732–740 (2012)
17. Li, G., Kwon, K.C., Shin, G.H., Jeong, J.S., Yoo, K.H., Kim, N.: Simplified integral imaging pickup method for real objects using a depth camera. J. Opt. Soc. Korea **16**(4), 381–385 (2012)
18. Jiao, X.X., Zhao, X., Yang, Y., Fang, Z.L., Yuan, X.C.: Dual-camera enabled real-time three-dimensional integral imaging pick-up and display. Opt. Express **20**(25), 27304–27311 (2012)
19. Cooperation Stereo Vision. http://www.cs.cmu.edu/clz/stereo.html

20. Kavehvash, Z., Mehrany, K., Bagheri, S.: Optimization of the lens-array structure for performance improvement of integral imaging. Opt. Lett. **36**(20), 3993–3995 (2011)
21. Srinivasan, V., Liu, H.C., Halioua, M.: Automated phase-measuring profilometry of 3-D diffuse objects. Appl. Opt. **23**(18), 3105–3108 (1984)
22. Kim, E.H., Hahn, J., Kim, H., Lee, B.: Profilometry without phase unwrapping using multi-frequency and four-step phase-shift sinusoidal fringe projection. Opt. Express **17**(10), 7818–7830 (2009)
23. Kim, J., Jung, J.H., Jang, C., Lee, B.: Real-time capturing and 3D visualization method based on integral imaging. Opt. Express **21**(16), 18742–18753 (2013)
24. Schaffer, M., Grosse, M., Kowarschik, R.: High-speed pattern projection for three-dimensional shape measurement using laser speckles. Appl. Opt. **49**(18), 3622–3629 (2010)
25. Su, L., Su, X., Li, W., Xiang, L.: Application of modulation measurement profilometry to objects with surface holes. Appl. Opt. **38**(7), 1153–1158 (1999)
26. Ou, P., Li, B., Wang, Y., Zhang, S.: Flexible real-time natural 2D color and 3D shape measurement. Opt. Express **21**(14), 16736–16741 (2013)
27. Zhang, S., Van Der Weide, D., Oliver, J.: Superfast phase-shifting method for 3-D shape measurement. Opt. Express **18**(9), 9684–9689 (2010)
28. Liu, K., Wang, Y., Lau, D.L., Hao, Q., Hassebrook, L.G.: Dual-frequency pattern scheme for high-speed 3-D shape measurement. Opt. Express **18**(5), 5229–5244 (2010)
29. Xu, Y., Jia, S., Bao, Q., Chen, H., Yang, J.: Recovery of absolute height from wrapped phase maps for fringe projection profilometry. Opt. Express **22**(14), 16819–16828 (2014)
30. Park, K.S., Min, S.W., Cho, Y.: Viewpoint vector rendering for efficient elemental image generation. IEICE Trans. Inf. Syst. **E 90-D**, 233–241 (2007)
31. Kang, H.H., Lee, J.H., Kim, E.S.: Enhanced compression rate of integral images by using motion-compensated residual images in three-dimensional integral-imaging. Opt. Express **20**(5), 5440–5459 (2012)
32. Lee, J.J., Shin, D.H., Lee, B.G.: Simple correction method of distorted elemental images using surface markers on lenslet array for computational integral imaging reconstruction. Opt. Express **17**(20), 18026–18037 (2009)

Eave Tile Reconstruction and Duplication by Image-Based Modeling

Li Ji Jun Nan, Geng Guo Hua[⊠], and Jia Chao

Visualization Lab, Northwest University, Xi'an, China
emre2005@sohu.com, ghgeng@nwu.edu.cn,
guaibaojc@163.com

Abstract. We present a pipeline for eaves tiles geometry reconstruction from single binary image, which collected in their monotype album. This pipeline consists of shape from shading based spatial points reconstruction, feature-preserved point cloud smoothing for high quality models, and 3D printing techniques to obtain the duplication of eaves tiles. Compared with other reverse engineering methods, we reduce the high demand of original point cloud data in modeling, efficiently reconstruct the large number of eaves tiles, and by duplicating we reappear the lost culture relic face after thousands of years. We illustrate the performance of our pipeline on Qin Dynasty eaves tiles.

Keywords: Geometry reconstruction · Image-based modeling · L1-norm · Shape from shading · 3D print

1 Introduction

As art works with unity of form and spirit, eaves tiles are the witnesses of Chinese early multiculturalism during the period of the Qin and the Han Dynasty. With today's widely spread of digital archaeological technology, the need of digitalization for eaves tiles became more and more urgent, which specifically instantiated in more efficient data collecting, from low level to high level modeling and processing, data driven analysis and retrieval. Compared with the 2-D information represented by images of eaves tiles, the 3-D information represented by models are difficult to obtain but scientifically reflect the whole picture of eaves tile system; and accompanied with the emergence of 3D printing technology, we can easily have the mass-produced reproductions of eaves tiles. Existing approaches for modeling and retrieval are either supervised requiring manual labeling; or labeling need tags for precise definition which are difficult obtained and thus are unsuited for analyzing large collections spanning many thousands of models. In this paper we propose an automatic pipeline that starts with the collection of eaves tiles' binary image and then optimizes for modeling to best translate the input image collection. As output, the pipeline produces a cluster of eaves tile models. We demonstrate our main contributions as follows: first, in order to obtain smooth convex edge and multilayer slice of the model, we implement image blurring on binary images, after that we can do linear interpolation by the gray information between the original image and what we called negative image, which generated for ground floor of eaves tiles model; second, we repair the generated models by L1-norm

© Springer International Publishing Switzerland 2015
Y.-J. Zhang (Ed.): ICIG 2015, Part II, LNCS 9218, pp. 219–225, 2015.
DOI: 10.1007/978-3-319-21963-9_20

based point cloud smoothing, further we propose an approach of constrained texture mapping by photograph of existed eaves tiles to strengthen the realism of the reconstruction results; at last, we duplicate the models by using the advanced 3D printing techniques. At the end of our work, we show the 3D printing object of eaves tile models which can only be found in museum nowadays.

The key technique in our pipeline is the Shape From Shading methods. All SFS based modeling methods are devised in terms of partial differential equations of the first order, the unknown of the problem being the depth function, which describes the height of each point in the scene. Classical methods of resolution such as: characteristic strips method [1]; level sets method [2]; search for viscosity solutions, through finite differences schemes [3, 4] or semi-Lagrangian schemes [5], or through the use of the fast marching algorithm [6]; resolution of an equivalent optimal control problem [7–9]. The common shortage of the above methods is that the problem is not well-posed in the absence of boundary conditions [10] even though they supposed to be regular. In order to render the problem well-posed, it is usual to add some priori knowledge on the depth function or on its gradient such as a less arbitrary boundary condition applied to real images [11]. In our scenario, the boundary condition is determined by the thickness of eave tiles, these parameters can be found in archaeological report, which bring us convenient on algorithm design and also accurate modeling results.

2   Model Reconstruction

2.1   Image Pre-processing

In order to figure out the target image from the real tile ends image. We need to segmentation the image. Thresholding-based image segmentation is a well-known technique that is used in a broad range of applications. We used a median-based extension method to segment the tile ends image.

Let $x = \{x_1, x_2, \ldots, x_N\}$ be the gray levels of the pixels of a tile ends image I. We choose one threshold t yields two classes $C_1(t) = \{x : 0 \leq x \leq t\}$ and $C_2(t) = \{x : t + 1 \leq x \leq T\}$, where T is the maximum gray level. A generalized formula to partition image into tow classes can be defined as follows:

$$\sigma_B^2(t) = \arg\min_t \{\omega_1(t)V_1(t) + \omega_2(t)V_2(t)\} \tag{1}$$

Where we have

$$\begin{cases} \omega_1(t) = \sum_{x=0}^{t} h(x) \\ \omega_2(t) = \sum_{x=t+1}^{T} h(x) = 1 - \omega_1(t) \end{cases} \tag{2}$$

And

$$\begin{cases} V_1(t) = \frac{1}{\omega_1(t)} \sum_{x=0}^{t} h(x) \|(x - m_1(t))\|_\beta \\ V_2(t) = \frac{1}{\omega_2(t)} \sum_{x=t+1}^{t} h(x) \|(x - m_2(t))\|_\beta \end{cases} \tag{3}$$

Where $\| \cdot \|$ is the norm symbol. Using this formulation, we get each class using the Laplacian distribution and by using the median for obtaining optimal thresholds when class-conditional distributions are skewed or contaminated by outliers. Figure 1 shows the gray histogram and the result of segmentation and binaryzation of eaves tiles monotype.

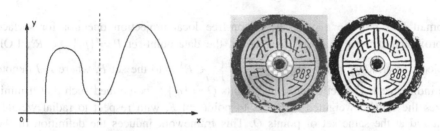

Fig. 1. Segmentation and binaryzation result of eaves tiles monotype.

2.2   SFS Methods

We use classical SFS method based on reflectance function to the first order at each point in the segmented image for modeling by following steps:

Gives the following system of equations:

$$r\left(\frac{u_{i,j} - u_{i-1,j}}{\delta}, \frac{u_{i,j} - u_{i,j-1}}{\delta}\right) = I_{i,j} \quad for(i,j) \in D \tag{4}$$

Developing to the first order in $u_{i,j}$ and denoting $u_{i,j}^{cur}$ the current estimate of height $u_{i,j}$ and $u_{i,j}^{new}$ a refinement, Eq. (4) becomes:

$$r_{i,j}^{cur} + \left(u_{i,j}^{new} - u_{i,j}^{cur}\right)\left[(\partial r/\partial p)_{i,j}^{cur} + (\partial r/\partial q)_{i,j}^{cur}\right] = I_{i,j} \quad for(i,j) \in D \tag{5}$$

Because there is no guarantee that the denominator in Eq. (5) will not vanish, we put forward the following modification:

$$u_{i,j}^{new} = u_{i,j}^{cur} - K_{i,j}^{cur}\left(r_{i,j}^{cur} - I_{i,j}\right) \quad for(i,j) \in D \tag{6}$$

In experiment we take the stopping criterion consists in fixing the value of $k_{max} = 2$, and make 5 times iteration to stop. Figure 2 shows the reconstruction result of Qin Dynasty eaves tiles by SFS method.

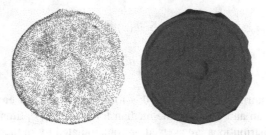

Fig. 2. Reconstruction of 9233 vertices model by SFS.

3 Point Cloud Smoothing

Lipman [12] propose a parameterization-free local projection operator for surface approximation from point-set data. Given the data point-set $P = \{p_j\}_{j \in J} \subset R^3$, LOP projects an arbitrary point-set $X^{(0)} = \left\{x_i^{(0)}\right\}_{i \in I} \in R^3$ onto the set P, where I, J denote the indices sets. The set of projected points $Q = \{q_i\}_{i \in I}$ be defined such that it minimizes the sum of weighted distances to points of P, with respect to radial weights centered at the same set of points Q. This framework induces the definition of the desired points Q as the fixed point solution of the equation:

$$Q = G(Q) \tag{7}$$

Where

$$
\begin{aligned}
G(C) &= \arg\min_{X=\{x_i\}_{i \in I}} \{E_1(X, P, C) + E_2(X, C)\} \\
E_1(X, P, C) &= \sum_{i \in I} \sum_{j \in J} \|x_i - p_j\| \theta(\|c_i - p_j\|) \\
E_2(X, C) &= \sum_{i' \in I} \lambda_{i'} \sum_{i \in I \setminus \{i'\}} \eta(\|x_{i'} - c_i\|) \theta(\|c_{i'} - c_i\|)
\end{aligned}
\tag{8}
$$

Here $\theta(r)$ is a fast-decreasing smooth weight function with compact support radius h defining the size of the influence radius, $\eta(r)$ is another decreasing function penalizing x_i which get too close to other points, and $\{\lambda_i\}_{i \in I}$ are balancing terms. If the distance between two points are very close, the above method will have a lot of overlap in k neighborhood which caused those two mid-values of L_1 defined by k neighborhood is likely to be the same one. We use Alexa's method [13] to avoid the mid-value of L_1 local clustering, by calculating the convexity-preserved interpolation in point cloud data to achieve the effect of the approximation as Fig. 3:

$$\bar{p}_i(x) = x - (n_i \circ (x - p_i))n_i \tag{9}$$

Use Eq. (8) into point cloud smoothing method, we define that:

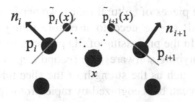

Fig. 3. Predictive value of the position and the convexity schematic diagram.

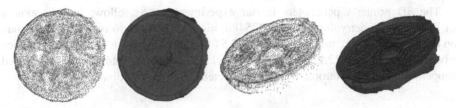

Fig. 4. Compared with Fig. 2, the model has been smoothed after convexity-preserved interpolation, 13786 vertices.

Fig. 5. The photo texture mapping result after triangulation.

$$E_1'(X, P, C) = \sum_{i \in I} \sum_{j \in J} \|x_i - \bar{p}_j(c_i)\| \circ \theta(\|c_i - p_j\|) \tag{10}$$

After the smoothing procedure above, we obtain the high quality models of eaves tiles, Fig. 4 shows our experiment result, and we take photograph as the mapping texture, result see in Fig. 5.

4   3D Printing

3D printing is any of various processes to make a three-dimensional object. In 3D printing, additive processes are used, in which successive layers of material are laid down under computer control. These objects can be of almost any shape or geometry, and are produced from a 3D model or other electronic data source. The current 3D printing technology has been widely used in the protection of cultural heritage, compared to traditional methods of rolling over, 3D printing technology can directly for nondestructive copy of 3D digital model to realize the cultural relics.

Before the printing the pieces of cultural relics, we need make sure that the surface of digital model is closed. so we need to use hole filling algorithm to repair the existence holes of model. In the processing of 3D printing, first step is make processed 3D model into rapid prototyping software. The second step is adjusting the size of the model, setting parameters such as the strength of the slice thickness and material and generated a file type which can be recognized by rapid prototyping equipment. The last is printing model by 3D printing machine and remove unnecessary support material and polishing the physical model, then, do some post-processing to complete the imitation of tile ends.

The 3D printer's parameters in our experiment are as follow: layer thickness 0.1 mm, shell binder/volume ratio 0.275486, binder/volume ratio core 0.137743, max top thickness 5.08 mm, min top thickness 2.54 mm, wall thickness 3.175 mm, distance between walls by X/Y 12.7 mm, base grid thickness 6.35 mm. Table 1 shows the bleed compensation and anisotropic scaling parameters on three coordinate axis (Fig. 6).

Table 1. The bleed compensation and anisotropic scaling parameters on coordinate axis.

Parameters	X axis	Y axis	Z axis
Bleed compensation (mm)	0.14224	0.12954	0.09906
Anisotropic scaling	1	1	1

Fig. 6. The 3D printer and printed material object in our experiment.

5   Conclusions

Due to the consideration of cultural heritage protection, typical methods of reverse engineering for eave tiles reconstruction is not allowed, the image-based modeling is a very efficient and feasible way to rebuild the entity of eave tiles. In this paper, We proposed a method of 3D reconstruction based on single image with gray scale information. Core idea is based on gray scale information of image to calculate each pixel surface normal vector and depth information to rebuild the 3D model. All in all, from the perspective of the research trends of visual development at abroad, SFS method is still a very young field, although in those years based on the research of the 3D prototype of single image reconstruction, both from visual mechanism and practical application of existing technology has obvious deficiencies, we need continue study in this field. In the future, we will improve the efficiency. Using 3D printing technology, we product the replica of tile ends in the Qin and Han Dynasty, that is big step for culture heritage protection, especially in tile ends in the Qin and Han Dynasty filed.

References

1. Farrand, A.B., Rochkind, M., Chauvet, J.M., et al.: Obtaining shape from shading information, the psychology of computer vision. Proc. Interchi Hum. Factors Comput. Syst. **8**(76), 193 (1993)
2. Kimmel, R., Bruckstein, A.M.: Tracking level sets by level sets: a method for solving the shape from shading problem. Comput. Vis. Image Underst. **62**(1), 47–58 (1995)
3. Lions, P., Rouy, E., Tourin, A.: Shape-from-shading, viscosity solutions and edges. Numer. Math. **64**(1), 323–353 (1993)
4. Faugeras, O., Prados, E.: Perspective shape from shading and viscosity solutions. In: ICCV, vol. 2, p. 826 (2003)
5. Falcone, M., Sagona, M.: An algorithm for the global solution of the shape-from-shading model. In: Del Bimbo, A. (ed.) ICIAP 1997. LNCS, vol. 1310, pp. 596–603. Springer, Heidelberg (1997)
6. Tankus, A., Sochen, N., Yeshurun, Y.: Perspective shape-from-shading by fast marching. In: IEEE Conference on Computer Vision and Pattern Recognition, vol. 1, pp. 43–49 (2004)
7. Bichsel, M., Pentland, A.P.: A simple algorithm for shape from shading. In: 1992 IEEE Computer Society Conference on Computer Vision and Pattern Recognition, Proceedings CVPR 1992, pp. 459–465. IEEE (1992)
8. Oliensis, J., Dupius, P. A global algorithm for shape from shading. In: Proceedings of the Fourth International Conference on Computer Vision, 1993, pp. 692–701. IEEE (1993)
9. Horn, B.K.P., Brooks, M.J.: The variational approach to shape from shading. Comput. Vis. Graph. Image Process. **33**(86), 174–208 (1986)
10. Durou, J.D., Piau, D.: Ambiguous shape from shading with critical points. J. Math. Imaging Vis. **12**(2), 99–108 (2000)
11. Prados, E., Faugeras, O.: Shape from shading: a well-posed problem?. In: IEEE Computer Society Conference on Computer Vision and Pattern Recognition, CVPR 2005, pp. 870–877. IEEE (2005)
12. Lipman, Y., Cohen-Or, D., Levin, D., et al.: Parameterization-free projection for geometry reconstruction. ACM Trans. Graph. **26**(3), 22(1–5) (2007)
13. Alexa, M., Adamson, A., Alexa, M., et al.: Interpolatory point set surfaces – convexity and hermite data. ACM Trans. Graph., 307–308 (2007)

Edge Directed Single Image Super Resolution Through the Learning Based Gradient Regression Estimation

Dandan Si, Yuanyuan Hu, Zongliang Gan$^{(\boxtimes)}$, Ziguan Cui, and Feng Liu

Jiangsu Provincial Key Lab of Image Processing and Image Communication, Nanjing University of Posts and Telecommunications, Nanjing 210003, China
{13010601,13010602,ganzl,cuizg,liuf}@njupt.edu.cn

Abstract. Single image super resolution (SR) aims to estimate high resolution (HR) image from the low resolution (LR) one, and estimating accuracy of HR image gradient is very important for edge directed image SR methods. In this paper, we propose a novel edge directed image SR method by learning based gradient estimation. In proposed method, the gradient of HR image is estimated by using the example based ridge regression model. Recognizing that the training samples of the given sub-set for regression should have similar local geometric structure based on clustering, we employ high frequency of LR image patches with removing the mean value to perform such clustering. Moreover, the precomputed projective matrix of the ridge regression can reduce the computational complexity further. Experimental results suggest that the proposed method can achieve better gradient estimation of HR image and competitive SR quality compared with other SR methods.

Keywords: Super resolution · Edge directed · Gradient estimation · Ridge regression

1 Introduction

Image super resolution (SR) is a fundamental and significant issue in image processing community and computer vision applications. Generally, single image SR aims to recover a high resolution (HR) image from the low resolution (LR) one [1, 2]. The SR problem is inherently ill-posed given that many different HR images can produce the same LR image when blurred and down-sampled.

Currently, approaches solving the SR problem, can be classified into four categories, i.e., interpolation based, learning based, reconstruction based and edge directed (for a good survey see in [18]). Interpolation based approaches estimate the

---

Z. Gan—This research was supported in part by the National Nature Science Foundation, P. R. China. (No. 61071166,61172118, 61071091, 61471201), Jiangsu Province Universities Natural Science Research Key Grant Project (No. 13KJA510004), Natural Science Foundation of Jiangsu Province (BK20130867), the Six Kinds Peak Talents Plan Project of Jiangsu Province (2014-DZXX-008), and the "1311" Talent Plan of NUPT.

Y.-J. Zhang (Ed.): ICIG 2015, Part II, LNCS 9218, pp. 226–239, 2015.
DOI: 10.1007/978-3-319-21963-9_21

high-resolution image by interpolating the unknown pixels based on the surrounding known LR pixels, such as MSI [3] and SAI [4]. The underlying assumption of learning based approaches [5–9] is that there exists an inherent relationship between LR and HR image patch pairs. Then the relationship is learned and applied to a new LR image to recover its HR version. In addition, reconstruction based approaches highlight a reconstruction constraint and back-projection [10] is a classical reconstruction based one. Due to the jaggy or ringing artifacts of this method, many improvements have been made with different priors and regularization terms imposed [11–17]. The last category is about edge directed approaches. Edge directed approaches refer to the methods based on the edge models, where effective image edge priors [11–15] are enforced as a gradient domain constraint to estimate the target HR image, such as the edge smooth prior [14] or the gradient profile prior [11]. Thanks to the new algorithm, many scholars pay much attention to improve it. Adaptive gradient magnitude self-interpolation method GMSI [18] and cross-resolution sharpness preserving model DFSR [19] appear in succession.

Drawing a conclusion from previous work, instead of making use of gradient relationship between LR and HR image patch pairs, most edge directed methods estimate HR gradients of images according to edge pixels position or gradient magnitude for whole image. Motivated by it, we propose a novel edge directed image SR method by learning based gradient estimation. In particular, the gradient of HR image is estimated through using the example based ridge regression model. The main step of our method is about gradient regression estimation and reconstruction. The step about gradient regression estimation can further be divided into sample training and gradient estimation specifically. Recognizing that the training samples of the given sub-set for regression should have similar local geometric structure based on clustering, we employ high frequency of LR image patches with removing the mean value to perform such clustering. Moreover, the precomputed projective matrix of the ridge regression can reduce the computational complexity greatly. In reconstruction, the estimated gradient is regarded as a gradient constraint to guarantee that the result HR image preserves sharpness and refrains from artifacts such as jaggy and blurring. Experimental results suggest that the proposed method can achieve better gradient estimation of HR image and competitive SR quality compared with other SR methods. We will describe the main step of our method in detail in following section.

2 Edge Directed Single Image Super Resolution

In conventional SR problem [10–12], one LR image is modeled as the Gaussian blurred and down sampled one of its HR version. Namely, given a HR image I_h, a LR one I_l is generated by

$$I_l = (I_h * G) \downarrow_s \tag{1}$$

where $*$ is a convolution operator, $\downarrow$ is a down-sampling operation, s is a scaling factor, G is a blur kernel which is commonly approximated as a Gaussian function. The edge directed single image super resolution methods [11, 18] usually model the SR problem as Eq. 2, that is, given the LR image I_l and the estimated HR gradient field ∇I_h^T, I_h can be reconstructed by minimizing the following energy function:

$$I_h^* = \arg \min_{I_h} E\left(I_h | I_l, \nabla I_h^T\right) = E_i(I_h | I_l) + \beta E_g(\nabla I_h | \nabla I_h^T) \tag{2}$$

where $E_i(I_h | I_l)$ is the reconstruction constraint in image domain, $E_g(\nabla I_h | \nabla I_h^T)$ is the gradient constraint in gradient domain, and parameter β is a weighting constant to balance these two constraints as a trade-off. In experiments, a larger β imposes more importance on the gradient domain, which contributes to producing sharp edges with little artifacts. Conversely, a smaller β places much importance on the image domain, resulting in better image color and contrast, yet with ringing or jaggy artifacts along edges. The reconstruction constraint measures the difference between the LR image I_l and the smoothed and down-sampled version of the HR image I_h, i.e.

$$E_i(I_h | I_l) = |(I_h * G) \downarrow_s - I_l|^2 \tag{3}$$

The gradient constraint requires that the gradient ∇I_h of the recovered HR image should be close to the estimated gradient ∇I_h^T as Eq. 4. This paper mainly focuses on the estimation of ∇I_h^T, which will be presented in Sect. 3.1.

$$E_g\left(\nabla I_h | \nabla I_h^T\right) = |\nabla I_h - \nabla I_h^T|^2 \tag{4}$$

3   Proposed Edge Directed Super Resolution Method

One motivation of our work is to estimate HR gradient of bicubic interpolated image patch with HR gradient of samples in the same cluster, based on the fact that image patches belonging to one cluster have similar local geometric structure. The main flow of our method is shown in Fig. 1, which includes gradient regression estimation and reconstruction.

Gradient regression estimation includes sample training and gradient estimation. First, in sample training (see Sect. 3.2), to generate meaningful clusters, we perform the clustering for image patches with removing their mean value. They are first classified into s^2 classes according to the central pixel position, where s is a scaling factor. Then K-means method is used to cluster patches into a lot of clusters for each class. After that, sparse filtering matrix W and sparse feature F is calculated for each cluster. Second, in gradient estimation, for each patch of high frequency in bicubic interpolated image, its sparse feature is calculated with sparse filtering matrix W. Then ridge regression method [7] is used to solve the coefficients of its sparse feature to all samples feature in the same cluster. And HR gradient of the patch is estimated with the coefficients and HR gradient of samples. In construction, the estimated gradient is regarded as the gradient domain constraint in the edge directed SR model as Eq. 2.

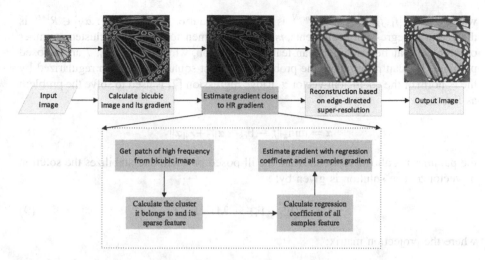

Fig. 1. Overview of our proposed method. First, bicubic interpolated image and its gradient is calculated. Second, HR gradient is estimated with regression coefficients and HR gradient of all samples. Last, the output image is reconstructed based on the edge directed SR model in Eq. 2 with the bicubic interpolated image as an initial.

3.1   Gradient Regression Estimation of Super Resolution Image

Based on the fact that gradients of similar samples in one cluster are alike, we can estimate gradient of a patch by HR gradient of samples in the same cluster with their feature regression coefficients. Given a LR image I_l, we upsample it to obtain bicubic interpolated one I_{bic}. For patches whose variance is larger than a threshold TH_1 in I_{bic}, we perform our gradient estimation method to reduce computational complexity. And for the other patches, we use gradient of bicubic images instead. For each cropped image patch x with size $n \times n$ in I_{bic}, $\hat{x}$ is the high-frequency component as x minus its mean value u. Then we find the cluster that $\hat{x}$ belongs to by the standard of minimum Euclidean distance as Eq. 5 and calculate its sparse feature as Eq. 6

$$k^* = \arg \min {}_k \|\hat{x} - C_{ck}\|_2^2, \ k = 1...K \tag{5}$$

$$f = W_{ck^*} * \hat{x} \tag{6}$$

where C_{ck} is cluster center of one cluster labeled by c and k (c and k is the label of cluster that will be introduced in Sect. 3.2), W_{ck^*} is sparse filtering matrix of the cluster that $\hat{x}$ belongs to, f is feature of $\hat{x}$. Supposing there are N exemplar patches belonging to the cluster, then regression coefficients of feature f with all exemplar features can be formulated as:

$$\alpha = \min_\alpha \|f - F_{ck^*} \cdot \alpha\|_2^2. \tag{7}$$

where $F_{ck^*} = [f_1, f_2, \ldots, f_N] \in R^{m*N}$ is matrix of feature, $\alpha = [\alpha_1, \alpha_2, \ldots \alpha_N] \in R^{1*N}$ is the vector of regression coefficients, m is feature dimension. For most clusters, number of exemplar patches is larger than feature dimension, which makes Eq. 7 an ill-posed problem. We can reformulate the problem as a least squares regression regularized by the l_2-norm of the coefficient vector α. Ridge regression [7] is used to solve the problem as Eq. 8:

$$\alpha = \min_\alpha \|f - F_{ck^*} \cdot \alpha\|_2^2 + \lambda\|\alpha\|_2 \tag{8}$$

the parameter λ allows us to alleviate the ill-posed problem and stabilizes the solution of vector α. The solution is given by:

$$\alpha = (F_{ck^*}^T \cdot F_{ck^*} + \lambda I)^{-1} F_{ck^*}^T f \tag{9}$$

where the projection matrix:

$$T = (F_{ck^*}^T \cdot F_{ck^*} + \lambda I)^{-1} F_{ck^*}^T \tag{10}$$

then gradient can be estimated using the same coefficients on HR gradient of samples by (11) and (12)

$$dx = DX_{ck^*} \cdot \alpha = \sum_{j=1}^{N} (dx)_j \alpha_j \tag{11}$$

$$dy = DY_{ck^*} \cdot \alpha = \sum_{j=1}^{N} (dy)_j \alpha_j \tag{12}$$

where dx and dy is respectively estimated gradient in horizontal and vertical direction for the patch x, DX_{ck^*} and DY_{ck^*} is respectively HR gradient matrix of all samples in these two directions, $(dx)_j$ and $(dy)_j$ is gradient of the j sample, which means that the estimated gradient is linear weighted sum of HR gradients of samples in the same cluster. For overlapped patches, two choices are alternative to estimate their gradients. First, only central pixel gradient is estimated. Second, we estimate gradient of each patch independently. Then to obtain the estimated image gradient, we average each pixel as it appears in the different patches. The second way yields better results so that we adopt it in our experiments. In implementation, in order to reduce the computational load, the projection matrix T is calculated offline, namely that we only need to multiply the precomputed projection matrix T with the sparse feature f.

3.2 Sample Training

(1) Clustering of Sample Sets. Since natural images are abundant and easily acquired, we can assume that there are sufficient exemplar patches available for each cluster. Same with the gradient estimation step, only meaningful image patches whose variance is greater than TH_1 are selected.

Firstly, as shown in Fig. 2, for a scaling factor 3, only the pixels on position 1 in I_{bic} are from LR image directly. While other pixels on positions 2–9 are interpolated by the surrounding pixels on position 1. Therefore overlapped patches in I_{bic} can be classified into 9 classes centered by the 9 kinds of pixels. From each I_h and the corresponding I_{bic}, a large set of patches $\hat{P}_c(c = 1, 2, \ldots, 9)$ of I_{bic} and corresponding HR gradient patches $\partial_x I_h$, $\partial_y I_h$ and can be cropped. For a patch P_c in I_{bic}, we compute its mean value as μ and extract the feature $\hat{P}_c$ as the intensity P_c minus μ. Denote the gradient field $\nabla I_h = (\partial_x I_h, \partial_y I_h)$, the image I_h is convolved respectively by discrete gradient operator $k_1 = [-(1/2), 0, (1/2)]$ and $k_2 = k_1^T$ to obtain $\partial_x I_h$ and $\partial_y I_h$. The similarity of two patches p_i and p_j, is defined as $\delta = \frac{\|p_i - p_j\|_1}{pixelnum}$. In order to avoid redundancy in one class, patches whose similarity is smaller than a threshold TH_2 are excluded.

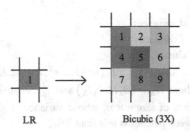

LR   Bicubic (3X)

Fig. 2. Patches are classified into 9 classes by central pixel position for a scaling factor 3

Secondly, we adopt the K-means method to partition $\hat{P}_c$ into K clusters $\{\hat{P}_{c1}, \hat{P}_{c2}, \ldots, \hat{P}_{cK}\}$ and denote by C_{ck} the center of $\hat{P}_{ck}$. For given image patch, the most suitable cluster can be selected to estimate its HR gradient. Here K is usually set as integer power of 2 so that classification can be implemented with binary tree to improve efficiency.

(2) Feature of Image Patches. Sparse filtering [20] is selected as the method of extracting feature, which is a simple but efficient algorithm with just one parameter. And the parameter presents the number of feature to learn. In order to learn the features of $\hat{P}_c$, we first note $\hat{P}_c$ as the data x. Supposing there are l LR exemplar patches belonging to the same cluster, feature of one sample is defined as soft-absolute function as Eq. 13, the sparse filtering objective function is as Eq. 14

$$F_j^{(i)} = \sqrt{\varepsilon + (W_j^T x^{(i)})^2} \approx |W_j^T x| \tag{13}$$

$$\min \sum_{i=1}^{l} \left\| \hat{F}^{(i)} \right\|_1 = \sum_{i=1}^{l} \left\| \frac{\tilde{F}^i}{\left\| \tilde{F}^i \right\|_2} \right\|_1 \tag{14}$$

where $F \in R^{m*l}$ is feature matrix and $W \in R^{m*n^2}$ is sparse filtering matrix. Each row of F is a feature and each column is a sample, namely, each entry $F_j^{(i)}$ is the activity of feature j on sample i. For a cluster labeled by c and k, $\hat{P}_{ck}$ means LR patches, DX_{ck} is horizontal HR gradient and DY_{ck} represents vertical HR gradient. Meanwhile cluster centered noted as C_{ck}, W_{ck} and F_{ck} mean sparse filtering matrix and sparse feature matrix separately. Our training process is summarized in Algorithm 1 (Table 1).

Table 1. Main flow of sample training.

Algorithm 1. Sample training
Input: the HR images $I_h^i (i = 1, \dots T)$

Initialize: s (scaling factor)
       n (patch size)
     TH_1 (threshold of variance)
     TH_2 (threshold of similarity)
     K (number of cluster)

Output: $\hat{P}_{ck}$、DX_{ck}、DY_{ck}、C_{ck}、W_{ck}、$F_{ck}(c = 1, \dots s^2, k = 1, \dots K)$
1. Calculate HR image gradient $\nabla I_h = (\partial_x I_h, \partial_y I_h)$ and I_{bic}^i as scaling factor is s.
2. Extract overlapped patches of size $n \times n$, whose variance is greater than TH_1. And we request the similarity ε between patches is less than TH_2.
3. Classify the sample sets into $s^2 \times K$ clusters according to central pixel position and K-means method.
4. Calculate sparse filtering matrix W and sparse feature F for each cluster.

3.3 Reconstruction of Super Resolution Image

The estimated ∇I_h^T above is regarded as the gradient constraint in edge directed SR model as Eq. 2. The objective energy function Eq. 2 is a quadratic function with respect to I_h, therefore it is convex and the global minimum can be obtained by the standard gradient descent by solving the gradient flow equation. In our implementation, we use the following iterative schemes to optimize it:

$$
I_h^{t+1} = I_h^t - \tau \cdot \frac{\partial E\left(I_h | I_l, \nabla I_h^T\right)}{\partial I_h}
$$

$$
= I_h^t - \tau \cdot \left[((I_h * G) \downarrow_s - I_l) \uparrow_s * G - \beta (\mathrm{div}(\nabla I_h) - \mathrm{div}(\nabla I_h^T)) \right] \quad (15)
$$

where $\mathrm{div}(\nabla \cdot) = \frac{\partial^2}{\partial x^2} + \frac{\partial^2}{\partial y^2}$ is the Laplacian operator, $\mathrm{div}(\nabla I_h) = \frac{\partial(\partial_x I_h)}{\partial x} + \frac{\partial(\partial_y I_h)}{\partial x}$. It can be carried out using standard finite difference scheme and τ is the step size.

4 Experiments

4.1 Settings

We select the Berkeley Segmentation Datasets [21] as our training set and test our method on a variety of natural images with rich edges. And 6 test examples are presented in Fig. 3. Note that, for color images, we transform them from RGB color space to YUV space. As human vision is more sensitive to luminance information, we only apply the proposed edge directed method on luminance channel (Y) and up-sample chrominance channels (UV) by bicubic interpolation. Finally, three channels are transformed into RGB as the final SR result. For a scaling factor 3, the patch size n is set as 11.

| Zebra | Lady | Horse | Plane | Lena | Butterfly |

Fig. 3. Six test example images (Color figure online).

Number of Clusters K: Because of memory limitation (8 GB) of the computer, we randomly collected 10^5 patches for 9 classes from the Berkeley Segmentation Datasets. The number of clusters is a trade-off between result quality and training computational complexity. In experiments, we compare super resolution results generated by 128 and 512 clusters. With more clusters, the most suitable cluster can be selected to estimate HR gradient for the given patch, so that the estimated gradient is close to HR gradient meanwhile high-frequency regions of the reconstructed image are better with less jaggy artifacts along edge. In other experiments, K is set as 512.

Parameters: The standard variance of Gaussian blur kernel is set as 1.4 for a scaling factor 3. We set TH_1 and TH_2 as 10 and 0.2 separately and feature dimension m as 100 in sample training. In gradient estimation step, the results on different λ are stable and we set it as 50 in our experiments. In construction, in terms of the objective indicator and visual effect, β and τ is respectively set as 0.1 and 1.5 with number of iterations set as 30.

4.2 Results

MSE between estimated gradient and HR gradient is calculated to evaluate their similarity and the fidelity of estimated gradient. We compare gradient MSE of results generated by 128 and 512 clusters. The gradient MSE results of bicubic, GMSI [18] and our method are listed in Table 2 and part images of estimated gradient maps are shown in Fig. 4. From Table 2, our error of estimated gradient is less than that of GMSI. With more clusters, the MSE are less. From Fig. 4, we can see the gradient of

234 D. Si et al.

Table 2. MSE of gradient compared to GMSI on six examples.

Test images	MSE			
	Bicubic	GMSI [18]	Our method	
			128 clusters	512 clusters
Zebra	10.90	12.34	8.09	**7.94**
Lady	8.22	8.98	6.18	**6.01**
Horse	6.96	7.68	5.58	**5.12**
Plane	3.49	4.09	2.75	**2.44**
Lena	5.80	6.22	4.59	**4.51**
Butterfly	15.44	18.22	11.46	**10.99**
Mean value	8.47	9.59	6.44	**6.17**

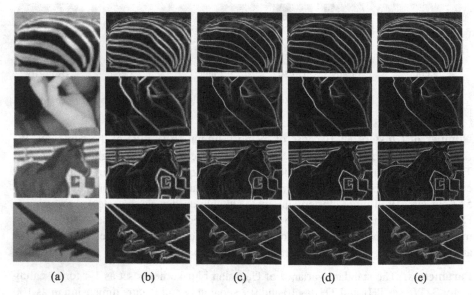

(a)   (b)   (c)   (d)   (e)

Fig. 4. Comparisons of estimated gradient with GMSI [18] and bicubic. (a) Part of bicubic interpolated image. (b) The gradient field of images in (a) (MSE: 8.47). (c) Transformed gradient of GMSI [18] (MSE: 9.59). (d) Estimated gradient of our method (MSE: 6.17). (e) Ground truth gradient.

our method is sharper and much closer to the HR gradient compared to GMSI, because we estimate patch gradient with HR gradient of similar samples in the same cluster. Figure 9 shows one example results generated by 128 and 512 clusters with all the other same settings. As shown, edges of the reconstructed image are better with less jaggy artifacts along edge with more clusters.

Moreover, the PSNR and SSIM [22] results are just calculated on Y channel, in order to measure the SR results qualitatively, which are separately listed in Tables 3 and 4. We compared our algorithm with IBP [10], GMSI [18], and DFSR [19]. Figures 6 and 7 present two comparisons of our method with GMSI and DFSR in gradient

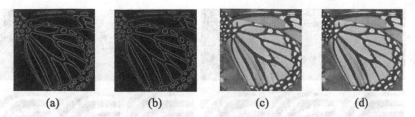

Fig. 5. Results using different cluster number. (a) and (c) are estimated gradient and results generated by 128 clusters. (b) and (d) are generated by 512 clusters. (a) GMSE: 11.46. (b) GMSE: 10.98. (c) PSNR: 25.83 dB, SSIM: 0.880. (d) PSNR: 26.10 dB, SSIM: 0.889.

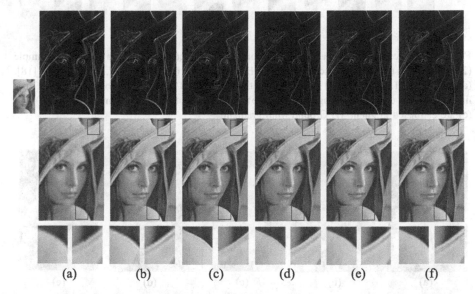

Fig. 6. Super resolution comparison (3×) of other edge directed methods. (a) Bicubic upsample (31.39 dB/0.870). (b) Back-projection (33.09 dB/0.899) [10]. (c) GSMI (33.07 dB/0.892) [18]. (d) DFSR (32.74 dB/0.893) [19]. (e) Our method (33.56 dB/0.903). (f) Ground truth. The first line is gradient domain. Among them, (a), (b) and (d) is gradient of the image result. (c) and (e) are estimated gradient. (f) Ground truth gradient.

domain. As shown in these two figures, images are blurred by bicubic interpolation and jagged along edges by back-projection. GMSI method estimates a much sharper gradient domain, leading to edges of the reconstructed image sharper yet unnatural and artificial (refer to close-ups). The main reason is that the goal of GMSI is to obtain gradient domain which is sharper but not close to HR Gradient. Figures 8 and 9 present two examples with the two methods in image domain. As shown, the results of DFSR are very sharp, with rare ringing and blurring. However, unreal parts begin to appear and small scale edges are not well recovered. For example, eye area of Lady face seems to be very unreal and textures on Butterfly wing are less obvious. Compared to DFSR, our method recovers details better, especially on salient edges.

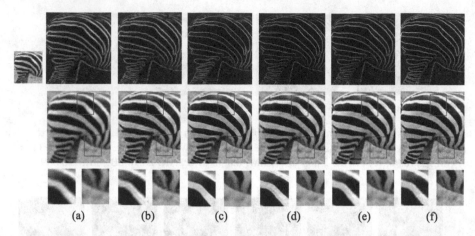

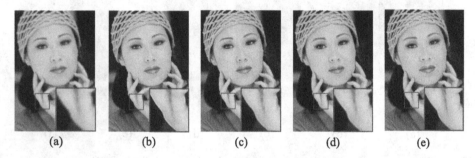

Fig. 7. Super resolution comparison (3×) of other edge directed methods. (a) Bicubic upsample (25.630/0.767). (b) Back-projection (27.67 dB/0.837) [10]. (c) GSMI: (27.37 dB/0.820) [18]. (d) DFSR: (27.12 dB/0.827) [19]. (e) Our method (28.46 dB/0.845). (f) Ground truth. The first line is gradient domain. Among them, (a), (b) and (d) is gradient of the image result. (c) and (e) are estimated gradient. (f) Ground truth gradient.

Fig. 8. Super resolution comparison (3×) of other edge directed methods. (a) Bicubic upsample (28.64 dB/0.8857). (b) GMSI (30.53 dB/0.913) [18]. (c) DFSR (30.44 dB/0.913) [19]. (d) Our method (31.29 dB /0.923). (e) Ground truth.

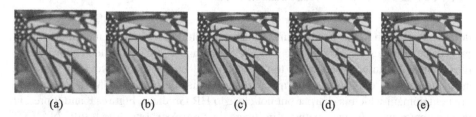

Fig. 9. Super resolution comparison (3×) of other edge directed methods. (a) Bicubic upsample (23.27 dB/0.804). (b) GMSI (24.60 dB/0.859) [18]. (c) DFSR (25.70 dB/0.882) [19]. (d) Our method (26.10 dB/0.889). (e) Ground truth.

Table 3. PSNR measurement on six examples.

Test images (3×)	IBP [10]	GMSI [18]	DFSR [19]	Our method	
				128 clusters	512clusters
Zebra	27.67	27.37	27.12	28.32	**28.46**
Lady	30.30	30.53	30.44	31.08	**31.29**
Horse	30.84	31.03	30.71	31.88	**32.77**
Plane	37.56	38.26	**39.43**	38.67	39.05
Lena	33.09	33.07	32.74	33.45	**33.56**
Butterfly	24.88	24.60	25.70	25.83	**26.10**
Mean value	30.72	30.81	31.02	31.54	**31.87**

Note: IBP, GMSI and our method is implemented on same parameters: $\tau = 1.5$, $\beta = 0.1$ and iterations = 30. Parameter of DFSR is the same with its paper: $\tau = 0.1$, $\beta = 0.2$ and iterations = 30 (Bold: best, underline: second best).

Table 4. SSIM measurement on six examples.

Test images (3×)	IBP [10]	GMSI [18]	DFSR [19]	Our method	
				128 clusters	512 clusters
Zebra	0.837	0.820	0.827	0.844	**0.845**
Lady	0.911	0.913	0.913	0.921	0.923
Horse	0.857	0.852	0.854	0.864	**0.871**
Plane	0.975	0.977	**0.981**	0.979	0.980
Lena	0.899	0.892	0.893	0.902	**0.903**
Butterfly	0.840	0.859	0.882	0.880	**0.889**
Mean value	0.887	0.886	0.892	0.898	**0.902**

4.3 Complexity

In implementation, the projection matrix T in gradient regression estimation step is precomputed offline, meaning that we only need to multiply the precomputed projection matrix T with the sparse feature f. Therefore, the computation time is only linear multiplication and linear addition for a patch. The total computation complexity is linearly dependent on the number of high frequency patches in the bicubic interpolated image (Fig. 5).

5 Conclusion

In this paper, a novel edge directed image SR method by learning based gradient estimation has been presented. In proposed method, the gradient of HR image is estimated by using the example based ridge regression model. Considering the fact that the training samples of the given sub-set for regression should have similar local geometric structure based on clustering, we employed bicubic interpolated image patches with removing the mean value to perform clustering. Moreover, the precomputed projective matrix of the ridge regression reduced the computational complexity further. In reconstruction, the estimated gradient was regarded as the gradient constraint to guarantee that the result HR image preserves sharpness and refrains from artifacts. Experimental results showed that estimated gradient of our proposed method is much close to the ground truth and recovered image can preserve sharper edge compared with other SR methods.

References

1. Elad, M., Feuer, A.: Super-resolution reconstruction of image sequences. IEEE Trans. Pattern Anal. Mach. Intell. **21**(9), 817–834 (1999)
2. Farsiu, S., Robinson, D., Elad, M., Milanfar, P.: Fast and robust multiframe super resolution. IEEE Trans. Image Process. **13**(10), 1327–1344 (2004)
3. Guo, K., Yang, X., Zha, H., Lin, W., Yu, S.: Multiscale semilocal interpolation with antialiasing. IEEE Trans. Image Process. **21**(2), 615–625 (2012)
4. Yang, B., Gao, Z., Zhang, X., et al.: Principal components analysis based edge-directed image interpolation. In: IEEE International Conference on Multimedia and Expo, pp. 580–585 (2012)
5. Freeman, W.T., Jones, T.R., Pasztor, E.C.: Example-based super-resolution. J. IEEE Comput. Graph. Appl. **22**, 56–65 (2002)
6. Bevilacqua, M., Roumy, A., Guillemot, C., Alberi Morel, M.-L.: Low-complexity single-image super-resolution based on nonnegative neighbor embedding. In: BMVC (2012)
7. Timofte, R., De Smet, V., Van Gool, L.J.: Anchored neighborhood regression for fast example-based super-resolution. In: ICCV, pp. 1920–1927 (2013)
8. Yang, J., Wright, J., Ma, Y., Huang, T.: Image super-resolution as sparse representation of raw image patches. In: Proceedings of IEEE Conference on Computer Vision Pattern Recognition, pp. 1–8 (2008)
9. Freedman, G., Fattal, R.: Image and video upscaling from local self-examples. ACM Trans. Graph. **28**(3), 1–10 (2010)
10. Irani, M., Peleg, S.: Motion analysis for image enhancement: Resolution, occlusion and transparency. J. Vis. Commun. Image Represent. **4**(4), 324–335 (1993)
11. Sun, J., Xu, Z., Shum, H.-Y.: Gradient profile prior and its application in image super-resolution and enhancement. IEEE Trans. Image Process. **20**(6), 1529–1542 (2011)
12. Hang, H., Zhang, Y., Li, H., Huang, T.S.: Generative bayesian image super resolution with natural image prior. IEEE Trans. on Image Process. **21**, 4054–4067 (2012)
13. Krishnan, D., Fergus, R.: Fast image deconvolution using hyper-Laplacian priors. In: Proceedings of Advances in Neural Information Processing System, pp. 1033–1041 (2009)
14. Dai, S., Han, M., Xu, W., Wu, Y., Gong, Y., Katsaggelos, A.K.: A soft edge smoothness prior for color image super-resolution. IEEE Trans. Image Process. **18**(5), 969–981 (2009)
15. Fattal, R.: Image upsampling via imposed edge statistics. J. ACM Trans. Graph. **26**(3), 95–102 (2007)
16. Sun, J., Zhu, J., Tappen, M.: Context-constrained hallucination for image super-resolution. In: Proceedings of IEEE Conference on Computer Vision Pattern Recognition, pp. 231–238 (2010)
17. Kim, K.I., Kwon, Y.: Single-image super-resolution using sparse regression and natural image prior.J. IEEE Trans. Pattern Anal. Mach. Intell. **23**(6), 1127–1133 (2010)
18. Wang, L., Xiang, S., Meng, G.: Edge-directed single-image super resolution via adaptive gradient magnitude self-interpolation. IEEE Trans. Circ. Syst. Video Technol. **23**(8), 1289–1299 (2013)

19. Wang, L., Wu, H.-Y., Pan, C.: Fast image up-sampling via the displacement field. IEEE Trans. Image Process. (TIP) **23**, 5123–5135 (2014)
20. Ngiam, J., Koh, P., Chen, Z., Bhaskar, S., Ng, A.Y.: Sparse filtering. In: NIPS (2011)
21. Martin, D., Fowlkes, C., Tal, D., Malik, J.: A database of human segmented natural images and its application to evaluating segmentation algorithms and measuring ecological statistics. In: ICCV, vol. 2, pp. 416–423 (2001)
22. Wang, Z., Bovik, A.C., Sheikh, H.R., Simoncelli, E.P.: Image quality assessment. From error measurement to structural similarity. IEEE Trans. Image Process. **13**(4), 600–612 (2004)

Evacuation Simulation Incorporating Safety Signs and Information Sharing

Yu Niu, Hongyu Yang, Jianbo Fu, Xiaodong Che, Bin Shui,
and Yanci Zhang[✉]

Sichuan University, Sichuan, China
yczhang@scu.edu.cn

Abstract. In this paper, we combine local and global technology to simulate the behaviors of crowd. In the local, an improved weighting method to calculate preferred velocity is proposed, which reflects the current motion trend of a pedestrian. In the global, a decision tree is implemented to model the dynamic decision-making process, which plays an important role in choosing between several paths to destination. At the same time, we consider the influence of safety signs and information sharing on the behavior of pedestrians and give good security analysis to evacuation planning.

Keywords: Crowd simulation · Evacuation planning · Information sharing · Safety signs

1 Introduction

Today, as we face more and more emergencies, effective evacuation has become much important. Although people try to move faster than normal, the radical competition will slow down the evacuation process in most case. In normal environment, pedestrians have plenty time to figure out the best chooses with least consumption. They will behave some intelligent attributes, such as, they can help each other or maximize the use of resources. However, the intelligence may disappear as the security of pedestrians is threatened by the emergency situations. Due to short time and intense pressure, escape in the limited space will cause fierce competition between evacuees. How to make a good evacuation planning through the study of crowd behavior is still an open question.

Emergency simulation is a good choice, which can be used to design and evaluate evacuation plans, and train relevant personnel to gain valuable experience. It overcomes the shortness of exposing pedestrians in danger in evacuation practice which may not be treated seriously as the real emergency. By using virtual agents to simulate the behavior of pedestrians, many computational model [6,13,24] are built to model the autonomous agent that move and interact with each other and the environment. A key novelty of these models is the ability to represent the dynamic decision-making functions, which enable individuals to make realistic behavioral decisions.

Y.-J. Zhang (Ed.): ICIG 2015, Part II, LNCS 9218, pp. 240–251, 2015.
DOI: 10.1007/978-3-319-21963-9_22

Many factors should be considered in emergency evacuation planning, such as signs and information sharing. Safety signs will give effective exit instruction to evacuees. Effective sharing exports information, on the one hand, can help people find the way to export, on the other hand, help ease the pressure of competition and promote the cooperation between each other. For the case of panic, people will follow the general trend, that is, to do what other people do or follow the instruction of signs, which is easy to get stuck at a bottleneck during evacuation especially at the door. Therefore, to study the effect of safety signs and information sharing becomes very important for evacuation planning.

The rest of this article is organized as follows. Section 2 reviews the related work. Section 3 provides an overview of our model. In Sect. 4, the local and global technology is discussed in detail. Section 5 is the dynamic decision-making process include both local behavior motivation and global behavior controlling, where the global controlling is realized through a behavior tree. Experimental Results and Discussions is presented in Sect. 6 and finally, concludes in Sect. 7.

2   Related Work

An extensive studies arise recently dealing with different emergencies [12–14, 21]. [22] presents an agent-based travel demand model system for hurricane evacuation simulation, which is capable of generating comprehensive household activity-travel plans. [18] presents the method of crowd evacuation simulation for bioterrorism in micro-spatial environments using the basic theory of Virtual Geographic Environments (VGE), combined with pathogen diffusion and crowd simulation modeling techniques.

A good simulation model should deal with both the collision avoidance problem and global path planning and navigation. The velocity-based model [2] derived from robotics tries to find a collision-free velocities by solving a geometric optimization problem. A planning framework that satisfied multiple spatial constraints imposed on the path is presented in [11]. [20] presents a prototype of a computer simulation system that uses agent-based model to simulate an emergency environment with crowd evacuation and provides for testing of multiple disaster scenarios at virtually no cost.

The study about evacuation planning [1,7,23] and disaster response [5] exists. The instruction study as well as the cooperative work in evacuation is necessary. A tool for guiding a group of people out of a public building when they are faced with dangerous situations that need immediate evacuation is designed in [8]. A study about human responses to the direction information like signs, moving crowd and memorized information when choosing exit routes is proposed [3]. To establish new building design guidelines, [15] aims to enhance safety through improved design of the built environment by investigating issues associated with emergencies and evacuations. Reference [9] use the Asymmetry Information Environment (AIE) to study cooperative works. Incorporating with asymmetric information, agents can make realistic behavioral decisions which help to simulate the dynamic of evacuation inequality.

The control strategy applied to the designed models is important in crowd simulation. Evacuees are modeled as an agent complying with a series of behavior rules and decision-making methods [1]. An adaptive affective social decision-making model is proposed in [16]. Different decision-making methods directly influence the intelligence and reality of simulation results. BDI is a model to represent both the human decision-making and decision-planning functions in a unified framework [10,17].

3   Overview

In the process of simulation, local collision avoidance as well as global path planning and navigation are two indispensable technologies. Collision avoidance consider the interaction between agents and obstacles and the classical method is the *Optimal Reciprocal Collision Avoidance (ORCA)* method [19]. Path planning and navigation are used to provide goal-seeking capability and to model individual intention. Global path planning is used to reach the destination with the preferred velocity which is managed by collision avoidance to keep the reality of simulation.

Dynamic decision-making includes two parts, which are corresponding to the technologies discussed above. A pedestrian's moving motivation is decided through the local interaction, which is not only for the sake of avoiding collision but also important to its local navigation. Its local behavior motivation will generate the behavior driven, which decides a pedestrian's current preferred velocity. The influence of safety signs and information sharing are important in this process. The decision tree will determine the agents' decision in current situation, which will generate their willingness of moving towards the destination. It will decide the global path it chooses to move.

4   Local and Global Technology

In local navigation, collision avoidance technique is used to deal with interactions between agents and obstacles, which can effectively avoid upcoming collision. In this paper, the collision avoidance problem is solved by applying the *Optimal Reciprocal Collision Avoidance (ORCA)* method presented in [19]. As shown in (1).

$$ORCA^\tau_{A|B} = \{v|(v - (v_A^{opt} + \frac{1}{2}u)) \cdot n \geq 0\} \tag{1}$$

Global path planning mainly solves the problem about how to reach the destinations with the preferred velocity. Based on the reality of collision avoidance between the moving agents, v^{CA} which means the velocity meets the requirement of collision avoidance is generated by filtering v^{pre} with the process of ORCA in (2). The detail of solving v^{pre} is in Sect. 5.1

$$P_{tar} = P_{cur} + v^{CA} * \Delta T \tag{2}$$

P_{tar} denotes the target position and P_{cur} denotes the current position.

5   Dynamic Decision-Making

Dynamic decision-making includes two parts, which are corresponding to the technologies discussed above. A pedestrian's moving motivation is decided through the local interaction, which is not only for the sake of avoiding collision but also important to its local navigation. The agent's willingness of moving towards the destination is generated through a decision tree which decides the global path it chooses.

5.1   Local Behavior Motivation

A pedestrian's moving motivation is its preferred velocity, which control its current moving direction and speed [4]. As shown in (3).

$$v_i^p = v_i^p \cdot e_i^p \tag{3}$$

The Speed of Preferred Velocity: The magnitude of the preferred velocity v_i^p is calculated in two kinds of pedestrians. The acquainted pedestrians who know the way to exit will move at maximum speed v_{max}, while the novice pedestrians who always follow others will move at average speed of its neighbors. Although this strategy can simplify calculation to a certain extent, it is not very reasonable, because of the ignorance of many factors.

Adjust the Speed: For the member in the acquainted group, they have different level of willingness to help others. If they help the others, they couldn't move at the maximum speed v_{max}. As a result, their preferred speed will be reduced correspondingly. In emergency, people move or try to move considerably faster than normal. The moving speed not only depends on its physical condition but also on psychological effect aroused by the hazards. However, members in the novice group will be more panic than those in the acquainted group.

Inspired by these situations, we unify the speed of the acquainted group and the novice group as follows (4):

$$v_i^p = \beta_i \cdot v_{max} + (1 - \beta_i) \cdot v_{mean} \tag{4}$$

where β_i, shown in (5) is used to control the weight of v_{max} and v_{mean}.

$$\beta_i = \exp -\frac{A + \rho_i^{will}}{B - \rho_i^{priori}} \tag{5}$$

We use parameters ρ_i^{priori} and ρ_i^{will} to denote its priori knowledge, and its willingness to help others respectively. Constants A and B are used to adjust the contributions of ρ_i^{will} and ρ_i^{priori}.

The Direction of Preferred Velocity: The moving direction e_i^p is influenced by different degree of extrinsic and intrinsic factors [4]. Illustrated in (6).

$$e_i^p = \alpha_i \cdot e_i^E + (1 - \alpha_i) \cdot e_i^I \qquad (6)$$

where $\alpha_i \in [0, 1]$ is the combination weight.

The extrinsic factor e_i^E is solved through a well constructed neighborhood Ψ_i. As shown in (7). It satisfies three conditions: (1) The neighbor being chosen should be within its maximum visual range $p_{ij} < R$; (2) The neighbor should not be blocked by the barrier, when condition one is met; (3) To handle the condition when the number of neighbors N' is larger or smaller than N. If N' is larger than N, then the N nearest neighbors are chosen. If N' is smaller than N, then the N' neighbors' information plus $N - N'$ pairs of $(0,0)$ are used to construct Ψ_i.

$$\Psi_i = \{(\boldsymbol{p}_{i1}, \boldsymbol{v}_{i1}), ..., (\boldsymbol{p}_{ik}, \boldsymbol{v}_{ik}), ..., (\boldsymbol{p}_{iN}, \boldsymbol{v}_{iN})\} \qquad (7)$$

where $\boldsymbol{p}_{ik}$ denotes the position of k_{th} neighbor of pedestrian i, and $\boldsymbol{v}_{ik}$ denotes the neighbor's velocity.

The intrinsic factor e_i^I is obtained through the exit choosing process, which follow the principle of the closer the exit the higher chance to be selected. The probability P_k of choosing exit k can be computed by (8).

$$P_k = \frac{L_k^{-1}}{\sum_{i=1}^{M} L_i^{-1}} \qquad (8)$$

Adjust the Direction: The method discussed above considers only one group of crowd, when signs exit or not to calculate the extrinsic factor e_i^E. When two groups of pedestrians moving in opposite directions, pedestrian at the boundary of the two groups will only be influenced by one side, as shown in Fig. 1.

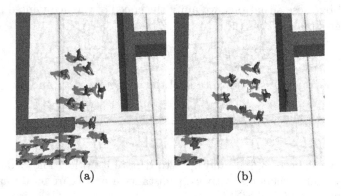

(a)   (b)

Fig. 1. (a) Two groups of pedestrians; (b) The pedestrian in red between the two groups chooses only one group to follow (Color figure online).

The neighbors are found simply according to the topology structure, that is not very reasonable. In addition, if it is influenced by two sides, neither groups will it follow. Then a strange phenomenon will appear, pedestrians at the boundary move in the direction perpendicular to the two directions of the two groups.

To avoid this situation, we first classify the pedestrians according to the target destination. In our common sense, a pedestrian will not change it destination easily, unless it find a better one or the previous one is impossible. If a pedestrian is at the boundary of N groups, only one direction of the groups will it choose to follow. D_{c_k} denotes the destination of most pedestrians in the k_{th} crowd within the maximum visual range of pedestrian i, D_i is the current destination of pedestrian i. The moving direction of a crowd is represent by e^{c_k}, and e^s is the safety signs instructive direction inside the maximum visual range.

1. When there is no sign instruction, D_i is equal to D_{c_k}, pedestrian i will choose its neighborhood in the k_{th} crowd and calculate e_i^E.
2. If D_i is equal to D_{c_k} and condition $e^{c_k} \cdot e^s > 0$ is met, which means the crowd is moving in the direction consistent with signs. In this situation, the pedestrian will follow the crowd naturally.
3. If safety signs exit and no crowd meeting the condition $e^{c_k} \cdot e^s > 0$, it will do the same operation like the no sign exits.
4. If the crowd destination which is different with it however consistent with signs, it will have a trend to change its direction or insist on the original direction. Details will be discussed in Sect. 5.2. If it changed its direction, then its neighborhood will be reconstructed.

5.2   Decision Tree

Decision tree plays an important role in choosing between several paths to destination. It generates the agent's current global goal, based on the private intention of the agent itself as well as the current situation. The agent executing the conditional judgment throughout the decision tree according to the *information set* collected from the environment. Meanwhile, a *behavior set* is introduced to tell the reaction of agents when an incident is triggered.

Behaviors illustrate in behavior tree between two kinds of agents, the novice agents and the acquainted agents. Novice agents who are unfamiliar with the scenario or environment make the decision mainly depend on the neighborhood. Acquainted agents obtain the knowledge of how to escape from the emergency and decide mainly by the prior knowledge but rarely focus on what the neighbor agents would behave.

Agents with the same condition may behave differently, which is showed in Figs. 2(b) and 3(b). The notes in Figs. 2 and 3 are illustrated as follows:

EXIT1: The exit in right bottom corner of the maze.
EXIT2: The exit in left top corner of the maze.
IMPASSE: The regions where cannot be got through.
START: The current location of the crowd, represented by red dot.
UNKNOWN REGION: The area where the agent is unfamiliar with.

In Figs. 2(a) and 3(a), the blue dots are T-junctions and the green ones are right-angle intersections. The black dots in right corner indicate the crowd. There are three probable paths to reach *EXIT1* and *EXIT2*, $Path_1 = \{START \rightarrow i \rightarrow j \rightarrow k \rightarrow h \rightarrow EXIT1\}$, $Path_2 = \{START \rightarrow a \rightarrow b \rightarrow c \rightarrow d \rightarrow e \rightarrow f \rightarrow g \rightarrow h \rightarrow EXIT1\}$, $Path_3 = \{START \rightarrow i \rightarrow j \rightarrow k \rightarrow l \rightarrow m \rightarrow n \rightarrow o \rightarrow p \rightarrow EXIT2\}$.

In Figs. 2(b) and 3(b) the blue dots are the branch node whose child nodes are the conditions represented by several green dots and actions represented by several orange dots. The information set consists of different conditions and the behavior set is composed of a sequence of actions.

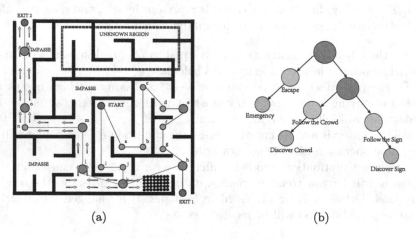

(a)   (b)

Fig. 2. (a) The maze scenario when the emergency happens and path from k to h is crowded; (b) Decision tree for novice agents (Color figure online).

Take novice agent A_n as an example, the information set {Emergency, Discover Crowd, Discover Sign}, the behavior set {Escape, Follow the Crowd, Follow the Sign}. The decision tree of the novice agent in Fig. 2(b) illustrates that when A_n arrived at k in Fig. 2(a) two behaviors will be carried out according to the conditions. If the condition of "Discover Crowd" is satisfied, A_n will take action of "Follow the Crowd" which means that the agent follows the crowd at the corner near *EXIT1* under the impact of crowds' moving trend. However, if the condition of "Discover Sign" is satisfied, A_n will take action of "Follow the Sign", this branch stands for the fact that the novice agent move along the direction as the yellow arrows tell and the neighborhood has far less effect on the agent's destination. With the satisfaction of these two decision branches, the novice agent chooses one of the two decisions with a comprehensive comparison.

For acquainted agent A_a, the behavior tree is shown in Fig. 3(b) with the information set {Emergency, Close to EXIT1, Close to EXIT2, EXIT1 Blocked, Crowded, Endure Time Unreached} and the behavior set {Escape, Run in EXIT1 Direction, Run in EXIT2 Direction, Give up EXIT1, Insist on EXIT1}. When A_a realizes the "Emergency" condition, A_a tries to escape from the maze. Because A_a notices the fact that it is closer to EXIT1, it will take the action of "Run in

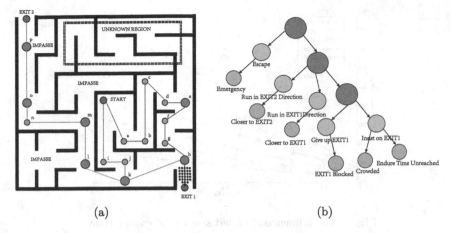

(a)   (b)

Fig. 3. (a) The maze scenario when the emergency happens and path from h to EXIT1 is crowded; (b) Decision tree for acquainted agents (Color figure online).

EXIT1 Direction" and move forward. When it arrives at position k in Fig. 3(a) it realised that the condition of "EXIT1 Blocked" and "Crowded" are satisfied. It faces the choices of "Give up EXIT1", "Run in EXIT2 Direction", or "Insist on EXIT1" by getting through the crowd until "Endure Time Unreached" is satisfied. The acquainted agent with strong confidence makes the decisions not on the neighborhood but on its own desires. It chooses one branch of the decision tree and makes the decision according to the probability about each branch.

6   Experimental Results and Discussions

In this section, we conducted several experiments with our dynamic-decision model. Agents will be influenced by so many factors, like safety signs, the crowds motion trend and the safety exit information.

First, we test the escape time of our model with different crowd size in a confined space, when the escape ratio reaches 80%. Escape ratio is defined as the ratio between the number of pedestrians get out the maze and the crowd size. The result is shown in Fig. 4. The escape time will increase with the increase of crowd size. At the beginning of evacuation, time increases in linear with the crowd size. When the escape ratio is higher, the relation ship of crowd size and escape time is no longer in linear relationship. This is because the influence of congestions, which hinders the escape process.

The second experiment is conducted to test the influence of signs on the evacuation process. We conduct several experiments with 400–500 agents to test the influence of signs to the escape time, when escape ratio reaches 80%.

As shown in Fig. 5, following the instruction of signs can significantly reduce the escape time. This result is consistent with the common sense that when emergency happens, it is better to actively seek the way to export than randomly

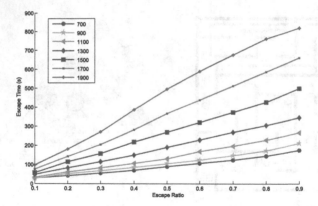

Fig. 4. The influence of crowd size to the escape time.

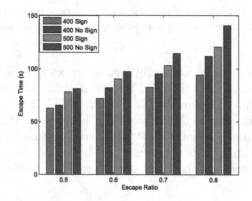

Fig. 5. The influence of safety signs to the escape time.

wander in the scenario with panic. Effective emergency evacuation signs play an important role in this respect.

The third experiment is conducted to test the influence of crowds motion trend on the agent moving direction. As shown in Fig. 6, a small group of agents in the right side find the crowd in front moving in the left direction. As a result, the condition of "Discover Crowd" is satisfied, they take action of "Follow the Crowd" and the agents follows the crowd under the impact of crowds' moving trend.

The last experiment is conducted to test the influence of agents' willingness to share information and help each other. We run the simulation with 400 pedestrians. A group of acquainted agents whose prior knowledge ρ^{priori} is high. We change the degree of the willingness of those agents to share information and help those novices.

As shown in Fig. 7, with the increase of the willingness of acquainted agents to share information the mean of the escape time will decrease with fairly small mean square time. We can conclude that when emergency happens, to share

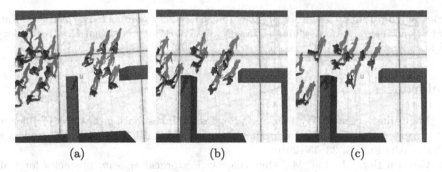

(a)   (b)   (c)

Fig. 6. (a) Two groups of agents; (b) The small group find the crowds moving trend; (c) Follow the crowd (Color figure online).

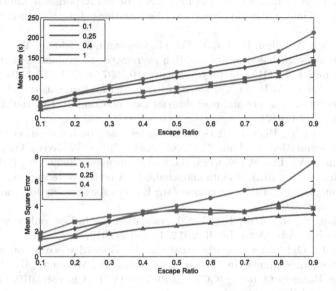

Fig. 7. The influence of increase willingness of share exit information to the escape time.

the information about the exit will help all the agents to get out and ease the pressure of competition.

7 Conclusions and Future Works

This paper proposes a model of dynamic decision-making for crowd simulation. This model shows the influence of safety sign and crowd on the agents' behavior. It also shows that easing the pressure of competition of people and helping people share information and help each other will have better evacuation effect.

Acknowledgments. The work presented in this paper is supported by National Natural Science Foundation of China (Grant No.61472261) and National Key Technology R&D Program of China (Grant No. 2012BAH62F02).

References

1. Augustijn-Beckers, E.W., Flacke, J., Retsios, B.: Investigating the effect of different pre-evacuation behavior and exit choice strategies using agent-based modeling. Procedia Eng. **3**, 23–35 (2010)
2. Van den Berg, J., Lin, M., Manocha, D.: Reciprocal velocity obstacles for real-time multi-agent navigation. In: IEEE International Conference on Robotics and Automation, ICRA 2008, pp. 1928–1935. IEEE (2008)
3. Bode, N.W., Wagoum, A.U.K., Codling, E.A.: Human responses to multiple sources of directional information in virtual crowd evacuations. J. R. Soc. Interface **11**(91), 20130904 (2014)
4. Che, X., Niu, Y., Shui, B., Fu, J., Fei, G., Goswami, P., Zhang, Y.: A novel simulation framework based on information asymmetry to evaluate evacuation plan. Vis. Comput, 1–9 (2015). http://dx.doi.org/10.1007/s00371-015-1119-6
5. Chen, X., Kwan, M.P., Li, Q., Chen, J.: A model for evacuation risk assessment with consideration of pre-and post-disaster factors. Comput. Environ. Urban Syst. **36**(3), 207–217 (2012)
6. Dong, T., Liu, Y., Bian, L.: A behavior model based on information transmission for crowd simulation. In: Pan, Z., Cheok, A.D., Müller, W. (eds.) Transactions on Edutainment VI. LNCS, vol. 6758, pp. 89–98. Springer, Heidelberg (2011)
7. Hector Jr, L., Lim, M.B., Piantanakulchai, M.: A review of recent studies on flood evacuation planning. In: Proceedings of the Eastern Asia Society for Transportation Studies, vol. 9 (2013)
8. Kamkarian, P., Hexmoor, H.: Crowd evacuation for indoor public spaces using coulomb's law. Adv. Artif. Intell. **2012**(4), 1–16 (2012)
9. Kusuda, T., Ogi, T.: Geospatial analysis of cooperative works on asymmetric information environment. In: Taniar, D., Gervasi, O., Murgante, B., Pardede, E., Apduhan, Bernady O. (eds.) ICCSA 2010, Part IV. LNCS, vol. 6019, pp. 336–345. Springer, Heidelberg (2010)
10. Lee, S., Son, Y.J., Jin, J.: An integrated human decision making model for evacuation scenarios under a BDI framework. ACM Trans. Model. Comput. Simul. (TOMACS) **20**(4), 23 (2010)
11. Ninomiya, K., Kapadia, M., Shoulson, A., Garcia, F., Badler, N.: Planning approaches to constraint-aware navigation in dynamic environments. Comput. Animation Virtual Worlds **26**, 119–139 (2014)
12. Patrix, J., Mouaddib, A.I., Gatepaille, S.: Detection of primitive collective behaviours in a crowd panic simulation based on multi-agent approach. Int. J. Swarm Intell. Res. (IJSIR) **3**(3), 50–65 (2012)
13. Peizhong, Y., Xin, W., Tao, L.: Retraction notice to agent-based simulation of fire emergency evacuation with fire and human interaction model [safety science 49 (2011) 11301141]. Saf. Sci. **50**(4), 1171 (2012). First International Symposium on Mine Safety Science and Engineering 2011
14. Pelechano, N., Malkawi, A.: Evacuation simulation models: challenges in modeling high rise building evacuation with cellular automata approaches. Autom. Constr. **17**(4), 377–385 (2008)

15. Sagun, A., Bouchlaghem, D., Anumba, C.J.: Computer simulations vs. building guidance to enhance evacuation performance of buildings during emergency events. Simul. Model. Pract. Theor. **19**(3), 1007–1019 (2011)
16. Sharpanskykh, A., Treur, J.: An adaptive affective social decision making model. In: Chella, A., Pirrone, R., Sorbello, R., Kamilla, R.J. (eds.) Biologically Inspired Cognitive Architectures 2012, vol. 196, pp. 299–308. Springer, Heidelberg (2013)
17. Shendarkar, A., Vasudevan, K., Lee, S., Son, Y.J.: Crowd simulation for emergency response using BDI agent based on virtual reality. In: Proceedings of the 38th Conference on Winter Simulation, pp. 545–553. Winter Simulation Conference (2006)
18. Song, Y., Gong, J., Li, Y., Cui, T., Fang, L., Cao, W.: Crowd evacuation simulation for bioterrorism in micro-spatial environments based on virtual geographic environments. Saf. Sci. **53**, 105–113 (2013)
19. Van Den Berg, J., Guy, S.J., Lin, M., Manocha, D.: Reciprocal n-body collision avoidance. In: Pradalier, C., Siegwart, R., Hirzinger, G. (eds.) Robotics Research, vol. 70, pp. 3–19. Springer, Heidelberg (2011)
20. Wagner, N., Agrawal, V.: Emergency decision support using an agent-based modeling approach. In: ISI, p. 186 (2012)
21. Wagner, N., Agrawal, V.: An agent-based simulation system for concert venue crowd evacuation modeling in the presence of a fire disaster. Expert Syst. Appl. **41**(6), 2807–2815 (2014)
22. Yin, W., Murray-Tuite, P., Ukkusuri, S.V., Gladwin, H.: An agent-based modeling system for travel demand simulation for hurricane evacuation. Transp. Res. Part C: Emerg. Technol. **42**, 44–59 (2014)
23. Zainuddin, Z., Aik, L.E.: Intelligent exit-selection behaviors during a room evacuation. Chin. Phys. Lett. **29**(1), 018901 (2012)
24. Zia, K., Riener, A., Ferscha, A., Sharpanskykh, A.: Evacuation simulation based on cognitive decision making model in a socio-technical system. In: Proceedings of the 2011 IEEE/ACM 15th International Symposium on Distributed Simulation and Real Time Applications, pp. 98–107. IEEE Computer Society (2011)

Facial Stereo Processing by Pyramidal Block Matching

Jing Wang[1], Qiwen Zha[1], Yubo Yang[2], Yang Liu[1(✉)], Bo Yang[1], Dengbiao Tu[1],
and Guangda Su[3]

[1] National Computer Network Emergency Response Technical Team/Coordination
Center of China, Beijing, China
wangjing8641@126.com, {zhaqiwen,tudengbiao}@163.com,
liuyang195753@sina.com, yangbo03@gmail.com
[2] Air Force Equipment Research Institute, Beijing, China
rechardyyb@126.com
[3] Department of Electronic Engineering, Tsinghua University, Beijing, China
susu@tsinghua.edu.cn

Abstract. This paper describes the Pyramidal Block Matching (PBM) stereo
method. It uses a pyramidal approach and a global energy function to obtain the
disparity image. First, the input images are rectified to obtain row-aligned epipolar
geometry. Then the face is segmented out of each image and a face pyramid is
generated. The main difference to our approach is that the first layer of pyramid
is the whole face. Matching result of the first layer provides input to the next layer,
where it is used to constrain the search area for matching. This process continues
on each layer. After that, a global energy function is designed to remove the wrong
pixels and get a smoother result. A comparison on face images shows that the
generated projection results of PBM are the closest to the ground truth images. A
face recognition experiment is also performed, and PBM achieves the best recognition rates.

Keywords: Face recognition · Stereo vision · Global optimization

1 Introduction

Face recognition has been a popular research topic in computer vision. Many face
recognition methods have been proposed [1, 2], such as Principal Components Analysis
(PCA) [3–5], Independent Components Analysis (ICA) [6], Hausdorff distance [7],
Elastic Graph-Matching (EGM) [8], Support vector Machine (SVM) [9], etc. These
monocular 2D face recognition methods evaluate 2D image regions, which are not
invariant under different lighting conditions, facial expressions, rotation and so on. Thus,
they suffer from limited input data and insufficient information. Tsalakanidou [10]
showed that depth information can be applied to improved face recognition. Afterwards,
many new algorithms based on 3D facial information were proposed [11, 12]. The depth
information is generated with passive 3D measurement techniques based on binocular
stereo vision, which are proven to be better than the traditional monocular 2D face
recognition methods [12].

© Springer International Publishing Switzerland 2015
Y.-J. Zhang (Ed.): ICIG 2015, Part II, LNCS 9218, pp. 252–260, 2015.
DOI: 10.1007/978-3-319-21963-9_23

The performance of passive 3D measurement is mainly determined by the accuracy of estimated disparity between corresponding points. Current methods of disparity estimation can usually be divided into four steps: matching cost computation, cost aggregation, disparity optimization, and disparity refinement [13]. Matching cost computation is always based on the absolute, squared, or sampling insensitive difference [13] of intensities. Cost aggregation connects the matching costs within a certain neighborhood [15, 16]. Methods of disparity computation are divided into two classes: local algorithm and global algorithm. The local algorithms select the disparity with the lowest matching cost, whereas the global algorithms define a global energy function to calculate the disparity.

Compared to the scene image matching, most of face images are very smooth, making the matching result ambiguous when the pixels are matched with each other. However, until now, few article concerns with a stereo matching algorithm that is suitable to face. This paper is concerned with the calculation of disparity between face images from binocular stereo cameras. A pyramidal approach is used in our algorithm, which is different from other algorithms. The pyramidal approach in other algorithms is always used to decrease the amount of data to be processed in which results at lower resolutions guide the matching at higher-resolutions. At each layer of the pyramid, each pixel is matched to find its corresponding point to give dense matches across the face. The main difference to our approach is that the first layer of pyramid is the whole face. The block of the whole face area is used directly to find the corresponding block in the other image. Then in the second layer of pyramid, the face area is divided into four blocks, and each block is matched to find its corresponding block separately. This process is performed on each pyramid layer. After the pyramidal approach, an original disparity image is obtained. A global energy function that includes a data term and a smoothness term is used to remove errors in the original disparity image so that a smoother result can be achieved.

The rest of this paper is organized as follows: Sect. 2 elaborates Semiglobal Matching method. Section 3 presents our method. Section 4 shows the experimental results. Section 5 concludes our work.

2   Semiglobal Matching

The Semiglobal Matching (SGM) [13] method is based on the idea of pixelwise matching of Mutual Information and approximating a global, 2D smoothness constraint by combining many 1D constraints. The algorithm is described in distinct processing steps. Some of them are optional, depending on the application.

The matching cost calculation of SGM can be based on Mutual Information (MI) [17], which is insensitive to recording and illumination changes. It is defined from the entropy H of two images (that is, their information content), as well as their joint entropy:

$$MI_{I1,I2} = H_{I1} + H_{I2} + H_{I1,I2} \tag{1}$$

The entropies are calculated from the probability distributions P of intensities of the associated images:

$$H_I = -\int_0^1 P_I(i) \log P_I(i) \, di \tag{2}$$

$$H_{I1,I2} = -\int_0^1 \int_0^1 P_{I1,I2}(i1, i2) \log P_{I1,I2}(i1, i2) \, di1 \, di2 \tag{3}$$

Kim et al. [18] transformed the calculation of the joint entropy $H_{I1,I2}$ into a sum over pixels using Taylor expansion:

$$H_{I1,I2} = \sum_p h_{I1,I2}\left(I_{1p}, I_{2p}\right) \tag{4}$$

$$h_{I1,I2}(i, k) = -\frac{1}{n} \log\left(P_{I1,I2}(i, k) * g(i, k)\right) * g(i, k) \tag{5}$$

$$P_{I1,I2}(i, k) = \frac{1}{n} \sum_P T\left[(i, k) = \left(I_{1p}, I_{2p}\right)\right] \tag{6}$$

Where $g(i, k)$ is a 2D Gaussian, the operator $T[] = 1$ when its argument is true, otherwise $T[] = 0$.

The resulting definition of Mutual Information is:

$$MI_{I1,I2} = \sum_p mi_{I1,I2}\left(I_{1p}, I_{2p}\right) \tag{7}$$

$$mi_{I1,I2} = h_{I1}(i) + h_{I2}(k) - h_{I1,I2}(i, k) \tag{8}$$

This leads to the definition of the MI matching cost:

$$C_{MI}(p, d) = -mi_{Ib, fD(Im)}\left(I_{bp}, I_{mq}\right) \tag{9}$$

$$q = e_{bm}(p, d) \tag{10}$$

An additional constraint is added that supports smoothness by penalizing changes of neighboring disparities. The pixelwise cost and the smoothness constraints are expressed by defining the energy $E(D)$ that depends on the disparity image D:

$$E(D) = \sum_p \left(C(p, D_p) + \sum_{q \in N_p} P_1 T[\left|D_p - D_q\right| = 1] + \sum_{q \in N_p} P_2 T[\left|D_p - D_q\right| > 1] \right) \tag{11}$$

The first term is the sum of all pixel matching costs for the disparities of D. The second term adds a constant penalty P_1 for all pixels q in the neighborhood N_p of p, for which the disparity changes a little bit (that is, 1 pixel). The third term adds a larger constant penalty P_2, for all larger disparity changes.

3 Our Method

3.1 Disparity Computation Process

Due to the smoothness of face image, traditional pixel to pixel or block to block match may lead to an ambiguous result. In order to cope with this problem, we use pyramidal block to block match. The first step is to rectify the images to obtain row-aligned epipolar geometry. After that, face in each image is segmented out based on the method of Adaboost [19]. A face pyramid is generated for each rectified face image. The first layer of the pyramid is a block of the whole face and the initial matching process is done on the first layer. There are many standard matching algorithms, such as normalized cross-correlation (NCC) [20], Sum of Squared Differences (SSD), Sum of Absolute Difference (SAD) and so on. We test these three algorithms on the whole face, and the matching results are very similar. When the face size is 150*150, the computation time for NCC is 409 ms, for SSD is 0.3 ms, and for SAD is 0.1 ms. As a result, we choose SAD as the matching method between the blocks in the pyramid. The matching result of the first layer provides an input to the next layer, where it is used to constrain the search area for matching. On the second layer, each block is divided into four equally sized blocks, and each block is matched near the position of the previous block. This process continues on each layer. The pyramidal matching process is shown in Fig. 1.

Rectified images   **Pyramidal matching process**

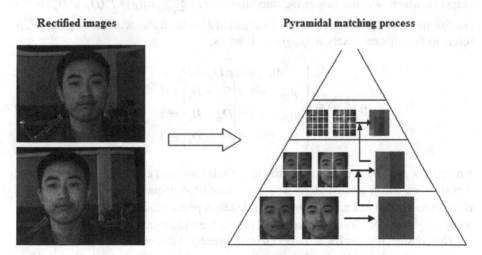

Fig. 1. Pyramidal matching process

We use five layers in our system, and for the fifth layer, the block size is 9*9. The result on the previous layer limits the matching process on the next layer within a small range, which not only accelerates the matching speed but also improves the matching accuracy. The disparity result of the pyramidal matching process is then used as the guidance to pixel-to-pixel matching. In the pixel-to-pixel process, NCC over a square window (3*3) is used as the matching algorithm. Pixel p in image I is matched against all pixels in image J within a given search area and the best match is retained. After that, a raw disparity image D_l that corresponds to the left image I_l is obtained.

The disparity image D_r that corresponds to the right image I_r can be obtained through the same process by exchanging the matching images. D_r should be consistent with D_l, that is, if p in image I matches to q in image J then q must also match to p. Each disparity of D_l is compared to its corresponding disparity of D_r. The disparity is set to invalid if both differ [13], as shown in Eq. (12).

$$\text{if } |D_r - D_l| > 1, \text{ then } D_l = -1 \tag{12}$$

3.2 Global Optimization

The original disparity image generated in the previous section contains many errors. An additional constraint is thus added to enforce smoothness by penalizing charges of neighboring disparities. We consider the following energy equation:

$$E(D) = \sum_{\{p,q\}\in N} u_1(p,q) \cdot T_1(p,q) + \mu \sum_{p\in D} u_2(p) \cdot T_2(D_P \neq D_P^0) \tag{13}$$

Where $\sum_{\{p,q\}\in N} u(p,q) \cdot T_1(p,q)$ is the smoothness penalty, which measures the extent to which D is not piecewise smooth, whereas $\sum_{p\in D} u_2(p) \cdot T_2(D_P \neq D_P^0)$ is the consistency penalty, which restrains the adjusted D to be in line with the original D^0. N refers to the adjacent pixels, $u_1(p,q)$ is defined as:

$$u_1(p,q) = \begin{cases} 0, & when\, D_p = D_q \\ p_1, & when\, |D_p - D_q| = 1 \\ p_2, & when\, |D_p - D_q| = 2 \\ p_3, & when\, |D_p - D_q| \geq 3 \end{cases} \tag{14}$$

where $p_3 > p_2 > p_1$. When the disparity in the neighborhood changes a little bit (that is, 1 pixel), we add a small penalty factor p_1; when the disparity in the neighborhood changes more (that is, 2 pixels), we add a little larger penalty factor p_2; when the disparity in the neighborhood changes more than 2 pixels, we add a much larger constant penalty p_3. The constant penalty for all larger changes preserves discontinuities [21]. The value of the smoothness penalty should be smaller for pairs $\{p, q\}$ with larger intensity differences $|I_p - I_q|$. So we define $T_1(p,q)$ as:

$$T_1(p,q) = 1 \Big/ (\propto |I_p - I_q| + 1) \tag{15}$$

In the consistency penalty, $T_2(\cdot)$ is 1 if its argument is true, and otherwise 0. $\sum_{p\in D} T_2(D_P \neq D_P^0)$ calculates the number of the pixels in the adjusted disparity image that disagree with those in the original disparity image. $u_2(p)$ is the judgment factor, if the pixel p in the disparity is set to be invalid according to Eq. (12), $u_2(p) = 0$, otherwise $u_2(p) = 1$.

We should find an appropriate D that is as smooth as possible and as consistent with D^0 as possible, that is, solve the energy Eq. (13) to get the minimum value. This energy optimization problem can be efficiently solved via Graph Cuts algorithm [21].

After that, sub-pixel disparity values are updated in order to remove the sudden change. A 7*7 Gaussian template is used to further smooth the disparity image, and a smoother result with sub-pixel value is efficiently obtained.

4 Experiment Results

4.1 Rotating Results

The Pyramidal Block Matching (PBM) method is designed for calculating accurate 3D information from face images. Since it is performed on pairs of face images that are acquired by the two calibrated cameras, to evaluate the accuracy of matching results, we established our own face database (TH-POSE face database). TH-POSE face database contains 200 persons, each person contains face images with 7 different views of left/right rotations under normal illumination condition. The angles of the faces are about −45, −30, −15, 0, 15, 20, 45 degrees. The rotation angles are restricted so that the two eyes are always visible.

In our experiment, 50 persons are chosen. We calculate 3D values of the frontal faces, rotate it by 15, 30 and 45 degrees, and compare the projections with the ground truth images. SGM and SAD algorithms are also done through the same process. The projection results of PBM are much better than SGM and SAD, as is shown in Fig. 2.

In Fig. 2, the frontal faces are rotated with different angles. The first row is the ground truth images with different angles, and the 2–4 rows are the projections of different algorithms. Results of SAD and SGM are corrupted with many wrong pixels around the nose and cheeks. Results of PBM look much better than those of SAD and SGM.

Table 1 shows the running times of the three methods. The testing platform is: Inter(R) Core™ i5-3470 CPU @3.2 GHz, with 4.0 GB RAM. Codes are written in VC++.

Table 1. Running time comparison

Method	Running time(s)
PBM	0.49
SAD	0.37
SGM	0.57

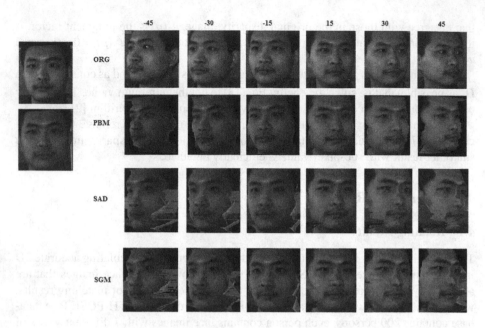

Fig. 2. Comparison of rotation results

From the Table 1, we can see that, PBM is faster than SGM, but a little slower than SAD. Considering the advantages of its performance, its time consuming is in the acceptable range.

4.2 Face Recognition Results

We also do a face recognition experiment to evaluate the quality of the rotating images. The frontal faces and the generated multi-pose faces form the training set, and the ground truth pose images form the testing set. Downsampled images [22] are used as the features, and Euclidean distance is used as the matching criteria. Simple feature extraction and face recognition methods are used in order to measure the similarity between the generated image and ground truth image. Recognition results are shown in Table 2.

Table 2. Recognition Accuracy [rank 1] on TH-POSE database

Method	Pose angles(°)		
	45	30	15
PBM	64.0 %	74.0 %	90.0 %
SAD	52.0 %	68.0 %	88.0 %
SGM	56.0 %	70.0 %	88.0 %

It can be seen from the Table 2 that through the increase of face angle, the recognition rates of SAD and SGM decline rapidly. PBM achieves the best performance, especially when face angle is large.

5   Conclusion

In this paper, we propose a new face stereo matching method based on pyramidal matching and energy minimization function. The algorithm well deals with a challenging limitation of pixel-to-pixel and block-to-block matching due to the smoothness of face, and achieves satisfactory performance. Face recognition experimental results show that our proposed algorithm achieves the best recognition rates.

References

1. Luo, Y., Tao, D., Geng, B., Xu, C., Maybank, S.J.: Manifold regularized multitask learning for semi-supervised multilabel image classification. IEEE Trans. Image Process. 22(2), 523–536 (2012). (NCBI)
2. Luo, Y., Tao, D., Xu, C., Xu, C., Liu, H., Wen, Y.: Multiview vector-valued manifold regularization for multilabel image classification. IEEE Trans. Neural Netw. Learn. Syst. 24(5), 709–722 (2013). IEEE Xplore
3. Turk, M., Pentland, A.: Eigenfaces for recognition. J. Cogn. Neurosci. 3(1), 71–86 (1991). NCBI
4. Yang, J., Zhang, D.: Two-dimensional PCA: a new approach to appearance-based face representation and recognition. IEEE Trans. Pattern Anal. Mach. Intell. 26(1), 131–137 (2004). Citeseer
5. Karamizadeh, S., Abdullah, S.M., Cheraghi, S.M., Randjbaran, E., Karamizadeh, F.: Face recognition by implying illumination techniques. J. Sci. Eng. 6, 1–7 (2015)
6. Bartlett, M.S., Movellan, J.R., Sejnowski, T.J.: Face recognition by independent component analysis. IEEE Trans. Neural Netw. 13(6), 1450–1464 (2002). NCBI
7. Beauchemin, M.: On the hausdorff distance used for the evaluation of segmentation results. Can. J. Remote Sens. 24(1), 3–8 (2014). Taylor & Francis
8. Wiskott, L., Fellous, J.-M., Kruger, N., Malsburg, C.V.D.: Face recognition by elastic bunch graph matching. Intell. Biometric Tech. Fingerprint Face Recogn. 19(7), 775–779 (1999). CRC Press, USA
9. Deniz, O., Castrillon, M., Hernandez, M.: Face recognition using independent component analysis and support vector machines. Pattern Recogn. Lett. 24(13), 2153–2157 (2003)
10. Tsalakanidou, F., Tzovaras, D., Strintzis, M.G.: Use of depth and color eigenfaces for face recognition. Pattern Recogn. Lett. 24(9–10), 1427–1435 (2003). Elsevier
11. Akihiro, H., Koichi, I., Takafumi, A., Hiroshi, N., Koji, K.: A robust 3d face recognition algorithm using passive stereo vision. IEICE Trans. 92-A(4), 1047–1055 (2009). JST
12. Kosov, S., Thormahlen, T., Seidel, H.P.: Rapid stereo-vision enhanced face recognition. In: ICIP, pp. 1221–1224. IEEEXplore, HongKong (2010)
13. Hirschmuller, H.: Stereo processing by semiglobal matching and mutual information. IEEE Trans. Pattern Anal. Mach. Intell. 30(2), 328–341 (2008)
14. Birchfield, S., Tomasi, C.: Depth discontinuities by pixel-to-pixel stereo. In: Proceedings of Sixth IEEE International Conference on Computer Vision, pp. 1073–1080. Springer, Berlin (1999)

15. Klaus, A., Sormann, M., Karner, K.: Segment-based stereo matching using belief propagation and a self-adapting dissimilarity measure. In: Proceedings of International Conference on Pattern Recognition, vol. 3, pp. 15–18. ACM (2006)
16. Yoon, K.-J., Kweon, I.-S.: Adaptive support-weight approach for correspondence search. IEEE Trans. Pattern Matching Mach. Intell. **28**(4), 650–656 (2006). ACM
17. Viola, P., Wells, W.M.: Alignment by maximization of mutual information. Int. J. Comput. Vis. **24**(2), 137–154 (1997)
18. Kim, J., Kolmogorov, V., Zabih, R.: Visual correspondence using energy minimization and mutual information. International Conference in Image Processing, pp. 1033–1040. ACM (2003)
19. Zhou, J.: Face recognition research in monitoring system. Thesis of Master's Degree, Tsinghua University, Beijing (2008)
20. Gonzalez, R.C., Woods, R.E.: Digital Image Processing, 3rd edn. Addison-Wesley, Boston (1992)
21. Boykov, Y., Veksler, O., Zabih, R.: Fast approximate energy minimization via graph cuts. IEEE Trans. Pattern Anal. Mach. Intell. **23**(11), 1222–1239 (2001). IEEEXplore
22. Wright, J., Yang, A.Y., Ganesh, A., Sastry, S.S., Ma, Y.: Robust face recognition via sparse representation. IEEE Trans. Pattern Anal. Mach. Intell. **31**(2), 210–227 (2009)

Fast Algorithm for Finding Maximum Distance with Space Subdivision in E^2

Vaclav Skala and Zuzana Majdisova[(✉)]

Faculty of Applied Sciences, University of West Bohemia,
Univerzitni 8, 30614 Plzen, Czech Republic
majdisz@kiv.zcu.cz

Abstract. Finding an exact maximum distance of two points in the given set is a fundamental computational problem which is solved in many applications. This paper presents a fast, simple to implement and robust algorithm for finding this maximum distance of two points in E^2. This algorithm is based on a polar subdivision followed by division of remaining points into uniform grid. The main idea of the algorithm is to eliminate as many input points as possible before finding the maximum distance. The proposed algorithm gives the significant speed up compared to the standard algorithm.

Keywords: Maximum distance · Polar space subdivision · Uniform 2D grid · Points reduction

1 Introduction

Finding a maximum distance of two points in the given data set is a fundamental computational problem. The solution of this problem is needed in many applications. A standard brute force (BF) algorithm with $O(N^2)$ complexity is usually used, where N is a number of points in the input dataset. If large sets of points have to be processed, then the BF algorithm leads to very bad time performance. Typical size of datasets in computer graphics is usually 10^5 and more points. Therefore the processing time of the BF algorithm for such sets is unacceptable.

However, our main goal is to find the maximum distance, not all the pairs of two points having a maximum distance. Therefore the complexity of this algorithm should be lower.

Various approaches, how to solve finding the maximum distance, are described in [9]. Other algorithms for finding the maximum distance of two points are in [1, 7].

1.1 Brute Force Algorithm

The standard BF algorithm for finding a maximum distance in set of points uses two nested loops. We can find such type of algorithms in many books dealing with fundamental algorithms and data structures, e.g. [4, 6]. In general, the BF algorithm can be described by Algorithm 1.

© Springer International Publishing Switzerland 2015
Y.-J. Zhang (Ed.): ICIG 2015, Part II, LNCS 9218, pp. 261–274, 2015.
DOI: 10.1007/978-3-319-21963-9_24

```
//Square of the distance
FUNCTION distance(A,B: point)
  distance := (A.x  - B.x)^2 + (A.y - B.y)^2;
END FUNCTION

dist := 0;
FOR i := 1 to N-1 do
  FOR j := i + 1 to N do
    dij := distance(X_i, X_j);
    IF dist < dij THEN
      dist := dij;
    END IF
  END FOR
END FOR
dist := SQRT(dist);
```

Algorithm 1. Brute force algorithm

Complexity of Algorithm 1 is clearly $O(N^2)$ and thus run time significantly increases with size of the input dataset.

In practice, we can expect that points in input set are not organized in a very specific manner and points are more or less uniformly distributed. In this case, we can use "output sensitive" algorithms which lead to efficient solutions. We propose such algorithm in Sect. 2.

2   Proposed Algorithm

In this section, we introduce a new algorithm for finding a maximum distance of two points in the given dataset in E^2. The main idea of this algorithm is to eliminate as many input points as possible using an algorithm with $O(N)$ complexity using space subdivision and determines the maximum distance for the remaining points with $O(k^2)$ complexity, where $k \ll N$. We use polar space subdivision for this elimination of points.

This section is organized as follows. In Sect. 2.1, we present the first step of the algorithm which is an axis aligned bounding box (AABB) and an initial convex polygon construction followed by the location of points inside the initial convex polygon. Section 2.2 describes how to divide the points into non-overlapping 2D triangular shape sectors. Section 2.3 presents reduction of the points [2] which have absolutely no influence on the value of maximum distance. In Sect. 2.4, we describe the division of remaining points into uniform 2D grid. Finally, the finding of the maximum distance of two points is made in Sect. 2.5.

2.1   Location of Points Inside Initial Polygon

An important property is that two points with maximal distance are lying on the convex hull of a given set of points [10]. This fact is apparent if we consider a case in which two points with the largest distance are part of the convex hull. It is then obvious that there are another two points with larger distance. We also know that the most extreme point on any axis is part of the convex hull. These properties are used to significantly speedup the proposed algorithm for finding the exact maximal distance.

At the beginning of our proposed algorithm, we need to find the exact extremal points in both axes, i.e. axis aligned bounding box (AABB) of a given dataset. The time complexity of this step is $O(N)$. So we generally get four distinct extremal points or less.

Now, we can create a convex polygon using these extremal points, see Fig. 1. One important property of this polygon is that any point lying inside has no influence on the value of maximal distance. Due to this fact, we can perform a fast and simple initial test for a point inside/outside the initial polygon and discard a lot of points.

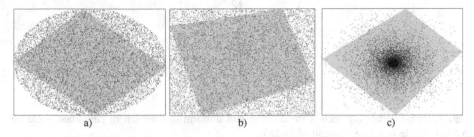

Fig. 1. Location of AABB and initial testing polygon for 10^4 points: (a) uniform points in ellipse, (b) uniform points in rectangle, (c) Gauss points.

The location test of a point inside a polygon can be performed as follows. Each edge of the polygon is an oriented line and so we can calculate outer product [10]:

$$f_i(x) = v_i \wedge (x - x_i) = \begin{vmatrix} v_{xi} & v_{yi} \\ x - x_i & y - y_i \end{vmatrix}, \qquad (1)$$

where x is the point and edge with index i is determined by point x_i and direction vector $v_i = (v_{xi}, v_{yi})$. If the polygon has an anticlockwise orientation and outer product $f_i(x) \leq 0$ for at least one $i \in \{0, 1, 2, 3\}$, then point x does not lie inside the polygon and has to be further processed. Otherwise, point x can be discarded as it is inside.

2.2 Division of Points into Polar Sectors

Only the points which lie outside or on the boundary of the initial convex polygon will be further processed. Firstly, we perform the division of AABB into eight non-overlapping $2D$ triangular shape sectors, i.e. polar subdivision. This division of AABB is using a center point and angular division, see Fig. 2. The center point C is determined as the average of all corners of the AABB.

When we do the division of points into non-overlapping sectors, we also determine angle between the x-axis and the vector $s = x - C$ for each point x. This can be performed using two different calculations. One way is to use an exact angle from 0 to 2π. For this approach, we have to calculate the angle using the following formula:

$$\varphi_e = \text{arctg2}(v_x, v_y). \tag{2}$$

However, calculation of function arctg2 takes a lot of computing time. Therefore, we use a simplified calculation of approximated angle. When the angle is determined, we have to locate the exact sectors (half of the quadrant for square AABB), where the point is located, and then calculate the intersection with the given edge. Calculation of the intersection with the given edge of AABB is easy. The distribution of simplified angle can be seen in Fig. 2. Calculation of simplified angle is faster than the formula (2).

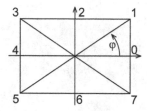

Fig. 2. Non-overlapping sectors for division and uniform distribution of simplified angle on AABB. Angle $\varphi \in [0, 8)$ instead of $[0, 2\pi)$.

Now we have the procedure how to calculate the simplified angle and therefore we are able to divide the points into sectors to which the given points belong.

For each sector with index i, one minimal point R_i^{min} is determined. This point has the minimum (from all points in a sector) distance from the nearest corner of AABB. (Note that the nearest corner of AABB lies in the same quadrant as the point.) The initial points R_i^{min} are lying on the edges of the initial polygon, see Fig. 3. These points can be calculated as an intersection point of the middle axis of a sector and the edge of the initial polygon.

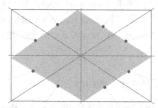

Fig. 3. Visualization of initial R_i^{min} points (red dots on the edges of the initial polygon) (Color figure online).

All minimum points R_i^{min} are connected into a polygon with vertices $R_1^{min}, \ldots, R_8^{min}$.

For each new point we have to check whether the distance from this point to the nearest corner of AABB is smaller than the distance from R_i^{min} to the same corner of

AABB. If this is true, then we have to replace point R_i^{min} with a processed point, add this point into the sector with index i and recalculate the test lines l^- and l^+, see Fig. 4. Otherwise we continue with the next step.

In the next step, we check whether the processed point lies over or under the test line segments l^- and l^+. We can compare the angle of the point with the angle of point R_i^{min}. If the angle is smaller, then we have to use the line l^-, otherwise we have to use the line l^+. If the point lies under the test line, it can be eliminated, because such a point has no influence on the value of maximum distance. Otherwise we add this point into the sector with index i.

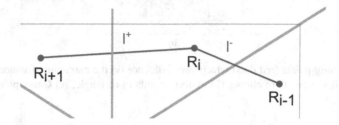

Fig. 4. Visualization of test lines l^- and l^+.

2.3 Reduction of Points for Testing

All points, which can have an influence on the value of maximum distance, are already divided into polar sectors. We gave points R_i^{min} some initial values before starting to divide the points into non-overlapping sectors and we used them to check whether to add or eliminate a point. Values of points R_i^{min} have changed during the division process; hence we recheck all remaining points using the final values of points R_i^{min}. Moreover, we perform union of the vertices of initial polygon and minimum points R_i^{min} before new testing and connect them into a polygon, see Fig. 5(a).

In this step, we check whether the processed point lies over or under the line segments l^{--}, l^-, l^+ and l^{++}, see Fig. 5(b). We select the concrete test line according to the angle again.

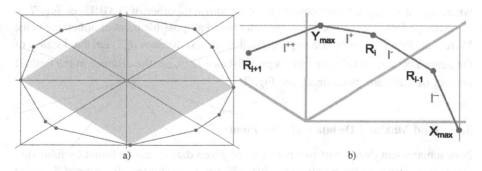

Fig. 5. Visualization of test lines for rechecking all remaining points

We minimize the number of points, which have an influence on the largest distance, using this step. Final sets of remaining points for input datasets with different distributions of points are shown in Fig. 6.

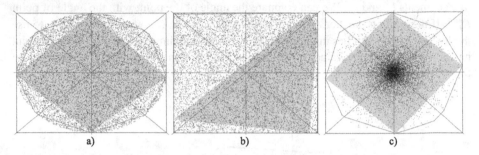

Fig. 6. Remaining points (red dots) which have influence on the maximum distance (10^4 input points): (a) uniform points in ellipse, (b) uniform points in rectangle, (c) Gauss points.

2.4 Division of Remaining Points into Uniform Grid

We have a set of suspicious points, i.e. points which can have an influence on the final maximum distance. In this step, these suspicious points will be further processed. Firstly, we define the uniform grid of AABB. This uniform grid contains $k \times k$ cells. Thus, each cell has index $i = row \cdot k + col$, width dx and height dy where:

$$dx = \frac{AABB_{width}}{k}, dy = \frac{AABB_{height}}{k}. \tag{3}$$

Now, we can perform the division of suspicious points into a defined uniform grid. We are able to calculate the exact index of a cell to which the given point x belongs using following formulae:

$$row = \left\lfloor \frac{y - y_{min}}{dy} \right\rfloor, col = \left\lfloor \frac{x - x_{min}}{dx} \right\rfloor, \tag{4}$$

where x_{min} and y_{min} are the coordinates of bottom left corner of AABB, see Fig. 7.

After performing previous step, we determined all possible pairs of nonempty cells. Moreover, for each pair of nonempty cells, the shortest distance d_{ij}^{cell}, i.e. the distance of the nearest corners of cells, and the largest distance D_{ij}^{cell}, i.e. the distance of the farthest corners of cells, are determined, see Fig. 7.

2.5 Find Maximal Distance of Two Points

Now a maximum distance of two points in the given dataset can be found by following steps. We determine the maximum value d_{max}^{cell} from the shortest distances d_{ij}^{cell} which

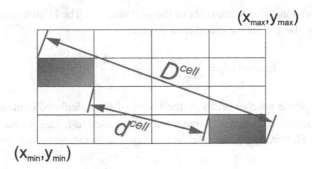

Fig. 7. Uniform grid of AABB. Value D^{cell} presents the largest distance of two cells and d^{cell} presents the shortest distance of two cells.

were calculated for all pairs of nonempty cells. When this value is known, we can eliminate all pairs of nonempty cells for which the largest distance D_{ij}^{cell} is smaller than d_{max}^{cell}.

For remaining pairs of nonempty cells, we perform the following. For each pair of nonempty cells, the maximum distance D_{ij} between points in these cells is determined, i.e. we calculate all distances from points in one cell to points in second cell and determine their maximum. Finally, we find the maximum value of these maximum distances D_{ij}.

3 Experimental Results

The proposed algorithm has been implemented in C# using.Net Framework 4.5 and tested on datasets using a PC with the following configuration:

- CPU: Intel® Core™ i7-2600 (4 × 3.40 GHz)
- Memory: 16 GB RAM
- Operating system Microsoft Windows 7 64 bits

3.1 Distribution of Points

The proposed algorithm for finding the maximum distance of two points has been tested using different datasets. These datasets have different types of distributions of points. For our experiments, we used well-known distributions such as randomly distributed uniform points in an ellipse, uniform points in a rectangle or points with a Gaussian distribution. Other distributions used were Halton points and Gauss ring points. Both of these distributions are described in the following text.

Halton Points. Construction of a Halton sequence is based on a deterministic method. This sequence generates well-spaced "draws" points from the interval $[0, 1]$. The sequence uses a prime number as its base and is constructed based on finer and finer prime-based divisions of sub-intervals of the unit interval. The Halton sequence [3] can be described by the following recurrence formula:

$$Halton(p)_k = \sum_{i=0}^{\lfloor \log_p k \rfloor} \frac{1}{p^{i+1}} \left(\left\lfloor \frac{k}{p^i} \right\rfloor \bmod p \right),\tag{5}$$

where p is the prime number and k is the index of the calculated element.

For the $2D$ space, subsequent prime numbers are used as a base. In our test, we used $\{2, 3\}$ for the Halton sequence and we got a following sequence of points in a rectangle:

$$Halton(2, 3, 5) = \left\{ \left(\frac{1}{2}a, \frac{1}{3}b\right), \left(\frac{1}{4}a, \frac{2}{3}b\right), \left(\frac{3}{4}a, \frac{1}{9}b\right), \left(\frac{1}{8}a, \frac{4}{9}b\right), \left(\frac{5}{8}a, \frac{7}{9}b\right), \right.$$
$$\left. \left(\frac{3}{8}a, \frac{2}{9}b\right), \left(\frac{7}{8}a, \frac{5}{9}b\right), \left(\frac{1}{16}a, \frac{8}{9}b\right), \left(\frac{9}{16}a, \frac{1}{27}b\right), \dots \right\}\tag{6}$$

where a is a width of the rectangle and b is a height of the rectangle.

Visualization of the dataset with 10^3 points of the Halton sequence from (6) can be seen in Fig. 8. We can see that the Halton sequence in $2D$ space covers this space more evenly than randomly distributed uniform points in the same rectangle.

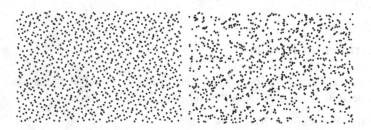

Fig. 8. $2D$ Halton points generated by $Halton(2, 3)$ (left) and $2D$ random points in a rectangle with uniform distribution (right). Number of points is 10^3 in both cases.

Gauss Ring Points. It is a special distribution of points in $2D$. Each point is determined as follows:

$$P = [a \cdot \varepsilon \cdot \cos(rand(0, 2\pi)), b \cdot \varepsilon \cdot \sin(rand(0, 2\pi))]$$

$$\varepsilon = 0.5 + 0.5 \cdot sign \cdot rand_{Gauss}\tag{7}$$

where a is a length of semi-major axis, b is a length of semi-minor axis, $sign$ is a randomly generated number from set $\{-1, 1\}$, $rand_{Gauss}$ is a randomly generated number with Gauss distribution from interval $[0, \infty)$ and $rand(0, 2\pi)$ is a random number with uniform distribution from 0 to 2π.

Visualization of the dataset with 10^3 Gauss ring points can be seen in Fig. 9. We can see that this dataset consists of a large set of points, which are close to the ellipse, and a small set of points, which are far from this ellipse.

Fig. 9. 2D Gauss ring points. Number of points is 10^3.

3.2   Optimal Size of Grid

In the proposed approach, the remaining points are divided into uniform grid $k \times k$ after their elimination by polar division. The size of the grid has significantly influence on the number of pairs of points for which their mutual distance is determined. Simultaneously the time complexity is increasing with growing size of the grid. Therefore, we need know an estimation of the optimal size of the grid, which should be dependent on the distribution of points and on the number of points. Therefore, we have to measure it for each type of input points separately.

We measured the time performance of our proposed algorithm for different distributions of points, different numbers of points and different sizes of grid. Measurement for 10^7 points is presented in Fig. 10. For all tested distributions of input points, we can see that the time performance decreases with the increasing size of grid until the optimal size of the grid is achieved. After that time, the complexity increases with the increasing number of divisions. Moreover, for all tested distributions of input points, except uniform points in the ellipse, it can be seen that the time complexity is practically independent on size of the grid. This is due to the fact that size of set of suspicious points is very small and the number of nonempty cells is small too, see Fig. 6(b, c). Thus the time complexity of division into uniform grid and consequent calculation is almost insignificant.

Figure 11 presents the optimal size of grid for different distributions of points and different numbers of points. It can be seen that the optimal size of grid increases with the increasing number of points. Moreover, we can see that for uniform distribution of points in the ellipse is needed larger size of the grid than for other tested distributions. This is due to the fact that for this distribution of points is the number of suspicious points substantially larger.

Evaluating experimental results for different distributions of points and different numbers of input points, i.e. 10^6, $\sqrt{10} \cdot 10^6$, 10^7, $\sqrt{10} \cdot 10^7$ and 10^8, including results from Figs. 10 and 11, we came to the following conclusion.

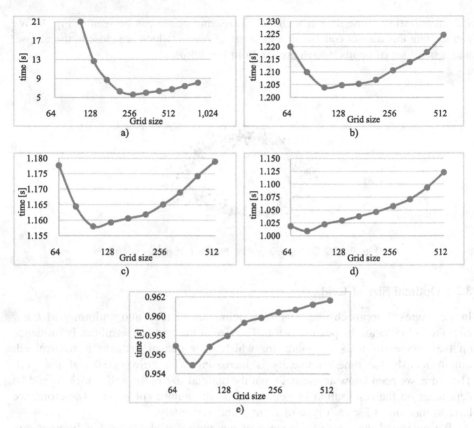

Fig. 10. The time performance of algorithm for finding maximum distance of two points for different points distributions and different size of grid. The size of grid denotes the number of cells in one axis. The number of input points is 10^7. Distribution of points are: (a) uniform points in ellipse, (b) uniform points in rectangle, (c) Halton points, (d) Gauss points, (e) Gauss ring points.

The optimal size of the grid is dependent on the number of input points, more precisely the size of the grid is dependent on number of suspicious point. Size of the grid has to increase with the increasing number of points.

3.3 Time Performance

In some applications, the time performance is one of an important criterion. Therefore, running times were measured for different number of input points with different distributions of points. Measurements were performed many times and average running times, calculated from the measured results, are in Table 1. Moreover, we can see these running times in Fig. 12.

It can be seen that the best time performance is for the Gauss ring points. The time performance for Halton points and for uniform distribution of points inside a rectangle is similar. Overall, we can say that for all tested distributions of input points, except

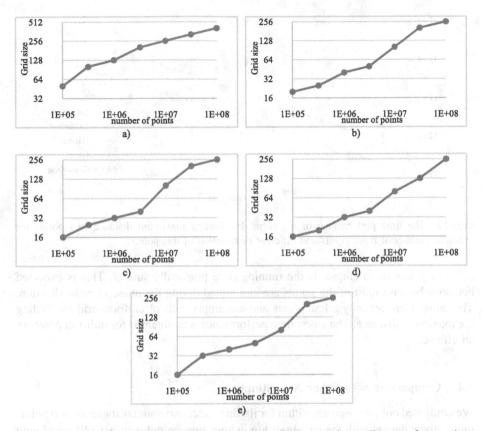

Fig. 11. Optimal number of grid size for algorithm for finding maximum distance of two points for different points distributions and different number of points. The size of grid denotes the number of cells in one axis. Distribution of points are: (a) uniform points in ellipse, (b) uniform points in rectangle, (c) Halton points, (d) Gauss points, (e) Gauss ring points.

Table 1. The time performance of convex hull for different number of input points and different distributions of points.

	Time [ms]				
Number of points	Uniform O	Uniform □	Halton	Gauss	GaussRing
1E+5	32.9	11.5	11.0	9.0	8.8
√10E+5	137.6	37.4	36.3	30.6	29.8
1E+6	466.2	119.1	113.5	93.3	93.4
√10E+6	1 745.5	367.8	355.8	315.0	296.0
1E+7	5 631.3	1 203.9	1 158.0	1 009.2	954.9
√10E+7	17 976.5	3 596.6	3 579.0	3 221.5	3 057.9
1E+8	56 769.0	11 154.0	11 505.0	12 004.0	9 680.0

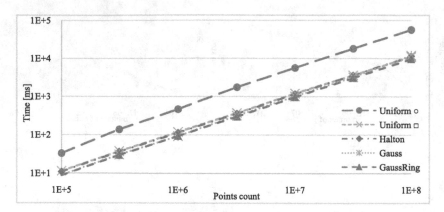

Fig. 12. The time performance of algorithm for finding maximum distance two points for different number of input points and different distribution of this points.

uniform points in an ellipse, is the running time practically similar. This is expected behavior because most of the points are eliminated during the phase of polar division. Therefore, there are only a few points and nonempty cells of uniform grid for finding the maximum distance. The worst time performance was obtained for uniform points in an ellipse.

3.4   Comparison with Other Algorithms

We compared our proposed algorithm for finding exact maximum distance of two points in the given dataset with the BF algorithm, whose time complexity is $O(N^2)$, and with the algorithm proposed in [8], which has expected time complexity $O(N)$, where N is the number of input points. It should be noted that the results for the algorithm in [8] are based on the use of the ratio of the BF algorithm to this algorithm.

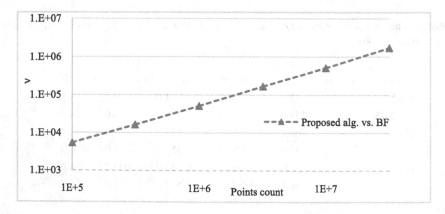

Fig. 13. The speed-up of our proposed algorithm for uniformly distributed points with respect to BF algorithm for the same datasets.

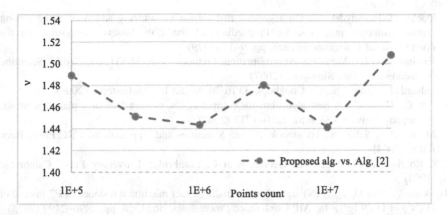

Fig. 14. The speed-up of our proposed algorithm for uniformly distributed points with respect to algorithm in [8] for the same datasets.

Running times were measured for different numbers of input points with uniformly distributed points. The resultant speed-up of our proposed algorithm with respect to the BF algorithm and algorithm in [8] can be seen in Figs. 13 and 14.

It can be seen that the speed-up of the proposed algorithm is significant with respect to BF algorithm and grows with the number of points processed. Moreover, our algorithm is in average 1.5 times faster than the algorithm in [8].

4 Conclusion

A new fast algorithm for finding an exact maximum distance of two points in E^2 with $\mathcal{O}_{expected}(N)$ complexity has been presented. This algorithm uses a space division technique. It is robust and can process a large number of points. The advantages of our proposed algorithm are simple implementation and robustness. Moreover, our algorithm can be easily extended to E^3 by a simple modification.

For future work, the algorithm for finding exact maximum distance of two points, can be easily parallelized, as most of the steps are independent. The second thing is to extend this algorithm to E^3.

Acknowledgments. The authors would like to thank their colleagues at the University of West Bohemia, Plzen, for their discussions and suggestions, and anonymous reviewers for their valuable comments and hints provided. The research was supported by MSMT CR projects LH12181 and SGS 2013-029.

References

1. Clarkson, K.L., Shor, P.W.: Applications of random sampling in computational geometry, II. Discrete Comput. Geom. **4**(1), 387–421 (1989)

2. Dobkin, D.P., Snyder, L.: On a general method for maximizing and minimizing among certain geometric problems. In: Proceedings of the 20th Annual Symposium on the Foundations of Computer Science, pp. 9–17 (1979)
3. Fasshauer, G.E.: Meshfree Approximation Methods with MATLAB. World Scientific Publishing Co., Inc., Singapore (2007)
4. Hilyard, J., Teilhet, S.: C# Cookbook. O'Reilly Media Inc., Sebastopol (2006)
5. Liu, G., Chen, C.: A new algorithm for computing the convex hull of a planar point set. J. Zhejiang Univ. Sci. A 8(8), 1210–1217 (2007)
6. Mehta, D.P., Sahni, S.: Handbook of Data Structures and Applications. CRC Press, Boca Raton (2004)
7. O'Rourke, J.: Computational Geometry in C. Cambridge University Press, Cambridge (1998)
8. Skala, V.: Fast $O_{expected}$ (N) algorithm for finding exact maximum distance in E2 instead of O (N^2) or O (N lgN). In: AIP Conference Proceedings, no. 1558, pp. 2496–2499 (2013)
9. Snyder, W.E., Tang, D.A.: Finding the extrema of a region. IEEE Trans. Pattern Anal. Mach. Intell. 2(3), 266–269 (1980)
10. Vince, J.: Geometric Algebra for Computer Graphics. Springer, Berlin (2008)

Fast Unconstrained Vehicle Type Recognition with Dual-Layer Classification

Xiao-Jun Hu[1], Bin Hu[1], Chun-Chao Guo[1], and Jian-Huang Lai[1,2](✉)

[1] School of Information Science and Technology,
Sun Yat-sen University, Guangzhou, China
{hux999m,chunchaoguo,huglenn232}@gmail.com
[2] Guangdong Key Laboratory of Information Security Technology,
Sun Yat-sen University, Guangzhou 510006, China
stsljh@mail.sysu.edu.cn

Abstract. This paper tackles the problem of vision-based vehicle type recognition, which aims at outputting a semantic label for the given vehicle. Most existing methods operate on a similar situation where vehicle viewpoints are not obviously changed and the foreground regions can be well segmented to extract texture, edge or length-width ratio. However, this underlying assumption faces severe challenges when the vehicle viewpoint varies apparently or the background is clutter. Thus we propose a dual-layer framework that can jointly handle the two challenges in a more natural way. In the training stage, each viewpoint of each type of vehicles is denoted as a sub-class, and we treat a pre-divided region of images as a sub-sub-class. In the first layer, we train a fast Exemplar-LDA classifier for each sub-sub-class. In the second layer of the training stage, all the Exemplar-LDA scores are concatenated for the consequent training of each sub-class. Due to introducing Exemplar-LDA, our approach is fast for both training and testing. Evaluations of the proposed dual-layer approach are conducted on challenging non-homologous multi-view images, and yield impressive performance.

Keywords: Vehicle type recognition · Exemplar-LDA · Dual-layer classification

1 Introduction

Vehicle type recognition based on vision has received great attention for its broad range of applications, including autonomous driving, intelligent transport and visual surveillance. It is an issue that aims to assign semantic labels to a vehicle image or video, such as truck, bus, sedan, or motorcycle. A framework for vehicle type recognition mainly consists of two components, namely vehicle representation and feature classification. Representation of vehicles is rather difficult comparing with that of other objects, since the appearance of different vehicles within the same type can vary drastically. This can be seen in Fig. 1. Even the appearance of the same type can change apparently with the angle.

© Springer International Publishing Switzerland 2015
Y.-J. Zhang (Ed.): ICIG 2015, Part II, LNCS 9218, pp. 275–283, 2015.
DOI: 10.1007/978-3-319-21963-9_25

To alleviate the difficulty on vehicle representation and classification, many existing methods mainly focus on constrained situations, for instance, video sequences captured from a single view [2,10,12,14,15,17]. In those sequences, intra-class appearance variations are not drastic and foreground regions can be segmented to further extract edge, length-width ratio, or other discriminative cues. This leads to easy representation and classification, as well as brings about an implicit deficiency that the model trained from a specific dataset is difficult to be applied to another scenario. For classification, hierarchical classification has shown its strength in saliency detection [16], face verification [1], and so on. However, previous works on vehicle type recognition usually rely on a single-level classification framework, including common AdaBoost [17], SVM [6,14] and KNN [9,12], which tends to be easily influenced by appearance changes.

Inspired by the recent fine-grained object categorization [1], we propose a unified framework for vehicle type recognition. Vehicles are represented in a higher level and unconstrained situation, which leads to that our representation can tolerate arbitrary viewpoint changes and large intra-class appearance variations. In the training stage, each viewpoint of each kind of vehicles is denoted as subset, and we treat a region of images in a subset as a sub-class. Different from [1] that trained one-vs-one SVM for each pair of sub-classes, we train a fast Exemplar-LDA classifier [7] for each sub-class firstly, also called region-based one-vs-one features. This is mainly due to the fact that Exemplar-LDA is much faster than Exemplar-SVM as well as achieving competing performance. In the second layer of the training stage, all the Exemplar-LDA scores are concatenated as a new feature vector for the consequent training of each vehicle type. Given a test image, scores of the first level are obtained from all the trained Exemplar-LDA classifiers. Then they are concatenated and fed into a SVM classifier for the final vehicle type output. The two layers are closely related, which can well handle both representation and classification.

(a)   (b)

Fig. 1. Challenges of vehicle type recognition. (a): Large intra-class appearance variation of 2 trucks caused by viewpoint change; (b): Type confusion caused by appearance similarity between a bus and a truck.

This paper aims to resolve two problems, including unconstrained vehicle recognition and fast vehicle recognition. The first problem is solved with the help of our dual-layer framework that generates a higher representation, and the second goal is achieved via the introduction of exemplar-LDA in the first layer. The main contributions of this work are three-fold. (1) We propose an approach to unconstraint vehicle type recognition, which jointly resolves larger intra-class variations within the same type as well as viewpoint-independent vehicle type recognition. (2) Our representation does not rely on any prior assumptions of a vehicle. Extraction of vehicle foreground regions is not deemed necessary, which allows our representation can be generalized to either video sequences or still images. (3) We leverage Exemplar-LDA to the first layer of our dual-layer classification, considering that the Exemplar-LDA is much faster than the conventional Exemplar-SVM and achieves competitive performacne. Thus our approach can be practicably implemented in real-world applications.

2 Related Work

Vehicle type recognition has drawn great attention in the past years. We will review closely related works following the two common components of this issue, namely vehicle feature representation and feature classification.

In terms of feature extraction, shape and texture features are more popular than color descriptors, since vehicle type is independent on color in most cases. An intuitive way to categorize vehicle types is to represent and classify the given vehicle with shape or edge cues. The contour and aspect ratio of vehicles are commonly exploited in [2,5,9,13] for representation. In [15], Tian et al. made use of color information and taxi symbols to detect taxi with the priori knowledge about the position of plate number. In [12,14], two new descriptors are introduced, named extract Square Mapped Gradients (SMG) and Locally Normalized Harris strengths (LNHS), respectively. However, both of them requires a frontal view for a car image. Reference [6,17] extracted SIFT and HOG to embed texture information of vehicle. Ma et al. [10] proposed modified-SIFT along with SIFT to demonstrate vehicles that made obvious performance improvements. It was extracted by first obtain SIFT on edge points, and then cluster them, which is followed by the final key point selection.

As for feature classification of vehicles, most common classification algorithms are employed in this field. SVM classifiers are ultilized in [6,14], while kNN is used in [9,12]. Also a Bayesian classifier was used by [10]. Moreover, Zhang [17] cascaded different strong classifier with Adaboost, which showed an obvious improvement.

Although extensive studies on vehicle type recognition have been presented, it remains a challenging problem for the reason that most existing approaches work in constrained scenarios. [2,10,12,13,17] are based on cameras whose positions are fixed, which means that their background is unchanged. [2,10,13] relies on foreground region extraction. It cannot achieve satisfactory performance if it confronts complicated background or the background is clutter. [2,10,12,14,15, 17] capture vehicles from an unchanged viewpoint. Hence they are sensitive to viewpoint variations and cannot work in realistic scenes, where diverse angles of vehicles occur frequently. [2,5,9,10,13] extract edge features and show impressive improvements on their testing data. However, their limitations emerge obviously when given images have low resolution or contain a clutter background.

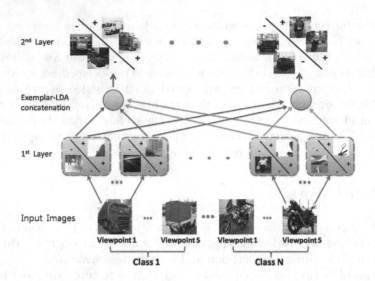

2nd Layer

Exemplar-LDA concatenation

1st Layer

Input Images

Viewpoint 1   Viewpoint 5   Viewpoint 1   Viewpoint 5

Class 1   Class N

Fig. 2. Sketch of the framework. Best viewed in color.

3   The Dual-Layer Framework

3.1   Overview of the Framework

Figure 2 demonstrates the sketch of our framework. In the vehicle classification dataset, we have four different types of vehicles (bus, car, motorcycle, truck). The training images of each vehicle category are further divided into five subsets according to the viewpoints. This division in training stage is critical, considering that intra-class appearance variations are extremely drastic. During feature learning, we treat each subset of vehicle as a sub-class, so that we totally have 20 classes in the final classification. Inspired by part-based models in many fine-grain classification works, we divide images into $n \times m$ overlapping windows, each of which plays the role of a part model. We extract HOG descriptors from each window and train a linear classifier $P_{i,j}$. Here i denotes a sub-class ranging from 1 to 20 in our experiment, and j indicates a window in the image. Please see Sect. 3.3 for details of training part classifiers. In fact, the underlying meaning of each trained part classifier is that the part classifier describes the local appearance attribute of a vehicle. In the feature extraction stage, each part models are applied to correspond location of image, and the detection scores in different sub-classes and different parts are concatenated to form our final feature representation

$$Ftr(H) = [\Phi(H_1, P_{1,1}), ..., \emptyset(H_{m*n}, P_{1,m*n}), ...,$$
$$\Phi(H_1, P_{20,1}), ..., \emptyset(H_{m*n}, P_{20,m*n})] \tag{1}$$

where $H_i \in [1, m*n]$ are HOG descriptors in each window, and Φ denotes the score function. Given this feature representation, we train 20 One-Vs-All classifiers with linear SVM. At testing stage, we obtain the predicted type of the vehicle by selecting the class with highest classification score ignoring the angle.

3.2 Training Exemplar-LDA for Each Part

Although POOF [1] has achieved significant performance improvement in fine-grained classification, it still shows some limitations, one of which is that training linear SVM for each part is time-expensive. The Exemplar-SVM method [11] in objet detection domain faces the same problem since it needs to train a SVM classifier for each training sample. In Exemplar-LDA [7], the authors replace the SVM with LDA which can be trained very efficiently. We can treat LDA model as a linear classifier with its weight given by $\omega = \Sigma^{-1}(\mu_1 - \mu_0)$. Here Σ is the class-independent covariance matrix and μ_i is corresponding to class-dependent mean. Exploiting the scale and translation invariance property of nature image [8], μ_0 and Σ in [7] are estimated offline, and then reused for all object categories.

Explicitly, given an image window of a fixed size, the HOG descriptor is a concatenation of gradient orientations histogram in each 8×8 cell. We denote x_{ij} as the feature vector of the cell in correspond location (i, j). We extract HOG descriptor from different scales and translations in training image, and compute the mean HOG feature $\mu = E[x_{ij}]$. Then we average the features over all locations and images. Exploiting the translation invariance property, for a category with size of N_0 cells, we can construct μ_0 by conveniently replicating μ over all N_0 cells.

Likewise, we can treat Σ as a block matrix with blocks $\Sigma_{(i,j),(l,k)} = E[x_{ij}x_{lk}^T]$. Under the assumption of translation invariance, we assume that $\Sigma_{(i,j),(l,k)}$ only depends on the relative offset $(i - k)$ and $(j - l)$, then we have

$$\Sigma_{(i,j),(l,k)} = \Gamma_{(i-l),(j-k)} = E\left[x_{uv}x_{(u+i-l),(v+j-k)}^T\right] \qquad (2)$$

Instead of learning $dN_0 \times dN_0$ matrix Σ, we only have to learn $d \times d$ matrices $\Gamma_{(s,t)}$ for all possible offset (s, t). Here d indicates the dimension of HOG descriptor. We learn the μ and matrices $\Gamma_{(s,t)}$ from all subwindows extracted from PASCALVOC 2010 dataset [3], which contains 10000 natural images. Σ can be reconstructed from Γ using Eq. 2.

3.3 Accelerating with Exemplar-LDA

As mentioned in Sect. 3.1, we need to train a linear classifier for each part of each sub-class. Here it is unpractical to employ conventional SVMs, which involve the hard sample mining procedure that is time-consuming. Therefore, we utilize the powerful Exemplar-LDA to train our part-based models. We average HOG descriptors of all positive samples of each part in order to obtain μ_1. The mean background μ_0 and the covariance matrix Σ are calculated following Sect. 3.2. The final weight of a trained linear classifier can be computed using

$$\omega = \Sigma^{-1}(\mu_1 - \mu_0). \qquad (3)$$

Table 1. Comparison results.

	Bus	Car	Motorcycle	Truck
BoW	66 %	67 %	81 %	64 %
HOG + RF	71 %	85 %	89 %	73 %
Ours	**91 %**	**93 %**	**99 %**	**92 %**

Fig. 3. Samples of the dataset.

4   Experimental Results

4.1   Dataset and Experiment Settings

There exists 4 vehicle types in our dataset, including car, bus, motorcycle and truck. 4000 images are contained in this dataset in total, with 5 different view-points for each type. Considering the symmetry of vehicles, only 5 viewpoints are collected, including 0 degree, 45 degree, 90 degree, 135 degree and 180 degree, which contains a circle from frontal view to rear view. 3600 images are used in the training stage, and the remaining 400 images are treated as the test set. This dataset is rather challenging for the reason that the backgrounds are clutter and the intra-class appearance variations are large. Samples of the dataset can be seen in Fig. 3. In our experiments, we denote each vehicle type as a class, each viewpoint of each class as a sub-class, and each region of each sub-class as a sub-sub-class. Here all the images are normalized into the same resolution with 224*224, and each image is divided into 4*4 regions. Consequently, there are 4 classes, 4*5 sub-classes, and 4*5*16 sub-sub-classes. In the first layer, 320 Exemplar-LDA classifiers are trained, while in the second layer, 20 SVMs are trained for all the sub-classes.

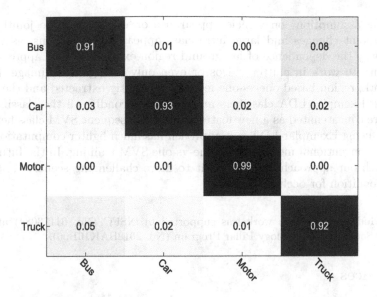

Fig. 4. The confusion matrix of our classification results.

4.2 Quantitative Results and Analysis

As can be seen in Fig. 4, our dual-layer approach achieves an average accuracy of 93 %. For every type, our recognition rate is over 90 %, especially for the motorcycle, whose accuracy even reaches 99 %. Besides the strength of our method, another reason of the high performance is that the appearance of motorcycles is obviously different form other vehicles. From Fig. 4, we can see that the main threaten comes from the classification of the buses and the trucks. This is mainly due to the fact that the two types are similar in appearance in some specific views, for instance, in the 135 degree.

In our experiments, we set two widely used models as the benchmark comparison methods, including the bag of words model (BoW) [4] and the Random Forest model using HOG features (HOG + RF). Table 1 gives the quantitative accuracy, from which we can see that our approach obviously outperforms the two benchmark methods.

Note that, our approach is rather fast in both training and testing, and thus it is appropriate to be implanted in real-world scenarios. The training time of per Exemplar-LDA consumes 0.3283 s, whilst the time of classification for each image only costs 0.0105 s.

5   Conclusion

This paper has presented a dual-layer framework for fast unconstrained vehicle type recognition. Unlike many existing methods, this work does not rely on strong assumptions on vehicle appearance or viewpoints. We jointly handle viewpoint changes and large intra-class appearance variations, as well as throw away the dependence of foreground region extraction. Our approach has the ability to work in clutter videos or even only a single-shot image. In our framework, region-based one-vs-one features are firstly extracted and the corresponding Exemplar-LDA classifiers are trained. Secondly, all the classification scores are concatenated as a new feature for the consequent SVM classifier. Due to introducing Exemplar-LDA, our approach has much lighter computation load than the conventional method using one-vs-one SVM training. In the future, we will enrich our approach and extend it to more challenging scenarios, such as type recognition for occluded vehicles.

Acknowledgement. This work was supported by NSFC (No. 61173084) and the National Science & Technology Pillar Program (No. 2012BAK16B06).

References

1. Berg, T., Belhumeur, P.N.: Poof: Part-based one-vs.-one features for fine-grained categorization, face verification, and attribute estimation. In: 2013 IEEE Conference on Computer Vision and Pattern Recognition (CVPR), pp. 955–962. IEEE (2013)
2. Chen, Z., Ellis, T., Velastin, S.A.: Vehicle type categorization: a comparison of classification schemes. In: 14th International IEEE Conference on Intelligent Transportation Systems (ITSC), pp. 74–79. IEEE (2011)
3. Everingham, M., Van Gool, L., Williams, C.K.I., Winn, J., Zisserman, A.: The pascal visual object classes (voc) challenge. Int. J. Comput. Vis. **88**(2), 303–338 (2010)
4. Fei-Fei, L., Perona, P.: A bayesian hierarchical model for learning natural scene categories. In: 2005 IEEE Computer Society Conference on Computer Vision and Pattern Recognition (CVPR), vol. 2, pp. 524–531. IEEE (2005)
5. Feris, R., Siddiquie, B., Zhai, Y., Petterson, J., Brown, L., Pankanti, S.: Attribute-based vehicle search in crowded surveillance videos. In: Proceedings of the 1st ACM International Conference on Multimedia Retrieval, p. 18. ACM (2011)
6. Gandhi, T., Trivedi, M.M.: Video based surround vehicle detection, classification and logging from moving platforms: issues and approaches. In: Intelligent Vehicles Symposium, pp. 1067–1071. IEEE (2007)
7. Hariharan, B., Malik, J., Ramanan, D.: Discriminative decorrelation for clustering and classification. In: Fitzgibbon, A., Lazebnik, S., Perona, P., Sato, Y., Schmid, C. (eds.) ECCV 2012, Part IV. LNCS, vol. 7575, pp. 459–472. Springer, Heidelberg (2012)
8. Hyvrinen, A., Hurri, J., Hoyer, P.O.: Natural Image Statistics: A Probabilistic Approach to Early Computational Vision. Springer, London (2009)
9. Iqbal, U., Zamir, S., Shahid, M., Parwaiz, K., Yasin, M., Sarfraz, M.: Image based vehicle type identification. In: 2010 International Conference on Information and Emerging Technologies (ICIET), pp. 1–5. IEEE (2010)
10. Ma, X., Grimson, W.E.L.: Edge-based rich representation for vehicle classification. In: 10th IEEE International Conference on Computer Vision (ICCV), vol. 2, pp. 1185–1192. IEEE (2005)

11. Malisiewicz, T., Gupta, A., Efros, A.A.: Ensemble of exemplar-svms for object detection and beyond. In: ICCV (2011)
12. Petrovic, V.S., Cootes, T.F.: Analysis of features for rigid structure vehicle type recognition. In: BMVC, pp. 1–10 (2004)
13. Rad, R., Jamzad, M.: Real time classification and tracking of multiple vehicles in highways. Pattern Recogn. Lett. **26**(10), 1597–1607 (2005)
14. Rahati, S., Moravejian, R., Mohamad, E., Mohamad, F.: Vehicle recognition using contourlet transform and SVM. In: 5th International Conference on Information Technology: New Generations. 2008 ITNG, pp. 894–898. IEEE (2008)
15. Tian, B., Li, B., Li, Y., Xiong, G., Zhu, F.: Taxi detection based on vehicle painting features for urban traffic scenes. In: 2013 IEEE International Conference on Vehicular Electronics and Safety (ICVES), pp. 105–109. IEEE (2013)
16. Yan, Q., Xu, L., Shi, J., Jia, J.: Hierarchical saliency detection. In: 2013 IEEE Conference on Computer Vision and Pattern Recognition (CVPR), pp. 1155–1162. IEEE (2013)
17. Zhang, B.: Reliable classification of vehicle types based on cascade classifier ensembles. IEEE Trans. Intell. Transp. Syst. **14**(1), 322–332 (2013)

Feature Matching Method for Aircraft Positioning on Airdrome

Jian Wang[1(✉)] and Yubo Ni[2]

[1] Civil Aviation ATM Institute, Civil Aviation University of China,
Tianjin 300300, China
caucwang@263.net
[2] Sino-European Institute of Aviation Engineering, Civil Aviation University of China,
Tianjin 300300, China

Abstract. The binocular stereoscopic vision technology could be used to locate targets on an aerodrome. To ensure positioning targets, the pixels on images from two vision sensors should be matched accordingly. Combining advantages of both SIFT (Scale-invariant feature transform) and an epipolar line constraint equation, a method of pixel matching is proposed. Roughly-matched points are first obtained using SIFT, in which some mismatched ones exist. Matched points are different from mismatched ones when an epipolar line constraint equation is introduced. Although matched points do not always meet the epipolar line constraint equation because of system measuring errors, the difference between the values of a matrix and critical threshold could be used to distinguish the mismatched pixels from roughly matched ones. This method can not only ensure the accuracy for the target matching, but also automatically find out feature points of the aircraft used for positioning.

Keywords: Binocular vision · SIFT · Epipolar line constraint · Mismatched points · Fundamental matrix · Threshold

1 Introduction

The airport complex operating environment needs means of surface surveillance to acquire transport traffic situations [1]. Nowadays, for hub airport surface surveillance, the S-mode radar and multi-point positioning sensors are used for the surveillance of cooperative targets. ICAO's (International Civil Aviation Organization) Advanced-Surface Movement Guidance and Control System (A-SMGCS) requires surveillance tools for non-cooperative targets [2]. Binocular stereo vision technology with good positioning accuracy has established the mathematical relationship between targets and their images. Using this technique, matching of targets of similar characteristics is important.

J. Wang—Professor, supervisor of postgraduate, main research field for high speed optical fiber communication system, photoelectric detection technology, air traffic control radar display technology.

Y.-J. Zhang (Ed.): ICIG 2015, Part II, LNCS 9218, pp. 284–291, 2015.
DOI: 10.1007/978-3-319-21963-9_26

In the field of image processing, methods of target matching based on image features have their own advantages, with good adaptability on the gray scale, the strain and the block [3]. Among these methods, the Scale Invariant Feature transform (SIFT) algorithm proposed by David Lowe has good robustness to most of the noise, brightness changes disturbances, etc. [3]. Although it can be used as a target matching method for the binocular stereo vision applications, it needs to be improved when used as a method for positing targets, since SIFT would produce easily error matching points. A proposal is put forwards by introducing an epipolar line constraint to remove mismatched points.

2 Matching Algorithm

2.1 SIFT

There are three main steps for SIFT: (1) detecting scale-space's extremas, localizing accurately key-points; (2) assigning orientation and establishing local image descriptors; (3) matching key-points.

The scale space of an image is defined as a function, which is generated from the convolution of a variable-scale Gaussian $G(x, y, \sigma)$ with an input image of $I(x, y)$ [4]:

$$L(x, y, \sigma) = G(x, y, \sigma) * I(x, y) \tag{1}$$

where, (x, y) is the position on an image, σ represents the degree of a smoothing scale parameter, showing the feature of an image. When the scale parameter is great, it can show the detail of the image. When the scale parameter is small, it can show the general information of the image [5]. To achieve rotation invariance and a high level of efficiency in scale space, the key location is selected at the maxima or the minima value of the difference of a Gaussian function [6], meaning that $\frac{\partial}{\partial \sigma}(\sigma^2 \nabla^2 L) = 0$. The efficient way of detecting keypoint locations in scale space is applying scale-space's extrema to the Difference-of-Gaussian (DoG) function convolved with the image. As DoG function has a strong response along edges, the edge response must be eliminated [7].

By assigning a consistent orientation to each keypoint based on local image features, the keypoint descriptor can be represented relative to this orientation and therefore achieve invariance to image rotation [8]. or image sampling on a certain scale, the gradient magnitude $m(x, y)$ and orientation $\theta(x, y)$ are computed using pixel differences:

$$m(x, y) = \sqrt{[L(x + 1, y) - L(x - 1, y)]^2 + [L(x, y + 1) - L(x, y - 1)]^2} \tag{2}$$

$$\theta(x, y) = \tan^{-1}[\frac{L(x, y + 1) - L(x, y - 1)}{L(x + 1, y) - L(x - 1, y)}] \tag{3}$$

After having assigned an image location, scale, and orientation to each keypoint, the gradient magnitude and the orientation are supplemented to a local 2D coordinate system, which can describe the local image region and provide these parameters with invariance [8]. The image gradient magnitude and orientation are sampled around the keypoint location. An orientation histogram is formed from the gradient orientations with sampled points within a region around the keypoint. The orientation histogram covers a range of orientations of 360°. Each sample added to the histogram is weighted by its gradient magnitude and a Gaussian-weighted circular window, with a σ being 1.5 times of the scale of the keypoint [9]. The descriptor is formed from the vector containing the values of all the orientation histogram entries. In order to achieve orientation invariance, the coordinates of the descriptor and the gradients are rotated relative to the keypoint orientation. For each keypoint, there are 16 array of histograms with 8 orientation bins in each and 128 element feature vectors, as shown in Fig. 1.

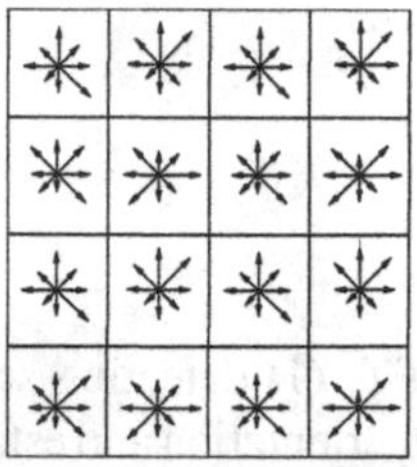

Fig. 1. SIFT keypoint descriptor

The best candidate for each keypoint is found by identifying its nearest neighbor in the database of keypoints from 2 images. The nearest neighbor is defined as the keypoint with minimum Euclidean distance for the invariant keypoint descriptor. Comparing the distance of the closest neighbor to that of the second-closest neighbor and supposing that the division of the closest neighbor to the second-closest neighbor is smaller than the global threshold, these 2 keypoints can be taken as the matched points. Otherwise, these 2 points are not matched [9].

2.2 Epipolar Line Constraint

For Binocular stereo vision, the two feature-matched points should locate in the same epipolar line. Using this idea, mismatched points can be found with the imaging formula [10]:

$$I_i = \begin{bmatrix} u_i \\ v_i \\ 1 \end{bmatrix} = \begin{bmatrix} k_{xi} & 0 & u_{0i} & 0 \\ 0 & k_{yi} & v_{0i} & 0 \\ 0 & 0 & 0 & 1 \end{bmatrix} \begin{bmatrix} R_i & p_i \\ 0 & 1 \end{bmatrix} \begin{bmatrix} x_w \\ y_w \\ z_w \\ 1 \end{bmatrix} = \begin{bmatrix} M_{3i} & m_{3i} \end{bmatrix} \begin{bmatrix} x_w \\ y_w \\ z_w \\ 1 \end{bmatrix} \quad (4)$$

where, (u_i, v_i) represents the coordinate on the image plan i. (u_{0i}, v_{0i}) is the coordinate of the camera in the image plan i. (k_{xi}, k_{yi}) represents the magnification in an image plan. R_i is the 3×3 rotation matrix of camera i. Vector p_i is the position vector of camera i. (x_w, y_w, z_w) is the coordinate of the target in the world coordinate system. M_{3i} is a 3×3 matrix and m_{3i} is a 3×1 vector. For surveillance using binocular stereo vision, i equals to 1 or 2. Simplifying the target position by using the formula above for camera 1 and 2, an equation could be obtained:

$$I_1 - M_{31}M_{32}^{-1}I_2 = -M_{31}M_{32}^{-1}m_{32} + m_{31} \tag{5}$$

Suppose the vector $\begin{bmatrix} m_x & m_y & m_z \end{bmatrix}^T = m_{31} - M_{31}M_{32}^{-1}m_{32}$, with the basic propriety of the matrix, there exists $m^+ = \begin{bmatrix} 0 & -m_z & m_y \\ m_z & 0 & -m_x \\ -m_y & m_x & 0 \end{bmatrix}$, so that $m^+ \begin{bmatrix} m_x \\ m_y \\ m_z \end{bmatrix} = 0$.

Equation 5 can be multiplied on left by m^+ and simplified as:

$$m^+I_1 - m^+M_{31}M_{32}^{-1}I_2 = 0 \tag{6}$$

Equation 6 can be multiplied on left by I_1^T and simplified as:

$$I_1^T m^+ M_{31}M_{32}^{-1}I_2 = 0 \tag{7}$$

Equation 6 is the epipolar line constraint equation. Denoting $F = m^+M_{31}M_{32}^{-1}$, which is usually called fundamental matrix, Eq. 6 will be simplified as:

$$I_1^T F I_2 = 0 \tag{8}$$

3   Aircraft Matching on an Aerodrome

Using the algorithm of SIFT to process the images from the airport surveillance, the simulation shows that most of the keypoints locate in such areas of aircraft as: head, nose landing gear (NLG), main landing gear (MLG), inlet of the engine, vertical tail, and wingtip.

For example, using an image size of 486 × 729, an 8-bit grayscale, and a global threshold set 0.4 or 0.9, results are shown in Fig. 2.

When the global threshold is set to 0.4, there are 44 matched points, with only 1 mismatched point, and about 93 % of the matched points locate on the aircraft. When the global threshold is set to 0.9, there 93 matched points, with 22 mismatched points, and about 52 % of matched points locate on the aircraft.

The global threshold is crucial, because the amount of matched points are not enough to describe the surveillance situation when the global threshold is a small value. When the global threshold is great, matched points will locate on the lamp of the apron, or vehicles, etc. These matched points are not located on the aircraft, and they are a kind of 'noise', which should be filtered out.

For civil aviation surveillance, especially for A-SMGCS policy, the method combines the algorithm of SIFT and the epipoplar line constraint for finding the mismatched points and remove them. As the error of the calibration, the matched points cannot always satisfy the epipoplar line constraint Eq. 7. To solve this problem, we define an operator $I_1^T F I_2$, and use this operator to calculate all matched points. The fundamental matrix is calculated during the calibration when the 2 camera are fixed. There will exist a threshold called critical threshold and all mismatched points will not

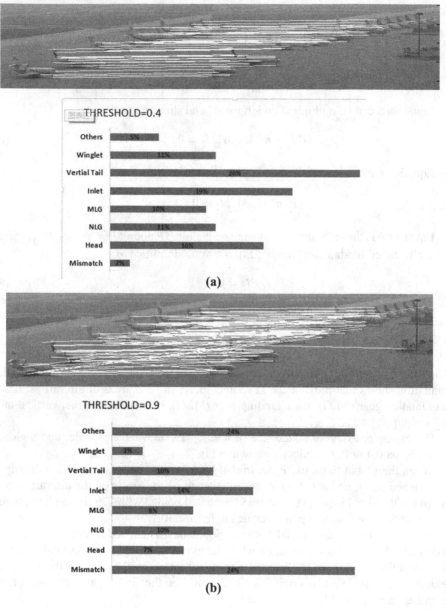

Fig. 2. (a). The statistics and the results when threshold is 0.4 (b). The statistics and the results when threshold is 0.9

satisfy the constrain $I_1^T F I_2 \leq \varepsilon$. By this judgment, we can easily find the mismatched points and remove them.

For the same surveillance case as the previous example, 8 matched points are used to calibrate the fundamental matrix (Table 1).

Table 1. The coordinate of 8 match points

Matched point	Camera 1 coordinate	Camera 2 coordinate
1	(289.76, 398.94)	(295.64, 565.95)
2	(271.71, 500.62)	(277.17, 671.55)
3	(273.01, 408.78)	(278.44, 576.18)
4	(245.68, 529.27)	(250.91, 663.35)
5	(247.36, 493.09)	(277.89, 498.46)
6	(272.47, 333,73)	(263.64, 699.68)
7	(258.48, 527.46)	(348.44, 271.92)
8	(342.56, 107.39)	(340.39, 263.58)

Putting these 8 matched points into Eq. 7, the fundamental matrix F can be found as:

$$F = \begin{pmatrix} -7.845 \times 10^{-6} & -6.356 \times 10^{-6} & 0.011738036 \\ 3.973 \times 10^{-6} & 1 \times 10^{-7} & 0.003476968 \\ -0.005120125 & -0.002781841 & 0.0476961799 \end{pmatrix}$$

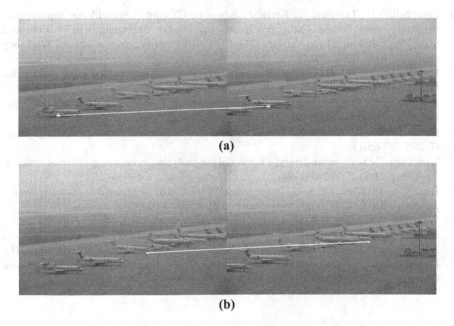

(a)

(b)

Fig. 3. (a). Mismatched point 1 (b). Mismatched point 2

When the global threshold is set to 0.7, 73 matched points are obtained by calculating the operator $I_1^T FI_2$, and two mismatched points are also obtained, shown in Fig. 3:

$$I_{21} = (398.97, 160.65), I_{11} = (356.10, 139.28), \text{ with } I_{11}^T FI_{21} = 1.046$$
$$I_{22} = (324.48, 495.09), I_{12} = (288.34, 486.61), \text{ with } I_{12}^T FI_{22} = 1.233$$

The matched point calculated by the operator $I_1^T FI_2 \in [0.39, 0.53]$. In this case, the critical threshold is defined as $\varepsilon = 0.8$, since the result calculated by the operator of the mismatched point is much bigger than the matched point. Checking by visual inspection, the result is correct.

4   Conclusion

Combining the SIFT and the epipolar line constrain, the method is for target matching of airport surveillance. The global threshold should not be great when targets to be positioned are the aircraft. Because of the error of calibration, the epipolar line constrain equation can't be used directly. Therefore an operator $I_1^T FI_2$ and the critical threshold should be defined and all matched points will satisfy the condition that the absolute value of $I_1^T FI_2$ is no large than ε. The simulation shows that this algorithm works well for the aircraft matching for airport surveillance.

References

1. Campbell, S.D., Londner, E., Keefe, J., Edwards, C.: Airport surveillance requirements validation using Monte Carlo simulation. In: Digital communications – Enhanced Surveillance of Aircraft and Vehicles (TIWDC/ESAV), Tyrrhenian International Workshop on, Roma, Italy, IEEE (2014)
2. Luo, X., Lu, Y., Wu, H.G.: A novel airport surface surveillance method using multi-video fusion. Telecommun. Eng. 7, 128–132 (2011)
3. Zeng, L., Wang, Y., Tan, J.: Improved algorithm for SIFT feature extraction and matching. Opt. Precis. Eng. 5, 1391–1397 (2011)
4. Cheng, D.Z., Li, Y.J., Yu, R.X.: Image matching method based on improved SIFT algorithm. 17, 285–287 (2011)
5. Lindeberg, T.: Scale-space theory: a basic tool for analyzing structures at different scales. J. Appl. Stat. 21(2), 225–270 (1994)
6. Hsu, C.-Y., Lu, C.-S., Pei, S.-C.: Image feature extraction in encrypted domain with privacy-preserving SIFT. IEEE Trans. Image Process. 21, 4593–4607 (2012)
7. Wang, H., Yang, K., Gao, F., Li, J.: Normalization methods of SIFT vector for object recognition. In: 2011 Tenth International Symposium on Distributed Computing and Applications to Business, Engineering and Science (DCABES), Wuxi, China. IEEE (2011)
8. Lowe, D.G.: Object recognition from local scale-invariant features. In: International Conference of Computer Vision, pp. 1150–1157 (1999)

9. Lowe, D.G.: Distinctive image features from scale-invariant keypoints. Int. J. Comput. Vision **60**(2), 91–110 (2004)
10. Sonka, M., Hlavac, V., Boyle. R.: Image Processing, Analysis, and Machine Vision, 3rd edn.

Flow Feature Extraction Based on Entropy and Clifford Algebra

Xiaofan Liu, Wenyao Zhang[✉], and Ning Zheng

Beijing Key Laboratory of Intelligent Information Technology,
School of Computer Science, Beijing Institute of Technology,
Beijing 100081, People's Republic of China
zhwenyao@bit.edu.cn

Abstract. Feature extraction is important to the visualization of large scale flow fields. To extract flow field features, we propose a new method that is based on Clifford algebra and information entropy theory. Given an input 3D flow field defined on uniform grids, it is firstly converted to a multi-vector field. We then compute its flow entropy field according to information theory, and choose high entropy regions to do the Clifford convolution with predefined multi-vector filter masks. Features are determined on the convolution results. With this method, we can locate, identify, and visualize a set of flow features. And test results show that our method can reduce computation time and find more features than the topology-based method.

Keywords: Flow visualization · Feature extraction · Clifford convolution · Flow field entropy

1 Introduction

Feature extraction is an important way to visualize flow fields in scientific computing. Feature visualization obtains meaningful structures from data fields, overcoming the disadvantages of traditional visualization methods. For 2D flow fields, topology analysis [1] is a traditional visualization based on feature extraction. Most methods based on topology analysis [2–4] work well in 2D feature extraction, but can not be simply extended to 3D flow fields. For example, the vortex core line reported in [5] can not be detected by topology analysis.

With such problems, methods based on Clifford algebra were developed to detect flow features [6], where multi-vector filter masks are predefined and used to convolve with the underlying flow fields to determine features. The main drawback of these methods is the heavy convolution, because it has to be applied on the whole field. Although Hitzer et al. [7] proposed the Clifford Fourier transformation to accelerate it, there is still an overhead to be cut down.

On the other hand, information theory was applied to measuring the complexity of streamlines [8]. And an information-theoretic framework was proposed and used for flow visualization [9–11]. With the information theory, flow field complexity can be measured with flow field entropy. The more complicated the areas are, the higher the entropy values are. This gives us some kinds of information about the structures in the underlying field.

© Springer International Publishing Switzerland 2015
Y.-J. Zhang (Ed.): ICIG 2015, Part II, LNCS 9218, pp. 292–300, 2015.
DOI: 10.1007/978-3-319-21963-9_27

With the motivation to make feature extraction easier, we propose a new method to extract features for 3D flow fields. In this method, we first compute the entropy of the flow field according to information theory, and then choose high entropy regions to do the Clifford convolution with multi-vector filter masks. Finally, features are determined on the convolution results. This method integrates information computing into flow field Clifford convolution, and increases the efficiency of feature extraction by avoiding most of unnecessary convolutions.

The remainder of this paper is organized as follows. Section 2 briefly reviews the related work. Section 3 gives our approach, including some basics about Clifford algebra and flow field entropy. Test results are included in Sect. 4. The final is the conclusions.

2 Related Work

In flow visualization, feature extraction is often used to simplify and visualize flow fields in large scale. And many methods have been proposed for flow feature extraction. Here, we only briefly review the work directly related to our method.

Based on the scalar product between two arbitrary vectors, Heiberg et al. [12] defined a scalar convolution on flow vector fields, and presented a template matching method to extract features in vector fields. It can detect most of flow features, for example, vortices, swirling flow, diverging, converging, etc. In [6], Ebling and Scheuermann proposed a pattern matching method based on Clifford convolution. This method can detect flow features, but its computation is heavy. In [7], Hitzer extended Fourier transform to Clifford algebra and got the accelerated Clifford convolution.

On the other hand, information theory was introduced for flow visualization. Chen and Jäenicke [8] presented an information-theoretic framework for flow feature analysis and visualization. Wang et al. [9] presented a block-wise technique to analyze the important aspect of time-varying data. In [10], Furuya and Itoh applied information theory to measure the complexity of existing streamlines based on the distribution of the tangent orientations. In [11], Xu et al. gave an information-theoretic framework for flow visualization, where the information of vector fields is measured by Shannon's entropy. In [13], Tao et al. proposed an information-theoretic framework, which applied dual information channels to solve streamline selection and viewpoint selection problems in flow visualization.

3 Our Approach

3.1 Overview

In this paper, we propose a feature extract method for 3D flow fields. This method shares the framework of pattern matching that is based on Clifford convolution, but includes a processing of region selection that is guided by flow field entropy. In the traditional pattern matching, convolution operator has to be applied on the whole input field. For some regions, however, there is no need to do convolution, since no meaningful features are contained in them. In order to reduce redundant overhead, we calculate the flow field entropy firstly, and then restrict the flow field convolution to regions with high entropy values. By this means, we can identify flow patterns and features precisely and efficiently. As a whole, our method works as followed.

(1) Initially, the input flow field is normalized and converted to a multi-vector field.
(2) Multi-vector filter masks are prepared for different flow patterns and features.
(3) Calculate the flow field entropy according to the information theory of flow field, and get the entropy field of the input field.
(4) Find out all local maxima in the entropy field, and put them into the candidates of potential feature points.
(5) For each candidate points, do the pattern matching using predefined multi-vector filter masks in the framework of Clifford convolution. If the neighborhood region of the candidate point matches with one mask, it is then recognized as a feature with the corresponding pattern.
(6) All flow patterns and features obtained in previous step are visualized with streamlines.

To help the understanding of our method, some concepts and processes are further described in the following subsections.

3.2   Vector Field Clifford Convolution

Convolution operator is usually applied to scalar fields. If X is a scalar field and Y is a scalar-value filter, the convolution between X and Y is defined as:

$$S_n(r) = \int \int \int <X_n(\xi), Y(r-\xi) > d\xi \tag{1}$$

Ebling and Scheuermann [6] extended the convolution operator to vector field by using the geometric product of multi-vectors given in the Clifford algebra framework [14]. In the Clifford algebra, there are 8 basis blades, $\{1, e_1, e_2, e_3, e_1e_2, e_1e_3, e_2e_3, e_1e_2e_3\}$, which form an eight-dimensional algebra space whose bases are in fact 3D vectors. The general elements in this algebra are called multi-vectors. A multi-vector of an n-dimensional Clifford algebra is a linear combination with real coefficients of the 2^n basis blades. The rule of multiplication operator is defined by the following equations:

$$1e_j = e_j, \quad j = 1, 2, 3 \tag{2}$$

$$e_je_j = 1, \quad j = 1, 2, 3 \tag{3}$$

$$e_je_k = -e_ke_j, \quad j, k = 1, 2, 3, j \neq k \tag{4}$$

$$(e_1e_2e_3)^2 = e_1e_2e_3e_1e_2e_3 = e_1e_1e_2e_3e_2e_3 = -e_2e_2e_3e_3 = -1 \tag{5}$$

The multiplication of two vectors **a** and **b** can be written as:

$$
\begin{aligned}
\mathbf{ab} &= (a_1 e_1 + a_2 e_2 + a_3 e_3)(b_1 e_1 + b_2 e_2 + b_3 e_3) \\
&= (a_1 b_1 + a_2 b_2 + a_3 b_3) + (a_1 b_2 - a_2 b_1) e_1 e_2 \\
&\quad + (a_2 b_3 - a_3 b_2) e_2 e_3 + (a_3 b_1 - a_1 b_3) e_3 e_1 \\
&= \;<\mathbf{a}, \mathbf{b}> + \mathbf{a} \wedge \mathbf{b}
\end{aligned}
\tag{6}
$$

The Clifford multiplication is in fact a convolution of a point in the vector field with a 1×1 filter mask. Therefore, if X is a 3D multi-vector filter mask and Y is a 3D multi-vector field, then the discrete convolution between X and Y can be defined as:

$$
C(j,k,l) = \sum_{p=-m}^{m} \sum_{q=-m}^{m} \sum_{r=-m}^{m} X(p,q,r) Y(j-p, k-q, l-r)
\tag{7}
$$

where j,k,l,p,q,r are coordinates of grid nodes, m is the dimension of the grid of the filter mask and $(j,k,l), (p,q,r)$ are grid nodes.

Given a filter mask with fixed direction, it will not match all the kind of the corresponding features in different directions. So we have to rotate the filter mask in a great deal of directions, which will cost too much computation time. As we can see in Eq. (6), however, $<\mathbf{a}, \mathbf{b}>$ is the inner product, and $\mathbf{a} \wedge \mathbf{b}$ is the outer product of the two vectors. So their multiplication gives us the sine and cosine of the angle between two vectors as follow:

$$
<\mathbf{ab}>_0 = \;<\mathbf{a}, \mathbf{b}> \; = \|\mathbf{a}\|\|\mathbf{b}\| \cos \alpha
\tag{8}
$$

$$
\|<\mathbf{ab}>_2\| = \|\mathbf{a} \wedge \mathbf{b}\| = \|\mathbf{a}\|\|\mathbf{b}\| \sin \alpha
\tag{9}
$$

where α is the angle between **a** and **b**. Therefore, when we get the discrete convolution between X and Y as shown in Eq. (7), we can estimate the angle between X and Y from the following equations:

$$
<C(j,k,l)>_0 \approx \eta \cos \alpha
\tag{10}
$$

$$
<C(j,k,l)>_2 \approx \eta \sin \alpha
\tag{11}
$$

where $\eta = \sum_{p,q,r} |X(p,q,r)| \leq \sum_{p,q,r} 1$, $|X(p,q,r)|$ is the magnitude of vector $X(p,q,r)$. With the estimated angle, we can directly rotate the filter mask to the desired direction, and do the Clifford convolution to detect features, avoiding checking all possible directions.

3.3 Flow Field Information Entropy

In our method, we introduce information entropy theory to reduce the calculation of Clifford convolution. Information theory provides a theoretical framework to quantitatively measure the information contained in a distribution of data values. In flow fields, flow directions around flow features are often in a high degree of variation, and then have high entropy values.

Given a random variable X with a sequence of possible values $\{x_1, x_2, \ldots, x_n\}$, if the probability for X to have the value x_i is $p(x_i)$, then the information content for the random variable X can be computed using Shannon's entropy:

$$H(x) = -\sum_{x_i} p(x_i) \log_2 p(x_i) \tag{12}$$

Xu et al. [11] took Shannon's entropy to compute the information of a vector field, where a map is created to approximate the probability mass function $p(x)$. For 3D vector fields in our consideration, a unit sphere is firstly divided into 642 uniform bins by the icosahedrons subdivision method [15]. Then a map is built from vectors to bins. With the map, the probability of the vectors in the bin x_i can be defined as:

$$p(x_i) = \frac{C(x_i)}{\sum_{i=1}^{n} C(x_i)} \tag{13}$$

where $C(x_i)$ is the number of vectors in the bin x_i. With the probabilities calculated here, we can get the flow field entropy according to the Eq. (12).

In practice, the flow field entropy is calculated in local regions. Given a grid point, a local neighborhood around the point, whose sizes are $3 \times 3 \times 3$, is used to build the map and get the estimated probability. By this means, we can get a scalar field which is called entropy field. The value in the entropy field shows the degree of vector variation in its neighborhood. Such a 2D example is given in Fig. 1, where regions with higher degree of variation have higher entropy values, and they are considered to contain more information than others. The entropy $H(x)$ is convex and reaches its maximum when $p(x_i)$ is equal for all x_i. We use this property of entropy field to reduce the overhead of Clifford convolution.

3.4 Multi-vector Filter Masks

Multi-vector filter masks can be regarded as very small vector fields, each of which contains a kind of flow patterns that is defined by the vectors. With predefined filter masks, we can detect the desired features through pattern matching. For 3D flow fields, interesting features [16] include as vortices, critical points, convergence, divergence, etc. We can design a representative filter masks for each of them. Two example masks are shown in Fig. 2. Due to the length limitation, other masks are not included in this paper.

4 Test Results

To evaluate the performance of our feature extraction method, we compared it with the topology-based method [17] where feature points are located by flow field interpolation.

Firstly, the flow field shown in Fig. 3(a) was used to test the method. This is a vortex field with a core line. Due to the fact that no critical point exists in this field, the

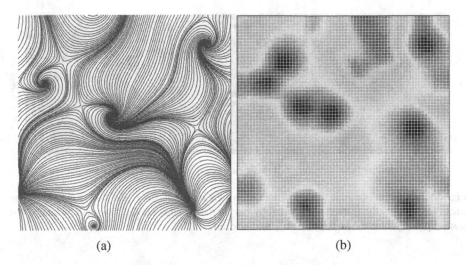

(a)   (b)

Fig. 1. Example of entropy field for a vector field (a) is the vector field visualized by streamlines, and (b) is its the entropy field, where warmer colors indicate higher entropy values.

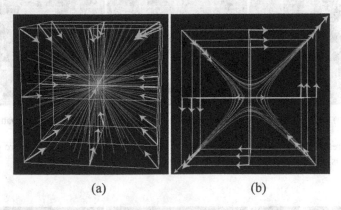

(a)   (b)

Fig. 2. Examples of multi-vector filter masks (a) is for sink point, (b) is for saddle point.

topology-based method can not find out the core line, which is the important feature of this field. For our method, it found the feature point as shown in Fig. 3(b). When a few streamlines associated with the feature point were rendered, we got the results in Fig. 3(c), where we can notice a straight line through the feature point. This line is the vortex core line.

For general flow fields, both our method and the topological method can find the same features, but our method is general faster than the later. For example, for the flow field in Fig. 4(a), it cost 926 ms for the topological method to find out the feature point shown in Fig. 4(b), while it was only 208 ms for our method. The flow pattern around the feature point was clearly disclosed by streamlines in Fig. 4(c).

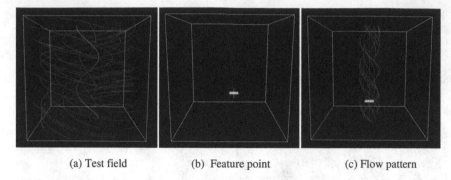

(a) Test field   (b) Feature point   (c) Flow pattern

Fig. 3. Test results for the flow field with a vortex core line (a) is the flow field shown by streamlines, (b) is the feature point found by our method, and (c) is the flow pattern around the feature point, where the vortex core line is disclosed.

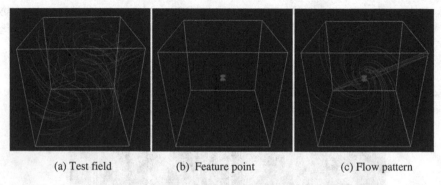

(a) Test field   (b) Feature point   (c) Flow pattern

Fig. 4. Test results for a simple flow filed (a) is the original field, (b) is the feature point in the field, and (c) is the flow pattern around the feature point.

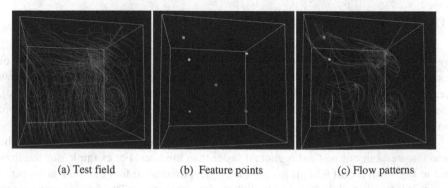

(a) Test field   (b) Feature points   (c) Flow patterns

Fig. 5. Test results for the complex flow field (a) is the original field, (b) is the feature points, and (c) is the flow patterns built with feature points and a few streamlines.

Figure 5 gives another test results for a complex flow field. This field was generally visualized by streamlines in Fig. 5(a), where it is hard to capture the flow pattern. For this field, our method got the feature points shown in Fig. 5(b), and further built the flow patterns in Fig. 5(c) with a few streamlines.

5 Conclusions

We present a new method in this paper to extract features in 3D flow fields. The main advantage of our method is that it can extract various types of flow features in a unified and efficiency way. Our method is based on the Clifford algebra convolution, but it reduces the cost of convolution by the computing of flow field entropy. Test results show that our method improves the extraction of flow features. Currently our method is only suitable for flow fields defined on rectangular grids. It would be extended to arbitrary grids in future.

Acknowledgments. This work was partially supported by the grants from the Natural Science Foundation of China (Nos.: 11472049, 11272066).

References

1. Gyulassy, A., Natarajan, V.: Topology-based simplification for feature extraction from 3D scalar fields. In: Visualization, 2005 VIS 2005, pp. 535–542. IEEE, Oct 2005
2. Zhang, W., Deng, J.: Topology-driven streamline seeding for 2D vector field visualization. In: IEEE International Conference on Systems, Man and Cybernetics, 2009, SMC 2009, pp. 4901–4905, Oct 2009
3. Reininghaus, J., Lowen, C., Hotz, I.: Fast combinatorial vector field topology. IEEE Trans. Vis. Comput. Graph. **17**(10), 1433–1443 (2011)
4. Otto, M., Germer, T., Hege, H.C., Theisel, H.: Uncertain 2D vector field topology. Comput. Graph. Forum **29**(2), 347–356 (2010)
5. Tricoche, X., Garth, C., Kindlmann, G., Deines, E., Scheuermann, G., Ruetten, M., Hansen, C.: Visualization of intricate flow structures for vortex breakdown analysis. In: Proceedings of the Conference on Visualization 2004, VIS 2004, pp. 187–194. IEEE Computer Society, Washington, DC (2004)
6. Ebling, J., Scheuermann, G.: Clifford convolution and pattern matching on vector fields. In: Visualization, 2003, VIS 2003, pp. 193–200. IEEE, Oct 2003
7. Hitzer, E., Mawardi, B.: Clifford fourier transform on multivector fields and uncertainty principles for dimensions n = 2 (mod 4) and n = 3 (mod 4). Adv. Appl. Clifford Algebras **18** (3–4), 715–736 (2008)
8. Chen, M., Jäenicke, H.: An information-theoretic framework for visualization. IEEE Trans. Vis. Comput. Graph. **16**(6), 1206–1215 (2010)
9. Wang, C., Yu, H., Ma, K.L.: Importance-driven time-varying data visualization. IEEE Trans. Vis. Comput. Graph. **14**(6), 1547–1554 (2008)
10. Furuya, S., Itoh, T.: A streamline selection technique for integrated scalar and vector visualization. In: Vis Š08: IEEE Visualization Poster Session, vol. 2, no. 4 (2008)

11. Xu, L., Lee, T.Y., Shen, H.W.: An information-theoretic framework for flow visualization. IEEE Trans. Vis. Comput. Graph. **16**(6), 1216–1224 (2010)
12. Heiberg, E., Ebbers, T., Wigstrom, L., Karlsson, M.: Three-dimensional flow characterization using vector pattern matching. IEEE Trans. Vis. Comput. Graph. **9**(3), 313–319 (2003)
13. Tao, J., Ma, J., Wang, C., Shene, C.K.: A unified approach to streamline selection and viewpoint selection for 3D flow visualization. IEEE Trans. Vis. Comput. Graph. **19**(3), 393–406 (2013)
14. Fernndez, V., Moya, A., Rodrigues, W.: Euclidean clifford algebra. Adv. Appl. Clifford Algebras **11**(3), 1–21 (2001)
15. Shen, L., Ford, J., Makedon, F., Saykin, A.: A surface-based approach for classification of 3D neuroanatomic structures. Intell. Data Anal. **8**(6), 519–542 (2004)
16. Ebling, J., Scheuermann, G.: Template matching on vector fields using clifford algebra. In: International Conference on the Applications of Computer Science and Mathematics in Architecture and Civil Engineering (IKM 2006) (2006)
17. Wang, Y., Zhang, W., Ning, J.: Streamline-based visualization of 3D explosion fields. In: 2011 Seventh International Conference on Computational Intelligence and Security (CIS), pp. 1224–1228, Dec 2011

Frame Rate Up-Conversion Using Motion Vector Angular for Occlusion Detection

Yue Zhao[1,2], Ju Liu[1(✉)], Guoxia Sun[1], Jing Ge[1], and Wenbo Wan[1]

[1] School of Information Science and Engineering,
Shandong University, Jinan 250100, China
{zhaoyue201211771,norling1,gjgjj1989}@163.com,
{juliu,sun_guoxia}@sdu.edu.cn
[2] Suzhou Research Institute of Shandong University, Suzhou 215021, China

Abstract. In this paper, we study on handling the issue of occlusions in frame rate up-conversion (FRUC), which has been widely used to reconstruct high-quality videos presented on liquid crystal display. Depending on different types of occlusion problems, adaptive motion estimation is carried out for reducing computational complexity. Luminance information based RGB angular distance color difference formula is proposed for improving Unsymmetrical-cross multi-hexagon grid search (UMHexagonS) motion estimation, which reduces the occlusion regions resulted by the wrong motion vectors. Non-occlusion regions are determined by motion vector angular, furthermore, exposed and occluded areas are located by comparisons of interpolated frames within directional motion estimation. Consequently, adaptive motion compensation is introduced to calculate interpolated frames. Experimental results demonstrate that our scheme has a superior performance compared with preciously proposed FRUC schemes. *abstract* environment.

Keywords: Frame rate up conversion · Adaptive motion estimation · Occlusion detection · Motion vector angular

1 Introduction

With the rapid development of computer and communication networks, FRUC has been widely studied as an essential means to increase temporal resolution in multimedia information processing. The basic principle of FRUC is liner interpolation according to neighboring sequence frames. FRUC not only can reduce flashings on screen which makes images clearer and steadier, but also save expensive costs of filming, storing and transferring high frame rate video [1]. Motion compensation frame interpolation (MCFI) has been an effective FRUC method, which can get the interpolated frame taking motion information into accounted.

However, MCFI faces many inevitable problems, such as block artifacts, hole problems, occlusion problems, etc. Naturally, these problems have affected the video quality and users' visual experience seriously. Hole problems can be solved by bi-directional motion estimation (ME) efficiently [2], and overlapped block

© Springer International Publishing Switzerland 2015
Y.-J. Zhang (Ed.): ICIG 2015, Part II, LNCS 9218, pp. 301–311, 2015.
DOI: 10.1007/978-3-319-21963-9_28

motion compensation can removal the edge artifacts around blocks [3]. Much research has been conducted over the years to address the issue of the occlusion problems.

Actually, occlusion is due to relative motion between motion objects or foreground and background, where occluded areas are covered while exposed areas are uncovered. Therefore, ignoring occlusion issue can result in annoying halo artifacts on object's edge [4]. A FRUC method combined true motion estimation and directionally adaptive motion compensated interpolation is proposed [5]. In [6], M. B. put forward a motion vector steered video in-painting method. An improved FRUC method based on dual ME and regional blending can also solve occlusion problems effectively [7]. In summary, detection and refinement of occlusion regions are two key steps for handling occlusion. In this paper, motion vector angle is firstly presented for locating non-occlusion regions. Secondly, adaptive motion compensation is given to modify occluded and exposed areas, which is merged with comparison of interpolated frames obtained by directional ME.

The contributions of this paper can be summarized as: (1) Adaptive motion estimation is used to handle different occlusion problems, which can fill up exposed areas caused by scene change in the simplest way. (2) Luminance information based UMHexagonS motion estimation [8] brings RGB angular distance color difference formula to decrease occlusion regions. (3) Comparison of interpolated frame from directional ME is to distinguish the occluded or exposed areas, and adaptive motion compensation makes modifications on occlusion regions. Subjective and objective evaluation results prove the proposed method can improve the quality of interpolated frame significantly with a low-complexity.

The rest of this paper is organized as follows. In Sect. 2, the proposed method is described in details. Experimental results and performance comparisons are provided in Sect. 3. Finally, we conclude the paper in Sect. 4.

2 Proposed Scheme

The proposed FRUC method is schematically shown in Fig. 1. The detail procedure are as follows: 1. Scene change detection based adaptive motion estimation [9]. 2. Detection of non-occlusion regions based on motion vector angular. 3. Location and modification on occlusion regions. In the first stage, adaptive ME can deal with the exposed areas introduced by scene change simply and effectively. In the second stage, luminance information based UMHexagonS ME guarantees for lowering occlusion regions firstly, then the use of motion vector angular results in detecting occlusion regions effectually. In the third stage, exposed and occluded areas are located and refined in terms of directional motion estimation.

Adaptive Motion Estimation Handling Different Occlusion Problems. There are three factors causing occlusion problems. It can be concluded from Fig. 2 on different sequences. The first one is exposed regions produced by scene change, as shown in *New*. The other one is static exposed background caused by

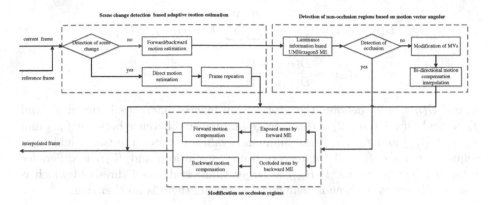

Fig. 1. Flowchart of the processed method

the motion of foreground, as illustrated in *Silent*. The last one, we can observe from *Ice* that occluded and exposed regions are induced by object motion. It is inescapably clear that the accurate motion vectors between sequence frames are absent when scene changes, so MCI method is not available. Taking computational complexity into account, frame repetition method is selected to obtain interpolated frames. Adaptive motion estimation is given by

$$f_{n+\frac{1}{2}}(x,y) = \begin{cases} f_{n+1}(x,y) \\ \frac{1}{2}f_n(x,y) + \frac{1}{2}f_{n+1}(x+v_x,y+v_y) \end{cases} \tag{1}$$

where $f_\otimes(\otimes)$ represents the frame, $f_{n+\frac{1}{2}}$, f_{n-1} and f_{n+1} are interpolated, previous and following frame relatively.

Generally, there is an relatively simple and efficient method based on average luminance difference for scene change detection [10], where the probability of scene change is small during FRUC. The formula is given by

Fig. 2. Different types of occlusion problems. From *left* to *right* and *up* to *down* video sequences (90th and 91th frames of *News*, 20th and 21th frames of *Silent*, 20th and 21th frames of *Ice*)

$$D(n, n+1) = \frac{1}{H \times W} \sum_{i=1}^{H} \sum_{j=1}^{W} |f_n(i,j) - f_{n+1}(i,j)|$$

$$R_{\Delta D} = \frac{D(n, n+1)}{D(n, n-1)} \tag{2}$$

where $D(n, n-1)$ denotes the average luminance difference between f_n and f_{n-1}, and $D(n-1, n-2)$ is the average luminance difference between f_{n-1} and f_{n-2}. $f_n(i,j)$ and $f_{n-1}(i,j)$ are luminance values between the two neighboring sequence images. $H \times W$ represents frame revolution, and $R_{\Delta D}$ is difference ratio of adjacent frames. If $R_{\Delta D}$ is larger than established threshold which is empirically set as 5, scene is changing, otherwise, there is no changing.

Luminance Information Based UMHexagonS Motion Estimation. In general, sum of absolute difference (SAD) is the most popular matching criteria for its simplicity and effectiveness. SAD accounts for the difference of three color components in RGB color space between current block and candidate block. It can be described as follows

$$SAD_B(x,y) = \sum_{(x,y) \in B} |f_n(x,y) - f_{n+1}(x,y)| \tag{3}$$

in essence, the calculation process is to acquire absolute difference of three channels, then tot up, and given in

$$SAD_B = \sum (|r_n - r_{n+1}| + |g_n - g_{n+1}| + |b_n - b_{n+1}|) \tag{4}$$

where (r_n, g_n, b_n) and $(r_{n+1}, g_{n+1}, b_{n+1})$ are the color value of current and reference pixel respectively. The above-mentioned formula ignores some important details and facts, as shows in the following. Firstly, it has different sensitive degree to eyes, when red, green, blue is changing; Secondly, the significance of three color occupies different positions in different images. At last, the space distance and vector angular is also the important factors. In this work, a color difference formula combining the characters of distance and angular [11] is applied to calculate SAD. There are two pixels in current frame and reference frame, where their values are (r_n, g_n, b_n), $(r_{n+1}, g_{n+1}, b_{n+1})$ respectively. SAD is calculated as following

$$SAD_B = \sqrt{\frac{S_r^2 w_r \Delta_r^2 + S_g^2 w_g \Delta_g^2 + S_b^2 w_b \Delta_b^2}{(w_r + w_g + w_b)255^2} + S_\theta S_{ratio}\theta^2} \tag{5}$$

where $\Delta_r = r_n - r_{n+1}$, $\Delta_g = g_n - g_{n+1}$, $\Delta_b = b_n - b_{n+1}$. (w_r, w_g, w_b) is $(1, 2, 1)$, and (S_r, S_g, S_b) is the significance of the three color components. θ stands for the motion vector angular normalized coefficient of the pixels in RGB color space regulated by S_θ, where S_θ is the gradient varies of three color components. S_{ratio} is an accommodation coefficient to avoid excessive value of θ. The above-mentioned formula has improved the accuracy of SAD, and, if luminance information is taken into accounted in UMHexagonS motion estimation, the preciseness will be better. Therefore, luminance information based UMHexagonS motion estimation using RGB angular distance color difference formula goes as follows:

Step 1. Transform from RGB to HSV, then abstract luminance information.

Step 2. Calculate the luminance difference ρ between the current block and candidate block, which is composed by original search point, then threshold $\phi = 1.5\rho$.

Step 3. During motion estimation, if luminance difference $\rho >= 1.5\phi$, improved RGB angular distance color difference formula is applied for figuring up SAD value. If not, carry on the next candidate block, in the same instant, update threshold.

An experiment has been conducted to test the validity of the proposed SAD algorithm under the environment of Matlab. YUV standard video sequence named soccer is selected for experiment, contrast tests are identical in algorithms and corrected experimental parameters besides calculation method of SAD. As can be seen from the comparison results in Fig. 3, proposed SAD algorithm is preferred to classical algorithm in both subjective and objective effects.

Fig. 3. Comparison of quality evaluation applying different SAD algorithm: From *left* to *right* SAD algorithm (conventional PSNR $= 27.2163$, proposed PSNR $= 28.5002$)

2.1 Detection of Non-occlusion Regions Based on Motion Vector Angular

For occluded and exposed areas, the correct pixel information is only available in previous or following frames. Occluded areas can achieve correct motion information by backward motion estimation and vice versa for exposed areas. Consequently, as for non-occlusion regions, motion vector angular from forward

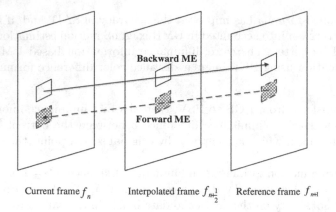

Fig. 4. A diagram of motion vector angular by directional motion estimation

and backward motion estimation is relative, where there reveals in Fig. 4. The specific process is concluded as follows. Firstly, forward and backward motion estimation provide motion vector field $F_{mv}(x, y)$ and $B_{mv}(x, y)$ separately. Secondly, motion vector angular is divided into eight fields according to rectangular coordinate system, which are X-axis, Y-axis and four quadrants. $F_{mv}(x, y)$ and $B_{mv}(x, y)$ are transformed to the motion vector field of the interpolated frame along respective motion trajectory. So two label matrices obtained to mark the directions of motion vector angular, which are denoted by F_{label} and B_{label}. Thirdly, If F_{label} and B_{label} belongs to the same relative direction, such as first quadrant and third quadrant, etc. The corresponding regions are regarded as non-occlusion areas. Otherwise, it needs further modifications.

2.2 Locations and Modifications on Occlusion Regions

The essence of occlusion is given in Fig. 5, occluded and exposed areas are judged as below. For occluded areas, the responding block in the interpolated frame acquired by backward ME should be similar to the block in previous frame f_n. Likewise, for exposed areas, the responding block obtained by forward ME in the interpolated frame should be similar to the block in the following frame f_{n+1}. The calculation formula are displayed in Eq. (6).

$$SAD_{F.exp}(x, y) = \sum (f_{F.(n+\frac{1}{2})}(x, y) - f_n(x + mv_{x.F}, y + mv_{y.F}))$$

$$SAD_{B.exp}(x, y) = \sum (f_{B.(n+\frac{1}{2})}(x, y) - f_n(x - mv_{x.B}, y - mv_{y.B}))$$

$$SAD_{F.occ}(x, y) = \sum (f_{F.(n+\frac{1}{2})}(x, y) - f_{n+1}(x - mv_{x.F}, y - mv_{y.F}))$$

$$SAD_{B.occ}(x, y) = \sum (f_{B.(n+\frac{1}{2})}(x, y) - f_{n+1}(x + mv_{x.B}, y + mv_{y.B}))$$

(6)

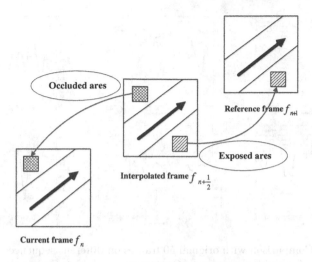

Fig. 5. A diagram of exposed and occluded areas.

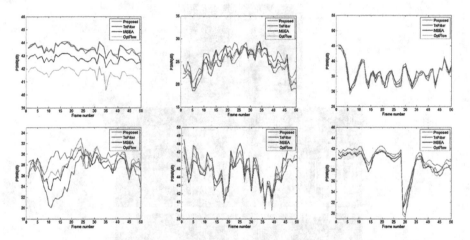

Fig. 6. PSNRs Comparison with original 50 frames on different sequences. From *left* to *right* and *up* to *down* video sequences (*Container, Ice, Silent, Soccer, Akiyo, Mother*)

where abbreviation 'F' and 'B' represents *forward ME, backward ME* respectively. Meanwhile, 'ex' and 'oc' stands for *exposed* and *occluded* areas. If $SAD_{F.oc} > SAD_{B.oc}$, it is located as occluded areas. While $SAD_{F.ex} < SAD_{B.ex}$, it belongs to exposed areas. Eventually, it can be drawn that forward MVs are suitable for exposed areas and backward MVs are appropriated for occluded areas. Hence, the interpolated frame is obtained as formula in Eq. (7)

$$f_{n+\frac{1}{2}}(x,y) = \frac{1}{2} \times (f_n(x - v_x, y - v_y) + f_{n+1}(x + v_x, y + v_y)). \tag{7}$$

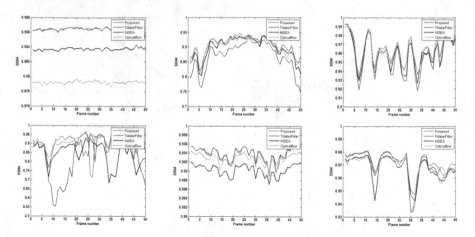

Fig. 7. SSIMs Comparison with original 50 frames on different sequences. From *left* to *right* and *up* to *down* video sequences (*Container, Ice, Silent, Soccer, Akiyo, Mother*)

Fig. 8. Visual comparison on frame 26th of Soccer sequence. The first line is original frame and the second line is interpolated frames. From *left* to *right* FRUC algorithms (*OptFlow, MSEA, TrilFilter, Proposed*)

3 Experimental Results

In the experiments, six test video sequences with standard CIF (352×288) are adopted, where these have different spatial details and movement complexity.

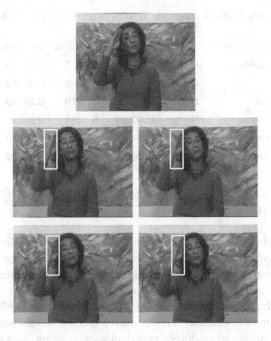

Fig. 9. Visual comparison on frame 26th of silent sequence. The first line is original frame and the second line is interpolated frames. From *left* to *right* FRUC algorithms (*OptFlow, MSEA, TrilFilter, Proposed*)

Table 1. Average PSNR comparison with original frames on 6 sequences

Test sequences	MSEA	OptFlow	TriFilter	Proposed
Container	42.7582	41.6684	43.4705	**43.5756**
Ice	24.9453	24.5195	23.8933	**25.9980**
Silent	36.0212	35.4738	35.3099	**36.4373**
Soccer	27.7633	28.4840	26.5814	**29.3107**
Akiyo	44.2779	44.5363	45.1194	**45.2931**
Mother	39.4248	39.3633	38.9698	**40.1008**

In order to evaluate the performance of proposed FRUC method, we make a comparison with three conventional FRUC methods, i.e., TriFilter [12], MSEA [13], and OptFlow [14]. Objective evaluation of the proposed method compared with above methods is on the principle of Peak signal-to-noise ratio (PSNR) and structural similarity index measurement (SSIM) [15]. Figures 6 and 7 give the results of the PSNRs and SSIMs of individual interpolated frame on different videos. Meanwhile the average PSNR and SSIM of different algorithms can be seen from Tables 1 and 2. On objective comparisons, the proposed algorithm has certain advantages over the conventional algorithms. Subjective quality can be evaluated by means of visual quality of local details, which is demonstrated in Figs. 8 and 9.

Table 2. Average SSIM comparison with original frames on 6 sequences

Test sequences	MSEA	OptFlow	TriFilter	Proposed
Container	0.9837	0.9792	0.9864	**0.9865**
Ice	0.8975	0.9020	0.8699	**0.9083**
Silent	0.9601	0.9630	0.9579	**0.9650**
Soccer	0.8468	**0.9126**	0.8286	0.9029
Akiyo	0.9903	0.9928	0.9938	**0.9939**
Mother	0.9682	0.9675	0.9701	**0.9722**

4   Conclusion

In this paper, a robust and fast FRUC method has been to address the occulsion problem. Adaptive motion estimation is first used for solving different types of occlusion problems, which reduces high complexity for filling exposed areas caused by scene change. Additionally, luminance information and RGB angular distance color difference formula union use into UMHexagonS ME is helpful to decrease the occlusion regions. What's more, motion vector angular based on directional ME is designed to detect non-occlusion regions, and the exposed and occluded areas is located according to the comparison of interpolated frames obtained by directional ME. In the end, we make use of adaptive MC to get the high quality interpolated frame. It can be supported that our newly proposed FRUC method improves the quality of interpolated frames both in objective and subjective evaluation by the results of experiments conducted.

Acknowledgments. This work was supported partially by Open Foundation of State Key Laboratory of Digital Multimedia Technology Laboratory (11131326) and Suzhou Science and technology plan (SYG201443).

References

1. Huang, C.L., Chao, T.T.: Motion-compensated interpolation for scan rate up-conversion. Opt. Eng. **35**(1), 166–176 (1996)
2. Li, R., Gan, Z., Cui, Z., Tang, G., Zhu, X.: Multi-channel mixed-pattern based frame rate up-conversion using spatio-temporal motion vector refinement and dual-weighted overlapped block motion compensation. J. Disp. Technol. **10**(12), 1010–1023 (2014)
3. Wang, D., Vincent, A., Blanchfield, P., Klepko, R.: Motion compensated framerate up-conversion-part ii: New algorithms for frame interpolation. IEEE Trans. Broadcast. **56**(2), 142–149 (2010)
4. Ozkalayci, B., Alatan, A.A.: Occlusion handling frame rate up-conversion. In: Proceedings of the ISPA, pp. 149–152 (2011)
5. Biswas, M., Namboodiri, V.: On handling of occlusion for frame rate up-conversion using video in-painting. In: Proceedings of the ICIP, pp. 785–788 (2010)

6. Guo, Y., Gao, Z., Chen, L., Zhang, X.: Occlusion handling frame rate up-conversion. In: Proceedings of the ICASSP, pp. 1424–1428 (2013)
7. Bellers, E. B., et al.: Solving occlusion in frame-rate up-conversion. In: Proceedings of the ICCE, pp. 1–2 (2007)
8. Zou, B., Shi, C., Xu, C.H., Chen, S.: Enhanced hexagonal-based search using direction-oriented inner search for motion estimation. IEEE Trans. Circuits Syst. Video Technol. **20**, 156–160 (2010)
9. Zhao, Y.: Frame rate up conversion method based on motion compensation. Master thesis, Shandong University (2015)
10. Ren, K., Jin, X.: Research on scene change detection algorithm based on H.264/SVC. In: Proceedings of the ICECC, pp. 1639–1642 (2011)
11. Yang, Z., Wang, Y., Yang, Z.: Vector-angular distance color difference formula in RGB color space. Broadcast. Comput. Eng. Appl. **46**, 154–156 (2010)
12. He, Y.H., Wang, C., Zhang, L., Tan, Y.P.: Frame rate up-conversion using trilateral filtering. IEEE Trans. Circuits Syst. Video Technol. **20**(6), 886–893 (2010)
13. Lee, Y. L., Nguyen, T.: Fast one-pass motion compensated frame interpolation in high-definition video processing. In: Proceedings of the ICIP, pp. 369–372 (2009)
14. Liu, C.: Beyond pixels: exploring new representations and applications for motion analysis. Doctoral thesis, Massachusetts Institute of Technology, pp. 369–372 (2009)
15. Wang, Z., Bovik, A.C., Sheikh, H.R., Simoncelli, E.P.: Image quality assessment: from error visibility to structural similarity. IEEE Trans. Image Process **13**(4), 600–612 (2004)

Fusion of Skeletal and STIP-Based Features for Action Recognition with RGB-D Devices

Ting Liu[✉] and Mingtao Pei

Beijing Laboratory of Intelligent Information Technology,
School of Computer Science, Beijing Institute of Technology, Beijing 100081,
People's Republic of China
{liuting1989,peimt}@bit.edu.cn

Abstract. Along with the popularization of the Kinect sensor, the usage of marker-less body pose estimation has been enormously eased and complex human actions can be recognized based on the 3D skeletal information. However, due to errors in tracking and occlusion, the obtained skeletal information can be noisy. In this paper, we compute posture, motion and offset information from skeleton positions to represent the global information of action, and build a novel depth cuboid feature (called HOGHOG) to describe the 3D cuboid around the STIPs (spatiotemporal interest points) to handle cluttered backgrounds and partial occlusions. Then, a fusion scheme is proposed to combine the two complementary features. We test our approach on the public MSRAction3D and MSRDailyActivity3D datasets. Experimental evaluations demonstrate the effectiveness of the proposed method.

Keywords: Human action recognition · Spatiotemporal interest points · HOGHOG descriptor · Skeletal feature · Feature fusion

1 Introduction

Human action recognition is a very hot research topic in computer vision community, aiming to automatically recognize and interpret human actions. It has a variety of applications in real world, such as Human Computer Interaction (HCI), security surveillance in public spaces, sports training and entertainment. Over the past decades, researchers mainly focused on learning and recognizing actions from either a single intensity image or an intensity video sequence taken by common RGB cameras [1, 2, 11]. However, the inherent limitations of this type of data source, such as sensitive to color and illumination changes, affect the development of action recognition. Recently, with the launch of the kinect sensor, 3D structural information of scene can be accessed by researchers and it opens up new possibilities of dealing with these problems. It brings a broader scope for human action recognition. Moreover, from the depth maps offered by kinect, the geometric positions of skeleton can also be detected [14]. The skeleton estimation algorithms are quite accurate under experimental settings, but not much accurate in reality

© Springer International Publishing Switzerland 2015
Y.-J. Zhang (Ed.): ICIG 2015, Part II, LNCS 9218, pp. 312–322, 2015.
DOI: 10.1007/978-3-319-21963-9_29

as shown in Fig. 1. It can hardly work when the human body is partly in view. The interaction with objects and occlusions caused by body parts in the scene can also make the skeleton information noisy. All these imperfections increase the intra-class variations in the actions.

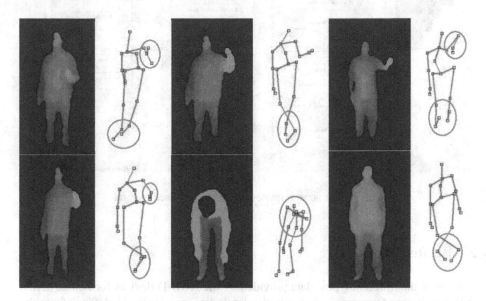

Fig. 1. Depth image and the extracted skeleton. Some skeleton points are disordered as shown in red ellipse (Color figure online).

The spatiotemporal interest points based features have shown good performance for action recognition in RGB videos [4, 5, 9]. It can handle partial occlusion and avoid possible problems caused by inaccurate segmentation. When the background of the scene is cluttered or the subject have interaction with surroundings, the STIPs features can capture more effective activity characteristics. That is to say, although good results can be obtained by skeletal features, the STIP features could provide useful additional characteristic value to improve the classification and robustness.

For this reason, in our work, the combination of skeletal and spatiotemporal based features is studied. First, 3D interest points are detected and a novel STIPs descriptor (HOGHOG) is computed in the depth motion sequence. Then the posture, motion and offset information are computed from skeleton joint positions. A fusion scheme is then proposed to combine them effectively after feature quantification and normalization. Support vector machine is served as the classifier for action recognition. Figure 2 shows the general framework of the proposed method.

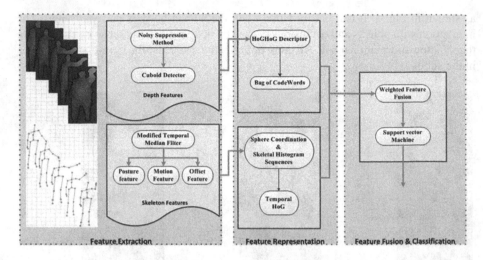

Fig. 2. The general framework of the proposed method

2   Related Work

The use of the different types' data provided by the RGB-D devices for human action recognition goes from employing only the depth data, or only the skeleton data, to the fusion of both the depth and skeleton data or the fusion of both the depth and RGB data. And in the development process, local spatiotemporal salient features have been widely applied.

Li et al. [10] employed the concept of BOPs (Bag of 3D points) in the expandable graphical model framework to construct the action graph to encode actions. The proposed method selects a small set of representative 3D points from the depth maps to reduce the dimension of the feature vector. Xia et al. [20] proposed an effective feature called HOJ3D based on the skeleton joints. They partition the 3D space to bins in a new coordination and formed a histogram by accumulating the occurrence of human body joints in these bins. A Hidden Markov Model is used for action classification and prediction. More recently, Oreifej and Liu [12] used a histogram (HON4D) to capture the distribution of the surface normal orientation in the 4D space of time, depth, and spatial coordinates. This descriptor has the ability of capturing the joint shape-motion cues in the depth sequence.

As for fusion data, Wang et al. [17] proposed to combine the skeleton feature and local occupation feature (LOP feature), then learned an actionlet ensemble model to represent actions and to capture the intra-class variance. A novel data mining solution is also proposed to discover discriminative actionlets. Ohn-Bar and Trivedi [11] characterized actions using pairwise affinities between view-invariant skeletal joint angles features over the performance of an action. They also proposed a new descriptor in which histogram of oriented gradients algorithm is used to model changes in temporal dimensions. Sung et al. [15] combined both the RGB and depth channels for action recognition.

In their work, spatio-temporal interest points are divided into several depth-layered channels, and then STIPs within different channels are pooled independently, resulting in a multiple depth channel histogram representation. They also proposed a Three-Dimensional Motion History Images (3D-MHIs) approach which equips the conventional motion history images (MHIs) with two additional channels encoding the motion recency history in the depth changing directions. Zhu et al. [23] combined skeletal feature and 2D shape based on the silhouette to estimate body pose. Feature fusion is applied in order to obtain a visual feature with a higher discriminative value.

Different spatiotemporal interest point (STIP) features have been proposed for action characterization in RGB videos with good performance. For example, Laptev [8] extended Harris corner detection to space and time, and proposed some effective methods to make spatiotemporal interests points velocity-adaptive. In Dollar's work [4], an alternative interest point detector which applied Gabor filter on the spatial and temporal dimensions is proposed. Willems et al. [18] presented a method to detect features under scale changes, in-plane rotations, video compression and camera motion. The descriptor proposed in their work can be regarded as an extension of the SURF descriptor. Jhuang et al. [6] used local descriptors with space-time gradients as well as optical flow. Klaser et al. [7] compared space-time HOG3D descriptor with HOG and HOF descriptors. Recently, Wang et al. [16] conducted an evaluation of different detectors and descriptors on four RGB/intensity action database. Shabani et al. [13] evaluated the motion-based and structured-based detectors for action recognition in color/intensity videos.

Along with the depth sensor popularization and the new type of data available, a few spatial-temporal cuboid descriptors for depth videos were also proposed. Cheng et al. [3] build a Comparative Coding Descriptor (CCD) to depict the structural relations of spatiotemporal points within action volume using the distance information in depth data. To measure the similarity between CCD features, they also design a corresponding distance metric. Zhao et al. [22] build Local Depth Pattern (LDP) by computing the difference of the average depth values between the cells. In Xia's work [19], a novel depth cuboid similarity feature (called DCSF) was proposed. DCSF describes the local "appearances" in the depth video based on self-similarity concept. They also used a new smoothing method to remove the noise caused by special reflectance materials, fast movements and porous surfaces in depth sequence.

3 Skeletal and STIP-Based Features

As has been mentioned above, we combine both skeletal and spatiotemporal features to recognize human action. The spatiotemporal features are local descriptions of human motions and the skeletal features are able to capture the global characteristic of complex human actions. The two features are detailed in this section.

3.1 Skeletal Feature

For each frame of human action sequence, human posture is represented by a skeleton model composed of 20 joints which is provided by the Microsoft kinect SDK. Among these points, we remove the point waist, left wrist, right wrist, left ankle and right ankle.

For the five points are close to others and redundant for the description of body part configuration.

As noted before, the skeleton information can be noisy caused by accident factors or faulty estimations. We use a modified temporal median filter on these skeleton joints to suppress noisy in the preprocess step.

Then we use these fifteen basic skeletal joints to form our representation of postures. The frame-based feature is the concatenation of posture feature, motion feature and offset feature. Denote the number of skeleton joints in each frame as N and the number of frames for the video is T. For each joint p, $p_i = \left(x_i(t), y_i(t), z_i(t) \right)$ at each frame t, the feature vector can be denoted as:

$$f^t = \left[f^t_{current}, f^t_{motion}, f^t_{offset} \right] \tag{1}$$

$$f^t_{current} = \left\{ p^t_i - p^t_j \,|\, i \neq j, ij = 1 \dots N \right\} \tag{2}$$

$$f^t_{motion} = \left\{ p^t_i - p^{t-1}_i \,|\, i = 1 \dots N \right\} \tag{3}$$

$$f^t_{offset} = \left\{ p^t_i - p^0_i \,|\, i = 1 \dots N \right\} \tag{4}$$

The posture feature $f^t_{current}$ is the distances between a joint and other joints in the current frame. The motion feature f^t_{motion} is the distances between joint in the current frame t and all joints in the preceding frame $t - 1$. The offset feature f^t_{offset} is the distances between joint in the current frame t and all joints in the initial frame $t = 0$.

In order to further extract the motion characteristics, we define Sphere Coordinate in each skeletal point and divide the 3D space around a point into 32 bins. The inclination angle is divided into 4 bins and the azimuth angle is divided into 8 equal bins with $45°$ resolution. The skeletal angle histogram of a point is computed by casting the rest joints into the corresponding spatial histogram bins.

Inspired by Ohn-Bar's work [11], we use Histogram of Gradients (HOG) to model the temporal change of histograms. We compute HOG features in a 50 % overlapping slide window in temporal space and it results in 15000-dimensional feature for an action.

3.2 HOGHOG Feature

Spatiotemporal features are used to capture the local structure information of human actions on depth data. In the preprocess step, a noisy suppression method is executed the same as the Xia' work [19].

We adopt the popular Cuboid detector proposed by Dollar [4] to detect the spatio-temporal interest points. We treat each action video as a 3D volume along spatial (x, y) and (t) temporal axes, and a response function is applied at each pixel in the 3D spatio-temporal volume. A spatiotemporal interest point can be defined as a point exhibiting saliency in the space and time domains. In our work, the local maximum of the response value in spatiotemporal domains are treated as STIPs.

First, a 2D Gaussian smoothing filter is applied on the spatial dimensions:

$$g\left(x,y\,|\sigma\right)=\frac{1}{2\pi\sigma^{2}}e^{-\frac{x^{2}+y^{2}}{2\sigma^{2}}} \tag{5}$$

Where σ controls the spatial scale along x and y.

Then apply 1D complex Gabor filter along the t dimension:

$$h\left(t\,|\tau,\omega\right)=e^{-\frac{t^{2}}{2\tau^{2}}}\cdot e^{2\pi i\omega t} \tag{6}$$

Where τ controls the temporal scale of the filter and $\omega=0.6/\tau$.

After the STIPs is detected, a new descriptor (called HOGHOG) is computed for the local 3D cuboid centered at STIPs. This descriptor is inspired by HOG/HOF descriptor and the temporal HOG.

To each 3D cuboid C_{xyt} (xy imply the size of each frame in cuboid and t is the number of frames in cuboid) which contains the spatiotemporally windowed pixel values around the STIPs, we use a modified histogram of oriented gradients algorithm to capture the detail spatial structure information in x, y dimensions. The algorithm capture the shape context information of each frame and generated t feature vectors. These feature vectors are collected into a 2D array and the same algorithm is applied to model the changes in temporal coordination. Then the 3D spatiotemporal cuboid is descripted as a vector by HOGHOG.

3.3   Action Description and Feature Fusion

Now we have two initial features: the spatiotemporal features representing local motions at different 3D interest points, and the skeleton joints features representing spatial locations of body parts.

To represent depth action sequence, we quantize the STIPs features based on bag-of-words approach. We use K-means algorithm with Euclidean distance to cluster the HOGHOG descriptors and build the cuboid codebook. Then the action sequence can be represented as a bag-of-codewords.

After this step, both depth sequence and skeletal sequence can be described by two different features. Then PCA is used to reduce the size of the feature vector. We choose a suitable number of dimensions to make the clustering process much faster as well as to obtain high recognition rate. Then we normalize them to make the max value of every feature to be 1.

Feature concatenation has been employed for feature fusion after dimension reduction and normalization. Finally, we also set a weight value to adjust the weights for STIPs and skeletal features. For the scene which include many interactions or the subject is partly in view, we can increase the weight of STIPs feature. And for scenes which background is clear and skeletal information captured has less noisy, we can increase the weight of skeleton feature. By means of feature fusion, we can retain the different characteristic data to improve the classification.

4 Experimental Evaluation

Experiments are conducted on two public 3D action databases. Both databases contain skeleton points and depth maps. We introduce the two databases and the experimental settings, and then present and analyze the experimental results in this section.

4.1 MSR - Action 3D Dataset

The MSR - Action 3D dataset mainly collects gaming actions. It contains 20 different actions, performed by ten different subjects and with up to three repetitions making a total of 567 sequences. Among these, ten skeletal sequences are either missing or wrong [17]. Because our fusion frame is noisy-tolerant to a certain degree, in our experiment we don't remove these action sequences.

Like most authors' work, we divide the dataset into three subsets of eight gestures, as shown in Table 1. This is due to the large number of actions and high computational cost of training classifier with the complete dataset. The AS1 and AS2 subsets were intended to group actions with similar movement, while AS3 was intended to group complex action together.

Table 1. Action in each of the MSR-Action3D subsets

AS1		AS2		AS3	
Label	Action name	Label	Action name	Label	Action name
A02	Horizontal arm wave	A01	High arm wave	A06	High throw
A03	Hammer	A04	Hand catch	A14	Forward kick
A05	Forward punch	A07	Draw cross	A15	Side kick
A06	High throw	A08	Draw tick	A16	Jogging
A10	Hand clap	A09	Draw circle	A17	Tennis swing
A13	Bend	A11	Two-hand	A18	Tennis serve
A18	Tennis serve	A14	Wave	A19	Golf swing
A20	Pick-up and throw	A12	Forward kick side boxing	A20	Pick-up and throw

On this dataset, we set $\sigma = 5$, $\tau = 30$, $N_p = 160$ and set the number of voxels for each cuboid to be $n_{xy} = 4$ and $n_t = 2$. We set the number of codebook to be 1800 and the number of dimension is 743.

Figure 3 shows the recognition rate obtained using only the skeleton, only the STIPs and fusing both of them. It can be observed that the worst results are always obtained using only the STIPs while the fusion of both skeletal features and STIPs features steadily improves the recognition rate. Despite the fact that the skeletal feature performs considerable better, for some specific action, the STIP-based feature obtains more useful additional information.

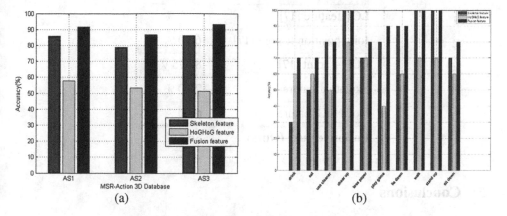

Fig. 3. Comparison of the proposed features in MSR - Action 3D (a) and MSR - Daily 3D (b)

Table 2 shows a comparison with other methods. Our method improves the results for subsets AS1 and AS3, as well as for the overall average. Our results are quite stable while other methods obtain good results only for specific subsets

Table 2. Performance evaluation of various algorithms on three subsets

Method	Dataset			
	AS1	AS2	AS3	Average
Bag of 3D points [10]	72.9 %	71.9 %	79.2 %	74.67 %
Histograms of 3D joints [20]	87.98 %	85.48 %	63.46 %	78.97 %
EigenJoints [21]	74.5 %	76.1 %	96.4 %	82.33 %
Our Methods	**91.55 %**	**84.67 %**	**93.06 %**	**89.76 %**

4.2 MSR - Daily 3D Dataset

The MSR-Daily 3D dataset collects daily activities in a more realistic setting, there are background objects and persons appear at different distances to the camera. Most action types involve human-object interaction. In our testing, we removed the sequences in which the subjects is almost still (This may happen in action type: sit still, read books, write on paper, use laptop and play guitar).

Table 3 shows the accuracy of different features and methods. We take $\sigma = 5$, $\tau = T/17$, $N_p = 500$ for STIP extraction and take the number of voxels for each cuboid to be $n_{xy} = 4$, $n_t = 3$.

Table 3. Recognition accuracy comparison for MSR-Daily 3D database

Method	Accuracy
LOP feature [17]	42.5 %
Joint position feature [17]	68.0 %
LOP + Joint [17]	85.75 %
Skeleton feature	77.0 %
HoGHoG feature	62.0 %
Fusion feature (Ours)	86.5 %

5 Conclusions

In this paper, the method of the combination of skeletal features and spatiotemporal features has been presented. Feature fusion is applied to obtain a more characteristic feature and improve human action recognition rate and robustness. During the experimentation, desirable results have been obtained both for the MSRAction3D dataset and the MSRDailyActivity3D dataset.

In view of the fact that the fused feature has achieved to improve the recognition rate with respect to the unimodal features, we can confirm that the STIPs information contained in the depth map can provide useful discriminative data, especially when the body pose estimation fails. These two features can be complementary to each other, and an efficient combination of them can improve the 3D action recognition accuracies.

References

1. Alnowami, M., Alnwaimi, B., Tahavori, F., Copland, M., Wells, K.: A quantitative assessment of using the kinect for xbox360 for respiratory surface motion tracking. In: SPIE Medical Imaging, p. 83161T. International Society for Optics and Photonics (2012)
2. Bobick, A.F., Davis, J.W.: The recognition of human movement using temporal templates. IEEE Trans. Pattern Anal. Mach. Intell. **23**(3), 257–267 (2001)
3. Cheng, Z., Qin, L., Ye, Y., Huang, Q., Tian, Q.: Human daily action analysis with multi-view and color-depth data. In: Fusiello, A., Murino, V., Cucchiara, R. (eds.) ECCV 2012 Ws/ Demos, Part II. LNCS, vol. 7584, pp. 52–61. Springer, Heidelberg (2012)
4. Dollár, P., Rabaud, V., Cottrell, G., Belongie, S.: Behavior recognition via sparse spatio-temporal features. In: 2nd Joint IEEE International Workshop on Visual Surveillance and Performance Evaluation of Tracking and Surveillance, pp. 65–72. IEEE (2005)
5. Harris, C., Stephens, M.: A combined corner and edge detector. In: Alvey Vision Conference, Manchester, vol. 15, p. 50 (1988)

6. Jhuang, H., Serre, T., Wolf, L., Poggio, T.: A biologically inspired system for action recognition. In: IEEE 11th International Conference on Computer Vision, ICCV 2007, pp. 1–8. IEEE (2007)
7. Klaser, A., Marszalek, M., Schmid, C.: A spatio-temporal descriptor based on 3d-gradients. In: BMVC 2008-19th British Machine Vision Conference, pp. 275:1–275:10. British Machine Vision Association (2008)
8. Laptev, I.: On space-time interest points. Int. J. Comput. Vis. **64**(2–3), 107–123 (2005)
9. Laptev, I., Lindeberg, T.: Velocity adaptation of space-time interest points. In: Proceedings of the 17th International Conference on Pattern Recognition, ICPR 2004, vol. 1, pp. 52–56. IEEE (2004)
10. Li, W., Zhang, Z., Liu, Z.: Action recognition based on a bag of 3d points. In: 2010 IEEE Computer Society Conference on Computer Vision and Pattern Recognition Workshops (CVPRW), pp. 9–14. IEEE (2010)
11. Ohn-Bar, E., Trivedi, M.M.: Joint angles similarities and HOG2 for action recognition. In: 2013 IEEE Conference on Computer Vision and Pattern Recognition Workshops (CVPRW), pp. 465–470. IEEE (2013)
12. Oreifej, O., Liu, Z.: Hon4d: histogram of oriented 4d normals for activity recognition from depth sequences. In: 2013 IEEE Conference on Computer Vision and Pattern Recognition (CVPR), pp. 716–723. IEEE (2013)
13. Shabani, A.H., Clausi, D.A., Zelek, J.S.: Evaluation of local spatio-temporal salient feature detectors for human action recognition. In: 2012 Ninth Conference on Computer and Robot Vision (CRV), pp. 468–475. IEEE (2012)
14. Shotton, J., Sharp, T., Kipman, A., Fitzgibbon, A., Finocchio, M., Blake, A., Cook, M., Moore, R.: Real-time human pose recognition in parts from single depth images. Commun. ACM **56**(1), 116–124 (2013)
15. Sung, J., Ponce, C., Selman, B., Saxena, A.: Unstructured human activity detection from rgbd images. In: 2012 IEEE International Conference on Robotics and Automation (ICRA), pp. 842–849. IEEE (2012)
16. Wang, H., Ullah, M.M., Klaser, A., Laptev, I., Schmid, C.: Evaluation of local spatio-temporal features for action recognition. In: BMVC 2009-British Machine Vision Conference, pp. 124–1. BMVA Press (2009)
17. Wang, J., Liu, Z., Wu, Y., Yuan, J.: Mining actionlet ensemble for action recognition with depth cameras. In: 2012 IEEE Conference on Computer Vision and Pattern Recognition (CVPR), pp. 1290–1297. IEEE (2012)
18. Willems, G., Tuytelaars, T., Van Gool, L.: An efficient dense and scale-invariant spatio-temporal interest point detector. In: Forsyth, D., Torr, P., Zisserman, A. (eds.) ECCV 2008, Part II. LNCS, vol. 5303, pp. 650–663. Springer, Heidelberg (2008)
19. Xia, L., Aggarwal, J.: Spatio-temporal depth cuboid similarity feature for activity recognition using depth camera. In: 2013 IEEE Conference on Computer Vision and Pattern Recognition (CVPR), pp. 2834–2841. IEEE (2013)
20. Xia, L., Chen, C.C., Aggarwal, J.: View invariant human action recognition using histograms of 3d joints. In: 2012 IEEE Computer Society Conference on Computer Vision and Pattern Recognition Workshops (CVPRW), pp. 20–27. IEEE (2012)
21. Yang, X., Tian, Y.: Eigenjoints-based action recognition using naive-bayes-nearest-neighbor. In: 2012 IEEE Computer Society Conference on Computer Vision and Pattern Recognition Workshops (CVPRW), pp. 14–19. IEEE (2012)

22. Zhao, Y., Liu, Z., Yang, L., Cheng, H.: Combing rgb and depth map features for human activity recognition. In: Signal and Information Processing Association Annual Summit and Conference (APSIPA ASC), 2012 Asia-Pacific, pp. 1–4. IEEE (2012)
23. Zhu, Y., Chen, W., Guo, G.: Fusing spatio temporal features and joints for 3d action recognition. In: 2013 IEEE Conference on Computer Vision and Pattern Recognition Workshops (CVPRW), pp. 486–491. IEEE (2013)

GA Based Optimal Design for Megawatt-Class Wind Turbine Gear Train

Jianxin Zhang$^{(\boxtimes)}$ and Zhange Zhang

Key Lab of Advanced Design and Intelligent Computing, Ministry of Education,
Dalian University, Dalian, People's Republic of China
zjx99326@163.com

Abstract. In this paper, we propose a novel megawatt-class wind turbine gear train optimal design method based on genetic algorithm. Firstly, we construct an objective function to obtain the optimal quality of gear train with the constrain conditions of ratio, adjacency, assemble, gear bending fatigue and gear surface contact fatigue limitations. Then, genetic algorithm is applied to achieve the optimal parameter of the objective function. Finally, the finite element analysis method is taken to verify the feasibility of the optimization results. One type of wind turbine gearbox is given as the detail example to verify the effective of proposed method, and the verification results show that the presented method can achieve good effect for wind turbine gearbox.

Keywords: Genetic algorithm · Wind turbine gear train · Optimal design · Finite element analysis

1 Introduction

Gearbox, which locates between the impeller and the generator, is one of the most important subsystem for wind turbine drive train. The main function of gearbox is to transfer power from the low speed impeller to the high speed generator, and converts a large torque to a low torque. Thus, a large ratio is needed between impeller and generator. To achieve the high transmission ratio requirement, megawatt-class wind turbine gear trains are commonly configured with three stages, such as one planetary stage followed by two parallel stages, or two planetary stages followed by one parallel stage [1]. Two specific gear train structures are given in Fig. 1. Generally speaking, the planetary gear train outperforms the parallel gear train under similar operation condition. The planetary gear also has advantages such as drive efficiency, small size, light weight, larger transfer ratio, steady and so on.

The design of the gear train in a traditional way mainly depends on the designer's intuition, experience and skills. The designer must determine the partial ratio, materials, the thermal treatment, the hardness, pinion teeth number and a large number operating parameters for every stage. They also have to ceaselessly check the root bending stress and tooth surface compressive stress. If these parameters do not meet the requirements, all of them must be redefined once by once [2]. Even if they are reasonable, we have no idea whether they are the best. There are lots of blindness to select the appropriate parameters on gears, which will result in the waste of time and manpower.

© Springer International Publishing Switzerland 2015
Y.-J. Zhang (Ed.): ICIG 2015, Part II, LNCS 9218, pp. 323–332, 2015.
DOI: 10.1007/978-3-319-21963-9_30

Fig. 1. Common megawatt-class wind turbine gear train

Thus, some optimal design approaches for gear trains have been studies by researchers and engineers. Qin et al. [3] studied the gear transmission optimization design and dynamic characteristics analysis method. Gologlu and Zeyveli [4] presented an automated preliminary design of gear drives by minimizing volume of parallel axis two stage helical gear trains using a genetic algorithm. Mendi et al. [5] proposed a genetic algorithm based dimensional optimization approach for spur gears design. In this paper, we present an optimization design method for megawatt wind turbine gear train based on genetic algorithm, and we make sure that the volume of designed gearbox is the minimum. The finite element method analysis is then taken to verify the feasibility of the proposed optimization method.

2   GA-Based Wind Turbine Gear Train Optimization Design Method

The Genetic Algorithm is perhaps the most well-known of all evolution-based search algorithms, and it has a well global search capability and suitable for solving the high complexity problems. It can search multiple non-inferior solutions simultaneously and problems which have a variety of nonlinear constraints. Furthermore, it has simple and low complexity requirements for optimization object.

2.1   The Objective Function

We take the minimum volume as objective function to optimize the drive train of the wind turbine which is constituted of three stages. In the paper, the total volume is composed by three parts, and respectively are sun gears, planetary gears and parallel gears [6]. Thus, the optimal objective can be given as:

$$\min V = \min \sum_{i=1}^{n} n_{wi} V_{wi}$$
$$= \min(n_{a1} V_{a1} + n_{b1} V_{b1} + n_{a2} V_{a2} + n_{b2} V_{b2} + n_{a3} V_{a3} + n_{b3} V_{b3}) \qquad (1)$$

In Eq. (1), V is the total volume of the drive train, n is the total number of the gears, V_{wi} is the volume of each gears, and n_{wi} is the number of corresponding gears.

2.2 The Design Variables

There are numerous parameters for gear train design [7]. In this paper, we select eight independent parameters as optimal variables, and they are respectively denoted as m_1, z_{a1}, z_{b1}, m_2, z_{a2}, z_{b2}, m_3, z_{a3}. m_1, m_2 and m_3 are the gear modulus of three stages. z_{a1}, z_{a2} and z_{a3} are the teeth number of pinion gears in the three stages, and z_{b1}, z_{b2} are the teeth number of big gears.

2.3 The Constraints

Gear train optimal design is a complex process with a large number of constraints [8], particularly when it considers the multiple interdependencies between the design variables. In this paper, we consider the design constraints as follows:

(1) **Concentric conditions.** To ensure the input and the output shaft on the same axis, the teeth number of the sun gear, planetary gear and the internal gear must meet the requirements: $z_a + 2 \times z_b = z_c$, where, z_c is the internal gears' teeth number.
(2) **Transmission ratio conditions.** Gear transmission ratio can be determined by the equation $i_{aH} = 1 + z_c/z_a$.
(3) **Adjacency conditions.** The planetary gears are mounted round the sun gear, and planetary gears can't collide with each other. Those require a certain distance between the planetary gears, that is $(z_a + z_b)\sin(180°/n_w) > z_b + 2 \times h_a^*$, where h_a^* is the addendum coefficient.
(4) **Assembly condition.** To make the planetary gears run smoothly, the sum of tooth number of annular gear and sun gear must be the integral multiple for the number of planetary gear.
(5) **Gear bending fatigue limit.** Gear bending fatigue limit can be represented by equation $\sigma_F = \frac{2 \times K \times T}{b \times d \times m} \times Y_{Fa}Y_{Sa}Y_\varepsilon \leq [\sigma_F]$, where Y_{Fa} is gear shape factor, Y_{Sa} is stress correction factor, Y_ε is gear overlap coefficient, K is dynamic load factor, T_{a1} is the driving torque of the stage and $[\sigma_F]$ is the maximum bending stress that material allows.
(6) **Gear surface contact fatigue strength limit.** This constrain can be denoted by equation $\sigma_H = Z_H Z_E Z_\varepsilon \times \sqrt{\frac{2 \times K \times T}{b \times d^2} \times \frac{u+1}{u}} \leq [\sigma_H]$. Z_H is pitch circle area coefficient, Z_E is material elasticity coefficient, Z_ε is coincidence coefficient, $[\sigma_H]$ is the maximum bending stress of the material, u is the gear transmission ratio of the stage.

2.4 Genetic Algorithm Settings

Objective function for wind turbine gearbox gear train is given in Eq. (1). The fitness function is the reciprocal of objective function, and is built as follows:

$$F = \frac{1}{V} \tag{2}$$

For the resolution process, the manner of selection, crossover and mutation operations are used as in reference [5]. The detail GA parameters include evolutionary generation, crossover probability, mutation probability, and they work as a criterion for algorithm running until the optimization terminated.

3 Application

A 3.3 MW wind turbine gearbox contained three stages is adopt to verify the proposed method. The input rotation speed of this gearbox is $r = 12.6$ r/min. The low speed stage uses standard NGW structure with four planet gears, and its ratio is $i_1 = 4.6$. The intermediate speed stage uses standard NGW structure with three planet gears, whose ratio is $i_2 = 5.7$. The planar gear with ratio being $i_3 = 3.5$ is adopted for the high speed stages. Then, we choose 17 $CrNiMo_6$ as the gear material. The structure of applied wind turbine gearbox is given in Fig. 2.

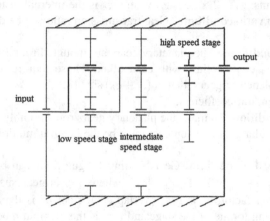

Fig. 2. A wind turbine gearbox structure

The variables are $X = [x_1, x_2, x_3, x_4, x_5, x_6, x_7, x_8]^T = [m_1, z_{a1}, z_{b1}, m_2, z_{a2}, z_{b2}, m_3, z_{a3}]^T$. The objective function can be denoted as

$$\min F(X) = f(x) = \frac{\pi \cdot \varphi}{4} x(1)^3 x(2)^3 + \pi \cdot \varphi x(1)^3 x(2) x(3)^2 + \frac{\pi \cdot \varphi}{4} x(4)^3 x(5)^3 +$$
$$\frac{3\pi\varphi}{4} x(4)^3 x(5) x(6)^2 + \frac{\pi \cdot \varphi}{4} x(7)^3 x(8)^3 + \frac{\pi \cdot \varphi \cdot (i_3^2 + 1)}{4} x(7)^3 x(8)^3$$

$$(3)$$

where, φ is the ratio of the diameter and the thickness.

Then, the constraint functions can be computed as follows:

$$\begin{cases} g_1(x) = |1 + (x_2 + 2 \cdot x_3)/x_2 - 4.6| - 0.04 \leq 0 \\ g_2(x) = |1 + (x_5 + 2 \cdot x_6)/x_5 - 5.7| - 0.04 \leq 0 \\ g_3(x) = \dfrac{2 \times 1.3 \times T_{a1}}{0.85 \times x_2^2 \times x_1^3} \times Y_{Fa} Y_{Sa} Y_\varepsilon - [\sigma_F] \leq 0 \\ g_4(x) = \dfrac{2 \times 1.3 \times T_{a2}}{0.85 \times x_5^2 \times x_4^3} \times Y_{Fa} Y_{Sa} Y_\varepsilon - [\sigma_F] \leq 0 \\ g_5(x) = \dfrac{2 \times 1.3 \times T_{a3}}{0.85 \times x_8^2 \times x_9^3} \times Y_{Fa} Y_{Sa} Y_\varepsilon - [\sigma_F] \leq 0 \\ g_6(x) = Z_H Z_E Z_\varepsilon \times \sqrt{\dfrac{2 \times 1.3 \times T_{a1}}{0.85 \times x_1^3 \times x_2^3} \times \dfrac{2 \cdot x_2 + 2 \cdot x_3}{x_2 + 2 \cdot x_3}} - [\sigma_H] \leq 0 \\ g_7(x) = Z_H Z_E Z_\varepsilon \times \sqrt{\dfrac{2 \times 1.3 \times T_{a2}}{0.85 \times x_4^3 \times x_5^3} \times \dfrac{2 \cdot x_5 + 2 \cdot x_6}{x_5 + 2 \cdot x_6}} - [\sigma_H] \leq 0 \\ g_8(x) = Z_H Z_E Z_\varepsilon \times \sqrt{\dfrac{2 \times 1.3 \times T_{a3}}{0.85 \times x_7^3 \times x_8^3} \times \dfrac{5}{7}} - [\sigma_H] \leq 0 \end{cases} \tag{4}$$

$$\begin{cases} h_9(x) = x_3 + 2 \times 1 - (x_2 + x_3) \sin(180°/4) < 0 \\ h_{10}(x) = x_6 + 2 \times 1 - (x_5 + x_6) \sin(180°/3) < 0 \\ h_{11}(x) = 2 \cdot (x_2 + x_3)/4 - c_1 = 0 \\ h_{12}(x) = 2 \cdot (x_5 + x_6)/3 - c_2 = 0 \end{cases} \tag{5}$$

Running the optimization algorithm based on Matlab genetic algorithm toolbox, we can get some non-integer results, as in Table 1.

Table 1. Optimal results

Groups	m_1	z_{a1}	z_{b1}	m_2	z_{a2}	z_{b2}	m_3	z_{a3}
Original	14	29	37	11	20	37	13	25
Optimal 1	14	28	36	11	20	37	14.5	22
Optimal 2	11.5	35	45	12.5	18	33	16	19
Optimal 3	21	19	24	11	20	36	16	19
Optimal 4	14	28	36	12	18	33	17	17
Optimal 5	14	28	36	12.5	18	33	16.5	18
Optimal 6	22	18	23	12.5	18	33	15.5	20
Optimal 7	15	26	33	10	22	41	16	19

In Table 1, we can see that all of the seven optimal results outperform the original gearbox. The volume of the original gearbox is 6.44×10^8 mm^3, and the volume of the optimal 4 is 5.42×10^8 mm^3. The weight of the optimal 4 reduces about 15.83 %, and its three stages' ratio are 4.57, 5.67 and 3.53 respectively. The result shows that there is a certain redundancy in original design. Comparing the optimal 1 with the optimal 4 and 5, we can see that their low-level gears adapt the same modulus and teeth number. However, the teeth number and the modulus of the intermediate and high stage are different. Thus, we can get the result that proper modulus increase can reduce the volume.

4   Finite Element Analysis

The appearance of finite element technique provides a powerful computational tool for engineering design, and it plays an important role in almost all areas of engineering. This method uses a finite model to represent the actual solid, and it uses the response of finite element model to represent the actual response [9].

The accurate models of gears are firstly built by using PRO/E with parametric design method [10], but they cannot be directly applied to perform the finite element analysis. Some small structure must be removed as they always make the meshing perish or complex [11]. In this paper, we import the reduced model into ANSYS. The element type of the model uses solid brick 8 nodes 185 and the model meshing in a smart size, whose linear density is 5. The material properties are set as same value as the actual operation. All gears' inner surfaces are imposed with full constraints and their two sides have the constraints in z axis. The forces are loaded tangential to the addendum circle. The actual work conditions for gears are complex. There are several pairs of teeth keeping in touch with each other at one time, and they share these forces. We perform an extreme condition that the force loads at one tooth. We select pinion gears of each stage for analysis, and some results are given as follows.

There are some similarities in Figs. 3 and 4. The strains at the middle are smaller than the two sides in z axis, and they are reduced from the top to root in x axis. The position of maximum strain is located at the tip of the teeth, and this can result in excessive wear or breakage of the teeth after a period of work [12], which is similar to

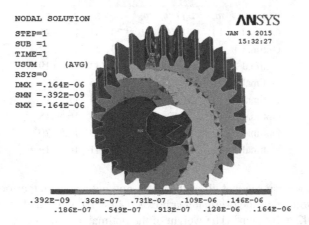

Fig. 3. Strain of original low stage sun gear

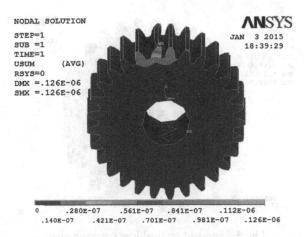

NODAL SOLUTION
STEP=1
SUB =1
TIME=1
USUM   (AVG)
RSYS=0
DMX =.126E-06
SMX =.126E-06

ANSYS
JAN 3 2015
18:39:29

0   .280E-07   .561E-07   .841E-07   .112E-06
   .140E-07   .421E-07   .701E-07   .981E-07   .126E-06

Fig. 4. Strain of optimal low stage sun gear

the real result. Furthermore, the situation of Fig. 3 is closer to the real result because the inner circle's constraints are limited as the actual situation. Some little effect constraints in other gears are not considered to simplify the computational. The detail number of these strains is given in Table 2.

Table 2. The strains of the teeth

Strain		Low speed stage sun gear (m)	Intermediate speed stage sun gear (m)	High speed stage pinion gear (m)
Original	Largest	0.164×10^{-6}	0.568×10^{-6}	0.863×10^{-6}
	Middle	0.913×10^{-7}	0.315×10^{-6}	0.479×10^{-6}
Optimized	Largest	0.126×10^{-6}	0.579×10^{-6}	0.809×10^{-6}
	Middle	0.703×10^{-7}	0.322×10^{-6}	0.449×10^{-6}

In Table 2, we know that the optimized tooth strains reduce in the low speed stage and the high speed stage is except the intermediate speed stage. The gears of the optimized low and high speed gears can well meet the requirement. The strain of the optimized intermediate stage gear is larger than original's, but the value is maintained in the permissible range. So, the optimized gears are feasible.

As it is shown in Figs. 5 and 6, the stress at the middle is smaller than the two sides in z axis, and the value increases from the middle to the top and root in x axis. The maximum stress is located at the tip of the tooth, and the root stress is bigger than other parts. This due to the most damage of the tooth root bending break and tooth fracture [13]. The details are given in Table 3.

In Table 3, we can see that the stress of the optimized tooth increases in all three stages. The largest stress of low speed stage maintains in the permissible range even though the optimal result increased, so the gears of the optimized low speed gears can meet the requirement. The largest stress of intermediate and high speed stage are larger

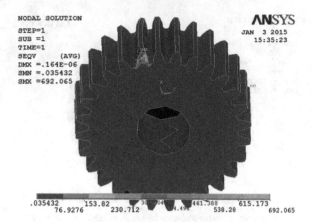

Fig. 5. Stress of original low stage sun gear

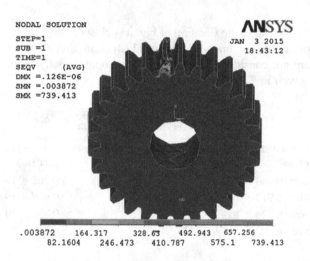

Fig. 6. Stress of optimal low stage sun gear

Table 3. The stress of the teeth

Stress		Low speed stage sun gear (MPa)	Intermediate speed stage sun gear (MPa)	High speed stage pinion gear (MPa)
Original	Largest	692.065	2695.72	3234.16
	Roots	230–400	900–1497	1078–1437
Optimal	Largest	739.413	3576.31	3465.14
	Roots	246–410	1192–1589	1155–1540

than permissible range, but we usually do some chamfer to avoid such local stress in practical applications, so they cannot reflect the real situation. The root stress value is close to the real, so we can use the root stress to certificate the gears feasibility, and this value maintains in the permissible range. Therefore, the optimal gears are feasible.

5 Conclusion

A GA based optimal design method for megawatt-class wind turbine gear train is proposed and certificated in this paper. It takes the minimum volume as objective function and the material selection, fabrication restrictions, assembly, bending stress, contact fatigue stress and fatigue life of gears as constrains according to the real requirement. The example shows that the given optimal method for the gear train design can obtain well result. The size of the gears in some places is smaller than before, while their strain and stress variation cannot affect the normal use of the gears. This proves that the method has a common sense in designing multi-stage planetary gear train.

Acknowledgements. This work is supported by the Program for Liaoning Excellent Talents in University (No. LJQ2013133).

References

1. Qiu, X.H., Han, Q.K., Chu, F.L.: Review on dynamic analysis of wind turbine geared transmission systems. J. Mech. Eng. **50**(11), 23–36 (2014)
2. Swantner, A., Campbell, M.I.: Automated synthesis and optimization of gear train topologies. In: ASME 2009 International Design Engineering Technical Conferences and Computers and Information in Engineering Conference, pp. 13–22 (2009)
3. Qin, D.T., Gu, X.G., Wang, J.H.: Dynamic analysis and optimization of gear trains in a megawatt level wind turbine. J. Chongqing Univ. **32**(4), 408–414 (2009)
4. Gologlu, C., Zeyveli, M.: A genetic approach to automate preliminary design of gear drives. Comput. Ind. Eng. **57**, 1043–1051 (2009)
5. Mendi, F., Baskal, T., Boran, K., Boran, F.E.: Optimization of module, shaft diameter and rolling bearing for spur gear through genetic algorithm. Expert Syst. Appl. **37**, 8058–8064 (2010)
6. Chen, T., Zhang, Z., Chen, D., Li, Y.: The optimization of two-stage planetary gear train based on mathmatica. In: Zu, Q., Hu, B., Elçi, A. (eds.) ICPCA 2012 and SWS 2012. LNCS, vol. 7719, pp. 122–136. Springer, Heidelberg (2013)
7. Tripathi, V.K., Chauhan, H.M.: Multi objective optimization of planetary gear train. In: Deb, K., Bhattacharya, A., Chakraborti, N., Chakroborty, P., Das, S., Dutta, J., Gupta, S.K., Jain, A., Aggarwal, V., Branke, J., Louis, S.J., Tan, K.C. (eds.) SEAL 2010. LNCS, vol. 6457, pp. 578–582. Springer, Heidelberg (2010)
8. Buiga, O., Tudose, L.: Optimal mass minimization design of a two-stage coaxial helical speed reducer with genetic algorithms. Adv. Eng. Softw. **68**, 25–32 (2014)

9. Li, Z., Chen, Y.: The computer simulation on wind turbine gearbox design. In: 2013 The International Conference on Technological Advances in Electrical, Electronics and Computer Engineering, pp. 454–458 (2013)
10. Bao, J.H., He, W.D., Li, L.X.: Finite element analysis of locomotive traction gear. In: 2010 International Conference on Mechanic Automation and Control Engineering, pp. 649–652 (2010)
11. Tong, H.L., Liu, Z.H., Li, Y.: The dynamic finite element analysis of shearer's running gear based on LS-DYNA. Adv. Mater. Res. **402**, 753–757 (2012)
12. Yang, S.H., Li, G.G.: 3D simulation on root stresses and tooth deformations of whole gear. Comput. Aided Eng. **22**(2), 36–40 (2013)
13. Tian, W., Fu, S.X., Li, C.Y.: Reasonable analysis of root stresses and teeth compliances based on ANSYS. J. Changsha Aeronaut. Vocat. Tech. Coll. **8**(4), 48–51, 63 (2008)

Generalized Contributing Vertices-Based Method for Minkowski Sum Outer-Face of Two Polygons

Peng Zhang and Hong Zheng[✉]

State Key Laboratory of Geomechanics and Geotechnical Engineering,
Institute of Rock and Soil Mechanics, Chinese Academy of Sciences, Wuhan, China
zhangpeng_50@163.com, hzheng@whrsm.ac.cn

Abstract. A new method is presented for computing the Minkowski sum outer-face of two polygons of any shape. Stemming from the contributing vertex concept, the concept of generalized contributing vertex is proposed. Based on the new concept, an efficient algorithm is developed, which starts from the construction of the superset of the Minkowski sum edges. The superset is composed of three types of edges: translated-corner edges, translated edges and corner edges. Then the Minkowski sum outer-face is extracted from the arrangement of the superset edges. The algorithm is implemented using C++ and the Computational Geometry Algorithms Library (CGAL). The experiments including very complicated polygons are conducted, suggesting that the proposed algorithm is more efficient than other existing algorithms in most cases.

Keywords: Computational geometry · Minkowski sum outer-face · Generalized contributing vertex · Translated-corner edge · Superset · Polygon

1 Introduction

The Minkowski sum of two objects A and B in an Euclidian space was defined by the German mathematician Hermann Minkowski (1864–1909) as the position vector addition of each point a in A and each point b in B

$$A \oplus B = \{a + b | a \in A, b \in B\} \tag{1}$$

where $a + b$ denotes the sum of position vector a and position vector b, corresponding to points in A and B respectively. The Minkowski sum can also be written as another form

$$A \oplus B = \bigcup_{a \in A} \{a + b | b \in B\} = \bigcup_{a \in A} \{a + b_0 + (b - b_0) | b \in B\} \tag{2}$$

where b_0 is the position vector of any selected point of B.

H. Zheng—This study is supported by the National Basic Research Program of China (973 Program), under the Grant Nos. 2011CB013505 and 2014CB047100; and the National Natural Science Foundation of China, under the Grant No. 11172313.

© Springer International Publishing Switzerland 2015
Y.-J. Zhang (Ed.): ICIG 2015, Part II, LNCS 9218, pp. 333–346, 2015.
DOI: 10.1007/978-3-319-21963-9_31

Since no transformation between coordinate systems is involved, in this study we do not differentiate between points and the position vectors of these points. For example, suppose point $b \in B$, by saying "vector b" we means the vector starting at the origin O of the coordinate system in use and ending at point b. In this way, Eq. 2 suggests that the Minkowski sum can be achieved by the following operations: (1) translate A by vector b_0, denoting by A'; and (2) sweep all points of A' with B by letting point b_0 traverse all points of A', the trace of sweeping is just $A \oplus B$. Since the polygons A and B are represented by their boundaries, it is sufficient to consider only the boundary points. Figure 1 illustrates the two operations.

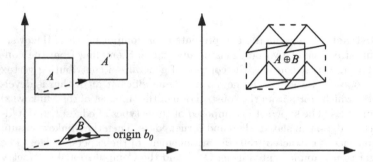

Fig. 1. The Minkowski sum of two polygons A and B is obtained by two operations. Firstly, translating A by vector b_0, A' is obtained; secondly, sweeping A' by letting point b_0 traverse all points of A', $A \oplus B$ is given by the trace of B.

The Minkowski sum is applied in many domains such as computer-aided design and manufacturing, image processing, motion planning in robotics. Shi [16] recently proposed a concept, the entrance block $E(A, B)$, to judge whether two blocks, represented by sets A and B, contact, which greatly simplifies the contact detection. The entrance block $E(A, B)$ is defined as

$$E(A, B) = \bigcup_{a \in A, b \in B} \{b - a + a_0\} \tag{3}$$

with a_0 an arbitrary point in A. By comparing Eqs. 1 and 3, we can immediately see that the entrance block $E(A, B)$ is actually the Minkowski sum $B \oplus \bar{A}$, where $\bar{A}$ is obtained through translating the centrally symmetric counterpart of A by vector a_0. So the Minkowski sum can be used to calculate the entrance block $E(A, B)$.

In most applications, the outer-face of the Minkowski sum rather than the interior is of interest. Therefore, we will propose an algorithm to compute the Minkowski sum outer-face.

This paper is organized as follows. Section 2 reviews the related literature. Section 3 introduces the original contributing vertices-based Minkowski sum algorithm. In Sect. 4, we expound in detail the algorithm based on the concept of generalized contributing vertices to calculate the Minkowski sum outer-face. In

Sect. 5, we present an implementation and make comparisons with the existing algorithms. Section 6 concludes the paper.

2   Related Works

There is one category of methods [2,8] for computing the Minkowski sum of two non-convex polygons based on convex decomposition: decomposing each non-convex polygon into convex sub-polygons, computing the Minkowski sum of each pair of sub-polygons, then performing the union of the pairwise Minkowski sums. These methods are time consuming because of the large size of the decomposition and union. Now, some other categories of methods are briefly reviewed below.

Ghost [9] presented a slope diagram algorithm to compute the Minkowski sum of polygons and polyhedrons. The polygons are represented in their slope diagram forms. The sum polygon can be obtained by merging the two slope diagrams. However, no implementations of the algorithm for non-convex polygons has been published.

Ramkumar [15] presented a method to compute the Minkowski sum outer-face of two simple polygons using convolution, which was introduced by Guibas et al. [10,11]. The method detects self-intersections for each cycle of the convolution, and snips off the loops thus created. The outer-face is obtained by connecting the cycles using paths inside the convolution. The convolution method is also used for computing the Minkowski sum of 2D curved objects [12], the Minkowski sum of ruled surfaces [13], and the Minkowski sum of boundary surfaces of 3D-objects [14].

Wein [18] described an efficient and robust method to compute the Minkowski sum using convolution too. The method keeps the faces with non-zero winding numbers from the arrangement of the convolution segments. The method is superior to the decomposition methods in most cases.

Behar and Lien [6] proposed a fast and robust method to compute the 2D Minkowski sum using reduced convolution. The arrangement computation time reduces since the number of convolution segments decreases, which takes a large portion of the total time. Several filters were proposed to extract the Minkowski sum boundaries. The method is faster than the convolution method.

Barki et al. [3–5] proposed the contributing vertices-based Minkowski sum algorithm. The algorithm will be reviewed in the next section since the new algorithm is improved from it.

3   Original Contributing Vertices-Based Minkowski Sum Algorithm

Barki et al. [3] proposed the contributing vertices-based Minkowski sum algorithm for convex polyhedrons (polygons). They showed that the Minkowski sum polygon S of two convex polygons A and B is a convex polygon composed of two types of edges: the edges parallel to the edges of A, named the "ranslated edges" of S; and the edges parallel to the edges of B, named the "corner edges" of S.

The two categories of edges are obtained from the edges of A and B by computing their contributing vertices. Here is the definition of a contributing vertex.

The **contributing vertex** $v_{k,B}$ of an edge $e_{i,A} \in A$ with an outer normal $n_{i,A}$ is a vertex of B that is farthest, in the sense of algebraic values, away from the line $e_{i,A}$, suggesting

$$v_{k,B} = argmax[\langle v_{l,B}, n_{i,A} \rangle | v_{l,B} \in B] \tag{4}$$

where $\langle \cdot, \cdot \rangle$ denotes the scalar product. An example is illustrated in Fig. 2.

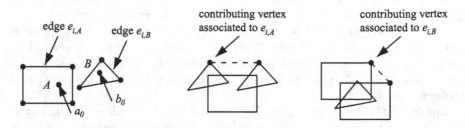

Fig. 2. The concept of contributing vertex

Interchanging A and B in Eq. 4, the contributing vertex $v_{k,A}$ of an edge $e_{i,B} \in B$ with an outer normal $n_{i,B}$ can be obtained See Fig. 2.

There is at least one contributing vertex for each edge of A or B. For some edges, there are two contributing vertices if they are equally farthest away from the line coinciding with these edges. In this case, the edge of A having two contributing vertices has the same orientation as the edge of B with the two vertices as the endpoints. Hereafter, by saying that edge $e_A \in A$ has the same orientation as edge $e_B \in B$, we mean that e_A and e_B have the same unit outward normal.

The process of contributing vertices-based Minkowski sum algorithm consists of the two main steps as follows.

- Determination of translated edges. For each edge $e_{i,A}$ of A, find out its contributing vertices $v_{k,B}$, deduce the translated edge corresponding to each $v_{k,B}$. If there are two contributing vertices that are two endpoints of some edge $e_{j,B}$, the translated edge is the Minkowski sum of $e_{i,A}$ and $e_{j,B}$. The edge $e_{j,B}$ will be ignored in the determination of corner edges because it has contributed once. If there is only one contributing vertex $v_{k,B}$, the translated edge is obtained through translating edge $e_{i,A}$ by vector $v_{k,B}$.
- Determination of corner edges. For each edge $e_{i,B}$ of B that has no the same orientation as any edge of A, find out its contributing vertex $v_{k,A}$, and deduce the corner edge which is obtained through translating edge $e_{i,B}$ by vector $v_{k,A}$.

An illustration of translated edges and corner edges is given in Fig. 3.

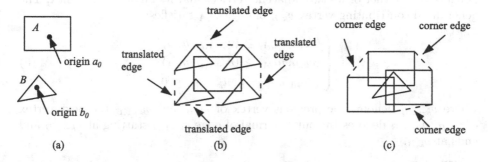

Fig. 3. (a) Two polygons A and B. (b) The translated edges. (c) The corner edges.

Select an arbitrary edge from the translated edges and corner edges as a seed edge, traverse other edges by neighborhood, then the Minkowski sum polygon is obtained.

Barki et al. adapted the contributing vertices-based Minkowski sum algorithm for a nonconvex-convex pair of polyhedra in [4]. Its implementation includes two main steps: (1) form the superset of the Minkowski sum edges through the use of the contributing vertex concept, and; (2) extract the Minkowski sum of the two polyhedra from the superset. However, it doesnt apply to the case of two non-convex polygons.

4   Generalized Contributing Vertices-Based Minkowski Sum Outer-Face Algorithm

In this section, we generalize the concept of contributing vertex to the concept of generalized contributing vertex. Then we use the new concept to develop an algorithm for computing the Minkowski sum outer-face of two polygons of any shape. The algorithm also has two main steps: first, construct the Minkowski sum superset edges; second, extract the Minkowski sum outer-face from the superset.

Lets define some notations here. For two polygons A and B in consideration, A has e_a edges and B has e_b edges; $v_{i,A}$ denotes the starting point of edge $e_{i,A}$, and $v_{i+1,A}$ the end point; similarly, $v_{j,B}$ denotes the starting point of edge $e_{j,B}$; $v_{j+1,B}$ denotes the end point.

4.1   Definition of Generalized Contributing Vertices and Translated-Corner Edge

In order to compute the Minkowski sum outer-face of two polygons of any shape, we generalize the contributing vertex concept to the generalized contributing vertex concept for the two polygons in consideration below.

Definition 1. The **generalized contributing vertex** $v_{k,B}$ of edge $e_{i,A}$ with an outer normal $n_{i,A}$ is a vertex of B whose distance away from the line $e_{i,A}$ is not less than either of its two adjacent vertices and its angle is non-reflex. The generalized contributing vertex $v_{k,B}$ of edge $e_{i,A}$ satisfies:

$$\begin{cases} \langle v_{k,B}, n_{i,A} \rangle \geq \langle v_{k-1,B}, n_{i,A} \rangle \\ \langle v_{k,B}, n_{i,A} \rangle \geq \langle v_{k+1,B}, n_{i,A} \rangle \\ \langle v_{k+1,B} - v_{k,B}, n_{k-1,B} \rangle \leq 0 \end{cases} \tag{5}$$

where $v_{k-1,B}$ denotes the previous vertex of $v_{k,B}$ and $v_{k+1,B}$ the next vertex of $v_{k,B}$; $n_{k-1,B}$ denotes the outer normal of edge $e_{k-1,B}$ starting at $v_{k-1,B}$ and ends at $v_{k,B}$.

When B is convex, generalized contributing vertices degenerate to contributing vertices. The generalized contributing vertices of the edges of B can be found out in a similar manner by interchanging A and B in Eq. 5. An illustration of the generalized contributing vertex concept is shown in Fig. 4.

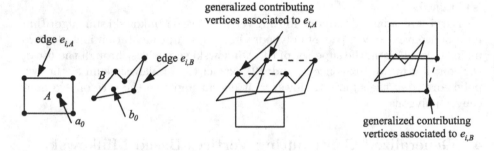

Fig. 4. The concept of generalized contributing vertex

When edge $e_{i,A}$ and edge $e_{j,B}$ have the same orientation, and at least one endpoint of each edge is the generalized contributing convex of the other, the translated edge and corner edge are collinear, have same orientation and will be joined or overlap, and should be merged into one edge, which will be called **"translated-corner edge"** subsequently. Three cases exist that are stated below to reduce the number of edges in the superset and decrease the complexity of the extraction of the Minkowski sum outer-face from the superset.

Case 1. If $e_{i,A}$ and $e_{j,B}$ have the same orientation, $v_{i,A}$ is the generalized contributing vertex of $e_{j,B}$, and $v_{j+1,B}$ is the generalized contributing vertex of $e_{i,A}$, then there is one translated-corner edge that starts at $v_{i,A} \oplus v_{j,B}$ and ends at $v_{i+1,A} \oplus v_{j+1,B}$.

Proof. Because $v_{j+1,B}$ is the generalized contributing vertex of $e_{i,A}$, there is the translated edge, $e_{i,A} \oplus v_{j+1,B}$. It starts at point $v_{i,A} \oplus v_{j+1,B}$, ends at point $v_{i+1,A} \oplus v_{j+1,B}$, and has the same orientation as $e_{i,A}$.

Because $v_{i,A}$ is the generalized contributing vertex of $e_{j,B}$, there is the corner edge, $v_{i,A} \oplus e_{j,B}$. It starts at point $v_{i,A} \oplus v_{j,B}$, ends at point $v_{i,A} \oplus v_{j+1,B}$, and has the same orientation as $e_{j,B}$.

The starting point of the translated edge $e_{i,A} \oplus v_{j+1,B}$ and the end point of the corner edge $v_{i,A} \oplus e_{j,B}$ are both $v_{i,A} \oplus v_{j+1,B}$. The translated edge $e_{i,A} \oplus v_{j+1,B}$ and the corner edge $v_{i,A} \oplus e_{j,B}$ are linked at $v_{i,A} \oplus v_{j+1,B}$, and accordingly merged into one translated-corner edge that starts at point $v_{i,A} \oplus v_{j,B}$, ends at point $v_{i+1,A} \oplus v_{j+1,B}$, and has the same orientation as $e_{i,A}$ or $e_{j,B}$. A case is illustrated in Fig. 5.

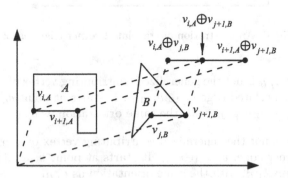

Fig. 5. An illustration of translated-corner edge case 1

Case 2. If $e_{i,A}$ and $e_{j,B}$ have the same orientation, $v_{i,A}$ is the generalized contributing vertex of $e_{j,B}$ but $v_{i+1,A}$ is not, and $v_{j,B}$ is the generalized contributing vertex of $e_{i,A}$ but $v_{j+1,B}$ is not, then there is the translated-corner edge that starts at $v_{i,A} \oplus v_{j,B}$, and ends at one of point $v_{i+1,A} \oplus v_{j,B}$ and point $v_{i,A} \oplus v_{j+1,B}$ that is farther away from the starting point $v_{i,A} \oplus v_{j,B}$.

Proof. Because $v_{j,B}$ is the generalized contributing vertex of $e_{i,A}$ but $v_{j+1,B}$ is not, there is the translated edge, $e_{i,A} \oplus v_{j,B}$. It starts at point $v_{i,A} \oplus v_{j,B}$, ends at point $v_{i+1,A} \oplus v_{j,B}$, and has the same orientation as $e_{i,A}$.

Because $v_{i,A}$ is the generalized contributing vertex of $e_{j,B}$ but $v_{i+1,A}$ is not, there is the corner edge, $v_{i,A} \oplus e_{j,B}$. It starts at point $v_{i,A} \oplus v_{j,B}$, ends at point $v_{i,A} \oplus v_{j+1,B}$, and has the same orientation as $e_{j,B}$.

As a result, the translated edge $e_{i,A} \oplus v_{j,B}$ and the corner edge $v_{i,A} \oplus e_{j,B}$ overlap since they start at the same point $v_{i,A} \oplus v_{j,B}$ and have the same orientation. The translated-corner edge should be the longer one, and accordingly ends at one of point $v_{i+1,A} \oplus v_{j,B}$ and point $v_{i,A} \oplus v_{j+1,B}$ that is farther away from the starting point $v_{i,A} \oplus v_{j,B}$. Figure 6 illustrates such a case.

Case 3. If $e_{i,A}$ and $e_{j,B}$ have the same orientation, and $v_{i,A}$ is not the generalized contributing vertex of $e_{j,B}$ but $v_{i+1,A}$ is; and $v_{j,B}$ is not the generalized contributing vertex of $e_{i,A}$ but $v_{j+1,B}$ is, then there is the translated-corner edge that ends at $v_{i+1,A} \oplus v_{j+1,B}$, and starts at one of $v_{i,A} \oplus v_{j+1,B}$ and $v_{i+1,A} \oplus v_{j,B}$ that is farther from the end point $v_{i+1,A} \oplus v_{j+1,B}$.

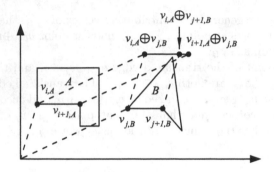

Fig. 6. An illustration of translated-corner edge case 2

Proof. Because $v_{j,B}$ is not the generalized contributing vertex of $e_{i,A}$ but $v_{j+1,B}$ is, we have the translated edge $e_{i,A} \oplus v_{j+1,B}$. It starts at point $v_{i,A} \oplus v_{j+1,B}$ and ends at point $v_{i+1,A} \oplus v_{j+1,B}$, with the same orientation as $e_{i,A}$.

Because $v_{i,A}$ is not the generalized contributing vertex of $e_{j,B}$ but $v_{i+1,A}$ is, we have the corner edge, $v_{i+1,A} \oplus e_{j,B}$. It starts at point $v_{i+1,A} \oplus v_{j,B}$ and ends at point $v_{i+1,A} \oplus v_{j+1,B}$, with the same orientation as $e_{j,B}$.

As a result, the translated edge $e_{i,A} \oplus v_{j+1,B}$ and the corner edge $v_{i+1,A} \oplus e_{j,B}$ overlap since they end at the same point $v_{i+1,A} \oplus v_{j+1,B}$ and have the same orientation. The translated-corner edge should be the longer one, and accordingly starts at one of point $v_{i,A} \oplus v_{j+1,B}$ and point $v_{i+1,A} \oplus v_{j,B}$ that is farther away from the ending point $v_{i+1,A} \oplus v_{j+1,B}$. Figure 7 illustrates such a case.

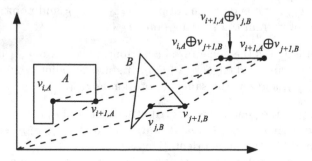

Fig. 7. An illustration of translated-corner edge case 3

4.2   Construction of the Minkowski Sum Edge Superset

The construction of the Minkowski sum edge superset starts with determining the translated-corner edges, translated edges and corner edges by finding out the generalized contributing vertices associated with all edges of A and B respectively. Four steps are involved in this operation.

1. Determination of generalized contributing vertices: For each edge $e_{i,A}$, find out its generalized contributing vertices. For each edge $e_{i,B}$, find out its generalized contributing vertices.

2. Determination of translated-corner edges: For each edge $e_{i,A}$, find out the edges $e_{j,B}$ having the same orientation. If such a pair of $e_{i,A}$ and $e_{j,B}$ falls into one of the three cases in the above, we can determine the translated-corner edge. The generalized vertices belonging to $e_{j,B}$ of $e_{i,A}$ and the generalized vertices belonging to $e_{i,A}$ of $e_{j,B}$ will not be considered in the rest, since they have been considered here.

3. Determination of translated edges: For each edge $e_{i,A}$, for each of the rest generalized contributing vertices $v_{k,B}$ which have not been considered, we have a translated edge, $e_{i,A} \oplus v_{k,B}$, which is obtained through translating it by vector $v_{k,B}$, and accordingly has the same orientation as $e_{i,A}$. Here, $v_{k,B}$ is a generalized contributing vertex.

4. Determination of corner edges: For each edge $e_{i,B}$, for each of the rest generalized contributing vertices $v_{k,A}$ which have not been considered, we have a corner edge, $e_{i,B} \oplus v_{k,A}$, which is obtained through translating it by vector $v_{k,A}$, and accordingly has the same orientation as $e_{i,B}$. Here, $v_{k,A}$ is a generalized contributing vertex.

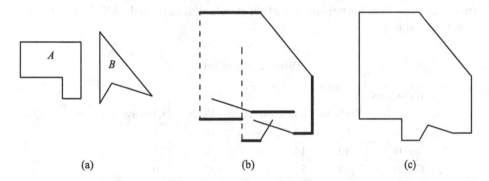

(a)   (b)   (c)

Fig. 8. (a) Two polygons A and B. (b) The Minkowski sum edges superset. The dashed lines are the translated-corner edges. The bold lines are the translated edges. The thin lines are the corner edges. (c) The Minkowski sum outer-face.

4.3 Extraction of the Minkowski Sum Outer-Face from the Superset Edges

There are two ways to extract the Minkowski sum outer-face from the superset: (1) compute the intersections of the superset edges and break the edges down at the intersections, from a seed edge containing the lexicographically smallest (or greatest) point among the superset vertices, traverse other outer-face edges by neighborhood, when there are multiple compatible edges adjacent to the end

point of the previous edge, we pick the one that makes a largest inner angle at
the point, and (2) compute the arrangement [7,17] of the superset edges, the
Minkowski sum outer-face is the resulted face with no boundary.

An example of a non-convex polygon A and a non-convex polygon B is
depicted in Fig. 8(a). The entire superset of the Minkowski sum edges is depicted
in Fig. 8(b). The Minkowski sum outer-face is depicted in Fig. 8(c).

5   Implementation and Comparison

In this section, we describe the implementation of the generalized contributing vertex-based Minkowski sum outer-face (GCVMSOF) algorithm. Then, we
compare the performance of this algorithm with other methods in the literature.

5.1   Implementation

The proposed algorithm has been implemented using C++ and the Computational Geometry Algorithms Library (CGAL) [1]. The extraction of the
Minkowski sum outer-face from the superset is the arrangement method, which is
done by the 2D arrangement package of CGAL, the outer-face is the unbounded
face. We select nine models, the first five from [18]: chain, stars, comb, fork and
knife; and the last four from [6]: g1g2, monkey, hand, bird. All data sets are
shown in Table 1.

Table 1. Input sets

Input sets	A		B	
	Vertices	Concave vertices	Vertices	Concave vertices
Chain	58	26	16	8
Starts	40	14	40	14
Comb	53	24	22	0
Fork	34	19	31	18
Knife	64	40	12	5
g1g2	30	13	34	19
Monkey	1204	577	24	11
Hand	57	15	84	16
Bird	275	133	57	15

All experiments were performed on a personal computer with 4 GB RAM
and 3.40 GHZ Intel Core i7 CPU. Figure 9 illustrates the input polygons and
their Minkowski sum outer-faces.

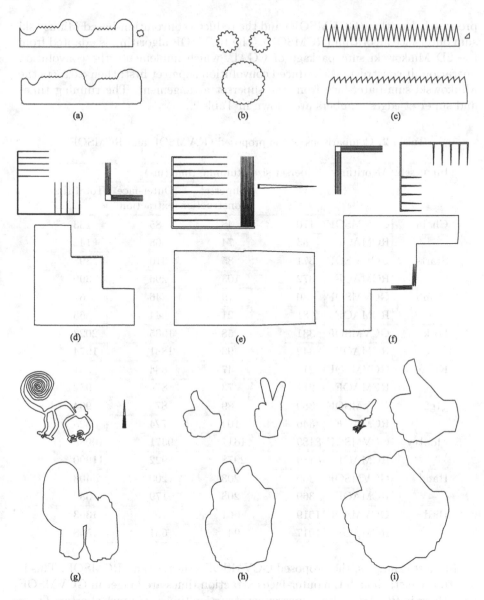

Fig. 9. Samples of input polygons (top) and their Minkowski sum outer-faces (bottom): (a) chain; (b) stars; (c) comb; (d) fork; (e) knife; (f) g1g2; (g) monkey; (h) hand; (i) bird.

5.2   Comparison

According to [18], the convolution-based Minkowski sum (CMS) algorithm is superior to the decomposition method in most cases. According to [6], the reduced convolution-based Minkowski sum algorithm is superior to the CMS algorithm. So the comparisons in the computation time are made between the proposed algorithm (GCVMSOF) and the reduced convolution-based Minkowski sum outer-face algorithm (RCMSOF). The RCMSOF algorithm is adapted from the 2D Minkowski sum package of CGAL, which implements the convolution operation. It constructs the reduced convolution superset first; then extracts the Minkowski sum outer-face from the superset arrangement. The running times and superset edges numbers are shown in Table 2.

Table 2. Comparisons of the proposed GCVMSOF and RCMSOF

Input sets	Algorithms	Superset size	Running time (ms)		
			Superset construction	Outer-face extraction	Total time
Chain	GCVMSOF	170	48	85	133
	RCMAOF	63	74	68	142
Starts	GCVMSOF	371	85	310	395
	RCMAOF	372	103	296	399
Comb	GCVMSOF	80	19	46	65
	RCMAOF	81	21	44	65
Fork	GCVMSOF	331	58	1965	2023
	RCMAOF	342	93	1881	1974
Knife	GCVMSOF	211	47	884	931
	RCMAOF	211	73	879	952
g1g2	GCVMSOF	389	89	875	964
	RCMAOF	346	104	724	828
Monkey	GCVMSOF	8189	1617	9371	10988
	RCMAOF	8189	2978	8922	11900
Hand	GCVMSOF	369	203	200	403
	RCMAOF	369	203	179	382
Bird	GCVMSOF	1019	661	702	1363
	RCMAOF	1017	947	651	1598

In most examples, the proposed GCVMSOF is faster than RCMSOF. This is due to the fact: though the outer-face extraction times are longer in GCVMSOF than those in RCMSOF, the superset construction times are much shorter. These experiments also suggest that the superset edges numbers of the two algorithms are almost equal, and the outer-face extraction time usually takes a large portion of the total time.

6 Conclusions

In this study, a new algorithm is developed to compute the Minkowski sum outer-face of two polygons of any shape by generalizing the contributing vertex concept. The new concept is straightforward and the algorithm is easy to implement. Three translated-corner edge cases associated with the new concept are found and proved. The experiments show that the new algorithm is superior to other methods for most input sets. The next work to develop the algorithm for calculating the Minkowski sum outer-face of two polyhedra based on the generalized contributing vertex concept.

References

1. The CGAL project homepage. http://www.cgal.org
2. Agarwal, P.K., Flato, E., Halperin, D.: Polygon decomposition for efficient construction of minkowski sums. Comput. Geom. **21**(1), 39–61 (2002)
3. Barki, H., Denis, F., Dupont, F.: Contributing vertices-based minkowski sum computation of convex polyhedra. Comput. Aided Des. **41**(7), 525–538 (2009)
4. Barki, H., Denis, F., Dupont, F.: Contributing vertices-based minkowski sum of a non-convex polyhedron without fold and a convex polyhedron. In: IEEE International Conference on Shape Modeling and Applications, 2009, SMI 2009, pp. 73–80. IEEE (2009)
5. Barki, H., Denis, F., Dupont, F.: Contributing vertices-based minkowski sum of a nonconvex-convex pair of polyhedra. ACM Trans. Graphics (TOG) **30**(1), 3 (2011)
6. Behar, E., Lien, J.M.: Fast and robust 2d minkowski sum using reduced convolution. In: IEEE/RSJ International Conference on Intelligent Robots and Systems (IROS), 2011, pp. 1573–1578. IEEE (2011)
7. De Berg, M., Van Kreveld, M., Overmars, M., Schwarzkopf, O.C.: Computational Geometry. Springer, Heidelberg (2000)
8. Flato, E.: Robust and efficient construction of planar minkowski sums. Master's thesis, Department of Computer Science, Tel-Aviv University (2000)
9. Ghosh, P.K.: A unified computational framework for minkowski operations. Comput. Graphics **17**(4), 357–378 (1993)
10. Guibas, L., Ramshaw, L., Stolfi, J.: A kinetic framework for computational geometry. In: 2013 IEEE 54th Annual Symposium on Foundations of Computer Science, pp. 100–111. IEEE (1983)
11. Guibas, L.J., Seidel, R.: Computing convolutions by reciprocal search. Discrete Comput. Geom. **2**(1), 175–193 (1987)
12. Lee, I.K., Kim, M.S., Elber, G.: The minkowski sum of 2D curved objects. Proceedings of Israel-Korea Bi-National Conference on New Themes in Computerized Geometrical Modeling, vol. 5, pp. 155–164 (1998)
13. Mühlthaler, H., Pottmann, H.: Computing the minkowski sum of ruled surfaces. Graph. Models **65**(6), 369–384 (2003)
14. Peternell, M., Steiner, T.: Minkowski sum boundary surfaces of 3d-objects. Graph. Models **69**(3), 180–190 (2007)
15. Ramkumar, G.: An algorithm to compute the minkowski sum outer-face of two simple polygons. In: Proceedings of the Twelfth Annual Symposium on Computational Geometry, pp. 234–241. ACM (1996)
16. Shi, G.h.: Basic equations of two dimensional and three dimensional contacts. In: 47th US Rock Mechanics/Geomechanics Symposium, American Rock Mechanics Association (2013)

17. Toth, C.D., O'Rourke, J., Goodman, J.E.: Handbook of Discrete and Computational Geometry. CRC Press, Boca Raton (2004)
18. Wein, R.: Exact and efficient construction of planar Minkowski sums using the convolution method. In: Azar, Y., Erlebach, T. (eds.) ESA 2006. LNCS, vol. 4168, pp. 829–840. Springer, Heidelberg (2006)

Handwritten Character Recognition
Based on Weighted Integral Image
and Probability Model

Jia Wu[1,2], Feipeng Da[1,2], Chenxing Wang[1,2], and Shaoyan Gai[1,2(✉)]

[1] College of Automation, Southeast University, Nanjing 210096, Jiangsu, China
{wj.bob, qxxymm}@163.com,
dafp@seu.edu.cn, w.chenxing@gmail.com
[2] Key Laboratory of Measurement and Control of Complex Systems
of Engineering, Ministry of Education,
Nanjing 210096, People's Republic of China

Abstract. A system of the off-line handwritten character recognition based on weighted integral image and probability model is built in this paper, which is divided into image preprocessing and character recognition. The objects of recognition are digitals and letters. In the image preprocessing section, an adaptive binarization method based on weighted integral image is proposed, which overcomes the drawbacks in the classic binarization algorithms: noise sensitivity, edge coarseness, artifacts etc.; In the character recognition section, combined with statistical features and structural features, an probability model based on the Bayes classifier and the principle of similar shapes is developed. This method achieves a high recognition rate with rapid processing, strong anti-interference ability and fault tolerance.

Keywords: Character recognition · Weighted integral image · Probability model · Statistical features · Structural features

1 Introduction

In 1929, Tausheck first filed a patent for the optical character recognition and pulled open the prelude of the character recognition. After decades of development, the character recognition technology has achieved rapid development and progressing. Among them, the recognition of the off-line handwritten characters are applied widely, but as a result of varieties of types and huge number of characters, as well as different writing styles, the recognition rate and speed need to be improved.

The off-line handwritten character recognition must conduct a series of image preprocessing operations, including binarization, de-noising, character segmentation, etc. Among them, the image binarization directly affects the efficiency and accuracy of the character recognition. Generally, in view of the selection methods of threshold for image pixels, the binarization methods can be categorized into two types: the global binarization and the adaptive binarization.

The global binarization methods attempt to define a single threshold for all pixels, the commonly-used global binarization methods are Otsu's method [1, 2], the iterative

© Springer International Publishing Switzerland 2015
Y.-J. Zhang (Ed.): ICIG 2015, Part II, LNCS 9218, pp. 347–360, 2015.
DOI: 10.1007/978-3-319-21963-9_32

method, etc. The adaptive binarization methods are combined the pixel values of the investigated point and its neighborhood points to determine the pixel value of the investigated point. Bernsen' method and Sauvola's method [1] are the representative algorithms.

Farrahi and Cheriet [2] propose AdOstu algorithm by combining the grid-based modeling and the estimated background map, the algorithm is applied to uneven illumination conditions. Bradley and Roth [3] put forward a technique for real-time adaptive binarization using the integral image, their method is robust to illumination changes in the images, but after binarization, sometimes, there exists some noises at the edge of the images, even appears artifacts (unexpected strokes obtained by the noises in the background). For this point, an adaptive binarization algorithm is presented by Nicolaou et al. [4] based on the local binary pattern, which gives different weights to the points around the investigated point and solves the phenomenon of artifacts effectively.

After image preprocessing, feature extraction and classifier are applied for character recognition. Feature extraction methods have been based mainly on two types of features: statistical derived from statistical distribution of points and structural. Methods based on statistical features, such as template matching, zoning method [5] etc., have a low complexity and the advantage of simple training, but their abilities to resist deformation are poor as well as inconformity for similar characters. Methods based on structure features, such as skeleton, outline, shape features, etc., are robust to deformation, but the complexity of algorithms are high.

Classification methods based on artificial neural network (ANN) [6], hidden markov model (HMM) [6], Bayesian network [7] or other technologies have been applied to the character recognition. Due to plenty of characters and the multiplicity of writing styles, using only a single feature extraction method has been unable to satisfy the demand of the character recognition. Therefore, zoning method based on Voronoi diagrams is used by Impedovo et al. [8], and the geometric features such as concave-convex features of the characters are made full use.

Giri and Bashir [9] suggest that combining statistical and structure features, building the characteristic matrix of the characters and using the decision tree classifier are favorable to the character recognition. Meanwhile, it is shown that approaches which employ a hierarchical recognition model combining multiple classifiers have considerable advantages compared to approaches with a single classifier, which can not only improve the recognition accuracy but also reduce the computational cost as well [10]. HMM and ANN are tight hang together by Espana-Boquera et al. [6], which achieves a high recognition rate. Pan et al. [11] combines statistic features and structure features, the preliminary classification is realized through designing four simple classifiers based on statistical features, and then the decision tree classifier based on structure features is applied to decide the final recognition result. The above studies show that different methods of feature extraction methods and classifiers are interactive designed for building the character recognition model, which can be helpful to improve the recognition accuracy and speed.

In our work, on the basis of Bradley's algorithm [3], combined with the grid-based model [2] and the weight-based model [4], the adaptive binarization method based on weighted integral image is presented in this paper, which overcomes the shortcomings of Bradley's algorithm. In the character recognition stage, the advantages of the statistic features and structure features [10] are integrated, the Bayes classifier based on zoning [5] is used to select range of characters first, and then, the probability model based on shape features [8, 9] is utilized to determine the final recognition result. The experimental results show that the character recognition system not only ensures the recognition efficiency but also improves the accuracy of the character recognition.

2 The Adaptive Binarization Algorithm

2.1 Bradley's Algorithm

In this section, a form of the adaptive binarization algorithms called Bradley's algorithm [3] is presented. The main idea in Bradley's algorithm is that the pixel value of each point is determined by the average pixel value of the surrounding points. An integral image (also known as a summed-area table) is applied in Bradley's algorithm, the value of the arbitrary point in the integral image refers to the sum of a rectangle region in the original image. The procedure of achieving an integrate image takes as follows: in the original image, we set the upper-left corner as the origin of coordinate and set the pixel value of the point $d_{(x,y)}$ as $P_{(x,y)}$, $S_{(x,y)}$ is the value in the integrate image and can calculate by the following formula:

$$S_{(x,y)} = \sum_{i=1}^{x} \sum_{j=1}^{y} P_{(i,j)} \qquad (1)$$

As shown in Fig. 1, the value of each rectangle in the left image represents the pixel value of each point in the original image, and the right image is its corresponding integral image.

After achieving the integral image, the pixel value of each point in the original image after binarization is determined by the integral image. The binarization rendering is shown in Fig. 2. The area of the shaded part is w × w (w is an eighth of the width of the original image). $S_{(a,b)}$, $S_{(c,d)}$, $S_{(c,b)}$ and $S_{(a,d)}$ in the integral image represent the corresponding value of the lower-right point $d_{(a,b)}$, the upper-left point $d_{(c,d)}$, the lower-left point $d_{(c,b)}$ and the upper-right point $d_{(a,d)}$ in the origin image. The procedure is as follows:

1	1	0	1
1	0	1	0
0	0	1	0
0	1	0	0

1	2	2	3
2	3	4	5
2	3	5	6
2	4	6	7

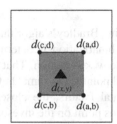

Fig. 1. Original image and integral image   **Fig. 2.** Binarization rendering

(1) The sum pixel of points in the shaded area:

$$sum = S_{(a,b)} - S_{(c-1,b)} - S_{(a,d-1)} + S_{(c-1,d-1)} \tag{2}$$

(2) The pixel value of the center point $d_{(x,y)}$ in the shaded area after binarization:

$$E_{(x,y)} = \begin{cases} 0 & P_{(x,y)} \times w^2 < sum \times 0.85 \\ 255 & others \end{cases} \tag{3}$$

2.2 The Adaptive Binarization Algorithm Based on the Weighted Integral Image

Bradley's algorithm is simple, efficient and especially suitable for images under the uneven illumination conditions, but the processed image is not perfect. As shown in Fig. 3, the left image is a gray image contained handwritten characters and the right image is the image binarized by Bradley's algorithm. Through observing the images, the upper edge of the right image exist a lot of noises and artifacts appear nearby the character of N, and same low-gray target points are lost (such as 6 and b in the upper-left corner).

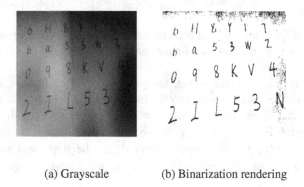

(a) Grayscale   (b) Binarization rendering

Fig. 3. Binarization renderings by Bradley's algorithm

Analyzing Bradley's algorithm can be found that, the pixel value of the investigated point after binarization is determined by the average pixel value of the surrounding points in the w × w region. That is to say, the impact of the surrounding points on the investigated point is the same, but in fact, taking into account the illumination and other environmental factors, the closer the point is to the investigated point, the greater impact of this point on the investigated point. Therefore, simply using the average pixel value of the surrounding points as the basis of binarization, due to uneven illumination etc., will inevitably lead that some low-gray target points which are similar to the surrounding points are misclassified as the background points, thus those target points are lost, and some high-gray background points which are similar to the target points are misclassified as the target points, thus appeared artifacts and noises. A more reasonable method should be chosen to achieve the pixel values of points after binarization. In addition, if the size of the original image is large, the value of the lower-right part in the integral image obtained by Bradley's algorithm may be too large to consume a great vast of computer memory space.

Combined with the weight-based model [4], a weighted integral image is proposed. As shown in Fig. 4, there are four points A, B, C and D in the origin image. The pixel value of each point is in order of A0, B0, C0 and D0. According to Bradley's algorithm, the corresponding value $S_{(x,y)}$ of point D in the integral image can be calculated as:

$$S_{(x,y)} = A0 + B0 + C0 + D0 \tag{4}$$

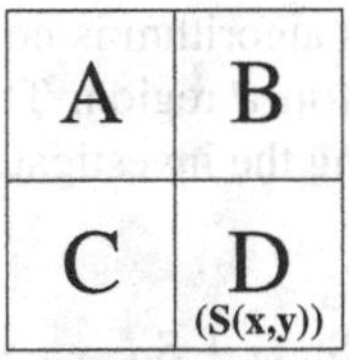

Fig. 4. Weighted integral image

In order to reflect the distances between the point D and other points which can influence the binarization results, we set the distances between points A, B, C to point D as m, n, k (here, points A, B, C and D adjoin each other, therefore, m = n = k = 1). The parameter t is the weighted value reflecting the distances between the points, t = 6 [4]. The corresponding value $S_{(x,y)}$ of point D in the weighted integral image can be given as:

$$S_{(x,y)} = \frac{\left(A0\left(1-\frac{1}{t}\right)^m + B0\left(1-\frac{1}{t}\right)^n + C0\left(1-\frac{1}{t}\right)^k + D0\right)}{\left(1-\frac{1}{t}\right)^m + \left(1-\frac{1}{t}\right)^n + \left(1-\frac{1}{t}\right)^k + \left(1-\frac{1}{t}\right)^0} \tag{5}$$

The general formula of the Eq. (5) is:

$$S_{(x,y)} = \frac{\sum_{i=0}^{N} P_i \times \left(1-\frac{1}{t}\right)^{A_i}}{\sum_{i=0}^{N} \left(1-\frac{1}{t}\right)^{A_i}} \tag{6}$$

where N is the number of points which are at the upper-left of point $d_{(x,y)}$ (including point $d_{(x,y)}$), A_i is the distance between each point to point $d_{(x,y)}$ and P_i is the pixel value of each point.

Apparently, according to the formula 6, the influence of different distances on the investigated point can be fully reflected by $S_{(x,y)}$.

In addition, for the sake of improving the efficiency of the algorithm and simplifying the algorithm implementation, the corresponding value $S_{(x,y)}$ of point $d_{(x,y)}$ in the weighted integral image can be simply achieved by the corresponding value $S_{(x-1,y)}$ of point $d_{(x-1,y)}$. The amount of recalculation is reduced by applying this iterative principle, namely:

$$S_{(x,y)} = \frac{\left(S_{(x-1,y)}\left(1-\frac{1}{t}\right) + \sum_{i=0}^{y}\left(P_{(x,i)} \times \left(1-\frac{1}{t}\right)^{(y-i)}\right)\right)}{\sum_{i=0}^{y}\left(1-\frac{1}{t}\right)^{(y-i)}+1} \tag{7}$$

After obtaining the weighted integral image, the pixel values of points after binarization can be determined. Because the values in the weighted integral image are weighted mean rather than sum, this algorithm is no longer like Bradley's algorithm to acquire the average value of points in a region. This algorithm seeks to the average value $T_{(x,y)}$ of nine points surrounding the investigated point (including the investigated point) in the weighted integral:

$$T_{(x,y)} = \left(\begin{array}{c} S_{(x,y)} + S_{(x-1,y-1)} + \\ S_{(x-1,y)} + S_{(x,y-1)} + \\ S_{(x+1,y+1)} + S_{(x+1,y)} + \\ S_{(x+1,y-1)} + S_{(x,y+1)} + \\ S_{(x-1,y+1)} \end{array} \right) \Big/ 9 \tag{8}$$

The pixel value $E_{(x,y)}$ of the investigated point after binarization can be acquired by the weighted average value $T_{(x,y)}$:

$$E_{(x,y)} = \begin{cases} 0 & P_{(x,y)} < T_{(x,y)} \times 0.85 \\ 255 & \text{others} \end{cases} \tag{9}$$

where 0.85 is reference to Bradley's algorithm.

Figure 5 is the processed image by our algorithm, artifacts nearby the character N disappear, the number of noises in the image is also less than the number of noises in the Fig. 3.

3 The Probability Model

3.1 The Training Phase

The system adopts the Bayes classifier, so the character training is necessary before recognition. The training process is the feature extraction and the procedure of saving the extracted eigenvalue to the training document. At first, the static zoning method [5] is applied. The sample images which contain a single character are divided into the

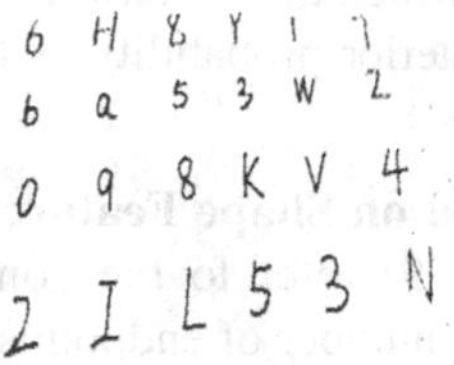

6 H 8 Y 1 1
b a 5 3 W 2
0 9 8 K V 4
2 I L 5 3 N

Fig. 5. Binarization rendering by our algorithm

regular grids 2 × 4. Namely, the sample images are divided into eight equal parts, and then the thirteen-dimensional feature extraction method [12] is applied to extract the statistical features of the characters, which can achieve thirteen eigenvalues of the characters. The concrete steps as follows: statistical of the percentage of the black points in the eight equal parts as eight eigenvalues; statistical of the number of black points in 1/3 and 2/3 horizontal direction of the image and divided by the height as two eigenvalues; statistical of the number of black points in 1/3 and 2/3 vertical direction of the image and divided by the height as two eigenvalues; statistical of the percentage of the black points in the whole image as the thirteenth eigenvalue.

The training samples of the system are from the special database 19 [13] by the United States National Institute of Standards and Technology (NIST). 6000 training images are chosen. In order to reduce the size of the training document and shorten the time of reading and processing training document, thirteen eigenvalues obtained by the thirteen-dimensional feature extraction method are made comparison with a selected decimal. This paper selects the decimal as 0.1. If the eigenvalue is bigger than 0.1, 1 is assigned to the eigenvalue, otherwise, 0 is assigned to the eigenvalue. Thirteen eigenvalues are converted to the binary code of 0 or 1.

3.2 Recognition Phase

The objects of character recognition are letters and digits which is a total of 62 characters. Combining with the statistic features and the structure features of characters, the Bayes classifier based on zoning is applied to the recognition firstly, and the Bayes classifier returns five similar characters, and then, the probability model based on shape features is applied to determine the final result.

3.2.1 The Bayes Classifier Based on Zoning
According to the principle of the Bayes [7], the Bayes classifier based on zoning is designed and steps of algorithm are as follows:

(1) Calculating the prior probability of each character, which is the number of each character divided by the total number of characters;
(2) Calculating the class conditional probability of each character, which is the probability density of the characters in the feature space of the known categories;
(3) The Bayes formula is applied to calculate the posteriori probability;

(4) Selecting five characters of which the posteriori probability are larger than others' and their corresponding posterior probability as the returned value.

3.2.2 Probability Model Based on Shape Features

Shape features of characters [8, 9] refer to the concave-convex characteristic, the number of the inner rings and the number of endpoints etc. Six characteristics are used in this paper, as shown in Fig. 6, which are the number of concaves, the right number of concaves, the number of grooves, the left number of concaves, the number of inner rings, the number of endpoints. The background-assignment method [14] is applied to detect the number of the concave-convex characteristic and the inner rings, the value of each characteristic is obtained by detecting the number of the corresponding inter-connected domain. If there is only one adjacent black point of the black investigated point in the image, the black investigated point is an endpoint. The system has been established the value table of shape features of 62 characters, as shown in Table 1, due to limited space, only part of the characters listed in Table 1. The remaining characters are similar.

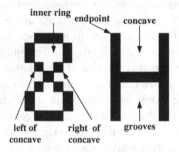

Fig. 6. Shape features of characters

Table 1. The value table of shape features of part of the characters

Characters	Concaves	Right of concaves	Grooves	Left of concaves	Inner rings	Endpoints
3	0	1	0	2	0	3
6	0	1	0	0	1	1
b	0	0	0	0	1	1
h	0	0	1	0	0	3
H	1	0	1	0	0	4
Z	0	1	0	1	0	2

The shape features of the handwritten characters are easily affected by the writers' writing styles. The shape features of the same characters writing by different people are not always exactly the same features. Therefore, the probability model based on shape features is applied to the character recognition.

The concrete implementation process is: first of all, six shape features of the character are extracted, and then, the six eigenvalues are respectively made comparison with the eigenvalues of the five characters selected by the Bayes classifier (set as 'a', 'b', 'c', 'd' and 'e'). For example, the six eigenvalues of 'a' are compared with the six eigenvalues of the character one by one. If the two eigenvalues are exactly the same, the value of probability is 100 %. If the difference value of the two eigenvalues is 1, the value of probability is 50 %. If the difference value of the two eigenvalues is 2, the value of probability is 25 %. Otherwise, the value of probability is 0. The values of 6 probability are added, and then, the sum is multiplied by the posteriori probability of 'a'. The product of the similar-probability of 'a', 'b', 'c', 'd' and 'e' are similar. Finally, the maximum is selected by comparing with the five similar-probabilities, and its corresponding character is the final recognition result.

4 Evaluation and Experimental Results

Experiment of this paper is based on VS2010 and OpenCV 2.31 (computer vision library) [15]. Respectively, the adaptive binarization method based on weighted integral image and the probability model based on the Bayes classifier and the principle of similar shapes have been analyzed in this section.

4.1 The Experiment of the Adaptive Binarization Method

A grayscale of uneven illumination is selected for this experiment, the experimental results are shown in Fig. 7. Figure 7(b) is the binary image using Otsu's method. Otsu's method belongs to the global binarization method. It is an inevitable problem that the binarization rendering is uncomplete when using the global binarization method. Figure 7(c) is the binary image using the CvAdaptiveThreshold function of OpenCV [15]. Gaussian smoothing is applied to the investigated point and its neighborhood points, and then the threshold is obtained by calculating the mean of those points. Figure 7(d) is the binary image using Bradley's algorithm [3]. Both cvAdaptive-Threshold function and Bradley's algorithm belong to the adaptive binarization algorithms. Contrasting images show that, when using cvAdaptiveThreshold function, some low-gray target points in the rendering are lost, and when using Bradley's algorithm, there are a lot of noises at the edge of the rendering and even exist artifacts nearby the character 'd', which affect the character recognition. Figure 7(e) is the binary image using the adaptive binarization method based on weighted integral image. The algorithm improves the quality of the image, removes the artifacts, largely reduces the number of noises and saves the complete character information.

A grayscale of even illumination is selected to illustrate the versatility of the algorithm, the results as shown in Fig. 8, it is not hard to see, this algorithm is less affected by the illumination conditions.

In order to reflect the influence of the algorithm on the recognition results, on the basis of the Fig. 7(d) and (e), after the processing of the de-noising and the character segmentation, the Fig. 9(a) and (b) are obtained respectively. It can be seen that,

(a) Grayscale   (b) Binarization rendering by Otsu   (c)Binarization rendering

by cvAdaptiveThreshold

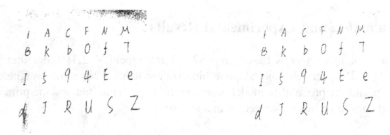

(d)Binarization rendering by Bradley's algorithm   (e) Binarization rendering by our algorithm

Fig. 7. Binarization renderings under the uneven illumination conditions by each algorithm

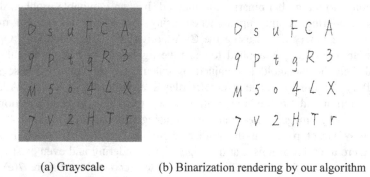

(a) Grayscale   (b) Binarization rendering by our algorithm

Fig. 8. Binarization renderings under the even illumination conditions by our algorithm

because of the existence of plenty of noises and artifacts in the Fig. 9(a), the characters cannot properly be divided (such as the character 'd') and the non- character infor- mations are erroneous segmented at the upper edge. In the guarantee of the integrity of the character informations, the simple de-noising algorithm cannot achieve great results. In order to obtain favorable character recognition results, a complex de-noising algorithm must be designed, which cannot offer a perfect guaranteed result. It is difficult to eliminate the artifacts nearby the character 'd'. On the other hand, it will undoubtedly increase the difficulty of designing the character recognition system and the recognition time as well as reduce the accuracy of the character recognition. The binary images which are obtained by our algorithm is shown in Fig. 9(b), and the excellent segmentation effect can be obtained by removing few of the isolated noises. Therefore, our algorithm can improve the accuracy of the character recognition and the recognition efficiency in a certain extent.

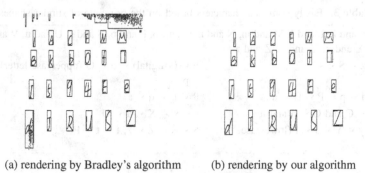

(a) rendering by Bradley's algorithm   (b) rendering by our algorithm

Fig. 9. Character segmentation renderings

4.2   The Experiment of the Probability Model

Under the premise that the characters have been trained, after a series of image pre-processing operations including image-graying, binarization, de-noising, smoothing, thinning, single-character segmentation, normalization etc., the character recognition can be carried out.

The test samples of this paper are 10000 test images selected from the NIST special database 19 and 100 handwritten character images collected from 100 people. The Table 2 is obtained by statistical analyzing the five most similar characters which are achieved by the Bayes classifier. The Table 2 shows us that the confusing lowercase and uppercase letters, such as C and c, V and v, Z and z etc., can be distinguished by the Bayes classifier according to their size. Because the image is full filled by the uppercase letters, but there is a great blank area at the top of the images contained the lowercase characters. The Table 3 is obtained by statistical analyzing the easily confusing characters which are achieved by the probability principle based on the similar shapes. The Table 3 shows us that the characters which have the same shape features, such as C and c, K and k etc., may be unable to be identified properly. A comparison with Tables 2 and 3 is made, which shows that the confusing characters of the two methods are scarcely overlapped. Finally, combining with the two methods, the probability model based on Bayes classifier and the principle of similar shapes is tested and analyzed by the confusing characters (each pair of the confusing characters have 100 samples). The results are shown in Table 4, it can be seen that this method has a superior recognition rate for the similar characters.

Table 2. Easily confused characters based on the Bayes classifier

1、1、J、I、i、j、7、T、f	2、3
5、S、8	6、b、h、G、k (lowercase letter)、E
A、8、B、6、9、R	a and e、2 and Z
0 (digital)、O (uppercase letter)、U、D、Q	V and U、V and X
r and t、7 and T	P and F、4 and A

Table 3. Easily confused characters based on the principle of similar shapes

C and c, K and k, L and l, M and m, N and n, O and o, P and p, S and s, U and u, V and v, W and w, X and x, Y and y, Z and z	
2、Z、z、S、s	b、0(digital)、o、O (uppercase letter)、Q、p
4、b、d、p、P、D、a	9、g、q、a
A and R、C and G、h and n	r、x、X、u、U
V、v、y、Y、J、l (lowercase letter)	S、s、Z、z; f、t、F

Table 4. Test results of easily confused characters

Confused character	Recognition rate/%	Confused character	Recognition rate/%	Confused character	Recognition rate/%
1 and l	93	S and 8	100	r and t	96
J and I	95	2 and Z	86	P and F	99
I and T	96	0 and O	85	V and U	96
5 and S	93	O and D	90	O and Q	98
8 and B	96	4 and A	99	i and j	97
C and G	98	9 and g	91	7 and T	93

The simulation is under an Intel Core2 E6550 (2.13 GHz), 4 GB DDR3, a GT 7300 graphics card and a 32-bit Windows 7 operating system. The Table 5 is obtained by testing 10000 images of NIST (among them, Ciresan et al. [16] realize the character recognition based on convolutional neural network(CNNs); Pawar et al. [17] present the extended fuzzy hyperline segment neural network algorithm (EFHLSNN. They all adopt the NIST database. The identify data come from the original experimental section). The Table 6 is obtained by testing 100 handwritten character images. It can be seen that after narrowing the scope of the recognition by the Bayes classifier, the characters are recognized by the principle of similar shapes finally. Our method, compared with the single method, can improve the recognition accuracy of the handwritten characters in the condition of guaranteeing the recognition efficiency. At the same time, this algorithm gains a higher accuracy of character recognition than the CNNs and EFHLSNN algorithms. Due to up to 196 features which extracted in the EFHLSNN algorithm, while there are 19 features in our algorithm, its recognition time is much longer than our algorithm's. Experimental results show that the probability model based on Bayes classifier and the principle of similar shapes, which realizes the

Table 5. Recognition accuracy by each algorithm (NIST)

Recognition methods	Recognition rate/%	The average time of single character recognition/ms
Bayes classifier	69.2	142
The principle of similar shapes	58.3	131
CNNs [16]	88.12	NULL
EFHLSNN [17]	76.6	1777
Our algorithm	90.3	155

Table 6. Recognition accuracy by each algorithm (actual images)

Recognition methods	Recognition rate/%	The average time of single character recognition/ms
Bayes classifier	63.6	159
The principle of similar shapes	56.7	162
CNNs [16]	83.6	140
EFHLSNN [17]	73.5	1962
Our algorithm	88.3	170

interactive design of different feature extraction methods (statistic features and structure features) and classifiers (the Bayes classifier and the probability method classifier), indeed improve the accuracy of character recognition in the premise of guaranteeing the efficiency.

5 Conclusion

In allusion to the two major difficulties in the process of the off-line handwritten character recognition: the binarization processing and the character recognition, this paper proposes the adaptive binarization algorithm based on weighted integral image and the probability model based on Bayes classifier and the principle of similar shapes. A practical system is developed by compiling the source codes, and plenty of images (10000 standard images and 100 actual images) are used in the experiment which can verify the correctness and operability of the theoretical model. The experimental results show that the recognition time is short (single character 155 ms (NIST), 170 ms (the actual images)) and the recognition rate is high (90.3 % (NIST), 88.3 % (the actual images)).

Acknowledgement. The authors gratefully thank the Scientific Research Program Funded by National Natural Science Foundation of China (51175081, 61405034), a Project Funded by the Priority Academic Program Development of Jiangsu Higher Education Institutions and the Doctoral Scientific Fund Project of the Ministry of Education of China (20130092110027).

References

1. Roy, S., Saha, S., Dey, A., et al.: Performance evaluation of multiple image binarization algorithms using multiple metrics on standard image databases. In: ICT and Critical Infrastructure: Proceedings of the 48th Annual Convention of Computer Society of India-Vol II, pp. 349–360. Springer International Publishing (2014)
2. Farrahi Moghaddam, R., Cheriet, M.: AdOtsu: an adaptive and parameterless generalization of Otsu's method for document image binarization. Pattern Recogn. **45**(6), 2419–2431 (2012)
3. Bradley, D., Roth, G.: Adaptive thresholding using the integral image. J. Graph. GPU Game Tools **12**(2), 13–21 (2007)
4. Nicolaou, A., Slimane, F., Maergner, V., et al.: Local binary patterns for arabic optical font recognition. In: 2014 11th IAPR International Workshop on Document Analysis Systems (DAS), pp. 76–80. IEEE (2014)
5. Impedovo, D., Pirlo, G.: Zoning methods for handwritten character recognition: a survey. Pattern Recogn. **47**(3), 969–981 (2014)
6. Espana-Boquera, S., Castro-Bleda, M.J., Gorbe-Moya, J., et al.: Improving offline handwritten text recognition with hybrid HMM/ANN models. IEEE Trans. Pattern Anal. Mach. Intell. **33**(4), 767–779 (2011)
7. Zhang, L.W.: Introduction to the Bayesian Network. Science Press, Beijing (2006). 张连文. 贝叶斯网引论
8. Impedovo, S., Lucchese, M.G., Pirlo, G.: Optimal zoning design by genetic algorithms. IEEE Trans. Syst. Man Cybern. Part A Syst. Hum. **36**(5), 833–846 (2006)
9. Giri, K.J., Bashir, R.: Character recognition based on structural analysis using code & decision matrix. In: 2013 International Conference on IEEE Machine Intelligence and Research Advancement (ICMIRA), pp. 450–453 (2013)
10. Vamvakas, G., Gatos, B., Perantonis, S.J.: Handwritten character recognition through two-stage foreground sub-sampling. Pattern Recogn. **43**(8), 2807–2816 (2010)
11. Pan, X., Ye, X., Zhang, S.: A hybrid method for robust car plate character recognition. Eng. Appl. Artif. Intell. **18**(8), 963–972 (2005)
12. Zhong, H.L., Hu, W.: A new feature extraction method on handwritten digits recognition system. J. Sichuan Univ. (Nat. Sci. Edn.) **44**(5), 1000–1004 (2007). 钟乐海, 胡伟. 手写体数字识别系统中一种新的特征提取方法[J]. 四川大学学报: 自然科学版
13. Grother, P.J.: NIST special database 19 handprinted forms and characters database. Nat. Inst. Stand. Technol. (1995)
14. Nikolaou, N., Makridis, M., Gatos, B., et al.: Segmentation of historical machine-printed documents using adaptive run length smoothing and skeleton segmentation paths. Image Vis. Comput. **28**(4), 590–604 (2010)
15. Liu, R.Z., Yu, S.Q.: Basic tutorials of OpenCV. Beijing University of Aeronautics and Astronautics Press, Beijing (2007). 刘瑞祯, 于仕琪. OpenCV 教程: 基础篇
16. Ciresan, D.C., Meier, U., Gambardella, L.M., et al.: Convolutional neural network committees for handwritten character classification. In: 2011 International Conference on Document Analysis and Recognition (ICDAR), pp. 1135–1139. IEEE (2011)
17. Pawar, D.: Extended fuzzy hyperline segment neural network for handwritten character recognition. In: Proceedings of the International MultiConference of Engineers and Computer Scientists, p. 1 (2012)

Hard Exudates Detection Method Based
on Background-Estimation

Zhitao Xiao[1], Feng Li[1], Lei Geng[1(✉)], Fang Zhang[1], Jun Wu[1], Xinpeng Zhang[1],
Long Su[2], Chunyan Shan[3], Zhenjie Yang[1], Yuling Sun[1], Yu Xiao[1], and Weiqiang Du[1]

[1] School of Electronics and Information Engineering, Tianjin Polytechnic University,
Tianjin, China
genglei@tjpu.edu.cn
[2] The Second Hospital of Tianjin Medical University, Tianjin, China
[3] Tianjin Medical University Metabolic Disease Hospital, Tianjin, China

Abstract. Hard exudates (HEs) are one kind of the most important symptoms
of Diabetic Retinopathy (DR). A new method based on background-estimation
for hard exudates detection is presented. Firstly, through background-estimation,
foreground map containing all bright objects is acquired. We use the edge information based on Kirsch operator to obtain HE candidates, and then we remove
the optic disc. Finally, the shape features, histogram statistic features and phase
features of the HE candidates are extracted. We use the SVM classifier to acquire
the accurate extraction of HEs. The proposed method has been demonstrated on
the public databases of DIARETDB1 and HEI-MED. The experiment results
show that the method's sensitivity is 97.3 % and the specificity is 90 % at the
image level, and the mean sensitivity is 84.6 % and the mean predictive value is
94.4 % at the lesion level.

Keywords: Hard exudates · Diabetic retinopathy · Background-estimation ·
SVM

1 Introduction

Diabetic Retinopathy (DR) is a severe complication of diabetes mellitus and one of the
most important causes of blindness. Early signs of DR include red lesions such as
microaneurysms (MA), intraretinal microvascular abnormalities (IRMA) and hemor-
rhages (HA), bright lesions like hard exudates (HEs) and cotton-wool spots (CW).
Among the early symptoms, HEs are main performance of macular edema, which appear
as bright structures with well-defined edges and variable shapes (as shown in Fig. 1).
Thus, the detection of HEs is very important for clinical diagnosis.

HE detection methods presented in literatures can be divided into three different
categories.

Mathematical morphology based methods: Welfer et al. [1] gave a method based on
mathematical morphology. Firstly, contrast of image was enhanced in LUV color space.
Then a set of morphological operations such as regional minima detection, morphological reconstruction and H-maxima transform were performed to detect exudates. At last,

Y.-J. Zhang (Ed.): ICIG 2015, Part II, LNCS 9218, pp. 361–372, 2015.
DOI: 10.1007/978-3-319-21963-9_33

Fig. 1. HE in fundus image and the enlarged area

SVM classifier was used to determine the severity of lesion. Gandhi et al. [2] identified HEs after blood vessels were removed by mathematical morphology methods.

Clustering-based methods: Jayakumari et al. [3] utilized contextual clustering algorithm to divide a fundus image into background and bright areas, then identified true exudates using Echo State Neural Network.

Machine learning methods: Sánchez et al. [4] detected HEs by Fisher linear classifier. High sensitivity and specificity are achieved in test of 58 images. García et al. [5] proposed a neural network based method for exudates extraction and tested it on 67 images (27 normal images and 40 DR images). Sae-Tang et al. [6] proposed a nonuniform illumination background subtraction method. Weighted surface fitting is used in fundus image background-estimation after performing image compensation. Estimated background is subtracted from the image and then exudates are detected from foreground of image using level-set evolution without re-initialization.

Mathematical morphology based methods detected exudates according to brightness characteristic without taking other characteristics into account, so that resulting in poor robustness and high noise sensitivity. Clustering-based methods are not only too sensitive to noise, but also much heavy in computation. On the other hand, it needs initial assumption due to unknown class center location and characteristics. Machine learning methods may get high miss-detection and false-detection rate if we can't choose suitable features and get all-sided training samples. According to the characteristics of HEs and the shortages of existing methods, this paper presents a method based on background-estimation and SVM classifier. Firstly, foreground map containing all bright objects is obtained by estimated background subtraction. After that, exudates candidates are gotten using edge information based on kirsch operator, and then optic disc is removed. Finally, the features of HE candidates are extracted and HEs are detected by SVM classifier. The block diagram of the proposed method is shown in Fig. 2.

2   HE Candidates Detection Based on Background-Estimation

HE candidates extraction includes two steps: (a) Due to high gray value of HEs, all bright targets of fundus image are extracted by estimating background; (b) According to the characteristics of HEs' sharp edge, the edge strength based on Kirsch operator of all bright objects are calculated. Then, final exudate candidates can be screened.

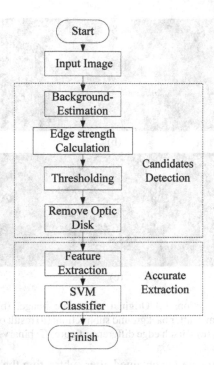

Fig. 2. Block diagram of the proposed method

2.1 Background-Estimation

Firstly, in order to improve efficiency, we resize the fundus images' height to 750 pixels while keeping width/height ratio of each images. For extracting foreground structure of fundus images, background need to be estimated. The procedure of background-estimation is shown in Fig. 3. A median filter, whose size is 25×25, is applied on grayscale image I_{gray} to estimate background I_{bg}. In order to make background more adapted to the original gray image, morphological reconstruction [7] is used on I_{bg}.

Morphological reconstruction is usually used to highlight the parts of mark image which is consistent with mask image, and ignore other parts. Here, the image after median filtering is a mark image. Mask image is the image whose pixel value is the maximum of corresponding original gray-scale image pixel and median filtered image pixel. A fundus image is shown in Fig. 4(a), and the background-estimation result is shown in Fig. 4(b).

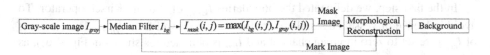

Fig. 3. Block diagram of background-estimation

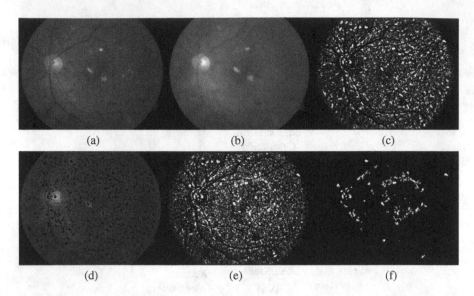

(a)   (b)   (c)

(d)   (e)   (f)

Fig. 4. HE candidates detection. (a) Original gray-scale image; (b) result of background-estimation; (c) foreground map after background subtraction; (d) result of removing bright targets from green channel image; (e) Kirsch edge difference figure; (f) binary image of HE candidates

A difference matrix image I is obtained after subtracting the estimated background from original gray image. In the resulting image, the peak of histogram is always centered on zero. The histogram shows a clear distinction between dark and bright structures. The former represents vasculature, macula, dark lesions and other structures. Bright structures are found in the positive side of histogram and include bright lesions and other structures. The pixels whose value is below zero are set to zero so that the exudate candidate image I_{cand} is obtained. However, there are still lots of false positive lesions, such as cotton wool spots and nerve fiber layer reflection. The image I_{cand} is shown in Fig. 4(c).

2.2 HE Candidates Extraction Based on Kirsch Operator

Compared to the false positive lesions, HEs have sharp edges. Hence edge intensity information is used to eliminate false positive lesions whose edges are fuzzy. Because fundus images show more clear structure characteristics in green channel of RGB color space, green channel image is used for calculating edge intensity. Here edge detector is based on Kirsch operator [8] at eight different directions on I_g. Kernel outputs are combined together by selecting the maximum value on each pixel output. Kirsch operator is fitted for HE extraction due to good performance on directivity, precision and anti-noise property.

In the first step, we delineated the boundaries I_{kirsch} of I_g using Kirsch operator. To avoid influence of vessel edges, these contours are removed from I_{kirsch}. The elements of I_{cand} are set to zero in green channel and I_{bge} is obtained (as shown in Fig. 4(d)), as following,

$$I_{bge}(i,j) = \begin{cases} I_g(i,j), & I_{cand}(i,j) = 0 \\ 0, & I_{cand}(i,j) \neq 0 \end{cases} \tag{1}$$

Then, image I_{bge} was performed morphological reconstruction using mask I_g. In this way, all the bright regions detected are removed from I_g. After applying Kirsch operator to the result, only the contours of blood vessels and dark elements are detected, that is $I_{0kirsch}$. The difference $I_{cankirsch}$ between I_{kirsch} and $I_{0kirsch}$ is calculated, hence the contours of bright regions are obtained. The result is shown in Fig. 4(e). The edge strength [9] δ of each candidate object θ_i in I_{cand} is defined as the mean intensity of the object in edge-enhanced image $I_{cankirsch}$, as following,

$$\delta(\theta_i) = \frac{\sum_{j \in \Pi_i} I_{cankirsch}(j)}{\sum_{j \in \Pi_i} 1} \tag{2}$$

Here, Π_i is the set of pixels in the candidate object θ_i using 8-connected neighborhood.

A candidate is considered HE if $\delta > Th$. Th represents a parameter of the algorithm. It determines the value which is used to consider if an edge has sharp boundary. If it is chosen low, more HEs are detected, meanwhile the number of false positives increases. After experiments, when $Th = 2$, the result can ensure less false positives and no miss-detection, as shown in Fig. 4(f).

2.3 Optic Disk Remove

In color retinal fundus images, Optic Disk (OD) usually shows as approximately circular spot, whose color is light yellow or white. Its color and brightness characteristic are very similar to HE, which means it usually appears in HE candidates. Therefore, accurate positioning and removing of OD is necessary.

OD is positioned and removed based on main vessels extraction. Firstly, main blood vessels are extracted using morphological method, and a cross map is obtained by vascular convergence direction. Then the optimal location of OD is determined by weighted convergent optimization. OD segmentation and removal is performed utilizing Hough transform. HE candidates are obtained after OD area is removed, as shown in Fig. 5.

3   Accurate Extraction of HE

Most of false targets can be removed, because of HE candidates' brightness and edge features. However, there are still some areas which are similar to true HEs on brightness level and edge shape. In this paper, shape features, histogram statistical features and phase features of HE candidate areas are utilized to distinguish true HEs from clear cotton wool spots, laser spot and serious macula reflection, and a SVM classifier is designed to complete HE accurate extraction.

Fig. 5. HE candidates after removing optic disk (area in green color) (Color figure online)

3.1 Feature Extraction

(1) Shape Features. For the easily mistaken laser spots, whose main characteristic is with regular shape of approximating circles, so the eccentricity and compactness are used to distinguish between HEs and laser spots.

Eccentricity: The ratio of long axis and short axis.

Compactness: The ratio of circumference's square and area.

(2) Histogram Statistical Features. HE's grayscale distribution is concentrated, but cotton-wool spots which are easy to be mistakenly identified present the characteristic that brightness changes lower from the center to around. Histogram is a powerful tool to describe images' grayscale distribution. Therefore, histogram statistical features are used to distinguish between cotton wool spots and HEs.

The calculation formula of image's histogram is shown below:

$$h(k) = \frac{n_k}{N}, \quad (k = 0, 1, 2, \dots, L-1) \tag{3}$$

where k is a variable represents gray scale levels, N is the pixel number of a gray image, n_k is the pixel number in gray scale level k, and L is the number of gray scale levels.

The utilized histogram statistical features are as follows:

(1) Variance: the secondary moment u_2 of mean value m. Where nth moment of m is defined as:

$$u_n = \sum_{k=0}^{L-1} (k-m)^n h(k) \tag{4}$$

The mean value m is defined as:

$$m = \sum_{k=0}^{L-1} kh(k) \tag{5}$$

(2) Smoothness: representation of texture depth degree of images. R is proportional to the range of regional gray value. It is defined as

$$R = 1 - [1 + \frac{u_2}{(L-1)^2}]^{-1} \tag{6}$$

(3) Third moment: histogram skewness measure. When $u_3 > 0$ histogram skews to the right, and when $u_3 < 0$ histogram skews to the left.

(4) Consistency: representation of gray value similarity. When gray values are equal in certain area, U reaches the maximum. When the difference degree increases, U decreases. It is defined as

$$U = \sum_{k=0}^{L-1} h^2(k) \tag{7}$$

(5) Entropy: Random measure. It reflects the roughness of texture. The greater the randomness, the bigger of e. It is defined as

$$e = - \sum_{k=0}^{L-1} h(k) \log_2(h(k)) \tag{8}$$

(3) Phase Features. The features explained above are all based on amplitude. Because of its sensitiveness to illumination change, the classification results are not ideal if only amplitude features are utilized. Phase information is stabilized to illumination and contrast, and it is with good noise immunity and in accordance with human visual perception.

Phase Congruency (PC) means that the most phase consistent points in Fourier component are set as the feature points. Morrone and Owens [10] defined the PC function as:

$$PC(x, y) = \max_{\bar{\phi} \in [0, 2\pi]} \frac{\sum_n A_n \cos(\phi_n(x) - \bar{\phi}(x))}{\sum_n A_n} \tag{9}$$

where A_n is amplitude of the nth harmonic cosine component. $\phi_n(x)$ is the Fourier series local phase in point of x. $\bar{\phi}(x)$ is the weighted average value of all Fourier items' local phase in this point. Finding out the maximum PC point equals to finding out the least changing point of local phase.

In fact, PC is a value which is difficult to calculate. It is found in reference [11] that local energy is the product of PC and the sum of Fourier amplitude, which means local energy is proportional to PC function. The peak value of local energy corresponds to the maximum PC. Therefore, seeking maximum PC is converted to seeking local energy. In this research, the local energy is calculated by log-Gabor wavelet function.

To apply PC to HE detection in fundus image, the PC expression needs to be converted to be two-dimensional. The method is: firstly, calculate the energy $E(x)$ of every point and compensate noise in each direction; then, sum up the values of all directions; finally, normalize the energy sum. The two-dimensional PC formula is as following

$$PC(x, y) = \frac{\sum_o \lfloor E_o(x, y) - T_o \rfloor}{\sum_o \sum_n A_{no}(x, y) + \varepsilon} \tag{10}$$

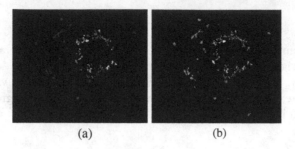

(a)   (b)

Fig. 6. Comparison between phase information and grayscale information of HE candidates. (a) phase information; (b) grayscale information

where E is the local energy, o means directions, n means the scale of wavelet function, ε is a small positive number preventing the denominator of formula to be 0, $PC(x, y)$ means the PC value in point (x, y), and T is the response of filter to noises in all scales. In order to balance the complexity of the method and the accuracy of results, in our research, o is 8, n is 3, ε is 0.0001.

Features like step, roof and Mach band are always appeared in high Phase Congruency [12] points. As shown in Fig. 5, in HE candidate areas, there are another common false target called reflective of the retina, in addition to the true HE, laser spots and cotton wool spots which are removed by shape and histogram features. HE whose brightness is high and boundary is clear is obviously different with fundus image background. It is easy to identify and its local energy is bigger, so that it has high phase congruency. Reflective of the retina is similar with HEs in gray-scale, but it is fused with healthy fundus background smoothly and with no obvious step, so the phase congruency is low. After phase congruency calculation, the result of HE candidate area is shown in Fig. 6(a), and the original gray level information is shown in Fig. 6(b). It is evident that the phase information can be used to distinguish between HEs and no HEs more effectively. In order to avoid the influence of other red lesions and blood vessels, each set of pixels in HE candidates are extracted, then calculate the following statistics: mean value, median value, variance, maximum value and minimum value.

A 12 dimension feature vector is formed by combining shape features, histogram statistical features and phase features.

3.2 SVM Classifier

According to the feature vector after feature extraction, HE candidate areas need to be divided into two classes: HE and no HE. So a two-class SVM classification model is adopted here. SVM classifier used in this method selects the Radial Basis Function (RBF) kernel, and adopts the method of cross validation to select the optimal parameters. In experiments, 510 samples of HE candidates were used for training and validation of the model, in which 345 samples were used for training and 165 samples were used for validation. Other fundus images containing HE candidates were tested with this model and accurate extraction of HEs was achieved. The final result is shown in Fig. 7.

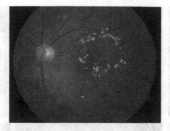

Fig. 7. Results of HE accurate detection

4 Experiments and Analysis

4.1 Experiment Material and Evaluation Parameters

This method is tested on public databases named DIARETDB1 [13] and HEI-MED [14]. DIARETDB1 database contains 89 color fundus images whose resolution is 1500×1152. Among them, 47 images are with HEs, 33 images are with cotton wool spots, hemorrhage or microaneurysm. HEI-MED database is a collection of 169 fundus images to train and test image processing algorithms for detection of exudates and diabetic macular edema.

The performance of the proposed method is measured using sensitivity (*SE*), specificity (*SP*), positive predictive value (*PPV*) and accuracy (*AC*) [15]. Their calculation formulae are as follows:

$$SE = TP / (TP + FN) \tag{11}$$

$$SP = TN / (FP + TN) \tag{12}$$

$$PPV = TP / (TP + FP) \tag{13}$$

$$AC = (TP + TN) / (TP + FP + TN + FN) \tag{14}$$

where,

TP - True Positives: Lesion regions which are correctly classified.

FP - False Positives: Non-lesion regions which are wrongly classified as lesion regions.

TN - True Negatives: Non-lesion regions which are correctly classified.

FN - False Negatives: Lesion regions which are wrongly classified as non-lesion regions.

4.2 Results and Analysis

Figure 8 shows HEs detection results and comparison results with groundtruth of different fundus images. It is better to declare that the groundtruth provided in database are areas labeled by experts manually (shown as purple block areas in the 3rd column of

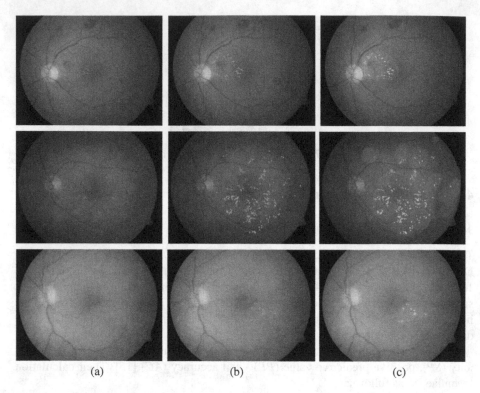

(a)   (b)   (c)

Fig. 8. Results of HEs detection. (a) Original images; (b) results by the proposed method; (c) contrast of results of experts labeled image

Fig. 8). In addition, accurate results are confirmed by experts from Tianjin Medical University Eye Hospital and Tianjin Medical University Metabolic Disease Hospital. It can be seen from Fig. 8 that whether low brightness images with more HEs (as show in 1st and 2nd row of Fig. 8), or high brightness images with less HEs (as shown in 3rd row of Fig. 8), this method can detect HEs accurately.

We evaluated the experimental results at the lesion level and the image level respectively. The parameter *SE* and *PPV*, which had higher discrimination, were used to evaluate the performance at lesion level, for the proportion of *FP* in recognition results is usually very low relative to the *TN*, and the parameter *SP* is close to 100 %, so that with no obvious discrimination. We used *SE*, *SP* and *AC* to evaluate the performance at image level. The comparison between our method and other typical HEs detection methods is shown in Table 1.

It shows that our method can achieve higher *SP* and *AC*. The method of Sánchez et al. can achieve 100 % in *SE*, *SP* and *AC* relies on his testing images. Although our method has lower sensitivity at lesion level, the missing detection of single HE is within tolerance for the distribution of HEs is always group by group. Our results improved the positive predictive value on the basis of getting better performance than the standard of diabetic lesion screening algorithm proposed by British Diabetic Association [16].

Table 1. Comparison of different methods

Methods	Results at lesion level		Results at image level		
	SE (%)	PPV (%)	SE (%)	SP (%)	AC (%)
Sánchez et al. [4]	88.0	–	100	100	100
García et al. [5]	87.6	83.5	100	77.7	91.0
Our method	84.6	94.4	97.3	90.0	93.7

5 Conclusion

A HEs detection method based on background-estimation and SVM classifier is presented in this paper. Firstly, foreground map containing all bright objects is obtained by background-estimation. HEs candidates are gotten by using edge information based on Kirsch operator. Then optic disc is removed. Finally, shape features, histogram statistic features and phase features of HE candidates are extracted before using SVM classifier, so that accurate extraction of HEs is realized. Compared with other methods, this method is based on brightness information and edge information, thus HEs candidates contain all HEs and the minimum false targets. In addition, fundus images have uncertain brightness and contrast because of different photographic environment. Phase information has great noise resistance and it is stabilized in brightness and contrast. So it has obvious advantages combining with Phase Congruency in feature extraction stage. The feasibility and superiority are demonstrated by the experiments on databases of DIARETDB1 and HEI-MED.

Acknowledgements. This work is supported by the Tianjin Science & Technology Supporting Project of China under grant No. 13ZCZDGX02100, Tianjin Research Program of Application Foundation and Advanced Technology of China under grant No. 15JCYBJC16600.

References

1. Welfer, D., Scharcanski, J., Marinho, D.R.: A coarse-to-fine strategy for automatically detecting exudates in color eye fundus images. Comput. Med. Imag. Graph. **34**, 228–235 (2010)
2. Gandhi, M., Dhanasekaran, R.: Diagnosis of diabetic retinopathy using morphological process and SVM classifier. In: International Conference on Communication and Signal Processing, pp. 873–877. IEEE Press, Washington (2013)
3. Jayakumari, C., Maruthi, R.: Detection of hard exudates in color fundus images of the human retina. Procedia Eng. **30**, 297–302 (2012)
4. Sánchez, C., Hornero, R., López, M.: A novel automatic image processing algorithm for detection of hard exudates based on retinal image analysis. Med. Eng. Phys. **30**, 350–357 (2008)
5. García, M., Sánchez, C., López, M.: Neural network based detection of hard exudates in retinal images. Comput. Meth. Prog. Biomed. **93**, 9–19 (2009)

6. Sae-Tang, W., Chiracharit, W., Kumwilaisak, W.: Exudates detection in fundus image using non-uniform illumination background subtraction. In: 2010 IEEE Region 10 Conference, pp. 204–209. IEEE Press, Piscataway (2010)
7. Vincent, L.: Morphological grayscale reconstruction in image analysis: applications and efficient algorithms. IEEE Trans Image Process. 2, 176–201 (1993)
8. Kirsch, R.A.: Computer determination of the constituent structure of biological images. Comput. Biomed. Res. 4, 315–328 (1971)
9. Sánchez, C.I., García, M., Mayo, A.: Retinal image analysis based on mixture models to detect hard exudates. Med. Image Anal. 13, 650–658 (2009)
10. Morrone, M.C., Owens, R.A.: Feature detection from local energy. Pattern Recogn. Lett. 6, 303–313 (1987)
11. Venkatesh, S., Owens, R.A.: An energy feature detection scheme. In: Proceedings of International Conference on Image Processing, pp. 553–557. IEEE Press, Singapore (1989)
12. Kovesi, P.: Image features from phase congruency. J. Comput. Vis. Res. 1, 1–26 (1999)
13. Kauppi, T., Kalesnykiene, V., Kamarainen, J.: The DIARETDB1 diabetic retinopathy database and evaluation protocol. In: Proceedings of the British Machine Vision Conference, pp. 61–65. British Machine Vision Association, Warwick (2007)
14. Giancardo, L., Meriaudeau, F.: Exudate-based diabetic macular edema detection in fundus images using publicly available datasets. Med. Image Anal. 16, 216–226 (2012)
15. Akobeng, A.: Understanding diagnostic tests 2: likelihood ratios, pre and post-test probabilities and their use in clinical practice. Acta Paediatr. 96, 487–491 (2007)
16. British Diabetic Association: Retinal Photography Screening for Diabetic Eye Disease. British Diabetic Association Report, London (1997)

Hierarchical Convolutional Neural Network for Face Detection

Dong Wang[✉], Jing Yang, Jiankang Deng, and Qingshan Liu

B-DAT Lab, School of Information and Control, Nanjing University of Information Science and Technology, Nanjing, China
{wangdong2013nuist,yang.xiaojing00,dengjiankang6}@gmail.com,
qsliu@nuist.edu.cn
http://bdat.nuist.edu.cn/

Abstract. In this paper, we propose a new approach of hierarchical convolutional neural network (CNN) for face detection. The first layer of our architecture is a binary classifier built on a deep convolutional neural network with spatial pyramid pooling (SPP). Spatial pyramid pooling reduces the computational complexity and remove the fixed-size constraint of the network. We only need to compute the feature maps from the entire image once and generate a fixed-length representation regardless of the image size and scale. To improve the localization effectiveness, in the second layer, we design a bounding box regression network to refine the relative high scored non-face output from the first layer. The proposed approach is evaluated on the AFW dataset, FDDB dataset and Pascal Faces, and it reaches the state-of-the-art performance. Also, we apply our bounding box regression network to refine the other detectors and find that it has effective generalization.

Keywords: Convolutional neural network · Hierarchical · Spatial pyramid pooling · Face detection

1 Introduction

In the field of computer vision, face detection achieved much success in these years. A capable face detector is a pre-condition for the task of facial keypoint localization and face recognition. In the anthropocentric world, face detection is widely used in a myriad of consumer products (e.g. social networks, smart mobile device applications, digital cameras, and even a wearable device).

In fact, detecting face "in the wild" is always to be a challenge to traditional detection methods due to large variations in facial appearances, occlusions, and clutters. As the textbook version of a face detector, the Viloa & Jones architecture [1] has been the source of inspiration for countless variants such as SURF cascades [2]. They support very fast face detection but the features have limited representation capacity. So, they cannot differentiate faces in uncontrolled environments. The part based models [3,4] have been proposed to address these problem. These models benefit from the fact that the part of an object often

© Springer International Publishing Switzerland 2015
Y.-J. Zhang (Ed.): ICIG 2015, Part II, LNCS 9218, pp. 373–384, 2015.
DOI: 10.1007/978-3-319-21963-9_34

presents less visual variations, and the global variation of the object can be modeled by the flexible configuration of different parts. However, they face the same issue as the previous feature-based holistic face detectors [1], because the part modeling is still based on the low level descriptors.

In recent years, convolution neural networks(CNNs) [5–7] became very popular. Convolution neural network has powerful learning ability and it has been widely used in the field of computer vision tasks such as image classification [8,9], object detection [10], scene parsing [11], facial point detection [12], and face parsing [13]. Studies in [9] show that a large, deep convolutional neural network was capable of achieving record-breaking results on a highly challenging dataset using purely supervised learning. The leading object detection method R-CNN [10] combines region proposals with CNNs and shows remarkable detection accuracy. Reference [14] proposed a new SPP-net, in which the spatial pyramid pooling (SPP) [15,16] layer is introduced to remove the fixed-size constraint of the network. Different from R-CNN [10] that repeatedly applies the deep convolutional networks to thousands of warped regions per image, SPP-net run the convolutional layers only once on the entire image, and then extract features by SPP on the feature maps. SPP-net is faster than R-CNN over one hundred times.

To address these challenges mentioned above, we propose a new face detector, which is based on a hierarchical convolution neural network. We consider a structure combination of deep convolutional neural network and the spatial pyramid pooling. This combination helps us to obtain powerful feature representation and fast running speed. We build the first layer of our architecture by applying the spatial pyramid pooling layer to a modification on the network in [9]. We make a structural modifications to the network in [9] by replacing the last pooling layer (e.g. $pool_5$, after the last convolutional layer) with a spatial pyramid pooling layer. SPP layer is applied on each candidate window of the $conv_5$ feature maps to pool a fixed-length representation of this window. The first layer of our structure in fact is a binary classifier of face and non-face. We name the binary classifier the "*FaceHunter*". We observe in the experiment that some bounding boxes of our *FaceHunter* deviate from the center of the face area after being integrated in the stage of non-maximum suppression [3]. So we introduce a CNN-based calibration layer (i.e. the second layer) to improve the localization effectiveness. It is a 2-level CNN-Refine structure for refining the relative high scored non-face output from our *FaceHunter*. Recent work [12] shows that a deep convolutional network based regression can reach top results in facial point detection task. Inspired by [12], we apply their approach in this paper and find that it can do well in face detection as well. The first level of our CNN-Refine structure, similar to [12], is a regression approach with a deep convolutional neural network. The second level is designed to judge the new boxes which come from the first level. In this level, we put the regressed boxes into the same classifier as *FaceHunter* to preserve the positive faces and delete the negative faces. See details in Sect. 3.2.

To evaluate our approach, we run our detector respectively on AFW [4], FDDB [17] and Pascal Faces dataset [18]. All the datasets contain faces in uncontrolled conditions with cluttered backgrounds and large variations in both face viewpoint and appearance, and thus bring forward great challenges to the current face detection algorithms. Surprisingly, our face detector puts up a good show and reach the state-of-the-art performance. We also evaluate our CNN-Refine structure that is applied to two different algorithms (i.e. Structured Models [18] and OpenCV [1]) on two public datasets. The result shows that it has effective generalization.

2 Overview

Figure 1 shows the construction of our two-layer hierarchical deep detector, which is a SPP-based face detector (i.e. *FaceHunter*) followed by a 2-level CNN-Refine structure. Once the picture is put into the *FaceHunter*, it will output initial face detecting results. The positive faces from *FaceHunter* will be directly output. However, the non-faces will not be deleted in general terms due to some ones of them in fact are close to the faces in the space of image. So we introduce a CNN-Refine structure to refine the negative output of first layer. The rects with relative high score, not all for efficiency, will be regressed by the first level of the CNN-Refine structure (i.e. *Deep CNN*). Then the regressed rects are fed to the second level which is a classifier the same as the first layer. It will finally delete the negatives and output the positives.

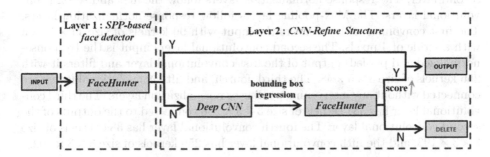

Fig. 1. The overview of our proposed face detector: a SPP-based face detector (i.e. *FaceHunter*) followed by a 2-level CNN-Refine structure.

3 Hierarchical Deep Detector

3.1 SPP-based Face Detector

We resize the image and extract the feature maps from the entire image only once. Then we apply the spatial pyramid pooling on each candidate window of the feature maps to pool a fixed-length representation. These representations are provided to the fully-connected layers of the network. Then we score these windows via a pre-trained binary linear SVM classifier and use non-maximum suppression on the scored windows.

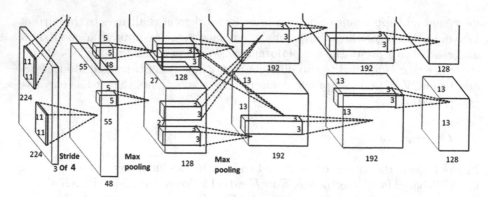

Fig. 2. The deep structure which is used for generating feature maps. One GPU runs the layer-parts at the top of the figure while the other runs the layer-parts at the bottom. The GPUs communicate only at certain layers.

Feature Maps. We consider a variant of the network in [9] to generate the feature maps, which removes the last pooling layer (i.e. $pool_5$). As depicted in Fig. 2, the net contains 5 layers. The kernels of the second, fourth, and fifth convolutional layers are connected only to those kernel maps in the previous layer. The kernels of the third convolutional layer are connected to all the kernel maps in the second layer. The response-normalization layers follow the first and second convolutional layers. The Max-pooling layers follow response-normalization layers. The first convolutional layer filters the input with 96 kernels of size $11 \times 11 \times 3$ with a stride of 4 pixels. The second convolutional layers input is the (response-normalized and pooled) output of the first convolutional layer and filters it with 256 kernels of size $5 \times 5 \times 48$. The third, fourth, and fifth convolutional layers are connected without any intervening pooling or normalization layers. The third convolutional layer has 384 kernels of size $3 \times 3 \times 256$ connected to the outputs of the second convolutional layer. The fourth convolutional layer has 384 kernels of size $3 \times 3 \times 192$, and the fifth convolutional layer has 256 kernels of size $3 \times 3 \times 192$.

The Spatial Pyramid Pooling Layer. Spatial pyramid pooling can maintain spatial information by pooling in local spatial bins. The size of these spatial bins is proportional to the image size, so the number of bins is fixed regardless of the image size. Spatial pyramid pooling uses the multi-level spatial bins, which has been shown to be robust to object deformations. After $conv_5$, as shown in Fig. 3, we use a 4-level spatial pyramid (1×1, 2×2, 3×3, 6×6, totally 50 bins) to pool the features on the feature maps. The $conv_5$ layer has 256 filters. So the spp layer generates a 12,800-d (i.e. 50×256) representation. We use the max pooling throughout this paper.

3.2   CNN-Refine Structure

Bounding Box Regression. Different detectors output different sizes and different styles of bounding boxes. We observe that some bounding boxes of our

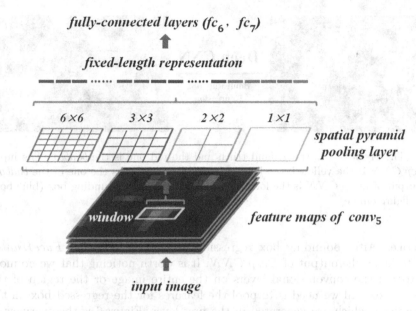

Fig. 3. The network with a spatial pyramid pooling layer: the feature maps are computed from the entire image and the pooling is performed in candidate windows.

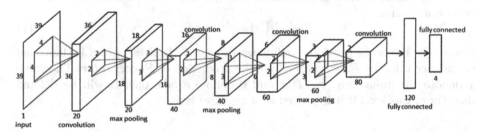

Fig. 4. The structure of *Deep CNN*: four convolutional layers followed by max pooling, and two fully connected layers.

FaceHunter deviate from the center of the face area after being integrated in the stage of non-maximum suppression. So, we introduce a CNN-based calibration layer to improve the localization effectiveness. We use a regression approach with a CNN structure to finely tune the bounding boxes which are not far from the faces in the space of image. We name these bounding boxes "*badbox*".

In this paper, we focus on the structural design of individual networks. Figure 4 illustrates the deep structure, which contains four convolutional layers followed by max pooling, and two fully connected layers. Figure 5 is the overview of this level. The green box is the ground truth, while the red one is a *badbox*. The input of Deep CNN is the yellow box whose side length is 1.8 times the one of the *badbox*.

Fig. 5. The green box is the ground truth and the red one is the *badbox*. The input of *Deep CNN* is the yellow box whose side length is 1.8 times the one of the *badbox*. The output of *Deep CNN* is the location of the finely tuned bounding box (blue box) (Color figure online).

Re-score. After bounding box regression we use the classifier *FaceHunter* again to judge the output of *Deep CNN*. It is worth noticing that we no more need to run the convolutional layers on the entire image or the region of the regressed box. All we need is to pool the features for the regressed box on the feature maps which are generated in the first layer. Figure 6 is the overview of this level. Once the classifier judge that the input is a positive one, the score of corresponding bounding box will be multiplied by a motivational factor α. It can be written as

$$S = \tfrac{s}{|s|}(|s| * \alpha), \mathrm{p} = 1. \tag{1}$$

where $\alpha > 1$, s is the previous confidence value of a *"badbox"* and S is the tuned confidence value by *FaceHunter*. p is the prediction of *FaceHunter*. The value 1 denote the input is a true face and 0 denote a fake one. It will be deleted directly in this level if it is judged as a negative face.

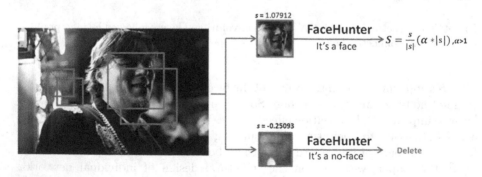

Fig. 6. The overview of the second level of our CNN-Refine structure: This level will encourage positive faces and delete the negative ones. "s" is the previous confidence value of a *"badbox"* and "S" is the tuned confidence value.

4 Experiments

4.1 Datasets and Experiment Setting

We use five datasets for our experiments: AFW [4] (205 images with bounding boxes), FDDB [17] (2845 images with ellipses annotations) Pascal Faces dataset [18] (851 Pascal VOC images with bounding boxes), AFLW [19] (26000 annotated faces), and a large face dataset of ourselves, which has a total of 980,354 annotated faces. All the datasets contain faces in uncontrolled conditions with cluttered backgrounds and large variations in both face viewpoint and appearance.

Training Setting. The training experiments are conducted in our own dataset and AFLW. 183,200 face images are selected from our own dataset to train *FaceHunter*, while the AFLW [19] dataset is used for valiation. Specially, to train the detector,we generate positive samples by cropping image patches which are centered at ground truth windows, and negative samples are those that overlaps a positive window by at most 25 % (measured by the intersection-over-union (IoU) ratio). To reduce redundant information resulting from overlapping negative samples, the negative sample that overlaps another negative sample by more then 75 % will be removed. Our implementation is based on the publicly available code of cuda-convnet [9] and Caffe [20]. We consider a single-size (i.e. 224×224) training mode. We use the 4-level spatial pyramid to generate the representation for each entire image. These representations are provided to the fully-connected layers of the network. Then we train a binary linear SVM classifier for each category on these features. Our implementation of the SVM training is shown as follows [10,14]. For the training of bounding box regression, we take training patches according to the face annotations, and augment them by small translation.

Testing Setting. In the general object detection task [10,14], they use the "fast" mode of selective search [21] to generate 2,000 candidate windows per image. In our experiments, we observe that such method is not suitable due to the fact that faces in datasets suffer from large variations in facial appearances and very small faces. To cope with challenges from appearance variance, in our experiments, a low threshold is set to achieve 99 % recall of the ACF [22] detector and each image output 500 windows on average. Then we resize the image to the size of 224×224 and extract the feature maps from the entire image. In each candidate window, we use the 4-level spatial pyramid to generate the representation for each window. These representations are provided to the fully-connected layers of the network. Then the binary SVM classifier is used to score the candidate windows. Finally, we use non-maximum suppression (threshold of 0.3) on the scored windows.

In order to solve the problem that faces appear at all scales in images, we improve our method by extracting feature at multi scales. We resize the image to five scales (i.e. 480, 576, 688, 864, 1200) and compute the feature maps of conv5 for each scale. Then we empirically choose a single scale such that the scaled candidate window has a number of pixels closest to 224×224 for each candidate window. Then we only use the feature maps extracted from this scale to compute the feature of this window.

4.2   Experiment Results

Results on Three Public Datasets. We respectively evaluate our "*Face Hunter*" only (expressed using the red curve) and "CNN-Refined *FaceHunter*" (expressed using the blue curve) on AFW [4], FDDB [17] and Pascal Faces dataset [18]. The PR curve of our approach on the AFW [4] and Pascal Faces [18] dataset and the Discrete ROC curve on the FDDB [17] dataset are shown in Figs. 7, 8 and 9 respectively. Our *FaceHunter* detector can already reach top performance. Then our CNN-Refined structure can slightly improve the performance. The average precision of our detector can be enhanced by more than 1 percent after our whole CNN-Refine structure being applied to the detector. Figure 10 shows some examples of our detection results. As we can see, our detector can detect faces with different poses, in severe occlusions and cluttered background, as well as blurred face images.

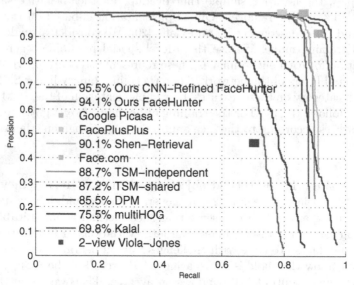

Fig. 7. PR Curve on AFW.

Evaluation about Our CNN-Refine Structure. Is the CNN-Refine structure only suitable for our *FaceHunter* detector? The answer is no. We evaluate it on two datasets for some other detectors and achieve exciting results. Figure 11 shows the evaluation about our CNN-Refine structure that is applied to two different algorithms (i.e. Structured Models [18] and OpenCV [1]) on two different datasets. Our CNN can also improve the performance of them.

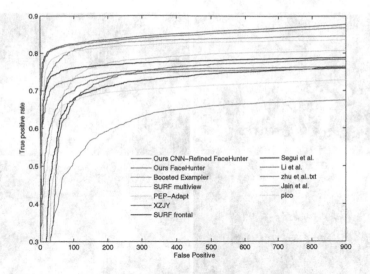

Fig. 8. Discrete ROC on FDDB.

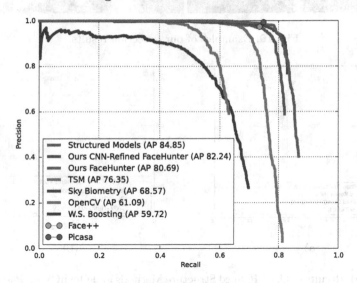

Fig. 9. PR Curve on Pascal Faces.

4.3 Computational Complexity Analysis

The complexity of the convolutional feature computation in ours *FaceHunter* is $O(r \cdot s^2)$ at a scale s (5-scale version in this work), where r is the aspect ratio and assume that r is about 4/3. In contrast, this complexity of R-CNN is $O(n \cdot 227^2)$ with the window number n (2000). In our single-scale version (e.g. s=688), this complexity is about 1/160 of R-CNN's. Even for our 5-scale version, this complexity is about 1/24 of R-CNN's. So our method is much faster than

Fig. 10. Examples of our detection results.

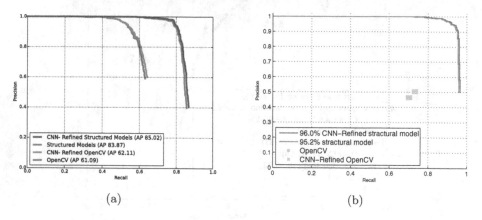

(a)   (b)

Fig. 11. (a). Results of CNN-Refined Structure Methods and OpenCV on Pascal Faces. (b). Results of CNN-Refined Structure Methods and OpenCV on AFW.

R-CNN. We evaluate the average time of 500 Pascal Faces [18] images using a single GeForce GTX Titan GPU (6 GB memory). Our 1-scale version takes only 0.05 s per image and the 5-scale version takes 0.29 s per image for convolutions. The GPU time of computing the 4,096-d fc7 features is 0.09 s per image.

5 Conclusion

In this work we propose a hierarchical convolutional neural network (CNN) face detector that can achieve state-of-the-art performance. We introduce the spatial pyramid pooling (SPP) layer to remove the fixed-size constraint of the network. With SPP layer we can run the convolutional layers only once on the entire image, and then extract features by SPP on the feature maps. The bounding box regression approach that we have introduced to refine the detection results proves to have effective generalization. It is the first time that spatial pyramid pooling (SPP) is used in the task of face detection and our results show that it can achieve good performance on highly challenging datasets.

References

1. Viola, P., Jones, M.J.: Robust real-time face detection. Int. J. Comput. Vis. **57**(2), 137–154 (2004)
2. Li, J., Zhang, Y.: Learning surf cascade for fast and accurate object detection. In: IEEE Conference on Computer Vision and Pattern Recognition (CVPR), pp. 3468–3475. IEEE (2013)
3. Felzenszwalb, P.F., Girshick, R.B., McAllester, D., Ramanan, D.: Object detection with discriminatively trained part-based models. IEEE Trans. Pattern Anal. Mach. Intell. **32**(9), 1627–1645 (2010)
4. Zhu, X., Ramanan, D.: Face detection, pose estimation, and landmark localization in the wild. In: IEEE Conference on Computer Vision and Pattern Recognition (CVPR), pp. 2879–2886. IEEE (2012)
5. Fukushima, K.: Neocognitron: A self-organizing neural network model for a mechanism of pattern recognition unaffected by shift in position. Biol. Cybern. **36**(4), 193–202 (1980)
6. LeCun, Y., Boser, B., Denker, J.S., Henderson, D., Howard, R.E., Hubbard, W., Jackel, L.D.: Backpropagation applied to handwritten zip code recognition. Neural Comput. **1**(4), 541–551 (1989)
7. Rumelhart, D.E., Hinton, G.E., Williams, R.J.: Learning internal representations by error propagation. Technical report, DTIC Document (1985)
8. Ciresan, D., Meier, U., Schmidhuber, J.: Multi-column deep neural networks for image classification. In: IEEE Conference on Computer Vision and Pattern Recognition (CVPR), pp. 3642–3649. IEEE (2012)
9. Krizhevsky, A., Sutskever, I., Hinton, G.E.: Imagenet classification with deep convolutional neural networks. In: Advances in Neural Information Processing Systems, pp. 1097–1105 (2012)
10. Girshick, R., Donahue, J., Darrell, T., Malik, J.: Rich feature hierarchies for accurate object detection and semantic segmentation. In: 2014 IEEE Conference on Computer Vision and Pattern Recognition, pp. 580–587. IEEE (2014)
11. Farabet, C., Couprie, C., Najman, L., LeCun, Y.: Learning hierarchical features for scene labeling. IEEE Trans. Pattern Anal. Mach. Intell. **35**(8), 1915–1929 (2013)
12. Sun, Y., Wang, X., Tang, X.: Deep convolutional network cascade for facial point detection. In: IEEE Conference on Computer Vision and Pattern Recognition (CVPR), pp. 3476–3483. IEEE (2013)

13. Luo, P., Wang, X., Tang, X.: Hierarchical face parsing via deep learning. In: IEEE Conference on Computer Vision and Pattern Recognition (CVPR), pp. 2480–2487. IEEE (2012)

14. He, K., Zhang, X., Ren, S., Sun, J.: Spatial pyramid pooling in deep convolutional networks for visual recognition, arXiv preprint arXiv:1406.4729

15. Grauman, K., Darrell, T.: The pyramid match kernel: Discriminative classification with sets of image features. In: IEEE International Conference on ICCV, vol. 2, pp. 1458–1465. IEEE (2005)

16. Lazebnik, S., Schmid, C., Ponce, J.: Beyond bags of features: Spatial pyramid matching for recognizing natural scene categories. In: IEEE Computer Society Conference on Computer Vision and Pattern Recognition, vol. 2, pp. 2169–2178. IEEE (2006)

17. Jain, V., Learned-Miller, E.G.: Fddb: A benchmark for face detection in unconstrained settings, UMass Amherst Technical report

18. Yan, J., Zhang, X., Lei, Z., Li, S.Z.: Face detection by structural models. Image Vis. Comput. **32**(10), 790–799 (2014)

19. Kostinger, M., Wohlhart, P., Roth, P.M., Bischof, H.: Annotated facial landmarks in the wild: A large-scale, real-world database for facial landmark localization. In: IEEE International Conference on Computer Vision Workshops (ICCV Workshops), pp. 2144–2151. IEEE (2011)

20. Jia, Y.: Caffe: An open source convolutional architecture for fast feature embedding. http://caffe.berkeleyvision.org

21. Van de Sande, K.E., Uijlings, J.R., Gevers, T., Smeulders, A.W.: Segmentation as selective search for object recognition. In: 2011 IEEE International Conference on ICCV, pp. 1879–1886. IEEE (2011)

22. Yang, B., Yan, J., Lei, Z., Li, S.Z.: Aggregate channel features for multi-view face detection. In: 2014 IEEE International Joint Conference on Biometrics (IJCB), pp. 1–8. IEEE (2014)

Human-Object Interaction Recognition
by Modeling Context

Qun Zhang$^{(\boxtimes)}$, Wei Liang, Xiabing Liu, and Yumeng Wang

Beijing Laboratory of Intelligent Information Technology, School of Computer
Science, Beijing Institute of Technology, Beijing 100081, People's Republic of China
{zhangqun,liangwei,liuxiabing,wangyumeng}@bit.edu.cn

Abstract. In this paper, we present a new method to recognize human-
object interactions by modeling the context between human actions and
manipulated objects. It is a challenging task due to severe occlusion
between human and objects during the interacting process. While human
actions and objects can provide strong context information, such as some
action happening is usually related to a certain object, by which we can
improve the accuracy of recognition for both of them. In this paper, we
use global and local temporal features from skeleton sequences to model
actions, and kernel features are applied to describe objects. We optimize
all possible solutions from actions and objects by modeling the context
between them. The results of experiments show the effectiveness of our
method.

Keywords: Human-object interaction · Action recognition · Object
classification · Context

1 Introduction

Human-object interaction recognition has been studied in the field of computer
vision for years and it has a broad prospective application. Although human can
distinguish interactions easily, it is still a difficult task for computers. The reasons
are: (1) The appearance of objects and human vary a lot due to occlusion between
objects and human during interactions, which leads to the failure of recognition.
As shown in Fig. 1(a), objects are occluded by hand. In this situation, it is
challenging for object recognition only by appearance. (2) There are ambiguities
in human actions if we only consider the pose from a single frame. Even for pose
sequences, it is not easy. Sometimes different actions have similar pose sequences.
In Fig. 1(b) and (c), *"calling"* and *"drinking"* can not be separated well from
skeleton sequences.

Inspired by the work of Yao and Fei-Fei [22], we propose a method to recognize human-object interactions by modeling the context between human actions
and manipulated objects with RGBD videos which are captured by Kinect sensor. Firstly, we train a classifier by SVM algorithm for actions with pose sequence
features, which can score each action, and then we search all possible manipulated objects by a sliding window near human hand region. We keep all possible

© Springer International Publishing Switzerland 2015
Y.-J. Zhang (Ed.): ICIG 2015, Part II, LNCS 9218, pp. 385–395, 2015.
DOI: 10.1007/978-3-319-21963-9_35

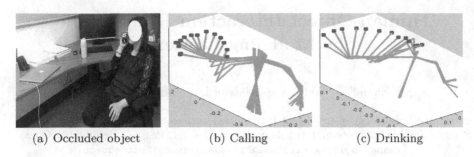

(a) Occluded object   (b) Calling   (c) Drinking

Fig. 1. Human-object interaction examples. (a) The manipulated objects are small and occluded in human-object interactions, (b) and (c) are ambiguous with similar pose sequences.

interpretations of action and object labels. By modeling the context between them, we get the most reasonable results of human actions and manipulated objects with optimization. Our framework is shown in Fig. 2.

The rest of this paper is organized as follows. In Sect. 2, we introduce the related works. In Sect. 3, more details of our method are presented. In Sect. 4, our dataset and experimental results are described. Finally, the paper is concluded in Sect. 5 with discussion.

2   Related Work

Action Recognition. Action recognition is very important in the field of computer vision. Researchers have proposed many different approaches to solve this problem. Most of traditional methods focused on 2D data. They used features like silhouettes and shapes to extract spatio-temporal feature descriptors to recognize actions [4,6,17,19]. Raptis and Soatto [17] proposed a hierarchical structure which included SIFT average descriptor, trajectory transition descriptor, and trajectory proximity descriptor. Some works [13,14] modeled actions with the coordinates of skeletons or the relative position of body parts. The approach in [13] extracted local joints structure as local skeleton features and histograms of 3D joints as global skeleton features for action recognition. In most of the above work, actions are performed without occlusion. When occlusions happen, the features usually tend to fail. It is one of the most difficult issues in many kinds of vision work.

Object Features. The "good" features are very important for object classification. Researchers have presented various kinds of features. For low-level image features, SIFT [8,15] and HOG [7,25] are the most popular features in vision tasks. Many researchers adopted multiple kinds of features to represent various aspects of objects for classification in [1,2,11]. Ito and Kubota [11] introduced three different co-occurrence features named color-CoHOG (color-Co-occurrence Histograms of Oriented Gradients), CoHED (Co-occurrence Histograms of pairs of Edge orientations and color Difference), and CoHD (Co-occurrence Histograms of color Difference) to classify objects. Benefitted from the performance of 3D sensors, such as the Kinect sensor, some researchers [1, 2] extracted features from RGBD data. Bo et al. [2] presented five depth kernel descriptors that captured different cues including size, shape and edges. Some other approaches used a set of semantic attributes to classify objects [12, 18]. Su et al. [18] used five groups of semantic attributes including scene, color, part, shape, and material, they demonstrated that the semantic attributes can be helpful to improve the performance of object classification.

Context. Psychology experiments have shown that context plays an important role in recognition in the system of human vision. It has been used for some tasks in computer vision, such as object detection, object classification, action recognition, scene recognition, and semantic segmentation [10, 16, 19, 20, 23]. Marszalek et al. [16] claimed human actions have relations to the purpose and scene. Hence, they modeled the context between human actions and scenes to recognize actions. Sun et al. [19] adopted a hierarchical structure to represent the spatio-temporal context information for action recognition. In [20], they proposed a 4D human-object interaction model to recognize the events and objects in the video sequences. Gupta et al. [10] combined the spatial with function constraint between human and objects to recognize actions and objects. Yao et al. [23] modeled the mutual context of objects and human poses in human-object interaction activities.

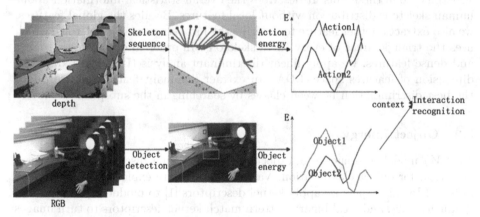

Fig. 2. An overview of our framework

3   Modeling Context of Actions and Objects

We define human-object interactions as $I = <A, O>$. Given a RGBD video V in time interval $T = [1, T]$, our goal is to recognize manipulated objects O and actions A respectively. We cast recognition into an optimization problem:

$$E(I, V) = \sum_{t=1}^{T} (\lambda_1 E(A, V_t) + \lambda_2 E(O, V_t) + E(A, O)). \tag{1}$$

Where $E(A, V_t)$ is the energy of human actions in temporal space. $E(O, V_t)$ is the energy of manipulated objects in spatial space. $E(A, O)$ is the energy of context between human actions and manipulated objects. λ_1 and λ_2 are weights to balance the contribution of each energy term.

3.1 Action Energy

$E(A, V_t)$ models the energy of human actions. We train a classifier by multi-class SVM [5] to score each skeleton sequence as class a. The energy is:

$$E(A, V_t) = \omega_a \theta_a. \tag{2}$$

Where ω_a is the template parameter of action class a. θ_a is the skeleton features of human action.

As shown in Fig. 3, we improve the method of global features in [21], histograms of 3D joints (HOJ3D), by combining local features. This feature is computed with aligned spherical coordinate system and it is independent of views. We denote features as $\theta_a = \{F_L, F_G\}$. The features include two parts: *local features* $F_L = (l_1, l_2, ..., l_{N_l})$ and *global features* $F_G = (g_1, g_2, ..., g_{N_g})$. For global feature, 3D space is firstly divided into many bins and we count how many skeletons are in these bins. It describes the overall statistical information about human skeletons distribution without local features. Besides the global features, we also extract another feature to describe the local structure of skeletons, which uses the triangle areas of every three skeletons. In order to obtain more robust and dense features, we apply linear discriminant analysis (LDA) to reduce the dimension of features space. LDA can extract dominant features and produce the best discrimination between classes by searching in the subspace.

3.2 Object Energy

$E(O, V_t)$ models the energy of object label. Extracting discriminative features is critical for object classification. Various features are explored by researchers [3,9,24]. In this paper, we apply kernel descriptors [1] to model objects. We use gradient, color, and local binary pattern match kernel descriptors to turn images into patch-level features. We sample the image patches with different sizes, such as 4×4 rectangle or 8×8 rectangle. Then, the gradient match kernel is used to measure gradient orientations similarity between patches from two different images. In the same way, the color match kernel and local binary pattern match kernel can represent image appearance and local shape respectively. We visualize these three types of kernel features in Fig. 4. As the number of image patches is large and evaluating kernels is time consuming, we utilize kernel principal component analysis to extract compact basis vectors. In human-object interactions, object is often small and occluded. Fortunately, benefitted from the Kinect, we

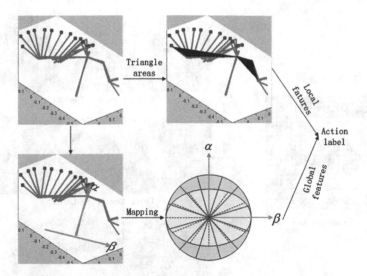

Fig. 3. The features for action recognition. (1) Extracting local features by computing triangle areas. (2) Extracting global features by mapping the skeleton coordinates into spherical bins.

can get more stable and reliable human pose. So we use sliding window to detect object near human hand region with several sizes. For each window, we extract above features and then compute the cost that assigning the label o to the object by a linear SVM classifier. The energy is defined as:

$$E(O, V_t) = \omega_o \theta_o. \tag{3}$$

Where ω_o is the template parameter of object class o. θ_o is the kernel features of manipulated object.

3.3   Context Between Actions and Objects

Human can recognize human-object interactions easily even some information is missing. There is the context between action and related object in human mind. The knowledge of context is helpful to get the most reasonable interpretation for action and the manipulated object together. For example, when someone is drinking, severe occlusion usually happened because of human's hand holding the cup. But, for human, it is easy to fill in the information of the object. It is supposed that there exists a cup in human hand when the human is doing the action of *"drink"*. Some kinds of action has a higher possibility to manipulate certain objects. That is to say, we can infer the human action with the related object and vice versa. The context between human actions and manipulated objects is defined as:

$$E(A, O) = \sum_{i=1}^{N_A} \sum_{j=1}^{N_O} N_{(A=i)} N_{(O=j)}. \tag{4}$$

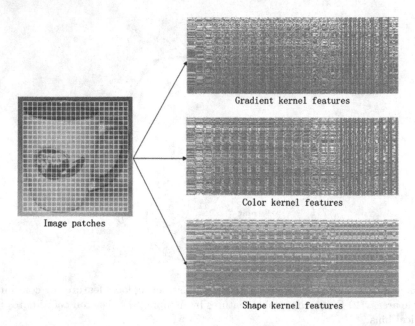

Fig. 4. The gradient, color, and shape kernel features of the cup (Color figure online)

Where N_A and N_O represent the number of action classes and object classes respectively. $N_{(A=i)}$ and $N_{(O=j)}$ represent the number of the ith category action and the jth category object respectively.

3.4 Learning and Inference

We adopt SVM algorithm to learn the action model parameter ω_a, defined by:

$$\min_{\omega, \xi_i} \quad \frac{1}{2}\omega^T\omega + C\sum_{i=1}^{N}\xi_i. \tag{5}$$

$$\text{s.t.} \quad y_i(\omega\theta + b_i) \geq 1 - \xi_i.$$

Where y_i is the label for data x_i. θ is the feature for data x_i. Similarly, we can learn the object model parameter ω_o by SVM.

Our final optimization function is to solve the minimum energy in Eq. (1), defined by:

$$I^\star = \arg\min_{I_1 I_2 \cdots I_t} \sum_{t=1}^{T} E(I_t, V_t). \tag{6}$$

We optimize the Eq. (6) via greedy algorithm framework. We always choose the locally optimal choice at each stage with the hope of finding a global optimum.

4   Experiments

We collect a human-object interaction dataset by Kinect sensor with RGB, depth and skeletons. There are ten subjects, six males and four females. Each person performs each interaction four or five times. In our dataset, there are eight different daily interactions including *calling with a phone, drinking with a cup, picking up a mouse, putting down a cup, opening a laptop, turning off a laptop, opening a soda can, and pouring into a cup*. Some examples from our dataset are shown in Fig. 5.

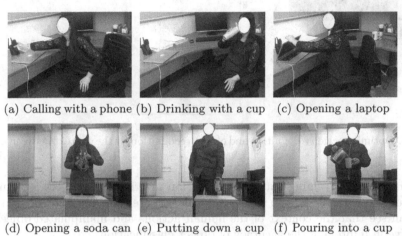

(a) Calling with a phone (b) Drinking with a cup   (c) Opening a laptop

(d) Opening a soda can (e) Putting down a cup   (f) Pouring into a cup

Fig. 5. Some examples of the human-object interactions in our dataset

Action Recognition. The human actions are ambiguous without manipulated objects, for example, making a call has similar skeleton sequences with drinking. We use global features and local features from skeleton data described in Sect. 3.1. The confusion matrix of the action recognition without and with the manipulated objects context are shown in Fig. 7(a) and (b). The results in Fig. 7(a) demonstrate that making a call, drinking, putting down and pouring water have a large confusion probability. In Fig. 6, the *"drink"* action energy is minimum, but considering the manipulated objects, it has a large chance to be the phone, we finally infer the action label is *"make a call"*. The results of our method show that the action recognition accuracy can be improved with the related objects as context.

Object Classification. In human-object interactions, related objects are always small or occluded by human hand. Occlusion is one of the most difficult issues in the field of computer vision. Bo et al. [1] designed a family of kernel features that described gradient, color and shape. Our dataset is randomly split into ten parts, and we adopt leave-one-sample-out cross validation strategy, namely, one original video sequence is used as the test data while the rest original video

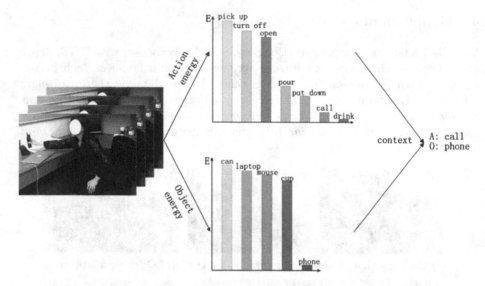

Fig. 6. Optimize action recognition and object recognition by the context between them.

sequences as the training data. The confusion matrix of the object recognition without and with the human actions information are shown in Fig. 8(a) and (b). We can see that the context of the human actions and manipulated objects is effective in improving the accuracy of object classification.

Human-Object Interaction Recognition. In addition to the results of human actions and objects from the RGBD video, we can also recognize human-object interaction. Figure 9 indicates the performance of the human-object interaction recognition of our method. We can see that our results demonstrate the effectiveness of human action recognition and object classification for better human-object interaction recognition.

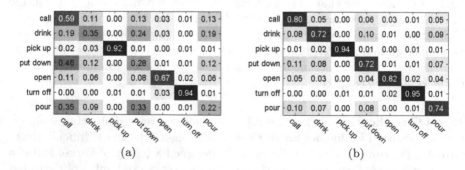

Fig. 7. (a) The confusion matrix of action recognition in [21]. (b) The confusion matrix of our method

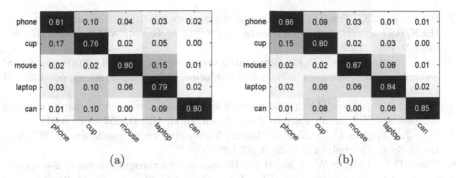

(a)   (b)

Fig. 8. (a) The confusion matrix of object recognition in [1]. (b) The confusion matrix of our method

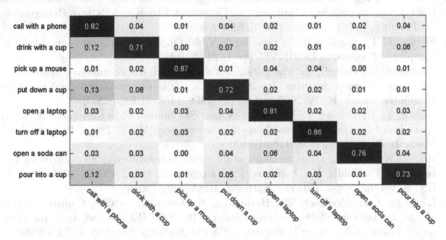

Fig. 9. The confusion matrix of human-object interaction recognition

5   Conclusions

Human-object interaction recognition is one of the most important topics in the field of computer vision. In this paper, we model human actions and manipulated objects in a unified framework for recognition. For human actions, we use local features together with global features to improve the accuracy of recognition. For object recognition, we apply kernel features. Experiments show that the features are more discriminative. Then we model the context between actions and manipulated objects. It is helpful to improve human-object interaction recognition. In the future, we will extend our dataset and consider more kinds of actions and objects.

References

1. Bo, L., Ren, X., Fox, D.: Kernel descriptors for visual recognition. In: Advances in Neural Information Processing Systems, pp. 244–252 (2010)

2. Bo, L., Ren, X., Fox, D.: Depth kernel descriptors for object recognition. In: 2011 IEEE/RSJ International Conference on Intelligent Robots and Systems (IROS), pp. 821–826. IEEE (2011)
3. Bo, L., Sminchisescu, C.: Efficient match kernel between sets of features for visual recognition. In: Advances in Neural Information Processing Systems, pp. 135–143 (2009)
4. Bobick, A.F., Davis, J.W.: The recognition of human movement using temporal templates. IEEE Trans. Pattern Anal. Mach. Intell. **23**(3), 257–267 (2001)
5. Chang, C.C., Lin, C.J.: Libsvm: a library for support vector machines. ACM Trans. Intell. Syst. Technol. (TIST) **2**(3), 27 (2011)
6. Chen, D.Y., Shih, S.W., Liao, H.Y.: Human action recognition using 2-d spatio-temporal templates. In: 2007 IEEE International Conference on Multimedia and Expo, pp. 667–670. IEEE (2007)
7. Dalal, N., Triggs, B.: Histograms of oriented gradients for human detection. In: 2005 IEEE Computer Society Conference on Computer Vision and Pattern Recognition, CVPR 2005, vol. 1, pp. 886–893. IEEE (2005)
8. Flitton, G.T., Breckon, T.P., Bouallagu, N.M.: Object recognition using 3d sift in complex CT volumes. In: BMVC, pp. 1–12 (2010)
9. Grauman, K., Darrell, T.: The pyramid match kernel: discriminative classification with sets of image features. In: 2005 Tenth IEEE International Conference on Computer Vision, ICCV 2005, vol. 2, pp. 1458–1465. IEEE (2005)
10. Gupta, A., Kembhavi, A., Davis, L.S.: Observing human-object interactions: using spatial and functional compatibility for recognition. IEEE Trans. Pattern Anal. Mach. Intell. **31**(10), 1775–1789 (2009)
11. Ito, S., Kubota, S.: Object classification using heterogeneous co-occurrence features. In: Daniilidis, K., Maragos, P., Paragios, N. (eds.) ECCV 2010, Part V. LNCS, vol. 6315, pp. 701–714. Springer, Heidelberg (2010)
12. Lampert, C.H., Nickisch, H., Harmeling, S.: Learning to detect unseen object classes by between-class attribute transfer. In: 2009 IEEE Conference on Computer Vision and Pattern Recognition, CVPR 2009, pp. 951–958. IEEE (2009)
13. Liang, Y., Lu, W., Liang, W., Wang, Y.: Action recognition using local joints structure and histograms of 3d joints. In: 2014 Tenth International Conference on Computational Intelligence and Security (CIS), pp. 185–188. IEEE (2014)
14. Lin, Z., Jiang, Z., Davis, L.S.: Recognizing actions by shape-motion prototype trees. In: 2009 IEEE 12th International Conference on Computer Vision, pp. 444–451. IEEE (2009)
15. Lowe, D.G.: Distinctive image features from scale-invariant keypoints. Int. J. Comput. Vis. **60**(2), 91–110 (2004)
16. Marszalek, M., Laptev, I., Schmid, C.: Actions in context. In: 2009 IEEE Conference on Computer Vision and Pattern Recognition, CVPR 2009, pp. 2929–2936. IEEE (2009)
17. Raptis, M., Soatto, S.: Tracklet descriptors for action modeling and video analysis. In: Daniilidis, K., Maragos, P., Paragios, N. (eds.) ECCV 2010, Part I. LNCS, vol. 6311, pp. 577–590. Springer, Heidelberg (2010)
18. Su, Y., Allan, M., Jurie, F.: Improving object classification using semantic attributes. In: BMVC, pp. 1–10 (2010)
19. Sun, J., Wu, X., Yan, S., Cheong, L.F., Chua, T.S., Li, J.: Hierarchical spatio-temporal context modeling for action recognition. In: 2009 IEEE Conference on Computer Vision and Pattern Recognition, CVPR 2009, pp. 2004–2011. IEEE (2009)

20. Wei, P., Zhao, Y., Zheng, N., Zhu, S.C.: Modeling 4d human-object interactions for event and object recognition. In: 2013 IEEE International Conference on Computer Vision (ICCV), pp. 3272–3279. IEEE (2013)
21. Xia, L., Chen, C.C., Aggarwal, J.: View invariant human action recognition using histograms of 3d joints. In: 2012 IEEE Computer Society Conference on Computer Vision and Pattern Recognition Workshops (CVPRW), pp. 20–27. IEEE (2012)
22. Yao, B., Fei-Fei, L.: Modeling mutual context of object and human pose in human-object interaction activities. In: 2010 IEEE Conference on Computer Vision and Pattern Recognition (CVPR), pp. 17–24. IEEE (2010)
23. Yao, B., Fei-Fei, L.: Recognizing human-object interactions in still images by modeling the mutual context of objects and human poses. IEEE Trans. Pattern Anal. Mach. Intell. **34**(9), 1691–1703 (2012)
24. Yu, K., Xu, W., Gong, Y.: Deep learning with kernel regularization for visual recognition. In: Advances in Neural Information Processing Systems, pp. 1889–1896 (2009)
25. Zhang, J., Huang, K., Yu, Y., Tan, T.: Boosted local structured HOG-LBP for object localization. In: 2011 IEEE Conference on Computer Vision and Pattern Recognition (CVPR), pp. 1393–1400. IEEE (2011)

Image Annotation Based on Multi-view Learning

Zhe Shi, Songhao Zhu[⊠], and Chengjian Sun

School of Automatic, Nanjing University of Posts and Telecommunications,
Nanjing 210046, China
njuptzsl@yeah.net

Abstract. With the explosive growth of image data collections on the web, labeling each image with appropriate semantic description based on the image content for image index and image retrieval has become an increasingly difficult and laborious task. To deal with this issue, we propose a novel multi-view semi-supervised learning scheme to improve the performance of image annotation by using multiple views of an image and leveraging the information contained in pseudo-labeled images. In the training process, labeled images are first adopted to train view-specific classifiers independently using uncorrelated and sufficient views, and each view-specific classifier is then iteratively re-trained using initial labeled samples and additional pseudo-labeled samples based on a measure of confidence. In the annotation process, each unlabeled image is assigned appropriate semantic annotations based on the maximum vote entropy principle and the correlationship between annotations with respect to the results of each optimally trained view-specific classifier. Experimental results on a general-purpose image database demonstrate the effectiveness and efficiency of the proposed multi-view semi-supervised scheme.

1 Introduction

With the rapidly increasing volume of image data collection uploaded to the Internet, the demand of developing content-based analysis technologies to effectively organize, manage and utilize such huge amount of information resources has become an important and challenging research topic in the field of intelligent multimedia analysis. Among these technologies, image annotation, which aims to build an exact correspondence between visual information at the perceptual level and linguistic descriptions at the semantic level, is an elementary step and a promising step for content-based image indexing, retrieval and other related multimedia applications. Therefore, automatic annotating an image with high-level semantic descriptions has emerged as an important and challenging research topic in recent years.

In the past couple of years, many novel algorithmic techniques have been proposed to deal with the problem of image annotation, such as nested deep belief nets based method [1], covariance discriminative based method [2], bilinear deep learning based method [3], local and global information based method [4], separable principal components analysis based method [5], graph theory based method [6], two-dimensional

Y.-J. Zhang (Ed.): ICIG 2015, Part II, LNCS 9218, pp. 396–406, 2015.
DOI: 10.1007/978-3-319-21963-9_36

multi-label active learning based method [7], Wavelet feature based metric [8], high order statistics based method [9], sparse coding based method [10].

The task of these existing algorithms is to assign appropriate labels to a given image with respect to the semantic contents of the image. There are two issues that should be considered when designing an effective and efficient image annotation algorithm: on one hand, the number of labeled images is often very small while the number of unlabeled images is often very large; on the other hand, an image is generally represented by a combination of feature set, such as color, shape and texture. The performance of image annotation is seriously affected by the above discussed two issues. To address the first issue, the semi-supervised methods are adopted to leverage the information contained in unlabeled images to improve the prediction performance [11, 12]. To address the second issue, the multi-view learning algorithms are utilized to achieve the informative and representative training images to reduce the amount of labeled samples required for training [13]. In multi-view learning, multiple classifiers are trained separately using several different views extracted from the labeled samples, then these view-specific classifiers assign labels to pseudo-labeled samples and the disagreement among different view-specific classifiers is utilized to selected additional pseudo-labeled samples, finally new view-specific classifiers are re-trained using the initial labeled samples and the newly pseudo-labeled unlabeled samples to improve the overall annotation performance. The idea of multi-view learning and semi-supervised learning can be effectively integrated, such as the method proposed by Zhang in [14].

In this paper, we propose a new multi-view semi-supervised learning scheme for automatic image annotation. The basic idea of the proposed scheme, as shown in Fig. 1, is described as follows. Firstly, uncorrelated and sufficient views, such as color histogram, wavelet texture and edge direction histogram, are extracted to train V view-specific classifier $\{h_1, h_2, ..., h_v, ..., h_V\}$ independently, and the labels of each pseudo-labeled image over each view is achieved by using the learned view-specific classifier. Secondly, initial labeled samples and pairs of pseudo-labeled samples with high confidence are utilized to iteratively re-train view-specific classifiers to build better classifiers for improving the model performance. Finally, unlabeled images are assigned the category annotation using the maximum vote entropy principle based one optimally trained view-specific classifiers, and other annotations on the annotation list can be obtained based on the correlationship between annotations. The experimental results show that by taking advantage of both multi-view and multi-view the proposed approach significantly outperforms state-of-the-art methods.

The rest of the paper is organized as follows. The proposed image annotation scheme is detailed in Sect. 2. The experimental results and some discussions of the proposed image annotation scheme are presented in Sect. 3. Finally, this paper is concluded in Sect. 4.

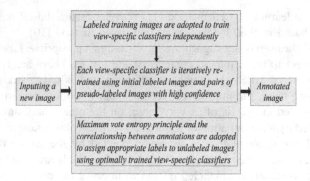

Fig. 1. The basic idea of the proposed scheme.

2 Multi-view Semi-supervised Annotation Scheme

In this section, we will detail the proposed multi-view semi-supervised learning scheme, which consists of multi-view classifiers learning process based on the uncorrelated and sufficient visual features, multi-view classifiers optimal process based on the initial labeled samples and pairs of pseudo-labeled samples with high confidence level, multi-view annotation process based on trained view-specific classifiers.

Before detailing the scheme of multi-view semi-supervised learning process, there are some notations that need to be pre-defined.

- An labeled image set LS with L images $\{x_1, x_2, ..., x_l, ..., x_L\}$ and a pseudo-labeled image set PS with U images $\{x_{L+1}, x_{L+2}, ..., x_{L+u}, ..., x_{L+U}\}$.
- An image x_l from labeled image set is attached with a set of annotations $Y = \{y_1, y_2, ..., y_k, ..., y_K\}$ where K is the number of annotations and each $y_k \in \{-1, 1\}$ indicates whether one semantic concept occurs (1) or not (−1).
- An image x_{L+u} from pseudo-labeled image set is represented as multi-view vector $\{x_{(L+u)1}, x_{(L+u)2}, ..., x_{(L+u)v}, ..., x_{(L+u)V}\}$ where V is the number of views.

2.1 Learning Process of Multi-view Classifiers

The process of each view-specific classifier learning is detailed as follows:

- Several distinct feature sets, such as color histogram, wavelet texture and edge direction histogram, are extracted and considered as uncorrelated and sufficient views of an image, then one view-specific classifier (Support Vector Machine) hv on the vth view is trained to predict decision boundaries between different categories using initial labeled image set $\{x_1, x_2, ..., x_l, ..., x_L\}$:

$$h_v : x_{lv} \rightarrow y_k, l \in (1, L), v \in (1, V), y_k \in Y \tag{1}$$

2.2   Semi-supervised Optimal Process of Multi-view Classifiers

The semi-supervised optimal process of multi-view classifiers is detailed as follows:

- Let p_{uv}^k denotes the probability of one pseudo-labeled sample $x_{(L + u)}$ belongs to the kth category in the vth view:

$$p_{uv}^k = p_u^k(h_v) = p(y_k = 1|x_{(L+u)v})$$

(2)

The prediction of the pseudo-labeled sample $x_{(L + u)}$ belonging to the kth category in the vth view can be computed using the following formula:

$$y_{uv}^k = \text{sgn}(p(y_k = 1|x_{(L+u)v}) - p(y_k = -1|x_{(L+u)v}))$$

(3)

For comprehensive evaluation of the confidence of each pseudo-labeled image's annotation results over all views, the Gaussian distance is here adopted to measure the disagreement level of annotation results over pseudo-labeled images using different view-specific classifier. Let $p_{uv} = \{p_{uv}^1, p_{uv}^2, ..., p_{uv}^k, ..., p_{uv}^K\}$ denotes the probability of the pseudo-labeled image $x_{(L + u)}$ belongs to each category in the vth view, and then a disagreement measurement between any two view-specific classifiers h_v and $h_{v'}$ over any a random pseudo-labeled image $x_{(L + u)}$ can be formulated as follows:

$$DL(h_v, h_{v'}) = \sum_{\{v,v'\} \subseteq V \wedge v \neq v'} \exp\left(-\|p_{uv} - p_{uv'}\|_2^2\right)$$

$$= \sum_{\{v,v'\} \subseteq V \wedge v \neq v'} \exp\left(-\left(\sqrt{\sum_{k \in (1,K)} (p_u^k(h_v) - p_u^k(h_{v'}))^2}\right)^2\right)$$

(4)

This notion of disagreement can then be extended to all view-specific classifiers by taking the average disagreement between any pair of view-specific classifiers:

$$\widetilde{DL}(h_1, h_2, ..., h_v, ..., h_V) = \frac{2}{V(V - 1)} \sum_{\{v,v'\} \subseteq V \wedge v \neq v'} DL(h_v, h_{v'})$$

(5)

- According to the multi-view learning framework proposed by Sridharan et al. [15] for classification, a set of classifiers $\{h_{(v)}\}$ over each v view is optimally re-trained by maximizing their consensus on the unlabeled data. Specifically, each view-specific classifier is iteratively re-trained using initial labeled images and additional pseudo-labeled images, and the optimal procedure over each v view is repeated until the disagreement level of pseudo-labeled image set does not decrease after re-training. The optimal process of the multi-view semi-supervised classifier is detailed in Table 1.

Table 1. Optimal process of each multi-view semi-supervised classifier

---

Input:
- Training image collection containing labeled image set LS $(x_1, x_2, ..., x_l, ..., x_L)$ and pseudo-labeled image set PS $(x_{L+1}, x_{L+2}, ..., x_{L+u}, ..., x_{L+u})$;
- Size of the pair of two pseudo-labeled images S;
- View-specific classifier set $\{h_1, h_2, ..., h_v, ..., h_V\}$;

Initialize:
- For each view v, train $h_v^k(0)$ using the labeled image set LS $(x_1, x_2, ..., x_l, ..., x_L)$;

Multi-View Semi-Supervised Classifier Learning:
- $t \leftarrow 0$;
- **repeat**
    for $s=1, ..., S$ **do**
      sample (u, u') from S
      if $p_u^k(h_v(t)) - p_u^k(h_v(t)) \geq 0.25$ **then**
        $LS \leftarrow LS \cup \{(x_{L+u}, +1), (x_{L+u'}, -1)\}$
      else if $p_u^k(h_v(t)) - p_u^k(h_v(t)) < -0.25$ **then**
        $LS \leftarrow LS \cup \{(x_{L+u}, -1), (x_{L+u'}, +1)\}$
      end if
    end for
    $t \leftarrow t + 1$;
    for each view v, train $h_v(t)$ over each category using the labeled image set LS;
  until $DL\big(h_1(t+1), ..., h_V(t+1)\big) \geq DL\big(h_1(t), ..., h_V(t)\big)$

output: $h_v(t), v \in \{1, 2, ..., V\}$

During the iterative process of optimally training each view-specific classifier, the pairs of pseudo-labeled images with distinct difference in view-specific property are added into the initial labeled images to re-train each view-specific classifier to improve prediction performance of assigning appropriate labels for unlabeled images.

2.3 Annotation Process Using Multi-view Classifiers

For each image, there are many semantic annotations can be assigned to it based on the image content. Among these semantic annotations, the first annotation on the annotation list, also considered as the category annotation, should be first achieved since it semantically describes the main visual content. Other annotations on the annotation list can then be successively achieved based on the correlationship between annotations. Therefore, the annotation process here consists of the following two steps: (1) The first annotation, namely the category annotation, can be achieved using the maximum vote entropy principle based on the results of optimally trained multi-view classifiers; (2) Other annotations on the annotation list can be successively obtained based on the correlationship between annotations.

2.3.1 Annotation Process of the Category Annotation

For each unlabeled image, the maximum vote entropy principle is employed to obtain the first annotation, namely the category annotation. Let l_{qv}^k denote that an unlabeled image xq from the unlabeled image set $\{x_1, x_2, \ldots, x_q, \ldots, x_Q\}$ is assigned the annotation k over the view v, and p_{qv}^k has the maximum value in the annotation probability set p_{qv}:

$$p_{qv}^k = \arg\max_k \left(p_{qv}^1, p_{qv}^2, \ldots, p_{qv}^k, \ldots, p_{qv}^K\right) \tag{6}$$

Vote entropy, as a measure of the level of disagreement, is here utilized to metric the purity of annotation results over all views:

$$VE_q = \sum_{k=1}^{K} \frac{vt\left(l_{q(.)}^k\right)}{V} \log \frac{vt\left(l_{q(.)}^k\right)}{V} \tag{7}$$

where $vt(l_{q(.)}^k)$ denotes the number of votes that the unlabeled image x_q is assigned to the annotation k in each view v.

The unlabeled image x_q can then be automatically assigned to the annotation which has a maximum number of votes when the following inequality is true:

$$VE_q \geq \mu - \phi^{-1}(\alpha) \times \delta \tag{8}$$

where Φ is standard normal distribution of annotation result over all unlabeled images as formulated in Eq. (9), μ and $\sigma\psi$ are the expectation and variance of the standard normal distribution respectively, and $\beta\psi$ is the level of disagreement confidence.

$$VE = \sum_{q=1}^{Q} VE_q \tag{9}$$

2.3.2 Annotation Process of Other Annotations

After achieving the category annotation, other annotations on the annotation list can then be successively obtained with respect to the correlationship between these annotations, which is formulated as follows:

$$corr(y_i, y_j) = \frac{num(y_i, y_j)}{\min(num(y_i), num(y_j))} \tag{10}$$

where $num(y_i)$ and $num(y_j)$ are defined as the number of images annotated by annotation y_i and y_j respectively, and $num(y_i, y_j)$ is defined as the number of images annotated by both y_i and y_j.

3 Data Set and Experimental Setup

In this section, we will first present the dataset used in our experiments, then describe the features selected to train multi-view classifiers, and finally discuss the evaluation measures for image annotation.

3.1 Dataset

All the experiments in this work are conducted on a dataset consisting of 50000 images, crawled from the image share website Flicker. Ten most popular tags, including bird, bear, cat, flower, fox, plane, tree, train, sky, and sunset, are selected to implement the annotation-based retrieval. The associated annotations of each retrieved image are ranked according to the option of interesting, and the top 5000 images for each type of retrieval tag are collected together with their associated information, including tags, uploading time, location, etc. Since many of the collected annotations are misspelling or meaningless, it is necessary to perform a pre-filtering for these annotations. More specifically, one annotation can be kept only when the annotation is matched with a term in the Wikipedia. In our case, 17226 unique annotations in total are obtained.

For quantitative evaluation, 24000 images randomly selected from the dataset are adopted as the training set and other 26000 images are selected as the testing set. To get the ground truth, ten volunteers are invited to view each image and exhaustively give their own annotations. Then, the ground truth annotations of each image are the intersection of the given annotations.

3.2 Feature Selection

The problem of feature selection has been an active research topic for many decades due to the fact that feature selection might have a great impact on the final annotation results. In the implementation, the following low-level features including color, texture, semantic description, and textual feature are extracted as the visual descriptors:

- 128-D histogram in HSV color space with 8 bins for Hue and 4 bins each for Saturation and Value;
- 44-D auto-correlogram in HSV color space with inhomogeneous quantization into 44 color bands;
- 225-D block-wise moments in LAB color space, which are extracted over 5×5 fixed grid partitions, each block is described by a 9-D feature;
- 18-D edge direction histogram in HSV color space with two 9-dimensional vectors in horizontal and vertical directions respectively;
- 36-D Pyramid Wavelet texture extracted over 6-level Haar Wavelet transformation, each level is described by a 6-D feature: mean and variance of coefficients in high/high, high/low, and low/high bands;
- A bag-of-words representation obtained using the scale-invariant feature transform method;

- A set of textual feature extracted from annotations associated to each image and a bag-of-words representation obtained using a tf.idf term weighting after filtering out those rare words.

3.3   Evaluation Measures

An annotation-based evaluation measure, normalized discounted cumulative gain at the top s ($NDCG@s$ for short), is here utilized to evaluate the annotation performance. In contrast to other measures, such as precision and recall which only measure the accuracy of annotation results, $NDCG@s$ can measure different levels of relevance and prefer optimal relevance as close as possible to actual relevance. Therefore, this evaluation metric can be utilized to better reflect users' requirement of ranking the most relevant annotations at the top of the annotation list, and is computed as:

$$NDCG@s = \frac{1}{\Gamma} \sum_{i=1}^{s} \frac{2^{rel(i)} - 1}{\log(1 + i)} \qquad (11)$$

where Γ, a normalization factor derived from the top s annotations on the annotation list, is here adopted to ensure the value of $NDCG@s$ is 1, and $rel(i)$ is the relevance of an assigned annotation at the location i.

Here, the relevance of each assigned annotation is divided into the following five levels: the most relevant is set as 5, relevant is set as 4, partially relevant is set as 3, weakly relevant is set as 2, and irrelevant is set as 1. The $NDCG@s$ of each unlabeled image is first computed, and then the mean of $NDCG@s$ over the whole unlabeled images are here reported as the final metric of performance evaluation.

3.4   Compared Algorithms

In the current implementation, the proposed multi-view semi-supervised classification approach is compared with other three annotation approaches: one supervised view-specific classification approach (SVS for short) [16], one semi-supervised view-specific classification approach (SSVS for short) [17], and one semi-supervised multi-view classification approach (SSMV for short) [18].

4   Experimental Results

In this section, we will first introduce the process of optimal training over each view-specific classifier, then present the experimental results and give some analysis.

4.1   Optimal Training Process

To simulate a semi-supervised learning scenario, the training dataset is manually divide into two subsets: one subset is utilized as the labeled set in which the labels are known, and the other subset is utilized as the pseudo-labeled set in which the labels are hidden. The split is performed randomly, and each experiment is repeated 50 times, over 50 different subsamplings of the training data. Four different split size of the labeled set are 1000, 2000, 5000, and 10000 respectively, and the corresponding split size of the pseudo-labeled set are 23000, 22000, 19000, and 14000 respectively. In each split, the proportion of each class is kept similar to what is observed in the training dataset. The test collection is left unchanged, and all reported experimental results apply to this test collection.

4.2   Experimental Results

Performance comparison with respect to average $NDCG@s$ of four different annotation methods with 1000 labeled and 23000 pseudo-labeled samples are illustrated in Fig. 2, where the experimental results are averaged over 50 random splits of the training samples and all the classes. It can be clearly seen from Fig. 2 that the proposed semi-supervised multi-view method outperforms the supervised view-specific annotation method SVS, the semi-supervised view-specific annotation method, as well as the semi-supervised multi-view annotation method SSMV. This improvement confirms the method from the following two aspects: one is that the performance of multi-view classifiers can be improved by adding pairs of pseudo-labeled images with high confidence into the initial labeled image set to iteratively retraining; the other is that the property of multi-view features can be utilized in the process of training stage and testing stage to improve the annotation performance.

The performance comparison between different methods with respect to different labeled samples is shown in Fig. 3, which shows the similar conclusions as in Fig. 2.

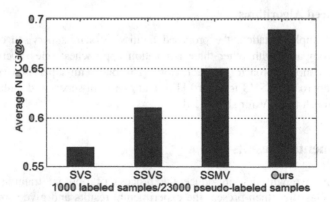

Fig. 2. Performance comparison of different annotation methods in terms of average $NDCG@s$ with 1000 labeled and 23000 pseudo-labeled samples.

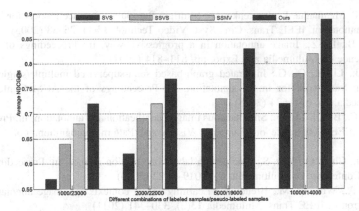

Fig. 3. Performance comparison of different annotation methods in terms of average *NDCG@s* with different labeled and pseudo-labeled samples.

5 Conclusion

In the training process, each view-specific classifier is first trained independently using uncorrelated and sufficient views, and each view-specific classifier is then iteratively re-trained using initial labeled samples and additional pseudo-labeled samples with high confidence. In the annotation process, each unlabeled image is assigned appropriate semantic annotations based on the maximum vote entropy principle and the correlationship between annotations. Experiments conducted on the Flicker dataset show that the proposed scheme can better reflect the images' visual content compared with state-of-the-art methods.

It is worth noting that although the performance of the annotation has been improved to some extent, there are several potential works for future development. Firstly, experiments will be conducted on larger datasets and different datasets using the proposed annotation method. Then, other features will be investigated to improve the performance of image annotation. Finally, we will explore annotation quality improvement problem in a more general scenario, such as annotation categorization, to construct the better lexical indexing for social images.

Acknowledgement. This work is supported by Postdoctoral Foundation of China under No. 2014M550297, Postdoctoral Foundation of Jiangsu Province under No. 1302087B.

References

1. Duygulu, P., Barnard, K., de Freitas, J.F.G., Forsyth, D.: Object recognition as machine translation: learning a lexicon for a fixed image vocabulary. In: Heyden, A., Sparr, G., Nielsen, M., Johansen, P. (eds.) ECCV 2002, Part IV. LNCS, vol. 2353, pp. 97–112. Springer, Heidelberg (2002)

2. Feng, S., Manmatha, R., Lavrenko, V.: Multiple Bernoulli relevance models for image and video annotation. IEEE Trans. Circ. Syst. Video Technol. **13**(1), 26–38 (2003)
3. Wang, B., Li, Z.: Image annotation in a progressive way. In: Proceedings of the IEEE Conference on Multimedia and Expo, pp. 811–814 (2007)
4. Tang, J., Li, H., Qi, G.: Integrated graph-based semi-supervised multiple/single instance learning framework for image annotation. In: Proceedings of the ACM Conference on Multimedia, pp. 631–634 (2008)
5. Wang, C., Blei, D., Li, F.: Simultaneous image classification and annotation. In: Proceedings of the IEEE Conference on Computer Vision and Pattern Recognition, pp. 1903–1910 (2009)
6. Tang, J., Chen, Q., Yan, S.: One person labels one million images. In: Proceedings of the ACM Conference on Multimedia, pp. 1019–1022 (2010)
7. Ulges, A., Worring, M., Breuel, T.: Learning visual contexts for image annotation from flickr groups. IEEE Trans. Multimedia **13**(2), 330–341 (2011)
8. Verma, Y., Jawahar, C.V.: Image annotation using metric learning in semantic neighbourhoods. In: Fitzgibbon, A., Lazebnik, S., Perona, P., Sato, Y., Schmid, C. (eds.) ECCV 2012, Part III. LNCS, vol. 7574, pp. 836–849. Springer, Heidelberg (2012)
9. Zhu, S., Hu, J., Wang, B., Shen, S.: Image annotation using high order statistics in non-euclidean spaces. Vis. Commun. Image Represent. **24**(8), 1342–1348 (2013)
10. Huang, J., Liu, H., Shen, J., Yan, S.: Towards efficient sparse coding for scalable image annotation. In: Proceedings of the ACM Conference on Multimedia, pp. 947–956 (2013)
11. Marin-Castro, H., Sucar, L., Morales, E.: Automatic image annotation using a semi-supervised ensemble of classifiers. In: Rueda, L., Mery, D., Kittler, J. (eds.) CIARP 2007. LNCS, vol. 4756, pp. 487–495. Springer, Heidelberg (2007)
12. Sayar, A., Vural, F.: Image annotation with semi-supervised clustering. In: Proceedings of the IEEE Symposium on Computer and Information Sciences, pp. 12–17 (2009)
13. Liu, W., Tao, D., Cheng, J., Tang, Y.: Multiview hessian discriminative sparse coding for image annotation. Comput. Vis. Image Underst. **118**(1), 50–60 (2014)
14. Zhang, X., Cheng, J., Xu, C., Lu, H., Ma, S.: Multi-view multi-label active learning for image classification. In: Proceedings of the IEEE Conference on Multimedia and Expo, pp. 258–261 (2009)
15. Sridharan, K., Kakade, S.: An information theoretic framework for multiview learning. In: Proceedings of the Annual Conference on Learning Theory, pp. 403–414 (2008)
16. Blum, A., Mitchell, T.: Combining labelled and unlabelled data with co-training. In: Proceedings of the IEEE Conference on Learning Theory, pp. 92–100 (1998)
17. Zhu, S., Liu, Y.: Semi-supervised learning model based efficient image annotation. IEEE Sig. Process. Lett. **16**(11), 989–992 (2009)
18. Amini, M., Usunier, N., Goutte, C.: Learning from multiple partially observed views-an application to multilingual text categorization. In: Proceedings of the IEEE Conference on Neural Information Processing Systems, pp. 28–36 (2009)

Image Denoising with Higher Order Total Variation and Fast Algorithms

Wenchao Zeng[1], Xueying Zeng[2]([✉]), and Zhen Yue[1]

[1] Jining First People's Hospital, Jining 272011, People's Republic of China
[2] School of Mathematical Sciences, Ocean University of China, Qingdao 266100, People's Republic of China
auwizeng@gmail.com

Abstract. In this paper, we propose an efficient higher order total variation regularization scheme for image denoising problem. By relaxing the constraints appearing in the traditional infimal convolution regularization, the proposed higher order total variation can remove the staircasing effects caused by total variation as well as preserve sharp edges and finer details well in the restored image. We characterize the solution of the proposed model using fixed point equations (via the proximity operator) and develop convergent proximity algorithms for solving the model. Our numerical experiments demonstrate the efficiency of the proposed method.

Keywords: Image denoising · Total variation · Infimal convolution · Proximity operator

1 Introduction

Noise removal is a long standing problem in image processing. Many different methods have been proposed for image denoising problem, among which the well-known Rudin-Osher-Fatemi (ROF) total variation (TV) model is one of the most popular methods [8]. This model restores the image by solving a minimization problem

$$\arg\min_{u}\{\frac{1}{2}\|u - f\|_2^2 + \lambda\,\mathrm{TV}(u)\}, \tag{1}$$

where f is the observed noisy image, $\mathrm{TV}(u)$ denotes the total variation of u and λ is the regularization parameter to balance both terms in (1). The distinctive feature of the total variation is that it can preserve sharp edges well. However, natural images usually contain smooth part that can be destroyed by TV, and therefore, the denoised image by total variation regularization often suffers the undesired staircasing effects in the flat region of the image [10]. Addressing this drawback of the total variation, many improved ROF models have been proposed in the recent literature. These approaches can be roughly divided into two categories. In the first category, some local gradient information is added to the total variation to make it differentiate different features of the image [4,5,11]. Another

© Springer International Publishing Switzerland 2015
Y.-J. Zhang (Ed.): ICIG 2015, Part II, LNCS 9218, pp. 407–416, 2015.
DOI: 10.1007/978-3-319-21963-9_37

category to reduce the staircasing effect in the restored image is to incorporate higher order derivatives into the regularization term. One successful approach in this direction was give in [2] who suggested to use the infimal convolution of functionals with first and second order derivatives as regularizer. The resulting image denoising model has the form of

$$\arg\min_u\{\frac{1}{2}\|u - f\|_2^2 + \text{ICTV}(u)\}, \tag{2}$$

where $\text{ICTV}(u)$ is the infimal convolution regularization that will be defined in Sect. 2. Although the staircaing effects caused by total variation can be alleviated to some extent, the infimal convolution regularization often penalizes the smooth regions of the image too much and may blur the sharp edges and finer details of the image.

In this paper, a novel higher order total variation regularization is proposed to remove the staircasing effects while still preserve sharp edges and finer details in the restored image. We first give an equivalent formulation of the traditional infimal convolution regularizer and motivate the proposed higher order total variation by relaxing the constrains appearing in traditional infimal convolution regularizer. This modification will not increase any difficulties for the numerical treatments of the resulting image denoising model. We characterize the solution of the proposed model via fixed points of fixed point equations in which the proximity operators of convex functions are involved. Based on the characterization, the convergent proximity algorithm is developed to solve the model.

The paper is organized as follows. We shall briefly introduce the difference matrices that are used to define total variation and the regularization terms in this paper in Sect. 2. In Sect. 3, we present the higher order total variation regularization term and the proposed image denoising model. We characterize the solution of the model via fixed point equations and develop numerical algorithms for the proposed model in Sect. 4. Numerical experiments showing the performance of our method is given in Sect. 5. Finally, we conclude our paper in Sect. 6.

2   Difference Matrices and Total Variation

In this section, we present the precise definition of the regularization terms appearing in model (1) and (2). For the sake of simplicity, we assume the image is an $n \times n$ square matrix for some integer n. To describe the problem in matrix algebra language, we treat the image as a vector in $\mathbb{R}^N$ by sequentially concatenating the columns of the image. Here we assume that $N = n^2$. To define the total variation of the image u, we need a $n \times n$ backward difference matrix

$$D := \begin{bmatrix} 0 & & & \\ -1 & 1 & & \\ & \ddots & \ddots & \\ & & -1 & 1 \end{bmatrix},$$

then $-D^\top D$ is the second order central difference matrix. Since we reshape the square image into a vector, we can use

$$D_x := I_n \otimes D, \quad D_y := D \otimes I_n$$

as the first order difference matrices for the image, where $\otimes$ denotes the Kronecker product of the matrices and I_n denotes the $n \times n$ identity matrix. Hence, by setting the gradient matrix

$$B_1 := [D_x; D_y]$$

which is formed by stacking two matrices into a single one, and $\varphi : \mathbb{R}^{2N} \to \mathbb{R}$ defined for $z \in \mathbb{R}^{2N}$ as

$$\varphi(z) := \sum_{i=1}^{N} \sqrt{z_i^2 + z_{i+N}^2}, \tag{3}$$

the composition $\varphi(B_1 u)$ computes the total variation $\mathrm{TV}(u)$ appearing in the model (1).

The second order difference matrices for the image can be defined as

$$D_{xx} := I_n \otimes (-D^\top D), \quad D_{yy} := (-D^\top D) \otimes I_n, \quad D_{xy} := (-D^\top) \otimes D, \quad D_{yx} := D \otimes (-D^\top),$$

using which we can get the second order gradient matrix

$$B_2 := [D_{xx}; D_{xy}; D_{yx}; D_{yy}].$$

The first and second order gradient matrices B_1 and B_2 are related by

$$B_2 = RB_1$$

where

$$R = \begin{bmatrix} I_n \otimes -D^t & 0 \\ -D^t \otimes I_n & 0 \\ 0 & I_n \otimes -D^t \\ 0 & -D^t \otimes I_n \end{bmatrix}.$$

Based on our notation, the regularizer $\mathrm{ICTV}(u)$ in (2) which use the infimal convolution of functionals with first and second order derivatives has the form of

$$\mathrm{ICTV}(u) := \min_{u=u_1+u_2} \{\lambda_1 \varphi(B_1 u_1) + \lambda_2 \psi(B_2 u_2)\}, \tag{4}$$

where λ_1 and λ_2 are positive parameters balancing between the first and second order derivatives, and $\psi : \mathbb{R}^{4N} \to \mathbb{R}$ is defined $z \in \mathbb{R}^{4N}$ as

$$\psi(z) := \sum_{i=1}^{N} \sqrt{\sum_{j=0}^{3} z_{i+jN}^2}. \tag{5}$$

3   The Proposed Model

In this section, we give the proposed higher order total variation regularization term and the resulting image denoising model. The proposed regularizer can be seen as the improved version of the infimal convolution regularizer in (4). The following lemma presents an equivalent form of the infimal convolution regularizer in (4) which facilitates us to motivate the proposed higher order total variation regularization term.

Lemma 1. *For any u, we have that*

$$\text{ICTV}(u) = \min_{\substack{B_1 u = d + x \\ d,\, x \in \mathcal{R}(B_1)}} \{\lambda_1 \varphi(d) + \lambda_2 \psi(Rx)\}, \tag{6}$$

where $\mathcal{R}(\cdot)$ denotes the range of a matrix.

Proof. Clearly, we can conclude that

$$\min_{\substack{B_1 u = d + x \\ d,\, x \in \mathcal{R}(B_1)}} \{\lambda_1 \varphi(d) + \lambda_2 \psi(Rx)\} = \min_{B_1 u = B_1 u_1 + B_1 u_2} \{\lambda_1 \varphi(B_1 u_1) + \lambda_2 \psi(B_2 u_2)\}$$

by setting $d = B_1 u_1$ and $x = B_1 u_2$.

Since $u = u_1 + u_2$ implies that $B_1 u = B_1 u_1 + B_1 u_2$, we can get

$$\min_{u = u_1 + u_2} \{\lambda_1 \varphi(B_1 u_1) + \lambda_2 \psi(B_2 u_2)\} \geq \min_{B_1 u = B_1 u_1 + B_1 u_2} \{\lambda_1 \varphi(B_1 u_1) + \lambda_2 \psi(B_2 u_2)\} \tag{7}$$

On the other hand, for any u_1, u_2 satisfying $B_1 u = B_1 u_1 + B_1 u_2$, there exists $v \in \mathcal{N}(B_1)$ such that $u = u_1 + u_2 + v$, and we can have

$$\lambda_1 \varphi(B_1 u_1) + \lambda_2 \psi(B_2 u_2) = \lambda_1 \varphi(B_1(u_1 + v)) + \lambda_2 \psi(B_2 u_2)$$
$$\geq \min_{u = u_1 + u_2} \{\lambda_1 \varphi(B_1 u_1) + \lambda_2 \psi(B_2 u_2)\}$$

which implies that

$$\min_{B_1 u = B_1 u_1 + B_1 u_2} \{\lambda_1 \varphi(B_1 u_1) + \lambda_2 \psi_2(B_2 u_2)\} \geq \min_{u = u_1 + u_2} \{\lambda_1 \varphi(B_1 u_1) + \lambda_2 \psi(B_2 u_2)\}$$

This together with (7) complete the proof.

The proposed higher order total variation regularization term can be seen as the improved version of the infimal convolution regularizer and has the form of

$$\text{HTV}(u) = \min_{B_1 u = d + x} \{\lambda_1 \varphi(d) + \lambda_2 \psi(Rx)\}. \tag{8}$$

As can be seen from Lemma 1, the difference between the original infimal convolution relarization and its modified version (8) consists in the relaxed conditions on the new regularizer. For $\text{HTV}(u)$ we no longer have the restriction that

$d, x \in \mathcal{R}(B_1)$ and $B_1 u$ can be decomposed into any components d and x. The authors in [9] showed that this modification can generally lead to better numerical results than the original model (4). This modification was given a theoretical fundament in [1] based on tensor algebra and the corresponding new regularizer was called total generalized variation.

Using the higher order total variation in (8) as the regularizer, the proposed image denoising model is

$$\arg \min_{u} \{\frac{1}{2}\|u - f\|_2^2 + \mathrm{HTV}(u)\}, \tag{9}$$

which can be reformulated as an equivalent unconstrained two variables minimization problem

$$\arg \min_{u,d} \{\frac{1}{2}\|u - f\|_2^2 + \lambda_1 \varphi(d) + \lambda_2 \psi(B_2 u - Rd)\}. \tag{10}$$

Both above models are equivalent in the sense that if the pair $(\hat{u}, \hat{d})$ is the solution of model (10) then $\hat{u}$ is the solution of model (9). Therefore, we can solve model (10) as an alternative of directly solving model (9).

4 Minimization Algorithm

The main focus of this section is to give numerical proximity algorithm that solve the proposed model (10). Proximity algorithm was proposed in [6] for solving the ROF model and outperformed the benchmarking split Bregman iteration method. The application of the proximity algorithm to other image models can be found in [3,7]. The main idea of this algorithm is firstly characterize the solution of the model via the fixed point of fixed point equations in which the proximity operators of the convex functions are included, and then develop efficient numerical algorithms via various fixed point iterations. The proximity operator of a real-valued function g is defined for $x \in \mathbb{R}^d$ and $\gamma > 0$ by

$$\mathrm{prox}_{\gamma g}(x) := \arg \min_{y} \{\frac{1}{2}\|y - x\|_2^2 + \gamma g(y)\}$$

For convenience of developing numerical algorithms, we can rewrite the proposed model into a general form of

$$\arg \min_{w} \{F(w) + \lambda_2 \psi(Bw)\}, \tag{11}$$

by defining the matrix B, the vector w and the function F as

$$B = [B_2, -R], w = [u; d]$$

and

$$F(w) = \frac{1}{2}\|u - f\|_2^2 + \lambda_1 \varphi(d)$$

respectively. The following proposition characterizes a solution of model (11) in terms of fixed point equations.

Proposition 1. *If $\hat{w}$ is a solution of model* (11), *then for any $\sigma, \gamma > 0$, there exist two vectors b, c such that*

$$\hat{w} = \text{prox}_{\frac{1}{\sigma}F}((I - \frac{\gamma}{\sigma}B^tB)\hat{w} - \frac{\gamma}{\sigma}B^t(b - c))$$

$$c = \text{prox}_{\frac{1}{\gamma}\psi}(b + B\hat{w}) \tag{12}$$

$$b = b + Bw - c$$

Conversely, if there exist positive parameters σ, γ and vectors b, c and $\hat{w}$ satisfying equations in (12), *then $\hat{w}$ is a solution of model* (11).

Proof. See Proposition 5 in [3].

According to Proposition 1, the solution of model (10) is characterized by the fixed point equations in (12). Based on these fixed point equations, we can naturally propose an iterative algorithm that generates the sequence $\{w^k, c^k, b^k\}$ from arbitrary initial vector (w^0, c^0, b^0). This iterative procedure may be stated as follows:

$$\begin{cases} w^{k+1} = \text{prox}_{\frac{1}{\sigma}F}((I - \frac{\gamma}{\sigma}B^tB)w^k - \frac{\gamma}{\sigma}B^t(b^k - c^k)) \\ c^{k+1} = \text{prox}_{\frac{1}{\gamma}\psi}(b^k + Bw^{k+1}) \\ b^{k+1} = b^k + Bw^{k+1} - c^{k+1} \end{cases} \tag{13}$$

The following theorem establishes a convergence result of the proposed iterative scheme (13), its proof can be found in Theorem 4.1 in [3].

Theorem 1. *If the positive numbers γ and σ are chosen to satisfy*

$$\frac{\sigma}{\gamma} < \frac{1}{\|B\|_2^2}, \tag{14}$$

then the sequence $\{(w^k, b^k, c^k)\}$ generated by the iterative scheme (13) *converges to the solution of model* (10).

Implementing the iterative procedure (13) requires the availability of explicit forms of two proximity operators $\text{prox}_{\frac{1}{\sigma}F}$ and $\text{prox}_{\frac{1}{\gamma}\psi}$. We next present explicit forms of these proximity operators. We first give the closed forms of the proximity operator of F. Remembering that $w = [u; d]$ and $F(w) = \frac{1}{2}\|u - f\|_2^2 + \lambda_1\varphi(d)$, the corresponding proximity operator of F in (13) reads

$$\begin{bmatrix} u^{k+1} \\ d^{k+1} \end{bmatrix} = \text{prox}_{\frac{1}{\sigma}F}((I - \frac{\gamma}{\sigma}B^tB)w^k - \frac{\gamma}{\sigma}B^t(b^k - c^k)) = \arg\min_{u,d}\{\frac{1}{2}\| \begin{bmatrix} u \\ d \end{bmatrix}$$

$$- \begin{bmatrix} (I - \frac{\gamma}{\sigma}B_2^tB_2)u^k - \frac{\gamma}{\sigma}B_2^t(b^k - c^k) \\ (I - \frac{\gamma}{\sigma}R^tR)d^k + \frac{\gamma}{\sigma}R^t(b^k - c^k) \end{bmatrix}\|^2 + \frac{1}{2\sigma}\|u - f\|^2 + \frac{\lambda_1}{\sigma}\varphi(d)\} \tag{15}$$

The minimization problem in (15) is very easy to compute since it can solved separately with respect to u^{k+1} and d^{k+1}, that is we have

$$u^{k+1} = \frac{1}{1+\sigma}f + \frac{\sigma}{1+\sigma}((I - \frac{\gamma}{\sigma}B_2^tB_2)u^k - \frac{\gamma}{\sigma}B_2^t(b^k - c^k))$$

$$d^{k+1} = \text{prox}_{\frac{\lambda_1}{\sigma}\varphi}((I - \frac{\gamma}{\sigma}R^tR)d^k + \frac{\gamma}{\sigma}R^t(b^k - c^k)). \tag{16}$$

Both of the proximity operators $\text{prox}_{\frac{1}{\gamma}\psi}$ and $\text{prox}_{\frac{\lambda_1}{\sigma}\varphi}$ appearing in (13) and (16) have the closed-form solutions respectively. For $t > 0$ and $x \in \mathbb{R}^{2N}$ and $\widetilde{x} \in \mathbb{R}^{4N}$, set $y := \text{prox}_{t\varphi}(x)$ and $z := \text{prox}_{t\psi}(\widetilde{x})$, writing $\bar{x}_i := [x_i; x_{i+N}]$, and $\bar{\widetilde{x}}_i := [\widetilde{x}_i; \widetilde{x}_{i+N}; \widetilde{x}_{i+2N}; \widetilde{x}_{i+3N}]$, for $i = 1, 2, \cdots, N$, we have

$$\begin{bmatrix} y_i \\ y_{i+N} \end{bmatrix} = \max\left\{\|\bar{x}_i\|_2 - t, 0\right\} \frac{\bar{x}_i}{\|\bar{x}_i\|_2} \tag{17}$$

and

$$\begin{bmatrix} z_i \\ z_{i+N} \\ z_{i+2N} \\ z_{i+3N} \end{bmatrix} = \max\left\{\|\bar{\widetilde{x}}_i\|_2 - t, 0\right\} \frac{\bar{\widetilde{x}}_i}{\|\bar{\widetilde{x}}_i\|_2} \tag{18}$$

respectively.

In summary, we have the following convergent algorithm for solving problem (10):

Algorithm 1. Proximity algorithm to solve the proposed model (10).

---

1. Given: f and positive parameters $\lambda_1, \lambda_2, \sigma, \gamma$ satisfies $\frac{\sigma}{\gamma} < \frac{1}{\|B\|^2}$
2. Initialization: $u^0 = 0, d^0 = 0, b^0 = 0, c^0 = 0$
3. For $k \in \mathbb{N}$,
   (a) $u^{k+1} = \frac{1}{1+\sigma}f + \frac{\sigma}{1+\sigma}((I - \frac{\gamma}{\sigma}B_2^t B_2)u^k - \frac{\gamma}{\sigma}B_2^t(b^k - c^k))$
   $d^{k+1} = \text{prox}_{\frac{\lambda_1}{\sigma}\varphi}((I - \frac{\gamma}{\sigma}R^t R)d^k + \frac{\gamma}{\sigma}R^t(b^k - c^k))$
   (b) $c^{k+1} = \text{prox}_{\frac{1}{\gamma}\psi}(b^k + B_2 u^{k+1} - Rd^{k+1})$
   (c) $b^{k+1} = b^k + B_2 u^{k+1} - Rd^{k+1} - c^{k+1}$
   (d) Stop, if u^{k+1} converges or satisfies a stopping criteria; otherwise, set $k \leftarrow k+1$.
4. Write the output from the above loop as: $\hat{u}, \hat{d}$

---

5   Experiments

In this section, we justify the proposed higher order total variation regularization term and image denoising model by its performance in removing Gaussian noise from images. The peak signal-to-noise ration(PSNR) is used to measure the quality of the restored image. We select the standard pepper and lena images and a CT image as our testing data. Both of the lena and pepper are with the size of 256×256, and the CT image is with the size of 555×555. All of the images are shown in Fig. 1. The regularization parameters are chosen to produce the highest PSNR values in all of the experiments. The stopping criterion of all of the algorithms is that the relative error between the successive iterates of the restored images should satisfy the following inequality

$$\frac{\|u^{i+1} - u^i\|_2^2}{\|u^i\|_2^2} \leq 10^{-4}$$

Lena   Pepper   CT

Fig. 1. The original images.

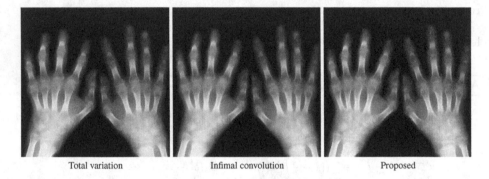

Total variation   Infimal convolution   Proposed

Fig. 2. The restored CT images in the case of Gaussian noise with $\delta=10$.

where u^i is the denoised image at the i-th iteration. Each PSNR value reported in this section is the averaged result of three runs.

We add additive white Gaussian noise with standard deviation $\delta = 10$ and $\delta = 20$ to the lena, pepper and CT images respectively. We use the ROF model (1), the infimal convolution model (2), and the model (9) which is based on our proposed higher order total variation to restore the images. The PSNR results of all restored images are shown in Table 1. We can see that our proposed model can produce the restored images with the higher PSNR values than those of the ROF model and infimal convolution model. To see the visual effects of the restored images, we show the CT images (the case of $\delta = 10$) in Fig. 2. Figure 3 is the zoomed version of Fig. 2. It can be clearly seen the staircasing effects caused by the total variation when the image is zoomed in. The infimal convolution regularization can remove the staircasing effects caused by TV, however, the visible blurring artifacts at the edges are introduced. Our proposed higher order total variation regularization can produce more favorable result without visual artifacts while still preserve sharp edges and finer details well.

Table 1. The summary of the restoration results of Models (1), (2), and (9).

Model	$\delta = 10$			$\delta = 20$		
	Lena	Pepper	CT	Lena	Pepper	CT
Model (1)	32.30	32.47	36.84	29.07	29.67	33.67
Model (2)	33.07	33.28	37.55	29.55	30.21	34.51
Model (9)	**33.52**	**33.69**	**37.98**	**30.06**	**30.75**	**34.86**

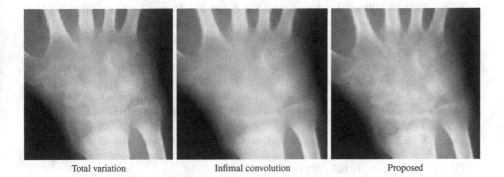

| Total variation | Infimal convolution | Proposed |

Fig. 3. Zoomed results of the restored CT images in the case of Gaussian noise with δ=10.

6 Concluding Remarks

We propose an higher order total variation regularization for image denoising problem. This regularization term can be seen as the improvement of the traditional infimal convolution type regularization and can alleviate the staircasing effects in the restored image caused by total variation. We use the proximity algorithm to solve the resulting model and establish the convergence result of the algorithm. Numerical results presented in this paper demonstrate the efficiency of the proposed method.

Acknowledgment. This work is supported by the Promotive Research Fund for Excellent Young Scientists of Shandong Province (No. BS2014DX003), by the Specialized Research Fund for the Doctoral Program of Higher Education of China (No. 20130132120022), and the Fundamental Research Funds of the Central Universities of Ocean University of China (No. 201313009).

References

1. Bredies, K., Kunisch, K., Pock, T.: Total generalized variation. SIAM J. Imaging Sci. **3**, 492–526 (2010)
2. Chambolle, A., Lions, P.: Image recovery via total variation minimization and related problems. Numer. Math. **76**, 167–188 (1997)

3. Chen, F., Shen, L., Yuesheng, X., Zeng, X.: The moreau envelope approach for the l1/tv image denoising model. Inverse Probl. Imaging **8**(1), 53–77 (2014)
4. Chen, Q., Montesinos, P., Sun, Q., Heng, P., Xia, D.: Adaptive total variation denoising based on difference curvature. Image Vis. Comput. **28**(3), 298–306 (2010)
5. Dong, Y., Hintermuller, M., Rincon-Camacho, M.: Automated regularization parameter selection in mutiscale total variation methods for image restoration. J. Math. Imaging Vis. **40**(1), 82–104 (2011)
6. Micchelli, C.A., Shen, L., Xu, Y.: Proximity algorithms for image models: Denosing. Inverse Probl. **27**(4), 045009(30pp) (2011)
7. Micchelli, C.A., Shen, L., Yuesheng, X., Zeng, X.: Proximity algorithms for the l_1/tv image denosing models. Adv. Comput. Math. **38**(2), 401–426 (2013)
8. Rudin, L., Osher, S., Fatemi, E.: Nonlinear total variation based noise removal algorithms. Phys. D **60**, 259–268 (1992)
9. Setzer, S., Steidl, G., Teuber, T.: Infimal convolution regularizations with discrete l1-type functionals. Commun. Math. Sci. **9**(3), 797–872 (2011)
10. Strong, D., Blomgren, P., Chan, T.: Spatially adaptive local feature-driven total variation minimizing image restoration. In: Proceedings of SPIE, vol. 3167, pp. 222–233 (1997)
11. Zeng, X., Li, S.: An efficient adaptive total variation regularization for image denoising. In: 2013 Seventh International Conference on Image and Graphics (ICIG), pp. 55–59. IEEE (2013)

Improve Neural Network Using Saliency

Yunong Wang[1,2(✉)], Nenghai Yu[1,2], Taifeng Wang[3], and Qing Wang[1,2]

[1] Department of Electronic Engineering and Information Science,
University of Science and Technology of China, Hefei, China
{wynd,wqing}@mail.ustc.edu.cn
[2] Key Laboratory of Electromagnetic Space Information,
Chinese Academy of Sciences, Hefei 230027, China
ynh@ustc.edu.cn
[3] Microsoft Research, Beijing 100000, China
taifengw@microsoft.com

Abstract. In traditional neural networks for image classification, every input image pixel is treated the same way. However real human visual system tends pay more attention to what they really focus on. This paper proposed a novel saliency-based network architecture for image classification named Sal-Mask Connection. After learning raw feature maps from input images using a convolutional connection, we use the saliency data as a mask for the raw feature maps. By doing an element-by-element multiplication with the saliency data on the raw feature maps, corresponding enhanced feature maps are generated, which helps the network to filter information and to ignore noise. By this means we may simulate the real human vision system more appropriately and gain a better performance. In this paper, we prove this new architecture upon two common image classification benchmark networks, and we verify them on the STL-10 datasets. Experimental results show that this method outperforms the traditional CNNs.

Keywords: Sal-Mask connection · Machine learning · Convolutional neural network · Saliency · Image classification

1 Introduction

Convolutional neural network (CNN) has been very popular and proved extremely effective in handling the problems of image recognition, object detection and image classification. In image classification, it has become the state-of-art. Li Wan [1] got an error rate of 0.21 % and Ciresan [2] got 0.23 % on the MNIST dataset, beating all other methods such as SVM, K-Nearest Neighbors, Boosted Stumps and those Neural Nets, none of which use convolutional connections.

The structure of CNNs is under fast and varied progress, but since LeNet-5 [3], it has become a typically standard structure for CNNs - stacked convolutional connections with one or more full connections at the end of the network. Within the net, convolutional connections are optionally followed by contrast normalization and

© Springer International Publishing Switzerland 2015
Y.-J. Zhang (Ed.): ICIG 2015, Part II, LNCS 9218, pp. 417–429, 2015.
DOI: 10.1007/978-3-319-21963-9_38

pooling connections. Many kinds of variants of this basic structure are proposed, and get the best results [4,5] so far on MNIST, CIFAR and ImageNet classification challenge. Network in Network (NIN) [6] and GoogleNet [7] reflect the trend that nets are becoming bigger and deeper while becoming more and more better. Using stacked convolutional connections as the main frame, researchers have discovered different ways to improve the performance. Alex came up with the local response normalization in NIPS 2012 [4]. Hinton proposed dropout [8] and then dropconnect [1] generalized after it. Also a novel way to train activation functions adaptively named Maxout [9] is proposed by Goodfellow. Despite all those variants of CNNs, they are all in fact the same - to stack and combine convolutional connections, pooling connections, full connections and others to form a net. A network like that can't simulate human visual system (HVS) well enough because the input image pixels of the CNNs are treated evenly. By that, it means that each pixel is treated as importantly as one another, which is handled quite differently in real HVS.

In real HVS, we tend to pay more attention to what we really focus on when we look. It is generally agreed that the HVS uses a combination of image driven data and prior models in its processing [11]. What HVS used is called Visual Saliency. The ability of the HVS to detect visual saliency is extraordinarily fast and reliable [10]. Saliency is a broad term that refers to the idea that certain parts of a scene are pre-attentively distinctive and create some form of immediate significant visual arousal within the early stages of the HVS [11]. It has been a central problem in many computer vision tasks, and helps to solve matching or correspondence problems such as object recognition, classification or tracking. Though the neural network is attempting to mimic how the HVS might be processing the images, computational modeling of this basic intelligent behavior remains a challenge.

To take further advantage of saliency information, we proposed a new connection named Sal-Mask Connection in this paper, which uses saliency data as an element-by-element mask for raw feature maps learned by convolutional connection from input images. The Sal-Mask Connection helps the neural networks work better. We call the network with a Sal-Mask Connection in it as a Sal-Mask Network.

In Sect. 2, we will explain the detail of a Sal-Mask Connection. Section 3 illustrates the structure of two traditional CNNs we used as benchmarks and the structure of the Sal-Mask Networks we used to verify the improvement. In Sect. 4, several experimental results will be presented. Section 5 will include a short conclusion and a precise introduction of some future work.

2   Sal-Mask Connection and Sal-Mask Network

2.1   Backgrounds of Saliency

It is observed that primates have a remarkable ability to interpret complex scenes in real time, despite the limited speed of the neuronal hardware available for such tasks [12]. It is generally acknowledged that the HVS uses a combination of image driven data and prior models in its processing, which means that intermediate and advanced visual processes select a subset of the available sensory information before further processing, most likely to reduce the complexity of scene analysis. This selection appears to be implemented in the form of a spatially circumscribed region of the visual field, the so-called focus of attention, which means that particular locations in the scene are selected based on their behavioral relevance or on local image cues [13]. Saliency is the metadata that describes the cues, it plays an important role in HVS, helps human to understand what they see.

Applying that procedure of HVS to a neural network system - the first convolutional connection is like the first routine of HVS, and the rest part of the network is like the further processing of HVS. As human will always select particular locations on the first routine using saliency information, it is natural to ameliorate the neural network in the same way. It is obvious that a better saliency will lead to a better performance. But it is hard to say which saliency is best for a neural network, as basically neural network is a black box lacking details inside. While there is no explicit rule to follow, it is a trade off to take a trial-way to judge the saliency algorithms. However, for lack of computation resources and time, we only tried out a few kinds of saliency data and we will chose two of them as testimony. One type of saliency we used is from Dani et al. [14], in the following paper, we will call it Alpha Saliency for short. The other is from Mingming Chen et al. [15], we will call it RC Saliency for short, as Chen called it so in [15]. Figure 1 has some examples.

(a)   (b)   (c)

Fig. 1. Saliencies. (a) is original image, (b) is Alpha saliency and (c) is RC saliency.

2.2 Structure of Sal-Mask Network

Before the discussion begins, as the concepts of layer and connection are often comprehended differently and confusing in different theses, we define the data of neurons within the same layer as a Layer in this paper, and the data of weights and computation along with it as a Connection, as shown in Fig. 2.

As described before, typically a CNN network starts with a convolutional connection. Based on that, we divide a convolution neural network into two parts. One includes the input layer, the first convolutional connection and the second layer - the feature maps learned by the first convolutional connection, which we named as raw feature maps. And the other one which includes the rest part of the network, we call it a Basic Neural Network (Basic NN).

To simulate the procedure of HVS as has been noted, the structure of so-called Sal-Mask Network is shown in Fig. 3. In Fig. 3, layer 1 is original image

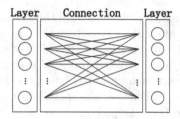

Fig. 2. Definition of layer and connection

data, layer 2 is saliency data which is generated using some pre-defined saliency algorithms. Layer 3 contains raw feature maps learned from layer 1 using a convolutional connection. Combine raw feature maps from layer 3 and saliency data from layer 2, we get the enhanced feature maps, as is layer 4. And the connection before layer 4 is is what we called Sal-Mask connection, which helps enhance the raw feature maps. Then the enhanced feature maps are input into the rest of the net. This is how a Sal-Mask Network works. More details about the Sal-Mask Connection and Sal-Mask Network will be introduced in Sect. 2.3.

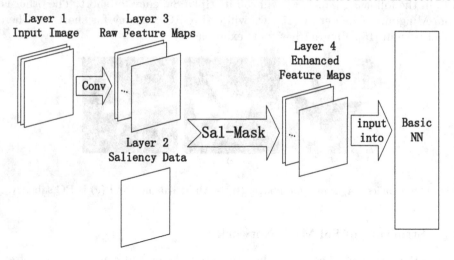

Fig. 3. Structure of Sal-mask network

2.3 Formulas and Deduction

As in layer 1, we use x_i to indicate the i-th pixel of the input image. Here we treat the two-dimension plus multi-channel image as a one-dimension array, as it is equivalent on math. Thus $i \in \{1, N\}$, where $N = imageWidth \cdot imageHeight \cdot imageChannel$.

Layer 2 is saliency data, which are obtained using some pre-defined algorithms. In this paper, it is either RC saliency or Alpha Saliency. Also, we treat the two-dimension saliency data as a one-direction array. Hence s_i indicates the i-th pixel of the saliency data. The width and height of saliency data is the same as that of the input image data, hence $i \in \{1, M\}$, where $M = imageWidth \cdot imageHeight$.

Layer 3 is raw feature maps learned from layer 1 using convolutional connection. y_{jk} is the value of the j-th neuron of the k-th raw feature map. As in this paper, we'll acquiesce to do a padding operation to keep the feature maps the same size as the input image. Here, each feature map, which is two-dimension, is treated as a one-direction array, while there are K raw feature maps, K depends on the detail of the convolutional connection. Then we expand the formula of the convolutional connection to a common format, using w_{ijk} to indicate the shared weight between x_i and y_{jk}:

$$z_{jk} = \sum w_{ijk} \cdot x_i + b_{jk}. \tag{1}$$

$$y_{jk} = f(z_{jk}). \tag{2}$$

f is the activation function of the convolutional connection, and z_{jk} is the value of neuron before activation function. b_{jk} is bias.

The most essential part is the Sal-Mask Connection before layer 4. It takes both layer 2 and layer 3 as inputs. For each raw feature map in layer 3, it makes an element-by-element multiplication with the saliency in layer 2, and generates a corresponding enhanced feature map in layer 4. Therefore, the enhanced feature maps are calculated as follows:

$$ez_{jk} = y_{jk} \cdot s_j. \tag{3}$$

$$ey_{jk} = h(ez_{jk}). \tag{4}$$

ey_{jk} is value the j-th pixel of the k-th enhanced feature map. ez_{jk} is the value before activation function and h is the activation function used.

As Eq. (3) described the feedforward of Sal-Mask Connection, we can deduce the the backpropagation formula using the definition of the backpropagation algorithm. δ_{jk} is the error backforwarded to layer 3 and layer 2 needs no feedback as it is an input layer. By expanding δ_{jk} using chain rule, we get:

$$\delta_{jk} = -\frac{\partial E}{\partial z_{jk}} = -\frac{\partial E}{\partial ez_{jk}} \cdot \frac{\partial ez_{jk}}{\partial y_{jk}} \cdot \frac{\partial y_{jk}}{\partial z_{jk}}. \tag{5}$$

According to the definition of Eq. (3), we know that

$$\frac{\partial ez_{jk}}{\partial y_{jk}} = s_j. \tag{6}$$

And with Eq. (2) we get

$$\frac{\partial y_{jk}}{\partial z_{jk}} = f'(z_{jk}). \tag{7}$$

Combining all the above, we get the formula for the backpropagation like this:

$$\delta_{jk} = e\delta_{jk} \cdot sy_j \cdot f'(z_{jk}). \tag{8}$$

$e\delta_{jk}$ is the error of layer 4, which is passed backward from the rest of the network, δ_{jk} is the error of layer 3.

It can be observed from the formulas before, that on both feedforward and backpropagation processes, the higher the value of saliency (s_j) is, the more it contributes to the output and the more effective feedback we will get. However, in original saliency data as shown in Fig. 1, there are too many pixels with value 0. Thus the corresponding neurons of raw feature maps will make no contribution to the feedforward result and gain no feedback during backpropagation. So we use the average of saliency data and a pure white image as the mask for Sal-Mask Connection to guarantee that the mask will not cause too many loss of the details of input images.

3 Network Structures

3.1 Benchmark Networks and Sal-Mask Networks Improved

As mentioned before, stacked convolutional layers have become a typical standard structure for a CNN since LeNet-5 [3]. We chose two typical examples out of them and do the experiments based on these two networks: AlexNet [4] and NIN [6]. However, due to the limit of GPU we used, we changed the structure slightly and used a simplified version with minor parameters. Besides, we skip the data augmentation which will take too much time on computation. So it may not perform as well as the state-of-art technology, still the comparison results are clear enough to prove the Sal-Mask Connection and Sal-Mask Network effective. The network structure of AlexNet and the corresponding Sal-Mask Network based on it are shown in Fig. 4. The structure of NIN and Sal-Mask Network based on it are shown in Fig. 5.

3.2 Connections and Parameters

In Figs. 4 and 5, a square frame stands for a Layer. As we use our networks on image classification problems, the size of a Layer is in format of $imageWidth \cdot imageHeight \cdot imageChannels$, except for the last frame, which is the output layer and the number stands for how many classes the dataset has. Texts nearby arrows between two layers stand for Connections, with the illustration of connection type, serial number and parameters.

Conv is short for convolutional connection. It has three parameters: kernel size $m \cdot n$, kernel number K and stride s. In Figs. 4 and 5, the parameters are in format of $m \cdot n \cdot K$ and the stride is set to 1. Before every convolutional connection, we do a padding to keep the corner pixels of the input images at the center of the kernels. That makes the feature maps the same size of image before the convolutional connection. Relu is short for Rectified Linear Units. It is used as activation function instead of sigmoid and linear. It is used by Alex [4] too. In the network, every convolutional connection and full connection used Relu.

Pool is short for pooling connection. It has three parameters: pooling size k, pooling stride s and pooling function - whether max-pooling(short as max) or

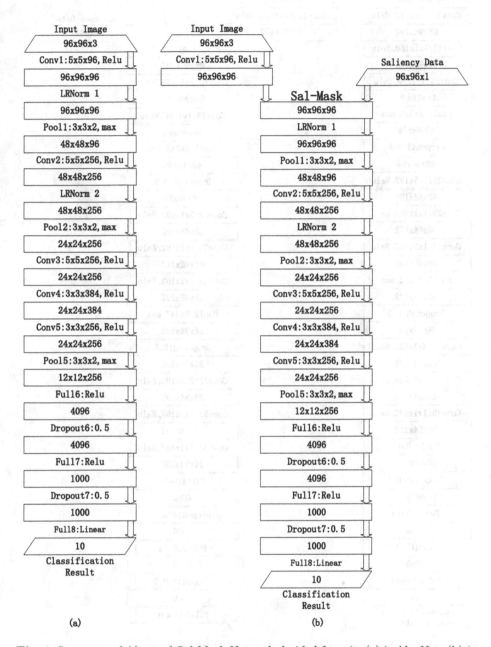

Fig. 4. Structure of Alex and Sal-Mask Network derided from it. (a) is AlexNet, (b) is the Sal-Mask Network derided from AlexNet.

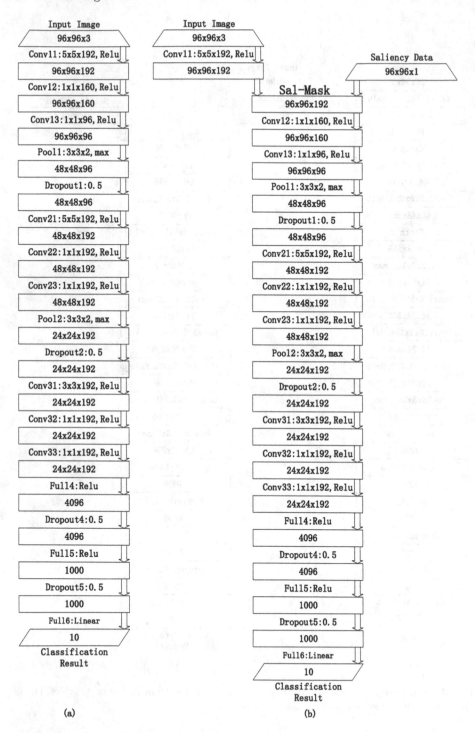

Fig. 5. Structure of NIN and Sal-Mask Network deride from it. (a) is NIN, (b) is the Sal-Mask Network derided from NIN.

average pooling(short as ave). In Fig. 4, the parameters are in format of $k \cdot k \cdot s$, and pooling function is described. Basically, all pooling connections we used have the parameter of $k = 3$, $s = 2$ and are max-poolings. They are overlapping pooling connections, as same as AlexNet [4].

LRNorm is short for local response normalization which is also proposed by Alex [4]. Denoted by $a_{x,y}^i$ the activity of a neuron computed by applying kernel i at position (x, y), the response-normalized activity $b_{x,y}^i$ is given by the expression

$$b_{x,y}^i = a_{x,y}^i / (k + \alpha \cdot \sum_{j=max(0,i-n/2)}^{min(N-1,i+n/2)} (a_{x,y}^i)^2)^\beta. \tag{9}$$

where the sum runs over n adjacent kernel maps at the same spatial position, and N is the total number of kernels in the layer. Local response normalization connection has four parameters : k, n, α and β. In our experiments, we set k as 1, n as 3, α as 0.00005 and β as 0.75.

Full is short for full connection, which depends on the size of both input layer and output layer. And Dropout is for dropout connection, which drops neurons of input layer radomly by ratio r. It is proposed by Hinton [8]. In our experiments, we set r as 0.5 for every dropout connection.

4   Experiments

4.1   Code and Dataset

Caffe [16] is a deep learning framework developed by the Berkeley Vision and Learning Center (BVLC) and by community contributors. We implemented our own code based on the design of Caffe, and we implemented the code for Sal-Mask Connection by our own.

As the memory and computation ability of GPU we used is limited, we are unable to afford a run on the ImageNet dataset. Therefore, we have to pick a minor dataset instead. However, saliency algorithms so far are not good enough for images that are too small, so the dataset we use cannot be too small. Taking these two points into consideration, we used STL-10 dataset [17]. It is an image recognition dataset inspired by the CIFAR-10 dataset but with some modifications. The size of images in it is 96×96 pixels, which is ok for saliency algorithms. The labeled data in it includes 5000 training images and 8000 test images, which makes the dataset not too big to run a network on it. As the name suggests, there are 10 classes of images in STL-10.

4.2   Improvement on AlexNet

Using structure described in Fig. 4, we use fixed learning rate 0.001 at the beginning and turn it down to 1/10 every 40 epochs. We do the test every epoch and get a benchmark on STL-10 using AlexNet, which is shown by solidline in Fig. 6. Then we put Sal-Mask Connection on AlexNet to improve it into a Sal-Mask Network. We get the result shown in Fig. 6, and it proved Sal-Mask Connection do make the performance better. The accuracy for Sal-Mask Network using RC Saliency is drawn by short dashed line, and the accuracy for Sal-Mask Network using Alpha Saliency is drawn by long dashed line in Fig. 6. It is clear to see that Sal-Mask Network do improve the AlexNet.

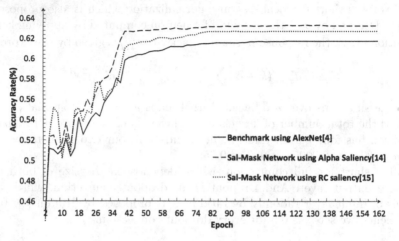

Fig. 6. Results for three different nerworks

Table 1 shows the best accuracy for each experiment, and the better results are highlighted in bold. Using RC Saliency as mask, the Sal-Mask Network based on AlexNet is 0.98 % better than original AlexNet. And the Sal-Mask Network using Alpha Saliency is 1.5 % better than original AlexNet.

Table 1. Improvement on AlexNet

Network	Accuracy(%)
Benchmark using AlexNet	61.74
Sal-Mask Network using RC saliency	**62.72**
Sal-Mask Network using Alpha saliency	**63.24**

4.3   Improvement on NIN

Using the structure described in Fig. 5, we use fixed learning rate 0.001 at the beginning and turn it down to 1/10 every 40 epochs. Again we do the test every epoch and get a benchmark on STL-10 using NIN, which is shown by solidline in Fig. 7. Then we put Sal-Mask Connection on AlexNet to improve it into a Sal-Mask Network. The accuracy for Sal-Mask Network using RC Saliency is drawn by the short dashed line, and the accuracy for Sal-Mask Network using Alpha Saliency is drawn by the long dashed line in Fig. 7. The Sal-Mask Connection also works well on the base of NIN.

Table 2 shows the best accuracy for each experiment, and the better results are highlighted in bold. The accuracy increased 2.10 % using RC Saliency and 0.70 % using Alpha Saliency.

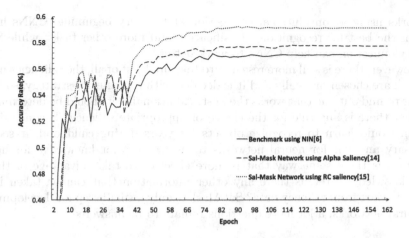

Fig. 7. Results for three different nerworks

Table 2. Improvement on NIN

Network	Accuracy(%)
Benchmark using NIN	57.13
Sal-Mask Network using RC saliency	**59.23**
Sal-Mask Network using Alpha saliency	**57.83**

4.4 Discussion

By results shown before, it is clear that with networks with Sal-Mask Connection work better than the benchmark networks. With different saliency data as mask, the performance may improve differently, varying from 0.70 % to 2.10 % as the results shows. With these two groups of experiments as proof, it is convinciable that Sal-Mask Connection will work on different CNNs.

5 Conclusion

In this paper, we proposed a novel connection called Sal-Mask Connection, which is build upon the idea that the HVS would select a subest of the input visual information. To simulate that procedure, we use saliency data as a element-by-element mask for raw feature maps learned from input images by the first convolutional connection of the network. The new connection helps the network to filter information and ignore noise. It is theoretically correct when designing the structure, according to saliency theory for HVS. And it is also proved correct by solid experiment results. In this paper, we use the proposed connecion on two common image classification benchmark networks, and experimental results show that this method is superior to the traditional CNNs. With the help of the experiemnts, Sal-Mask Connection is proved useful as it can work on neural networks using a convolutional connection at the very beginning. CNNs have proven the best for recognition, classification and more other tasks, while Sal-Mask Connection can help CNNs to work better.

However, there is still more research to take up. First of all, the saliencies used as mask are chosen manually and it is decided with a trial-error strategy, so it is urgent to find out one that works the best. Additionally, it should be determined whether there is any rule for the choice of appropriate saliency? Second, since human would learn to recognize objects for years during childhood, it seems necessary and fair for neural networks to use some prior knowledge for help. However, is there some way that is more effective to take advantage of these prior knowledge? Yet, is there any other information that can be taken into account apart from saliency data? Sal-Mask is only a small step for development of neural networks, a lot more questions remain to be answered.

Acknowledgments. This work is supported by the National Science Foundation of China (No.61371192, No.61103134).

References

1. Wan, L., Zeiler, M., Zhang, S., et al.: Regularization of neural networks using dropconnect. In: International Conference on Machine Learning, pp. 1058–1066 (2013)
2. Ciresan, D., Meier, U., Schmidhuber, J.: Multi-column deep neural networks for image classification. In: Computer Vision and Pattern Recognition, pp. 3642–3649 (2012)
3. LeCun, Y., Boser, B., Denker, J.S., Henderson, D., Howard, R.E., Hubbard, W., Jackel, L.D.: Backpropagation applied to handwritten zip code recognition. Neural Comput. 1(4), 541–551 (1989)
4. Krizhevsky, A., Sutskever, I., Hinton, G.E.: Imagenet classification with deep convolutional neural networks. In: Neural Information Processing Systems, pp. 1097–1105 (2012)
5. Zeiler, M.D., Fergus, R.: Visualizing and understanding convolutional networks. In: European Conference on Computer Vision, pp. 818–833 (2014)
6. Lin, M., Chen, Q., Yan, S.: Network in network (2013). arXiv preprint arXiv:1312.4400
7. Szegedy, C., Liu, W., Jia, Y., Sermanet, P., Reed, S., Anguelov, D., Rabinovich, A., et al.: Going deeper with convolutions (2014). arXiv preprint arXiv:1409.4842
8. Hinton, G.E., Srivastava, N., Krizhevsky, A., Sutskever, I., Salakhutdinov, R.R.: Improving neural networks by preventing co-adaptation of feature detectors (2012). arXiv preprint arXiv:1207.0580
9. Goodfellow, I.J., Warde-Farley, D., Mirza, M., Courville, A., Bengio, Y.: Maxout networks (2013). arXiv preprint arXiv:1302.4389
10. Hou, X., Zhang, L.: Saliency detection: a spectral residual approach. In: Computer Vision and Pattern Recognition (CVPR), pp. 1–8 (2007)
11. Kadir, T., Brady, M.: Saliency, scale and image description. Int. J. Comput. Vis. 5(2), 83–105 (2001)
12. Itti, L., Koch, C., Niebur, E.: A model of saliency-based visual attention for rapid scene analysis. IEEE Trans. Pattern Anal. Mach. Intell. 20(11), 1254–1259 (1998)

13. Itti, L., Koch, C.: A saliency-based search mechanism for overt and covert shifts of visual attention. Vis. Res. **40**(10), 1489–1506 (2000)
14. Levin, A., Lischinski, D., Weiss, Y.: A closed-form solution to natural image matting. IEEE Trans. Pattern Anal. Mach. Intell. **30**(2), 228–242 (2008)
15. Cheng, M.M., Zhang, G.X., Mitra, N.J., Huang, X., Hu, S.M.: Global contrast based salient region detection. In: Computer Vision and Pattern Recognition (CVPR), pp. 409–416 (2011)
16. Jia, Y., Shelhamer, E., Donahue, J., Karayev, S., Long, J., Girshick, R., Darrell, T., et al.: Caffe: convolutional architecture for fast feature embedding. In: ACM International Conference on Multimedia, pp. 675–678 (2014)
17. Coates, A., Ng, A.Y., Lee, H.: An analysis of single-layer networks in unsupervised feature learning. In: International Conference on Artificial Intelligence and Statistics, pp. 215–223 (2011)

Improved Spread Transform Dither Modulation Using Luminance-Based JND Model

Wenhua Tang[1,2], Wenbo Wan[1], Ju Liu[1(✉)], and Jiande Sun[1]

[1] School of Information Science and Engineering, Shandong University,
Jinan 250100, China
meilirensheng5896@163.com, zeyzff23@qq.com
{juliu,jd_sun}@sdu.edu.cn
[2] State Key Laboratory of Integrated Services Networks, Xidian University,
Xian 710071, China

Abstract. In the quantization-based watermarking framework, perceptual just noticeable distortion (JND) model has been widely used to determine the quantization step size to provide a better tradeoff between fidelity and robustness. However, the perceptual parameters computed in the embedding procedure and the detecting procedure are different, as the image has been altered by watermark embedding. In this paper, we incorporate a new DCT-based perceptual JND model, which not only shows better consistency with the HVS characteristics compared to the conventional models, but also can be invariant to the changes in the watermark framework. Furthermore, an improved spread transform dither modulation (STDM) watermarking scheme based on the new JND model is proposed. Experimental results show that the proposed scheme provides powerful resistance against common attacks, especially in robustness against Gauss noise, amplitude scaling and JPEG compression.

Keywords: STDM · Luminance · JND model · Watermarking

1 Introduction

Digital watermarking has attracted extensive attention for the multimedia copyright protection, data authentication, fingerprinting, multimedia indexing, and so on. Recently spread transform dither modulation (STDM), proposed by Chen and Wornell [1], is a representative one owing to its advantages in implementation and computational flexibility.

J. Liu—Project was partially supported by the Special Development Fund of Shandong Information Industry (2011R0116), Research Fund for the Doctoral Program of Higher Education under Grant (20130131110029) and Open Fund of State Key Laboratory of Integrated Services Networks under Grant (ISN14-03).
J. Sun—Project was partially supported by Natural Science Foundation of Shandong Province (ZR2014FM012).

Y.-J. Zhang (Ed.): ICIG 2015, Part II, LNCS 9218, pp. 430–437, 2015.
DOI: 10.1007/978-3-319-21963-9_39

In order to improve the performance of STDM, the perceptual character of the human visual system (HVS) is widely adopted to obtain the optimal trade-off between imperceptibility and robustness. As is well known, the improvement in fidelity can be achieved by adapting the watermark strength according to Just Noticeable Distortion (JND) model, the maximum distortion that the HVS can not perceive. Various perceptual STDM watermarking schemes have been proposed over the years [2–10]. In [2], Watsons perceptual model [3] is initially introduced within the STDM framework. In their framework, the projection vectors used in STDM are assigned as the slacks computed by Watsons perceptual model, so as to ensure that more changes are directed to coefficients with larger perceptual slacks. However, it is not robust enough for valumetric scaling attackTo further improve the capability of the framework, an improved algorithm termed as STDM-OptiMW was proposed [4], where the perceptual model was not only used to determine the projection vector, but also to select the quantization step size. But this scheme must use lots of DCT coefficients to embed one bit, which results in a low embedding rate. An improved method [5] is proposed to compute the quantization steps by adopting the perceptual slacks from Watsons model and the projection vector. Unfortunately, Watsons JND model is image-dependent and can rely on adapting to local image properties. Therefore, the perceptual slacks calculated in the original image and in the watermarked image are inconsistent. Based on the luminance-effect only part of Watsons model, X. Li et al. [6]. Proposed a step-projection based scheme that can ensure the values of quantization step size used in the watermark embedder and detector are identical while the attacks are absent. But the simple perceptual model used is not well-correlated with the real visual perception characteristics of HVS.

In order to obtain an optimal balance between imperceptibility and robustness, we present an improved STDM watermarking scheme based on a novel luminance-based JND model [7], which is better correlated with the real visual perception characteristics of HVS and can be directly applied within the STDM watermarking framework. The rest of this paper is organized as follows. Section 2 provides a brief introduction to STDM. The novel JND model is detailed in Sect. 3. Section 4 gives proposed STDM framework using the novel JND model. In Sect. 5, experimental results are provided to demonstrate the superior performance of the proposed scheme. Finally, Sect. 6 summarizes the paper.

2   Spread Transform Dither Modulation

As the proposed watermarking algorithm is based on STDM, introduction of STDM is necessary. STDM applies the Dither Modulation (DM) quantizer to modify the projection of the host vector along a given direction [1]. It has both the effectiveness of QIM and the robustness of a spread-spectrum system; thus, the improvements are significant.

STDM differs from regular QIM in terms of its signal, where the host vector x is projected onto a randomly generated vector u to get the projection x_u firstly.

Then the resulting scalar value is quantized and added to the components of the signal that are orthogonal to u. We can obtain the watermarked vector y as follows:

$$y = x + (Q(x_u, \Delta, m, \delta) - x_u) \cdot u, \quad m \in \{0, 1\}, \tag{1}$$

and the quantization function $Q(\cdot)$ is expressed as

$$Q(x_u, \Delta, m, \delta) = \Delta \cdot round\left(\frac{x_u + \delta}{\Delta}\right) - \delta, \quad m \in \{0, 1\}, \tag{2}$$

where Δ is the quantization step and δ is the dither signal corresponding to the message bit m.

In the detecting procedure, the received vector $\tilde{x}$ is projected onto the random vector u and the message bit $\tilde{m}$ is estimated from the projection given by

$$\tilde{m} = \arg \min_{b \in \{0,1\}} |\tilde{x}_u - Q(\tilde{x}_u, \Delta, b, \delta)|, \tag{3}$$

3 Luminance-Based JND Model for STDM Watermarking

In the STDM watermarking framework, the error introduced by the watermark embedding should not exceed the distortion visibility thresholds (slack) s, otherwise the watermark will become perceptible. Here, a new luminance-based JND model is employed to calculate the s associated with each DCT coefficient within the 8×8 block. The sophisticated perceptual JND model not only includes both contrast sensitivity function (CSF) and the luminance adaptation (LA) effect [7], but also remains invariant with watermark embedding procedure.

As discussed by M. Kim [7], The luminance adaptation (LA) effect of the HVS relies not only on the background luminance of an image but also on DCT frequency. The frequency characteristics are taken into account from the corresponding psychophysical experiment results, and consists of two factors: the base threshold J_{base}, and the modulation factor M_{LA} for LA, respectively. The complete model is expressed as

$$JND(n, i, j) = s \cdot N \cdot J_{base} \cdot M_{LA}, \tag{4}$$

where the parameter n is the index of a DCT block, and (i, j) is the position of $(i, j) - th$ DCT coefficient. s is intended to account for summation effect of individual JND thresholds over a spatial neighborhood for the visual system and is set to 0.14 [7]. N is the dimension of DCT (8, in this case). The parameters J_{base} and M_{LA} will be detailed later.

3.1 Spatial CSF Effect

HVS has a band-pass property and is more sensitive to the noise injected in the DCT basis function along the horizontal and vertical directions than the diagonal direction in spatial frequency. The spatial CSF model describes the sensitivity of human vision for each DCT coefficient. The base threshold J_{base} is generated by spatial CSF based on a uniform background image [7] and can be given by considering the oblique effect [8] as

$$J_{base}\left(\omega_{i,j}, \varphi_{i,j}\right) = \left(J_d\left(\omega_{i,j}\right) - J_v\left(\omega_{i,j}\right)\right) \cdot \sin\left(\varphi_{i,j}\right)^2 + J_v\left(\omega_{i,j}\right), \tag{5}$$

where $J_d\left(\omega_{i,j}\right)$ and $J_v\left(\omega_{i,j}\right)$ is empirically found as

$$\begin{cases} J_d\left(\omega_{i,j}\right) = 0.0293 \cdot \omega_{i,j}^2 + (-0.1382) \cdot \omega_{i,j} + 1.75 \\ J_v\left(\omega_{i,j}\right) = 0.0238 \cdot \omega_{i,j}^2 + (-0.1771) \cdot \omega_{i,j} + 1.75, \end{cases} \tag{6}$$

where $\omega_{i,j}$ is cycle per degree (cpd) in spatial frequency for the $(i,j)-th$ DCT coefficient and is given by

$$\omega = \omega = \sqrt{i^2 + j^2}\big/(2N\theta), \tag{7}$$

and

$$\theta = \tan^{-1}\left[1/2 \cdot R_{VH} \cdot H\right], \tag{8}$$

where θ indicates the horizontal/vertical length of a pixel in degrees of visual angle [9], R_{VH} is the ratio of the viewing distance to the screen height, H is the number of pixels in the screen height, and $\varphi_{i,j}$ stands for the direction angle of the corresponding DCT component, which is expressed as

$$\varphi_{i,j} = \sin^{-1}\left(2 \cdot \omega_{i,0} \cdot \omega_{0,j}\big/\omega_{i,j}^2\right). \tag{9}$$

3.2 Luminance Adaptation Effect

The minimally perceptible brightness difference increases as background brightness increases. It means that higher luminance level leads to higher JND values [9]. Because the proposed JND thresholds were detected at the intensity value of 128, a modification factor should be included for other intensity values. This effect is called the luminance adaptation (LA) effect [10], and is a function of the average pixel intensity. However, The LA factor previously described remains sensitive to valumetric scaling since the average intensity does not scale linearly with amplitude scaling, so we needed the average intensity to scale linearly with valumetric scaling for robustness.

We introduced the pixel intensity to be μ_p, and it is expressed as

$$\mu_p = \frac{\sum\limits_{x=0}^{N-1}\sum\limits_{y=0}^{N-1} I\left(x,y\right)}{KN^2} \cdot \frac{128}{C_0}, \tag{10}$$

where N is the DCT block size, $I\left(x,y\right)$ is the pixel intensity at the position (i,j) of the block, K is the maximum pixel intensity (255, in this case) and the term C_0 denotes the mean intensity of the whole image. Thus, the improved average pixel intensity scales linearly with amplitude scaling and it is theoretically invariant to valumetric scaling attacks.

M. Kim [7] performed a psychophysical experiment for JND measurement with respect to the LA effect in DCT domain, and a novel empirical luminance adaptation factor M_{LA} that employed both the cycles per degree (cpd) $\omega_{i,j}$ for spatial frequencies and the average intensity value of the block μ_p can be formulated as

$$M_{LA}\left(\omega_{i,j},\mu_p\right)$$
$$= \begin{cases} 1+\left(M_{0.1}\left(\omega_{i,j}\right)-1\right)\left|\frac{\mu_p-0.3}{0.2}\right|^{0.8}, \mu_p \le 0.3 \\ 1+\left(M_{0.9}\left(\omega_{i,j}\right)-1\right)\left|\frac{\mu_p-0.3}{0.6}\right|^{0.6}, \mu_p > 0.3, \end{cases} \tag{11}$$

where the $M_{0.1}\left(\omega_{i,j}\right)$ and $M_{0.9}\left(\omega_{i,j}\right)$ are empirically set as

$$M_{0.1}\left(\omega_{i,j}\right) = 2.468 \times 10^{-4}\omega_{i,j}{}^2 + 4.466 \times 10^{-3}\omega_{i,j} + 1.14$$
$$M_{0.9}\left(\omega_{i,j}\right) = 1.230 \times 10^{-3}\omega_{i,j}{}^2 + 1.433 \times 10^{-2}\omega_{i,j} + 1.34. \tag{12}$$

4   Proposed JND Model-Based STDM Watermarking Scheme

We applied the proposed novel JND models to calculate the quantization step size during STDM-based watermark embedding and detection procedures. As illustrated in Fig. 1, our proposed scheme consisted of two parts, the embedding procedure and the detection procedure. The embedding procedure of the proposed scheme can be described as follows:

(1) Divide the image into disjointed 8 × 8 blocks of pixels, and perform DCT transform to determine the DCT coefficients. Select a part of these coefficients (from the 4-th to the next L-th zig-zag-scanned DCT coefficients) to form a single vector, denoted as the host vector x with length L.
(2) As described in Sect. 3, the proposed JND model are used to calculate the slack vector s.

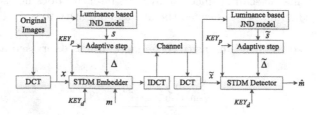

Fig. 1. Block diagram of proposed spread transform dither modulation (STDM) watermarking scheme based on Luminance-based JND Model.

(3) Use the two secret keys, KEY_p and KEY_d to generate the random projection u. Project the host vector x and the slack vector s onto to get the u projections x_u and s_u, respectively. The corresponding quantization step Δ is then obtained via s_u, which is multiplied by a factor to adjust for the embedding strength in practice.

(4) Embedded one bit of the watermark message m into the host projection x_u, according to Eq. (1). Finally, the modified coefficients are transformed to create the watermarked image.

The watermarked image may sustain certain attacks during transmission. The received image is used to detect the watermark as follows:

(1) Determine the received host vector $\tilde{x}$ of the disjoint block in step (1) of the embedding procedure.
(2) Calculate the perceptual slack vector $\tilde{s}$ via the proposed JND model mentioned in Sect. 3.
(3) Project the received host vector $\tilde{x}$ and slack vector $\tilde{s}$ onto the project vector u to get the projection $\tilde{x}_u$ and $\tilde{s}_u$. Note that, the corresponding quantization step Δ can be obtained via $\tilde{s}_u$ multiplied by the factor.
(4) Use the STDM detector to extract the watermark message $\tilde{m}$ according to Eq. (3).

5 Experimental Results and Analysis

To verify the robustness of the proposed JND model guided STDM watermarking scheme, a serial of tests are conducted to evaluate the performance of the proposed scheme. Furthermore, comparison experiments are performed with the former proposed STDM improvements, termed as STDM-RW [2], STDM-OptiWM [10], STDM-AdpWM [5], and STDM-RDMWm [6].

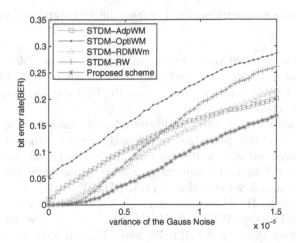

Fig. 2. BER versus Gaussian noise for different watermarking algorithms.

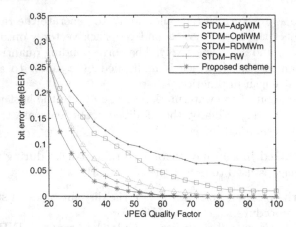

Fig. 3. BER versus JPEG compression for different watermarking algorithms.

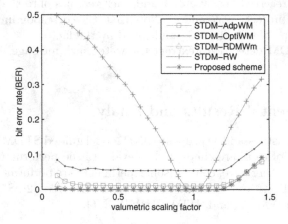

Fig. 4. BER versus valumetric scaling factor for different watermarking algorithms.

In these tests, we used various standard images of size 256×256 from the USC-SIPI image database [11], and take the average results. The simulation results listed in Figs. 2, 3 and 4 demonstrate the better robustness performance of our proposed schemes.

Figure 2 shows the response to additive white Gaussian noise. The STDM-OptiWM and STDM-RW performed significantly worse because of the mismatch problem. Our proposed scheme did not exceed 17 % for the Gaussian noise with variance 1.5×10^{-3} of and outperformed other schemes in the noise-adding attacks-in particular, 5 % lower than STDM-RDMWm scheme.

The sensitivity to JPEG compression is shown in Fig. 3. From the robustness results, both STDM-OptiWM and STDM-AdpWM have average BER values 5 % and 2 % higher than the STDM-RW and STDM-RDMWm schemes, which have similar results. Our proposed scheme, on the other hand, has average BER values 4.3 % lower than the STDM-RW and 4.7 % lower than the STDM-RDMWm scheme. The superior performance of the proposed scheme is achieved by the superior robustness properties of our proposed JND model.

As shown in Fig. 4, all the schemes except STDM-RW, do have robustness to valumetric scaling. STDM-OptiWM and STDM-AdpWM have average BER values 10 % and 2 % higher than our proposed scheme due to the mismatch problem within the watermark embedding. Although the other three algorithms showed passable robustness to this attack, our proposed scheme had the best performance.

6 Conclusion

In this paper, a new luminance-based JND model, which gave us a novel way to take full advantage of the HVS researches and can remain invariant within the STDM watermarking framework, is employed to design an improved STDM watermarking scheme. In this way, a better tradeoff between robustness and fidelity is obtained. Experimental results have demonstrated that the proposed watermarking scheme was superior to other state-of-the-art methods against common image processing attacks with a fixed transparency.

References

1. Chen, B., Wornell, G.: Quantization index modulation: a class of provably good methods for digital watermarking and information embedding. IEEE Trans. Inf. Theor. **47**(4), 1423–1443 (2001)
2. Li, Q., Doerr, G., Cox, I.J.: Spread transform dither modulation using a perceptual model. In: Proceedings of the IEEE International Workshop on Multimedia Signal Processing, May 2006, pp. 98–102 (2006)
3. Watson, A.B.: DCT quantization matrices optimized for individual images. In: SPIE. Proceedings of the Human Vision Processing and Digital Display IV, vol. 1913, pp. 202–216, June 1993
4. Li, Q., Cox, I.J.: Improved spread transform dither modulation using a perceptual model: robustness to amplitude scaling and JPEG compression. In: Proceedings of IEEE ICASSP, vol. 2, pp. 185–188 (2007)
5. Ma, L.: Adaptive spread-transform modulation using a new perceptual model for color image. IEICE Trans. Info. Sys. **E93–D**(4), 843–856 (2010)
6. Li, X., Liu, J., Sun, J., Yang, X.: Step-projection-based spread transform dither modulation. IET Inf. Secur. **5**(13), 170–180 (2011)
7. Bae, S.H., Kim, M.: A novel DCT-based JND model for luminance adaptation effect in DCT frequency. IEEE Signal Process. Lett. **20**, 893–896 (2013)
8. Rust, B., Rushmeier, H.: A new representation of the contrast sensitivity function for human vision. In: Proceedings of the International Conference on Image, Science System, Technology, January 1997, pp. 1–15, (1997)
9. Ahumada, A.J., Peterson, H.A.: Luminance-model-based DCT quantization for color image compression. Proc. SPIE **1666**, 365–374 (1992)
10. Wei, Z., Ngan, K.N.: Spatio-temporal just noticeable distortion profile for grey scale image/video in DCT domain. IEEE Trans. Circ. Systs. Video Technol. **1913**, 337–346 (2009)
11. USC-SIPI Image Database. http://sipi.usc.edu/database/

Incorporation of 3D Model and Panoramic View for Gastroscopic Lesion Surveillance

Yun Zong[1,2], Weiling Hu[3], Jiquan Liu[1,2(✉)], Xu Zhang[1,2], Bin Wang[1,2], Huilong Duan[1,2], and Jianmin Si[3]

[1] College of Biomedical Engineering and Instrument Science, Zhejiang University, Hangzhou 310027, China
{21315039,liujq,zhangxu_bme,11015021,duanhl}@zju.edu.cn
[2] Key Laboratory for Biomedical Engineering, Ministry of Education, Zhejiang University, Hangzhou 310027, China
[3] Institute of Gastroenterology, Sir Run Run Shaw Hospital, Zhejiang University, Hangzhou 310016, China
ringwh@hotmail.com, sijm@zju.edu.cn

Abstract. Natural Orifice Transluminal Endoscopic Surgery (NOTES) is widely used for clinical diagnoses. However, NOTES has two main problems: difficulties brought by endoscope's flexibility and narrow view of endoscope. Image-guided system is helpful to deal with these problems. In our previous work, a computer aided endoscopic navigation system (CAEN) was developed for gastroscopic lesion surveillance. In this paper, 3D model and panoramic view are incorporated into CAEN with three improvements: selection of reference and tracking features; perspective projection for constructing local and global panoramic view; 3D surface modeling using structure from motion. The system is evaluated from three clinic applications: broadening the view, non-invasive retargeting, and overall lesion locations. The evaluation results show that the mean accuracy of broadening the view is 0.43 mm, the mean accuracy of non-invasive retargeting is 7.5 mm, and the mean accuracy for overall lesion diagnosis is 3.71 ± 0.35 mm.

Keywords: 3D surface modeling · Feature selection · Image-Guided system · NOTES · Panoramic view

1 Introduction

In minimally invasive surgery, a new form named Natural Orifice Transluminal Endoscopic Surgery (NOTES) was proposed by the Natural Orifice Surgery Consortium for Assessment and Research (NOSCAR) in 2005. As NOTES reduces patients' pain and promotes postoperative recovery, it's regarded as a new evolution of minimally invasive surgery [1]. However, many problems of NOTES are proposed: first, as NOTES is carried out by surgeons, endoscope's flexibility troubles surgeons. Without assistance to achieve triangulation or to obtain consistent images, performing a complex surgery is difficult [2]; second, endoscope provides narrow view for surgeons, space orientation of surgical sites and image orientations both make troubles for surgeries [3].

© Springer International Publishing Switzerland 2015
Y.-J. Zhang (Ed.): ICIG 2015, Part II, LNCS 9218, pp. 438–445, 2015.
DOI: 10.1007/978-3-319-21963-9_40

To solve these problems, Image-guided system is employed, which is an assistant part of surgery. Tracking device of Image-guided system combined with image processing methods guide the experts to locate and target lesions in surgery. Bimanual manipulation was applied to assist NOTES, a standard dual channel endoscope (DCE) was compared with the combination of the R-Scope and the direct drive endoscope system (DDES) in [4]. In paper [5], Da Vinci Surgical System, which was firstly employed for gastric cancer in 2002 [6], was combined with 2D and 3D vision to confirm the orientations of images. Real-time tracking of the endoscope camera was proved helpful to locate surgical sites with a reference coordinate system [7], image-registration techniques improved excellent performance of surgery task in laparoscopy [8, 9]. 3D reconstruction and image stitching methods were beneficial for these tasks. To recover 3D depth information under endoscopy, new methods were developed, including the Gaussian mixture model [10], the non-rigid SFM theory [11]. In a word, Image-guided system was proved useful in NOTES.

In our previous work, a computer aided endoscopic navigation system (CAEN) was developed for non-invasive biopsy [12]. The system consists of a 6-DOF tracking endoscope device and a computer simulated work station. In the process, the tip of the tracking endoscope was used to touch the lesion; then the work station recorded the lesion's location; in the follow-ups, the lesion's location would guide the endoscopist in retargeting the lesions. We devoted to 3D reconstruction, it was proposed in paper [13], feature tracking was a start; then SFM was applied to reconstruct local patches; finally, all those patches were merged, which showed a prominent performance in endoscopy navigation. Panorama is another promising methodology to solve the narrow field of view (FOV) problem. In this paper, we improve the CAEN system by merging 3D model and panoramic view into the system. The improved system consists of three parts: feature selection, perspective projection, and 3D surface modeling. It has three clinic applications: broadening the view, non-invasive retargeting, and overall lesion diagnosis. The system is described as follows: methods are described in Sect. 2, results of this system are described in Sect. 3, and conclusion is described in Sect. 4, acknowledgement is in the last section.

2 Methods

2.1 Overview

The improved system consists of: a work station, an endoscope, and a 6-DOF position tracking device, as mentioned in CAEN. The 6-DOF position tracking device is made up of an electronic unit device, a sensor probe, and a magnetic transmitter. The system is devoted to assisting the endoscopist in operating on the stomach accurately. Figure 1 depicts the workflow of the system. Feature selection is the first step, and then perspective projection and 3D surface modeling are employed.

2.2 Feature Selection

Reference features and tracking features are selected during the gastroscopy. The standard of selecting reference points is that they can be easily found and touched by

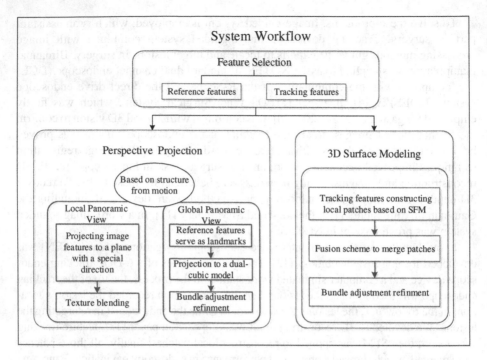

Fig. 1. System workflow: including feature selection, perspective projection, and 3D surface modeling

the endoscopist. According to anatomic characteristics of the stomach, the cardia, pylorus, junction of the anterior body wall and angularis, junction of the posterior body wall and angularis, middle of the antrum are selected as reference points. Reference points have to be touched at the beginning, and locations of them should be recorded for follow-up examinations. Tracking features are selected by endoscopist from images during the gastroscopy procedure. Image registration method is applied during tracking feature selection procedure. Reference features and tracking features are both employed to the following perspective projection and 3D surface modeling procedures.

2.3   Perspective Projection

The system implements perspective projection to construct the panoramic view. Panoramic view is one of the main methods in solving narrow FOV, including local panoramic view and global panoramic view.

During intra-operation, local panoramic view uses perspective projection. First, the position information of camera and images are transformed by tracking device; then images are projected onto a plane to construct a wider view based on SFM. Relationship between an image point $p_i = (x_i, y_i)^T$ and its corresponding 3D point $P_i = (X_i, Y_{i,}, Z_i)^T$ is described in the following equation:

$$M^{2*3} P_i = p_i \tag{1}$$

Projection matrix M^{2*3} is multiplied by internal matrix and external matrix. Internal matrix denotes internal information of camera, external matrix denotes the rotation and translation. Tracking feature points are selected and recorded by the 6-DOF tracking device. These image points are projected onto a plane based on Eq. (1). To achieve minimal errors, the plane is parallel with the camera's scope. We only select images adjacent to the current displayed image, and these images are captured using an endoscope with a very small skew angle. Finally, the composited image should be mapped with the texture information from the native gastroscopic images. We employ the multi-resolution pyramidal algorithm to blend the composited images [14]. With local panoramic view, the endoscopist is able to get a broadened view.

In post-operation, the endoscopist reviews images in order to reduce misdiagnoses. In this paper, we use global panoramic view to assist the endoscopist in reviewing. The global panoramic view uses a dual-cubic projection model which is similar to hemicubic model employed in [15]. As soon as the tracking endoscope enters the stomach, three of the reference points (including the cardiac orifice, angular incisures and pylorus) are marked as landmarks, then the position information captured by device starts to match with the dual-cubic model, and the corresponding images are projected onto the faces of dual-cubic model based on Eq. (1). Finally, the bundle adjustment algorithm is adopted to refine the model. As global panoramic view devotes to unfolding the surface of stomach, endoscopists are able to find overall lesions with reference points, so that misdiagnoses can be reduced.

2.4 3D Surface Modeling

In gastroscopy, to assist the endoscopist in accurate retargeting of lesions, 3D model is used for gastric navigation. Similar to the reference points, the biopsy sites are touched as tracking features, then the global coordinates are recorded by the work station. Using Eq. (1), SFM theory is adopted to reconstruct the local 3D gastric internal patches; subsequently, a novel fusion scheme is introduced to merge the local 3D patches; finally, BA algorithm is employed to refine the reconstructed model. This method renders a real-time gastric 3D scene as well as updates the local scene according to current displayed image frames, which indicates that the 3D scene can represent actual gastric deformation. With this model, some detailed information are displayed, surgical navigation is more accurate.

The procedure of non-invasive retargeting involves first examination and follow-up examinations. In all examinations, all five reference points has to be touched with the tip of the 6-DOF endoscope device and recorded, they are used for global coordinate registration. In the follow-up examinations, the global coordinate's registration is estimated. Afterwards, the recorded biopsy sites' positions are transformed and then marked in real endoscopic videos in order to guide the endoscopist in retargeting the biopsy sites.

3   Results

For this study, 35 patients with histories of gastric diseases were enrolled, and 15 patients of them had follow-up examinations. All patients provided a written informed consent for all examinations. The gastroscopy examination was performed by a skilled endoscopist (Table 1).

Table 1. Clinical characteristics

Variables	Number
Median age, year (range)	57.6 (38–77)
Sex (female/male)	21/14 Smoking
Smoking	13
Alcohol	15

As the system works in both intra-operation and post-operation. During the intra-operation, the system has two applications, broadening the view and navigation; in the post-operation procedure, the system contributes to overall lesion diagnosis. The results of these applications are evaluations of the system.

3.1   Broadening the View

In gastroscopy, the local panoramic view was rendered in real time. A 1500 * 500 pixels size canvas was created for the purpose of depicting complete neighbor environment of the lesions; according to the gastroscopic camera's motion and the distance between camera and the projection plane, neighbor images were selected. The local panoramic view used four sites, which include antral, stomach body, pylorus and angularis. They were projected onto the center of the canvas. Texture blending algorithm showed a good performance. The mosaicking error for local panoramic was 0.43 mm.

3.2   Non-invasive Retargeting

In order to compare the results between the non-invasive retargeting and tattooing, the selected biopsy sites were marked by tattooing and the 6-DOF endoscopy device respectively. In the first examination, a 3D model was built. Three months after the first examination, a follow-up endoscopy was performed with the system, and the global coordinates' registration was estimated between the two examinations. The distance between the targeted points and the tattooing area's center was designated as the accuracy of non-invasive retargeting. Moreover, the system's touching time and tattooing time were recorded. The mean accuracy was 7.5 mm, and the operation time was much shorter than the tattooing time (see Table 2).

Table 2.   Accuracy of the retargeting.

Biopsy location	Accuracies: (mean_SD) mm	Marking time: (mean_SD) s (Tattooing/CAEN)
Angularis	5.2 ± 2.8	12 ± 4.1/3 ± 1.8
Antral lesser curvature	7.2 ± 2.0	12 ± 4.4/2 ± 0.8
Antral greater curvature	6.3 ± 3.1	11 ± 3.6/2 ± 0.7
Antral posterior wall	8.2 ± 1.6	12 ± 5.5/2 ± 0.7
Antral anterior wall	7.9 ± 1.3	13 ± 5.2/2 ± 0.7

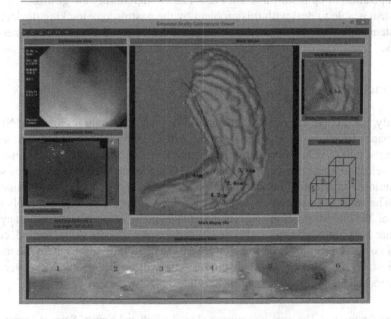

Fig. 2.   UI of the system

3.3   Overall Lesion Diagnosis

To validate the performance of the global panoramic view, 1000 points were randomly selected from panoramic view and re-projected onto the original frames. Euclidean distances for the corresponding points were regarded as the accuracy and the direct measured distance's unit was the pixel. To measure clinical physical measure result, biopsy forceps with a span diameter of 6 mm was used to touch the stomach, and the captured images provided a standard for converting the accuracy from pixel to millimeter. The mean error for global panoramic view was 3.71 ± 0.35 mm.

In Fig. 2, the top-left displays the current gastroscopy view seen by the endoscopist; local panoramic view shows the broadening view of images around the camera; probe information is also transmitted on UI; 3D model reconstructed by SFM is displayed in Mesh Model, marked biopsy sites are shown on both mesh model and local biopsy scene; global panoramic view is also shown on the bottom of UI.

Compared with the other computer-aided systems, our system has the following advantages: first, most systems only focus on intra-operation, such as the pathological site retargeting which uses affine deformation modelling [16], while the lesion diagnosis of our system works in both intra-operation and post-operation; second, as the operation of gastroscopy is flexible, many systems with geometry constraints are not accurate enough. For example, because the epipolar lines have many constraints on the camera parameters, the biopsy site re-localization method proposed in [17], which is based on the computation of epipolar lines, isn't accurate enough during the gastroscopy, while our system is able to deal with this problem by the gastroscopy tracking device; third, our system is easy to operate, as it has less operation steps than lots of computer-aided systems.

4   Conclusion

Currently, endoscope's flexibility and narrow view are two main problems of NOTES. In this paper, based on our previous system CAEN, 3D Modeling and Panoramic View are merged into CAEN. The developed system's workflow has three parts, including feature selection, perspective projection, and 3D modeling. The system makes several contributions: broadening the view, non-invasive retargeting, and overall lesion diagnosis. The results show that this system is likely suitable for clinical applications. However, the limitations of the current system should be emphasized: first, many operations are semi-automatic and associated with the endoscopist's skills; second, computational cost and accuracy need to be improved. In the future, more automatic methods will be involved; accuracy and consuming time will be improved; Moreover, more volunteers and endoscopists should be enrolled.

Acknowledgements. The work was supported by the National Natural Science Foundation of China (No. 31470955) and Zhejiang province key science and technology innovation team (2013TD13).

References

1. Coughlin, G., Samavedi, S., Palmer, K.J., Patel, V.R.: Role of image-guidance systems during NOTES. J. Endourol. **23**, 803–812 (2009)
2. Bardaro, S.J., Swanstrom, L.: Development of advanced endoscopes for natural orifice transluminal endoscopic surgery (NOTES). Minim. Invasive Ther. Allied Technol. **2006**(15), 378–383 (2006)
3. Swanstrom, L., Swain, P., Denk, P.: Development and validation of a new generation of flexible endoscope for NOTES. Surg. Innov. **16**, 104–110 (2009)

4. Spaun, G.O., Zheng, B., Martinec, D.V., Cassera, M.A., Dunst, C.M., Swanstrom, L.L.: Bimanual coordination in natural orifice transluminal endoscopic surgery: comparing the conventional dual-channel endoscope, the R-Scope, and a novel direct-drive system. Gastrointest. Endosc. **69**, 39–45 (2009)
5. Blavier, A., Gaudissart, Q., Cadiere, G.B., Nyssen, A.S.: Impact of 2D and 3D vision on performance of novice subjects using da Vinci robotic system. Acta Chir. Belg. **106**, 662–664 (2006)
6. Hashizume, M., Shimada, M., Tomikawa, M.: Early experiences of endoscopic procedures in general surgery assisted by a computer -enhanced surgical system. Surg. Endosc. **16**(8), 1187–1191 (2002)
7. Cleary, K., Peters, T.M.: Image-guided interventions: technology review and clinical applications. Annu. Rev. Biomed. Eng. **12**, 119–142 (2010)
8. Vosburgh, K.G., San, J.E.R.: Natural orifice transluminal endoscopic surgery (NOTES): an opportunity for augmented reality guidance. Stud. Health Technol. Inform. **125**, 485–490 (2007)
9. Vosburgh, K., Stylopoulos, N., Thompson, C., Ellis, R., Samset, E., San, J.E.R.: Novel real time tracking interface improves the use of laparoscopic and endoscopic ultrasound in the abdomen. Int. J. Comput. Assist. Radiol. Surg. **1**, 282–284 (2006)
10. Giannarou, S., Yang, G.-Z.: Tissue deformation recovery with gaussian mixture model based structure from motion. In: Linte, C.A., Moore, J.T., Chen, E.C.S., Holmes III, D.R. (eds.) AE-CAI 2011. LNCS, vol. 7264, pp. 47–57. Springer, Heidelberg (2012)
11. Zhu, S., Zhang, L., Smith, B.M.: Model evolution: an incremental approach to non-rigid structure from motion. In: 2010 IEEE Conference on Computer Vision and Pattern Recognition (2010)
12. Liu, J.Q., Wang, B., Hu, W.L., Zong, Y., Si, J.M., Duan, H.L.: A non-invasive navigation system for retargeting gastroscopic lesions. Biomed. Mater. Eng. **24**(6/2014), 2673–2679 (2014)
13. Wang, B., Liu, J.Q., Zong, Y., Duan, H.L.: Dynamic 3D reconstruction of gastric internal surface under gastroscopy. J. Med. Imaging Health Inform. **4**, 797–802 (2014)
14. Burt, P.J., Adelson, E.H.: A multiresolution spline with application to image mosaics. ACM Trans. Graph. (TOG) **2**(4), 217–236 (1983)
15. Behrens, A., Stehle, T., Gross, S., Aach, T.: Local and global panoramic imaging for fluorescence bladder endoscopy. In: Annual International Conference of the IEEE on Engineering in Medicine and Biology Society, EMBC 2009, pp. 6990–6993 (2009)
16. Ye, M.L., Giannarou, G., Patel, N., Teare, J., Yang, G.Z.: Pathological site retargeting under tissue deformation using geometrical association and tracking. In: The 16th International Conference on Medical Image Computing and Computer Assisted Intervention (2013)
17. Allain, B., Hu, M.X., Lovat, L.B., Cook, R., Ourselin, S., Hawkes, D.: Biopsy site re-localisation based on the computation of epipolar lines from two previous endoscopic images. In: The 12th International Conference on Medical Image Computing and Computer Assisted Intervention (2009)

Interactive Browsing System of 3D Lunar Model with Texture and Labels on Mobile Device

Yankui Sun[✉], Kan Zhang, and Ye Feng

Department of Computer Science and Technology, Tsinghua University, Beijing 100084, China
syk@mail.tsinghua.edu.cn

Abstract. This paper devotes to developing an interactive visualization system of 3D lunar model with texture and labels on mobile device. Using OpenGL ES 2.0 and Osg for android, we implement 3D lunar mesh model construction, lunar texture and mapping, GPU shader illumination programming, multi-level terrain labels and interactive browsing. In particular, a technique of terrain labels for mobile device is presented by developing a vertex shader and fragment shader which is dedicated to render texture, where the vertex shader is mainly used to determine the vertex's position attribute of the texture while the fragment shader is responsible for the color, font and transparency of the text, etc. The developed browsing system can be rendered on mobile device in real-time.

Keywords: Mobile device · Lunar model · Lunar texture · Terrain labels · OpenGL ES 2.0 · Osg for android · Chang'E-1

1 Introduction

China launched her own unmanned, lunar-orbiting spacecraft, CE-1 (Chang'E-1) in October 2007. CE-1 got 1.37 TB original research data which contain about 8.6 million LAM elevation values and 1,073 tracks of 2C-level CCD image data. In interactive visualization of lunar model, a series of research works have been done based on PC and/or internet [1–4]. In [1, 2], Sun et al. used the LAM data to construct an interactive lunar model using bicubic subdivision-surface wavelet and transmitted it through network using a client-server mode. In [3], Dong et al. constructed a lunar surface model, using the LAM data, the CCD data and hundreds of labels, and visualized it on personal computer with the converging problem in the polar regions being solved. Sun et al. further proposed and implemented an internet-based interactive visualization method of 3D lunar model with texture and labels [4]. In this paper, we devoted to developing the interactive browsing system of 3D lunar model with texture and labels on mobile device. It should be pointed out that, with the fast development of computing ability of mobile devices, rendering complex scene efficiently on portable device becomes an important research topic. Many researches in this aspect have been done based on client/service architecture [5, 6], where part of rendering work is done on the mobile devices. Recently, the research on doing rendering work completely on mobile devices has been done. [7] presented a technique which can manage the level-of-detail of 3D meshes in portable

© Springer International Publishing Switzerland 2015
Y.-J. Zhang (Ed.): ICIG 2015, Part II, LNCS 9218, pp. 446–452, 2015.
DOI: 10.1007/978-3-319-21963-9_41

devices. Here we will develop techniques to run 3D lunar model interactively on mobile device using OpenGL ES 2.0 and OSG for android. This is not straightforward to do, and there are some technical difficulties to overcome, including: (1) The implementation of the terrain label could not be done directly on mobile device because OpenGL ES 2.0 has different rendering pipeline from OpenGL; (2) The texture size loaded into the memory once time is limited,where the maximum texture size is 4096×4096 for OpenGL ES 2.0; (3) GPU programming of programmable pipeline shader for mobile device is more difficult. The above difficulties will be overcome here. The main contributions of this paper include: (1) Proposing a transparent literal texture mapping technique to implement multi-level terrain labels for 3D lunar model on mobile device. (2) Developing a real-time browsing system of 3D lunar model with texture and labels on mobile device by realizing 3D lunar mesh model construction, texture mapping, illumination calculation, human-machine interaction.

The rest of this paper is organized as follows. The Sect. 2 gives the systematic flow chart, and introduces the key implementation techniques. Section 3 describes the system development and implementation. Conclusions are made in Sect. 4.

2 Algorithm Description

Our systematic flow chart is shown in Fig. 1. It consists of some models including lunar mesh modeling, texture mapping, illumination calculation, terrain labels and human-machine interactive.

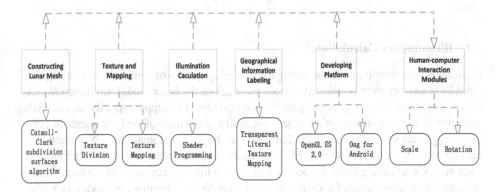

Fig. 1. Flow chart of our system

2.1 Lunar Mesh Modeling

A semi-regular lunar mesh with 50 thousand quadrilaterals was constructed by denoising, Catmull-Clark subdivision and resampling from the 8,610,511 data points obtained by CE-1, as was done in [3]. Its low resolution lunar 3D model with 24576 triangles and 12290 vertices is also obtained so that they can be browsed in multi-resolution. To render them on mobile device, the quadrangles of the lunar models are divided into triangles, and vertex array mapping method provided by OpenGL ES 2.0 is used to render the triangle mesh of the lunar models. More specifically, all the vertex information and the rendering information of the lunar triangle mesh are transmitted to GPU at once, and they are accessed and rendered sequentially according to vertex array.

2.2   Texture Division and Mapping

In [8], a lunar map with size of 18024×9012 has been effectively completed from CE-1 CCD image data. The texture size is about 120 M, which is impossible to load it into the memory of a mobile device once time since the texture size loaded into the memory once time is limited, where the maximum texture size is 4096×4096 for OpenGL ES 2.0. To solve this problem, a texture division method is proposed to load large size texture. First, the original lunar texture is divided into four parts: South Polar texture and North Polar texture with size of 5740×5740; Eastern and Western Hemisphere textures with size of 9100×3640. Then, these textures are all divided into two patches further so that the total texture size 122 M can be loaded into the memory in small patch sizes.

For the lunar mesh models mentioned above, each vertex's texture coordinate is calculated by using the texture mapping method used in [3], and they are stored in vertex array by allocating storage space for them. Texture rendering is realized in OpenGL ES 2.0 as follows. The function InputStream is used to decode a texture bitmap, and the texture is bound to a serial number by the function glBindTexture in OpenGL ES 2.0. Then, specifying the filling mode as texture filling when texture rendering is done in shader.

2.3   Illumination Calculation

Lighting is very important for enhancing the rendering quality of a lunar model. In [3], two point light sources were positioned in front and back of the lunar model. Lighting calculation is not complex in programming on PC because OpenGL support specifying materials and reflection characteristics of the object, location and intensity of the light source directly in the application, so illumination calculation can be done automatically. Yet the things become very different for OpenGL ES 2.0 because it renders pixel one by one. In this case, each vertex's rendering mode is specified by setting light source, normal, material attributes, and then illumination for each vertex is computed by illumination model. In particular, a normal parameter is computed and stored in a vertex array, and then it is transferred to GPU to be used in illumination calculation by shader code.

2.4   Terrain Labels

Terrain labels can be implemented on PC using the text information output function DrawListText() and Chinese byte stream reading function fread() in OpenGL. Unfortunately, these two functions are cut down in OpenGL ES 2.0, so there are some difficulties to realize terrain labels on 3D lunar models in mobile terminals. This paper designs and implements a technique to tag terrain information on the lunar model by using OpenGL

ES 2.0, called transparent literal texture mapping technique. Here a set of specific vertex shader and fragment shader are developed to render texture, which are different from the vertex shader and fragment shader for rendering the lunar mesh. In the new design, the vertex shader is mainly used to determine the vertex position attribute of a texture while the fragment shader to realize the color, font and transparent attributes of a text. Then, terrain text information is added into a texture bitmap, and it is output by using texture mapping embedded with the text. The following steps show how to realize text information labeling in 3D space by texture mapping using OpenGL ES 2.0.

Step 1: Merging Terrain Text Information into a Texture Bitmap. For each geographical name, a new bitmap and a new canvas are created. Then, the canvas is set to be transparent, and the attributes of the landmark such as font, color and size, are set. After all the settings are completed, we begin to draw the landmarks.

Step 2: Displaying the Text in Transparency on the Merged Bitmap. Get a vertex's color by Bitmap.getPixel and Bitmap.SetPixel functions. For each vertex, the corresponding alpha channel is set 0 to assure the text can be seen. Transparent attribute is the inherent attribute of the vertices. By setting the transparency, we can set the background color to be transparent, and show the text information in the texture.

Step 3: Labelling Geographical Names in a Right Position. Obtain 3D position coordinate of a texture and label geographical names in the right position of the lunar model. Bind texture rendering and camera so that terrain labels can be rotated and scaled together with viewpoint. In the meanwhile, backface cutting technique is used to hide invisible landmark to speed up the rendering speed.

Because of quantity of geographical names and small display screen of a mobile device, we propose a multi-level terrain label technique. In our application, we classified the geographical labels into different levels according to the distance, denoted distance by D, between a viewpoint and the center of the lunar model. The smaller the distance, the more labels displayed.

2.5   Human-Machine Interaction

Human-computer interaction is an important part for an interactive browsing system on mobile device. For Android application, the class used to correspond to user's gesture definition is OnTouchEvent. We realized three kinds of gesture interaction functions in our browsing system: rotation, zoom in and zoom out so that we can browse the lunar model from all directions and various perspectives.

3   System Development and Experimental Results

With the aforementioned techniques, we developed a lunar interactive visualization system with texture and labels under lighting environment by using OpenGL ES 2.0 and

OSG for android. One Plus mobile phone (5.5 inch screen, 1920 × 1080 resolution, four core processor, 3 Gb of memory, 64G external memory), which runs Android 4.3 operating system, is used as a mobile device to test the performance of our system.

OpenGL ES 2.0 uses programmable pipeline instead of fixed one in rendering, where GPU running code needs be written and loaded into the video card to compile when the program runs. In programming with OpenGL ES 2.0, how to render every pixel needs to be specified by developers. Obviously the great degree of freedom in programming also means more difficulties to meet. Compared with OpenGL ES 2.0, Osg for android is an advanced 3D interactive graphics development engine, where some powerful functions are provided so that the programming for developers is simplified greatly. In our application development, Osg is mainly used to manage 3D viewpoint (camera) including setting up and modifying the parameters of the camera such as location and direction. In human-computer interaction module, camera class in Osg engine is applied to make the camera do actions according to what we need, such as rotating around an orbit and so on, which simplifies the programming greatly compared to using OpenGL ES 2.0 directly.

An integrated software development framework for mobile device is designed and implemented, which is showed in Fig. 2. A cpp file programmed by VS2010 is loaded into Osg for android and complied in local computer (PC). To make the local codes run correctly in Java virtual machine, modify CMake List file by adding header files and cpp files, and then run it in NDK command line to generate .so file (a dynamic link library in Linux kernel) in target folder. Finally, compile the Java program by Java SDK to generate APK file, a set up file which can be installed in the mobile terminal.

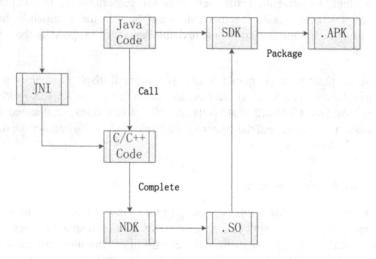

Fig. 2. An integrated software development framework in our system

Our experimental data is the same as that used in [3], including lunar mesh data, texture and label information. Here two-resolution lunar mesh models are used, one is the model with 24576 triangles when the viewpoint is far from the moon; the other is the one with 98304 triangles when the viewpoint is near the moon. The original lunar texture is divided into eight patches in all, as is described in Sect. 2.2. The number of geographical names is 468 in total both in English and Chinese, including 367 craters, 1 plain, 3 cliffs, 15 ridges, 20 mountains, 1 ocean, 2 valleys, 22 lunar mares, 17 lunar lacuses, 11 lunar sinuses, 3 lunar paluses and 6 capes. Three labelling levels are used, which correspond to $D < L_1$, $L_1 \leq D \leq L_2$ and $D > L_2$ respectively for the thresholds L_1 and L_2. Let r denote the lunar radius, we chose the threshold $L_1 = 2r$ and $L_2 = 5r$. Some experimental results are given in Fig. 3, where D is the distance between a viewpoint and the center of lunar model. By the way, our method can also label Chinese geographical names in corresponding coordinates.

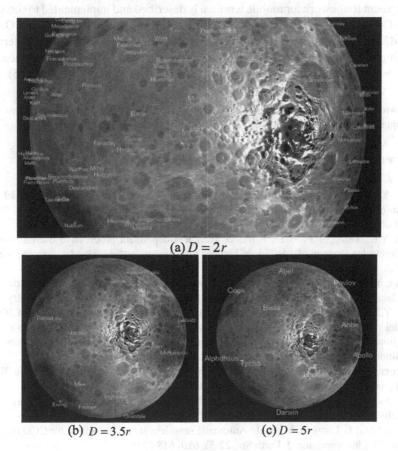

(a) $D = 2r$

(b) $D = 3.5r$ (c) $D = 5r$

Fig. 3. Lunar model visualization with label geographical names at different levels

Our browsing system supports three kinds of gesture interactions including rotation, zoom in and zoom out, which can make us browse the lunar model on mobile device in all-round and multi-angle. The average frame rate of the system is 62 fps for the lunar mesh with 24576 triangles and 33 fps for the model with 98304 triangles.

4   Conclusions

We developed an interactive visualization system of 3D lunar model with texture and labels on mobile device successfully. The system achieves real-time rendering frame rate. Specifically, we develop a vertex shader and fragment shader to render texture so that a technique of terrain labels for mobile device is provided for OpenGL ES 2.0. It is also provide a way to process a large size texture to overcome the limit of OpenGL ES 2.0 programming in texture loading size once time. In addition, a general software development framework for mobile terminal is described and implemented to show how to call C++ project by Java Virtual Machine based on OpenGL ES 2.0 and Osg for android. Therefore, our work provides a typical application for mobile terminal rendering. Everyone can download the lunar browsing system for mobile device from http://www.115.com/?lang=en (username: 13581683182; password: 19850415).

Acknowledgments. This work was supported by the National High Technology Research and Development Program of China ("863" Program) under Grant No. 2013AA013702.

References

1. Sun, Y.K., Mao, K.M., Zhang, T., et al.: A 3D multiresolution lunar surface model using bicubic subdivision-surface wavelets, with interactive visualization tools. Comput. Geosci. **37**(9), 1460–1467 (2011)
2. Sun, Y.K., Dong, Y.F., Mao, K.M., et al.: View-dependent progressive transmission and rendering for lunar model based on bicubic subdivision-surface wavelet. Adv. Space Res. **53**(12), 1848–1857 (2014)
3. Dong, Y.F., Sun, Y.K., Tang, Z.S.: Interactive visualization of 3D lunar model with texture and labels, using Chang'E-1 data. Sci. China Phys. Mech. Astron. **56**(10), 2002–2008 (2013)
4. Sun, Y.K., Dong, Y.F., Tang, Z.S.: Internet-based interactive visualization method of 3D lunar model with texture. Multimedia Tools Appl. (2014). doi:10.1007/s11042-014-1863-z
5. Noguera, J.M., Segura, R.J., Ogáyar, C.J., Joan-Arinyo, R.: Navigating large terrains using commodity mobile devices. Comput. Geosci. **37**(9), 1218–1233 (2011)
6. Noguera, J.M., Segura, R.J., Ogáyar, C.J., Joan-Arinyo, R.: A scalable architecture for 3D map navigation on mobile devices. Pers. Ubiquit. Comput. **17**(7), 1487–1502 (2013)
7. Francisco, R., Oscar, R., Miguel, C.: Efficient visualization of 3D models on hardware-limited portable devices. Multimedia Tools Appl. **73**(2), 961–976 (2014)
8. Ye, M.J., Li, J., Liang, Y.Y., et al.: Automatic seamless stitching method for CCD images of Chang'E-1 lunar mission. J. Earth Sci. **22**(5), 610–618 (2011)

Interactive Head 3D Reconstruction Based Combine of Key Points and Voxel

Yanwei Pang, Kun Li[✉], Jing Pan, Yuqing He, and Changshu Liu

School of Electronic Information Engineering, Tianjin University,
Tianjin 300072, China
dalikun0@sina.com

Abstract. In the 3D reconstruction of the head, we can extract a large number of key points from the face, but not enough key points from the hair. The 3D reconstruction method based key points do well in the facial reconstruction, but not be able to reconstruction the hair part. Because the traditional 3D reconstruction method based voxel exploit more silhouette information, the method can reconstruct the hair better than the method based key points. A method based the combine of key points and voxel is presented to reconstruct head models. The main process: first of all, extract key points and silhouette; secondly, reconstruct the head by key points method and get the space needed to be reconstruct by voxel method interactive; finally, reconstruct the space which we get in last step; Through this combination 3D reconstruction method, we can reconstruct a good head.

Keywords: 3D reconstruction · Key-points · Voxel · Interactive · Silhouette

1 Introduction

Reconstructing three-dimensional models from two-dimensional images has a hot research topic in the field of computer vision. The algorithm for computer three-dimensional reconstruction is usually divided into the following three: (a) silhouette-based algorithm [1]. Such algorithm use the object's silhouette projected on the image plane to reconstruct three-dimensional model of the object. (b) voxel-based algorithm [2]. Such algorithm divide the object into a lot of small cube (voxel), and then reconstruct the object based on these voxels; (c) key point based algorithm [3, 4]. Firstly, this algorithm obtains the sparse point clouds of the object's surface through the image sequence; and then, obtains the dense point clouds of the object's surface by the expansion step; finally, point clouds triangulation and texture mapping [5]. The reconstructed model has clear details. In the process of reconstruction the head three-dimensional by the key point based algorithm, because facial features have different colors and facial skin has diffuse reflection for incident light, we can extracted from the face a lot of key points. But hair is thick, thin and has low resolution textures. In some angles hair has a strong reflect because of the smooth surface of hair so that we obtain very different textures from different viewpoints. Because of all the above, we cannot extract enough key points from hair part. In response to these problems, we proposed an interactive head three-dimensional reconstruction system based combine

© Springer International Publishing Switzerland 2015
Y.-J. Zhang (Ed.): ICIG 2015, Part II, LNCS 9218, pp. 453–461, 2015.
DOI: 10.1007/978-3-319-21963-9_42

of key points and voxel. In the system, we extract the silhouette by a fast GrabCut algorithm and exploit the silhouette information in the key points based algorithm.

2   Related Work

2.1   3D Reconstruction Algorithm Based Key Points

Key points based three-dimensional method mainly includes following key steps: image feature extraction and image matching, camera calibration and pose estimation, sparse point clouds reconstruction, dense point clouds reconstruction, point clouds registration, point clouds triangulation and texture mapping. Camera's optical axis direction change when we shoot pictures from different viewpoints, so that there exist affine deformation between different pictures. We exploit a fully affine invariant image comparison method, Affine-SIFT (ASIFT) [6], to extract the image feature key points. While SIFT [7] is fully invariant with respect to only four parameters namely zoom, rotation and translation, the new method treats the two left over parameters: the angles defining the camera axis orientation (Fig. 1). For camera calibration, pose estimation and sparse point clouds reconstruction, our system integrates Bundler [8, 9]. Bundler takes a set of images, image features, and image matches as input, and produces a 3D reconstruction of camera and (sparse) scene geometry as output. The system reconstructs the scene incrementally, a few images at a time, using a modified version of the Sparse Bundle Adjustment package [10] of Lourakis and Argyros as the underlying optimization engine. Bundler has been successfully run on many Internet photo collections, as well as more structured collections. Finally, for dense reconstruction we use the execution of Yasutaka Furukawa's PMVS [11]/CMVS [12] tool chain. PMVS is a multi-view stereo software that takes a set of images and camera parameters, then reconstructs 3D dense point clouds of an object. PMVS stands for Patch-based Multi-view Stereos. Only rigid structure is reconstructed, in other words, the software automatically ignores non-rigid objects such as pedestrians in front of a building.

2.2   3D Reconstruction Algorithm Based Voxel

Three-dimensional reconstruction algorithm based voxel mainly includes the following key steps: dividing the object three-dimensional space into a voxel grid (Fig. 2)(a), dividing the image into foreground and background according to the outline of the object and projecting the voxels to the image. It will be part of the object if the voxel can be projected in the foreground in all of images (Fig. 2)(b), finally texture mapping of the voxel. We can obtain a realistic reconstructed three-dimensional model when the voxel is small enough. For the object silhouette extraction, we use a sample interactive fast GrabCut [13]. The projection matrix can be obtained in the bundler step mentioned before.

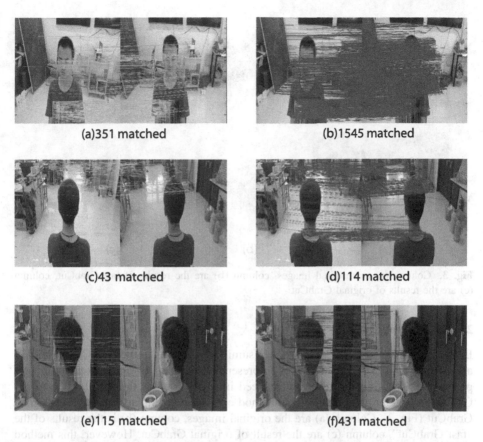

(a)351 matched   (b)1545 matched

(c)43 matched   (d)114 matched

(e)115 matched   (f)431 matched

Fig. 1. (a, c, e) Show the number of matched SIFT key points and the connection between the two image in different viewpoint, (b, d, f) show the number and connection of ASIFT key points. (a, b) Show the front of head, (c, d) show the back of the head, (e, f) show the side. As can be seen that ASIFT can extract more matched key points than SIFT in images at different viewpoints. Meanwhile, two method extract very small amounts matched key points in hair section.

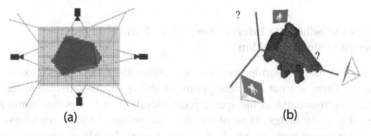

(a)   (b)

Fig. 2. (a) Dividing the object three-dimensional space into a voxel grid, (b) retain the voxel which can be projected into foreground of all images

Fig. 3. Column (a) are original images, column (b) are the results of fast GrabCut, column (c) are the results of original GrabCut

2.3 Fast GrabCut

Because the original GrabCut is time-consuming, to accelerate the GrabCut algorithm, a modified GrabCut algorithm [14] is presented by using resolution reduction pre-processing. The GrabCut result on reduced image is used as the initial value of the GrabCut on the original image. The method can obtain a similar result as the original GrabCut (Fig. 3). Column (a) are the original images, column (b) is the results of the "fast GrabCut", column (c) are the result of original GrabCut. However, this method interactive on the reduced image, we cannot specify foreground and background points but interactive by the rectangle on the image when the image is small. Because the operation of specifying foreground and background points is very necessary for extracting the silhouette when the color of foreground and the color of background is close. We improve it by interaction on the original image, and reduce the mask image obtained by interaction. We can make better use of interactive information.

2.4 Apply the Silhouette Information in Key Point-Based 3D Reconstruction Algorithm

In the key point-based algorithm process, we obtain the sparse point clouds after the bundler step. There are not only the points of the reconstructed object but also the points of the surroundings in the sparse point clouds. The key points come from the object and the surroundings. Most of the time the points of the surroundings account for most of the sparse point clouds. In this case, a considerable amount of time will be spent in dealing with the surrounding environment when performing PMVS step. Every point in the sparse point clouds is projected to the images, we count the number **n** of the images which one point is projected into the foreground and the **N** is the number of all

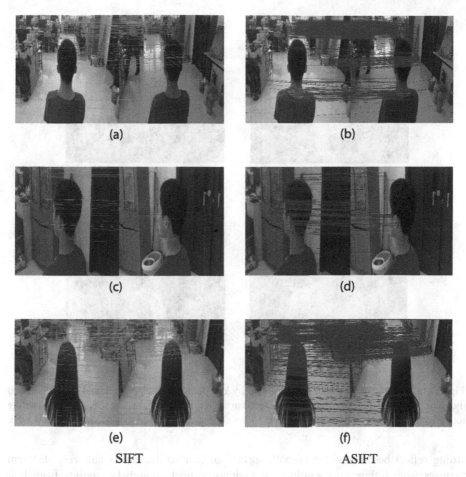

Fig. 4. (a, c, c) Are the matched SIFT key points in two images, (b, d, f) are the matched ASIFT key points in two images. Among them, (a, b) are the short hair, (c, d) are the longer hair, (e, f) are the long hair. As can be seen in the picture that neither SIFT nor ASIFT can extract enough key points from hair part, thus hair cannot be reconstructed by key point based algorithm.

images, if **n/N** > 35/37 (35/37 is an experience value) the point will be retained, otherwise the point will be delete. In this case, PMVS will just deal with the points belong to object and will save some time than dealing with all points. We don't filter the key points at the extracting key points step because the key points of surroundings make the camera calibration, pose estimation and sparse reconstruction more accurate in bundler step.

2.5 3D Reconstruction Based Combine of Key Point and Voxel

In the key point based 3D reconstruction method process, because of the special hair texture (smooth surface does not produce diffuse reflection, in some angles hair has a

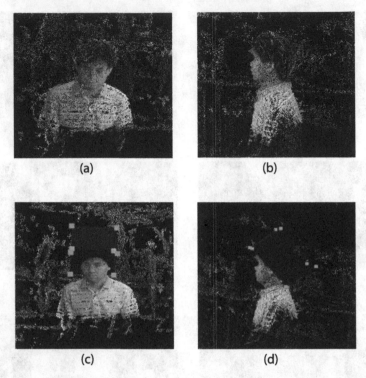

(a)   (b)

(c)   (d)

Fig. 5. (a, b) Is the dense cloud reconstructed by key point based algorithm, and we can see that the hair part don't get a satisfactory reconstruction result (there are cavities and wrong reconstruction). In (c, d), we use the cube to get the space which cannot be reconstructed well.

strong reflect because of the smooth surface of hair so that we obtain very different textures from different viewpoints), we cannot extract enough key points from hair (Fig. 4), meanwhile the rate of matching error if very high. So we cannot reconstruct hair part correctly in bundler step. But the silhouette of head can reflect the general three-dimensional shape of the hair. Our system implement a user controlled cubes which able to rotate freely, zooming, moving location in space (Fig. 5). We exploit the cube to obtain the space used to reconstruct the object by voxel based algorithm, and update the reconstructed three-dimensional model by the result of voxel based three-dimensional reconstruct algorithm. Finally, we reconstruct a good head model.

3   Results

Visual SFM [15, 16] is a GUI application for 3D reconstruction using structure from motion (SFM). This application extract and match SIFT key points in images, reconstruct sparse point cloud by bundler. For dense reconstruction, this program integrates the execution of Yasutaka Furukawa's PMVS/CMVS tool chain. The main steps of Visual SFM:

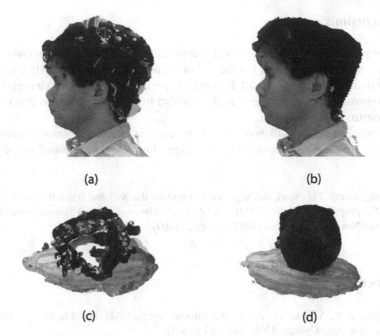

(a)   (b)

(c)   (d)

Fig. 6. Show the results of Visual SFM and our system, (a, c) is the result of Visual SFM, (b, d) is the result of our system. Because there is not matched key points, (a, c) have many wrong reconstruction and cavities in the hair area, and our system reconstruct a good head model with less wrong reconstruction and no cavities.

1. Input images
2. Extract SIFT and match key points
3. Reconstruct sparse point cloud by Bundler
4. Reconstruct dense point cloud by PMVS/CMVS
5. Point clouds triangulation and texture mapping

The main steps of our three-dimensional system based key points and voxel:

1. Input images
2. Extract and match key points and extract silhouette
3. Reconstruct sparse point cloud and filter the point belong to surroundings
4. Reconstruct dense point cloud
5. Obtain the space which to be reconstructed
6. Reconstruct the space obtained in last step by the voxel based algorithm
7. Update the reconstructed model
8. Point clouds triangulation and texture mapping

We reconstruct an object by Visual SFM and our system. As can be seen from the reconstruction results (Fig. 6), there exist many wrong reconstruction and cavities in the result of Visual SFM and there less wrong reconstruction and no cavities in the result of our system. The result of our system reconstructs a good head model.

4   Conclusions

Our paper proposed a three-dimensional reconstruction method based combine of key point and voxel and this method has the following features: exploiting ASIFT to extract more key points than traditional SIFT, user can specify the space (the hair part) needed to be reconstruct, using the voxel based algorithm to reconstruct hair so that obtain a good reconstructed head model.

Of course, there are still some problem: there is a discontinuous phenomenon between the two part reconstructed by two algorithm. We will improve in the future work.

Acknowledgement. This work was supported in part by the National Basic Research Program of China 973 Program (Grant No. 2014CB340400), the National Natural Science Foundation of China (Grant Nos. 61472274, 61271412, and 61222109).

References

1. Mülayim, A.Y., Yilmaz, U., Atalay, V.: Silhouette-based 3-D model reconstruction. IEEE Trans. Syst. Man Cybern. **33**(4), 582–591 (2003)
2. Wang, Y.: Research on Profile Extraction and Key Technologies for 3D Reconstruction, pp. 63–74. University of Chongqing, Chongqing (2010). (in Chinese)
3. Pons, J.P., Keriven, R., Faugeras, O.D.: Multi-view stereo reconstruction and scene flow estimation with a global image based matching score. Int. J. Comput. Vis. **72**(2), 179–193 (2007)
4. Seitz, S.M., Curless, B., Diebel, J.: A comparison and evaluation of multi-view stereo reconstruction algorithms. Comput. Vision Pattern Recogn. **1**, 519–528 (2006)
5. Kazhdan, M., Bolitho, M., Hoppe, H.: Poisson surface reconstruction. In: Symposium on Geometry Processing, pp. 61–70 (2006)
6. Morel, J.M., Yu, G.: ASIFT: A new framework for fully affine invariant image comparison. SIAM J. Imaging Sci. **2**(2), 438–469 (2009)
7. Lowe, D.G.: Distinctive image features from scale-invariant keypoints. Int. J. Comput. Vis. **60**(2), 91–110 (2004)
8. Snavely, N., Seitz, S.M., Szeliski, R.: Photo tourism: exploring image collections in 3D. ACM Trans. Graph. **25**(3), 835–846 (2006)
9. Snavely, N., Seitz, S.M., Szeliski, R.: Modeling the world from internet photo collections. Int. J. Comput. Vis. **80**(2), 189–210 (2007)
10. Lourakis, M., Argyros, A.: SBA: a software package for generic sparse bundle adjustment. ACM Trans. Math. Softw. **36**(1), 2 (2009)
11. Furukawa, Y., Curless, B., Seitz, S.M., Szeliski, R.: Towards internet-scale multi-view stereo. In: IEEE Conference on Computer Vision and Pattern Recognition, pp 1434–1441 (2010)
12. Furukawa, Y., Ponce, J.: Accurate, dense, and robust multi-view stereopsis. IEEE Trans. Pattern Anal. Mach. Intell. **32**(8), 1362–1376 (2010)
13. Rother, C., Kolmogorov, V., Blake, A.: "GrabCut" — interactive foreground extraction using iterated graph cuts. ACM Trans. Graph. **23**(3), 309–314 (2004)

14. Ding, H., Zhang, X.: Object abstraction algorithm with fast GrabCut. Comput. Eng. Des. **33** (4), 1477–1481 (2012). (in Chinese)
15. Wu, C.: Towards linear-time incremental structure from motion. In: International Conference on 3D Vision, pp. 127–134 (2013)
16. Wu, C., Agarwal, S., Curless, B., Seitz, S.M.: Multicore bundle adjustment. In: IEEE Conference on Computer Vision and Pattern Recognition, pp. 1063–6919 (2011)

Lighting Alignment for Image Sequences

Xiaoyue Jiang$^{(\boxtimes)}$, Xiaoyi Feng, Jun Wu, and Jinye Peng

School of Electronics and Information, Northwestern Polytechnical University,
Xi'an 710072, China
xjiang@nwpu.edu.cn

Abstract. Lighting is one of the challenges for image processing. Even though some algorithms are proposed to deal with the lighting variation for images, most of them are designed for a single image but not for image sequences. In fact, the correlation between frames can provide useful information to remove the illumination diversity, which is not available for a single image. In this paper, we proposed a 2-step lighting alignment algorithm for image sequences. Based on entropy, a perception-based lighting model is initialized according to the lighting condition of first frame. Then the difference between frames is applied to optimize the parameters of the lighting model and consequently the lighting conditions can be aligned for the sequence. At the same time, the local features of each frame can be enhanced. Experimental results show the effectiveness of the proposed algorithm.

Keywords: Lighting alignment · Entropy-based model · Perception-based model · Tracking

1 Introduction

Lighting can cause dramatic variance for images. Thus it is considered as one of the challenges for image processing tasks, such as object detection, recognition, and tracking. Algorithms that deal with the illumination variance can be classified as invariant feature-based and model-based methods. Those feature-based methods attempt to extract illumination invariant features from images, such as edge-based algorithm [1], quotient image-based algorithms [2–5], and Retinex theory-based algorithms [6–9]. For these algorithms, they remove the illumination at the cost of removing all low-frequency information of the images. Actually the low-frequency information is always very useful for the tasks of recognition and detection. On the other hand, the model-based algorithms try to describe the lighting variance. Low-dimensional subspace can be applied to model the complete lighting space with the theory proposed by Basri et al. [10] and Ramamoorith et al. [11]. In order to build up lighting subspace, 3D model is always required for the object [12–17]. Recently, Sparse representation-based algorithm also showed its effectiveness in dealing with illumination problem [18,19], while the lack of training images always limited its application.

© Springer International Publishing Switzerland 2015
Y.-J. Zhang (Ed.): ICIG 2015, Part II, LNCS 9218, pp. 462–474, 2015.
DOI: 10.1007/978-3-319-21963-9_43

There are a lot of algorithms to deal with the lighting problem for single images, but a few are designed for image sequences. Even though these algorithms that deal with lighting problems for single images can be applied to each frame in image sequences, they are always too complex to satisfy the time requirement of tasks performed on image sequences, such as tracking. Also, these algorithms do not consider the information that is provided by each frame. In fact the correlation between frames can be used to minimize the lighting variance. Meanwhile, to enhance the original features in images is also very crucial for the achievement of image-processing tasks. For most lighting preprocessing algorithms [20], they focused on removing lighting components from images and at the same time losing some object information. Therefore an effective lighting preprocessing method should minimize the lighting variation and keep or even enhance the intrinsic features of the objects as well.

In this paper, we propose a perception-based lighting alignment algorithm for image sequences. For each image frame, to ensure convergence, the algorithm works in two steps. First initial values of the lighting model parameters are estimated using the entropy of the current image as measure. These values are then used as initial guesses for a constrained least squares optimization problem, considering the correlation between two successive frames. Also, we adjusted the global lighting conditions of image sequences to be more uniform and enhance the local features of the image as well.

The perception based lighting model is introduced in Sect. 2. In Sect. 3 we give an overview of the proposed lighting adjustment algorithm for image sequence. Section 4 discusses qualitative and quantitative results of the lighting adjustment in the case of facial features detection and tracking. Finally, conclusions are drawn in Sect. 5.

2 Perception-Based Lighting Model

The Human Vision System (HVS) can adapt very well under enormously changed lighting conditions. People can see well at daytime and also at night. That is due to the accurate adaptation ability of the HVS. However, image capturing devices seldom have this adaptation ability. For an image taken under extreme lighting conditions, such as the images shown in first row of Fig. 2(b), a proper lighting adjustment algorithm should not only adjust the brightness of the images, but also enhance the features of the image, especially for the dark regions. To reach this goal, we propose to reduce the light variations by an adaptive adjustment of the image. Here, we employ a model of photoreceptor adaptation in Human Vision System [21] in which three parameters (α, f, m) control the lighting adjustment. The adjusted image Y is modeled as a function of these lighting parameters and the input image X as:

$$Y(\alpha, m, f; X) = \frac{X}{X + \sigma(X_a)} V_{max} \qquad (1)$$

where σ, referred to as *semi-saturation constant*, X_a the adaptation level, and V_{max} determines the maximum range of the output value (we use $V_{max} = 255$ to

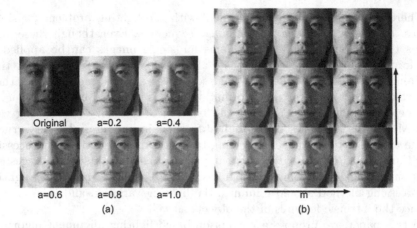

Fig. 1. (a) Adaptation level v.s. α parameter (b) lighting adjustment v.s. m and f parameters.

have grey image output in the range of $[0, 255]$). The semi-saturation constant σ describes the image intensity and its contrast through the parameters f and m, respectively [21]:

$$\sigma(X_a) = (fX_a)^m \tag{2}$$

Adaptation Level. I_a If we choose the average intensity of the image as the adaptation level I_a, the adjustment is global. It does not perform any specific processing to the darker or brighter region and some details in those regions may be lost. To compensate the details, the local conditions of every point should be considered. We can use the bi-linear interpolation to combine the global adaptation I_a^{global} and local adaptation $I_a^{local}(x, y)$ as,

$$I_a(x, y) = \alpha I_a^{local}(x, y) + (1 - \alpha)I_a^{global} \tag{3}$$

$$I_a^{local}(x, y) = K(I(x, y)) \tag{4}$$

$$I_a^{global} = mean(I) \tag{5}$$

Different kernel $K(\bullet)$ can be applied to extract the local information. Gauss kernel is the most commonly used one. The interpolation of the global and local information will adjust the details. In Fig. 1(a), with the increasing of the parameter α, the details become notable gradually. When $\alpha = 1$, i.e. $I_a = I_a^{local}$, all the details are expressed out including the noise.

Parameter f and m. The other two parameters f and m control the intensity and contrast, respectively. Parameter f is the multiplier in the adaptation function, i.e. to every point's adaptation level $I_a(x, y)$, f magnifies them with the same scale. The brightness of the whole image will be enhanced or suppressed accordingly.

The alternation of brightness can be shown only when changes on f is large enough. In [21], the parameter f is suggested to be rewritten in the following form

$$f = exp(-f')$$ (6)

With a comparative smaller changing range of f', f can alter the brightness of the image.

Parameter m is an exponent in the adaptation function. Different from the parameter f, m magnifies every $I_a(x,y)$ with a different scale based on its adaptation value. Therefore, parameter m can emphasize the difference between every point, i.e. the contrast. In Fig. 1(b), the parameter α is fixed. With the increment of m, the contrast of the image is enhanced in every row. And in every column, the brightness of the image is enhanced with the increase of f.

3   Image Sequence Lighting Adjustment

In capturing an image sequence the influence of the scene lighting may not be neglected. Often the variations of the lighting conditions cannot be avoided while recording, and therefore lighting adjustment methods must be used before further processing. In this paper, we propose a tow-steps lighting adjustment approach. First, the initial optimal parameters, α_k^0, f_k^0, m_k^0 of each frame X_k; $k = 1, \cdots N$ are calculated using entropy as an objective function. These values are then used as initial guesses for a constrained least squares optimization problem for further refinement of those parameter. In this step, the objective function is the difference between the adjusted previous frame Y_{k-1} and the current frame X_k. The two steps are detailed in the following sections, and experimental results are presented in Sect. 4.

3.1   Single Image Enhancement

It is well known that an image with large entropy value indicates that the distribution of its intensity values is more uniform, i.e. each intensity value has almost the same probability to appear in the image. Hence, the image cannot be locally too bright or too dark.

Entropy $H(x)$, defined as:

$$H(X) = -\sum_{i=0}^{255} p(i)log_2(p(i))$$ (7)

where $p(i)$ is the probability of the intensity values i in the whole image, can be employed to evaluate image lighting quality. When all the intensity values have the same probability in the image, the entropy can reach its maximum value 8. However, not all the images can reach the entropy $H(X) = 8$ when they are in their best situation. The optimal entropy value, H_o, is image content dependent. In this paper, we set $H_o = 7$ as the expected optimal entropy for all the images. Therefore the objective function for the lighting adjustment of every single image is

$$J_1(\alpha, m, f) = \underset{\substack{a\in[0,1];m\in[0.3,1) \\ f\in[\exp(-8),\exp(8)]}}{\arg\min} |H(Y(\alpha, m, f; X)) - H_o| \tag{8}$$

The lighting parameter α controls the adaptation level of the images, as in Eq. 4. It can adjust the image much more than the other two parameters (f, m). Therefore an alternate optimization strategy is used [22]. First, the parameter α is optimized with fixed m and f. Then the parameter m and f are optimized with fixed α. These two optimizations are repeated until convergence. To initialize, we estimate $\hat{\alpha}$ with fixed m and f which are selected according to the luminance situation of the image. The contrast-control parameter m can be determined by the key k of the image [21], as

$$m = 0.3 + 0.7k^{1.4} \tag{9}$$

The key of the image evaluates the luminance range of the image and is defined as

$$k = \frac{L_{max} - L_{av}}{L_{max} - L_{min}} \tag{10}$$

where L_{av}, L_{min}, L_{max} are the log average, log minimum and log maximum of the luminance respectively. For color images, we use the luminance image computed as $L = 0.2125I_r + 0.7154I_g + 0.0721I_b$, where I_r, I_g, I_b are the red, green, blue channels. The brightness-control parameter f is set to 1. Then the simplex search algorithm [23] is applied for determining the optimal $\hat{\alpha}$. Fixing the value $\hat{\alpha}$ in J_1, the simplex search algorithm is then used to search for optimal $\hat{m}$ and $\hat{f}$. The alternate optimization will stop when the objective function J_1 is smaller than a given threshold.

This approach can adjust an image to have suitable brightness and contrast. Also, it can enhance the local gradient features of the image due to the adjustment of the parameter α. However, entropy does not relate to intensity directly. Different images can have the same entropy value while their brightness is different. For example, the images in the second row of Fig. 2(a) and (b), being the lighting adjusted results of the images of the first row, have the same entropy values, but their lighting conditions are not similar. Consequently, for a sequence of images, we still need to adjust the brightness and contrast of successive frames to be similar and therefore enhance their features.

3.2   Lighting Adjustment of Successive Images

In video sequences, the difference between successive frames is due to object and/or camera motions and lighting changes. Whereas the former differences are exploited in object tracking and camera motion estimation, the latter, i.e. lighting differences, are such that the required brightness constancy assumption for tracking gets violated. In this paper, we show that for tracking of slow movement in a sequence captured by a fixed camera, the lighting problem can be reduced by applying a lighting adjustment method. Indeed, the lighting of the overall sequence could be made more uniform (in a sequential manner) by considering the changes between successive frames. We propose to use the difference between successive frames as an objective function to estimate the optimal lighting parameters of the current frame X_j, provided that the previous frame X_{j-1} has been adjusted, i.e. given Y_{j-1}:

$$J_2(\alpha, m, f) = \underset{\substack{\alpha\in[0,1];m\in[0.3,1) \\ f\in[\exp(-8),\exp(8)]}}{\arg\min} \sum_x \sum_y \left(Y(\alpha, m, f; X_j(x,y)) - Y_{j-1}\right)^2 \quad (11)$$

With Eq. 1, the difference $e(\alpha, m, f) = Y(\alpha, m, f; X_j) - Y_{j-1}$ between frames can be written as (for simplicity we drop the pixel index (x,y)):

$$e = \frac{X_j}{X_j - (f_j X_{a_j})^{m_j}} - \frac{X_{j-1}}{X_{j-1} - (f_{j-1} X_{a_{j-1}})^{m_{j-1}}} \quad (12)$$

When searching for the optimal parameters for the objective function J_2, the derivatives over different parameters need to calculate.

If the two images concerned are the same, the difference between these images is minimum, at the same time, the difference between the inverse of images will also reach to its minimum value. Therefore, we calculate the difference between the inverse of adjusted images to simplify the computation of derivatives, as

$$\tilde{e} = \frac{X_j - (f_j X_{a_j})^{m_j}}{X_j} - \frac{X_{j-1} - (f_{j-1} X_{a_{j-1}})^{m_{j-1}}}{X_{j-1}}$$

$$= \frac{(f_j X_{a_j})^{m_j}}{X_j} - \frac{(f_{j-1} X_{a_{j-1}})^{m_{j-1}}}{X_{j-1}} \quad (13)$$

Let $\hat{Y}_{j-1} = (f_{j-1} X_{a_{j-1}})^{m_{j-1}}/X_{j-1}$ and apply log to both side of Eq. 13, we can simplify the difference between frames further as

$$\hat{e} = \log \frac{(f_j X_{a_j})^{m_j}}{X_j} - \log \hat{Y}_{j-1}$$

$$= m_j \log f_j + m_j \log X_{a_j} - \log X_j - \log \hat{Y}_{j-1} \quad (14)$$

Then the objective function J_2 can be rewriten as

$$\hat{J}_2(\alpha_j, m_j, f_j) = \underset{\substack{\alpha\in[0,1];m\in[0.3,1) \\ f\in[\exp(-8),\exp(8)]}}{\arg\min} \sum_x \sum_y \left(m_j \log f_j + m_j \log X_{a_j} - \log X_j - \log \hat{Y}_{j-1}\right)^2 \quad (15)$$

This formulation allows easily estimating the partial derivatives, and we apply the interior-point algorithm [24] to solve the optimization problem $\hat{J}_2$, with initial values of the lighting parameters α_j^0, f_j^0 and m_j^0 obtained by minimizing Eq. 8.

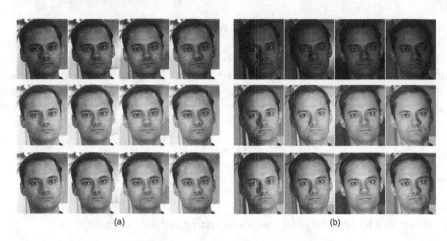

Fig. 2. Lighting adjustment results of frame 1 to 4 in L1 and L2. (a) and (b) are results of L1 and L2: from top to bottom are original images, entropy-based optimization, and 2-step optimization results, respectively.

4   Experiments on Lighting Adjustment

The proposed lighting adjustment algorithms of the previous section have been tested on the PIE facial database [25], from which we selected images under different lighting conditions to compose 3 test sequences, here referred to as L1, L2 and L3. We intend to take these sequences as typical examples to demonstrate the performance of the algorithm in slight lighting variations (L1), overall dark sequences (L2) and suddenly changing light variations (L3). To show the benefits of the proposed image sequence lighting adjustment approach, we compare it to state-of-art lighting adjustment methods for single images, namely, the quotient image (QI) algorithm [3], and the well known histogram equalization (HE) approach.

The lighting conditions of the test sequences can be described as follows. Sequence L1 and L2 are composed of 19 frames taken from the same person. The first row of Fig. 2 shows the first 4 frames of L1 and L2. The images in L1 are taken with ambient lighting and 19 different point light sources. The positions of these light points, are 10, 07, 08, 09, 13, 14, 12, 11, 06, 05, 18, 19, 20, 21, and 22, respectively. The images in L2 are taken under the same light point source but without ambient lighting, so they appear to be more dark. Sequence L3 is composed of 39 images which come from L1 and L2 alternately. Thus the lighting condition of the images in L3 is ambient lighting on and off alternately. The first row of Fig. 4 shows the frames 9 to 14 of L3.

To evaluate the lighting quality of the adjusted images, the *key value* (Eq. 10) and entropy are depicted in Fig. 3. The *key value* of an image evaluates the luminance range of the image. The entropy, being the mean entropy of the 3 color channels, relates to the distribution of the intensity values in each channel. The key value of all adjusted frames and the original sequence of L3 are shown

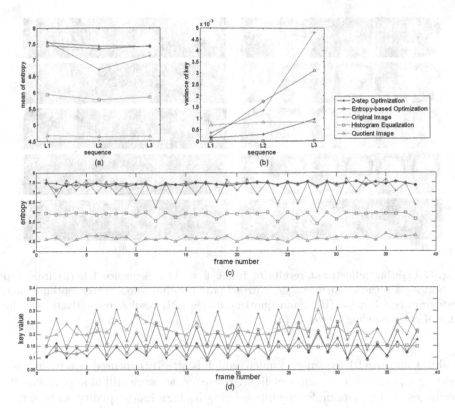

Fig. 3. Entropy and image key curves. (a) and (b) are the mean entropy and the variance of key of all the frames in the original sequences and adjusted results of the sequences, respectively. (c) and (d) are the entropy value and key value of every frame in L3 and different adjusted results of L3, respectively.

in Fig. 3(d). The key value zigzags due to the alternate brightness of the original sequence L3. For a sequence with reduced lighting variation the key value should stay constant throughout the sequence. Therefore, we show the variance of the key value in Fig. 3(b). For all the 3 test sequences, the variance of the key value of the results of the proposed 2-step optimization algorithm is smaller than that of the other algorithms except HE algorithm. However, HE algorithm costs the entropy value of images, whose results are even worse than the original images (Fig. 3(a)). The reason is that HE algorithm can make the intensity distribution uniform only by skipping values in the intensity range [0, 255] of the adjusted images, thereby leaving many gaps in the histogram of the adjusted images. The entropy value of the QI results are the smallest because of the loss of the low frequency information in the images. The proposed algorithm is the largest in the mean of entropy, Fig. 3(a), and we can also see from Fig. 4(a) that these resemble most the intensity value distribution of the original images. Our goal is indeed not to change the image appearance dramatically (as compared to QI) but only to obtain a good lighting quality. Therefore, it is quite normal that we

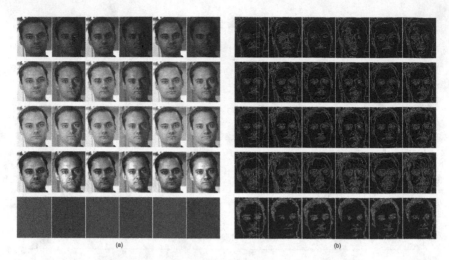

Fig. 4. Lighting adjustment results of frame 9 to 14 in sequence L3. (a) from top to bottom are the original images, entropy-based optimization, 2-step optimization, histogram equalization (HE), and quotient image (QI) results, respectively. (b) the edge of corresponding images in (a).

couldn't improve L1 sequence so much, which is already captured at a reasonable lighting quality with the ambient light. However, we were still able to adjust its brightness to be more uniform while keeping its high image quality, as shown in Fig. 2(a). On the other hand, our 2-step algorithm enhanced the image lighting quality significantly for the sequences L2 and L3 containing images taken under extreme lighting conditions.

Next, we examine the effect of the lighting adjustment methods on the object's edges of Fig. 4(b) to determine if the methods are appropriate as pre-processing for feature detection methods. Considering the edges in the adjusted images, our proposed algorithm enhances the feature of images. This is especially the case for those images taken in a dark environment. Also, highlight are compensated and the influence of shadows on the edges are reduced. The HE algorithm was able to enhance the contrast of the image but at the same time it enhanced noise as well. As we already mentioned, the QI algorithm removed most low frequency information of the image thereby included some important features of the image.

The advantage of the image difference-based optimization step is illustrated for facial feature tracking (on the sequences L1 to L3). We demonstrate that the difficulty of tracking a modified object appearance due to lighting changes can be overcome by employing our proposed algorithm as pre-processing. In this paper, we focus on the results of a template-based eye and mouth corner tracker. That tracker is part of a previously developed approach to automatically locate frontal facial feature points under large scene variations (illumination, pose and facial expressions) [26]. This approach consisted of three steps: (i) we use a

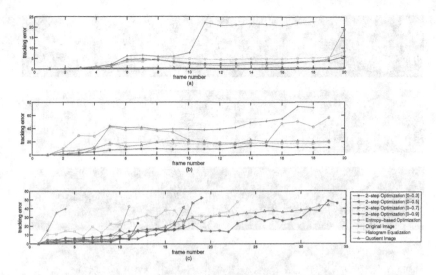

Fig. 5. Feature points tracking error

kernel-based tracker to detect and track the facial region; (ii) we constrain a detection and tracking of eye and mouth facial features by the estimated face pose of (i) by introducing the parameterized feature point motion model into a Lukas-Kanade tracker; (iii) we detect and track 83 semantic facial points, gathered in a shape model, by constraining the shapes rigid motion and deformation parameters by the estimated face pose of (i) and by the eyes and mouth corner features location of (ii).

The performance of the tracking of the eyes and mouth corners (6 feature points) on the original and adjusted image sequences L1 to L3 is displayed in Fig. 5. The tracking error per frame is calculated as the average distance between the real positions (manually identified) and the tracked positions of the 6 feature points in the image. When tracking was lost, the graph is truncated. Figure 5(a) shows that all adjustments of the sequence L1 allow to track until the end of that sequence. The QI shows the smallest tracking error because it enhances the gradient features in the image, but at the cost of obtaining visually unpleasant images (see last row of Fig. 4(a)). Compared to the HE results, our two-step optimization does reach a better tracking performance. Because the initial lighting variations in sequence L1 are not that big, the entropy-step alone may already improve the tracking. The benefit of the image difference-based optimization step becomes obvious via the tracking error graphs of the dark sequence L2 in Fig. 5(b). Here, the tracking errors on the 2-step optimization are the smallest. This shows that local features are enhanced very well, but also that taking care of correspondences between images is indeed important. QI and HE adjustments perform worse in tracking. For QI, the reason is that it may enhance the local features (gradients) only when the noise level is not high, i.e. images taken in good lighting conditions such as in L1. On the alternating dark and light

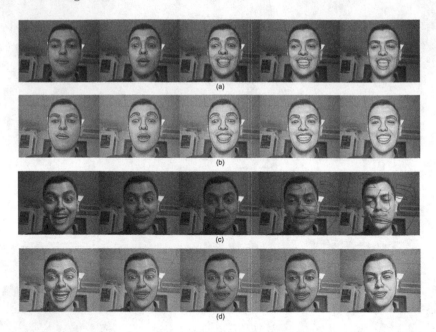

Fig. 6. Shape model results. (a) results on original sequence M1 with 10 frames (there are frame 1, 3, 5, 7, 10 from left to right), (b) corresponding results on adjusted sequence M1; (c) results on original sequence M2 with 14 frames (there are frame 1, 4, 6, 9, 14 from left to right), (d) corresponding results on adjusted sequence M2.

sequence L3 the tracking of the original and entropy-optimized sequence is very quickly lost, as shown in Fig. 5(c). It is thus crucial to take into account the sequence aspects in lighting adjustment. It is worth noting that the tracking for our proposed algorithm results was lost only when a part of the image were in deep shadow (such as frame 12, 17 and 19). Although no adjustment method can track until the end of the sequence, we see that a larger enhancement of the local features may allow to track longer (reduced entropy). That was done by enlarging the alpha range from $[0, 0.3]$ to $[0, 0.9]$ in the 2-step optimization (Eqs. 8 and 11). When comparing the errors before tracking was lost, we see that reducing frame differences, especially with small alpha range, increases the accuracy of the tracking. This shows that enhancing image sequence quality can also help to track.

Then we tested the constrained shape model tracking (step (iii) of [26]) on a sequence [27] adjusted by the 2-step lighting optimization. Before adjustment, shown in Fig. 6(a), (c), some tracked features could not be well delineated due to the illumination changes in the image sequence. The intensity and texture of the face image were improved by our lighting adjustment and therefore all shape points were tracked more efficiently as shown in Fig. 6(b), (d).

5   Conclusion

Lighting is always a crucial problem for image based pattern recognition. Lighting is the main factor that makes the image. Therefore when lighting changes, images of objects will also change such that difficulties arise in detecting, recognizing and tracking them throughout images. Currently, most of the algorithms that deal with the lighting problems are only aimed at adjusting the lighting conditions of one image. However, in tracking the problems arise at the lighting difference between frames.

For the application of tracking, we proposed a 2-step lighting adjustment algorithm to reduce the influence of the variation oflighting conditions in an image sequence. First, an entropy-based algorithm is applied to calculate initial lighting parameters of a perceptual lighting model. Then the difference between current and previous frames is employed as an objective function for the further optimization of those lighting parameters. Using this criteria, successive frames are adjusted to have similar brightness and contrast. Image lighting quality, measured by entropy and key value, but also local features are enhanced. We did demonstrate the effectiveness of the proposed algorithm for subsequent image processing, such as detection and tracking.

References

1. Gao, Y., Leung, M.K.: Face recognition using line edge map. IEEE Trans. Pattern Analy. Mach. Intell. **24**(6), 764–779 (2002)
2. Shashua, A., Riklin-Raviv, T.: The quotient image: class-based re-rendering and recognition with varying illuminations. IEEE Trans. Pattern Anal. Mach. Intell. **23**(2), 129–139 (2001)
3. Wang, H., Li, S.Z., Wang, Y.: Generalized quotient image. In: Computer Vision and Pattern Recognition, CVPR 2004, vol. 2, pp. 498–505. IEEE (2004)
4. Xie, X., Zheng, W.S., Lai, J., Yuen, P.C., Suen, C.Y.: Normalization of face illumination based on large-and small-scale features. IEEE Trans. Image Process. **20**(7), 1807–1821 (2011)
5. Zhao, X., Shah, S.K., Kakadiaris, I.A.: Illumination normalization using self-lighting ratios for 3D2D face recognition. In: Fusiello, A., Murino, V., Cucchiara, R. (eds.) ECCV 2012 Ws/Demos, Part II. LNCS, vol. 7584, pp. 220–229. Springer, Heidelberg (2012)
6. Tan, X., Triggs, B.: Enhanced local texture feature sets for face recognition under difficult lighting conditions. IEEE Trans. Image Process. **19**(6), 1635–1650 (2010)
7. Chen, T., Yin, W., Zhou, X.S., Comaniciu, D., Huang, T.S.: Total variation models for variable lighting face recognition. IEEE Trans. Pattern Anal. Mach. Intell. **28**(9), 1519–1524 (2006)
8. Chen, W., Er, M.J., Wu, S.: Illumination compensation and normalization for robust face recognition using discrete cosine transform in logarithm domain. IEEE Trans. Syst. Man Cybern. Part B: Cybern. **36**(2), 458–466 (2006)
9. Xie, X., Lam, K.M.: An efficient illumination normalization method for face recognition. Pattern Recogn. Lett. **27**(6), 609–617 (2006)
10. Basri, R., Jacobs, D.W.: Lambertian reflectance and linear subspaces. IEEE Trans. Pattern Anal. Mach. Intell. **25**(2), 218–233 (2003)

11. Ramamoorthi, R., Hanrahan, P.: On the relationship between radiance and irradiance: determining the illumination from images of a convex lambertian object. J. Opt. Soc. Am. A **18**(10), 2448–2459 (2001)
12. Zhang, L., Samaras, D.: Face recognition under variable lighting using harmonic image exemplars. In: IEEE Computer Society Conference on Computer Vision and Pattern Recognition, CVPR 2003, vol. 1, pp. 19–25. IEEE (2003)
13. Wen, Z., Liu, Z., Huang, T.S.: Face relighting with radiance environment maps. In: IEEE Conference on Computer Vision and Pattern Recognition, vol. 2, pp. 158–165. IEEE (2003)
14. Zhang, L., Wang, S., Samaras, D.: Face synthesis and recognition from a single image under arbitrary unknown lighting using a spherical harmonic basis morphable model. In: IEEE Conference on Computer Vision and Pattern Recognition, vol. 2, pp. 209–216. IEEE (2005)
15. Lee, J., Moghaddam, B., Pfister, H., Machiraju, R.: A bilinear illumination model for robust face recognition. In: Tenth IEEE International Conference on Computer Vision, ICCV 2005, vol. 2, pp. 1177–1184. IEEE (2005)
16. Wang, Y., Liu, Z., Hua, G., Wen, Z., Zhang, Z., Samaras, D.: Face re-lighting from a single image under harsh lighting conditions. In: IEEE Conference on Computer Vision and Pattern Recognition, pp. 1–8. IEEE (2007)
17. Zhao, X., Evangelopoulos, G., Chu, D., Shah, S., Kakadiaris, I.A.: Minimizing illumination differences for 3D to 2D face recognition using lighting maps. IEEE Trans. Cybern. **44**(5), 725–736 (2014)
18. Wagner, A., Wright, J., Ganesh, A., Zhou, Z., Mobahi, H., Ma, Y.: Toward a practical face recognition system: Robust alignment and illumination by sparse representation. IEEE Trans. Pattern Anal. Mach. Intell. **34**(2), 372–386 (2012)
19. Zhuang, L., Yang, A.Y., Zhou, Z., Sastry, S.S., Ma, Y.: Single-sample face recognition with image corruption and misalignment via sparse illumination transfer. In: 2013 IEEE Conference on Computer Vision and Pattern Recognition (CVPR), pp. 3546–3553. IEEE (2013)
20. Han, H., Shan, S., Chen, X., Gao, W.: A comparative study on illumination preprocessing in face recognition. Pattern Recogn. **46**(6), 1691–1699 (2013)
21. Reinhard, E., Devlin, K.: Dynamic range reduction inspired by photoreceptor physiology. IEEE Trans. Vis. Comput. Graph. **11**(1), 13–24 (2005)
22. Jiang, X., Sun, P., Xiao, R., Zhao, R.: Perception based lighting balance for face detection. In: Narayanan, P.J., Nayar, S.K., Shum, H.-Y. (eds.) ACCV 2006. LNCS, vol. 3852, pp. 531–540. Springer, Heidelberg (2006)
23. Nelder, J.A., Mead, R.: A simplex method for function minimization. Comput. J. **7**, 308–313 (1965)
24. Waltz, R.A., Morales, J.L., Nocedal, J., Orban, D.: An interior algorithm for nonlinear optimization that combines line search and trust region steps. Math. Program. **107**(3), 391–408 (2006)
25. Sim, T., Baker, S., Bsat, M.: The CMU pose, illumination, and expression (PIE) database. In: Proceedings. Fifth IEEE International Conference on Automatic Face and Gesture Recognition, pp. 46–51. IEEE (2002)
26. Hou, Y., Sahli, H., Ilse, R., Zhang, Y., Zhao, R.: Robust shape-based head tracking. In: Blanc-Talon, J., Philips, W., Popescu, D., Scheunders, P. (eds.) ACIVS 2007. LNCS, vol. 4678, pp. 340–351. Springer, Heidelberg (2007)
27. Dornaika, F., Davoine, F.: Simultaneous facial action tracking and expression recognition in the presence of head motion. Int. J. Comput. Vision **76**(3), 257–281 (2008)

Modelling and Tracking of Deformable Structures in Medical Images

Saïd Ettaïeb[1](✉), Kamel Hamrouni[1], and Su Ruan[2]

[1] Research Laboratory of Signal, Image and Information Technology,
University of Tunis El Manar, Tunis, Tunisia
settaieb@gmail.com, kamel.hamrouni@enit.rnu.tn
[2] LITIS, Quantif University of Rouen, Rouen, France
su.ruan@univ-rouen.fr

Abstract. This paper presents a new method based both on Active Shape Model and a priori knowledge about the spatio-temporal shape variation for tracking deformable structures in medical imaging. The main idea is to exploit a priori knowledge of shape that exists in ASM and introduce new knowledge about the shape variation over time. The aim is to define a new more stable method, allowing the reliable detection of structures whose shape changes considerably in time. This method can also be used for the three-dimensional segmentation by replacing the temporal component by the third spatial axis (z). The proposed method is applied for the functional and morphological study of the heart pump. The functional aspect was studied through temporal sequences of scintigraphic images and morphology was studied through MRI volumes. The obtained results are encouraging and show the performance of the proposed method.

Keywords: Active shape model · A priori knowledge · Spatio-temporal shape variation · Deformable structures · Medical images

1 Introduction

In medical imaging, tracking dynamic structures has a major interest in some clinical applications to aid in the diagnosis. Examples include the study of the function of the heart pump. This study requires the detection of the left ventricle during the cardiac cycle in order to estimate the quantity of blood pumped in the corresponding time interval. Three-dimensional segmentation by slices (known as $2d + \frac{1}{2}$ segmentation) can also join the problem of dynamic structures segmentation, insofar as the shape of an anatomical structure can vary according to the third spatial dimension (z). In both cases, the fundamental theoretical problem is to track a structure whose shape changes via a set of images; whether it is in temporal sequences of images or in successions of three-dimensional slices. Compared to other fields of object tracking, this problem remains difficult because of the poor quality of medical images (low contrast, low resolution, the presence of noise, etc.).

To address this issue, we plan to develop a method based on Active Shape Model – ASM [5]. Indeed, the ASM is a particular class of deformable models which is based

© Springer International Publishing Switzerland 2015
Y.-J. Zhang (Ed.): ICIG 2015, Part II, LNCS 9218, pp. 475–490, 2015.
DOI: 10.1007/978-3-319-21963-9_44

on a forte a priori knowledge of the shape. This reduces the solutions space and leads always to acceptable shapes. The key idea in this paper is to integrate, in this model, new a priori knowledge about the shape variation over time. The objective is to define a new method well adapted for tracking dynamic structures, incorporating a priori knowledge on the spatio-temporal shape variation. The proposed method requires two main phases: a training phase which aims to model, from a set of sample sequences, the spatio-temporal variation of the shape of interest and a tracking phase, which is based on the obtained model to find the studied structure in all images of a new sequence. This paper is organized as follows: in Sect. 2, we present a short state of the art on the segmentation of deformable structures in medical imaging. Section 3 is devoted to detail the steps of the proposed method. In Sect. 4, the proposed approach is applied to the functional and morphological study of the heart pump.

2 Related Work

The deformable models [1–6] are certainly the most popular approach in the field of medical images segmentation, due to their flexibility and ability to integrate a priori knowledge about the anatomical structures. The basic idea is to start with an initial coarse segmentation that will evolve gradually, according to several constraints, towards the target contours. These models have the advantage of segmenting an image by integrating a global vision of the shape of the structure to be extracted. They are widely studied and applied to the static segmentation of rigid structures, whether in the 2D case or the 3D case [7]. However, in some medical applications, it is sometimes necessary to follow up the spatio-temporal variation of non-rigid structures, whose shape varies over time. In this aim, several extensions of deformable models were proposed. For example, in [8], the authors propose to track anatomical structures in sequences of images by active contour [1] whose initialization in the image i is deduced automatically from the previous result in the image $i - 1$. In several other works [9–13], the sequence of images is treated in a global way and the studied shape variation is described by a single model that evolves over time. The majority of these works is focused mainly on the spatio-temporal tracking of cellular structures [7, 9] and the left ventricle of the heart [10, 11, 14, 15]. However, despite the success obtained in some cases, the quality of the results depends on the initialization step and the choice of propagation parameters. In addition, the used a priori knowledge has generally a global criterion.

3 Proposed Method

The proposed method requires three main steps: a step of spatio-temporal shape modelling, a step of grey levels modelling and a tracking step (spatio-temporal segmentation), which is based on the results of both first ones to locate the target structure in a new sequence.

3.1 Spatio-Temporal Shape Modelling

The objective of this step is to build a statistical spatio-temporal shapes model which describes precisely the variation over time of the deformable structure to be segmented. It requires, first of all, the preparation of a spatio-temporal training set, which includes all the possible configurations of this structure.

Preparation of a Spatio-Temporal Training Set. First, we have to collect a set of sequences of different images. Every sequence must contain the same structure in the same period of time and with the same number of images. Then, we have to extract the spatio-temporal shapes by putting on the contour of every sequence, a sufficient number of landmark points on the wished contour (Fig. 1).

Fig. 1. Extraction of spatio-temporal shape

Given F the number of images by sequence and L the number of landmark points put on each image, the spatio-temporal shape that models a sequence i can then be represented by a vector S_i:

$$S_i = [u_{i1}, u_{i2}, u_{i3}, \ldots \ldots u_{iF}] \tag{1}$$

With $u_{ij} = [x_{ij1}, y_{ij1}, x_{ij2}, y_{ij2}, \ldots x_{ijL}, y_{ijL}]$ is a vector that models the jth shape in the ith sequence. Thus, the spatio-temporal training set will be represented by a set of spatio-temporal shapes:

$$\{S_i \text{ with } i = 1 \ldots N \text{ (N number of sequences)}\}$$

Aligning Spatio-Temporal Shapes. After extracting spatio-temporal shapes from samples of sequences, an alignment step of shapes is required in order to put the corresponding vectors $\{S_i\}$ at a centered position. This allows to eliminate the problem of variation in position and in size and to study only the most important variation in shape between the various configurations of the studied structure. The alignment procedure of the spatio-temporal shapes has the same idea of shapes alignment in the ASM. First, it consists in taking, randomly, a spatio-temporal shape on which are aligned all the others. Then, in every iteration, a mean spatio-temporal shape is calculated, normalized and on which the others will be realigned. This process is stopped when the mean spatio-temporal shape reach some stability.

Generation of the Statistical Spatio-Temporal Shapes Model. The aligned vectors $\{S_i\}$, resulting from the two previous steps, can be arranged in an observation matrix M (Fig. 2) whose size is $(2lF, N)$. This matrix describes both the spatial and temporal variation of the shape of the studied structure:

Spatial variation →

Temporal variation ↓

$M =$

	Sequence1	Sequence2	Squence3	....	SequenceN	
	x_{111}	x_{211}	x_{311}	....	x_{N11}	
	y_{111}	y_{211}	y_{311}	....	y_{N11}	
	....	....	....	....	....	shape1
	x_{11l}	x_{21l}	x_{31l}	....	x_{N1l}	t_1
	y_{11l}	y_{21l}	y_{31l}	....	y_{N1l}	
	x_{121}	x_{221}	x_{321}	....	x_{N21}	
	y_{121}	y_{221}	y_{321}	....	y_{N21}	
	....	....	....	....	....	shape2
	x_{12l}	x_{22l}	x_{32l}	....	x_{N2l}	t_2
	y_{12l}	y_{22l}	y_{32l}	....	y_{N2l}	
	....	....	....	....	....	
	x_{1F1}	x_{2F1}	x_{3F1}	....	x_{NF1}	
	y_{1F1}	y_{2F1}	y_{3F1}	....	y_{NF1}	
	....	....	....	....	....	shapeF
	x_{1Fl}	x_{2Fl}	x_{3Fl}	....	x_{NFl}	t_F
	y_{1Fl}	y_{2Fl}	y_{3Fl}	....	y_{NFl}	

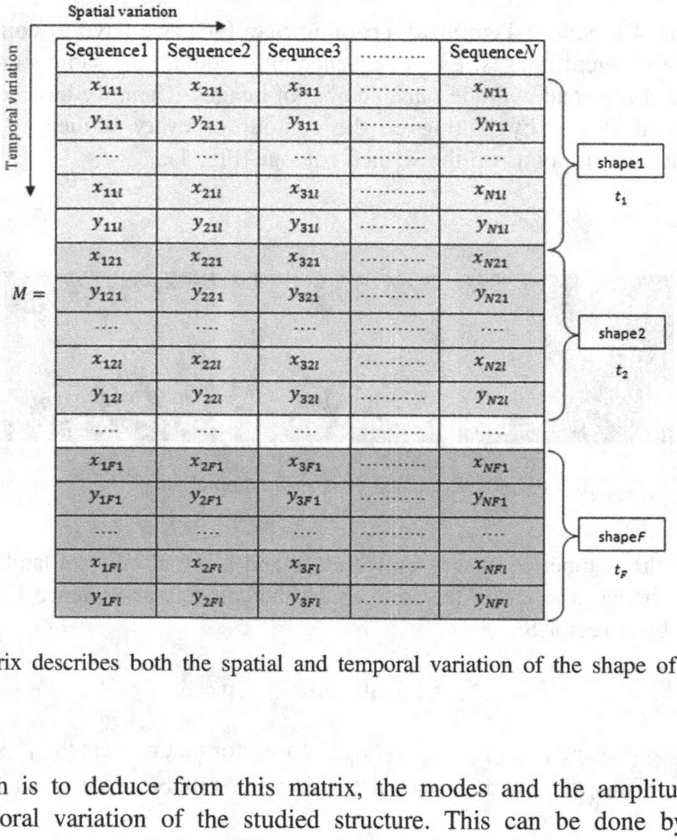

Fig. 2. Matrix describes both the spatial and temporal variation of the shape of the studied structure

The aim is to deduce from this matrix, the modes and the amplitudes of the spatio-temporal variation of the studied structure. This can be done by applying principal component analysis (PCA) on the raw data. Indeed, the main modes of spatio-temporal variation of the studied structure will be represented by the principal components deduced from the covariance matrix C_s associated with the observation matrix (Eq. 2).

$$C_s = \frac{1}{N}\sum_{i=1}^{N} dS_i dS_i^t \tag{2}$$

where $dS_i = S_i - \bar{S}$ is the deviation of the ith spatio-temporal shape S_i compared to a mean spatio-temporal shape, that is calculated:

$$\bar{S} = \frac{1}{N}\sum_{i=1}^{N} S_i \tag{3}$$

These principal components are given by the eigenvectors of the matrix C_s, such as:

$$C_s P_k = \lambda_k P_k \qquad (4)$$

P_k is the Kth eigenvector of C_s and λ_k is the corresponding eigenvalue. Each vector represents a variability percentage of the variables used to build the covariance matrix. The variability percentage represented by each vector is equal to its corresponding eigenvalue. In general, we can notice a very fast decreasing of the eigenvalues, which is used to classify the corresponding vectors in decreasing order. Therefore, we can choose the first t eigenvectors, which represent the important variability percentage, as principal components. Every spatio-temporal shape S can be simply represented by the mean spatio-temporal shape and a linear combination of principal components (main deformation modes):

$$S = \bar{S} + Pb \qquad (5)$$

where $\bar{S}$ is the mean spatio-temporal shape, $P = (p_1, p_2, p_3, \ldots, p_t)$ is the base of t principal components and $b = (b_1, b_2, b_3, \ldots, b_t)^t$ is a weight vector representing the projection of the spatio-temporal shape S in the base P. Generally, the amplitude of the allowable deformation following a principal component P_k is limited as follows:

$$-3\sqrt{\lambda_k} \le b_k \le 3\sqrt{\lambda_k} \qquad (6)$$

As a result, from the basic equation (Eq. 5) we can deduce infinity of shapes describing the spatio-temporal studied structure by choosing correctly the b_k values (Eq. 6). Equation 5 defines, then, the statistical spatio-temporal shapes model, which defines an allowable deformation space for spatio-temporal studied structure. This model will be used in the spatio-temporal localization stage to guide the evolution in such a way that it is only in the allowable space.

3.2   Grey Levels Modelling

In the tracking step, the proposed method is based on intensities information of the treated sequence. It is about finding an optimal correspondence between the properties of luminance of the treated sequence with information of luminance collected from sequences samples. For that purpose, in addition to the spatio-temporal shape modelling, it is necessary to model the grey levels information from the training sequences. The grey levels modelling consists in extracting, for each landmark point i on each image j of the sequence k and then through all the training sequences, the grey levels profile g_{ijk} from a segment of length n, centered in this point i and carried by its normal:

$$g_{ijk} = [g_{ijk0}, g_{ijk1}, g_{ijk2}, \ldots, g_{ijkn-1}] \qquad (7)$$

$g_{ijkt}(t = 0 \ldots n - 1)$ is the grey level of the tth pixel of the examined segment.

The derivative of this grey levels profile is defined by the expression 8:

$$dvg_{ijk} = [g_{ijk1} - g_{ijk0}, \ldots, g_{ijkn-1} - g_{ijkn-2}] \tag{8}$$

dvg_{ijk} is a vector of size $(n - 1)$, including the differences in grey levels between two successive points of the examined segment.

The normal derivative of this profile is defined by:

$$y_{ijk} = \frac{dvg_{ijk}}{\sum_{k=0}^{n-2} |dvg_{ijkt}|} \tag{9}$$

Through all the images in a sequence and then through all the training sequences, we can define for each landmark point i, a mean normal derivative of the grey levels given by the expression 10.

$$\bar{y}_i = \frac{1}{FN} \sum_{j=1}^{F} \sum_{k=1}^{N} y_{ijk} \tag{10}$$

This mean normal derivative related to the point i, will be used in the stage of spatio-temporal localization to move the same point towards a better position.

3.3   Tracking Step

The objective now is to tracking the studied structure in a new sequence. A way to achieve this is to start with an initial spatio-temporal shape, which will gradually evolve towards the contours of the studied structure in all images simultaneously. This idea can provide a procedure of tracking, which consists in repeating iteratively the following four steps.

Initialization. This step consists in putting an initial spatio-temporal shape S_i on the treated sequence. This shape can be built from a spatio-temporal shape S_a belonging to the training set:

$$S_i = M(k_i, \theta_i)[S_a] + t_i \tag{11}$$

with:

$$M(k_i, \theta_i) = \begin{bmatrix} k_i \cos \theta_i & -k_i \sin \theta_i \\ k_i \sin \theta_i & k_i \cos \theta_i \end{bmatrix} \text{ a matrix } (2 * 2)$$

$t_i = (t_{xi}, t_{yi}, t_{xi}, t_{yi}, t_{xi}, t_{yi} \ldots \ldots t_{xi}, t_{yi})$ a translation vector of size $2 * F * N$.

k_i, θ_i and t_i are respectively the homothety, rotation and translation to be applied to every point of S_a in order to build the initialization S_i.

Search for the Elementary Movement. We will first address the problem of moving a single landmark point. Then, we will show how to calculate the elementary movement of the initial estimate dS_i. Indeed, A is a particular landmark point of S_i. To move the point A to the borders of the studied structure, the idea is to extract from each image j of the processed sequence, a search grey levels profile of length m pixels (with $m \gg (n - 1)$) which is centered in A and supported by the normal to the edge passing through this point.

Then, the point A will be represented by a matrix H_A, defined as follows:

$$H_A = \begin{array}{c|c|c|c|c|} & 1 & 2 & \cdots & F \\ \hline 1 & g_{A11} & g_{A21} & \cdots & g_{AF1} \\ \hline 2 & g_{A12} & g_{A22} & \cdots & g_{AF2} \\ \hline 3 & g_{A13} & g_{A23} & \cdots & g_{AF3} \\ \hline \vdots & \vdots & \vdots & (g_{Ajk}) & \vdots \\ \hline m & g_{A1m} & g_{A2m} & \cdots & g_{AFm} \\ \hline \end{array}$$

H_A is a matrix of $m * F$ combinations where each column represents the search profile on the image j. Knowing that each landmark point A is defined by a mean normal derivative of the grey levels $\bar{y}_A$, we can calculate, from the matrix H_A, a new matrix $H'_A(j, l)$ which represents the difference between the grey level information surrounding the current point A and that related to the same point during the grey levels modelling. This matrix can be defined as follows:

$$H'_A(j, l) = (g_{Aj}(l) - \bar{y}_A)^t I^t_{n-1} I_{n-1} (g_{Aj}(l) - \bar{y}_A) \tag{12}$$

with j from 1 to F, l from 1 to m and I_{n-1} is the identity matrix $(n - 1)$. $g_{Aj}(l)$ is the sub-profile of length $(n - 1)$ centered at the lth position of the search profile g_{Aj} that contains the normal derivative of the intensities. (It is necessary to remind that $g_{Aj}(l)$ and $\bar{y}_A$ have the same size $(n - 1)$). The best positions to which has to slide the point A. on the treated sequence are given as follows:

$$p_{Aj} = [\min(H'_A(j, l))]. \tag{13}$$

with j from 1 to F, l from 1 to m

p_{Aj}: is the position to which has to slide the point A on the jth image.

Therefore, we can calculate the elementary movements of the particular point A in all the images of the sequence, such as:

$$\left\{ dp_{Aj} = distance\left(A, p_{Aj}\right) \text{ with } j \text{ from 1 to } F \right\}. \tag{14}$$

dp_{Aj}: is the elementary movement of point A in the jth image.

By applying the same principle for the other landmark points of the initial spatio-temporal shape S_i, we can deduce finally the elementary movement dS_i:

$$dS_i = \left[dp_{Aj}\right] \tag{15}$$

with A from 1 to L, j from 1 to F

L: Number of landmark points.
F: Number of images by sequence.

Determining the Parameters of Position and Shape. After determining the elementary movement dS_i, we must now determine the parameters of position and shape to make this movement, while respecting the constraints of spatio-temporal deformation imposed by the modelling step.

Determining the Position Parameters: We suppose that the initial estimate S_i is centered in a position (x_c, y_c) with an orientation θ and an homothety k. Determining the position parameters means determining the parameters of geometric operations $1 + dk$, $d\theta$ and $dt = (d\,x_c, dy_c)$ to be applied to each point of S_i in order to reach the new position $(S_i + dS_i)$. A simple way to determine these parameters is to align the two vectors S_i and $(S_i + dS_i)$.

Determining the Shape Parameters: If we suppose that the initial estimate S_i is defined in the base of the principal components by a weight vector b, we seek to determine the variation db in order to trace $(S_i + dS_i)$ in the same base. Given that the initial estimate is built from a spatio-temporal shape S_a belonging to the training set, determining the shape parameters db is to solve first in dx the following equation:

$$M(k_i(1 + dk), \theta_i + d\theta)[S_a + dx] + t_i + dt = S_i + dS_i \tag{16}$$

which means

$$M(k_i(1 + dk), \theta_i + d\theta)[S_a + dx] = S_i + dS_i - (t_i + dt) \tag{17}$$

But we have $S_i = M(k_i, \theta_i)[S_a] + t_i$
    If we replace S_i by its value in the Eq. (17), we find:

$$M(k_i(1 + dk), \theta_i + d\theta)[S_a + dx] = M(k_i, \theta_i)[S_a] + t_i + dS_i - (t_i + dt) \tag{18}$$

But we know that:

$$M^{-1}(k, \theta)[\ldots] = M(k^{-1}, -\theta)[\ldots] \tag{19}$$

By applying this rule to the Eq. (18), we obtain

$$S_a + dx = M\left((k_i(1 + dk))^{-1}, -(\theta_i + d\theta)\right)[M(k_i, \theta_i)[S_a] + dS_i - dt \tag{20}$$

what means that:

$$dx = M((k_i(1 + dk))^{-1}, -(\theta_i + d\theta))[M(k_i, \theta_i)[S_a] + dS_i - dt] - S_a \qquad (21)$$

dx is determined in $2 * L*F$ size. However, we have t modes of variation. Then, we have to calculate dx', the projection of dx in the base of principal components P. This can be done by adopting the approach of least squares. Indeed, $dx' = wdx$ with $w = P(P^tP)^{-1}P^t$ is a projection matrix. However, the principal components of P are pairwise orthogonal, meaning that $P^tP = I$. This, then, gives $dx' = PP^tdx$. We know $dx' = Pdb$, if we multiply both sides of this equation by P^t, we can deduce finally the shape parameters $db = P^tdx'$.

$db = (db_1, db_2, db_3, \ldots, db_t)$ is a weight vector allowing to build and to limit the new vector $(S_i + dS_i)$ in the base of principal components.

Movement of the Spatio-Temporal Shape and the Limitation of the Shape Parameters. This last step consists in moving S_i to the new position $(S_i + dS_i = S_i^1)$, by using the already calculated parameters. We obtain:

$$S_i^1 = M(k_i(1 + dk), \theta_i + d\theta)[S_a + Pdb] + t_i + dt \qquad (22)$$

We should note that the shape parameters $db = (db_1, db_2; db_3, \ldots db_t)$ must be limited in the allowable intervals of variation defined by the Eq. (6), to produce acceptable spatio-temporal shapes. Indeed, if for example a value db_k $(1 \leq k \leq t)$ exceeds the maximum value in a component k, it will be limited as follows:

$$\left\{ \begin{array}{l} \text{if } db_k > v_{max_k} \\ \text{then } db_k = v_{max_k} \\ \text{if } db_k < -v_{max_k} \\ \text{then } db_k = -v_{max_k} \end{array} \right. \qquad (23)$$

with $v_{max_k} = 3\sqrt{|\lambda_k|}$ is the maximum value of allowable variation following the component k. λ_k is the eigenvalue related to the component k. Now, from S_i^1, we will repeat the same steps to build S_i^2 then S_i^3 ... and so on, until no significant change is detected or the maximum number of iterations is reached.

4 Experimental Results

In this section, we show the application of our contribution for the functional and morphological study of the heart pump (left ventricle). The functional aspect was studied through temporal sequences of scintigraphic images and morphology was studied through MRI volumes.

4.1   Tracking of the Left Ventricle in Scintigraphic Sequences of Images of the Heart

In this application, the used image database contains 25 scintigraphic sequences of images of the heart from 25 different patients. Each sequence shows a heart beat cycle, represented by 16 images of 128 * 128 pixels. We have selected 8 sequences for the training step. After showing the selected sequences to a specialist doctor, we concluded that the details of the left ventricle can be represented by 20 landmark points. The variability percentage of the initial data is fixed to 95 % and the length of the grey levels profile in the training step is 7 pixels. In the tracking step, the length of profile search is 19 pixels. The maximum number of iterations is fixed at 60 iterations. The used test sequences are selected from the 17 remaining sequences in the original database. Figure 3 shows an example of the result of tracking that is obtained on a test sequence. Figure 4 shows the activity-time curve of the left ventricle calculated using the obtained result. The ventricular ejection fraction found in this experiment is 52 %, which seems to be normal (healthy cases).

We note that the final spatio-temporal shape succeeded generally in locating the shape of the left ventricle. This can show the performance of the method even in the presence of contours that are difficult to identify. This result is qualitatively considered satisfactory by the medical specialists.

4.2   2d + ½ Segmentation of the LV in MRI Volumes

In this section, we present the second application of the proposed method: the $2d + \frac{1}{2}$ segmentation, where the temporal component will be considered as the third spatial axis (z). We are interested in studying the left ventricle morphology via the extraction of its three-dimensional shape from MRI volumes.

For that purpose, we first built a training set, composed of 10 volumes. Each volume is divided into 10 slices (short axis) of size 192 * 160, covering the left ventricle from apex to the base. During the modelling phase, 20 landmarks are placed on each slice of each volume in order to extract the three-dimensional shapes of the left ventricle (Fig. 5). Each volume is thus modelled by a three-dimensional vector of size 2 * 20 * 10. After the aligning step and using 95 % as a variability percentage of the initial data, the CPA application on these data provided five principal variation modes. The length of the grey levels profile in the modelling step is equal to 30 % of the length of the search profile. The maximum number of iterations is fixed at 60 iterations. In the following, Fig. 6 shows a plane representation of the initialization of the mean three-dimensional shape on each slice on a treated volume. Figure 7 shows the result of corresponding segmentation. 3D visualization of some obtained results is given in Fig. 8.

We can notice, in Fig. 7, that the contours have succeeded to correctly delineate the shape of the left ventricle (endocardium) in all slices, even with the presence of the pillars muscle (black point) in some cases. This demonstrates that the proposed method can be effectively used for three-dimensional segmentation. Indeed, the forte a priori knowledge of shape used following the third spatial component (in each slice

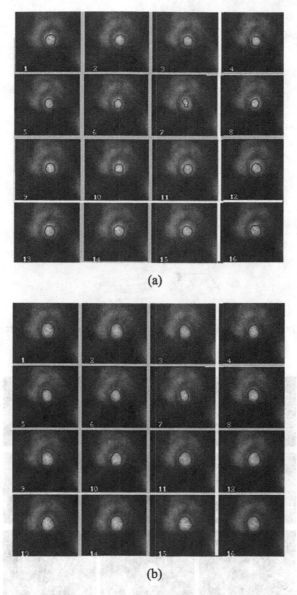

Fig. 3. Result of the spatio-temporal tracking of the LV. (a) Initialization of the mean spatio-temporal shape on a treated sequence. (b) Final result of the tracking

separately), helped to easily exceed the heterogeneity of intensities (pillars) and thus lead to a satisfactory result. In Fig. 8, we can see a significant variation of the three-dimensional size of the left ventricle. This can provide information about the moment of acquisition of the volume in question (acquisition phase: diastolic or systolic phase). This three-dimensional representation of the left ventricle shape can be useful to specialists for detecting morphological abnormalities of the heart. We should

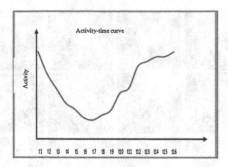

Fig. 4. activity-time curve

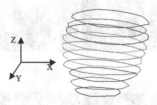

Fig. 5. Three-dimensional shape of the LV determined during the training step

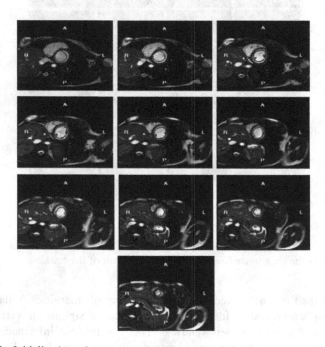

Fig. 6. Initialization of the mean three-dimensional shape on a treated volume

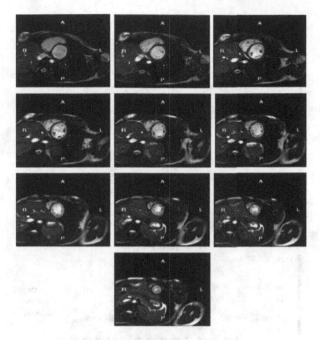

Fig. 7. Result of 2d $+\frac{1}{2}$ segmentation

Fig. 8. 3D visualization of some obtained results

note that, in this application, the proposed method was used with some hypotheses. Indeed, we used, in both modelling and tracking step, volumes with the same number of slices (10 slices), that ideally match. However, that is not always true in clinical practice, because of the distance parameter between slices at the moment of acquisition. It is then necessary to define a pre-processing step in order to make correspondence, automatically, between slices of training volumes and those of the volume to be segment.

Quantitative Results. In order to evaluate quantitatively the proposed method, we selected four sequences of the test database, which are manually pre-segmented by an expert and are used as a ground truth. Then, we decided to compare our contribution ASMT with the ground truth, the basic model ASM and with another method that is proposed by Fekir et al. [8]. This method allows the tracking of non-rigid objects in

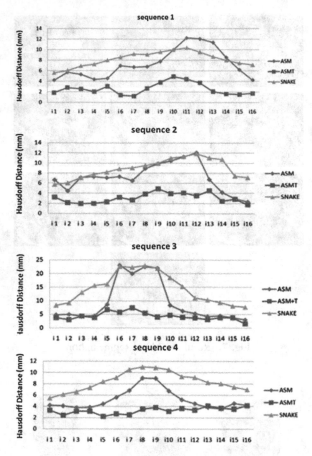

Fig. 9. Hausdorff distance between each method (ASM, ASMT and SNAKE) and the reference segmentation of the four sequences

sequences of images using active contour SNAKE [1] whose initialization in the image i is automatically deduced from the result in the image i − 1.

Since the compared methods are contour-based methods, we chose the Hausdorff distance as a measure of segmentation quality [16]. Figure 9 shows the Hausdorff distance between each method (ASM, ASMT and SNAKE) and the reference segmentation of the four sequences.

Looking at the four diagrams, we can see clearly that the red curve (ASMT) has some stability compared to the other curves (blue and green). Indeed, for the red curve and through the four diagrams, the values of the Hausdorff distance are between 1.18 and 7.38 (mm). By cons, for both blue and green curves, the values of the Hausdorff distance often represent great variations, which rose from 2.3 (mm) and reach 23.06 (mm). Through these measures, and although that in some cases the ASM and SNAKE provide acceptable results (especially in diastole images), we can deduce that our method provides for all images in each sequence an overall result that is more stable and closer to manual segmentation. This proves the effectiveness of the integration of a priori knowledge about the spatio-temporal shape variation of the left ventricle. Indeed, the stage of spatio-temporal shape modelling provides more precise information on the spatial shape variation of the left ventricle at every moment of the cardiac cycle. This is what influences, consistently and in each image of the sequence, the accuracy of the results of the localization stage. The poor results obtained by ASM and SNAKE may be explained by the imprecision of the initialization in some images of the sequences and the generality of the a priori information about the shape. Besides, these results are mainly obtained in systole images (contraction stage) where the size of the left ventricle becomes very small and difficult to detect. In conclusion, it is clear that the integration of a priori knowledge about the spatio-temporal shape variation of the left ventricle improved significantly the results of segmentation. This increases the reliability of diagnostic parameters such as the activity-time curve and the ventricular ejection fraction, whose calculation is based on these results.

5 Conclusion

In this paper, we proposed to incorporate a new a priori knowledge about the spatio-temporal shape variation in the active shape model in order to define a new simple and more stable method for detecting structures whose shape change over time. The proposed method is based on two types of a priori knowledge: the spatial and temporal variation of the studied structure. It has also the advantage of being applicable on sequences of images. The experimental validation of the proposed method, whether on temporal sequences or three-dimensional images shows the interest of the integration of a priori knowledge on shape variation according to the third component (temporal or spatial). Indeed, using precise information (geometry and deformation modes) about the shape to be detected each time (respectively in each slice) provided more stable results. We are convinced of the relevance of the used method, however, some improvements can be added and the validation should be pursued. Indeed, the most difficult step in our approach is the labelling step. It consists in manually extracting the spatio-temporal shapes from training sequences. That is why, it is usually performed by an expert. The complexity of this step is in function of the number of training sequences, the number of images by sequence and the number of landmark points needed to represent the target structure details. Once, these parameters become important, this task becomes tedious and time consuming. Then, we should think to make this task semi-automatic or fully automatic. A way to make it semi-automatic is to consider that the shape of the studied structure at instants $t - 1$, t and $t + 1$ has a low variation. The manual training can be thus done on a reduced number of images which correspond to well chosen moments of the sequence. Then, the result of this training will be used for the automatic segmentation of the remaining images. This segmentation is then considered as training. Thus, the complexity of the labelling task can be reduced at least 70 %. Moreover, it is possible to enrich and further validate this approach for other types of applications. For example, if we replace the temporal component by the third spatial axis (z), this method can be effectively used for volume segmentation that is based on an important a priori knowledge of shape. In this case, we must solve some additional issues such as correspondence between the slices of training volumes and the slices of the volume to be segmented as well as the automatic determination of the slices that contain the studied structure during the segmentation.

References

1. Kass, M., Witikin, A., Terzopoulos, D.: Snakes: active contour models. Int. J. Comput. Vis. **1**, 321–331 (1988)
2. Cohen, L.D.: Active contour models and balloons. CVGIP Image Underst. **53**, 211–218 (1991)
3. Osher, S., Sethian, J.A.: Fronts propagating with curvature-dependent speed: algorithms based on Hamilton-Jacobi formulations. J. Comput. Phys. **79**, 12–49 (1988)
4. Caselles, V., Kimmel, R., Sapiro, G.: Geodesic active contours. Int. J. Comput. Vis. **22**, 61–79 (1997)
5. Cootes, T.F., Taylor, C.J., Cooper, D.H., Graham, J.: Active shape models - their training and application. Comput. Vis. Image Underst. **61**, 38–59 (1995)
6. Cootes, T.F., Edwards, G.J., Taylor, C.J.: Active appearance models. IEEE Trans. Pattern Anal. Mach. Intell. **23**, 681–685 (2001)
7. Singh, A., Goldgof, D., Terzopoulos, D.: Deformable Models in Medical Image Analysis. IEEE Computer Society, Silver Spring (1998)
8. Fekir, A., Benamrane, N., Taleb-Ahmed, A.: Détection et Suivi d'Objets dans une Séquence d'Images par Contours Actifs. In: Proceedings of CIIA (2009)
9. Leymarie, F., Levine, M.: Tracking deformable objects in the plane using an active contour model. IEEE Trans. Pattern Anal. Mach. Intell. **15**, 617–634 (1993)
10. McInerney, T., Terzopoulos, D.: A dynamic finite element surface model for segmentation and tracking in multidimensional medical images with application to cardiac 4D image analysis. Comput. Med. Imaging Graph. **19**, 69–83 (1995)
11. Niessen, W., Duncan, J., Viergever, M., Romeny, B.: Spatio-temporal analysis of left ventricular motion. In: SPIE Medical Imaging, pp. 250–261. SPIE Press, Bellingham (1995)
12. Sclaroff, S., Isidoro, J.: Active blobs. In: Proceedings of the Sixth IEEE International Conference on Computer Vision, pp 1146–1153 (1998)
13. Hamarneh, G., Tomas, G.: Deformable spatio- temporal shape models: extending active shape models to 2D + time. J. Image Vis. Comput. **22**, 461–470 (2004)
14. Lelieveldt, B., Mitchell, S.C., Bosch, J.G., van der Geest, R.J., Sonka, M., Reiber, J.H.C.: Time-continuous segmentation of cardiac image sequences using active appearance motion models. In: Insana, M.F., Leahy, R.M. (eds.) IPMI 2001. LNCS, vol. 2082, pp. 446–452. Springer, Heidelberg (2001)
15. Signh, A., Von Kurowski, L., Chiu, M.: Cardiac MR image segmentation using deformable models. In: SPIE Proceedings of the Biomedical Image Processing and Biomedical Visualization, pp. 8–28 (1993)
16. Huttenlocher, D., Klanderman, D., Rucklige, A.: Comparing images using the Hausdorff distance. IEEE Trans. Pattern Anal. Mach. Intell. **15**, 850–863 (1993)

Moving Object Extraction in Infrared Video Sequences

Jinli Zhang[1,2(✉)], Min Li[1], and Yujie He[1]

[1] Xi'an Research Institute of Hi-Tech,
Hongqin Town, Xi'an, Shaanxi Province, China
jlz_007@sina.com, {clwn,ksy5201314}@163.com
[2] Department of Information Engineering, Engineering University of CAPF,
Sanqiao Town, Xi'an, Shaanxi Province, China

Abstract. In order to extract the moving object in infrared video sequence, this paper presents a scheme based on sparse and low-rank decomposition. By transforming each frame of the infrared video sequence to a column and combine all columns into a new matrix, the problem of extracting moving objects in infrared video sequences is converted to a sparse and low-rank matrix decomposition problem. The resulted nuclear norm and L_1 norm related minimization problem can also be efficiently solved by some recently developed numerical methods. The effectiveness of our proposed scheme is illustrated on different infrared video sequences. The experiments show that, compared to ALM algorithm, our algorithm has distinct advantages in extracting moving object from infrared videos.

Keywords: Infrared video sequence · Moving object · Extraction · L_1 norm · Low-rank · Sparse

1 Introduction

With the prevalence of infrared cameras and infrared sensors, the infrared video plays an increasing important role on human life and production. For example, the infrared videos about the wild animal activity which were obtained from infrared video surveillance equipments have brought great convenience for the wild animal researchers. When the target and background brightness have not a distinct difference in the infrared video sequences or people's some need, it is very necessary to separate the moving object from the backgrounds. How to effectively extract the moving target in an infrared video is a problem worthy of studying.

This paper aims at developing an effective scheme to extract the moving objects in infrared video sequences. Motivated by the regularization models proposed in [1, 2] for other applications, we take a similar regularization approach for moving objects extraction from background.

Foundation Item: The National Natural Science Foundation of China (61102170).

Y.-J. Zhang (Ed.): ICIG 2015, Part II, LNCS 9218, pp. 491–499, 2015.
DOI: 10.1007/978-3-319-21963-9_45

2 Detailed Algorithm

In this section, we present the algorithm in details. First, each frame of the infrared video sequences is reformed to a column, then combining all columns to a new matrix $D \in \mathbb{R}^{m \times n}$. Because the video content is composed of the background and moving objects, the matrix D can be represented as the sum of background and moving objects. If we represent the background component as $A \in \mathbb{R}^{m \times n}$ and represent moving object component as $E \in \mathbb{R}^{m \times n}$, then the matrix D can be expressed as

$$D = A + E. \tag{1}$$

In video sequences, the adjacent frames have most of the same background information, especially in the video with high frame rate. Thus, matrix A has many same columns and it is a low-rank matrix. Because the size of the moving objects in each frame is far less than the size of frame, the number of nonzero is far less than the element number in matrix E. Thus, matrix E is a sparse matrix. Based on these observations, if we can accurately decompose the matrix D into the sum of a low-rank matrix and a sparse matrix, the moving objects can be extracted from background.

2.1 Notation

Before presenting the details of decomposing D into a low-rank matrix A and a sparse matrix E, we first define some notations for the simplicity of discussions. The L_1 norm and the Frobenius norm of a matrix $X \in \mathbb{R}^{n_1 \times n_2}$ are defined by:

$$\|X\|_1 = \sum_{i=1}^{n_1} \sum_{j=1}^{n_2} |x_{i,j}| \text{ and } \|X\|_F = (\sum_{i=1}^{n_1} \sum_{j=1}^{n_2} |x_{i,j}|^2)^{1/2}, \tag{2}$$

respectively. Where $x_{i,j}$ is the (i,j)-th element of X. Assuming that r is the rank of X, the singular value decomposition of X is then defined by

$$X = U \sum V^T, \quad \sum = diag(\{\sigma_i\}_{1 \le i \le r}). \tag{3}$$

Where U and V are $n_1 \times r$ and $n_2 \times r$ matrices with orthonormal columns respectively. The nuclear norm of X is defined as the sum of singular values, i.e.

$$|X|_* = \sum_{i=1}^{r} |\sigma_i|. \tag{4}$$

The shrinkage operator $S_\tau : \mathbb{R} \to \mathbb{R}$ is defined by

$$S_\tau(x) = sgn(x) \max(|x| - \tau, 0). \tag{5}$$

Where $\tau \ge 0$. When S_τ is extended to matrices by applying it element-wise.

The singular shrinkage operator $D_\tau(x)$ is defined [3] by

$$D_\tau = US_\tau(\Sigma)V^T.\tag{6}$$

It is noted that $S_\tau(X)$ and $D_\tau(x)$ are the solutions of the following two minimization problems respectively

$$\min_Y \tau\|Y\|_1 + \frac{1}{2}\|Y - X\|_F^2, \ \min_Y \tau\|Y\|_* + \frac{1}{2}\|Y - X\|_F^2.\tag{7}$$

2.2 Sparse and Low-Rank Decomposing

In order to exactly extract the sparse matrix E and low-rank matrix A, we can solve the following minimization problem to estimate A and E:

$$\min_{A,E\in\mathbb{R}^{n_1\times n_2}} rank(A) + \lambda\|E\|_0 \text{ s.t. } D = A + E.\tag{8}$$

Where λ is a suitable regularization parameter. $rank(\cdot)$ denotes the rank for a matrix. $\|\cdot\|_0$ denotes the pseudo-norm that counts the number of non-zeros.

The minimization problem (8) is a non-convex problem. In general, it is very hard to solve. Referring to the approaches in [4, 5], we try to solve the follow minimization to estimate A and E.

$$\min_{A,E\in\mathbb{R}^{m\times n}} \|A\|_* + \lambda\|E\|_1 \text{ s.t. } D = A + E.\tag{9}$$

Where $\|\cdot\|_1$ is the element-wise sum of absolute values for a matrix.

The minimization model (9) above has been proposed in [1, 2] to extract low-dimensional structure from a data matrix. It could be viewed as a replacement of the Principal Component Analysis (PCA) method. The minimization approaches is termed as Principal Component Pursuit (PCP) for solving the problem of background subtraction in video surveillance. In their approach, the observed video matrix (array of image frames) is decomposed into the low-rank matrix structure (static background) and the sparse matrix structure (moving objects).

In our approach, we convert the minimization question (9) to an augmented Lagrange multiplier form:

$$\min_{A,E\in\mathbb{R}^{m\times n}} \|A\|_* + \lambda\|E\|_1 + \frac{1}{2\mu}\|D - A - E\|_F^2.\tag{10}$$

Here, the value of λ is set the same as [1] suggested:

$$\lambda = 1\big/\sqrt{\max(m,n)}.\tag{11}$$

Where m, n are the number of rows and columns of the matrix D.

In recent years, there are some good methods on how to efficiently solve L_1 norm related minimization problem. One of them is the accelerated proximal gradient (APG) method, which shows a very good performance on solving L_1 norm and nuclear norm related minimization problems (e.g. [6–9]). Another promising approach is the ADMM (alternating directions method of multipliers) which also can efficiently solve such problems (e.g. [10–12]). In our approach, we used the APG method to solve the minimization problem (10).

The general APG method aims at solving the following minimization problem:

$$\min_X \quad g(X) + f(X) \tag{12}$$

Where g is a non-smooth function, f is a smooth function. Algorithm 1 describes the specific scheme of APG.

Algorithm 1.   APG method

1.   do

2. $Y_k = X_k + \dfrac{t_{k-1} - 1}{t_k}(X_k - X_{k-1})$;

3. $G_k = Y_k + \dfrac{1}{L_f}\nabla f(Y_k)$;

4. $X_{k+1} = \arg\ \min_X g(X) + \dfrac{L_f}{2}\|X - G_k\|_F^2$;

5. $t_{k+1} = \dfrac{1 + \sqrt{1 + 4t_k^2}}{t_k}$, $k = k+1$;

6.   until converged

Based on the APG method, the minimization problem (10) can be converted to (12) by setting

$$\begin{cases} X = (A, E) \\ g(X) = \mu\|A\|_* + \lambda\mu\|E\|_1 \\ f(X) = \frac{1}{2}\|D - A - E\|_F^2 \end{cases} \tag{13}$$

When applying Algorithm 1 to solve the (10), the minimization problem in Step 4 of Algorithm 1 becomes (noticing $L_f = 2$ in our case)

$$\min_{A,E}\ \mu\|A\|_* + \lambda\mu\|E\|_1 + \|A - G_k^A\|_F^2 + \|E - G_k^E\|_F^2. \tag{14}$$

Since A and E are separable in the above minimization, their solutions can be obtained separately by applying singular value shrinkage operator on G_k^A and soft shrinkage operator on G_k^E, i.e. $A_{k+1} = D_{\mu/2}(G_k^A)$, $E_{k+1} = S_{\lambda\mu/2}(G_k^E)$.

The detailed algorithm for solving the minimization problem (10) is described in Algorithm 2.

Algorithm 2. APG method for solving the minimization problem (10)

1. Initialization: $E_0 = A_0 = O^{m \times n}, Y_0^A = Y_0^E = \dfrac{D}{\sigma_1}, k = 0$

   $\mu_0 = \dfrac{5}{4}\sigma_1$, ($\sigma_1$ is the largest singular value of D);

   Set $\varepsilon > 0$, $K > 1$, $\rho > 1$, $\mu_{max} \gg 1$;

2. do

3. $Y_k^A = A_k + \dfrac{t_{k-1}-1}{t_k}(A_k - A_{k-1})$, $Y_k^E = E_k + \dfrac{t_{k-1}-1}{t_k}(E_k - E_{k-1})$;

4. $G_k^A = Y_k^A - \dfrac{1}{2}(Y_k^A + Y_k^E - D)$, $G_k^E = Y_k^E - \dfrac{1}{2}(Y_k^A + Y_k^E - D)$;

5. $(U, \Sigma, V) = svd(G_k^A)$, $A_{k+1} = US_{\mu k/2}(\Sigma)V^T$, $E_{k+1} = S_{\lambda k/2}(G_k^E)$;

6. $t_{k+1} = \dfrac{1+\sqrt{1+4t_k^2}}{t_k}$, $\mu_{k+1} = \min(\rho\mu_k, \mu_{max})$, $k = k+1$;

7. until $\dfrac{\|D - A_{k+1} - E_{k+1}\|_F}{\|D\|_F} < \varepsilon$ or $k \geq K$.

After the low-rank matrix A and the sparse matrix E are obtained by Algorithm 2, the low-rank matrix A and the sparse matrix E will be reformed to the format of the original infrared video sequences.

3 Experimental Results and Analysis

In this section, we evaluate the performance of the proposed method on three infrared video sequences "irw1", "irw2" and "plane". In order to facilitate the evaluation, our algorithm is compared with the inexact augmented Lagrange multipliers (ALM) algo-rithm [11] for its high efficiency in solving minimization problems. For a fair com-parison, in each algorithm, the error tolerance ε is set to 1.0×10^{-7} and the maximal iterations number K is set to 1000. 30 frames of each infrared video sequence were input to two algorithms in experiments. The sizes of each frame of the infrared video "irw1", "irw2" and "plane" are 240×320, 240×320 and 200×256 respectively. All the experiments are performed on a desktop computer (CPU 2.30 GHz, RAM 3.25 GB) with the MATLAB R2012b software. Figures 1, 3 and 5 show the results of extracted

<table>
<tr><td>(a) one original frame</td><td>(b) extracted background from (a)</td><td>(c) extracted object from (a)</td></tr>
</table>

Fig. 1. Extracting result of background and object from "irw1" by Algorithm 2

objects and background in three infrared videos by the Algorithm 2. Figures 2, 4 and 6 show the results of extracted objects and background by the ALM algorithm. The performance of two algorithms in terms of the runtime, iteration number and the rank of the extracted low-rank matrix A are listed in Table 1.

From above figures, it can be seen that, no matter big or small, quick or slow, the moving objects can be completely extracted by the Algorithm 2. In Fig. 2, one foot of the man had not been extracted to the moving object opponent by ALM algorithm. From Figs. 3 and 4, we can find that, for the small object plane, the extracted plane has clear edge by Algorithm 2 than that by ALM algorithm. From Figs. 5 and 6, it can be seen that, for the slow moving man, partial contour of the man was not extracted to the object opponent by ALM algorithm. As can be seen from Table 1, compared to ALM algorithm, Algorithm 2 has the following distinct advantages: the rank of the recovered

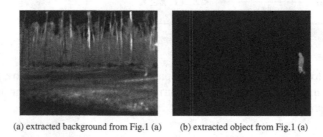

(a) extracted background from Fig.1 (a)   (b) extracted object from Fig.1 (a)

Fig. 2. Extracting result of background and object from "irw1" by ALM algorithm

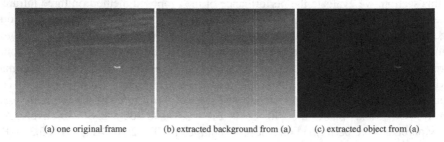

(a) one original frame   (b) extracted background from (a)   (c) extracted object from (a)

Fig. 3. Extracting result of background and object from "plane" by Algorithm 2

(a) extracted background from Fig.3 (a)   (b) extracted object from Fig.3 (a)

Fig. 4. Extracting result of background and object from "plane" by ALM algorithm

(a) one original frame   (b) extracted background from (a)   (c) extracted object from (a)

Fig. 5. Extracting result of background and object from "irw2" by Algorithm 2

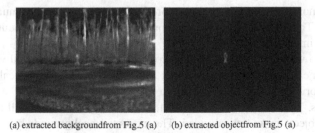

(a) extracted backgroundfrom Fig.5 (a)   (b) extracted objectfrom Fig.5 (a)

Fig. 6. Extracting result of background and object from "irw2" by ALM algorithm

Table 1. Comparison of the results of extracting objects in different infrared video sequence by two algorithms.

Infrared video	Algorithm	Rank (A*)	Iteration number	Time (s)
"irw1"	Algorithm 2	10	20	12.7310
	ALM	15	34	21.6427
"irw2"	Algorithm 2	9	19	12.3445
	ALM	15	33	21.4404
"plane"	Algorithm 2	9	28	13.0447
	ALM	12	36	16.7718

(a) one original frame   (b) extracted background from (a)   (c) extracted object from (a)

Fig. 7. Extracting result of background and object from optical video "highway" by Algorithm 2

(a) extracted background from Fig.7 (a)   (b) extracted object from Fig.7 (a)

Fig. 8. Extracting result of background and object from optical video "highway" by ALM algorithm

background more lower, running time more less and fewer iteration number to reach convergence. These advantages for rapid analysis and process large amounts of infrared video data is important.

In order to verify the validity of the proposed algorithm for optical videos, Figs. 7 and 8 show the results of extracted object and background in an optical video "highway" by Algorithm 2 and ALM algorithm respectively.

From Figs. 7 and 8, it can be seen that, the two algorithms are still able to extract the moving objects in an optical video. The extracted backgrounds by two algorithms have no obvious difference from the visual point of view, but there are more car tracks which belong to the background in Fig. 8(b) than that in Fig. 7(c).

4   Conclusions

In this paper, we presented a scheme to extract the moving objects from infrared video sequence. We convert the problem of extracting the moving object from videos to a sparse and low-rank matrix decomposition problem. The resulting L_1 norm related minimization problem can also be efficiently solved by many recently developed numerical methods. The effectiveness of our proposed algorithm is also validated to other types of video (e.g., optical videos). The experiments show that, compared to ALM algorithm, our algorithm has distinct advantages in extracting moving object from infrared videos and optical videos.

References

1. Candes, E.J., Li, X.D., Yi, M., Wright, J.: Robust principal component analysis? J. ACM **58** (3), 1–37 (2011)
2. Zhou, Z., Li, X., Wright, J., Candes, E.J., Ma, Y.: Stable principal component pursuit. In: IEEE International Symposium on Information Technology (ISIT) (2010)
3. Cai, J.F., Candes, E.J., Shen, Z.: A singular value thresholding algorithm for matrix completion. SIAM J. Optim. **20**(4), 1956–1982 (2010)
4. Chandrasekaran, V., Sangavi, S., Parrilo, P.A., Willsky, A.S.: Sparse and low-rank matrix decompositions. In: IEEE 47th Annual Allerton Conference on Communication, Control, and Computing, pp. 962–967 (2009)
5. Wright, J., Ganesh, A., Rao, S., Peng, Y., Ma, Y.: Robust PCA: exact recovery of corrupted low-rank matrices via convex optimization. In: NIPS 2009, Whistler, BC, Canada (2009)
6. Beck, A., Teboulle, M.: A fast iterative shrinkage-thresholding algorithm for linear inverse problems. SIAM J. Imaging Sci. **2**(1), 183–202 (2009)
7. Shen, Z.W., Toh, K.C., Yun, S.: An accelerated proximal gradient algorithm for frame based image restoration via the balanced approach. SIAM J. Imag. Sci. **4**(2), 573–596 (2011). Technical report
8. Toh, K.C., Yun, S.: An accelerated proximal gradient algorithm for nuclear norm regularized least squares problems. Pac. J. Optim. **6**, 615–640 (2010)
9. Lin, Z., Ganesh, A., Wright, J., Wu, L., Chen, M., Ma, Y.: Fast convex optimization algorithms for exact recovery of a corrupted low-rank matrix. UIUC Technical report UILU-ENG-09-2214 (2009)
10. Yuan, X.M., Yang, J.F.: Sparse and low-rank matrix decomposition via alternating direction methods. Pac. J. Optim. **9**(1), 167–180 (2013)
11. Lin, Z.C., Chen, M.M., Wu, L.Q., Ma, Y., The augmented lagrange multiplier method for exact recovery of corrupted low-rank matrices. UTUC Technical report UILU-ENG-09-2215 (2010)
12. Tao, M., Yuan, X.M.: Recovering low-rank and sparse components of matrices from incomplete and noisy observations. SIAM J. Optim. **21**(1), 57–81 (2011)

Moving Object Segmentation
by Length-Unconstrained Trajectory Analysis

Qiyu Liao[✉], BingBing Zhuang, Jingjing Wang, and Nenghai Yu

CAS Key Laboratory of Electromagnetic Space Information,
University of Science and Technology of China, Hefei, China
{fisher8,bbzhuang,kkwang}@mail.ustc.edu.cn
ynh@edu.ustc.cn

Abstract. Background subtraction for moving cameras is an unsolved
key problem in intelligent video analysis. Trajectory analysis has demonstrated a significant difference between background and foreground
motion model. But under limitation of trajectory-tracking technique,
long-term trajectories are hardly dense and well distributed enough,
which may cause inaccuracy in boundary discrimination. Addressed to
these problems, in this paper we proposed a robust algorithm of "length
unconstrained trajectory analysis" (LUCTA), to recapture "invalid"
information of short trajectories. Extensive experiments demonstrate
competitive performance of our frame work on both accuracy and
time cost.

Keywords: Background subtraction · Moving cameras · Trajectories

1 Introduction

Background subtraction is the very first step in intelligent video analysis. It aims
to find independent moving objects in a relatively static scene. In order to achieve
the detection of moving objects in video sequences, many previous works [1–3]
have been proposed to construct background model to find the motion region.
Recently many works [4,5] applied smoothness and arbitrariness constraints to
strengthened the framework, which have achieved success in many situations.
however, assuming that the scene is captured by fixed cameras, they fail to
accommodate video taken by moving cameras.

Dealing with moving cameras, work [6] presents a method for modeling in a
panoramic view, which is based on some literatures on image mosaic techniques
for constructing panoramic views (e.g., [7]). But, they all have an assumption
that the camera movement only contains rotation about its optical center which
can guarantee no significant parallax, which is proved to be unrealistic in engineering applications. Approach in [8] estimates the motion of some key-points
in video by finding and tracking feature points, without constructing an explicit

Q. Liao—This work is supported by National Natural Science Foundation of China
(NO. 61371192).

Y.-J. Zhang (Ed.): ICIG 2015, Part II, LNCS 9218, pp. 500–509, 2015.
DOI: 10.1007/978-3-319-21963-9_46

background model. Work [9] finds the trajectories of some key-points, and then tries to construct a panorama with affine camera model. There are still some ways achieve their goal by reconstructing a 3-D scene [10,11]. But to obtain a 3-D scene, multi-view shooting is necessary. All of these works only consider the relative motion between two frames, which may cause instability in classification.

Some works, however, is based on long-term trajectory analysis (LTTA). They estimate the dominant background motion to distinguish unmatched foreground motions. Reference [12] combines trajectory analysis with appearance model to distinguish feature points, and then complete bayesian modeling with these points. Instead of simply applying RANSAC, two constraints are reasonably applied to background and foreground, i.e., low rank and group sparsity constraints [13–15]. Work [16] introduced superpixel to improve the segmentation accuracy. Long-term trajectory analysis, however, is not robust enough to handle dynamic or nonrigid scene, because all of these works require that trajectories must be long enough to construct an accurate low-rank model. As a compromise, what we usually do is simply abandon trajectories last less than required, which means that we have to abandon useful information from occluded region (Fig. 1.). Worse still, occlusion usually happens on the boundaries between moving objects and background. As a consequence, such missing information may cause serious inaccuracy of the final result. Different from all previous works, this paper propose a novel framework called "length-unconstrained trajectory analysis" (LUCTA), which make full use of short trajectories without influencing the property of matrix decomposition. In our framework, a stable model of background motion is constructed with long-term analysis, and applied to separate short trajectories. By doing this, the number of available trajectories is significantly raised, and we can easily improve the accuracy of the boundary of moving object in pixel-level labeling.

Fig. 1. Trajectory distribution: Magenta and green points represent for full length ($P = 50$) and short ($P < 50$) trajectories.

2   Methodology

Our background subtraction algorithm takes a raw video sequence as input, and generates a binary labeling at the pixel level. Figure 2 shows our framework. It has three major steps: low-rank modeling, trajectory classification and pixel level labeling. In the first step, we form dense trajectories of featured points (b), and separate them into tow group: full-length and short trajectories. With

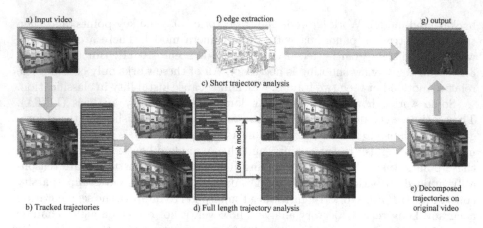

a) Input video

f) edge extraction

g) output

c) Short trajectory analysis

Low rank model

b) Tracked trajectories

d) Full length trajectory analysis

e) Decomposed
trajectories on
original video

Fig. 2. The framework takes a raw video sequence as input, produces a trajectory matrix (red line is the interrupted parts), analyse this trajectories respectively and produces a binary labeling as the output (Color figure online).

trajectories that pass through all frames, a low-rank motion model is formed (d). With this model, all trajectories are proposed to decomposed into foreground and background (e). Finally, we combine the trajectory information with original graph to produce a pixel level labeling map (g).

2.1 Notations

For a F frame video sequence, P points are tracked. Each trajectory is presented as $p_i = [x_i^1, y_i^1, x_i^2, y_i^2, ..., x_i^F, y_i^F] \in \mathbb{R}^{1 \times 2F}$, where x and y denote the 2D coordinates in each frame. If the ith point doesn't appear in frame k, x_i^k and y_i^k will be set to 0. The collection of P trajectories can be represented as a $P \times 2F$ matrix, $\Phi = [p_1^T, p_2^T, ..., p_P^T]^T$, and $\Phi \in \mathbb{R}^{P \times 2F}$. Φ may contain many zeros, because when camera moves, new scene comes into view and old one becomes invisible. Also, trajectory interruption caused by occlusion is another important reason. Similarly, we denote tow subset matrixs of Φ, Φ_L, presents for trajectories that appear in all F frames, and Φ_S for those less than F. Φ can be decomposed as: $\Phi = B + E$, Where $B, E \in \mathbb{R}^{P \times 2F}$ denote matrices of background and error. Similarly, we have $\Phi_L = B_L + E_L$ and $\Phi_S = B_S + E_S$, where B_L, E_L, B_S, E_S respectively present for background and error matrices of full-length and short trajectories.

2.2 Motion Model of Background

If environment is static, the motion in video depends only on the motion of moving objects, the 3D structure of the scene and the motion of the camera. What we need to do is separate motion information caused by moving object from those caused by camera motion. Trajectories of background tend to be consistent, while those of foreground are relatively different from primary motion pattern. Generally, full length trajectory matrix B_L can be factored as a $P_L \times 3$ structure matrix of 3D points and a $3 \times 2F$ orthogonal matrix [17]. In other words, background trajectories are proposed to be linearly represented by no more than 3 basis vectors.

Without any prior information, it's not easy to find these basis vectors in a hybrid trajectory matrix. A reasonable solution is to take advantage of low rank and group sparse property. It can be transformed into a convex optimization problem:

$$argmin_{B_L, E_L} \parallel \Phi_L - B_L - E_L \parallel_F^2$$
$$s.t. Rank(B_L) < 3, \parallel E_L \parallel < \alpha k \tag{1}$$

This equation can be solved by applying two stages iteratively [15]:

Stage 1: Fix B_L, preserve the αP_L rows with largest values of matrix $\Phi_L - B_L$ as E_L, while the rest rows are set to zero;

Stage 2: Fix E_L, apply SVD to the matrix $(\Phi_L - E_L) = U\Sigma V^T$, preserve three largest eigenvalues and the rest set zero to form Σ'; update $B_L = U\Sigma' V^T$.

After convergence, $\Psi = \Sigma' V^T = [\omega_1^T, \omega_2^T, \omega_3^T]$ is the component trajectory matrix we want, where $\omega_1, \omega_2, \omega_3$ represent for 3 component motion of the background.

2.3   Trajectory Level Classification

For full-length trajectories, a fitting function used to establish consensus is the projection error on the three dimensional subspace spanned by the component trajectories. The matrix of component trajectories Ψ is then used to construct a projection matrix, $\Theta = \Psi(\Psi^T\Psi)^{-1}\Psi^T$. By measuring the projection error $f(p_i|\Psi) = \frac{2}{F}\parallel\Theta p_i - p_i\parallel_2$, the likelihood that a given trajectory p_i belongs to the background can be easily evaluated.

Short trajectories, however, is not fit for this function. Because some of it's elements is factitiously set to zero, applying such function will lead to huge projection error. Essentially, setting zeros to a trajectory vector is a dimension reducing process. In order to fit for this function, target subspace should have the same dimension. Assuming that p_i is a short trajectory vector, corresponding component trajectories are proposed to be:

$$\omega_j(k)' = \begin{cases} 0 & \text{if } p_i(k) = 0, \\ \omega_j(k) & \text{if } p_i(k) \neq 0. \end{cases} \tag{2}$$

where $k = 1, 2, 3$. Background motion model is presented as $\Psi' = [\omega_1'^T, \omega_2'^T, \omega_3'^T]$, and similarly the low-dimensional projection matrix $\Theta' = \Psi'(\Psi'^T\Psi')^{-1}\Psi'^T$, the likelihood that a short trajectory p_i belongs to the background can be evaluated as $f(p_i|\Psi') = \frac{2}{\parallel p_i \parallel_0}\parallel\Theta' p_i - p_i\parallel_2$. For convenience, errors under different projection matrices $f(p_i|\Psi')$ and $f(p_i|\Psi')$ will be all named as "$f(p_i)$" in the remainder

of this paper. Uniform standard can be applied on both full-length and short trajectories: If $f(p_i) > \delta$, p_i is sentenced to foreground trajectory, else sentenced to
background trajectory. Given a data matrix of $P \times 2F$ with P trajectories over F
frames, the major calculation is $O(PF^2)$ for SVD on each iteration. Considering
that we add a short trajectory analysing step, the projection calculation for P'
trajectories is $O(PF)$, so the total calculation of the classification is $O(PF^2)$.

2.4   Pixel Level Labeling

The labeled trajectories from the previous step are then used to segment all
frames at pixel level. First, the image edge information is abstracted to form
a edge map $C(x, y)$ by applying canny operator. For stronger edge detection
responses in (x,y), the lower $C(x, y)$ is. Labels are supposed to be separated
on these edges, and minimize the mistakes in calibrations on trajectory level.
Now we can transform the labeling question into a combinatorial optimization
problem, which minimizes the energy function:

$$\min_{x_p}\{ \sum_{p \in G} (V_p(x_p)) + \lambda \sum_{pq \in E} (V_{pq}(x_p, x_q)) \} \qquad (3)$$

where p represents for pixels in a single frame, and x_p for different labels of
these pixel. G is set of tracked points appeared in this frame, while E represents
for the neighbouring relation between pixel p and q. Data cost $V_p(x_p)$ can be
described by errors of trajectory level calibration, and smooth cost $V_{pq}(x_p, x_q)$
by the edge map. The globally optimal solution can be efficiently computed using
graph-cuts [18].

3   Experiments

Given space limitations, this article only lists 4 typical examples to demonstrate the performance of our framework. Three (Vcars, VPerson and VHand) is
from video source provided by Sand and Teller, and one (people) is recorded
by ourselves. Performances are evaluated by F-Measure: $F = 2recall \times$
$precision/(recall + precision)$. F_T is for trajectory level and F_P is for pixel
level. Comparison will mainly be made between results of full-length (LTTA)[15]
and proposed length-unconstrained trajectory analysis (LUCTA). Here, "full-
length" is defined as a reasonable value of 30 [13], which is neither too long to
be tracked nor too short to conduct matrix decomposition; In the other side,
"length-unconstrained" means making use of all trajectories lasting between 3
to 50 frames.

3.1   Property of Short Trajectories

In this part, we take video VPerson for example to clarify the effectiveness of
short trajectories (Fig. 3). In (a), the amount of trajectories of each length are
counted. As shown, number of trajectories lasts more than 50 frames is 6386,

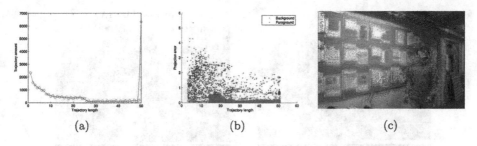

Fig. 3. Performance of short trajectories on test video VPerson: (a). Quantity-length distribution; (b). Projection error-length distribution; (c). Length-position distribution.

while number of short trajectories that lasts between 3 to 49 frames is 20495, most of which (55.2 %, 11348) are extremely short (lasts over 3 to 10frames). Mid-term trajectories only take 16.2 % (3388). (b) shows the projection errors distribution in each length. Blue points presents for foreground and magenta ones for background (confirmed by ground truth). The distance of two colors at each column can estimate how well foreground points can be detected. For this sequence, trajectories that lasts more than 27 frames are easily clarified. While length drops to 5 or even 3, although several points may be misjudged, the same threshold is still effective.

In (c) trajectories are set to different colors. If a trajectory is full-length, then it is set to green. And it shades to blue as it's length decreases. Short trajectories often appear on such positions: (1). The edge of the vision; (2). The edges between background and foreground; (3). Nonrigid foreground. We can intuitively tell that (2) and (3) may cause great inaccuracy of the detection.

We also test our framework on three video sequences, and compare classification results. As shown in Fig. 4, been affected by occlusions, there are lots of blank areas in upper lines. By taking short trajectories into consideration, the majority of these areas are made up, which makes description of boundaries between foreground and background more precisely. In our framework, most of short trajectories are correctly classified, and errors are evenly distributed across the frames, which has little influence on the final result.

3.2 Pixel Level Labeling Performance

Since that our work is mainly focused on the contribution of short trajectories, in this part, we will do comparisons between performances with and without applying short trajectories. We also take the two state-of-art algorithms as reference: RANSAC-based [12] and RPCA-based [13] background subtraction. The quantitative and qualitative results are shown in Fig. 5 and Table 1, respectively. Compared with LTTA, LUCTA has lower accuracy but vastly improved quantity (about 3 to 4 times). The reason for decreased accuracy can mainly be attributed as short trajectories often appear around the boundary. Generally, misjudgments of short trajectories often occur as noise points and spread all over the frame.

LTTA   Proposed LUCTA

Fig. 4. Performance comparison between LTTA and LUCTA on four video sequences. The upper and below line shows distribution of full length and unconstrained length trajectories in video fames, respectively. By using short trajectories, blank areas caused by occlusion between background and foreground are made up.

In fact, in our experiments we find the effect of such misjudgments on the pixel-level labeling to be small or non-existent. Moreover, although the property of trajectories degenerate as the length decrease, it's still better and more robust than some classic algorithms.

We also compared **time cost** of LTTA and LUCTA. Because the number of 50-length trajectories is much less than number of 30-length ones, the calculation for matrix decomposition is reduced. Taking consideration of time spent on

Trajectory classification LTTA LUCTA

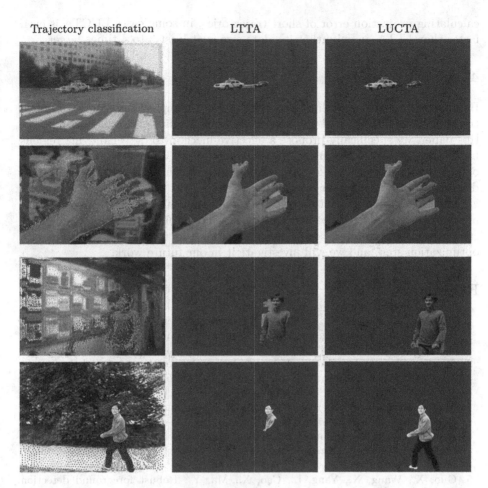

Fig. 5. Result comparison on pixel level labeling: The first column is trajectory classification results. Magenta and blue points represent for detected full-length and short background trajectories; While green and yellow points represent for detected full-length and short foreground trajectories. The second and third column is pixel level labeling results of LTTA and proposed LUCTA (Color figure online).

Table 1. Result comparison

Video	RANSAC F_T	RPCA F_T	LTTA				Proposed LUCTA			
			Number	Time	F_T	F_P	Number	Time	F_T	F_P
VCars	95.5 %	82.5 %	10826	1.41	97.1 %	91.8 %	**15506**	2.15	95.3 %	**98.9 %**
VHand	92.0 %	64.5 %	7501	2.99	95.2 %	89.0 %	**26789**	4.10	86.2 %	**95.6 %**
VPerson	70.3 %	74.0 %	6386	6.90	93.0 %	73.6 %	**23005**	**5.22**	87.6 %	**96.5 %**
People1	85.2 %	92.4 %	1377	0.88	96.3 %	29.8 %	**7242**	**0.73**	87.7 %	**94.6 %**

Compared with LTTA, our LUCTA shows great advantage in trajectory number, while the accuracy decreases insignificantly.

calculating projection error of short trajectories, in some cases LUCTA is even faster than LTTA, in spite that it's data size is at least 3 to 4 times larger.

4 Conclusion

Because of dimensionality limitation on matrix decomposition process, classical tracking based background subtraction can not acquire accurate boundary. In this paper, we specifically propose a effective method to detect moving regions from video sequences. By using "short trajectories", we get the information of occluded areas, which makes our labeling step much easier. Experiences also demonstrate the competency of our work.

Still and all, we can see that in trajectory classification step, the performance of extreme short trajectories is not satisfying enough. In fact, such misjudgment can be solved by adding constraints of spatial and temporal correlation into optimization step, and we will investigate it in our future work.

References

1. Cristani, M., Bicego, M., Murino, V.: Integrated region-and pixel-based approach to background modelling. In: Workshop on Motion and Video Computing, Proceedings, pp. 3–8. IEEE (2002)
2. Stauffer, C., Grimson, W.E.L.: Learning patterns of activity using real-time tracking. IEEE Trans. Pattern Anal. Mach. Intell. **22**(8), 747–757 (2000)
3. Mittal, A.: Huttenlocher, D.: Scene modeling for wide area surveillance and image synthesis. In: IEEE Conference on Computer Vision and Pattern Recognition, Proceedings, vol. 2, pp. 160–167. IEEE (2000)
4. Zhou, X., Yang, C., Weichuan, Y.: Moving object detection by detecting contiguous outliers in the low-rank representation. IEEE Trans. Pattern Anal. Mach. Intell. **35**(3), 597–610 (2013)
5. Guo, X., Wang, X., Yang, L., Cao, X., Ma, Y.: Robust foreground detection using smoothness and arbitrariness constraints. In: Fleet, D., Pajdla, T., Schiele, B., Tuytelaars, T. (eds.) ECCV 2014, Part VII. LNCS, vol. 8695, pp. 535–550. Springer, Heidelberg (2014)
6. Mittal, A., Paragios, N.: Motion-based background subtraction using adaptive kernel density estimation. In: Proceedings of the 2004 IEEE Computer Society Conferenceon Computer Vision and Pattern Recognition, CVPR 2004, vol. 2, pp. II-302–II-309. IEEE (2004)
7. Irani, M., Anandan, P., Hsu, S.: Mosaic based representations of video sequences and their applications. In: Fifth International Conference on Computer Vision, Proceedings, pp. 605–611. IEEE (1995)
8. Sand, P., Teller, S.: Particle video: long-range motion estimation using point trajectories. Int. J. Comput. Vis. **80**(1), 72–91 (2008)
9. Jin, Y., Tao, L., Di, H., Rao, N.I., Xu, G.: Background modeling from a free-moving camera by multi-layer homography algorithm. In: 15th IEEE International Conference on Image Processing, ICIP 2008, pp. 1572–1575. IEEE (2008)
10. Taneja, A., Ballan, L., Pollefeys, M.: Modeling dynamic scenes recorded with freely moving cameras. In: Kimmel, R., Klette, R., Sugimoto, A. (eds.) ACCV 2010, Part III. LNCS, vol. 6494, pp. 613–626. Springer, Heidelberg (2011)

11. Brutzer, S., Hoferlin, B., Heidemann, G.: Evaluation of background subtraction techniques for video surveillance. In: 2011 IEEE Conference on Computer Vision and Pattern Recognition (CVPR), pp. 1937–1944. IEEE (2011)
12. Sheikh, Y., Javed, O., Kanade, T.: Background subtraction for freely moving cameras. In: 2009 IEEE 12th International Conference on Computer Vision, pp. 1219–1225. IEEE (2009)
13. Candès, E.J., Li, X., Ma, Y., Wright, J.: Robust principal component analysis? J. ACM (JACM) **58**(3), 11 (2011)
14. Yuan, M., Lin, Y.: Model selection and estimation in regression with grouped variables. J. R. Stat. Soc.: Ser. B (Stat. Methodol.) **68**(1), 49–67 (2006)
15. Cui, X., Huang, J., Zhang, S., Metaxas, D.N.: Background subtraction using low rank and group sparsity constraints. In: Fitzgibbon, A., Lazebnik, S., Perona, P., Sato, Y., Schmid, C. (eds.) ECCV 2012, Part I. LNCS, vol. 7572, pp. 612–625. Springer, Heidelberg (2012)
16. Liao, Q., Liu, B., Yu, N.: Moving object detection for moving cameras on superpixel level. In: Seventh International Conference on Image and Graphics, pp. 307–312 (2013)
17. Tomasi, C., Kanade, T.: Shape and motion from image streams under orthography: a factorization method. Int. J. Comput. Vis. **9**(2), 137–154 (1992)
18. Boykov, Y., Kolmogorov, V.: An experimental comparison of min-cut/max-flow algorithms for energy minimization in vision. IEEE Trans. Pattern Anal. Mach. Intell. **26**(9), 1124–1137 (2004)

Multidimensional Adaptive Sampling and Reconstruction for Realistic Image Based on BP Neural Network

Yu Liu[(✉)], Changwen Zheng, and Fukun Wu

Science and Technology on Integrated Information System Laboratory,
Institute of Software, Chinese Academy of Sciences, Beijing, China
15600602128@163.com, changwen@iscas.ac.cn,
1024057620@qq.com

Abstract. A novel adaptive sampling and reconstruction algorithm is presented to address the noise artifacts of Monte Carlo rendering. BP neural network is adopted to estimate per pixel error that guides sampling rate in the multidimensional spaces. In sampling stage, coarse samples are firstly generated to train BP network. Then per pixel error is estimated by the BP predicted value. Additional samples are distributed to the slices of pixels which have large errors. These slices are extracted through a heuristic distance. A warping procedure is then carried out to remove individual light paths that result in significant spikes of noise. In reconstruction stage, the final image is reconstructed by filtering each pixel with appropriate anisotropic filter. Filters with small scales are used to keep clarity while the large ones smooth out noise. Compared to the state-of-the-art methods, experimental results demonstrated that our algorithm achieves better results in numerical error and visual image quality.

Keywords: Adaptive sampling and reconstruction · BP neural network · Anisotropic filter · Multidimensional analysis

1 Introduction

Monte Carlo technique computes pixel colors by analyzing the multidimensional integral at every pixel. This method distributes samples into the multidimensional domain and then integrates them into the final pixel value. Though its simplicity, Monte Carlo technique suffers serious noise because of limited sampling rate. In order to reduce noise with sparse samples, kinds of adaptive sampling and reconstruction methods are employed.

Adaptive sampling methods distribute samples with an optimal fashion that sampling rate is determined by per pixel error. Therefore regions with large errors acquire more samples. The pioneering work of Mitchell [1] laid the foundation for this method. There are two strategies to address this: image space sampling and multidimensional spaces sampling. The first strategy relies only on a local measure of variance, which fails to simulate effects such as motion blur and soft shadow. For instance, Rigau [2] and Xu [3] construct criterions by f-divergence and fuzzy uncertainty respectively. Bala et al. [4] perform an edge-aware interpolation to reduce noise. However, their quality is

© Springer International Publishing Switzerland 2015
Y.-J. Zhang (Ed.): ICIG 2015, Part II, LNCS 9218, pp. 510–523, 2015.
DOI: 10.1007/978-3-319-21963-9_47

restricted by the accuracy of edge detection. The second strategy takes lens, time and other non-image spaces into account to render a wide range of realistic effects. Hachisuka et al. [5] sample the multidimensional spaces to simulate special effects, but it is limited by the curse of dimensionality. Recently, algorithms which operate in the transform domain generate pleasing images, and Durand et al. [6] firstly analyze the frequency content of radiance and how it is altered by numerous phenomena. Through performing Fourier transform, Soler [7] and Egan [8] render high-quality depth of field and motion blur respectively. Overbeck et al. [9] harbor the idea that signal yields large wavelet coefficients while noise yields small coefficients, and they propose an iterative denoising framework by wavelet shrinkage. However, it is still challenging for these existing transform methods to analyze non-image spaces together.

Reconstruction algorithms are employed to construct a smooth result by applying appropriate filters. Bilateral filter is applauded for its feature preservation and Tomasi and Manduchi [10] combine spatial kernel and range kernel to construct bilateral filter. However, their efficiency is limited by the color term. Isotropic filters [11] which use symmetric kernels for all pixels cause a blurred result. Recently, anisotropic reconstruction methods have been widely developed. Greedy method proposed by Rousselle et al. [12] presents a pleasing result through selecting Gaussian filters for different pixels, but they didn't take much visual quality into consideration. Non-local mean filter [13] which splits samples into two buffers is also adopted to estimate per pixel error. Li et al. [14] employ anisotropic bilateral filters to better handle complex geometric, but it needs expensive auxiliary information such as depth and normal. The core idea for anisotropic reconstruction is the choice of filter scale. However, a robust criterion is challenging.

Recently, regression analysis functions [15, 16] have been widely used in realistic rendering for their compactness and ease of evaluation. The major shortage for the existing methods is to deal with high-dynamic multidimensional content. Most previous algorithms only analyze local variance of samples. RRF [15], for instance, returns the indirect illumination through giving viewing direction and lighting condition, and for this reason it fails to predict pixel error accurately.

In this paper, we propose a novel two-stage adaptive sampling and reconstruction method based the BP neural network (Fig. 1). The key idea is to design BP network as a nonlinear function of multidimensional content such that it is a global representation and fast to converge. Firstly, multidimensional content of coarse samples is used to train per pixel BP network and then per pixel error is estimated by the BP predicted value. Additional samples are then distributed to the pixels with large errors. A warping algorithm is also carried out to recognize outliers and removes them to further avoid spikes of noise. In reconstruction stage, per pixel error obtained in the former stage is chosen as a robust criterion to select filter scale. All the pixels are reconstructed by suitable anisotropy bilateral filter. Finally, a second reconstruction is recommended to make up the discontinuity caused by abrupt change of filter scales. Important notations and their experimental values are summarized in Table 1.

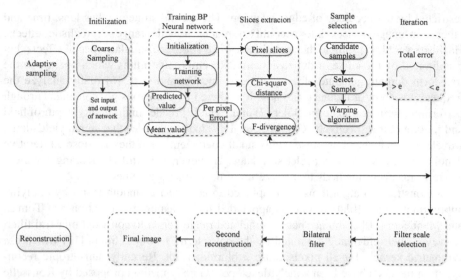

Fig. 1. Algorithm framework

Table 1. Notations and their experimental values

Notations	Content	Value
$\omega_{ih}\ \omega_{ho}$	Connected weights	$(-1,1)$
Nit	Training times	$(10,100)$
e	Error thresholding	0.1
$b_h\ b_o$	Output thresholding	0.01 0.01
μ	Learning rate	$(0.02,0.08)$
Ψ	Pixel contrast thresholding	0.05
N_{candi}	Number of candidate sample	4
r	Reconstruction radius	4
$\alpha\ \sigma_c$	Reconstruction shape parameters	$\alpha = \{0.1, 1, 3, 5, 10\}\ \sigma_c = 0.3$
$\Phi = \{\Phi_1\Phi_2\Phi_3\Phi_4\}$	Filter scale thresholding	$\Phi = \{0.3, 0.45, 0.7, 0.85\}$
$f(\mathrm{x})$	Reward function	$f(x) = \frac{1}{1+e^{-x}}$
m	Quantized levels	5

2   Adaptive Sampling Based on BP Neural Network

BP neural network is a back propagation process that predicts output values. It is a universal function approximator and we use it for its relative compactness and high speed in evaluation. Illustrated as Fig. 2, three layers are presented in the network. Each layer has a number of nodes connected by defined weights. The multidimensional content is regarded as input layer: two image positions, two lens positions and one time position. Additional dimensions such as light source can be easily transplanted into our

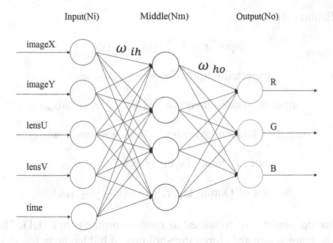

Input(Ni)   Middle(Nm)   Output(No)

imageX

ω_{ih}

ω_{ho}

imageY   R

lensU   G

lensV   B

time

Fig. 2. Per pixel BP neural network (Color figure online)

framework for more effects, and we only describe five dimensions for simplicity. The output layer is constructed by the three components of pixel spectral value: red, green and blue.

2.1 Initialization

At the beginning of sampling stage, coarse samples are distributed to train network. The node numbers in three layers are $Ni = 5$, Nm and $No = 3$ respectively, where Nm is a user-defined parameter. Our algorithm distributes coarse samples by standard Monte Carlo method such as Low Discrepancy [17]. Only one hidden layer is set to balance training cost.

The training number Nit is a critical factor for accuracy. Traditional training methods take only one sample each iteration, which limit the prediction accuracy because only sparse samples are available. Our algorithm guarantees accuracy through employing the patch training model. In this model, all sample errors are added up to form a global error. Partial derivatives of this global error are then computed to adjust node weights $(\Delta\omega_{ih}, \Delta\omega_{ho})$. In theory, the effect of training Nit times with patch model equals to the effect of training $Nit \times Ncoarse$ times with traditional model, where $Ncoarse$ is current sample number. Besides, patch model results in a rapid convergence nature that reduce time.

2.2 Training BP Neural Network

Training BP neural network needs expected outputs which are used to compute training error. Since the actual pixel value are not available, mean value of coarse samples is utilized instead. One of our BP training iteration is described as follows:

Step1: Initialization BP network:

$$\text{input: } x = (x_1, x_2, x_3, x_4, x_5) \tag{1}$$

$$\text{expected output: } do = (do_1, do_2, do_3) \tag{2}$$

$$\text{input of Hidden layer: } hi = (hi_1, hi_2, hi_3 \ldots hi_{Nm}) \tag{3}$$

$$\text{output of Hidden layer: } ho = (ho_1, ho_2, ho_3 \ldots ho_{Nm}) \tag{4}$$

$$\text{input of Output layer: } yi = (yi_1, yi_2, yi_3) \tag{5}$$

$$\text{output of Output layer: } yo = (yo_1, yo_2, yo_3) \tag{6}$$

The connected weights are initialized as random numbers in $(-1,1)$. The max error thresholding is denoted as e and output thresholding of hidden layer (output layer) is b_h (b_o). Learning rate is μ.

Step 2: Value propagation:

$$\text{input of Hidden layer: } hi_h = \sum_{i=1}^{5} \omega_{ih} x_i - b_h \quad (h = 1, 2, 3, \ldots Nm) \tag{7}$$

$$\text{output of Hidden layer: } ho_h = f(hi_h) \tag{8}$$

$$\text{input of Output layer: } yi_o = \sum_{i=1}^{Nm} \omega_{ho} ho_i - b_o \quad (o = 1, 2, 3) \tag{9}$$

$$\text{output of Output layer: } yo_o = f(yi_o) \tag{10}$$

Step 3: Adjust the weights:

$$\omega_{ih} = \omega_{ih} + \Delta\omega_{ih} \quad \omega_{ho} = \omega_{ho} + \Delta\omega_{ho} \tag{11}$$

Each training process is built on the basis of last iteration. When all the Nit training processes come to an end, our method set $imageX$, $imageY$ to 0 and $lensU$, $lensV$, $time$ to random numbers in $(0,1)$ to calculate the predicted value I'. The current pixel error is then estimated as the contrast between I' and expected value I.

$$I = \frac{\sum_{x=1}^{n} I_x}{n} \tag{12}$$

$$bias = \frac{|I' - I|}{I} \tag{13}$$

n is the total number of samples. If $bias > \Psi$, the current pixel is determined to be in a high frequency region (such as edge or texture) that further sampling is needed.

2.3 Slices Extraction

The high frequency pixels obtained in Sect. 2.2 usually locate in complex regions (Fig. 3(a)) which mainly cause noise. It is critical to choose new sample positions for these pixels. Our algorithm distributes new samples as follows. Firstly, these pixels are divided into slices (Fig. 3(b)). We focus on the truth that different slices present different complexities due to the nature of high frequency. For example, slice B has a lower complexity than slice C that locates in the boundary of two different surfaces. We extract the two slices which has the strongest contrast. This is achieved by considering Chi-square distance [18]:

$$diff(X, Y) = \frac{1}{N(X) + N(Y)} \sum_{i=1}^{m} \frac{(\sqrt{\frac{N(Y)}{N(X)}} hi(X) - \sqrt{\frac{N(X)}{N(Y)}} hi(Y))^2}{hi(X) + hi(Y)} \tag{14}$$

$diff(X, Y)$ is the contrast between slice X and Y. Pixel value is quantized to m levels and $hi(X)$ is the current sample number of level i for slice X. $N(X) = \sum_i hi(X)$ $(N(Y) = \sum_i hi(Y))$ is the total sample number of slice $X(Y)$.

The two slices extracted above has the strongest contrast. Important notation is that one of them (slice B) is usually far away from the boundary while another one contain it (slice C). To locate more samples in the vicinity of this boundary, a warping algorithm is described in Sect. 2.4. Before our warping algorithm, the less complex slice is recognized in the light of f-divergence [2]:

$$fdiver(X) = \frac{1}{N(X)} \bar{L} \sqrt{\frac{1}{2} \sum_{i=1}^{N(X)} (\sqrt{p_i} - \sqrt{\frac{1}{N(X)}})^2} \tag{15}$$

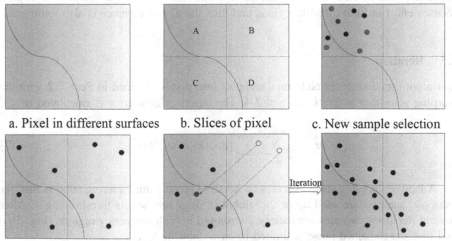

a. Pixel in different surfaces   b. Slices of pixel   c. New sample selection

d. New samples distribution   e. Warping algorithm   f. Final sample distribution

Fig. 3. New sample selection

where $\overline{L} = \frac{1}{N(X)} \sum\limits_{i=1}^{N(X)} L_i$ is the mean value of slice X and $p_i = \frac{L_i}{\sum\limits_{i=1}^{N(X)} L_i}$. Slice with a smaller

$fdiver(X)$ is determined to be the less complex slice.

2.4 Sample Selection

To approximate Poisson disk distribution for new samples, N_{candi} (Fig. 3(c)) candidates are generated and the one which minimizes per slice error is finally selected to distribute into the image space:

$$S(x) = \frac{1}{N} \sum_{i=1}^{N(X)} \frac{|I_i - I_{can}|}{I_i} \tag{16}$$

$S(x)$ is the slice error for candidate I_{can}. The main difference between ours and naive Poisson disk distribution is the metric choice: per slice error used in this paper performs better in visual image quality while the traditional methods use image space distance. These newly selected samples commonly appear in the vicinity of complex geometries that relate to low-probability yet high-energy light paths. They are recognized as outliers and removed to further reduce noise. Besides, only local variance is minimized if same amount of samples are distributed into all slices, since that it can't focus effort in the most difficult part. New samples which possess smallest slice error are distributed into all the slices of difficult pixels obtained in Sect. 2.2 (Fig. 3(d)).

After suitable sample is chosen (red dot in Fig. 3(c)) from candidates (yellow dots in Fig. 3(c)), our algorithm transfers (Fig. 3(e)) new samples in the slice with a smaller f-divergence (slice B) into the slice with a larger f-divergence (slice C). These samples are transferred symmetrically by the local positions. Finally, the warping algorithm focuses effort in local difficult regions and thus the global variance is also minimized.

2.5 Iteration

Our algorithm distributes additional samples into pixels obtained in Sect. 2.2 with the warping algorithm in Sects. 2.3 and 2.4. The current global error is calculated as:

$$er = \frac{1}{2} \sum_{k=1}^{Ncoarse} \sum_{o=1}^{3} (do_o(k) - yo_o(k))^2 \tag{17}$$

Adaptive sampling stage executes an iterative process until a termination is met, for example, samples are used up or the global error er reaches its thresholding e. After several iterations, samples are mainly distributed in high-frequency regions (Fig. 3(f)) and thus the remained noise is limited to an acceptable level.

3 Reconstruction

Our reconstruction method make a trade-off between noise reduction and keeping clarity through filter scale selection. Pixels with large errors are suitable for small scale filters to keep clarity, and vice versa. We focuses on the fact that filters with small scale have little bias but much noise while the large ones have little noise but much bias. Therefore, large scale filters are selected for pixels in low frequency regions to denoise and small ones in the remain regions to reduce bias.

3.1 Bilateral Filter

Image distance $d()$ and color distance $c()$ are combined to construct the bilateral kernel $\omega_{pq} = d(|p - q|)c(|I_p - I_q|)$:

$$I_p = \frac{\sum_{q\in\Omega_p} \omega_{pq} I_q}{\sum_{q\in\Omega_p} \omega_{pq}} = \frac{\sum_{q\in\Omega_p} e^{-\alpha\frac{|p-q|^2}{2}} e^{-\frac{|I_p-I_q|^2}{2\sigma_c^2}} I_q}{\sum_{q\in\Omega_p} e^{-\alpha\frac{|p-q|^2}{2}} e^{-\frac{|I_p-I_q|^2}{2\sigma_c^2}}} \tag{18}$$

The final pixel value I_p is calculated by averaging pixels over a neighborhood window Ω_p with radius r. α and σ_c control the rate of falloff for $d()$ and $c()$ respectively. In practice, the same σ_c is used for all filters since the related work [14] pointed out that color term doesn't help much. A key observation is that the filter scale increases when the α goes from coarser to finer, and thus filter with a coarser α is selected to reconstruct pixels with larger error.

3.2 Filter Scale Selection

Our filterbank is composed of five spatially-varying bilateral filters, which denoted as $\alpha = \{\alpha_1, \alpha_2, \alpha_3, \alpha_4, \alpha_5\}$ that goes from finer to coarser. The choice thresholding is accumulated as $\Phi = \{\Phi_1\Phi_2\Phi_3\Phi_4\}$. We utilizes the BP pixel error as a robust criterion, and therefor filter scale is simply chosen by considering the *bias*:

$$
\begin{aligned}
&\text{if} &&0 < bias < \Phi_1 &&\alpha = \alpha_1 \\
&\text{else if} &&\Phi_1 < bias < \Phi_2 &&\alpha = \alpha_2 \\
&\text{else if} &&\Phi_2 < bias < \Phi_3 &&\alpha = \alpha_3 \\
&\text{else if} &&\Phi_3 < bias < \Phi_4 &&\alpha = \alpha_4 \\
&\text{else} &&&&\alpha = \alpha_5
\end{aligned}
$$

With suitable filter choice, output pixels are reconstructed. As shown in Fig. 4, filters with coarse α are selected in edges to keep clarity while finer ones are selected in background to denoise. However, this reconstruction may presents discontinuity (or Ringing artifact) in boundaries since the abrupt change of filter scale. As illustrated in

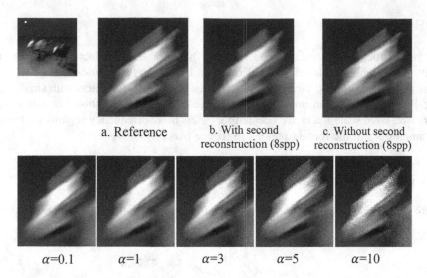

a. Reference   b. With second   c. Without second
                    reconstruction (8spp)   reconstruction (8spp)

$\alpha=0.1$ $\alpha=1$ $\alpha=3$ $\alpha=5$ $\alpha=10$

Fig. 4. Filter scale selection

Fig. 4(c), image without second reconstruction exhibits more discontinuity and visual artifacts in edges. Through its low probability, it may cut down smoothness. We treat this problem by filtering all pixels again with the same scale α_3. This second reconstruction balances the discontinuity to a pile of nearby pixels. As shown in Fig. 4(b), the second reconstruction leads to a more smoothness result.

4 Experimental Results

Our algorithm and previous approaches are implemented on the top of PBRT [17]. All the images were rendered by an Intel(R) Core(TM) i7-3630 QM CPU with 8 GB RAM. Rendered images are compared to previous methods including Low Discrepancy [17], F-divergences [2], Fuzzy [3] and GEM [12]. The rendering time and MSE (mean square error) is also compared under the same experimental environment. Learning rate is a variable controlled by the global error er. In addition, we also explain how the effect of noise removal is altered by the critical parameter Nit. In our experiments, node number of input layer is set to 4 for simplicity:

$$\{image = \sqrt{(imageX)^2 + (imageY)^2}, lensU, lensV, time\} \tag{19}$$

4.1 Scenes

Figure 5(a) is a global illumination scene which is rendered with 16 samples per pixel. The images rendered by Low Discrepancy and Fuzzy suffer serious noise both in low frequency regions (red block and green block) and high frequency regions (yellow

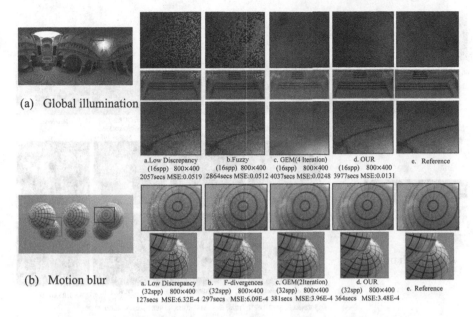

a.Low Discrepancy   b.Fuzzy   c. GEM(4 Iteration)   d. OUR   e. Reference
(16spp) 800×400   (16spp) 800×400   (16spp) 800×400   (16spp) 800×400
2057secs MSE:0.0519 2864secs MSE:0.0512 4037secs MSE:0.0248 3977secs MSE:0.0131

a. Low Discrepancy   b.   F-divergences   c. GEM(2Iteration)   d. OUR   e. Reference
(32spp) 800×400   (32spp) 800×400   (32spp) 800×400   (32spp) 800×400
127secs MSE:6.32E-4 297secs MSE:6.09E-4 381secs MSE:3.96E-4 364secs MSE:3.48E-4

Fig. 5. Global illumination and motion blur effects (Color figure online)

block). In this scene, the noise level of GEM is as good as ours. However, our method presents better details than GEM in high frequency regions such as stair. Besides, our result presents a smoother and less block effect result.

Figure 5(b) demonstrates a motion blur scene consists of three moving balls. This scene is rendered with 32 samples per pixel. Three balls rotates with different speed increasing from left to right. The red block shows that our method is able to sample the motive details better than Low Discrepancy and F-divergences, which generate much more noise. Pay attention to the static ball (yellow block), our method remove the outliers that mainly cause spikes of noise and produce a clearer detail while the GEM obviously causes an overly blurred image. This scene indicates that our warping algorithm is more sensitive to the high frequency details.

In the car scene render by 16 samples per pixel in Fig. 6(a), a soft shadow effect is simulated under the occlusion of tire (red block). GEM performs better than Low Discrepancy, but it failed to capture the texture on tire. Our algorithm suffers the least noise and is smoother on the soft shadow region. Besides, our image is closest to the reference image. Because of the BP neural network used in this article, we captures the details accurately. In addition, our denoising effect is as good as Low Discrepancy (Fig. 6(a).c) which consumes four times samples (64spp).

Figure 6(b) is a dragon scene with depth of field effect. We compared images both in the focus region (red block) and blur region (yellow block). The Low Discrepancy method suffers serious noise in the blur region because of its single sampling rate. Different with the GEM which uses Gaussian filters to reconstruct pixels, our bilateral filter take more visual image quality into account and produce a smoother result in the

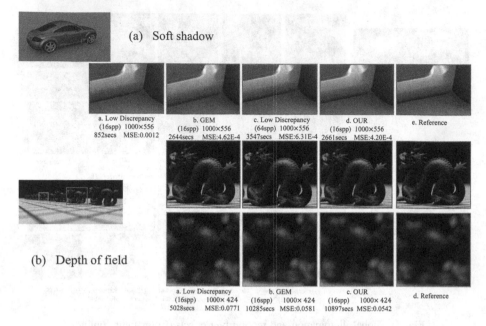

Fig. 6. Soft shadow and depth of field effects (Color figure online)

blur region. Besides, the second reconstruction procedure makes up the discontinuity which is more obvious in the boundaries of GEM.

4.2   Analysis

Figure 7 compares the MSE of Low Discrepancy and our algorithm for the scene in Fig. 5(b). This figure indicates that our method achieves a much lower MSE with the same sample number. The MSE and rendering time in Figs. 5 and 6 also indicate that our algorithm generates images with a lower MSE and better visual quality than previous methods. In summary, our algorithm is more sensitive to high frequency content both in the local and non-local variances and therefore we can handle a vast body of realistic effects.

The parameter *Nit* is critical to efficiency of our algorithm. In theory, the more times we training the more accurate results we obtain. However, time consumption limits the training number. Figure 8 analyze the change of MSE and rendering time when *Nit* goes from 10 to 100 for scene in Fig. 4. This scene is rendered with 8 samples per pixel. The blue line indicates that training time increases violently between (10–30) and (90–100) while gently between (30–90). The green line shows that MSE is relatively high when a small training number (10–40) is employed. Based on the above analysis, a large *Nit* (70–90) is recommended for simple scenes while a small *Nit* (50–60) for complex scenes to make a trade-off between time and MSE.

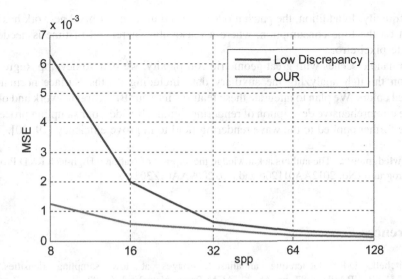

Fig. 7. Mean square error

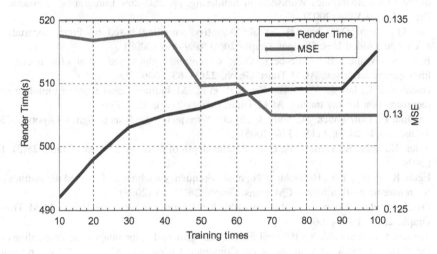

Fig. 8. Parameter analysis

5 Conclusion and Future Work

This paper proposes an efficient two-step rendering algorithm. We vary sampling rate according to the per pixel error calculated through BP analysis. Adaptive samples are distributed to the high frequency regions both in local and non-local regions. Besides, high light noise is also reduced through a warping algorithm. With our BP network analysis, suitable filter scales are selected to keep clarity while limit the noise artifacts. Experiments results indicates that our algorithm handles a wide range of effects and achieves a better result over many state-of-the-art algorithm in terms of MSE and visual image quality. In addition, the patch model we used to train per pixel network has little impact on the time consumption, where a reasonable increment of time is needed to estimate pixel error.

To handle scenes with great geometric complexity, we plan to develop Regression function through analyzing the auxiliary data including depths, surface normal and textured colors. We plan to integrate these features into our BP neural network and obtain a more comprehensive description of rendering details. Besides, our sampling procedure will be further applied to the wave rendering field to improve efficiency [19, 20].

Acknowledgments. The authors acknowledge the support of National High-tech R&D Program (863 Program) (No. 2012AA011206 and No. 2009AA01Z303).

References

1. Mitchell, D.P.: Generating antialiased images at low sampling densities. In: ACM SIGGRAPH 1987, pp. 65–72. ACM Press, New York (1987)
2. Rigau, J., Feixas, M., Sbert, M.: Refinement criteria based on f-divergences. In: Proceedings of the 14th Eurographics Workshop on Rendering, pp. 260–269. Eurographics Association Press, Aire-la-Ville (2003)
3. Xu, Q., Chen, D., Chen, H., et al.: Adaptive sampling based on fuzzy uncertainty. J. Comput. Aided Des. Comput. Graph. 20(6), 689–699 (2008)
4. Bala, K., Walter, B., Greenberg, D.P.: Combining edges and points for interactive high-quality rendering. ACM Trans. Graph. 22(3), 631–640 (2003)
5. Hachisuka, T., Jarosz, W., Weistroffer, R.P., et al.: Multidimensional adaptive sampling and reconstruction for ray tracing. ACM Trans. Graph. 27(3), 33 (2008)
6. Durand, F., Holzschuch, N., Soler, C., et al.: A frequency analysis of light transport. ACM Trans. Graph. 24(3), 1115–1126 (2005)
7. Soler, C., Subr, K., Durand, F., et al.: Fourier depth of field. ACM Trans. Graph. 28(2), 18 (2009)
8. Egan, K., Tseng, Y.T., Holzschuch, N., et al.: Frequency analysis and sheared reconstruction for rendering motion blur. ACM Trans. Graph. 28(2), 93 (2009)
9. Overbeck, R.S., Donner, C., Ramamoorthi, R.: Adaptive wavelet rendering. ACM Trans. Graph. 28(5), 1–12 (2009)
10. Tomasi, C., Manduchi, R.: Bilateral filtering for gray and color images. In: Proceedings of the Sixth International Conference on Computer Vision, pp. 839–846. IEEE Computer Society Press, Washington, D.C. (1998)
11. Cook, R.L.: Stochastic sampling in computer graphics. ACM Trans. Graph. 5(1), 51–72 (1986)
12. Rousselle, F., Knaus, C., Zwicker, M.: Adaptive sampling and reconstruction using greedy error minimization. ACM Trans. Graph. 30(6), 159 (2011)
13. Rousselle, F., Knaus, C., Zwicker, M.: Adaptive rendering with non-local means filtering. ACM Trans. Graph. 31(6), 195 (2012)
14. Li, T.M., Wu, Y.T., Chuang, Y.Y.: SURE-based optimization for adaptive sampling and reconstruction. ACM Trans. Graph. 31(6), 194 (2012)
15. Ren, P., Wang, J., Gong, M.: Global illumination with radiance regression functions. ACM Trans. Graph. 32(4), 130 (2013)

16. Liu, X.D., Zheng, C.W.: Adaptive cluster rendering via regression analysis. Vis. Comput. **31**(1), 105–114 (2015)
17. Pharr, M., Humphreys, G.: Physically Based Rendering: From Theory to Implementation. Morgan Kaufmann, San Francisco (2010)
18. Delbracio, M., Musé, P., Buades, A., et al.: Boosting monte carlo rendering by ray histogram fusion. ACM Trans. Graph. **33**(1), 8 (2014)
19. Wu, F., Zheng, C.: A comprehensive geometrical optics application for wave rendering. Graph. Models **75**(6), 318–327 (2013)
20. Wu, F., Zheng, C.: Microfacet-based interference simulation for multilayer films. Graph. Models **78C**, 26–35 (2015)

Modeling and Simulation of Multi-frictional Interaction Between Guidewire and Vasculature

Dongjin Huang[1]([✉]), Yin Wang[1], Pengbin Tang[1], Zhifeng Xie[1], Wen Tang[2], and Youdong Ding[1]

[1] School of Film and TV Arts and Technology, Shanghai University,
Shanghai 200072, People's Republic of China
djhuang@shu.edu.cn
[2] Department of Creative Technology, University of Bournemouth,
Fern Barrow, Poole, Dorset BH12 5BB, UK

Abstract. In the cardiovascular interventional operation, the surgeon steers the tip of a long-thin guidewire to reach the clinical targets while traveling through the inner of blood vessels, and performs a wide range of minimally invasive procedures. However, real-time simulating the physical deformation behaviours of guidewire caused by a large areas of frictional contact between guidewire and vasculature during insertion is a challenge task. From the microscopic view, this paper built a novel multi-frictional contact dynamics model based on flexible multi-body system to address the multi-frictional interaction between them. In the model, guidewire and vascular formed a flexible multi-body system and the process of contact and collision could be divided into three stages, including contact detection, contact handling and separation. In the first stage, a continuous collision detection algorithm based on an adaptive layer was proposed to obtain a set of "point-surface" contact pairs quickly. After confirming the contact areas, a multi-frictional contact dynamics algorithm based on nonlinear equivalent spring damping was put forward. In the normal direction, nonlinear spring damping model was used to compute the spring restoring force and nonlinear damping force. In the tangential direction, sliding friction, static friction and rolling friction were calculated during the collision between two bodies by coulomb friction model. Finally, all frictional forces in the contact areas were added to the physical models of guidewire for further simulating various non-linear deformation behaviors. The experimental results show that this algorithm is feasible and could simulate the multi-frictional interaction between guidewire and blood vessles very well with real-time performance.

Keywords: Flexible multi-body system · Guidewire · Multi-frictional contact · Equivalent spring-damper model · Physical simulation

1 Introduction

Minimally invasive vascular surgery(MIVS) is a revolutionary breakthrough in modern medical procedures, which has received more and more attention in

Y.-J. Zhang (Ed.): ICIG 2015, Part II, LNCS 9218, pp. 524–537, 2015.
DOI: 10.1007/978-3-319-21963-9_48

recent years. MIVS uses vascular interventional instruments, such as guidewire, catheter, etc. to insert into blood vessels and perform the operation under the guidance of medical imaging equipments like X-ray, CT, MRI and ultrasound. Attribute to the advantages of little hemorrhage, minimal wound, fast rehabilitation and less complications comparing to traditional open surgery, MIVS has been widely adopted to treat angiographic, angioplasty, thrombectomy, treatment of cancer, vascular malformation and so on [1].

With the rapid development of virtual reality technology, VR systems have been increasingly applied in almost every industry by virtual of its own advanced technology, especially in medical field. Introducing VRT into clinical skills training of MIVS, the virtual training simulator provides a realistic virtual environment to trainees with visual, hearing and haptic sense interface, and makes junior doctors master kinds of clinical performance skills and hand-eye co-ordination in a short time for the purpose of achieving better training effect. In the system, the models of guidewire and vasculature are the most important components. Simulating the contact interaction between them not only could reproduce the living clinical operation situation in the visual, but also could make doctors apperceive the inner structure of blood vessels by the haptic devices for hand-sense training. Beyond all doubt, it is extremely significant to do the dynamics simulation for the contact and collision between guidewire and blood vessels using effective and high-precision methods.

In the flexible multi-body system, it is needed to regard objects as the flexible bodies with large overall motion and nonlinear deformation due to the complex dynamics behaviors [2]. Obviously, guidewire and vasculars both are deformable objects. They form a flexible multi-body system during the process of guidewire insertion and their contact interaction is a typical multi-frictional contact of flexible multi-body system. In the microscopic view, the surfaces of guidewire and vasculature are consist of a number of polygons. When guidewire inserting, the contact areas between them are generated by many contact pairs and the contact forces appear at the same time. Just under such contact forces, guidewire and vascular happen to do the nonlinear deformation. The whole process of collision and contact between them could be summed up as follow. At the moment of contacting, the contact areas are small and disperse along the shaft of guidewire and only few contact-pairs work. In the compression stage, contact areas increase gradually and more and more contact-pairs take effect. In the separating process, contact areas become smaller and contact-pairs are separated gradually.

Until now, many researchers all over the world have researched the interaction between guidewire and vascular deeply and made a lot of achievements. However, most of the studies focused on the guidewire physical model and only considered the collision contact situation on the control nodes of guidewire [3–5]. In fact, the collision contacts between them not only occurs at the control nodes, but also at the shaft between two adjacent control nodes. This paper does the further discuss on the collision and contact between guidewire and blood vessels from the microscopic view, and make dynamics simulation of their multi-frictional interaction in real time.

There are three impediments that make it difficult to model and simulate the multi-frictional interaction between guidewire and blood vessels. First of all, a robust physical model of guidewire is needed to simulate various nonlinear deformation behaviors under the action of external forces accurately, including bending, twisting and stretching. Secondly, a continuous collision detection algorithm based on flexible multi-body system is needed to be proposed, which could obtain the contact areas during guidewire insertion quickly. Finally, a multi-frictional contact dynamics model based on flexible multi-body system is needed to calculate the contact forces accurately by the dynamics information of contact-pairs, especially the friction force.

In order to address these problems, we proposed a new multi-frictional interactive algorithm between guidewire and vascular based on flexible multi-body system. From the microscopic view, we introduced an adaptive layer into a continuous collision detection algorithm for obtaining the set of "point-surface" contact pairs quickly. Then a multi-frictional dynamics model based on nonlinear equivalent spring damping was proposed for calculating the friction force under various conditions, including sliding friction force, static friction force and rolling friction force. The experimental results show that this algorithm could simulate an insertion procedure very well with complex structure of vasculature in real time.

2   Related Work

Physical Models for Guidewire: guidewire is a kind of long-thin flexible object. Building its physical model is the same as simulations for 1D flexible objects, such as hair, tubes, ropes and cables. Its geometric structure is constrained controlled by a complex physical system in space, and it should not only take the bending deformation into account, but also the twisting deformation and stretching deformation around its centreline. In addition, the numerical stability and computation efficiency of the physical model are also needed to be considered.

In the recent years, foreign and domestic researchers have put forward a lot of good deformation algorithms for guidewire simulation based on physical model, which could be classified three main types, including hybrid mass-spring model [4,6,7], finite element based model [8–10] and elastic rod model [3,11,12]. On the basis of traditional mass-spring model, hybrid mass-spring methods add the bending force and the rotation of nodes into model. These algorithms are simple and good performance in real time, but the accuracy is low and it is easy to cause the oscillation. In the finite element based model, guidewire, with long-thin structure, is separated into several simple units, and it analyzes the dynamics of these discrete units instead of the whole structure. Though various deformation behaviors of guidewire could be simulated precisely by finite element methods, it is not suitable for some VR systems with real time requirement because of its complex calculation. The third kind of modeling approach is based on elastic rod model. As shown in Fig. 1, the discrete setting of centreline is used to describe a guidewire as a set of control nodes $x_0, x_1, \cdots, x_n$, which are connected by edges $e_0, e_1, \cdots, e_{n-1}$, meeting $e_{i-1} = x_i - x_{i-1}$. The calculation speed of elastic rod model is depended on the number of these nodes. So, the adaptive method of node number is proposed in paper [3] for achieving both simulation efficiency and accuracy.

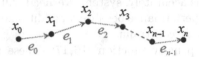

Fig. 1. Elastic rod model

The calculation principle of elastic rod model is introduced as follow. Let x_i^k, v_i^k be the current position and velocity of node i at the time step k respectively, $x_i^k \in \Re^{3n}$, $v_i^k \in \Re^{3n}$. So the position and velocity at the next time step $k+1$ are:

$$x_i^{k+1} = x_i^k + \Delta t v_i^k + \Delta t^2 ((\frac{1}{2} - \beta)a_i^k + \beta a_i^{k+1}) \tag{1}$$

$$v_i^{k+1} = v_i^k + \Delta t ((1 - \gamma)a_i^k + \gamma a_i^{k+1}) \tag{2}$$

where $0 \le \beta \le 1, 0 \le \gamma \le 1$ are constants for calculating the integration, a_i^{k+1} is acceleration, which could be obtained by Eq. (3):

$$F(x_i^{k+1}, v_i^{k+1}) = M a_i^{k+1} \tag{3}$$

Then, Eq. (3) is linearized by Newton-Raphson iteration.

$$F(x_i^k, v_i^k) + \frac{\partial F}{\partial x}(x_i^{k+1} - x_i^k) + \frac{\partial F}{\partial v}(v_i^{k+1} - v_i^k) \approx M a_i^{k+1} \tag{4}$$

Finally, substituting Eqs. (1) and (2) into Eq. (4), we could get the values of a_i^{k+1}, x_i^{k+1} and v_i^{k+1}.

Considering the above, we can draw a conclusion that elastic rod model could simulate all kinds of complex contact deformations in real time with the advantages of precision and efficiency. Therefore, combining with the features of flexible multi-body system, we have further improved the physical model of guidewire based on our previous work [3], particularly discuss the collision detection of flexible multi-body system in depth from the microscopic view for obtaining the multi-contact areas between guidewire and blood vessels.

Collision Dynamics Models: Fast and accurate collision response is a key difficulty to compute multi-frictional contact forces. And this kind of algorithms mainly include three categories:

(1) Impulse-momentum methods [13]. These methods can easily and effectively get the system motion state after colliding by solving generalized impulse-momentum equation and coefficient of restitution equation. However, it cannot obtain collision forces and system dynamics state with time changing during the collision.

(2) Methods based on additional constraints [14,15]. Generally, these methods introduce a Lagrange multiplier to build all kinds of constraint boundary conditions of collision and friction, and substitute these conditions into differential-algebraic equations of multi-body system to obtain the dynamical variables and contact forces. Though these methods could satisfy contact constraint conditions accurately, system overhead will increase substantially with poor real time performance because an additional degree of freedom will be introduced for every constraint.

(3) Methods based on penalty function [16,17]. These methods assume that the deformation is constrainted in the neighborhood of contact areas, and use the penetration depth and penetration velocity as the parameters for collision force computation between two bodies by introducing quasi-static contact theory. So penalty-based methods are the approximate methods to use contact force element to replace the complex deformation in contact areas.

Let x be a point of object A, and $\delta(x)$ is the penetration depth into object B, the penalty-based equation is:

$$F(x) = k\delta(x) \tag{5}$$

Where k is contact stiffness, the higher value of that, the smaller value of $\delta(x)$. From the equation (5), it is obvious that the computation of penalty-based methods is easy without adding freedom degree of constraint equations and updating the stiffness matrix for every object. But the accuracy of these methods largely depend on the choosing of penalty factor. In order to solve this problem, augmented Lagrange method [18] is adopted wildly, which is shown in Eq. (6). Due to the additional factor λ, augmented Lagrange method becomes insensitive to contact stiffness k.

$$F(x) = k\delta(x) + \lambda \tag{6}$$

In conclusion, if using constraints-based methods(like LCP algorithms) to process collision response between guidewire and blood vessels, it will need large additional computation to calculate LCP equations and hard to run in real-time, even though it could simulate the multi-frictional contact between them accurately. Therefore, we adapt penalty-based method as the dynamics model to address their collision for achieving the real time performance of virtual training system for MIVS.

3   Fast Continuous Collision Detection

To calculate multi-frictional contact forces between guidewire and blood vessels during insertion, the contact areas should be obtained firstly. In other words, it needs to get the set of "point-surface" contact pairs in the contact areas.

In our virtual training simulator, the physical model for guidewire is based on discrete elastic rod model, as shown in Fig. 1. The body of that is constructed by many standard structure of cylinders with radius r. The vasculature model is a 3D polygon mesh with thousands of irregular triangular faces, which is reconstructed by 3D rotational X-ray images captured from a real patient. From the microscopic view, when guidewire inserting into blood vessels, the contact areas may appear under the surface of control nodes and the shaft of guidewire between two adjacent control nodes.

In order to get the set of "point-surface" contact pairs between guidewire and vasculature quickly, taking the section of guidewire between two adjacent control nodes x_i and x_{i+1} as a example, we construct a size-adaptive layer at the bottom of the cylinder for accelerating continuous collision detection with size $(L_i' \times w \times h)$ and orientation $\overrightarrow{nl_i}$, which is shown in Fig. 2. Where the adaptive value L_i' is the length of bounding box of layer, which is computed by recursion dichotomy algorithm. The adaptive value w is the width of bounding box of layer and related to the size of lumen of blood vessels at the control node x_i, which could be got by pre-extracting the centreline of blood vessels. The experiential value range is $0.25r \leq w \leq 2r$, the bigger size of lumen, the smaller value of w. The value h is the height of bounding box of layer, which is set as a constant.

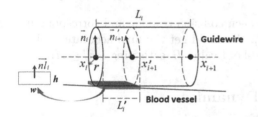
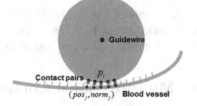

Fig. 2. The size and orientation of layer

Fig. 3. "point-surface" contact pairs

After confirming the size and orientation of layer, we proposed a layer-based continues collision detection algorithm to obtain the set of "point-surface" contact pairs between guidewire and vascular quickly. Next, we will use the section of guidewire between two adjacent control nodes x_i and x_{i+1} to describe this algorithm as following:

Step 1: Building an AABB hierarchical bounding volume tree by recursion to divide the whole vascular model into several mesh units.

Step 2: Using Sphere-AABB collision detection method to check the collision and contact situation at the control node x_i and x_{i+1}.

There are three cases in collision detection with the radius of sphere r the same as the guidewire:

① If the collision spheres at x_i and x_{i+1} both collide with vascular, the large contact area under the surface of cylinder may appear.

② If only the collision sphere at x_i collides with vascular, the small contact area under the surface of cylinder near the x_i may appear. And it needs to resize the layer in this circumstance.

③ The same as ②. If only the collision sphere at x_{i+1} collides with vascular, the small contact area under the surface of cylinder near the x_{i+1} may appear. And it needs to resize the layer in this circumstance.

Step 3: Computing L_i' by recursion dichotomy algorithm to build the size-adaptive of layer.

Let x_{i+1}' be the midpoint of x_i and x_{i+1}, $x_{i+1}' = \frac{1}{2}(x_i + x_{i+1})$. We set $x_{i+1}' = x_{i+1}$ to do the recursive computation by step 2 until convergence to the extreme right node $x_{i+1_{max}}'$. Then, we could get the normal vectors of collision triangles $\overrightarrow{n}_i$ and $\overrightarrow{n}_{i+1_{max}}$ at node x_i and $x_{i+1_{max}}'$, the length of layer $L_i' = p(x_{i+1_{max}}') - p(x_i)$ and the orientation of layer $nl_i = \overrightarrow{n}_i + \overrightarrow{n}_{i+1_{max}}$.

Step 4: Getting the set of collision triangles with center position and normal vector by the method of layer-AABB collision detection.
Step 5: Finally, we use these collision triangles information $(pos_j, norm_j)$ to create corresponding rays, and do the intersection computation between rays and guidewire to obtain the set of "point-surface" contact pairs.

As shown in Fig. 3, the distance between collision triangle and corresponding intersection point p_i is $len_i = p_i - pos_j$. We could get the final accurate "point-surface" contact pairs by setting a threshold value H, satisfying $len_i \leq H$.

4 Multi-frictional Contact Dynamics

Guidewire slides on the vascular wall by external force after insertion, and multi-frictional interaction between them happens as shown in Fig. 4. With guidewire inserting slowly, the amount of "point-surface" contact pairs increasing gradually and more and more contact pairs work. In the contact area Ω, the reaction forces from vascular wall to guidewire contain the normal constraint force F_N^i and the tangential constraint force F_T^i, where F_N^i is the normal pressure of contact pair i along the normal direction of collsion triangle, and F_T^i is tangential resultant force of contact pair i, including sliding friction force, static friction force and rolling friction force.

From Sect. 3 we have obtained the accurate contact areas which are consisted of a few "point-surface" contact pairs. Then we add two directions resultant forces F_N and F_T as a total resultant forces $F = F_N + F_T$, to the control nodes of guidewire for simulating various nonlinear deformation behaviors, where F_N is the normal resultant constraint force in Ω near the control node of guidewire with $F_N = \sum F_N^i$, and F_T is the tangential resultant constraint force with $F_T = \sum F_T^i$. F_N and F_T form a friction cone with 2φ apex angle, meeting $\tan\varphi = \frac{F_T}{F_N}$, as shown in Fig. 4. When one of control node of guideiwre and vascular is under the stable critical state in Ω, the apex angle of that reaches the maximum $2\varphi_f$. Here φ_f is called the frictional angle, satisfying:

$$\tan \varphi_f = \frac{F_{max}}{F_N} = \frac{\mu_{static} \cdot F_N}{F_N} = \mu_{static} \tag{7}$$

Where μ_{static} is static friction coefficient, which is relative to the material property of guidewire and vascular. When the angle θ between the normal direction and the external resultant forces acting on the control node i meeting $\theta < \varphi_f$, the node i will under viscous status because of satisfying the frictional self-locking condition.

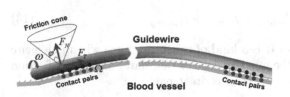

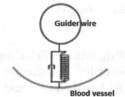

Fig. 4. Multi-frictional contact dynamics

Fig. 5. Equivalent spring damping model

4.1 Contact Dynamics in the Normal Direction

In the normal direction of contact area, we build a nonlinear equivalent spring damping model to compute the continues collision contact force between guidewire and blood vessels quickly with time, as shown in Fig. 5. In this algorithm, the collision contact model is taken as spring damping model, the collision force is used to describe spring contact force and the damper is adopted to simulate energy loss during the contact process. In fact, the equivalent spring damping model is using penalty function method to deal with constrains.

The equations of nonlinear equivalent spring damping model is:

$$F_N = \Sigma F_N^i \tag{8}$$

$$F_N^i = (f_k^i + f_d^i) \cdot L(\partial_i) \tag{9}$$

$$L(\partial_i) = \begin{cases} 0, \partial_i \geq 0 \\ 1, \partial_i < 0 \end{cases} \tag{10}$$

$$f_k^i = k \cdot |\partial_i|^n \tag{11}$$

$$f_d^i = -c_i \cdot |\partial_i|^n \cdot \dot{\partial}_i \tag{12}$$

Where f_k^i is the spring contact force of contact pair i with contact stiffness k, which is relative to the material of contact surface and geometry. $L(\partial_i)$ is logic function to make a judgement on whether contact or not according to the penetration depth ∂_i. $\dot{\partial}_i$ is the penetration velocity of contact pair i. f_d^i is nonlinear damping force. c_i is damping coefficient which is relative to coefficient of restitution and the initial velocity of collision. According to [19], we set $c_i = 3(1 - e^2)/4v_{i-}$, where e is coefficient of restitution and v_{i-} is the initial velocity of collision point i.

4.2   Contact Dynamics in the Tangential Direction

In the tangential direction of contact area, the frictional contacts between guidewire and vascular mainly contain sliding contact, adhesive contact and rolling contact. Therefore, frictional contact force of contact pair i in the tangential direction originates from three parts: sliding friction force $f^i_{sliding}$, static friction force f^i_{static} and rolling friction force $f^i_{rolling}$, the equation of that is listed as below:

$$F^i_T = f^i_{sliding} + f^i_{static} + f^i_{rolling} \tag{13}$$

Sliding/static Friction Force: It is a kind of resistance force when guidewire slides or has a sliding trend on the inner-surface of vascular. So coulomb friction model based sliding/static friction force of contact pair i is:

$$f^i_{sliding/static} = sgn(v_i) \cdot \mu \cdot F^i_N \tag{14}$$

Where $sgn(v_i)$ is a sign function, which is relative to the relative velocity of collision point, μ is friction coefficient, including sliding or static friction coefficient, and F^i_N is normal contact force of contact pair i. When guidewire sliding on the blood vessels, if some of control nodes are under viscous status, the friction coefficient of contact area near these nodes should be set from sliding friction coefficient to static friction coefficient because of $\mu_{sliding} < \mu_{static}$.

About the friction coefficient μ, J. Schroder [20] have published the friction coefficient between guidewire and cather with different types and different materials. However, there are no relative literatures have been published about the friction coefficient between guidewire with different materials and blood vessels with different types of lesions. Because the friction coefficient of guidewire almost the same as vascular, we refer to [20] and set the sliding and static friction coefficient to compute sliding/static friction force between guidewire and blood vessels, $\mu \in [0.01, 0.48]$.

Rolling Friction Force: Rolling friction is more complex. Modern rolling friction theory considers that when a object is rolling under external force, it not only exists normal pressure but also tangential force in contact area, so the contact area is divided into the micro-sliding area, where only exists rolling, and adhesive area, where exists rolling and sliding. And rolling friction force is mainly produced by two factors: elastic hysteresis and viscous effect [21]. That is to say, rolling friction force is a kind of resistance on the surface between guidewire and vascular when they happens relative motion or the trend of relative motion by the normal force and torque.

Guidewire has a standard cylinder structure with radius r and length l between two adjacent nodes. The rolling frictional moment M_i of contact pair i is directly proportional to the normal contact force F^i_N between two contact bodies:

$$M_i = K_i \cdot F^i_N \tag{15}$$

$$K_i = [\frac{2\alpha}{3\pi} + \frac{\sigma_b + \sigma_{s/2}}{6H_{vessel}}][\frac{4rF^i_N}{\pi l}(\frac{1 - v_1^2}{E_1} + \frac{1 - v_2^2}{E_2})] \tag{16}$$

Where K_i is rolling friction coefficient, and its value is set in literature [21], α is elastic hysteresis coefficient, H_{vessel} is hardness of vascular wall, σ_b is maximum tensile stress of adhesive point, σ_s is tensile stress of center contact point, v_1 and v_2 are Poisson ratio of two contact bodies, E_1 and E_2 are elastic modulus of two contact bodies.

Finally, the resultant moment $M = \sum M_i$ of all contact pairs near the control node is calculated and added to guidewire model for further simulating twisting deformation of guidewire caused by rolling.

5 Experimental Results

We have developed a virtual training system for MIVS to verify the algorithm of multi-frictional contact between guideswire and blood vessels. The system mainly includes guidewire dynamics module, continuous collision detection module, multi-frictional contact dynamics response module, virtual force feedbacks module etc., and the architecture of that is shown in Fig. 6.

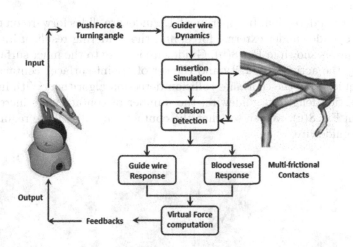

Fig. 6. System architecture of virtual training simulator

In this paper, based on previous work [3], we further improve the multi-area continuous collision detection from the microscopic view, and the rendering results of guidewire physical deformations including bending, twisting and stretching deformation are shown in Fig. 7.

We design two experiments to test our algorithm. Experiment 1: guidewire is inserted into a straight regular cylinder model, which is a standard 3D mesh made by 3dmax with r 1.8 cm and 35000 triangles, as shown in Fig. 8(a). Experiment 2: guidewire is inserted into a blood vessels model, which is reconstructed 3D rotational X-ray images captured from a real patient with 30420 triangles. This vasculature model is a part of aorta near the heart including aortic arch,

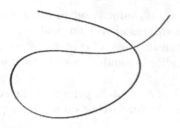 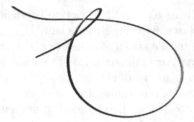

(a) node number: 24; bend parameter: 3.50; twist parameter: 5.00; stretch parameter: 2.00; radius: 0.1

(b) node number: 24; bend parameter: 2.00; twist parameter: 2.50; stretch parameter: 2.00; radius: 0.1

Fig. 7. Rendering results of guidewire

as shown in Fig. 9(a). Then we will analysis the multi-frictional contact between guidewire and blood vessels from two aspects: collision detection, multi-frictional contact forces.

(1) Collision detection. In experiment 1, guidewire slides forward on the inner surface of cylinder under external force, and the rendering result of its physical deformations as shown in Fig. 8(b). Guidewire is close to the inner surface of the cylinder by the action of gravity and the set of "point-surface" contact pairs is obtained quickly by the continues collision detection algorithm. With increasing of the insertion length of guidewire, the number of contact pairs increases linearly. From Fig. 8(c), we can see that the contact pairs distribute regularly just below the guidewire.

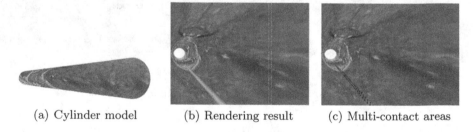

(a) Cylinder model   (b) Rendering result   (c) Multi-contact areas

Fig. 8. Simulation of multi-frictional interaction between guidewire and cylinder

In experiment 2, guidewire slides on the vascular wall under the external force, the rendering result of that as shown in Fig. 9(b). The same as Exp. 1, with increasing of the insertion length of guidewire, the number of "point-surface" contact pairs increases linearly. From Fig. 9(c), we can see that the contact pairs distribute irregularly under the guidewire due to the irregular triangles of blood vessel model.

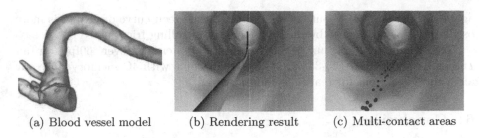

(a) Blood vessel model   (b) Rendering result   (c) Multi-contact areas

Fig. 9. Simulation of multi-frictional interaction between guidewire and blood vessels

(2) Multi-frictional contact forces. In experiment 1, guidewire is inserted into cylinder with a constant speed of 2.0 cm/s. As in the Fig. 10 of Exp. 1, before the inserted length less than 3.0 cm, the total friction is close to zero because guidewire does not collide with the cylinder. Then, guidewire is inserted continually and the friction is almost growing linearly with the slop of about 0.005. From the curve of Exp. 1, we can see that adding rolling friction has an influence on computing the multi-frictional contact forces between them. The green curve shows the result of adding rolling friction, which is more oscillating than the blue curve without rolling friction because of viscous effect.

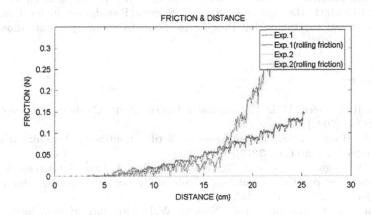

Fig. 10. The relationship between friction and distance (Color figure online)

In experiment 2, guidewire is inserted into blood vessel with a constant speed of 2.0 cm/s. As in the Fig. 10 of Exp. 2, the same as Exp. 1, before the insertion length less than 5.0 cm, the total friction is close to zero because guidewire does not collide with the blood vessel. Then, guidewire is inserted continually and the friction almost growing linearly at the straight anterior of the blood vessel with the slop of about 0.004, but the friction suddenly increases when guidewire reaches the first turning of the blood vessel at the insertion length 16.0 cm. Then guidewire is inserted continually and the friction almost growing linearly again with the slop of about 0.032. Similarly, the green curve of Exp. 2 is more oscillating than red curve by the viscous effect of rolling friction.

The frame rate of our virtual training system is over 60fps on an $Intel\textregistered Core^{TM}$ 4 CPU i5-3337U @1.8 GHz machine with 4G memory since our algorithm is efficient for real-time computations.

6 Conclusion

The real-time multi-frictional contact simulation has important significance in the training system of cardiovascular interventional operation. From the microscopic view, our paper proposed a multi-frictional contact algorithm between guidewire and blood vessels based on the flexible multi-body dynamics. The algorithm computes the frictions from normal direction and tangential direction in the contact areas. In normal direction we get the normal contact force by nonlinear spring damping model, and in tangential direction we calculate the sliding, static and rolling friction by the Coulomb friction model. The experimental results show that this algorithm could simulate the multi-frictional contact between guidewire and blood vessels very well in real time, especially in the complex vascular structures.

Acknowledgements. his work was supported by NSFC of China under Grant No. 61402278, 61303093, the Shanghai Natural Science Foundation under Grant No. 14ZR1415800 and the Innovation Program of Shanghai Municipal Education Commission (No. 14YZ023).

References

1. Safian, R.D., Freed, M.S.: The Manual of Interventional Cardiology. Science Press, Royal Oak (2004)
2. Han, S., Hong, J.: Several key issues in flexible multibody dynamics with contact/impact. Mech. Eng. **33**(2), 1–7 (2011)
3. Tang, W., Lagadec, P., Gould, D., Wan, T.R., Zhai, J., How, T.: A realistic elastic rod model for real-time simulation of minimally invasive vascular interventions. Vis. Comput. **26**(9), 1157–1165 (2010)
4. Alderliesten, T., Konings, M.K., Niessen, W.J.: Modeling friction, intrinsic curvature, and rotation of guide wires for simulation of minimally invasive vascular interventions. IEEE Trans. Biomed. Eng. **54**(1), 29–38 (2007)
5. Spillmann, J., Harders, M.: Inextensible elastic rods with torsional friction based on lagrange multipliers. Comput. Animation Virtual Worlds **21**(3), 561–572 (2010)
6. Luboz, V., Blazewski, R., Gould, D.: Real-time guidewire simulation in complex vascular models. Vis. Comput. **25**(9), 827–834 (2009)
7. Huang, P., Chao, J., Xuewen, C., et al.: Cather modering in vr simulation of cather ablation of atrial fibrillation. J. Comput. Aided Des. Comput. Graph. **24**(9), 1139–1144 (2012)
8. Nowinski, W.L., Chui, C.K.: Simulation of interventional neuroradiology procedures. In: Proceedings of International Workshop on Medical Iamging and Augmented Reality, pp. 87–94 (2001)

9. Ma, X., Jianhuang, W., Wang, S., et al.: Simulation training system for cerebrovasuclar interventional surgery. Chin. J. Dial. Artif. Organs **21**(3), 25–31 (2010)

10. Wan, T.R., Tang, W., Huang, D.: Real-time simulation of long thin flexible objects in interactive virtual environments. In: Proceedings of the 18th ACM Symposium on Virtual Reality Software and Technology (VRST 2012), pp. 85–92 (2012)

11. Bertails, F., Audoly, B., Cani, M.P., et al.: Super-helices for predicting the dynamics of natural hair. ACM Trans. Graph. **25**(3), 1180–1187 (2006)

12. Bergou, M., Wardetzky, M., Robinson, S., et al.: Discrete elastic rods. ACM Trans. Graph. (SIGGRAPH 2008) **27**(3), 63:1–63:12 (2008)

13. Zhang, D., Angeles, J.: Impact dynamics of flexible-joint robots. Comput. Struct. **83**, 25–33 (2005)

14. Otaduy, M.A., Tamstorf, R., Steinemann, D., et al.: Implicit contact handling for deformable objects. Comput. Graph. Forum (EUROGRAPHICS 2009) **28**(2), 559–568 (2009)

15. Allard, J., Faure, F., Courtecuisse, H., et al.: Volume contact constraints at arbitrary resolution. ACM Trans. Graph. (SIGGRAPH 2010) **29**(4), 82:1–82:10 (2010)

16. Tang, M., Manocha, D., Otaduy, M.A., et al.: Continuous penalty forces. ACM Trans. Graph. (SIGGRAPH 2012) **31**(4), 107:1–107:9 (2012)

17. Harmon, D., Zhou, Q., Zorin, D.: Asynchronous integration with phantom meshes. In: Proceedings of the 2011 ACM SIGGRAPH/ Eurographics Symposium on Computer Animation, pp. 247–256 (2011)

18. Laursen, T.A.: Computational Contact and Impact Mechanics: Fundamentals of Modeling Interfacial Phenomena in Nonlinear Finite Element Analysis. Springer, Heidelberg (2002)

19. Hunt, K.H., Crossley, F.R.E.: Coefficient of restitution interpreted as damping in vibroimpact. J. Appl. Mech. **42**(2), 440–445 (1975)

20. Schroder, J.: Technology assessment: the mechanical properties of guidewirespart iii: Sliding friction. CardioVasc. Intervent. Radiol. **16**, 93–97 (1993)

21. Guo, J.: The mechanism of producing rolling friction force and its calculaton. Lubr. Eng. **01**, 19–24 (1998)

Multi-modal Brain Image Registration Based on Subset Definition and Manifold-to-Manifold Distance

Weiwei Liu, Yuru Pei[✉], and Hongbin Zha

Peking University, Beijing China
peiyuru@cis.pku.edu.cn

Abstract. Image registration is an important procedure in multi-modal brain image processing. The main challenge is the variations of intensity distributions in different image modalities. The efficient SSD based method cannot handle this kind of variations. And other approaches based on modality independent descriptors and metrics are usually time-consuming. In this article, we propose a novel similarity metric based on manifold-to-manifold distance imposed on the subset of original images. We define a subset for a compact representation of the original image. Manifold learning technique is employed to reveal the intrinsic structure of the sampled data. Instead of comparing the images in the original feature space, we use the manifold-to-manifold distance to measure the difference. By minimizing the distance between the manifolds, we iteratively obtain the optimal registration of the original image pair. Experiment results show that our approach is effective to deal with the multi-modal image registration on the BrainWeb dataset.

Keywords: Multi-modal registration · Subset definition · Manifold-to-manifold distance

1 Introduction

Multi-modal image registration is essential to brain image processing, e.g. the image fusion, which can provide comprehensive information of multi-modal images. Conventional registration methods based on sum of squared difference (SSD) cannot be directly applied since the intensity distributions are obviously different. Some modality-independent metrics such as mutual information (MI) [15] and cross correlation (CC) [1] were proposed for the multi-modal image registration. The registration methods based on MI and CC are generally time consuming. Moreover, the modality-independent feature descriptors can be used for multi-modal image registration via the landmark-based methods. However, the calculation of modality independent descriptors can be complicated. Efforts were also made to figure out a common representation of the reference and moving images and then use L2 norm as the similarity metric to optimize the transformation. One example is the registration method built upon the Laplacian image [22]. However, the nonlinear embedding of the original images often involves a large computation cost considering the image dimensionality.

© Springer International Publishing Switzerland 2015
Y.-J. Zhang (Ed.): ICIG 2015, Part II, LNCS 9218, pp. 538–546, 2015.
DOI: 10.1007/978-3-319-21963-9_49

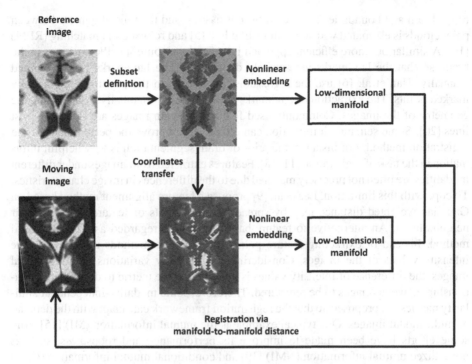

Fig. 1. The framework of our proposed registration method

We propose our registration framework based on the subset definition and the manifold-to-manifold distance as illustrated in Fig. 1. A subset is defined for the compact representation of the original image. We calculate the low-dimensional manifolds of the extracted subsets and use the manifold-to-manifold distance to estimate the image difference. First, we define a subset via edge detection on the reference image. And the coordinates of the sampled points are transferred to the moving image. Image patches centered on these points from both moving and reference images are used to describe the context information. Second, we use the dimensionality reduction technique to deal with the sampled subset. Considering the complicated structures of medical images, we use Laplacian eigenmaps [2] for the low-dimensional embedding with preservation of locality. Instead of measuring the similarity in the original feature space, we estimate the image difference via the distance between manifolds of the subsets. The registration is optimized iteratively by minimizing the manifold-to-manifold distance.

2   Related Work

Multi-modal image registration plays an important role in the field of brain image processing. It has been studied for years and many approaches have been proposed to solve the problem. One type of solution is to sample a dense point cloud on the surface of the brain and boundaries between different tissues, and then the alignment between point clouds is estimated with algorithms like ICP [5] and robust point matching (RPM) [16]. A similar but more efficient approach is to focus on some specific positions in the brain, so that the landmarks are sparsely distributed. The landmarks can be defined manually. Han et al. [6] use the regression forest to learn the positions of manually marked points. The extraction of landmarks can also be automatically by analyzing the geometry of the images. Commonly used features in brain images are ridges or crest lines [20]. Some semantic information can effectively improve the performance of the registration method. For instance, the prior of brain segmentation is very helpful information in the task of registration [11, 18]. Features extracted from images under different modalities are often not precisely matched due to the differences in image characteristics. To cope with this limitation, Lee et al. [9] propose a feature alignment method based on Gaussian-weighted distance map by spreading the weights of feature points to their neighborhood. An alternative to feature-based method is regarded as intensity-based method. Instead of extracting feature points, this type of methods uses directly the intensity values of the images. Considering the intensity variations of multi-modal images, the difference of intensity values is not an effective metric to describe the relationship between images to be registered. Therefore, some modality-independent similarity metrics are proposed so that the registration framework can adapt with the demand of multi-modal images. One typical example is the mutual information (MI) [15]. And some efforts have been made to improve its performance and robustness, such as normalized mutual information (NMI) [19] and conditional mutual information (CMI) [14]. Recently, methods that combine geometric and intensity features are proposed to make the intensity based registration more robust. Sulcal information can be used to constraint the registration of brain images [4, 8]. The cortical surface is considered in the processing of brain volume data [13]. The method of MI is also extended by combining the gradient field calculated in the images [12].

Further related work includes some registration approaches based on internal similarity and manifold learning. Instead of exploring the relationship of the original images, some preprocessing steps are involved to make the images comparable. The already mentioned work of Penney et al. [17] considers the internal similarity in local areas to obtain modality-independent descriptors. The similar idea is also used by Heinrich et al. [7] in their work of modality independent neighborhood descriptor (MIND). Vectors that consist of differences between each pixel and its neighbors are organized as the descriptors of local structures. A second group of techniques seek to figure out a common representation for multi-modal images so that mono-modal registration based on L1 and L2 metrics can be applied. Wachinger et al. [21] use entropy image to represent the structures of input images. Locations with obvious anatomic structures have high entropy, while the entropy values of smooth areas are low. Finally, we want to refer to the method of Laplacian image [22]. Manifold learning technique is applied on image patches sampled across the whole image and a new intensity value is assigned to each pixel according to the corresponding coordinate in the low-dimensional space. Given the number of pixels in an image, this processing can be very time consuming.

3 Subset Definition

Due to the high dimensionality of the image data, we define a subset of the original image for a compact representation. In this article, we use the Canny operator [3] to extract points on edges from the brain image. We observe that the extracted points almost cover all the contours of sulcus and gyrus as well as the boundaries between white and grey matters.

The edge points are still densely distributed on the image. We further randomly downsample the detected points so that the final subset contains no more than 1000 samples. Image patches around these points are used as the subset to represent the original image.

We only use the Canny edge detector on the reference image and transfer the coordinates of the sampled points to the moving image. The transferred coordinates on the moving image actually deviate from the real boundaries. We use image patches around the sampled points to depict their context.

4 Metric Based on Manifold-to-Manifold Distance

Our subset definition is still a modality-related representation since the intensity values are directly used. We employ Laplacian eigenmaps [2] to get low-dimensional manifolds of the defined subsets to reveal their intrinsic structure and eliminate. The intrinsic structure describes the internal similarity of patches within each image and provides modality-independent information.

Let $\mathcal{M}^r, \mathcal{M}^m$ denote the low-dimensional manifolds of the subsets defined in the reference and moving images respectively. Laplacian eigenmaps starts with the construction of a neighborhood graph that describes the structure of the data. An image patch can be represented with a high-dimensional vector, where each entry corresponds to the intensity value of a pixel. We denote the data point corresponding to the ith image patch as p_i, and its counterpart in the low dimensional space as q_i. The Euclidean norm $\left\| p_i - p_j^2 \right\|$ is used to estimate the distance between two patches in the high-dimensional space. This distance is only defined when the patches are close to each other. In this work, we choose the implementation that searches for the k nearest neighbors and connects the corresponding nodes with weights assigned to the edges in the form of heat kernel $W_{ij} = e^{\left\| -P_i - P_j \right\|^2 / (2 \cdot \sigma^2)}$, where σ^2 indicates the variance. Subsequently, the low-dimensional manifold with locality best preserved on average is obtained by minimizing $\sum_{i,j} W_{ij} \left\| p_i - p_j \right\|^2$.

In the neighborhood graph, edges only connect nodes that are close to each other, and the number of neighbors should not be too large. But when the value of k is too small, the neighborhood graph may be separated into several isolated subgraph. To avoid the emergence of undefined relationship between any pair of data points, we set k = 100 so that there is only one connected subgraph. And this selection does not severely contradict with the assumption of locality.

The dimension of the low-dimensional space is set to 2. The mapping results of Laplacian eigenmaps only guarantee that the local structures are preserved. We need to put the low-dimensional manifolds of the subsets into a mutual space before estimating the distance between the manifolds. Here, we figure out an affine transformation by minimizing the distance

$$\|T \cdot \mathcal{M}^m - \mathcal{M}^r\|^2 . \tag{1}$$

where T indicates the transformation imposed on the manifold of the moving image.

Subsequently, the distance between two manifolds is formulated as

$$d(\mathcal{M}^m, \mathcal{M}^r) = \frac{1}{2} \left\| \widehat{T} \cdot \mathcal{M}^m - \mathcal{M}^r \right\|^2 , \tag{2}$$

where $\widehat{T}$ is the optimal transformation that minimize the distance in Eq. 1. This manifold-to-manifold distance is used as the image distance measurement in our registration approach.

5   Image Registration

The registration is calculated in an iterative way. In every iteration, the transformation parameters are updated to lower the difference between the reference and moving images measured with the manifold-to-manifold distance. The updated transformation is performed on the moving image. We use the Laplacian eigenmaps to calculate the low-dimensional manifold of the moving image. And then, the distance between the manifolds of the subsets defined on the reference and moving images is calculated. The iteration ends when the manifold-to-manifold distance reaches the convergence. Based on our proposed similarity metric, the problem of image registration can be converted to the minimization of the manifold-to-manifold distance defined in Eq. 2.

$$\widehat{T}_I = argmin_{T_I} d\left(\mathcal{M}^m\left(T_I \right), \mathcal{M}^r \right). \tag{3}$$

We use T_I to denote the transformation of the original image. $\mathcal{M}^m\left(T_I \right)$ indicates the low dimensional manifold of the moving image when transformation T_I is imposed on it.

We consider the rigid transformation on 2D images with 3 registration parameters to be optimized: the rotation r, the translations on x and y directions t_x, t_y, respectively. The registration is optimized with BFGS [10]. The gradient of the objective function can be written as

$$\frac{\partial d}{\partial T_I} = \left(\frac{\partial d}{\partial r}, \frac{\partial d}{\partial t_x}, \frac{\partial d}{\partial t_y} \right)^T , \tag{4}$$

where d is short for $d\left(\mathcal{M}^m\left(T_I \right), \mathcal{M}^r \right)$. The partial derivatives are estimated as follows,

$$\frac{\partial d}{\partial r} = \left\| \widehat{T} \cdot \mathcal{M}^m - \mathcal{M}^r \right\| \frac{\partial \left(\widehat{T} \cdot \mathcal{M}^m \right)}{\partial r}. \tag{5}$$

$$\frac{\partial d}{\partial r} = \left\| \widehat{T} \cdot \mathcal{M}^m - \mathcal{M}^r \right\| \frac{\partial \left(\widehat{T} \cdot \mathcal{M}^m \right)}{\partial t_x} \tag{6}$$

$$\frac{\partial d}{\partial r} = \left\| \widehat{T} \cdot \mathcal{M}^m - \mathcal{M}^r \right\| \frac{\partial \left(\widehat{T} \cdot \mathcal{M}^m \right)}{\partial t_y} \tag{7}$$

6 Experiments

We apply our method on the brain MRI images provided by BrainWeb database[1], which includes modalities of T1, T2 and PD. The images have been adjusted and they are well aligned. In order to demonstrate the effectiveness of our proposed similarity metric, we show plots of the similarity between slices selected from the T1- and T2-weighted images for rotation and translations in Fig. 2. Three different slices are tested. It can be seen that the image difference measured by the manifold-to-manifold distance approaches the minimum when two images are well aligned.

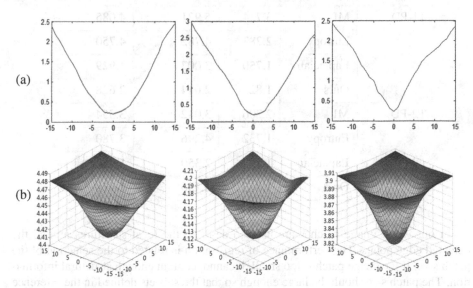

Fig. 2. Plots of the similarity respect to rotation (a) and translations in x and y directions (b)

---

[1] http://www.bic.mni.mcgill.ca/brainweb/.

We also test our method in registration experiments. The transformation parameters are calculated for all combinations of image modalities. We first make a random rigid transformation on one of the images, with rotations in the range of $\pm15°$ and translations ±15 mm. The calculated parameters are compared with them and the errors are shown in Table 1. For each configuration in Table 1, the registration is calculated 100 times with random starting positions. The registration methods proposed in [21] based on the entropy image and Laplacian image as well as the approach based on MI [15] are compared in this table. The experiments prove that the Laplacian eigenmaps for the defined subset can effectively depict the brain images and lead to accurate registration results.

Table 1. Registration errors for all combinations of the three MR modalities. Rotation in degree and translation in mm. The results of the registration based on the Entropy image and Laplacian image are from [21]

Modalities	Metric	Rotation	Translation x	Translation y
T1-T2	MI	3.026	4.785	5.513
	Entropy	2.084	4.539	5.231
	Laplacian	2.584	2.061	2.168
	Ours	**1.937**	**1.596**	**1.882**
T1-PD	MI	3.734	5.921	4.085
	Entropy	2.283	4.782	4.750
	Laplacian	**1.750**	3.007	**1.929**
	Ours	1.823	**2.014**	2.628
T2-PD	MI	2.206	3.042	3.554
	Entropy	1.732	4.296	3.780
	Laplacian	1.171	2.350	1.984
	Ours	**1.065**	**2.136**	**1.778**

In our work, image patches are used to describe the local structures around the detected edge points. The performance of registration is related to the selection of the patch size. If the image patch is too small, it cannot contain enough structural information. The patch size should be large enough so that the subsets defined in the reference and moving images have sufficient overlap, but too large patches also lead to high computational cost. The setting of the patch size is application related. In our experiments, we consider the rotation up to $15°$ and the translations 15 mm. We set the patch size to 31×31, and the dimension of the image patch is 961. In Fig. 3, we illustrate the changes of similarity respect to translation in y direction with different patch sizes. When the patch size is too small, a lot of local minima show up as the translation is obvious. Without a proper initial value, the result is likely to be trapped in the local minima.

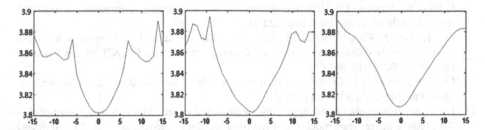

Fig. 3. The similarity respect to translation in y direction with patch sizes of 5×5 (left), 15×15 (middle) and 31×31 (right).

7   Conclusion

In this article, we proposed a novel similarity metric for multi-modal brain images based on subset definition and manifold-to-manifold distance, and utilize it to solve the registration of brain images. We use a subset made up of patches around the sampled edge points to depict the structure of the brain images. Then, Laplacian eigenmaps is employed to calculate the low-dimensional manifold of the subset. The image difference is estimated via the manifold-to-manifold distance. Our results demonstrate that this metric provides a good measurement for the image difference and leads to effective image registration.

References

1. Avants, B.B., Epstein, C.L., Grossman, M., Gee, J.C.: Symmetric diffeomorphic image registration with cross-correlation: evaluating automated labeling of elderly and neurodegenerative brain. Med. Image Anal. **12**(1), 26–41 (2008)
2. Belkin, M., Niyogi, P.: Laplacian eigenmaps and spectral techniques for embedding and clustering. In: NIPS, vol. 14, pp. 585–591 (2001)
3. Canny, J.: A computational approach to edge detection. IEEE Trans. Pattern Anal. Mach. Intell. **6**, 679–698 (1986)
4. Collins, D.L., Le Goualher, G., Venugopal, R., Caramanos, A., Evans, A.C.: Cortical constraints for non-linear cortical registration. In: Höhne, K.H., Kikinis, R. (eds.) VBC 1996. LNCS, vol. 1131, pp. 307–316. Springer, Berlin Heidelberg (1996)
5. Feldmar, J., Malandain, G., Declerck, J., Ayache, N.: Extension of the ICP algorithm to non-rigid intensity-based registration of 3D volumes. In: Proceedings of the Workshop on Mathematical Methods in Biomedical Image Analysis, pp. 84–93. IEEE (1996)
6. Han, D., Gao, Y., Wu, G., Yap, P.-T., Shen, D.: Robust anatomical landmark detection for MR brain image registration. In: Golland, P., Hata, N., Barillot, C., Hornegger, J., Howe, R. (eds.) MICCAI 2014, Part I. LNCS, vol. 8673, pp. 186–193. Springer, Heidelberg (2014)

7. Heinrich, M.P., Jenkinson, M., Bhushan, M., Matin, T., Gleeson, F.V., Brady, M., Schnabel, J.A.: MIND: modality independent neighbourhood descriptor for multi-modal deformable registration. Med. Image Anal. **16**(7), 1423–1435 (2012)

8. Hellier, P., Barillot, C.: Coupling dense and landmark-based approaches for nonrigid registration. IEEE Trans. Med. Imag. **22**(2), 217–227 (2003)

9. Lee, H., Lee, J., Kim, N., Kim, S.J., Shin, Y.G.: Robust feature-based registration using a Gaussian-weighted distance map and brain feature points for brain PET/CT images. Comput. Biol. Med. **38**(9), 945–961 (2008)

10. Liu, D.C., Nocedal, J.: On the limited memory BFGS method for large scale optimization. Math. Prog. **45**(1–3), 503–528 (1989)

11. Liu, J.: Segmentation-assisted registration for brain MR images. Multi Modality State-of-the-Art Medical Image Segmentation and Registration Methodologies, pp. 335–353. Springer, New York (2011)

12. Liu, J., Tian, J.: Registration of brain MRI/PET images based on adaptive combination of intensity and gradient field mutual information Copyright © 2007 J. Liu and J. Tian. This is an open access article distributed under the Creative Commons Attribution License (2007)

13. Liu, T., Shen, D., Davatzikos, C.: Deformable registration of cortical structures via hybrid volumetric and surface warping. NeuroImage **22**(4), 1790–1801 (2004)

14. Loeckx, D., Slagmolen, P., Maes, F., Vandermeulen, D., Suetens, P.: Nonrigid image registration using conditional mutual information. IEEE Trans. Med. Imag. **29**(1), 19–29 (2010)

15. Maes, F., Collignon, A., Vandermeulen, D., Marchal, G., Suetens, P.: Multimodality image registration by maximization of mutual information. IEEE Trans. Med. Imag. **16**(2), 187–198 (1997)

16. Papademetris, X., Jackowski, A.P., Schultz, R.T., Staib, L.H., Duncan, J.S.: Computing 3D non-rigid brain registration using extended robust point matching for composite multisubject fMRI analysis. In: Ellis, R.E., Peters, T.M. (eds.) MICCAI 2003. LNCS, vol. 2879, pp. 788–795. Springer, Heidelberg (2003)

17. Penney, G.P., Griffin, L.D., King, A.P., Hawkes, D.J.: A Novel Framework for Multi-modal Intensity-based Similarity Measures Based on Internal Similarity. Medical Imaging. International Society for Optics and Photonics, Bellingham (2008)

18. Pohl, K.M., Fisher, J., Levitt, J.J., Shenton, M.E., Kikinis, R., Grimson, W.L., Wells, W.M.: A unifying approach to registration, segmentation, and intensity correction. In: Duncan, J.S., Gerig, G. (eds.) MICCAI 2005. LNCS, vol. 3749, pp. 310–318. Springer, Heidelberg (2005)

19. Pradhan, S., Patra, D.: Nonrigid image registration of brain MR images using normalized mutual information. In: Proceedings of the Second International Conference on Soft Computing for Problem Solving, pp. 1069–1077. Springer, India (2014)

20. Subsol, G., Roberts, N., Doran, M., Thirion, J.P., Whitehouse, G.H.: Automatic analysis of cerebral atrophy. Magn. Reson. Imag. **15**(8), 917–927 (1997)

21. Wachinger, C., Navab, N.: Entropy and Laplacian images: Structural representations for multi-modal registration. Med. Image Anal. **16**(1), 1–17 (2012)

22. Wachinger, C., Navab, N.: Manifold learning for multi-modal image registration. In: BMVC, pp. 1–12 (2010)

Multimodal Speaker Diarization Utilizing Face Clustering Information

Ioannis Kapsouras, Anastasios Tefas, Nikos Nikolaidis[(✉)], and Ioannis Pitas

Department of Informatics, Aristotle University of Thessaloniki,
54124 Thessaloniki, Greece
{jkapsouras,nikolaid}@aiia.csd.auth.gr

Abstract. Multimodal clustering/diarization tries to answer the question "who spoke when" by using audio and visual information. Diarization consists of two steps, at first segmentation of the audio information and detection of the speech segments and then clustering of the speech segments to group the speakers. This task has been mainly studied on audiovisual data from meetings, news broadcasts or talk shows. In this paper, we use visual information to aid speaker clustering. We tested the proposed method in three full length movies, i.e. a scenario much more difficult than the ones used so far, where there is no certainty that speech segments and video appearances of actors will always overlap. The results proved that the visual information can improve the speaker clustering accuracy and hence the diarization process.

Keywords: Multiomodal · Diarization · Clustering · Movies

1 Introduction

Speaker diarization/clustering tries to detect speech segments and cluster similar segments in order to group together segments of the same speakers. Diarization can automatically answer the question "who spoke when" when used together with speaker recognition systems, by providing the speakers true identity. Alternatively the same question can be answered in a semi-automatic way by combining diarization with the manual labelling of the speaker clusters with their true identity. Speaker diarization is a process that automatically produces semantic information from audio data.

Movies contain both audio and video information. Usually, video and audio are considered as different modalities and are analysed separately. In this paper, the combination of the two modalities (audio and video) for the task of speaker clustering/diarization is investigated. The intuition behind the modalities fusion is that one can perform a similar to speaker diarization analysis upon the visual data: face clustering. In more detail, assume that faces are detected in the frames of a movie and then the detected faces are tracked over time, resulting in a number of video facial trajectories [2,5,13]. A representative face is selected to represent a facial trajectory. The selected faces can then be clustered into

© Springer International Publishing Switzerland 2015
Y.-J. Zhang (Ed.): ICIG 2015, Part II, LNCS 9218, pp. 547–554, 2015.
DOI: 10.1007/978-3-319-21963-9_50

clusters, each ideally corresponding to a single actor/person. The face clustering results and/or video information can be used in the audio based diarization process in order to improve the speaker clustering accuracy.

In the proposed method, audio speech segments and video facial trajectories were used as high level features to improve speaker clustering. In more detail, the similarity of two speech segments was increased when these segments have overlap with visual appearances of the same actor and was decreased otherwise.

The proposed multimodal approach was tested in 3D feature length movies. Multimodal analysis of movies content has certain inherent difficulties since unlike meetings or talk shows audio (speech) and video are often not coherent in movies, for example the person depicted in the video might not be the one that is speaking.

2   Previous Work

Multimodal speaker diarization, which is closely related to multimodal person clustering has already been studied in the literature, but mainly on audiovisual data from meetings or talk shows, which impose far less difficulties than movie content. The video information can enhance the audio information during the speaker diarization, hence a multimodal approach to diarization (audio + video) can improve the answer in the diarization question "who spoke when". In [4], Khoury et al. proposed a framework for audio-visual diarization. The authors combined audiovisual information using co-occurrence matrices. Moreover, they used information, such as face size and lip activity rates to improve the audiovisual association. Their method improves all audio, video and audiovisual diarization. The authors evaluated their method in a number of news videos, meetings videos and movies. In [8], Noulas et al. proposed a probabilistic framework to perform multimodal speaker diarization. The proposed method uses a Dynamic Bayesian Network (DBN) to model the people as multimodal entities that are involved in audio and video streams and also in audiovisual space. The model is generated by using the Expectation Maximization algorithm. The proposed DBN, also called factorial HMM, can be treated as an audiovisual framework. The factorial HMM arises by forming a dynamic Bayesian belief network composed of several layers. Each of the layers has independent dynamics, but the final observation vector depends upon the state in each layer. Their method was tested in meetings and news videos. Multimodal speaker diarization is also addressed by Friedland et al. in [6]. The method combines audio and video low level features, by using agglomerative clustering, where GMMs are used to model the clusters. The method proposed by [6] was tested on meetings video.

To our knowledge, there are no methods that use multimodal information for speaker diarization on 3D video and multichannel audio data. Moreover, the task of diarization is much easier, when the input data are from meetings or talk shows. In such setups, the visual appearance of a speaker (i.e., its clothing or facial appearance) does not change within the duration of the meeting/show. The composition of the group of participating persons typically does not change either. For talk shows, one can further assume that the speaker is in a close-up view. Moreover, the possibility that the speaker is the person that is shown (actor) is very high. These observations do not apply in the case of 3D films or films in general. In this case, the speaker/actor visual appearance may change over the duration of the movie. Furthermore, the group of people may change over time. Finally, the coherence between visual and audio scene is not guaranteed, since, for example, 3DTV video and audio scenes often capture only a part of the real scene (there may be people speaking that are not displayed or displayed people may speak but one may hear the voice of somebody else). Due to the above, the situation is much less constrained in the case of 3DTV content and person identification is more difficult than in the previously discussed setups.

3 Method Description

The proposed methods use information derived from video to improve the speaker clustering. In order to combine video and audio information, video facial trajectories and speech segments were used. Video trajectories are series of facial images in consecutive frames (usually depicting the same person) and speech segments are segments where speech has been detected in the audio channel of a movie.

3.1 Audio Processing

The first step in speaker diarization is speech detection. Speech segments are detected and subsequently segmented in the audio channel of a video. Finally speaker clustering is performed in order to group together speech segments in clusters that are homogeneous. Each cluster should ideally correspond to a single speaker. In more detail the three steps of the speaker diarization approach used in this paper are:

- **Speech Detection:** using Mel Frequency Cepstral Coefficients (MFCC) features and SVM classifiers.
- **Change Point Detection:** in order to further segment the speech segments to homogeneous parts.
- **Spectral Clustering:** to group speech segments that belong to the same speaker.

Features are extracted from the segmented speech segments. The audio features used were the Mel Frequency Cepstral Coefficients (MFCC) and the Spectral Flatness Measures (SFM). In speaker diarization, the standard score is based on the Bayesian Information Criterion (BIC) using Gaussian models [3]. A distance matrix $\mathbf{D}$ of dimensions $N \times N$ is derived using the MFCC features and the BIC criterion where N is the number of the audio segments. A novel variant [10] of the spectral clustering proposed in [7] was used for clustering.

3.2 Video Processing

The first step in video processing is face detection and tracking. Faces are detected using [11] and tracked in the video channel or channels (in the case of

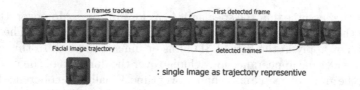

Fig. 1. Face trajectory computed by using face detection and tracking.

3D videos) of a movie using the algorithm proposed in [14]. In more detail, each detected face is tracked for K frames. A series of tracked images of a detected face form a facial trajectory (Fig. 1). Each facial trajectory is represented by any of the images included in it and these trajectories are clustered by using their representative images. It is obvious that all faces included in a trajectory belong to the same actor unless tracking error occur. Local Binary Patterns (LBP) [9] were used as features to represent the facial images.

Calculating LBPs for all pixels of an image is not the best solution neither in terms of effectiveness nor in terms of calculation time. In our case we have chosen to calculate LBPs only in pixels that carry important information (i.e. mouth, eyes, etc.), thus two passes of fiducial points detectors were used. The first one is for the calculation of 66 fiducial points, such as outline of eyes, eyebrows, mouth etc., [1] and the second one [12] for better localization of these points. Moreover, these fiducial points are used in order to scale and align the detected images. LBPs are calculated upon patches around these 66 aligned points. Final, a histogram with K bins is calculated for each of these features. By this way a descriptor of dimension $66 \times K$ is calculated for each image.

In order to perform face clustering, similarities between each pair of images (each image representing a facial trajectory) have to be computed. The χ^2 distance was used to calculate the distances between two corresponding LBP histograms on a pair of images i, j and the final d_{ij} distance value was computed as the sum of the 66 distances (one per histogram). The similarity between the two images was calculated as $1/d_{ij}$ and a similarity matrix $\mathbf{V}$ between facial images (or more precisely facial image trajectories) was computed. Finally the clustering method in [10] is used to perform face clustering by utilizing $\mathbf{V}$. The result of face clustering can be used to improve speaker clustering (Sect. 3.3).

3.3 Multimodal Approach

As can be seen in Sects. 3.1 and 3.2, speaker clustering and face clustering group the speakers and the actors in the audio and visual data of a movie respectively. The speakers and the (visible) actors of a movie are in general the same people (people that speak in a movie, usually appear in it also), thus face clustering can improve most probably the speaker clustering i.e. the diarization process.

The input of the algorithm used for multimodal speaker clustering is the similarity matrix of the audio segments. The main idea is to (a) increase the similarity of two speech segments, when these segments overlap with visual appearances of the same actor or (b) decrease the similarity value, if no such overlap exists. The matrix derived by audio features (Sect. 3.1) is actually a speech segments distance/dissimilarity matrix, i.e., has small values when two speech segments are similar and high values otherwise. Therefore, the first step towards combining audio and video information was to transform this matrix to a similarity matrix $\mathbf{S}$. This was done by using a sigmoid function:

$$S_{i,j} = \frac{1}{1 + exp(4 * (D_{i,j} - \bar{D})/\sigma)}, \tag{1}$$

where $D_{i,j}$ is an element of the distance matrix $\mathbf{D}$, $\bar{D}$ the mean value of $\mathbf{D}$ and σ the standard deviation of $\mathbf{D}$. To combine information from video and audio, in order to enhance speaker clustering using video, a new matrix $\mathbf{Q}$ is created with dimensions equal to those of the speech similarity matrix $\mathbf{S}$. The next step is to find, for each element (i, j) of the matrix $\mathbf{Q}$, the video trajectories that overlap in time with the speech segments that correspond to this element. Then, if the same actor appears in the corresponding video trajectories, the corresponding element of $\mathbf{Q}$ is increased, otherwise it is decreased. The final similarity matrix $\mathbf{F}$ is formed by combining the speech similarity matrix $\mathbf{S}$ and matrix $\mathbf{Q}$:

$$\mathbf{F} = \mathbf{S} + \alpha\mathbf{Q}, \ 0 \leq \alpha \leq 1. \tag{2}$$

Two different approaches were implemented and tested (see Sect. 4), in order to create the matrix $\mathbf{Q}$, i.e., to change the elements of $\mathbf{Q}$ that correspond to speech segments which overlap with video trajectories. In the first approach, the ground truth for the actors depicted in the video trajectories was used, in order to check performance when the face clustering is perfect, i.e., it contains no errors. In more detail, for each pair of audio segments, the overlapping facial trajectories are found and, if the same actor appears in these trajectories according to the ground truth information, then the value in the corresponding element in matrix $\mathbf{Q}$ is multiplied with q where $q > 1$, otherwise it is multiplied with $1/q$. In the second more realistic approach, the same procedure is used, but instead of using the ground truth for the actors, the results of the face clustering algorithm are used. In other words, the results of face clustering described in Sect. 3.2 are used to check if the same actor appears in the overlapping facial trajectories.

Finally, after the calculation of matrix $\mathbf{F}$ using (2), the clustering algorithm in [10] is used for speaker clustering.

4 Experimental Results

The evaluation of the proposed multimodal speaker clustering approach was made by using a modified F-measure. F-measure punishes the erroneous split of a class into 2 parts quite strictly. In the modified version of F-measure used in this paper, overclustering is performed by creating more than the needed clusters and then the clusters that correspond to the same speaker are merged. The final F-measure is evaluated upon this merged clustering result. By this way, F-measure becomes less strict in the evaluation of splitted classes and evaluates more the purity of clusters.

The proposed approach was tested in three full length 3D feature films of different duration, size of cast and genre. These movies were selected in order to test the proposed approach in a difficult and realistic scenario. Stereo information of the video channels was exploited in two ways. Face detection [11] was applied on both channels (left and right), mismatches between the two channels were rejected and a stereo tracking algorithm [14] was applied in both channels. By using the above approaches we end up with a number of facial trajectories, namely series of consecutive facial images. As stated in previous section, each of these trajectories is represented by a single facial image for each channel (Left-Right). For 2 trajectories represented each one by 1 (in case of a mismatch) or 2 images (in case of left-right channel) the following similarity is calculated:

$$Simlarity = max_{ij}LBP(x_i, x_j)x_i \in T_k, x_j \in T_m \qquad (3)$$

where x_i is an image belonging to the T_k trajectory and x_j is an image belonging to T_m trajectory and $1 \leq k, m \leq 2$.

It should be noted that only a relatively small number of speech segments overlap with facial trajectories, which is a usual phenomenon in movies and makes multimodal diarization difficult in such content.

Experiments have been conducted to verify the performance of the proposed method. The results can be seen in Table 1 alongside with the performance of the clustering when only audio modality was taken into account. As can be seen in this Table 1, the use of video ground truth information for the actors depicted in each facial trajectory (Multimodal 1 column) improves the clustering performance by approximately 8 % in every movie, in terms of the modified F-measure compared to audio only diarization. Since the ground truth was used, it can be deducted that this is the best possible improvement for speaker clustering by using the video information with the proposed approach. When using information derived from actual facial image clustering in video the improvement, as can be seen in Table 1 (column Multimodal 2), is approximately 5 %.

As can be seen from the experimental results, information derived from video data can help the audio-based speaker diarization. The increase in performance is higher when ground truth information is used, which leads to the obvious conclusion that the better the face clustering in the video, the better the effect of multimodal speaker clustering in the speaker diarization. It should be noted that, face clustering is not the only way to cluster the actors facial images in a video. Face recognition or label propagation can also be used to cluster the actors to groups and use this information for multimodal speaker clustering.

Table 1. Speaker Clustering F-measure, when video information is incorporated.

	Audio only	Multimodal 1	Multimodal 2
Movie 1	0.51	0.59	0.56
Movie 2	0.48	0.57	0.51
Movie 3	0.45	0.53	0.5

5   Conclusions

In this paper we proposed a method to improve speaker diarization through a multimodal approach. The improvement of speaker clustering can be done by using video information derived from video data through face clustering. Experiments in three full stereo movies have shown that multimodal speaker clustering achieves better results that single modality speaker clustering.

Acknowledgment. The authors wish to thank A. Roebel, L. Benaroya and G. Peeters (IRCAM, France) for providing speech analysis data (speech segments similarity matrices) used in this work.

The research leading to these results has received funding from the European Union Seventh Framework Programme (FP7/2007–2013) under grant agreement number 287674 (3DTVS). This publication reflects only the authors views. The European Union is not liable for any use that may be made of the information contained therein.

References

1. Asthana, A., Zafeiriou, S., Cheng, S., Pantic, M.: Robust discriminative response map fitting with constrained local models. In: Proceedings of 2013 IEEE Conference on Computer Vision and Pattern Recognition (CVPR), pp. 3444–3451 (2013)
2. Baltzakis, H., Argyros, A., Lourakis, M., Trahanias, P.: Tracking of human hands and faces through probabilistic fusion of multiple visual cues. In: Gasteratos, A., Vincze, M., Tsotsos, J.K. (eds.) ICVS 2008. LNCS, vol. 5008, pp. 33–42. Springer, Heidelberg (2008)
3. Chen, S., Gopalakrishnan, P.: Speaker, environment and channel change detection and clustering via the bayesian information criterion. In: Proceedings of DARPA Broadcast News Transcription and Understanding Workshop (1998)
4. El Khoury, E., Snac, C., Joly, P.: Audiovisual diarization of people in video content. Multimedia Tools Appl. **68**(3), 747–775 (2014)
5. Elmansori, M.M., Omar, K.: An enhanced face detection method using skin color and back-propagation neural network. Eur. J. Sci. Res. **55**(1), 80 (2011)
6. Friedland, G., Hung, H., Yeo, C.: Multi-modal speaker diarization of real-world meetings using compressed-domain video features. In: Proceedings of the IEEE International Conference on Acoustics, Speech and Signal Processing, ICASSP 2009, pp. 4069–4072 (2009)
7. Ng, A.Y., Jordan, M.I., Weiss, Y.: On spectral clustering: Analysis and an algorithm. In: Proceedings of NIPS, pp. 849–856. MIT Press (2001)
8. Noulas, A., Englebienne, G., Krose, B.: Multimodal speaker diarization. IEEE Trans. Pattern Anal. Mach. Intell. **34**(1), 79–93 (2012)
9. Ojala, T., Pietikainen, M., Harwood, D.: Performance evaluation of texture measures with classification based on kullback discrimination of distributions. In: Proceedings of the 12th IAPR International Conference on Pattern Recognition, 1994. Vol. 1 - Conference A: Computer Vision amp; Image Processing, vol. 1, pp. 582–585 (1994)
10. Orfanidis, G., Tefas, A., Nikolaidis, N., Pitas, I.: Facial image clustering in stereo videos using local binary patterns and double spectral analysis. In: IEEE Symposium Series on Computational Intelligence (SSCI) (2014)

11. Stamou, G., Krinidis, M., Nikolaidis, N., Pitas, I.: A monocular system for person tracking: Implementation and testing. J. Multimodal User Interfaces **1**(2), 31–47 (2007)
12. Uricar, M., Franc, V., Hlav, V.: Detector of facial landmarks learned by the structured output svm. In: Proceedings of VISAPP 2012, pp. 547–556 (2012)
13. Zoidi, O., Nikolaidis, N., Tefas, A., Pitas, I.: Stereo object tracking with fusion of texture, color and disparity information. Signal Proc. Image Commun. **29**(5), 573–589 (2014)
14. Zoidi, O., Nikolaidis, N., Pitas, I.: Appearance based object tracking in stereo sequences. In: Proceedings of the 2013 IEEE International Conference on Acoustics, Speech and Signal Processing (ICASSP), pp. 2434–2438 (2013)

Multi-object Template Matching Using Radial Ring Code Histograms

Shijiao Zheng, Buyang Zhang, and Hua Yang[✉]

State Key Laboratory of Digital Manufacturing Equipment and Technology,
Huazhong University of Science and Technology, Wuhan, China
huayang@hust.edu.cn

Abstract. In this paper, a novel template matching algorithm named radial ring code histograms (RRCH) for multi-objects positioning is proposed. It is invariant to translation, rotation and illumination changes. To improve the identification ability of multi objects with different rotation angles, radial gradient codes using relative angle between gradient direction and position vector is proposed. Adjustable weights in different regions make it possible to adapt various type objects. Experiments using a LED sorting equipment demonstrate that our algorithm results in correct positioning for multi objects in complicated environments with noise and illumination invariance.

Keywords: Multi-object · Rotation invariance · Illustration changes · Radial ring code histograms

1 Introduction

In industrial automation, template matching is a well-known machine vision approach for estimating the pose of object. As demands for production efficiency have increased, the ability to match multi object with different rotation angles in an image efficiently has become increasingly important, especially in integral circuit (IC) manufacturing fields. Traditional matching algorithms can't already meet these demands, when the objects arranged closely under different illumination conditions.

Over the last two decades, various template matching algorithms have been proposed [1–3]. The most popular algorithm is the normalized cross correlation (NCC) [4]. It compensates for both additive and multiplicative variations under the uniform illumination changes. Because of lacking rotation invariance, when an object in the target image is rotated with respect to the template, a set of templates at different orientations is required. This procedure is brute-force and time-consuming. In order to increase the searching speed under different rotation angles, different algorithms by using salient and distinctive features such as regions, edges, contours and points, are proposed to get the rotation invariant. Invariant moments matching methods [5–7] are effective especially for rotated binary patterns, but its poor performance to noise and occlusion. Geometric

© Springer International Publishing Switzerland 2015
Y.-J. Zhang (Ed.): ICIG 2015, Part II, LNCS 9218, pp. 555–564, 2015.
DOI: 10.1007/978-3-319-21963-9_51

hashing (GH) [8] is a good method in matching the objects with simple geometric structure, but it is limited to noise and complex shape objects. Generalized Hough transform (GHT) [9] is robust against rotation, scaling, which utilizes voting through local edges evidences. However, it needs enormous memory to store the voting space for selecting the maximum score point and it is unable to deal with the problem of multi rotation objects matching.

Many algorithms using gradient information extracted from the image are proposed. These algorithms are stably resistant to light transformation and widely used in object recognition [10]. Histograms of Oriented Gradient (HOG) [11] has significantly existing feature sets for human detection, but it has limit of recognizing large-angles-rotation objects. The latest matching algorithms based on scale and rotation invariant key-points with histograms of gradient information, like SIFT [12,13], PCA-SIFT [14], SURF [15] and GLOH [16,17], present very spectacular recognition performance. However, they fail to find some simple shapes with little grayscale variations. These algorithms have a prohibitive complexity so that they are difficult to be applied in industry.

Orientation codes [18] are based on the utilization of gradient orientation histograms for searching rotation-invariant object in the case of illumination fluctuations. The method consists of two stages. The first stage estimates the approximate rotation angle of the object image by using histograms of the orientation codes. Second, orientation code matching at the right orientation is applied only to the best histogram matches. Marion [19] presented a much faster technique by using integral histograms. The gradient orientation histograms are not intrinsically rotation invariant and a histogram shifting is necessary in order to find the best angle. Thus, this algorithm cannot deal with the condition of array-arranged multi objects.

This paper proposes a radial ring code histograms (RRCH) algorithm for multi-object template matching. The algorithm has the robustness against position translation, angle rotation and illumination changes. By using radial gradient codes which is the relative angle between gradient direction and position vector, it performs better than the original orientation codes algorithm, and the identification ability of multi objects is also improved. Distance ring projections are essentially adopted to improve the restriction of surrounding objects clutter. Various type objects can be matched by adapting adjustable weights in different regions. The proposed method is invariant to illumination owing to utilization of gradient information rather than pixel brightness directly. In addition, the method is more suitable used in multi-object coarse-search step to get the small candidate area and combined with other fine-matching steps.

The rest of this paper is organized as follows: Sect. 2 presents the problem about conventional orientation codes and describes the proposed RRCH algorithm. The implementation details and experimental results are given in Sect. 3. Conclusions follow in Sect. 4.

2   Matching with Radial Ring Code Histograms

The gradient orientation histograms [19] applied in coarse-search is not effective for searching multi objects. As shown in Fig. 1(a), the subimages under the blue circle and blue circle are obviously different. However, the gradient orientation histograms of the two subimages are similar, as showed in Fig. 1(b). This figure proves that the gradient orientation histogram can not match well, when the multi objects arranged closely.

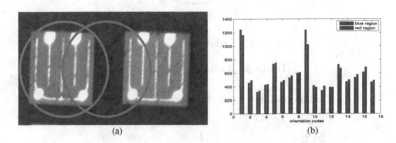

(a)   (b)

Fig. 1. The problem in searching multi objects: (a) Two circle regions in sample object image, (b) Orientation histograms of the two regions (Color figure online).

Radial ring code histogram is proposed to tackle the problem. It is based on gradient information combining with the spatial structure. Firstly, gradient direction is transformed into radial gradient codes by the principle of statistics. Then, ring distance projection is utilized to acquire radial ring codes. Next, radial ring code histograms are calculated. Through comparing the histograms similarity between template image and the target image, the positions of multi objects are estimated. The detail procedure is described in this section.

2.1   Radial Ring Codes

Gradient information is chosen to generate the descriptor because of the little sensitivity to illumination changes. There are various operations, like Sobel operator, to calculate horizontal derivatives ∇f_x and vertical derivatives ∇f_y for computing the gradient direction $\Phi(x,y) = \tan^{-1}(\nabla f_y / \nabla f_x)$ and gradient magnitude $\Omega(x,y) = \sqrt{\nabla f_y^2 + \nabla f_x^2}$.

A circle effective region is selected to obtain the rotation invariance. The center of the circular region is regarded as a rotation reference point. The present point P in the region and the reference point O are linked to a straight line. The angle between this line and the gradient direction of the present point P is called as radial gradient angle α, as shown in Fig. 2. If the image is rotated counterclockwise angle θ, P is transformed into P'. Obviously, the relative angle α does not change with the rotation.

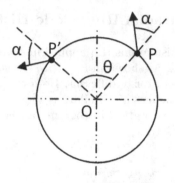

Fig. 2. Radial gradient angle

Table 1. Radial gradient codes

Radial gradient angles	Radical gradient codes
$[0, \frac{\pi}{N})$	0
$[\frac{\pi}{N}, \frac{2\pi}{N})$	1
...	...
$[\frac{(N-1)\pi}{N}, \pi]$	$N-1$

The range of the gradient direction is $[-\pi, \pi]$, while the radial gradient angle is $[0, \pi]$. To reduce the amount of computation, the radial gradient angles are quantified as the radial gradient codes using Eq. 1

$$\Upsilon(x,y) = round(\frac{\alpha(x,y)}{\triangle\alpha}), \; when \quad \Omega(x,y) > T \tag{1}$$

The radial angle is divided into N groups, which can not be chosen too large or small, considering the rotation errors. To suppress the effective of noise, the radial gradient code is computed, when the magnitude is larger than the threshold T. The angle step is $\triangle\alpha = \pi/N$, the relationship between radial gradient angles and radial gradient codes is shown in Table 1.

The radial gradient angle at one point changes with the different reference point. In Fig. 3, the relative angles between g_1 and the line OA or the line $O'A$ are distinct. Therefore, the amplitude of the angle change is related to the radial distance (between the reference point and the present point). The radial distance is closer, the radial gradient angle changes more sharp. The evidence is that $\angle O'AO$ and $\angle O'BO$ are different. Thus, its essential to take a separate treatment with different radial distance.

The ring distance projection is a process as a partition step in our approach. As shown in Fig. 4, the effective region is segmented into two parts: inner circle and outer ring. If a reference point moves one pixel, the change value of radial gradient angle in outer ring should be littler than $\triangle\alpha$. The radius of inner circle r can be calculated in Eq. (2).

$$r \geq \frac{1}{\tan^{-1}(\triangle\alpha)}$$
$$r \leq R \tag{2}$$

r is chosen as $\frac{1}{2}R$ here. If there is only one region with radial gradient codes, the descriptor size is N, else the descriptor dimension is $2N$. Sometimes, N dimensional vectors to represent an image is finite to achieve reliable matching. The descriptor with radial ring codes increases the vector dimension to improve the feature representation capability and ensure the rotation invariant feature description. Certainly, the more the dimensions are, the more computational cost is.

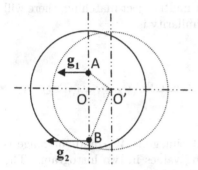

Fig. 3. A contrast with two different reference point

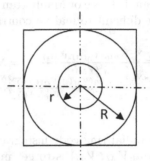

Fig. 4. Illustration of ring distance projection

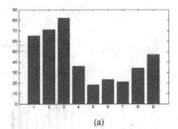

(a)

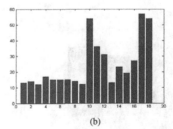

(b)

Fig. 5. (a) Radial ring code Histograms in N, (b) Radial ring code Histograms in 2N.

2.2   Radial Ring Code Histograms for Matching

In a region, codes are counted respectively to be expressed as radial ring code histograms. Histograms of the different regions are arranged according to a certain order. There is an example about two kinds of histograms in $N = 9$. In Fig. 5(b), the first N histograms are from inner circle, while the second N histograms are from outer ring. The radial ring code histograms can be written as

$$V = [\nu(0), \nu(1), \ldots, \nu(k)], \quad (k = N - 1 \quad or \quad k = 2N - 1) \qquad (3)$$

RRCH is a real rotation invariant feature description, which does not depend on the main direction. It is stronger and more adaptable than the traditional method including nonlinear illumination changes. The weight of inner circle is ω and the weight of outer ring is $1 - \omega$. Generally, ω is less than 0.5, when there are two regions.

Template image and subimage (part of object image with the same size of template image) are transformed into a vector in form of radial ring code histograms. There are some approaches to compare the correspondence with two vectors by distance or similar metric [20], such as the Chi-Square statistic, Euclidean distance or Manhattan distance. For multi object matching, there will be more difficult to make a contrast. So the similarity is

$$S = \frac{\sum_{i=0}^{N-1} min(V_M(i), V_O(i))}{\sum_{i=0}^{N-1}(V_M(i))}, (k = N - 1)$$
$$S = \frac{\sum_{i=0}^{N-1} w \cdot min(V_M(i), V_O(i)) + \sum_{i=N}^{2N-1}(1-w) \cdot min(V_M(i), V_O(i))}{\sum_{i=0}^{N-1}(w \cdot V_M(i)) + \sum_{i=N}^{2N-1}((1-w) \cdot V_M(i))}, (k = 2N - 1, 0 \leq \omega \leq 1)$$
$$(4)$$

The radial ring code histograms of template image is V_M and subimage is V_O. $min(V_M, V_O)$ is to get max overlapping values in two histograms. The formula is different when k is $N - 1$ or $2N - 1$ and can be changed for various objects.

Ultimately, template image is sliding window through the entire image to search objects and get the score matrix. According to the threshold, the candidate areas are inquired with local maximum score.

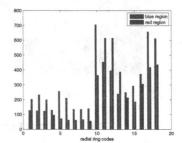

Fig. 6. LED machine

Fig. 7. The histogram of the object image in Fig. 1

3   Experiment

This section verifies the performance of the proposed method. First of all, a test for rotation-variance is shown. Secondly, the computation time is in comparison with some similar techniques. Thirdly, the multi object detection is essential to be validated. Finally, there are some experiments about the robustness of illumination varying. The images for this test are grabbed from LED machines in Fig. 6.

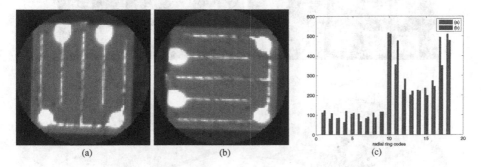

Fig. 8. IC chips for rotation-variant test: (a) Template image, (b) Rotation image, (c) the histograms of the IC chips (a)(b).

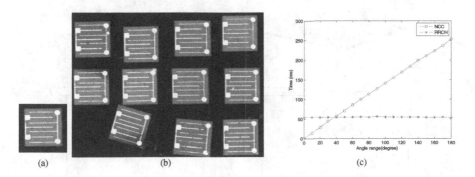

Fig. 9. Time test: (a) Template image (19×19 pixels), (b) Object image (60×80 pixels), (c) The computation time of NCC and RRCH in different angle searching ranges.

To confirm rotation-variance of the presented algorithm, IC chips were rotated with various arbitrary angles. An example is shown in Fig. 8. As can be seen, the histograms of the IC chips are closely resembled with high similarity. Meanwhile, the picture proves that when the patterns are rotated, the histograms are similar. Figure 8 shows that the proposed method plays a good performance on matching the object with rotation.

As explained above, NCC is the method to search objects by a set of templates with different rotation angles. The computational time of the proposed algorithm was also compared with NCC in different angle ranges, shown in Fig. 9.

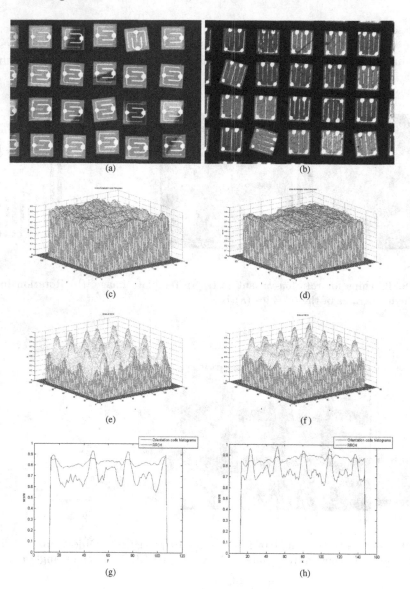

Fig. 10. IC chips for robust test: (a) LED chips with illumination-fluctuations, (b) LED chips with illumination-fluctuations and noise, (c) Orientation Code Histograms Score matrix for figure (a), (d) Orientation Code Histograms Score matrix for figure (b), (e) RRCH Score matrix for figure (a), (f) RRCH Score matrix for figure (b), (g) x = 26, score contrast for figure (a), (h) y = 76, score contrast for figure (b).

All the computations were performed with C language under the same conditions without any acceleration or speed promotion. From the experiment results, it can be seen that the computation time of NCC is increasing with the angle searching range, while the computation time of RRCH is remain unchanged due to the rotation invariance.

There is a problem presented in Sect. 2.1, the conventional method cannot recognize the difference between the red and the blue region in Fig. 1. However, RRCH is used for the two regions, the result shown in Fig. 7 is that histograms are larger different than the method. It means that RRCH is adaptable to solve the problem in multi objects matching.

There are same multi arrayed chips. The template images were extracted one of them in Fig. 10(a)(b), and Orientation Code Histograms and RRCH were used to get the results of score, shown in Fig. 10(c)(d)(e)(f). Chips were in illumination-invariant condition with different angles in Fig. 10(a). The environment for the image in Fig. 10(b) was more complicated, multi chips with illumination-fluctuations and noise. Figure 10(g)(h) verifies that the RRCH can be used to distinguish the position of the object with the other disturbing factors better than Orientation Code Histograms. If the score threshold is set appropriately, the small candidate areas can be selected quickly.

4   Conclusion

In this paper, a new method for multi-object matching method, called RRCH, is proposed. It is achieved with the utilization of gradient information in the form of radial ring codes. The method is robust for detecting objects in noisy environments in spite of illumination changes. Experiments demonstrate the rotation- and brightness invariance of the proposed method for object search. However, there is much room to promote in speed and optimal parameters and the method can be combined with other template matching algorithms. The method is more suitable used in multi-object coarse-search step to get the small candidate area and combined with other fine-matching steps.

Acknowledgments. The work described in this paper is partially supported by National Natural Science Foundation of China under grant Nos. 51327801, 51475193. The authors would like to thank the reviewers for their constructive comments that improved the presentation of the paper.

References

1. Zitov, B., Flusser, J.: Image registration methods: a survey. Image Vis. Comput. **21**, 977–1000 (2003)
2. Ashburner, J.: A fast diffeomorphic image registration algorithm. Neuroimage **38**, 95–113 (2007)
3. Jenkinson, M., Bannister, P., Brady, M., Smith, S.: Improved optimization for the robust and accurate linear registration and motion correction of brain images. Neuroimage **17**, 825–841 (2002)
4. Lewis, J.: Fast normalized cross-correlation. Vis. Interface **10**, 120–123 (1995)
5. Wood, J.: Invariant pattern recognition: a review. Pattern Recogn. **29**, 1–17 (1996)

6. Liao, S.X., Pawlak, M.: On image analysis by moments. IEEE Trans. Pattern Anal. Mach. Intell. **18**, 254–266 (1996)
7. Flusser, J., Suk, T.: Pattern recognition by affine moment invariants. Pattern Recogn. **26**, 167–174 (1993)
8. Wolfson, H.J., Rigoutsos, I.: Geometric hashing: an overview. Comput. Sci. Eng. **4**, 10–21 (1997)
9. Ratnasamy, S., Karp, B., Yin, L., Yu, F., Estrin, D., Govindan, R., et al.: GHT: a geographic hash table for data-centric storage. In: Proceedings of the 1st ACM International Workshop on Wireless Sensor Networks and Applications, pp. 78–87 (2002)
10. Kovalev, V.A., Petrou, M., Bondar, Y.S.: Using orientation tokens for object recognition. Pattern Recogn. Lett. **19**, 1125–1132 (1998)
11. Dalal, N., Triggs, B.: Histograms of oriented gradients for human detection. In: IEEE Computer Society Conference on Computer Vision and Pattern Recognition, CVPR 2005, pp. 886–893 (2005)
12. Lowe, D.G.: Object recognition from local scale-invariant features. In: Proceedings of the Seventh IEEE International Conference on Computer vision, pp. 1150–1157 (1999)
13. Lowe, D.G.: Distinctive image features from scale-invariant keypoints. Int. J. Comput. Vis. **60**, 91–110 (2004)
14. Juan, L., Gwun, O.: A comparison of sift, pca-sift and surf. Int. J. Image Process. (IJIP) **3**, 143–152 (2009)
15. Bay, H., Tuytelaars, T., Van Gool, L.: SURF: speeded up robust features. In: Leonardis, A., Bischof, H., Pinz, A. (eds.) ECCV 2006, Part I. LNCS, vol. 3951, pp. 404–417. Springer, Heidelberg (2006)
16. Mikolajczyk, K., Schmid, C.: Indexing based on scale invariant interest points. In: Proceedings of the Eighth IEEE International Conference on Computer Vision, ICCV 2001, pp. 525–531 (2001)
17. Mikolajczyk, K., Schmid, C.: A performance evaluation of local descriptors. IEEE Trans. Pattern Anal. Mach. Intell. **27**, 1615–1630 (2005)
18. Ullah, F., Kaneko, S.I.: Using orientation codes for rotation-invariant template matching. Pattern Recogn. **37**, 201–209 (2004)
19. Marimon, D., Ebrahimi, T.: Efficient rotation-discriminative template matching. In: Rueda, L., Mery, D., Kittler, J. (eds.) CIARP 2007. LNCS, vol. 4756, pp. 221–230. Springer, Heidelberg (2007)
20. Swain, M.J., Ballard, D.H.: Color indexing. Int. J. Comput. Vis. **7**, 11–32 (1991)

Novel DCT Features for Detecting Spatial Embedding Algorithms

Hao Zhang$^{(\boxtimes)}$, Tao Zhang, Xiaodan Hou, and Xijian Ping

Zhengzhou Information Science and Technology Institute, Zhengzhou, China
haozhang78@126.com,
{brunda,hxd2305,pingxijian}@163.com

Abstract. Traditionally, discrete cosine transform (DCT) features and Cartesian calibration are mainly utilized in joint picture expert group (JPEG) steganalysis. As well known, the steganalyzer without any modification can also work for spatial steganography. However, since JPEG and spatial embedding have different influences on DCT coefficients, this direct generalization is not quite reasonable. This essay studies the statistical moments and histogram variances of DCT coefficients under pixel domain modification. A novel steganalyzer for detecting spatial steganography is established by all alternating current (AC) coefficient features and Cartesian calibration. The experimental results state that the proposed steganalyzer outperforms the old DCT feature based method, as well as several spatial and wavelet feature based methods.

Keywords: Steganalysis · Steganography · Discrete cosine transform

1 Introduction

Image steganography is the art of secret communication in which messages are embedded in an image without drawing suspicion. There are several common choices for cover formats, mainly containing JPEG and bitmap. Secret messages are usually hidden by modifying coefficients for JPEG or by changing pixel values for bitmap.

Steganalysis, as an opposite technique, is to detect the presence of hidden data. In the earlier, Farid [1] utilized a classifier to establish a supervised learning based steganalysis framework. The study, with the help of some powerful classifier, can be converted into finding effective steganalytic features by statistical analysis. Since the embedding algorithms have different kinds of influences on cover data, a well-concerned question is how to establish a universal feature set. To make a try, Shi [2], Goljan [3], and Wang [4] extracted various features in wavelet domain, Li [5] and Pevný [6] selected several feature sets in spatial domain. A work [7] in the famous BOSS competition state that the merged DCT feature set, originally designed for JPEG steganalysis, is also useful to detect spatial steganography. Nowadays, the sets of rich model [8–10] in these three domains are brought forward to design powerful steganalyzers.

Noticing that DCT feature sets in references are designed for JPEG, we argue that they are not so appropriate for spatial algorithms. In fact, since the energy of natural image concentrates in low and middle frequency parts, the high frequency coefficient

© Springer International Publishing Switzerland 2015
Y.-J. Zhang (Ed.): ICIG 2015, Part II, LNCS 9218, pp. 565–571, 2015.
DOI: 10.1007/978-3-319-21963-9_52

distribute closely around zero and had better not be changed for safety. Consequently, both merged DCT features and rich model features are mostly extracted from middle and low frequency coefficients. This character makes the feature set neglect the high frequency variance in spatial embedding scheme.

In this paper, we discuss how to propose a suitable DCT feature set for detecting spatial steganography. First, the model along with the corresponding statistical analysis is given and the novel feature set is proposed in Sect. 2. Next, the experimental results are shown to verify the effectiveness of new features. Finally, the paper is concluded.

2 Model and Analysis

2.1 Model Establishment

Divide the image into blocks of size 8×8. For any pixel block $\{c_{p,q}\}_{0 \leq p,q \leq 7}$, the stego noise $\{n_{p,q}\}_{0 \leq p,q \leq 7}$ is set to be additive and the stego block $\{s_{p,q}\}_{0 \leq p,q \leq 7}$ is obtained by the formula $s_{p,q} = c_{p,q} + n_{p,q}$. Compute the two dimensional DCT transform by

$$C_{u,v} = \frac{A_u A_v}{4} \sum_{0 \leq p,q \leq 7} c_{p,q} \cos \frac{(2p+1)u\pi}{16} \cos \frac{(2q+1)v\pi}{16}, \qquad (1)$$

where $0 \leq u, v \leq 7$ and $A_u = 1/\sqrt{2}$ when $u = 0$ or otherwise $A_u = 1$. Similarly, $N_{u,v}$ and $S_{u,v}$ can be obtained and the formula $S_{u,v} = C_{u,v} + N_{u,v}$ holds.

Now we come to study the statistical difference between $C_{u,v}$ and $S_{u,v}$. Given (u, v), let the probability density function (PDF) of $C_{u,v}$ be f_C, and that of $N_{u,v}$ be f_N. The PDF of $S_{u,v}$ can be calculated by convolution

$$f_S = f_C * f_N, \qquad (2)$$

as the noise is independent from cover. Model $C_{u,v}$ by generalized Gaussian distribution. Next, to make clear the PDF of $S_{u,v}$, we need to know how $N_{u,v}$ is distributed.

Since there are many kinds of embedding algorithms, which could produce distinct influences on covers, an ideal noise model are not so easy to get. Note that the traditional work relies on Gaussian distribution, we figure that it is not quite reasonable. In much earlier research, people focus on least significant bit (LSB) replacement and LSB matching algorithms. The hypothesis that stego noises are independent from pixel to pixel was soundly suitable. Observing that $N_{u,v}$ is a weighted summation of 64 random variables, the central limit theorem guarantees the accuracy of Gaussian model. In recent years, content-based adaptive algorithms are largely used. The range or intensity of modification usually depends on some preseted measurement, such as L^p norm for residues by directional filters [10], absolute values of subtractive pixels [11]. Noises among adjacent pixels could have close but complex relationship. So it should be rather difficult to select a distribution with a concrete form.

Nevertheless, we find some commonness which fits for all types of embedding schemes as far as we known. This general character can be describe by

$$f_N(x) > f_N(y), 0 < x < y \text{ or } 0 > x > y. \tag{3}$$

The random variable $N_{u,v}$ which satisfies the inequality will be single-peak distributed but not necessarily symmetrical. Compared with Gaussian distribution, the model is much more universal. In addition, we can show it really matches the generally acknowledged embedding principle.

In a spatial embedding scheme, the pixel modification is always demanded to be as smaller as possible to ensure security. As a common example, the LSB algorithms limit the alteration to the range $[-1, 1]$, and the probability of 0 is theoretically bigger than that of -1 or 1. Even in an adaptive scheme, such as PVD [12], no matter what range the pixel difference belongs to, the alteration ranges from 0 to some fixed integer k, and the distribution also satisfies the property described by the inequality (3).

Furthermore, this property can be naturally generalized to multidimensional cases. Let $X = (x_1, x_2, \cdots, x_L)$ be the vector of multiple noise variables, the density $f_N(X)$ could be larger when some x_i makes bigger in $[0, +\infty)$ or makes smaller in $(-\infty, 0]$. If we choose the 64 noises $\{n_{p,q}\}_{0 \leq p,q \leq 7}$ as the vector, then the corresponding DCT noise vector Y of $\{N_{u,v}\}_{0 \leq u,v \leq 7}$ will be obtained by a orthogonal transformation T. Note that $Y = 0$ if and only if $X = T^{-1}Y = 0$, the vector Y will be also single-peak distributed. In another word, under the transform, the property still holds for Y as well as for each component $N_{u,v}$. Therefore, this single-peak model is assumed to be appropriate for analyzing the statistical differences between f_C and f_S.

2.2 Statistical Analysis

Two classes of features are utilized here to characterize the distribution alteration, one is the histogram, the other is the PDF absolute moment. The conclusions with the associated proofs are detailed as follows.

Theorem 1. If C is generalized-Gaussian distributed and N is single-peak distributed subjected to the inequality (3), then f_C and f_S satisfy that

$$\begin{cases} f_S(0) \leq f_C(0), \\ \frac{f_S(x) + f_S(-x)}{f_S(0)} \geq \frac{f_C(x) + f_C(-x)}{f_C(0)}. \end{cases} \tag{4}$$

Proof. Consider symmetrical histogram variables

$$\begin{cases} \tilde{f}_N(x) = \frac{1}{2}(f_N(x) + f_N(-x)), \\ \tilde{f}_S(x) = \frac{1}{2}(f_S(x) + f_S(-x)). \end{cases} \tag{5}$$

Utilizing the linearity of convolution, we obtain $\tilde{f}_S = f_C * \tilde{f}_N$. Then the proof of (4) is equivalent to the proof of the equalities

$$\begin{cases} \tilde{f}_S(0) \le \tilde{f}_C(0), \\ \dfrac{\tilde{f}_S(x)+\tilde{f}_S(-x)}{\tilde{f}_S(0)} \ge \dfrac{\tilde{f}_C(x)+\tilde{f}_C(-x)}{\tilde{f}_C(0)}. \end{cases} \tag{6}$$

These can be gotten by using the theorems in [13].

Theorem 2. Denote the mathematical expectation by $E[\cdot]$. Under the same hypothesis of theorem 1, the inequality $E[|C|^n] \le E[|S|^n]$ always holds for each $n \ge 1$.

Proof. First, we obtain

$$E[|S|^n] = \int_{-\infty}^{+\infty} f_S(x)|x|^n dx = \int_{-\infty}^{+\infty}\int_{-\infty}^{+\infty} f_C(x-y)f_N(y)|x|^n dxdy \tag{7}$$

according to the definition of mathematical expectation. For each $n \ge 1$, the inner integral satisfies that

$$\begin{aligned} \int_{-\infty}^{+\infty} f_C(x-y)|x|^n dx &= \int_{-\infty}^{+\infty} f_C(x)|x-y|^n dx \\ &= \frac{1}{2}\int_{-\infty}^{+\infty} f_C(x)(|x-y|^n + |x+y|^n)dx \\ &\ge \frac{1}{2^n}\int_{-\infty}^{+\infty} f_C(x)(|x-y|+|x+y|)^n dx \\ &\ge \int_{-\infty}^{+\infty} f_C(x)|x|^n dx \\ &\ge E[|C|^n], \end{aligned} \tag{8}$$

where the second equality uses the symmetry of f_C and the first inequality uses the convexity of $x^n (x > 0)$. Then we have

$$E[|S|^n] \ge \int_{-\infty}^{+\infty} E[|C|^n]f_N(y)dy = E[|C|^n].\# \tag{9}$$

These two theorems imply that, although the embedding schemes are changeable, different stego noises invariably have the same influences on both the histogram f_C and the PDF absolute moment $E[|C|^n]$.

2.3 Proposed Feature Set

Under the guide of above results, a novel steganographic feature set can be designed. Given an image, we use non-overlapping 8×8 block DCT to get the samples of 64 coefficient random variables $\{D_{u,v}\}_{0 \le u,v \le 7}$. Then the integer value histograms $\{h_{u,v}(\cdot)\}_{0 \le u,v \le 7}$ and PDF absolute moments $\{E[|D_{u,v}|^n]\}_{0 \le u,v \le 7}$ can be estimated by routine calculation, including rounding and averaging.

For each coefficient $D_{u,v}$, three central values of histogram and first two PDF absolute moments constitute a useful subset:

$$\mathcal{F}_{u,v} = \left\{ h_{u,v}(0), \frac{h_{u,v}(1) + h_{u,v}(-1)}{h_{u,v}(0)}, \frac{h_{u,v}(1) + h_{u,v}(-1)}{h_{u,v}(0)}, E\left[|D_{u,v}|\right], E\left[|D_{u,v}|^2\right] \right\}. \quad (10)$$

Note that the direct current coefficient $D_{0,0}$ dependents on mean value of pixel block, its distribution will be significantly influenced by cover content. So we only consider 63 AC coefficients in the basis feature set:

$$\mathcal{F} = \bigcup_{0 \le u,v \le 7} \mathcal{F}_{u,v} - \mathcal{F}_{0,0}. \quad (11)$$

Furthermore, the set is enhanced by so-called Cartesian calibration. The calibration technique was initially applied in JPEG steganalysis [14]. It could make the stegana-lyzer much more sensitive to the blockiness produced by steganography. Since the image has already been in spatial domain, we directly remove the first 4 columns and arrays of pixels. A new feature set $\tilde{\mathcal{F}}$ is then obtained by using the rest of image. Finally, the steganalyzer will be established by feature set $\tilde{\mathcal{F}} \cup \mathcal{F}$ and support vector machine (SVM) classifier with the same setup as in [6].

3 Experiment and Analysis

Ten thousand 256 gray-scale images with size 512×512 are downloaded from BOWS-2 database [15]. Then we take several algorithms containing LSBMR [16], BPCS [17], PVD, AE-LSB [11], EA [18] to produce stego images. For any algorithm, select three embedding rate (ER) between 0.1 bits per pixel (bpp) and 0.4 bpp. Exact features specified by $\mathcal{F} \cup \tilde{\mathcal{F}}$ from cover or stego image.

Each time we propose a steganalyzer, we execute a binary classification for given algorithm and ratio. That is to say, only ten thousand stego samples along with the cover samples are considered in one experiment. Half of the cover-stego sample pairs are randomly chosen for training and the left for testing.

To verify the advantage of new feature set, we would like to compare it with several other ones in references. They are two spatial feature sets named "Li110 [5]" and "Pevný686 [6]", two wavelet feature sets named "Wang156 [4]" and "Shi78 [2]", and two DCT feature sets named "Pevný548 [14]" and "Liu70 [19]". They are also utilized to design six kinds of steganalyzers by SVM. The area under receiver operating characteristic curve (AUC) will be used to compare the ability of these detectors.

The results are presented in Table 1, from which we can see the proposed features always outperform the traditional merged DCT features by Pevný. This indicates that the high frequency features really contribute to detection of spatial algorithms. Note that Liu take all DCT modes as an average and the corresponding results are relatively pretty bad, we figure that this simple mixture of different frequency features degrades the classification performance. For the LSBM and BPCS algorithms, although our proposed sets are not superior to the spatial domain feature sets, they clearly outper-form the wavelet domain ones.

Table 1. AUC comparison

Algorithm	ER	Li110	Pevný686	Wang156	Shi78	Pevný548	Liu72	Proposed630
LSBMR	10 %	91.41	**93.49**	84.62	82.48	80.50	60.85	88.05
	20 %	97.13	**97.74**	94.63	93.89	92.43	75.44	95.98
	30 %	**98.88**	98.11	97.54	97.17	96.57	82.69	97.78
BPCS	10 %	72.05	**98.16**	69.88	50.00	79.72	51.36	87.95
	20 %	86.38	**99.67**	84.96	62.98	91.58	55.81	96.38
	30 %	92.72	**97.48**	91.10	72.92	94.80	60.49	96.82
PVD	10 %	79.24	67.51	50.00	83.57	85.28	60.10	**99.85**
	20 %	92.99	78.92	65.44	90.02	92.87	70.05	**99.94**
	30 %	97.56	87.42	78.26	94.32	96.36	77.08	**99.98**
AE-LSB	10 %	62.71	67.53	50.00	68.28	77.43	56.47	**95.84**
	20 %	75.25	76.50	56.95	77.16	88.69	65.44	**98.68**
	30 %	84.10	85.78	66.14	82.90	93.80	72.97	**99.51**
EA	20 %	72.15	69.40	72.04	59.32	66.61	56.48	**75.66**
	30 %	**85.74**	80.58	84.49	71.97	78.87	62.03	85.23
	40 %	93.47	91.33	**93.85**	83.97	87.23	67.67	91.77

In addition, we are glad to show that the new feature set takes advantage in detecting edge adaptive algorithms, containing PVD, AE-LSB and EA (at 0.2bpp). Especially for PVD and AE-LSB, although the algorithms modifies less pixels than LSBMR and BPCS at the same embedding level, which reduces the effectiveness of spatial methods, they should have significantly influenced the coefficient distribution in frequency domain.

In summary, the novel feature set is well appropriate for detecting these algorithms with quite different embedding schemes. This result is consistent with the statistical analysis.

4   Conclusion

In this paper, a novel DCT feature set is proposed, and has been experimentally verified to be more effective than traditional methods, especially for detecting several edge adaptive algorithms. These results show the significance of model analysis and the effectiveness of high frequency information. However, the detection ability at low embedding rates is still not satisfying. In the future, we plan to explore better steganalyzer by using more powerful transformations.

Acknowledgments. This work was supported by the National Natural Science Foundation of China (No. 61272490). The authors would like to thank the reviewers for their insightful comments and helpful suggestions.

References

1. Farid H.: Detecting hidden messages using higher-order statistical models. In: Proceedings of the IEEE International Conference on Image Processing, pp. 905–908. IEEE Press, New York (2002)

2. Shi, Y.Q., Xuan, G., Zou, D., Gao, J.: Image steganalysis based on moments of characteristic functions using wavelet decomposition, prediction-error image, and neural network. In: Proceedings of the IEEE International Conference on Multimedia and Expo, pp. 269–272. IEEE Press, New York (2005)
3. Goljan, M., Fridrich, J., Holotyak, T.: New blind steganalysis and its implications. In: Proceedings of the SPIE Electronic Imaging, Security, Steganography, and Watermarking of Multimedia Contents VIII, 607201, SPIE, Bellingham (2006)
4. Wang, Y., Moulin, P.: Optimized feature extraction for learning-based image steganalysis. IEEE Trans. Inf. Foren. Sec. **2**, 31–45 (2007)
5. Li, B., Huang, J.W., Shi, Y.Q.: Textural features based universal steganalysis. In: Proceedings of the SPIE Security, Forensics, Steganography, and Watermarking of Multimedia Contents X, 765817, SPIE, Bellingham (2008)
6. Pevný, T., Bas, P., Fridrich, J.: Steganalysis by subtractive pixel adjacency matrix. IEEE Trans. Inf. Foren. Sec. **5**, 215–224 (2010)
7. Fridrich, J., Kodovský, J., Holub, V., Goljan, M.: Steganalysis of content-adaptive steganography in spatial domain. In: Filler, T., Pevný, T., Craver, S., Ker, A. (eds.) IH 2011. LNCS, vol. 6958, pp. 102–117. Springer, Heidelberg (2011)
8. Fridrich, J., Kodovský, J.: Rich models for steganalysis of digital images. IEEE Trans. Inf. Foren. Sec. **7**, 868–882 (2012)
9. Kodovský, J., Fridrich, J.: Steganalysis of JPEG images using rich models. In: Proceedings of the SPIE Media Watermarking, Security, and Forensics, 83030A, SPIE, Bellingham (2012)
10. Holub, V., Fridrich, J.: Designing steganographic distortion using directional filters. In: Proceedings of the IEEE International Workshop on Information Forensics and Security, pp. 234–239. IEEE Press, New York (2012)
11. Yang, C.H., Weng, C.Y., Wang, S.J., Sun, H.M.: Adaptive data hiding in edge areas of image with spatial LSB domain systems. IEEE Trans. Inf. Foren. Sec. **3**, 488–497 (2008)
12. Cai, K., Li, X., Zeng, T., Yang, B., Lu, X.: Reliable histogram features for detecting LSB matching. In: Proceedings of the IEEE Image Conference of Image Processing, pp. 1761–1764. IEEE Press, New York (2010)
13. Kodovský, J., Pevný, T., Fridrich, J.: Modern steganalysis can detect YASS. In: Proceedings of the SPIE Media Forensics and Security II, 754102, SPIE, Bellingham (2010)
14. Mielikainen, J.: LSB matching revisited. IEEE Signal Process. Lett. **13**, 285–287 (2006)
15. Bas, P., Furon, T.: BOWS-2. http://bows2.gipsa-lab.inpg.fr
16. Kawaguchi, E., Eason, R.O.: Principle and applications of BPCS-steganography. In: Proceedings of the SPIE Multimedia Systems and Applications, 3528-464, SPIE, Bellingham (1998)
17. Wu, D.C., Tsai, W.H.: A steganographic method for images by pixel-value differencing. Pattern Recog. Lett. **24**, 1613–1626 (2003)
18. Luo, W.Q., Huang, F.J., Huang, J.W.: Edge adaptive image steganography based on LSB matching revisited. IEEE Trans. Inf. Foren. Sec. **5**, 201–214 (2010)
19. Liu, Q., Sung, A.H., Qiao, M.: Neighboring joint density-based JPEG steganalysis. ACM TIST. 2, Article 16 (2011)

Novel Software-Based Method to Widen Dynamic Range of CCD Sensor Images

Wei Wen[✉] and Siamak Khatibi

Department of Communication System, Blekinge Technical Institute,
Karlskrona, Sweden
{wei.wen,siamak.khatibi}@bth.se

Abstract. In the past twenty years, CCD sensor has made huge progress in improving resolution and low-light performance by hardware. However due to physical limits of the sensor design and fabrication, fill factor has become the bottle neck for improving quantum efficiency of CCD sensor to widen dynamic range of images. In this paper we propose a novel software-based method to widen dynamic range, by virtual increase of fill factor achieved by a resampling process. The CCD images are rearranged to a new grid of virtual pixels com-posed by subpixels. A statistical framework consisting of local learning model and Baye-sian inference is used to estimate new subpixel intensity. By knowing the different fill factors, CCD images were obtained. Then new resampled images were computed, and compared to the respective CCD and optical image. The results show that the proposed method is possible to widen significantly the recordable dynamic range of CCD images and increase fill factor to 100 % virtually.

Keywords: Dynamic range · Fill factor · CCD sensors · Sensitive area · Quantum efficiency

1 Introduction

Since the first digital cameras equipped with charge-coupled device (CCD) image sensors in 1975 [1] the investigation on human visual system has been affecting the digital camera design and their development. In human visual system the retina, formed by the rod and cone photoreceptors, initiates the visual process by converting a contin-uous image to a discrete array of signals. Curcio et el. [2] investigation on human photo-receptor revealed that the properties of the rods and cones mosaic determine the amount of information which is retained or lost by sampling process, including resolution acuity and detection acuity. The photoreceptor layer specialized for maximum visual acuity is in the center of the retina, the fovea, which is 1.5 mm wide and is composed by cones entirely. Figure 1 shows a close up of the fovea region. The shape of cones is much closed to hexagonal and the cones in fovea are densely packed, where no gap between each two cones can be considered. Due to this configuration the visual acuity and neural sampling in fovea are optimized [3].

The image sensor array in a CCD digital camera is designed by modelling the fovea in human eyes for capturing and converting the analog optical signal from a scene into a

© Springer International Publishing Switzerland 2015
Y.-J. Zhang (Ed.): ICIG 2015, Part II, LNCS 9218, pp. 572–583, 2015.
DOI: 10.1007/978-3-319-21963-9_53

digital electrical signal. Over the past twenty years, the quality of digital camera sensors has made tremendous progress, especially in increasing resolution and improving low-light performance [4]. This has been achieved by reducing the pixel size and improving the quantum efficiency (QE) of the sensor [4, 5]. Assuming each pixel corresponding to one cone in fovea, the pixel density in camera sensor should be close to 199,000/mm2 which is the average density of the peak fovea cones in human eyes [2]. Todays the pixel density can be 24,305/mm2 in a common commercial camera such as Canon EOS 5D Mark II or the pixel density can be even higher as 480,000/mm2 in a special camera such as Nokia 808. However the quality of the image is not affected only by the pixel size or quantum efficiency of the sensor [6]. As the sensor pixel size becomes smaller this results to detect a smaller die size, gain higher spatial resolution and obtain lower signal-to-noise ratio (SNR); all in cost of lower recordable dynamic range (DR) and lower fill factor (FF). Hardware solutions in image sensor technologies as a respond to increase of mobile imaging applications try to compensate for the performance degradation with decrease of the pixel size. On the other hand the only standard post-processing solution for obtaining a nearly infinite displayable dynamic range is to use the high dynamic range imaging technology which implements a combination of several images captured with different exposure times or different sizes of aperture sensor [7, 8].

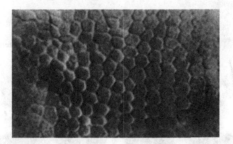

Fig. 1. A close up of the fovea region [2].

In this paper we propose a novel software-based method to compensate the performance degradation of the recordable dynamic range, with decrease of the pixel size, by virtual increase of fill factor. In our method the original fill factor is known and the processing is done on the captured image. The virtual increase of fill factor is achieved by a statistical resampling process which initiates the estimation of each new pixel intensity value. Our results show that it is possible to widen the dynamic range significantly by software solution. Although there are software technologies to improve the displayable dynamic range using only one image, such as the histogram equalization and image contrast enhancement [9], to the best of our knowledge, our approach is the first work that tries to improve the recordable dynamic range by virtually increase of the fill factor of a CCD sensor.

The rest of paper is organized as follow; in Sect. 2 the effect of fill factor is explained, in Sect. 3 the details of the method are described, Sect. 4 explains the experimental setup, the results are shown and discussed in Sect. 5, and finally we conclude and discuss potential future work in Sect. 6. Here it is worth to mention that we distinguish between recordable and displayable dynamic range where the recordable dynamic range represents the raw input dynamic range obtained after capturing of an image and the displayable dynamic range is considered a post-processing operation on the raw captured image.

2 Effect of Fill Factor

CCD sensor has reigned supreme in the realm of imaging with the steady improvement of performance, especially on scientific area [5] due to its advantage of high quantum efficiency. The QE which is defined as the number of signal electrons created per incident photon is one of the most important parameters used to evaluate the quality of a detector which affects the DR and SNR of captured images. Figure 2 is the graphical representation of a CCD sensor showing some buckets and rain drops shown as blue lines. Each bucket represents storage of photoelectrons, by modelling a photodiode and a well of one pixel in the CCD sensor and the rain drops, blue lines, represent the incident photons that fall into the sensor. By having bigger bucket more rain drops, number of photons, is collected, which can be seen as increase of the spatial quantum efficiency [10] resulting in DR quality improvement of captured images. The temporal quantum efficiency is related to accumulation of photoelectrons during the exposure time and is regulated by the fill factor [5].

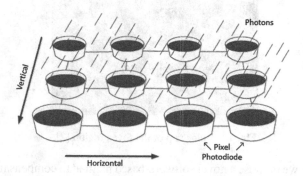

Fig. 2. Graphical representation of a CCD sensor.

The quantum efficiency is affected by fill factor as in $QE_{eff} = FF \times QE$, where QE_{eff} is the effective QE and FF is the fill factor which is the ratio of light sensitive area versus total area of a pixel [5]. A typical dynamic range, the ratio of the brightest accurately detectable signal to the faintest, of CCD sensors is proportional to the number of detected photons. The fill factor of non-modified CCD sensor varies from 30 % to 75 %. Figure 3(a) and (b) show light incident on a sensor with high and low fill factor pixels respectively. In a sensor with the high fill factor pixels more number of photons is captured in comparison to a sensor with the low fill factor pixels. Hardware innovations in image sensor technologies (e.g. decrease of occupied area of the pixel transistors, increase of the photodiode area within maintaining small pixel size and use of micro-lenses) are achieved to increase the fill factor. An effective way to increase the fill factor is to put a microlens above each pixel which converges light from the whole pixel unit area into the photodiode in order to capture more number of photons as shown in Fig. 3(c). Since 90 s, various microlens have been developed for increasing fill factor and they are widely used in CCD sensors [12, 13]. But it is still impossible to make fill factor 100 % in practical production due to the physical limits in digital camera development [4]. Our proposed method compensates the loss of input signal, caused by incident light on non-sensitive area, in each sensor pixel to achieve a fill factor of 100 %.

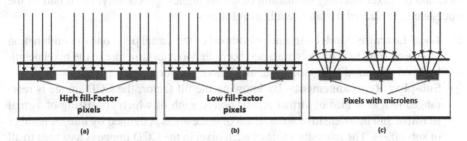

Fig. 3. Light incident on sensor with high and low fill factor pixels are shown in (a) and (b) respectively. (c) Pixel with the micro-lens is used to compensate the entering light [11].

3 Methodology

By collecting incoming photons into a sample grid, a CCD sensor samples an image. Figure 4 illustrates such conventional sampling grid on a CCD sensor array of four pixels. The white and black areas represent the sensitive areas and non-sensitive areas in pixels respectively. The blue arrows in the figure represent the positions of sampled signal. Let assume the size of each pixel is Δx by Δy. Then Δx and Δy, the sample interval in x and y directions, are the spatial resolution of the output image. The sampling function can be expressed as $F\left(x',y'\right) = \sum_{i=0}^{M} \sum_{j=0}^{N} \delta\left(i\Delta yx, j\Delta y\right) f\left(x,y\right)$ where x, y, x' and y' are pixel coordinates in the input optical image f and the output sampled image F, with size of M by N, respectively [14]. Let also assume the size of the sensitive area is $\Delta x'$ by $\Delta y'$ as shown in Fig. 4. Thus when the incident light is not in the sensitive area with size of $\Delta x'$ by $\Delta y', F\left(x',y'\right) = 0$.

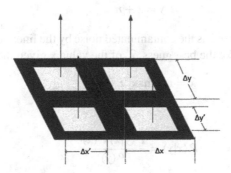

Fig. 4. The conventional image sampling on a CCD sensor.

Based on the discussion in Sect. 2 the fill factor is lower than 100 %, in that case the region of support corresponding to the sensitive area is not the whole area of one pixel. A signal resampling procedure is used in order to expand the region of support and improve the captured signal. For each pixel the resampled procedure consists of following parts: (a) local learning model, (b) sub-pixel rearrangement, (c) model simulations on sub-pixel grid, (d) intensity estimating of sub-pixels based on Bayesian inference, and (e) pixel intensity estimation based on highest probability. Each part of the procedure is explained in more details as it follows.

(a) **Local Learning Model** – In a neighborhood of the actual pixel one or combination of several statistical models are tuned according to data structure in the pixel neighborhood. We used a Gaussian statistical model in our experiments.

(b) **Sub-pixel Rearrangement** - By knowing the fill factor, the CCD image is rearranged in a new grid of virtual sensor pixels, each of which consisting of virtual sensitive and non-sensitive areas. Each of these areas is defined by integer number of sub-pixels. The intensity value of each pixel in the CCD image is assigned to all of sub-pixels in the virtual sensitive area. The intensity values of all sub-pixels in non-sensitive area in virtual sensor pixels were assigned to zero. An example of such rearrangement of sampled data to sub-pixel level is presented in Sect. 4.

(c) **Model Simulations on Sub-pixel Grid** – In a sub-pixel rearranged neighborhood of the actual pixel, the local learned model is used to simulate all intensity values of the sub-pixels. The known intensity values of virtual sensitive sub-pixels and result of linear interpolation on the sub-pixel grid for obtaining the unknown intensity values of virtual non-sensitive sub-pixels are used to initiate the intensity values in the simulation. Several simulations are accomplished where in each one the number of actual sub-pixels varies from zeros to total number of sub-pixels of the actual virtual sensitive area. In this way each sub-pixel of the actual virtual sensor obtains, after a number of simulations, various random intensity values.

(d) **Intensity Estimating of Sub-pixels Based on Bayesian Inference** – Bayesian inference is employed to estimate the intensity of each sub-pixel by having the model simulations values as the observation values. Let y be the observed intensity value of each sub-pixel after simulations and x be the true intensity value of the sub-pixel, then

$$y = x + n$$

where n can be considered as the contaminated noise by the linear interpolation process. Here the goal is to make the best guess, $\hat{x}$, of the value x given the observed values by

$$\hat{x} = \arg\max_x P(x|y),$$

and

$$P(x|y) = \frac{P(y|x)P(x)}{P(y)}$$

where $P(x|y)$ is the probability distribution of x given y, $P(y|x)$ is the probability distribution of y given x, $P(x)$ and $P(y)$ are the probability distribution of x and y.

By assumption of having a Gaussian noise yields

$$P(y|x) = P(x|x+n) = \frac{1}{\sqrt{2\pi}\sigma_n} e^{-\frac{(y-x)^2}{2\sigma_n^2}}$$

where σ_n is the variance of the noise; i.e. the variance of interpolated data from simulations for each sub-pixel. The educated hypothesis $P(x)$ is obtained by the local learning model which here has a Gaussian distribution with the mean μ_x and standard deviation of σ_x as following

$$P(x) = \frac{1}{\sqrt{2\pi}\sigma_x} e^{-\frac{(x-\mu_x)^2}{2\sigma_x^2}}$$

For posterior probability on x yields

$$P(x|y) \approx P(y|x)P(x) = \frac{1}{\sqrt{2\pi}\sigma_n} e^{-\frac{(y-x)^2}{2\sigma_n^2}} \times \frac{1}{\sqrt{2\pi}\sigma_x} e^{-\frac{(x-\mu_x)^2}{2\sigma_x^2}}$$

The x which maximizes $P(x|y)$ is the same as that which minimizes the exponent term in the above equation. Thus if $f(x) = -\frac{(y-x)^2}{2\sigma_n^2} - \frac{(x-\mu_x)^2}{2\sigma_x^2}$, when the derivative $f'(x) = 0$, the minimum value or the best intensity estimation of the corresponding subpixel is

$$\hat{x} = \frac{y\sigma_x^2 + \mu_x\sigma_n^2}{\sigma_x^2 + \sigma_n^2}$$

(e) **Pixel Intensity Estimation Based on Highest Probability** – The histogram of intensity values of the actual virtual sensor sub-pixels is calculated which indicates

Fig. 5. The virtual CCD image sensor pixel composed by subpixels whose fill factor is set as 81 % (left) and the optical image (right).

a tendency of intensities probability. The multiplication of inverse of fill factor with highest value of such probability is considered as the estimated intensity value of the actual virtual sensor as the result of resampling procedure.

4   Experimental Setup

Several optical and CCD images for different fill factor values were simulated using our own codes and Image Systems Evaluation Toolbox (ISET) [15] in MATLAB. ISET is designed to evaluate how image capture components and algorithms influence image quality, and has been proved to be an effective tool for simulating the sensor and image capturing [16]. Five fill factor values of 25 %, 36 %, 49 %, 64 % and 81 %, were chosen for five simulated CCD sensors, having the same resolution of 128 by 128. All sensors had a pixel area of 10 by 10 square microns, with well capacity of 10000 e-. The read noise and the dark current noise were set to 1 mV and 1 mV/pixel/sec respectively. Each CCD sensor was rearranged to a new grid of virtual sensor pixels, each of which was composed of 40-by-40 sub-pixels. Figure 5 shows an example of the rearranged CCD sensor pixel with fill factor value of 81 %. The light grey and the dark grey areas represent the sensitive and the non-sensitive areas respectively. The sensitive area in each pixel was located in the middle of each pixel. The intensity value of subpixels in the virtual sensitive area was assigned by correspondent output image pixel intensity. The intensity values of all sub-pixels in non-sensitive area were assigned to zero. One type of optical and sensor image were generated and called as sweep frequency image. The intensity values of the sweep frequency image were calculated, in each row, from a linear swept – frequency cosine function. For generation of CCD sensor images, the luminance of the sweep frequency image was set to 100 cd/m^2 and the diffraction of the optic system was considered limited to ensure to obtain the brightness of the output as close as possible to the brightness of scene image. The exposure time was also set to 0.9 ms for all simulated five sensors to ensure constant number of input photons in the simulations.

5   Results and Discussion

The conventional sampled images from the sweep frequency optical images are shown in the first row of Fig. 6, the second row of images show the resampled images with our method. The result images from histogram equalization and image enhancement methods are shown in the third and fourth rows. The images of each row are related to different fill factor values, which are 25 %, 36 %, 49 %, 64 % and 81 % from left to right. All the images in Fig. 6 are displayed in unsigned 8 bits integer (uint8) format without any DR normalization. It can be seen that the DR of the conventional sampled images are very different from each other. When the fill factor is increasing, the DR is increased as well and approaching to the DR level of optical image shown in the Fig. 5. This is according to proportional relation of fill factor to number of photons which results to the intensity value changes of each pixel. The appearance of all resampled images with our proposed method is shown in Fig. 6 respectively. The top row of each image related to the sweep frequency optical image is chosen to visualize a typical comparison of pixel intensity values in these images. Figure 7 shows such pixel intensity values from conventional sampled images with the label of fill factor (FF) percentage, the optical and the resampled image from the image of 25 % fill factor with our method. The results in Fig. 7 are consistent with the image appearance in Fig. 6. These also verify that the pixel intensity values are increased as a consequence of virtual increase of fill factor by our method.

The dynamic range and root mean square error (RMSE) are used for comparison of the conventional sampled images, our resampled images and the respective optical image. The dynamic range is calculated by $DR = 20 \times \log_{10} p_{max}/p_{min}$, where p_{max} and p_{min} are the maximum and minimum pixel intensity values in an image. In uint8, there are 256 grey levels, which it means the maximum DR is 48.13 based on the above equation. The RMSE is defined as

$$RMSE = \sqrt{\frac{1}{n} \sum_{i=1}^{n} \left(P_i - Q_i\right)^2}$$

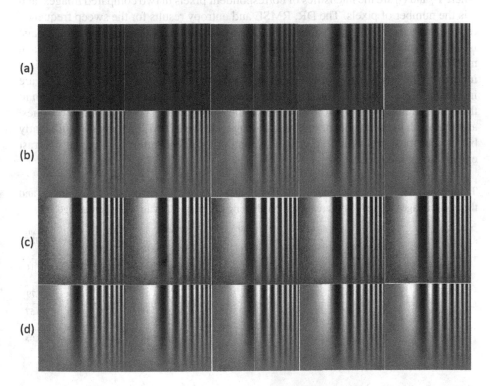

Fig. 6. The conventional sampled images (a) from the sweep frequency optical image having different fill factors, and the resampled image with our method (b), and the result images from histogram equalization (c) and image contrast enhancement (d). From left to right, the sensor fill factors are 25 %, 36 %, 49 %, 64 % and 81 %.

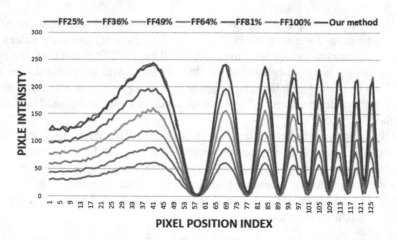

Fig. 7. The row wise comparison of pixel intensity values in sweep frequency related images.

where P_i and Q_i are the intensities of correspondent pixels in two compared images, and n is the number of pixels. The DR, RMSE and entropy results for the sweep frequency related images are shown in Tables 1 and 2 respectively, where the entropy of an image is used to evaluate the amount of information preservation after implementation of each method. Generally when the fill factor is increasing, the RMSEs between the optical image and the other images are decreasing, on the contrary entropy values and DRs are increasing. The tables also show that our method not only widen DRs in comparison to the conventional method but also preserve the information, shown in entropy values, and approach the truth data of the optical image, shown in RMSEs values, significantly better than post-processing solutions of histogram equalization and image contrast enhancement methods.

Table 1. The RMSE and dynamic range (DR in dB) comparison between the optical image and the result images related to different methods having different fill factor (FF) percentage.

Methods	FF25 %		FF36 %		FF49 %		FF64 %		FF81 %		Mean RMSE
	RMSE	DR	RMSE	DR	RMSE	DR	RMSE	DR	RMSE	DR	
Conventional method	102.54	36	87.51	39	69.5	42	49.63	44	26.4	46	67.16
Our method	4.69	48	9.79	48	3.6	48	3.09	48	2.79	48	4.79
Histogram Equalization	36.24	48	38.13	48	36.13	48	36.25	48	36.11	48	36.57
Image Contrast enhancement	12.08	48	14.84	48	11.39	48	10.95	48	10.87	48	12.03

Table 2. The Entropy comparison between the optical image and the result images related to different methods having different fill factor (FF) percentage.

Methods	FF25 %	FF36 %	FF49 %	FF64 %	FF81 %	Standard deviation
Conventional method	5.34	5.90	6.29	6.67	7.00	0.64
Our method	7.31	7.35	7.33	7.33	7.33	0.02
Histogram Equalization	5.1	5.42	5.59	5.77	5.80	0.27
Image Contrast enhancement	5.28	5.84	6.22	6.64	6.92	0.64

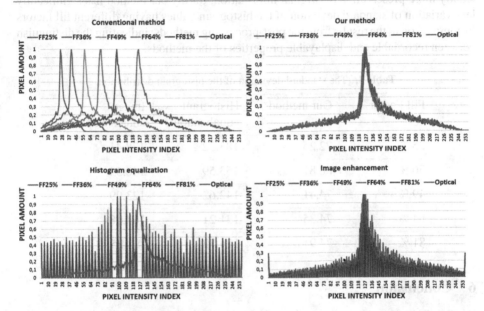

Fig. 8. The normalized histogram envelopes of conventional sampled images related to the sweep frequency optical image and correspondent our proposed resampled images, the images created with histogram equalization and image contrast enhancement.

Figure 8 shows the histograms envelopes of the conventional sampled images and the resampled images by our method and another two post-processing methods for improving the dynamic range. The results in the figures verify as well our statement that the dynamic range is widening by our method. The top left plot in Fig. 8 shows the histogram envelopes of the conventional sampled images and the truth optical image. The dynamic range varies with the change of fill factor for the conventional sampled images and by increase of fill factor the width of dynamic range is also increased. However the histogram envelopes of the resampled images by our method, shown in top right plot in Fig. 8, have the same width of dynamic range, independent of fill factor changes, and the DR is significantly close to DR of the truth optical image. The histograms envelopes of images by the post-processing methods, shown in bottom left plot in Fig. 8, have wider range than the conventional method, but fewer numbers of gray level indexes in comparison to our method, which is also consistent with result of the entropy in Table 2 indicating unsuccessfulness of such methods in preservation of information. The obtained results from the resampling images by our method show that the dependency of the method to fill factor is not significant, see Table 3. In the table the standard deviation of the histograms of result images by different methods are presented which indicating three issues: first the changes in the standard deviation of histograms are correlated to the preservation of original information, see the Table 2; secondly our method has significantly lower standard deviation of the histogram value than the values obtained by the post-processing methods within each fill factor value, indicating significantly more preservation of original information; thirdly our method has significantly less variation of standard deviation of the histogram values having different fill factors in comparison to the results from the post-processing methods; indicating the distinguish between recordable and displayable properties of the methods.

Table 3. The standard deviation of the histogram distribution.

Fill Factor	Our method	Histogram equalization	Image enhancement
25 %	72.25	183.52	178.41
36 %	68.87	153.59	140.54
49 %	74.41	142.62	123.99
64 %	74.35	131.21	104.08
81 %	74.91	124.72	88.95

6   Conclusion

In this paper, a novel software-based method is proposed for widening the dynamic range in CCD sensor images by increasing the fill factor virtually. The experimental results show that the low fill factor causes high RMSE and low dynamic range in conventional sampling images and increase of fill factor causes increase of dynamic range. Also the results show that 100 % fill factor can be achieved by our proposed method; obtaining low RMSE and high dynamic range. In the proposed method, a CCD image and a known value of fill factor are used to generate virtual pixels of the CCD sensor where the intensity value of each pixel is estimated by considering an increase of fill factor to 100 %. The stability and fill factor dependency of the proposed method were examined in which the results showed a maximum of 1.6 in RMSE and 0.02 in entropy of all resampled images for standard deviation in comparison to the optical image from the proposed method and fill factor dependency was insignificant. In the future works we will apply our methodology on CMOS sensors and the color sensors.

References

1. Prakel, D.: The Visual Dictionary of Photography. AVA Publishing, 91 (2013). ISBN 978-2-940411-04-7
2. Curcio, C.A., Sloan, K.R., Kalina, R.E., Hendrickson, A.E.: Human photoreceptor topography. J. Comp. Neurol. **292**, 497–523 (1990)
3. Rossi, E.A., Roorda, A.: The relationship between visual resolution and cone spacing in the human fovea. Nat. Neurosci. **13**, 156–157 (2010)
4. Goldstein, D.B.: Physical Limits in Digital Photography (2009). http://www.northlight-images.co.uk/article_pages/guest/physical_limits_long.html
5. Burke, B., Jorden, P., Vu, P.: CCD Technology. Exp. Astron. **19**, 69–102 (2005)
6. Chen, T., Catrysse, P., Gamal, A.E., Wandell, B.: How small should pixel size be? In: Proceedings of the SPIE, vol. 3965, pp. 451–459 (2000)
7. Reinhard, E., Ward, G., Pattanaik, S., Debevec, P.: High Dynamic Range Imaging: Acquisition, Display and Image-Based Lighting. Morgan Kaufmann Publishers, San Francisco (2005)
8. Yeganeh, H., Wang, Z.: High dynamic range image tone mapping by maximizing a structural fidelity measure. In: IEEE International Conference on Acoustics, Speech and Signal Processing, pp. 1879–1883 (2013)
9. Abdullah-Al-Wadud, M., et al.: A dynamic histogram equalization for image contrast enhancement. IEEE Trans. Consum. Electron. **53**(2), 593–600 (2007)
10. Sebastiano, B., Arcangelo R.B., Giuseppe, M., Giovanni, P.: Image Processing for Embedded Devices: From CFA Data to Image/video Coding, p. 12. Bentham Science Publishers (2010). ISBN 9781608051700
11. Dalsa, Image sensor architectures for digital cinematography (2003). http://www.teledynedalsa.com/public/corp/PDFs/papers/Image_sensor_Architecture_Whitepaper_Digital_Cinema_00218-00_03-70.pdf
12. Deguchi, M., Maruyama, T., Yamasaki, F.: Microlens design using simulation program for CCD image sensor. IEEE Trans. Consum. Electron. **38**, 583–589 (1992)
13. Donati, S., Martini, G., Norgia, M.: Microconcentrators to recover fill- actor in image photodetectors with pixel on-board processing circuits. Opt. Express **15**, 18066–18075 (2007)
14. Potmesil, M., Chakravarty, I.: Modelling motion blur in computer-generated images. Comput. Graph. **17**(3), 389–399 (1983)
15. Farrell, J., Xiao, F., Catrysse, P., Wandell, B.: A simulation tool for evaluating digital camera image quality. In: Proceedings of the SPIE International Society for Optical Engineering, vol. 5294, p.124 (2004)
16. Farrell, J., Okincha, M., Parmar, M.: Sensor calibration and simulation. In: Proceedings of the SPIE International Society for Optical Engineering, vol. 6817 (2008)

Object Contour Extraction Based on Merging Photometric Information with Graph Cuts

Rongguo Zhang[1(✉)], Meimei Ren[1], Jing Hu[1], Xiaojun Liu[2], and Kun Liu[2]

[1] School of Computer Science and Technology,
Taiyuan University of Science and Technology, Taiyuan 030024, Shanxi, China
rg_zh@163.com
[2] School of Mechanical and Automotive Engineering,
Hefei University of Technology, Hefei 230009, China
liuxjunhf@163.com

Abstract. Graph cuts algorithm is one of high effective optimal methods in image segmentations. To improve the effect of segmentation caused by uneven illumination, a contour extraction method which merges photometric information with graph cuts is proposed. Firstly, the method gets the color values and brightness values of pixel depending on the color image, represents photometric values with the average of these values. Then, the photometric information is integrated into the energy function of active contour model, and a new energy function is built. Finally, we can get the optimal solution for solving new energy function with max-flow/min-cut algorithm, obtain global and local contours of the target object. Experimental results show that the proposed method can make initial contour convergence to the target object more accurately and faster.

Keywords: Photometric information · Energy function · Graph cuts · Contour extraction

1 Introduction

Image segmentation is a key issue in image processing, pattern recognition and computer vision. It is to make full use of the color, brightness, texture and shape feature information. Through image segmentation, the image is divided into a plurality of small areas. So that, image has some identical or similar characteristics in the same region, and has larger differences between different regions. Contour extraction can be understood as the image region of interest to the user to be split, and then extract the contour of the object target. The accuracy of the segmentation results directly affects image analysis and contour extraction. However, because of the influence of illumination, the reflection of object's surface and other aspects, the results of segmentation often appear deviation. Thus, the segmentation of non-uniform illumination on image has become an important research topic in recent years.

For various methods of image segmentation, people put forward different classifications from different view. According to two basic properties of the image– non continuity and homogeneity [1], people can realize image segmentation. Non continuity refers to a sudden change in gray level, so it can be detected by dot, line and side

© Springer International Publishing Switzerland 2015
Y.-J. Zhang (Ed.): ICIG 2015, Part II, LNCS 9218, pp. 584–599, 2015.
DOI: 10.1007/978-3-319-21963-9_54

to complete image segmentation. Homogeneity is refers to the similarity in the region of the gray level, so it can be cut by thresholding, clustering, region growing and region merging and splitting method to realize segmentation. Some methods are presented by the literature [2]. Using these methods, the image can be segmented based on the image space method, feature space method and the physical characteristics method, Lucchese has made very good summary in the literature [2].

Traditional image segmentation methods, such as threshold, edge detection, region growing, splitting and merging, although simple, shortcut, but poor robustness, are easy to leak in weak point of boundary. The pertinence of these methods is strong. With the rapid development of computer technology, people not only hope to be able to develop segmentation methods more efficient, robust, but also hope to find a general unified framework for these methods.

In recent years, people put forward the framework of image segmentation based on energy minimization. The framework can fuse the upper visual information and context information, in order to get better segmentation of interesting targets. Its basic feature is to construct an energy function, then according to the energy function, select the appropriate optimization technology, which makes the function minimization. According to the continuity of energy function method based on the framework, image segmentation methods can be divided into two categories [3].

(1) The optimization is defined on the functional of a continuous contour or surface. This kind of method is a continuous functional to infinity in space R. It uses the variational method, gradient descent method and other optimization technology to optimize energy function. The basis of its value calculation is mainly the finite difference, finite element method. The method mainly comprises the snake, geodesic active contour model [4–10], regional competition and some segmentation method based on level set method [11–15]. Its characteristics are: The continuous functional integrates region and boundary information to segment the target, some properties of these information are formed by the geometric expression [16, 17]. Optimization technology of the method can only ensure that local optimal variable values for the energy function, cannot get the global optimization.

(2) The cost function is defined on a discrete variable set optimization. This kind of method is directly transformed the problem into a combinatorial optimization in finite dimensional integer space, and using dynamic programming, maximum flow minimum cut algorithm to optimize. The methods mainly include the path based method and graph cuts method. The path based method uses dynamic programming to calculate the optimal path, such as intelligent scissors [18] and live-wire [19] using the Dijkstra algorithm, DP-snake [20] algorithm using Viterbi algorithm. Its characteristics are: the boundary information can be naturally expressed very well, but it is difficult for regional information expression [21]. Because the three dimensional goal cannot be used to describe the path, so the segmentation problem was defined in the two dimensional space.

The method based on graph cuts can be very good to overcome the above shortcomings, not only the problem can be extended to the N dimension space, but also provides a general cost function. Region and boundary information and some topological restrictions can naturally add into the cost function. The graph cuts theory is introduced into the field of computer vision for the first time by Yuri Boykov and Maric-Pierre Jolly [22, 23]. They put forward and realized a method that using the max-flow/min-cut algorithm [24] to minimize the energy function and then gain the contour of object. Many researchers proposed different segmentation methods for the shortcoming of graph cuts algorithm. Rother et al. put forward GrabCut algorithm [25], which is better currently a method to extract the target. Liu et al. propose a method of interactive graph cuts in [26]. Jain et al. extract object contour by predicting sufficient annotation strength model based on graph cuts theory [27]. Literature [28] use super-pixel Gaussian model to build graph cuts model to improve the efficiency of the graph cuts algorithm. Wang et al. combine fuzzy C-means clustering algorithm with graph cuts to segment image [29]. Liu et al. combine graph cuts theory and wavelet transform algorithm to improve the efficiency and quality of the graph cuts segmentation and improve shrinking bias phenomena that occur during the extraction [30]. Xu et al. proposed an active contour algorithm based on graph cuts (GCBAC) theory since the traditional active contour algorithm is easy to fall into local optimum [31]. Zhang et al. put forward active contour edge method based on conjugate gradient B-spline [32]. Zheng et al. use active contour algorithm based on graph cuts to achieve the selective extraction of local and global contours [33].

Based on the work mentioned above, we present a novel contour extraction method which merges photometric information into the energy function, and construct a new energy function. The photometric information of pixels in the image is expressed with the mean values of the brightness information and color information of the image. The gray values of pixels are replaced by the photometric information of pixels. This method uses the maximum flow/minimum cut algorithm to enable initial contour converge to the target profile, finally extracts global contour of image object. Then using partial segmentation method, the average values of luminosity in each local area of the image are obtained. Adjusting the value of illumination, the appropriate threshold of photometric in an area of image is selected. Against the problem of the target surface of image with different brightness, it can be assigned with different photometric thresholds in different surface, and can achieve the accurate local contour of the subject image with little light on it. The method is based on active contour model and graph cuts algorithm, can overcome the shortcomings occurred in previous literatures. This algorithm integrates luminosity information into the energy function, expands the scope of application. The experiment results demonstrate that the method can extract the global contour and local contour selectively more accurately and faster for more images.

2   Basic Theory and Method

2.1   Basic Theory of Active Contours

We know that C is a closed subset in Ω which is made up of a finite set of smooth curves, if Ω_i denotes the connected components of $\Omega \backslash C$, then the segmentation problems in computer vision can be defined as follows: give an image I_0, find a decomposition Ω_i of Ω and an optimal piecewise smooth approximation I of I_0, such that

I varies smoothly with each Ω_i, and rapidly or discontinuously across the boundaries of Ω_i. So the curve evolution formulation based on active contours model can be represented as follow:

$$E_{ACM}(I, C) = \iint_{\Omega} (I - I_0)^2 dxdy$$
$$+ \mu \iint_{\Omega \backslash C} |\nabla I|^2 dxdy \tag{1}$$

Where I_0 is the initial image on Ω to be segmented, I is an piecewise smooth approximation image of I_0 with discontinuities on interface curve C, $|C|$ is the length of C, μ is a positive parameters which control the amount of smoothness.

2.2 Basic Theory of Graph Cuts

The main idea of graphic cuts is: the image is mapped to a network diagram with terminal nodes. Each adjacent pixel in the image is corresponded to the network node in the graph. The weight of edge in the network diagram shows the similarity of adjacent pixels. According to this weight, a suitable energy function is designed. By minimizing the energy function, the image segmentation can be finished, finally achieve the contour of object.

Setting $G = (V, E)$ is an undirected graph. Where, V is a set of vertices, E is a set of edges. In the set of vertices V, connection (x, y) is called an edge e, which have two different directions, i.e., from x to y and from y to x, respectively. It is denoted by (e, x, y) and (e, y, x). Every edge of the network graph G is obtained using this operation. Thus the edge obtained is denoted as E, and define a capacity function c in E. Then graph G and capacity function c form a network is denoted by $N = (G, s, t, c)$. Were s, t are called source and sink. A function $\Phi: E \rightarrow R$ is called a stream of network which meets the following conditions:

(1) $\Phi(e,x,y) = -\Phi(e,y,x)$, for any $(e,x,y) \in E(x \neq y)$;
(2) $\Phi(x,v) = \Sigma(e,x,y) \in E\Phi(e) = 0$, for any $x \in V\backslash\{s,t\}$;
(3) $\Phi(e) \leq c(e)$, for any $e \in E$.

In this case, $\Phi(x, v) = \Sigma(e, x, y) \in E\Phi(e)$ is called flow for the stream Φ. According to Ford-Fulkerson maximum flow/minimum cut theorem, network diagram can obtain the minimum cut by calculating the maximum flow of the network.

3 Construction of New Model

3.1 Photometric Model Establishing

The surface brightness and color rendering are determined by surface radiation to gaze into the eyes. A mathematical model is built to simulate the phenomenon of surface illumination. According to mathematical model, through calculating the surface brightness of radiation to gaze into the eyes, we can get the color and brightness of each pixel in the image.

When light arrives the surface, only the transmitted light and reflected light can be seen by the human's eyes, and produce visual effects, the light absorbed by the object is converted into heat, so the last object rendered in color and brightness is controlled by the transmitted light and reflected light. If the object is opaque, with the absence of transmitted light, the color of the object is only determined by the reflected light. In light model, simple lighting model considers only the reflective case of the surface under the direct rays of light. Simple lighting model is expressed as:

$$I = I_e + I_d + I_s \tag{2}$$

In (2), I expresses that the light intensity of the surface of the object reflect to the viewpoints; I_e indicates the intensity of ambient light; I_d represents the intensity of diffuse light and I_s expresses light intensity of specula reflected.

There are many representations of the color image, such as RGB, color format YCbCr, LAB and HSB. In color format YCbCr, Y represents the image brightness, Cb, Cr represent blue component and yellow component of an image, which represent color degrees of pixel. Integrated color image consists of the three components, the average value of which represented the photometric value of the pixel.

First, we consider the image represented with RGB form, the individual components of YCbCr for each pixel can be obtained using the following equations.

$$\begin{cases} Y = 0.257 \times R + 0.504 \times G + 0.098 \times B + 16 \\ Cb = -0.184 \times R - 0.291 \times G + 0.493 \times B + 128 \\ Cr = 0.439 \times R - 0.368 \times G - 0.071 \times B + 128 \end{cases} \tag{3}$$

Then, L_i represents the photometric value of the pixel I,

$$L_i = (Y_i + Cb_i + Cr_i)/3 \tag{4}$$

Where, Y_i, Cb_i and Cr_i respectively represent lightness, blue component and red component of the pixel i.

3.2   Global Contour Model

Graph cuts is a powerful combinatorial optimization method. It can solve discrete labeling problems by minimizing energy function. The model can be written in the following standard form:

$$E(f) = \sum_{p \in P} D_p(f_p) + \sum_{(p,q) \in N} V_{p,q}(f_p, f_q) \tag{5}$$

Where, f is a labeling function from set of pixels P map to set of labels L. N is a neighborhood system. The term $D_p(f_p)$ is used to measure the penalty of assigning label

f_p to pixel p. The term $V_{p,q}(f_p,f_q)$ is used to measure the penalty of assigning labels f_p, f_q to the pixels p and q.

In this paper, we want to use graph cuts method to optimize the active contour model. The goal is to find a labeling which can minimize the energy function like (5). Now based on continuous active contour model, we rewrite the energy function (1) in discrete form as follows:

$$E = \mu \times E_{smooth}(p,q) + E_{data}(p) \tag{6}$$

Where, μ is the regularizing parameter. $E_{smooth}(p,q)$ is used to measure the extent to which pixels (p,q) are not piecewise smooth. $E_{data}(p)$ is used to measure the disagreement between pixel p and the observed data.

Taking into account the impact caused by the photometric value of the image, the final contour of object should be inaccurate, and existing methods only consider removing the shaded area to get the overall outline of the image. This paper attempts to integrate photometric information into energy function based on active contour model and graph cuts, in order to improve the method proposed in literature [33] about splitting the images affected large by light. Since the regularizing parameter μ in energy (6) is used to balance the edge and region terms. It often influences the segmentation results. In order to simplify the problem, we set the regularizing parameter μ as a constant value 1, then energy function can be written as:

$$E = E_{smooth}(p,q) \times E_{data}(p,q) \tag{7}$$

Where, $E_{data}(p,q)$ indicates the penalty for assigning pixels p and q different labels.

$$E_{smooth}(p,q) = \sum_{p,q \in \Omega} \sum_{p \in N(q)} \frac{\omega_{pq} \times ((1 - x_p)x_q + x_p(1 - x_q)}{1 + \beta|I(p) - I(q)|}$$
$$E_{data}(p,q) = \sum_p Min((I_{ps} + I_{qt}), (I_{pt} + I_{qs})) \tag{8}$$

Where, $\beta > 0$ is a scaling parameter, pixel p is in the vicinity of pixel q, i.e. $N(q)$, N denotes a 4-connected neighborhood, and $\omega_{pq} = \sigma^2 \Delta\theta_{pq}/|e_{pq}|$ with the angular differences $\Delta\theta_{pq}$ between the nearest edge lines and the length$|e_{pq}|$ of edge e_{pq}. I_{ps}, I_{qt}, I_{pt}, and I_{qs} can be calculated as follow

$$I_{ps} = (I(p) - c_s)^2; I_{qt} = (I(q) - c_t)^2$$
$$I_{pt} = (I(p) - c_t)^2; I_{qs} = (I(q) - c_s)^2 \tag{9}$$

In (9), c_s and c_t can be calculated by formula (10) based on the corresponding relations in Table 1. Figure 1 shows the RGB color value corresponding to the pixel position in Table 1. $I(p)$ is the photometric information of the pixel p:

Table 1. The conversion process of color pixel values

Pixel number	R	G	B	Gray value	Photometric value	S/T	x_p(1/0)	B/O
1	101	98	79	97	116.32	S	0	B
2	210	208	211	209	151.06	T	1	O
3	176	180	183	179	141.94	T	1	O
4	67	66	46	64	106.64	S	0	B
5	47	56	35	51	101.79	S	0	B
6	98	91	72	91	115.05	S	0	B
7	47	48	32	46	101.74	S	0	B
8	219	214	220	216	153.79	T	1	O
9	205	203	206	204	149.62	T	1	O

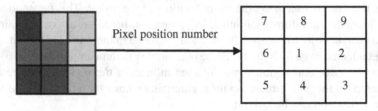

Fig. 1. RGB color value corresponding to the pixel position number (Color figure online)

$$c_s = (\sum_p I(p)(1 - x_p))/(\sum_p (1 - x_p))$$

$$c_t = (\sum_p I(p)x_p)/(\sum_p x_p)$$
(10)

According to Table 1 and formula (7), the network graph can be constructed. The weights of edges connecting neighboring pixel nodes are assigned as $E_{smooth}(p,q) \times E_{data}(p,q)$; for terminals S/T links, if the following definition for each pixel p is true

$$I_{ps} > I_{pt} + |I_{ps} - I_{pt}|/2$$
(11)

Then add link pT with a big weight. if the following definition for each pixel p is true

$$I_{pt} > I_{ps} + |I_{ps} - I_{pt}|/2$$
(12)

Then add link Sp with a big weight.

3.3   Local Contour Model

In general, we conduct the research to the image, not on the entire image, but further on a part of an image. Therefore, the research on local image segmentation has more practical significance. We study on the image of the object surfaces with different luminosities, each face contour can be extracted by changing photometric values of image intensity. From previous analysis, we know that every pixel value of local area in the image can be calculated as follow:

$$c_s(\phi) = \frac{\int_\Omega u_0(x,y) H_\varepsilon(\phi(x,y)) dxdy}{\int_\Omega H_\varepsilon(\phi(x,y)) dxdy}$$

$$c_t(\phi) = \frac{\int_\Omega u_0(x,y)(1 - H_\varepsilon(\phi(x,y))) dxdy}{\int_\Omega (1 - H_\varepsilon(\phi(x,y))) dxdy} \tag{13}$$

To obtain surface contour extraction in the image based on photometric information, photometric value is as follow.

$$L(i,j) = \begin{cases} c_s & L(i,j) > c_{thl} \\ c_t & otherwise \end{cases} \tag{14}$$

Where, (i, j) represents image position of the pixel. c_{thl} represents threshold value of the c_s. $L(i, j)$ represents photometric value of the image pixel in the position (i, j).

After converted graph cuts format, every average photometric value of local area can be calculated as follow:

$$c_{ls} = \left(\sum_p L(p)(1 - x_p)\right) / \left(\sum_p (1 - x_p)\right)$$

$$c_{lt} = \left(\sum_p L(p)x_p\right) / \left(\sum_p x_p\right) \tag{15}$$

Then use the following local energy equation to extract evolution contours.

$$E_l = E_{lsmooth}(p,q) \times E_{ldata}(p,q) \tag{16}$$

Where $E_{lsmooth}$ and E_{ldata} can be calculator as following

$$E_{lsmooth}(p,q) = \sum_{p,q \in \Omega} \sum_{p \in N(q)} \frac{\omega_{pq} \times ((1 - x_p)x_q + x_p(1 - x_q)}{1 + \beta|L(p) - L(q)|}$$

$$E_{ldata}(p,q) = \sum_p Min((L_{ps} + L_{qt}), (L_{pt} + L_{qs})) \tag{17}$$

$L_{ps}, L_{qt}, L_{pt},$ and L_{qs} can be calculated as following

$$L_{ps} = (L(p) - c_{ls})^2; L_{qt} = (L(q) - c_{lt})^2$$

$$I_{pt} = (L(p) - c_{lt})^2; L_{qs} = (L(q) - c_{ls})^2 \tag{18}$$

For terminals S/T links, we have the following definitions

$$L_{ps} > L_{pt} + | L_{ps} - L_{pt} | / 2 \qquad (19)$$

And

$$I_{pt} > I_{ps} + | I_{ps} - I_{pt} | / 2 \qquad (20)$$

For each pixel p, if the definition (19) is true and xp is 1, then add link pT with a big weight. if the definition (20) is true and xp is 0, then add link Sp with a big weight.

4 Experimental Results and Analysis

With the above algorithm, we will respectively carry on experiments with light affected on different initial contour curves. Experimental platforms are as follow. Operating system is Win7, development tool is Matlab R2012a. Main parameters of computer hardware are CPU: Intel (R) Core (TM) i3, RAM: 2G. On these platforms, four color images are used to test global contour extraction. Two color images are used to test local contour extraction.

4.1 Global Contour Extraction

Four color images are illustrated in Fig. 2. First row is the process for synthetic image, second row is the process for lotus image, third row is the process for sand pot image, fourth row is the process for stone image. The images in Fig. 2(a) and (b) represent the original image and the initial contour line. Figure 2(c) and (d) are respectively the results of the original algorithm for image not affected by light and the proposed algorithm for image affected by light.

Table 2 is the effect comparison of segmentation for illumination influence images. It shows that the perimeter of the target is represented by the number of pixels of the contour line, and the area of the target is represented by the number of pixels in the contours, with which to compare the effect of segmentation. The target perimeter and area obtained by proposed method are close to the original from the data in Table 2. It can be seen from Fig. 2 also, the contour obtained by the original method is not the exact contour of the object, but also part of the target.

Table 3 is the efficiency comparison of segmentation for illumination influence images in the above experiments. The ratio of the target perimeter and area of the original algorithm and the proposed method against that of the desired target, represents the results of image segmentation. The time in Table 3 represents the segmentation efficiency. It can be seen from the image called stone in Fig. 2, the more complex the background image, the more extraction time. It can be seen from the data of Table 3 that, the results obtained from proposed method are close to the ideal result, and the error is about 1 %.

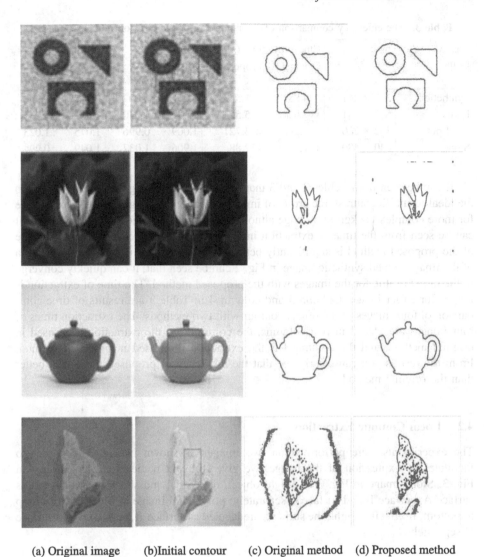

(a) Original image   (b)Initial contour   (c) Original method   (d) Proposed method

Fig. 2. The comparison of segmentation result for illumination influence image

Table 2. The effect comparison of segmentation for illumination influence images

Image name	The ideal state		The original method		The proposed method	
	Perimeter (pl_0)	Area (as_0)	Perimeter (pl_1)	Area (as_1)	Perimeter (pl_2)	Area (as_2)
Synthetic	8251	84560	8536	84263	8269	84465
Lotus	3539	84014	3855	86553	3825	86582
Sand pot	5915	18166	5967	19534	5893	18588
Stone	5474	211970	10436	222267	5676	210611

Table 3. The efficiency comparison of segmentation for illumination influence images

Image Name	Image Size	Efficiency (time (s))		Results			
		Original	Proposed	$pl_1/$ pl_0	$pl_2/$ pl_0	$as_1/$ as_0	$as_2/$ as_0
Synthetic	349 × 261	4.859	1.543	1.035	1.002	0.997	0.998
Lotus	517 × 341	7.624	5.567	1.089	1.030	1.081	1.031
Sand pot	392 × 280	5.299	4.721	1.009	0.996	1.075	1.023
Stone	640 × 480	171.99	152.88	1.906	1.037	1.049	0.994

It can be seen from Tables 2 and 3 that the results of two algorithms are similar to the ideal result. In contrast, the errors of image called lotus is large, so the error is large for more complex background image although contour of an object can be obtained; It can be seen from the time of extraction in Table 3 that the speed of the convergence of the proposed method is significantly better than the original method. From the data of the image named synthetic image in Fig. 2 can be seen that, it can quickly converge to the target profile for the images with the proposed method. The time of extraction is longer for larger image. Column 3 and column 4 in Table 3 are results of time comparison of four images of the object contour with two methods. The extraction times of four images are placed in two columns, the column 3 is the extraction time used in original method, and the column 4 is the extraction time used in proposed method. From the results you can clearly see that the efficiency of proposed method is better than the original method.

4.2 Local Contour Extraction

The experiments were performed on two images as shown in Fig. 3. In order to facilitate the expression of the image, we give different names for each surface in Fig. 3. Stone image in Fig. 3(a), bright object, dark side, and shadows are labeled as surface A, surface B and surface C separately; polyhedral image in Fig. 3(b), from top to bottom, from left to right, the surfaces are labeled as surface A, surface B and surface C separately.

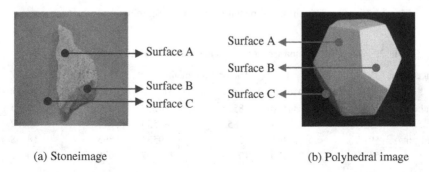

(a) Stoneimage   (b) Polyhedral image

Fig. 3. The images to be processed

Table 4. The average photometric value of the local surface

Image name	Image size	Foreground/Background	Average photometric value		
			Surface A	Surface B	Surface C
Stone	640 × 480	C_s	171.799	141.967	142.020
		C_t	168.095	134.755	137.828
Polyhedron	500 × 375	C_s	145.547	200.331	96.619
		C_t	110.702	109.142	111.607

Using the formula (13), we can get different average photometric values as target surface calculation results of foreground and background values. As shown in Table 4, shows the average photometric value of the local surface in different images, the foreground average brightness value C_s and background average brightness value C_t.

Now on the average photometric values obtained in the previous section analysis, we take the name stone image in Fig. 3(a) as an example to conduct a detailed analysis.

Figure 4 is a process of local contour extraction for the stone image in Fig. 3(a). From Table 4, we can get some results just like following. When using surface A as target, the average photometric value of surface A is 171.799, the average photometric value of other remaining part of the surface is 168.095. When the surface B for the prospects, the average photometric value of surface B is 142.020, the average photometric value similarly in other parts of the surface is 137.828. The average photometric value of surface C is 141.967, the average photometric value of the other part of the surface is 134.755. Now to obtain the surface A in the image contour extraction based on photometric information, the image of the photometric value is as follow according to the previous analysis.

$$L(i,j) = \begin{cases} 171.799 & L(i,j) > 170 \\ 168.095 & otherwise \end{cases} \tag{21}$$

Where, (i, j) represents the pixels in the image position; $L(i, j)$ represents (i, j) pixel photometric value.

Because the photometric values of surface B and surface C are close, so need for two groups of photometric data to change a pixel value, and then extract the contours. The photometric value of surface B and C can be obtained respectively according to following equations.

$$L(i,j) = \begin{cases} 134.755 & L(i,j) < 137.828 \\ 141.967 & otherwise \end{cases} \tag{22}$$

$$L(i,j) = \begin{cases} 142.020 & L(i,j) > 141.967 \\ 137.828 & otherwise \end{cases} \tag{23}$$

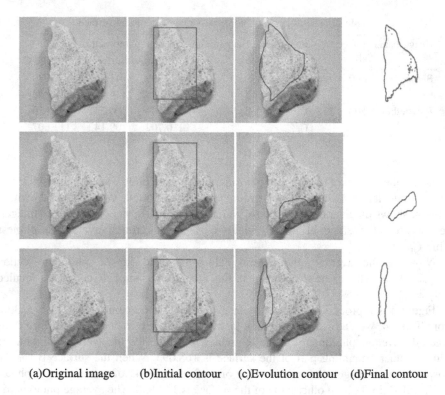

(a)Original image   (b)Initial contour   (c)Evolution contour   (d)Final contour

Fig. 4. Local contour extraction for the stone image

According to the process of local contour extraction of the pictures above, the extraction results are shown in Fig. 4. First row is the process of local contour extraction for surface A. Second row is the process of local contour extraction for surface B. Third row is the process of local contour extraction for surface C.

Figure 5 is the result of partial contour extraction of the image polyhedron. As can be seen from the figure, the proposed method may be the local contour extraction image accurately. Because the map polygon A has three surface photometric values, but they are very closely, so in the contour extraction, can obtain one surface contour. Surface B and surface C have different photometric values, so can accurately obtain the contour lines separately. In Fig. 5, first row is the process of local contour extraction for surface A. Second row is the process of local contour extraction for surface B. Third row is the process of local contour extraction for surface C. Therefore, the difference of the image photometric value is more big, the proposed method can obtain more accurate local contour.

The photometric values of other pictures can be processed using same method. The contour extraction of the processed image can be done using previous method.

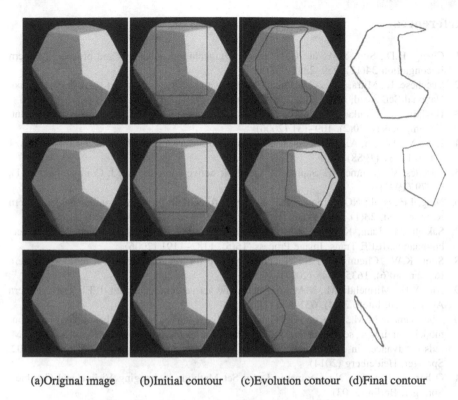

(a)Original image   (b)Initial contour   (c)Evolution contour (d)Final contour

Fig. 5. Local contour extraction for the polyhedron image

5 Conclusions

In this paper, photometric information is integrated into the energy function, with active contour model based on graph cuts to extract contour of the object. We can see that it has certain constraints for complex background images in global division. Therefore, to improve the method again, and expand the use of the method, the local division is used in the next contents of this paper. The method can extract contours of selective part of the image, such as bright side part, the shaded part and the dark side part. It can be seen from the results that regardless of the image large or little affected by light, the proposed method can obtain more accurate contour, and the proposed algorithm is better than the original algorithm in convergence time.

Acknowledgement. This work was financially supported by National Natural Science Foundation of China (51375132), Shanxi Provincial Natural Science Foundation (2013011017), Jincheng Science and Technology Foundation (201501004-5), Ph.D Foundation of Taiyuan University of Science and Technology (20122025).

References

1. Cheng, H.D., Sun, Y., et al.: Color image segmentation: advances and prospects. Pattern Recongnition **34**(12), 259–2281 (2001)
2. Lucchese, L., Mitra, S.K.: Color Image segmentation: a state-of-the-art survey. Proc. Indian National Sci. Acad. **67**(2), 207–221 (2001)
3. Boykov, Y., Funka-Lea, G.: Graph cuts and efficient N-D image segmentation. Int. J. Comput. Vis. **70**(2), 109–131 (2006)
4. Kass, M., Witkin, A., Terzopoulos, D.: Snakes: active contour models. Int. J. Comput. Vis. **1** (4), 321–331 (1988)
5. Caselles, V., Kimmel, R., Sapiro, G.: Geodesic active contours. Int. J. Comput. Vis. **22**(1), 61–79 (1997)
6. Ning, J.F., et al.: NGVF: an improved external force field for active contour model. Pattern Recogn. Lett. **28**(1), 58–63 (2007)
7. Sakalli, M., Lam, K.M., Yan, H.: A faster converging snake algorithm to locate object boundaries. IEEE Trans. Image Process. **15**(5), 1182–1191 (2006)
8. Sum, K.W., Cheung, P.Y.S.: Boundary vector for parametric active contours. Pattern Recogn. **40**(6), 1635–1645 (2007)
9. Xie, X.H., Mirmehdi, M.: MAC: magnetostatic active contour model. IEEE Trans. Pattern Anal. Mach. Intell. **30**(4), 632–646 (2008)
10. Abdelsamea, M.M., Gnecco, G., Gaber, M.M.: A survey of *SOM*-based active contour models for image segmentation. In: Villmann, T., Schleif, F.-M., Kaden, M., Lange, M. (eds.) Advances in Self-Organizing Maps and Learning. AISC, vol. 295, pp. 293–302. Springer, Heidelberg (2014)
11. Osher, S., Paragios, N.: Geometric Level Set Methods in Imaging Vision, and Graphics. Springer, Berlin (2003)
12. Lie, J., Lysaker, M., Tai, X.C.: A binary level set model and some applications for mumford-shah image segmentation. IEEE Trans. Image Process. **15**(5), 1171–1181 (2006)
13. Zhang, K., Zhang, L., Song, H., Zhang, D.: Reinitialization-free level set evolution via reaction diffusion. IEEE Trans. Image Process. **22**(1), 258–271 (2013)
14. Tai, X.C., Li, H.W.: A piecewise constant level set methods for elliptic inverse problems. Appl. Numer. Math. **57**(5–7), 686–696 (2007)
15. Zhang, R.G., Yang, L., Liu, K.: Moving objective detection and its contours extraction using level set method. In: International Conference on Control Engineering and Communication Technology, Shenyang, China, pp. 778–781 (2012)
16. Yezzi, A.J., Kichenassarny, S., Kumar, A., et al.: A geometric snake model for segmentation of medical. IEEE Trans. Med. Imaging **16**(2), 199–209 (1997)
17. Vasilevskiy, A., Siddiqi, K.: Flux maximizing geometric flows. IEEE Trans. Pattern Anal. Mach. Intell. **24**(12), 1565–1578 (2002)
18. Mortensen, E.N., Barrett, W.A.: Interactive segmentation with iintelligent scissors. Graph. Models Image Process. **60**, 349–384 (1998)
19. Falcao, A.X., Udupa, J.K., Samarasekera, S., et al.: User-steered image segmentation paradigms: live wire and live lane. Graph. Models Image Process. **60**, 233–260 (1998)
20. Amini, A.A., Weymouth, T.E., Jain, R.C.: Using dynamic programming for solving variational problems in vision. IEEE Trans. Pattern Anal. Mach. Intell. **12**(9), 855–867 (1990)
21. Jermyn, I., Ishikawa, H.: Globally optimal regions and boundaries. In: International Conference on Computer Vision, II, pp. 904–910 (1999)

22. Boykov, Y.Y., Jolly, M.P.: Interactive graph cuts for optimal boundary & region segmentation of objects in ND images. In: Proceedings of the IEEE International Conference on Computer Vision, II, pp. 105–112 (2001)
23. Boykov, Y.Y., Funka-Lea, G.: Graph cuts and efficient ND image segmentation. Int. J. Comput. Vis. **70**(2), 109–131 (2006)
24. Boykov, Y.Y., Kolmogorov, V.: An experimental comparison of min-cut/max-flow algorithms for energy minimization in vision. IEEE Trans. Pattern Anal. Mach. Intell. **26**(9), 1124–1137 (2004)
25. Rother, C., Kolmogorov, V., Blake, A.: Grabcut: Interactive foreground extraction using iterated graph cuts. ACM Trans. Graph. **23**(3), 309–314 (2004)
26. Liu, J., Wang, H.Q.: An interactive image segmentation method based on graph cuts. J. Electron. Inf. Technol. **30**(8), 1973–1976 (2008)
27. Jain, S.D., Grauman, K.: Predicting sufficient annotation strength for interactive foreground Segmentation. In: Proceedings of the IEEE International Conference on Computer Vision, pp. 1–8 (2013)
28. Han, S.D., Zhao, Y., Tao, W.B., et al.: Gaussian super-pixel based fast image segmentation using graph cuts. Acta Automatica Sinica. **37**(1), 11–20 (2011)
29. Wang, X.F., Guo, M.: Image segmentation approach of combining fuzzy clustering and graph cuts. J. Comput. Aplications **29**(7), 1918–1920 (2009)
30. Liu, Y., Feng, G.F., Jiang, X.Y., et al.: Color image segmentation based on wavelet transform and graph cuts. J. Chin. Comput. Syst. **10**(10), 2307–2310 (2012)
31. Xu, N., Ahuja, N., Bansal, R.: Object segmentation using graph cuts based active contours. Comput. Vis. Image Underst. **107**(3), 210–224 (2007)
32. Zhang, R.G., Liu, X.J., Liu, K., et al.: B-spline active contours boundary extraction based on conjugate gradient vector. J. Image Graph. **15**(1), 103–108 (2010)
33. Zheng, Q., Dong, E.Q., Cao, Z.L.: Graph cuts based active contour model with selective local or global segmentation. Electron. Lett. **48**(9), 490–491 (2012)

Object-Based Multi-mode
SAR Image Matching

Jie Rui[1,2,3]([⊠]), Chao Wang[1], Hong Zhang[1], Bo Zhang[1], Fan Wang[3],
and Fei Jin[3]

[1] Institute of Remote Sensing and Digital Earth,
Chinese Academy of Sciences, Beijing, China
ruijie@radi.ac.cn
[2] University of Chinese Academy of Sciences, Beijing, China
[3] Zhengzhou Institute of Surveying and Mapping, Zhengzhou, China

Abstract. Owing to the effect of imaging mechanism and imaging conditions in synthetic aperture radar (SAR) image, inconsistent features and relationship correspondence constitute key problems using traditional image matching algorithms because of significant differences between the images. This study proposes an object-based SAR image matching method. Two images are matched through same ground objects, by means of property and shape information of objects, which are obtained via object extraction and morphological operations. We utilize a shape context descriptor to compare contours of objects and detected invariant control points. The experimental results show that the proposed method achieves reliable and stable matching performance, and can alleviate deformation and nonlinear distortion effects of different systems.

Keywords: Image matching · Object-based · Shape matching · Shape context

1 Introduction

Image matching technology is an extremely important modern information processing technology, especially in the field of image processing, to integrate multisource and multitemporal data. It has been widely used in multispectral classification, object recognition, image fusion, change detection, image mosaicking, image sequence analysis, and cartography updating.

Image matching focuses on searching similar objects or scenes in mass images. It is different to image registration, which focuses on geometrically aligning two images of the same scene. Most methods of both image matching and image registration are same because both need to find similar features in images, except the differences of emphasis on search strategy and geometric precision. Image matching is considered to be pre-processing or preliminary work for image registration in most applications, primarily because relationship of features or objects between different images is difficult to establish, which is usually referred to as correspondence problem in literatures. Although a lot of work has been done, automatic image matching still remains an open problem. Until now, it is still rare to find a rapid, robust, and automatic image matching method, and most existing image matching methods are designed for particular

© Springer International Publishing Switzerland 2015
Y.-J. Zhang (Ed.): ICIG 2015, Part II, LNCS 9218, pp. 600–610, 2015.
DOI: 10.1007/978-3-319-21963-9_55

applications. The performance of a methodology is always limited to a specific application, or sensor characteristics and the terrain characteristic of the imaged area [1].

2 Image Matching

Image matching methods can be broadly classified into two main categories: area-based and feature-based. Area-based methods measure region correlation directly using information of image intensities, e.g., correlation coefficient (CC), mutual information (MI), without any structural analysis. Consequently, they are sensitive to the intensity changes and have large amount of data to be processed. The limitations are optimal size of window and nonlinear transformation between two images. Feature-based methods do not consider the pixel grey values as a primitive to correlate, but extract other structural information (e.g. points, edges, linear structures, regions) [2, 3]. The feature-based methods have relative small computation, and the distinguished advantages are high reliability and speed, which are more appropriate for areas with poor information. The drawback of the feature-based methods is that the respective features might be hard to detect and/or unstable in time.

Sophisticated approaches have been developed based on multi-features or multi-layer feature [4]. Meanwhile, matching methods using both area-based and feature-based approaches simultaneously are received more attention [5, 6]. The integrated methods mainly include two steps: roughly match images based on feature extraction, and further improve reliability and precision based on correlation-like method. Moreover, some optimization approaches (e.g. Genetic algorithm, colony optimization) and matching strategies (e.g. tree/graph matching) also be used in matching process [7, 8].

The significant differences between the multisource images and most of the inherent speckle noise in the SAR images appear when matching multi-mode SAR images due to different imaging mechanisms and imaging conditions. For multisource imagery, the texture and grey levels at the location of conjugate positions will not likely be similar. Consequently, relationships between extracted points or lines features in different images will be difficult to establish, which cannot be solved perfectly through the sophisticated methods or optimization approaches.

The features extracted automatically using computer vision techniques are mostly low-level features (e.g. point, edge, color, texture), which is coarse understanding of image scenes. Although low-level features can accurately be extracted by various methods, they cannot readily be utilized to describe human visual perception of an image. Human beings tend to use high-level features, such as objects, scenes, to interpret images and measure their similarity. Objects and scenes are real understanding of image semantics [9]. For remote sensing images, semantic perception focusses on objects rather than scenes in most applications. At present, a lot of research is about the object-based methods in computer vision and pattern recognition, e.g., content-based image retrieval (CBIR) [10, 11]. In the field of remote sensing, image segmentation, classification, and change detection using object-based methods has attracted much attention [12]. Very little research has explored the topic in image matching. Object extraction using segmentation technology and shape matching between complex and incomplete contours of objects are key problems. Some earlier literatures [13, 14] exploit special objects (e.g. water regions, roads) for image matching, however, the purpose is only to detect distinct points (e.g., corners, centroids, intersections) as control point candidates. References [15, 16] exploit homogeneous closed region for multisource image matching and only edge or shape feature is used. In other words, these methods do not use semantic features of images and still belong to conventional feature-based methods.

In this paper, a novel object-based matching method is proposed. Obvious ground objects are extracted and two images are matched based on same objects or scenes by means of property and shape information of these objects, which belongs to high-level semantic features of images. We are interested in the application of object-based method and focus on robust shape matching algorithm. Curve smoothing, shape matching, and other related technology are used in matching process. The method has reliable and stable matching performance, and can alleviate the effect of deformation (rotation, translation, and scale) and nonlinear distortion caused by different sensors and different incident angles.

3   Proposed Method

3.1   Rationale

The idea of using ground objects for matching sensed images originally came from human visual perception where fast recognition between two images is compared via obvious ground objects. These ground objects are processed as integral object, and subsequently, properties, geometry information, and relations between different objects are combined and comprehensively utilized. Contours of objects in different images are not completely coincident and have local difference due to various reasons, especially in multisource imagery. It is not a problem since similar objects can be matched by its main body (Fig. 1a). In contrast, meaningless points or lines are very difficult to establish the relationship, especially in the case of different number (Fig. 1b). Obviously, a great number of points or lines may be a more difficult problem, which is so-called correspondence problem mentioned previously.

(a)   (b)

Fig. 1. (a) Objects are easy to match even with local deformations. (b) Points (centroids of lakes) are difficult to match.

The key advantage of the proposed method is that extracted objects include some properties (e.g., category, contour length, size, etc.) and these properties are also used for matching. This is main difference, also important difference, from the methods based on simple shape information. The ground objects, as high-level semantic features, are real understanding of images. In this sense, the proposed method can be considered as high-level image processing based on image interpretation, accords with human visual perception. Thus, stability and reliability of object-based matching method exceed the traditional methods based on meaningless point, line and edge features.

Compared with point or line features, the object-based matching method has distinct advantages. Information content of objects is huge and information content is a well-known criterion to judge about the feature distinctiveness. The most important point is that correspondence problem can be easily solved by conjugate object pairs. Moreover, the number of objects extracted from images is very small and the search space is restricted to same category, e.g., lake-to-lake, vegetation-to-vegetation. It can rapidly reduces the computation of searching and avoids false matching between similar shapes from different category, e.g. lake and vegetation.

3.2   Matching Process

The proposed matching method is divided into three steps.

(1) Objects extraction. First, the interest ground objects, e.g., lake, river, road, village, and vegetation, are extracted from the reference and the sensed image, respectively. The objects with different category use different segmentation algorithms. The extracted objects are marked with its category. Morphological Processing and data vectorization should be used to get shapes of objects.

(2) Object matching. All properties (e.g., category, contour length, size) are used for object coarse matching. Shape processing is essential for shape matching and curve smoothing can reduce the difference of object shapes in different images. Then, object shapes between two datasets are compared one by one based on shape context descriptor. Of course, the shape matching is limited to same category, e.g., lake-to-lake, vegetation-to-vegetation. The two shapes matched successfully are conjugate object pairs.

(3) Geometric transformation. Control points are selected from conjugate object pairs and the transformation estimation is solved via the least squares technique based on these control points. Matching precision is evaluated by computing residual error of check points.

The flowchart of the proposed method is presented in Fig. 2.

3.3   Shape Matching Using Shape Context

Shape is an important visual feature of an image, which provide most easy and obvious recognition information. However, shape matching is still a challenging task, especially, the objects in the sensed images often have a complex irregular shapes. The key

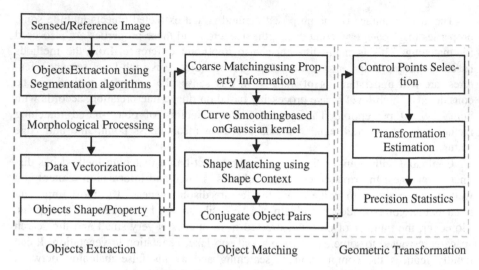

Fig. 2. Image matching flowchart.

point is to develop an appropriate descriptor to characterize the object shape and tolerate local deformations simultaneously. Therefore, the robust matching method for variform objects in remote sensing images is required.

Although numerous shape representation and analysis methods based on contour information exist, the most suitable tool to use for object contours is the shape context [17]. The shape context at a reference point captures the distribution of remaining points relative to it, thus generating a globally discriminative characterization. The shape context uses a log-polar histogram of coordinates and is tolerant of local deformations. The shape context can be used to quickly match a search for similar shapes via recognition.

For a point p_i on the shape, the histogram h_i is defined to be the shape context as follows

$$h_i(k) = \#\{q \neq p_i : (q - p_i) \in bin(k)\} \tag{1}$$

Where $k \in \{1, 2, \ldots, K\}$ and K is the number of histogram bins. We use 5 bins for polar radius *and* 12 bins for polar angle. $(q - p_i) \in bin(k)$ means that the vector originating from p_i to another point q belongs to the k th bin.

Note visual similarities among shape contexts shown in Fig. 3. Corresponding points on two same shapes will have similar shape contexts (Fig. 3a and c), enabling us to solve for correspondences as an optimal assignment problem, also can be used for shape similarity measurement.

The shape context descriptor is based on the characteristics of histogram, and the $\chi 2$ test statistics is used to measure the difference of two points. The cost of matching two points is defined as

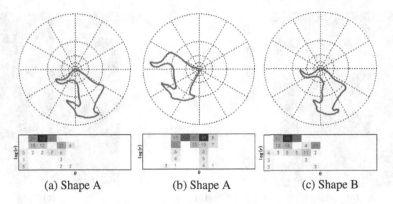

(a) Shape A   (b) Shape A   (c) Shape B

Fig. 3. Sampled edge points of two contours and example histogram of shape contexts.

$$C_{ij} = C\left(p_i, q_j\right) = \frac{1}{2}\sum \frac{\left[h_i(k) - h_j(k)\right]^2}{h_i(k) + h_j(k)} \tag{2}$$

where p_i is a point on the first shape and q_j is a point on the second shape. $h_i(k)$ and $h_j(k)$ denote the K-bin normalized histogram at p_i and q_j, respectively.

For p_i, traversing all points of the second shape and computing the point-to-point cost, the minimum value (which is less than the threshold) corresponding to the point is the matched point. Similarly, we can get the matching point of q_j.Two points are best paired if they correspond to one another.

In this case, the shape context descriptor is only used to match conjugate pairs of object contours between the two datasets, i.e., to find similar contours, regardless of correspondence between the points of the two shapes. In the design of our algorithm, two contours to determine whether similar based on matched point, that is to say that most are paired case, for example, more than 2/3, can be considered that the two contours are similar. While conventional algorithms compute shape similarities based on the shape context, such computations are complex and the threshold of similarity is difficult to determine. The proposed algorithm is simple to compute and presents a suitable similarity threshold, as few contours in different objects are similar.

4   Experimental Results

Two SAR satellite remote sensing image in Beijing, China, are used for our experiment. Radarsat-2 image, acquired in 2008 with the spatial resolution of 1.5 m, is regarded as the reference image. TerraSAR image, acquired in 2011 with the spatial resolution of 1.25 m, is regarded as the sensed image. Features in urban area from multi-mode SAR images are obviously inconsistent and relationship of features is difficult to established, indicates that the match will be a challenge.

In this experiment, we only select water region as the matching object since there are few constant distinct objects in urban area. Appropriate merge strategy is used after

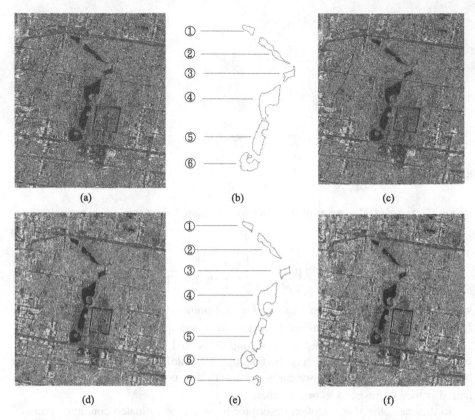

Fig. 4. SAR images in Beijing, China, and extracted objects. (a) Radarsat-2, 2008, (b) extracted result and (c) contours overlay on the original image (a). (d) TerraSAR, 2011, (e) extracted result and (f) contours overlay on the original image (d).

segmentation for whole objects. Two images with extracted objects are shown in Fig. 4. It can be seen that shapes of same object have distinct local difference.

The contours of objects extracted using segmentation and vectorization algorithms are quite coarse and have a lot of burrs. Thus, curve smoothing is essential to remove these burrs and details, i.e., reduce the difference of object shapes, which is useful for shape matching. An example of Gaussian smoothing is shown in Fig. 5.

We select a contour of the sensed objects and compute the maximum distance between all points. This distance is as the radius of the shape context descriptor, and the shape context is computed in accordance with a uniform radius for all contours of the reference objects. We match shapes between this object and all reference really objects individually and find optimal or suboptimal matching results (i.e., a similar shape cannot be found). Every contour of the sensed objects has a different radius during matching processing, and histogram distributions and the costs of all reference contour points are re-evaluated for each sensed object. The diagrams of object matching using shape context descriptor are shown in Fig. 6.

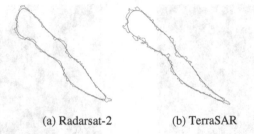

(a) Radarsat-2   (b) TerraSAR

Fig. 5. Curve smoothing of Object 2. Red line is original extracted contour and blue line is Gaussian smoothing result (Color figure online).

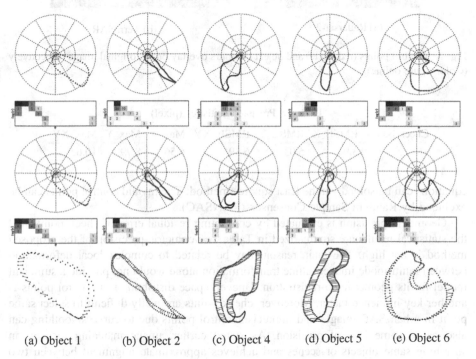

(a) Object 1   (b) Object 2   (c) Object 4   (d) Object 5   (e) Object 6

Fig. 6. Shape context matching. The first and second rows correspond to reference and sensed objects respectively. The red points on the contours indicate the matched point and black points indicate the unmatched point. The third row represents correspondences between best pairs, wherein costs are minimal for two shapes (Color figure online).

Control point candidates are selected from best point pairs of matched objects. Control points are uniformly distributed in contours of objects (see Fig. 7). Affine transformation can be used as the matching transformation function for satellite images when the demand of precision is not very high. To estimate transformation parameters, the number of control points should be greater than the number of parameters to be determined (i.e., three points at least). The resulting over-determined system of linear

(a) Radarsat-2   (b) TerraSAR

Fig. 7. Control points (red circle) and object contours overlay on the original image respectively (Color figure online).

Table 1. Precision statistics (pixel)

Check points	RMSE_X	RMSE_Y	RMSE_XY	Max_X	Max_Y	Max_XY
16	3.94	5.03	6.39	6.56	8.79	10.65

equations can be solved via the least squares method. The invalid control points can be excluded by Random Sample Consensus (RANSAC).

Geometric precision is evaluated by computing residual error of check points and the statistical results are summarized in Table 1. Geometric precision of the proposed method is not high. The main reason may be related to complex local deformation between multi-mode images, affine transformation alone would not provide a sufficient model for its geometric co-registration. Uneven space distribution of control points is another key influence factor. Moreover, check points are really difficult to select same point in urban SAR images and imprecise control points due to curve smoothing can also cause some loss of precision. As stated earlier, image matching focuses on searching same objects or scenes and achieves approximate alignment between two images. This study emphasizes the stable and reliable capability of object matching to solve correspondence problem. Of course, the matching result can be utilized as preliminary information for strict images registration.

5   Conclusion

This paper presents a novel object-based SAR image matching method, which can be considered as high-level image processing based on image interpretation and accords with human visual perception. Comparing with traditional feature-based methods, the main advantage of the proposed method is that object-based matching can avoid correspondence problem between features. The geometric shape and property information of the ground objects can be used in the matching, rather than meaningless point, line and edge features. The shape context descriptor is used for shape matching between objects with local deformations and exhibits globally discriminative characterization for variform objects. The proposed method also can be used in matching between SAR and optical image, even image and map.

Our method is illustrated by areal water regions, which have distinct shape and are easy to segment. The experiment and many other studies not listed here for reasons of space, demonstrate water regions are more suited for multi-mode image matching even shapes of same object are inconsistent and have local deformation. Besides, other typical ground objects, such as farmland, vegetation, villages, and roads, are also can be used in image matching. Of course, these objects are more difficult to extract and may have greater difference. Moreover, shape context descriptor is not suitable for linear water region, e.g. river, and sequence matching algorithms should be adopted. All of these problems need our further endeavor.

Acknowledgment. This work is supported by the National Natural Science Foundation of China (No. 41331176, No. 41271425).

References

1. Zitova, B., Flusser, J.: Image registration methods: a survey. Image Vis. Comput. **21**(11), 977–1000 (2003)
2. Li, H., Manjunath, B.S., Mitra, S.K.: A contour-based approach to multisensor image registration. IEEE Trans. Image Process. **4**(3), 320–334 (1995)
3. Suri, S., Schwind, P., Uhl, J., et al.: Modifications in the SIFT operator for effective SAR image matching. Int. J. Image Data Fusion **1**(3), 243–256 (2010)
4. Wang, Z., Zhang, J., Zhang, Y., et al.: Automatic registration of SAR and optical image based on multi-features and multi-constraints. In: 2010 IEEE International Geoscience and Remote Sensing Symposium (IGARSS), pp. 1019–1022 (2010)
5. Han, Y., Kim, Y., Yeom, J., et al.: Automatic registration of high-resolution optical and SAR images based on an integrated intensity-and feature-based approach. In: 2012 IEEE International Geoscience and Remote Sensing Symposium (IGARSS), pp. 6107–6110 (2012)
6. Ye, Y., Shan, J.: A local descriptor based registration method for multispectral remote sensing images with non-linear intensity differences. ISPRS J. Photogrammetry Remote Sens. **90**, 83–95 (2014)
7. Duan, X., Tian, Z., Ding, M., et al.: Registration of remote-sensing images using robust weighted kernel principal component analysis. AEU-Int. J. Electron. Commun. **67**(1), 20–28 (2013)
8. Yao, J., Goh, K.L.: A refined algorithm for multisensor image registration based on pixel migration. IEEE Trans. Image Process. **15**(7), 1839–1847 (2006)
9. Hong, D., Wu, J., Singh, S.S.: Refining image retrieval based on context-driven methods. In: Electronic Imaging 1999, pp. 581–592. International Society for Optics and Photonics (1998)
10. Liu, Y., Zhang, D., Lu, G., et al.: A survey of content-based image retrieval with high-level semantics. Pattern Recogn. **40**(1), 262–282 (2007)

11. Philbin, J., Chum, O., Isard, M., et al.: Object retrieval with large vocabularies and fast spatial matching. In: IEEE Conference on Computer Vision and Pattern Recognition, CVPR 2007, pp. 1–8 (2007)
12. Blaschke, T.: Object based image analysis for remote sensing. ISPRS J. Photogrammetry Remote Sens. **65**, 2–16 (2010)
13. Ton, J., Jain, A.K.: Registering Landsat images by point matching. IEEE Trans. Geosci. Remote Sens. **27**(5), 642–651 (1989)
14. Sheng, Y., Shah, C.A., Smith, L.C.: Automated image registration for hydrologic change detection in the lake-rich Arctic. IEEE Geosci. Remote Sens. Lett. **5**(3), 414–418 (2008)
15. Dare, P., Dowman, I.: An improved model for automatic feature-based registration of SAR and SPOT images. ISPRS J. Photogrammetry Remote Sens. **56**(1), 13–28 (2001)
16. Xiong, B., He, Z., Hu, C., et al.: A method of acquiring tie points based on closed regions in SAR images. In: 2012 IEEE International Geoscience and Remote Sensing Symposium (IGARSS), pp. 2121–2124 (2012)
17. Belongie, S., Malik, J., Puzicha, J.: Shape matching and object recognition using shape contexts. IEEE Trans. Pattern Anal. Mach. Intell. **24**(4), 509–522 (2002)

OCR with Adaptive Dictionary

Chenyang Wang[1], Yanhong Xie[2], Kai Wang[1](✉), and Tao Li[1]

[1] College of Computer and Control Engineering, Nankai University, Tianjin, China
wangk@nankai.edu.cn
[2] Shenzhouhaotian Technology Co., Ltd., Tianjin, China

Abstract. It has been proven by previous works that OCR is beneficial from reducing dictionary size. In this paper, a framework is proposed for improving OCR performance with the adaptive dictionary, in which text categorization is utilized to construct dictionaries using web data and identify the category of the imaged documents. To facilitate comparison with other existing methods that focus on language identification, an implementation is presented to improve the OCR performance with language adaptive dictionaries. Experimental results demonstrate that the performance of OCR system is significantly improved by the reduced dictionary. Compared with other existing methods for language identification, the proposed method shows a better performance. Also, any other categorization methodology is expected to further reduce the dictionary size. For example, an imaged document with specific language can be further categorized into sport, law, entertainment, etc. by its content.

Keywords: Dictionary size · Text categorization · Language identification · OCR

1 Introduction

Dictionary driven OCR is popular for text recognition from both document image [1] and imagery [2]. In previous works, it has been proven that OCR is beneficial from reducing dictionary size, e.g. about 40 % of fail-to-recognized words are corrected in [3,4] with a reduced dictionary. Manual or automated categorization of images into predefined categories is a natural way to reduce the size of the dictionary by the text embedded in images. For example, an image can be categorized into English, France, German, etc. with the different language, and it also can be categorized into sport, law, entertainment, etc. with the different content. A reduced dictionary with the specified category is expected for an improving OCR performance.

This work is supported by the National Natural Science Foundation of China under Grant No. 61201424, 61301238, 61212005, the Fundamental Research Funds of Tianjin, China under Grant No. 14JCTPJC00501, 14JCTPJC00556, and the Natural Science Foundation of Tianjin, China under Grant No.12JCYBJC10100, 14ZCDZGX00831.

© Springer International Publishing Switzerland 2015
Y.-J. Zhang (Ed.): ICIG 2015, Part II, LNCS 9218, pp. 611–620, 2015.
DOI: 10.1007/978-3-319-21963-9_56

As an application of text categorization [5], automated script and language identification has been studied in past decades for improving the performance of OCR. A. L. Spitz [6] first classifies the script of a document image as being either Han- or Latin-based with the vertical position distribution of upward concavities. Then language identification for Han images is conducted by optical density distribution. And language identification for Latin images is conducted by the most frequently occurring word shapes characteristic proposed in [7]. Rotation invariant texture features is used by T. N. Tan [8] for automated script identification, whose effectiveness is verified by the experiments on six languages that include Chinese, English, Greek, Russian, Persian, and Malayalam. A novel word shape coding scheme is proposed by S. Lu et al. [9] for language identification, in which a document vector is constructed by using the high-frequency word shape codes and then it is used to identify the language of the imaged document. The scheme is extended for the identification of both script and language in [10]. A comprehensive survey is presented by D. Ghosh et al. [11] on the developments of script identification. I. H. Jang et al. [12] propose a texture feature based method that combines Gabor and MDLC features for script identification. The Orientation of the Local Binary Patterns (OLBP) is proposed by M. A. Ferrer et al. [13] for line-wise script identification. Previous works on script and language identification can be categorized into texture-based such as [8,12,13] and shape coding-based such as [6,7,9,10]. Texture-based methods are used for script identification, in which the texture features are extracted from the text patches and a classifier is applied to identify the script of the imaged documents. Shape coding-based methods are used for both script identification and language identification, in which word shapes are coded and the statistics of word shapes are utilized to identify the script or the language of the imaged documents.

Previous works have only focused on script and language identification. The methods are difficult to be extended for the imaged document categorization by other categorization methodology. And the performance of OCR with the reduced dictionaries is not concerned. In this paper, a framework is proposed for improving OCR performance with the adaptive dictionary, in which text categorization is utilized to construct dictionaries using web data and identify the category of the imaged documents. The proposed framework is suitable for the reduction of dictionary size by any categorization methodology. To facilitate comparison with other existing methods that focus on language identification, an implementation is presented to improve the OCR performance with language adaptive dictionaries. Experimental results demonstrate that the performance of OCR system is significantly improved by the reduced dictionary. Compared with other existing methods for language identification, the proposed method shows a better performance.

The rest of the paper is organized as follows. The framework is proposed in Sect. 2 for OCR with adaptive dictionary. An implementation is presented in Sect. 3 to improve the OCR performance with language adaptive dictionaries. Experiments are conducted in Sect. 4 to verify our work. Summary of the paper are shown in Sect. 5.

2   Framework

The proposed framework is shown in Fig. 1, which consists of dictionary learning and OCR.

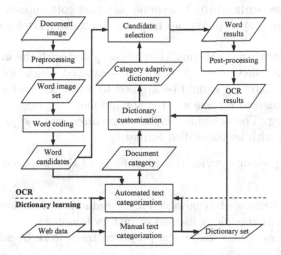

Fig. 1. The proposed framework

2.1   Dictionary Learning

In dictionary learning module, the data scratched from web is categorized by manual or automated text categorization. Then each dictionary in the dictionary set is initialized by manual categorized data and updated by automated categorized data. The real-time web data makes the proposed framework be adaptive for new words and new phrases.

2.2   OCR

In OCR module, preprocessing, word coding, automated text categorization, dictionary customization, candidate selection and post-processing are sequentially conducted to obtain the OCR results, which are briefly introduced as follows.

Preprocessing. Word image set is generated by analyzing the document image. The method can be top-down or bottom-up. Also, image processing such as binarization, noise removal, deskewing and auto-orientation should be applied on the document image for better OCR results.

Word Coding. Each word is coded by its shape. And then all candidate results for the word are generated, which always consist of some wrong results and no or a correct result.

Automated Text Categorization. All candidates are used for categorizing the imaged document to a specific category. To reduce the negative influence of noises for categorization, some candidates should be dropped if they are not matched with the words or the phrases in the dictionaries.

Dictionary Customization. The dictionary that corresponds to the detected document category is picked up from the dictionary set for the subsequent processing.

Candidate Selection. Each candidate is compared with the words in the category adaptive dictionary. And the mis-matched candidates are dropped. The phrases matching should be applied to select the best candidate if the candidate remained for one word is not unique.

Post-processing. The document layout is restored and the processing results are exported with user-specified format.

Compared with previous works, the advantages of the proposed framework are as follows.

- The proposed framework is suitable for the reduction of dictionary size by any categorization methodology instead of just by language.
- The real-time web data makes the proposed framework be adaptive for new words and new phrases.

3   Implementation

To facilitate comparison with other existing methods that focus on language identification, an implementation is presented to improve the OCR performance with language adaptive dictionaries. Only the methods for word coding and automated text categorization are introduced here. Other steps are just the same with that in a general OCR framework, thus they are ignored in this paper.

3.1   Word Coding

Simple shape features have been used for word coding in [6,7,9,10], and the proposed methods have been verified by experiments to be effective for script and language identification. Particularly, the method proposed in [9,10] is free of character segmentation. However, a high repetition coding rate always exists in the methods. That is, numerous candidate results are often generated for a word image, so that the negative influence of noises is inevitable for text categorization. To reduce the noises, only high-frequency words are used and only script/language identification is considered in previous works. It is difficult to adapt the methods for text categorization instead of just for language identification.

Character segmentation has been well studied in past decades [14]. It is not difficult to find the possible segmentation positions, but it is difficult to determine the correct segmentation positions. Sliding window based segmentation method is often used for the character recognition in imagery [2], which is always time consuming due to multi-scale scanning. In this paper, an individual characters based method is used for word coding, in which all possible segmentation positions are considered to find all possible candidates. To be efficient, contour based segmentation [15] is applied to obtain the over-segmentation results. And then each possibly correct segmentation or the combination of segmentations is represented by a vector that consists of the optical density [6] of n*n cells. Finally, the vector is matched with each pre-defined template. A character may be the result that the vector corresponds to as long as the match distance is small enough. As a result, a word image always corresponds to multiple candidates by different segmentations combination and different matched characters. For example, it is possible that a word "me" is coded as (m|rn)(e|c). That is, the candidates of the word include "me", "rne", "mc" and "rnc". Compared with the character recognition in OCR, the coding method used in this paper is simple and more candidate results are generated.

3.2 Automated Text Categorization

To reduce the negative influence of noisy candidates for text categorization, the candidates are dropped if they are not matched with any word in the dictionaries. For example, "rne", "mc" and "rnc" should be removed from the candidates of the word "me" as they are not correct spelled words. The same idea is also used in [6,7,9,10], and only relative high frequency codes are remained for script and language identification.

Correct spelled words are used for subsequent text categorization. In this paper, the number of words is counted for each specific category. And the category with the most words is set as the text categorization result. The method used here is very simple, and it is expected to improve the performance of text categorization by using a more complex one such as the methods in [5].

4 Experiments

4.1 Dataset

As is shown in Table 1, 12807 document images with eleven languages are collected for the verification of the proposed method, which are captured by scanning from magazines, books and printed documents. Some images used in experiments are given in Fig. 2(a).

To be compared with the methods in [9,10], the original images are corrupted by Gaussian noise (mean = 0, variance = 0.02), salt & pepper noise (noise ratio = 0.05) and low scanning resolution (150 dpi), respectively. The degraded images that correspond to Fig. 2(a) are given in Fig. 2(b) and (c). The images with low resolution look similar with the original ones, thus they are ignored here.

Table 1. An overview on document images used in experiments

Language	Abbreviation	The number of images
English	EN	2,500
French	FR	963
German	DE	1,151
Italian	IT	1,112
Swedish	SW	1,082
Spanish	ES	1,096
Portuguese	PT	1,400
Norwegian	NO	659
Dutch	NL	844
Polish	PL	1,000
Finnish	FI	1,000
Total		12,807

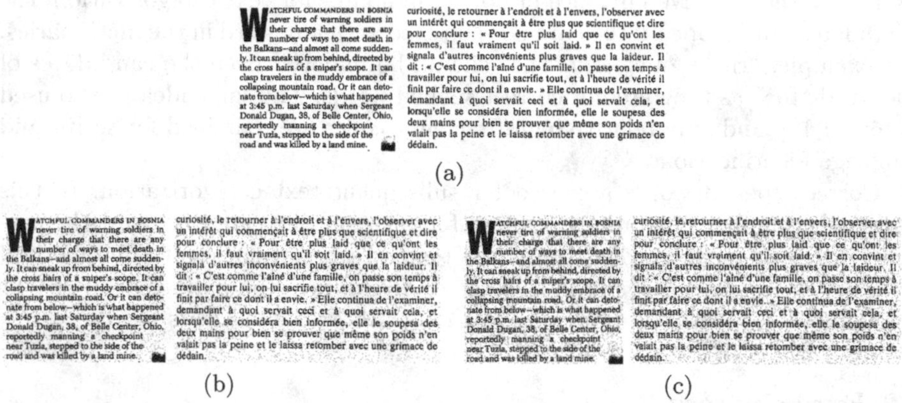

(a)

(b)

(c)

Fig. 2. Some images used in experiments. (a) Original images. (b) Images degraded by Gaussian noise (mean = 0, variance = 0.02). (c) Images degraded by salt & pepper noise (noise ratio = 0.05).

4.2 OCR Performance

To verify the performance of OCR with the reduced dictionary, two OCR systems are implemented, in which full dictionary and adaptive dictionary are respectively used for candidate selection. As is shown in Table 2, performance of OCR with full dictionary and that with adaptive dictionary are compared on the images with eleven languages. The total error rate is reduced from 1.96 % to 0.77 % by replacing the full dictionary with the adaptive dictionary, 60.91 % of mis-recognized characters being corrected.

Table 2. Performance of ocr with full dictionary and that with adaptive dictionary

Language	The number of total characters	OCR with full dictionary		OCR with adaptive dictionary		Reduction rate of errors by replacing full dictionary with adaptive dictionary (%)
		The number of mis-recognized characters	Error rate (%)	The number of mis-recognized characters	Error rate (%)	
English	4,404,992	78,148	1.77	67,695	1.54	13.38
French	3,715,867	94,334	2.54	61,284	1.65	35.04
German	3,848,309	64,128	1.67	33,092	0.86	48.40
Swedish	3,598,688	125,077	3.48	7,534	0.21	93.98
Spanish	3,877,759	46,649	1.20	31,308	0.81	32.89
Portuguese	4,380,493	85,771	1.96	11,872	0.27	86.16
Norwegian	1,963,128	50,168	2.56	5,990	0.31	88.06
Dutch	2,402,851	7,062	0.29	4,008	0.17	43.25
Polish	2,367,747	17,235	0.73	14,055	0.59	18.45
Finnish	2,236,520	96,879	4.33	9,340	0.42	90.36
Total	36,599,857	717,860	1.96	280,597	0.77	60.91

Table 3. Accuracy comparison for language identification (%)

Method	Salt and pepper noise	Gaussian noise	Low resolution	Three degradation combined
Spitz's [10]	83.53	86.90	78.77	72.22
Nobile's [10]	83.77	86.28	78.36	71.67
Suen's [10]	82.91	86.42	79.13	71.84
Lu's [10]	96.32	96.47	91.18	88.31
Ours	98.85	99.00	97.39	96.31

4.3 Language Identification

As is shown in Table 3 the proposed method outperforms other methods for language identification.

The detailed results between languages are given in Table 4, 5, 6 and 7. There are mainly two types of errors for language identification on images with salt and pepper noise or Gaussian noise. One is Portuguese being mis-identified as French, and another is English being mis-identified as Finnish. The samples with mis-identified language are analyzed and the mis-identified reasons are as follows.

Table 4. Identification results between languages on images with salt and pepper noise

True language	Detected language											Error
	EN	FR	DE	IT	SW	ES	PT	NO	NL	PL	FI	
EN	2433									67		67
FR	4	959										4
DE	3		1148									3
IT	15	1	7	1089								23
SW					1082							0
ES		1				1095						1
PT		45					1355					45
NO								659				0
NL									844			0
PL	2									998		2
FI	2										998	2

Table 5. Identification results between languages on images with gaussian noise

True language	Detected language											Error
	EN	FR	DE	IT	SW	ES	PT	NO	NL	PL	FI	
EN	2441										59	59
FR	2	961										2
DE			1151									0
IT	13	1	7	1091								21
SW					1082							0
ES		1				1095						1
PT		45					1355					45
NO								659				0
NL									844			0
PL										998		0
FI											998	0

- Some samples marked as Portuguese are the multi-lingual documents, e.g. the first two text lines in Fig. 3(a) are detected as Portuguese by Google Translate, while the last three text lines are detected as French.
- The text fonts in some English samples are special, e.g. Fig. 3(b).

   More errors are generated when the images are corrupted by low scanning resolution, the results being consistent with previous methods. To ensure the performance, an image resolution of at least 300DPI is suggested.

Table 6. Identification results between languages on images with low resolution

True language	Detected language											Error
	EN	FR	DE	IT	SW	ES	PT	NO	NL	PL	FI	
EN	2328		1			1					170	172
FR	2	961										2
DE	2		1149									2
IT	16	1	7	1088								24
SW					1082							0
ES	2	1				1093						3
PT		45					1355					45
NO								659				0
NL									844			0
PL	52									948		52
FI	33							1			966	34

Table 7. Identification results between languages on images with three degradation combined

True language	Detected language											Error
	EN	FR	DE	IT	SW	ES	PT	NO	NL	PL	FI	
EN	2255	2	1	1		1						245
FR	8	955										8
DE	2		1149									2
IT	25	1	7	1069								33
SW					1082							0
ES	3	1				1092						4
PT		45					1355					45
NO								659				0
NL									844			0
PL	79									921		79
FI	56										944	56

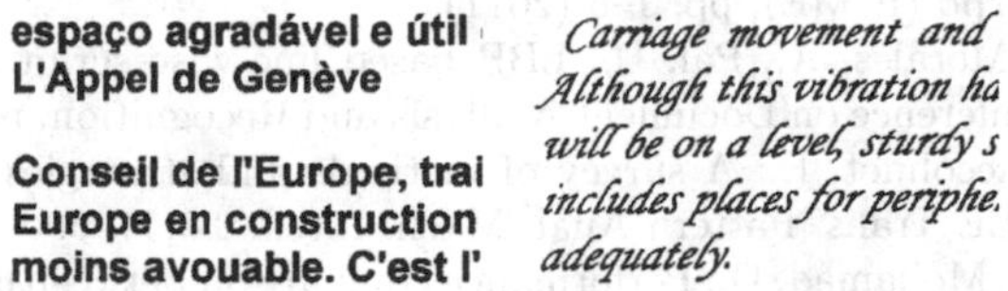

espaço agradável e útil
L'Appel de Genève

Conseil de l'Europe, trai
Europe en construction
moins avouable. C'est l'

(a)

Carriage movement and
Although this vibration ha
will be on a level, sturdy s
includes places for periphe.
adequately.

(b)

Fig. 3. Samples with mis-identified language. (a) Portuguese is mis-identified as French. (b) English is mis-identified as Finnish.

5 Conclusion

A framework is proposed for improving OCR performance with the adaptive dictionary, which is suitable for the reduction of dictionary size by any categorization methodology instead of just by language. And the real-time web data makes the proposed framework be adaptive for new words and new phrases. One of our future works is to improve the OCR performance with the further reduced dictionary by other categorization methodology instead of just by language.

References

1. Nagy, G.: Twenty years of document image analysis in PAMI. IEEE Trans. Pattern Anal. Mach. Intell. **22**(1), 38–62 (2000)
2. Ye, Q., Doermann, D.: Text detection and recognition in imagery: a survey. IEEE Trans. Pattern Anal. Mach. Intell. **37**, 1480–1500 (2015)
3. Yao, C., Bai, X., Shi, B., liu, W.: Strokelets: a learned multi-scale representation for scene text recognition. In: 2014 IEEE Conference on Computer Vision and Pattern Recognition (CVPR), pp. 4042–4049 (2014)
4. Shi, C., Wang, C., Xiao, B., Zhang, Y., Gao, S., Zhang, Z.: Scene text recognition using part-based tree-structured character detection. In: 2013 IEEE Conference on Computer Vision and Pattern Recognition (CVPR), pp. 2961–2968 (2013)
5. Sebastiani, F.: Machine learning in automated text categorization. ACM Comput. Surv. **34**(1), 1–47 (2002)
6. Spitz, A.L.: Determination of the script and language content of document images. IEEE Trans. Pattern Anal. Mach. Intell. **19**(3), 235–245 (1997)
7. Nakayama, T., Spitz, A.L.: European language determination from image. In: IEEE Conference on Document Analysis and Recognition (ICDAR), pp. 159–162 (1993)
8. Tan, T.N.: Rotation invariant texture features and their use in automatic script identification. IEEE Trans. Pattern Anal. Mach. Intell. **20**(7), 751–756 (1998)
9. Lu, S., Li, L., Tan, C.L.: Identification of Latin-based languages through character stroke categorization. In: 2007 International Conference on Document Analysis and Recognition (ICDAR), pp. 352–356 (2007)
10. Lu, S., Tan, C.L.: Script and language identification in noisy and degraded document images. IEEE Trans. Pattern Anal. Mach. Intell. **30**(1), 14–24 (2008)
11. Ghosh, D., Dube, T., Shivaprasad, A.P.: Script recognition review. IEEE Trans. Pattern Anal. Mach. Intell. **32**(12), 2142–2161 (2010)
12. Jang, I.H., Kim, N.C., Park, M.H.: Texture feature-based language identification using Gabor and MDLC features. In: 2011 IEEE International Conference on Multimedia and Expo (ICME), pp. 1–6 (2011)
13. Ferrer, M.A., Morales, A., Pal, U.: LBP based line-wise script identification. In: 2013 IEEE Conference on Document Analysis and Recognition, pp. 369–373 (2013)
14. Casey, R.G., Lecolinet, E.: A survey of methods and strategies in character segmentation. IEEE Trans. Pattern Anal. Mach. Intell. **18**(7), 690–706 (1996)
15. Kurniawan, F., Mohamad, D.: Performance comparison between contour-based and enhanced heuristic-based for character segmentation. In: 2009 Fifth International Conference on Signal-Image Technology & Internet-Based Systems (SITIS), pp. 112–117 (2009)

One Simple Virtual Avatar System Based on Single Image

Lanfang Dong[1][✉], Jianfu Wang[1], Kui Ni[1], Yatao Wang[1], Xian Wu[1], and Mingxue Xu[2]

[1] School of Computer Science and Technology,
University of Science and Technology of China, Hefei, China
lfdong@ustc.edu.cn
{wangjf55,nique,ythwang,wuxian}@mail.ustc.edu.cn
[2] College of Geophysics and Information Engineering,
China University of Petroleum (Beijing), Bejing, China
xumingxue2008@yeah.net

Abstract. To establish virtual avatar systems at the computing environments with limited resources, we design such a system based on single image which can generate speech animation with different facial expressions. Firstly, facial feature points are extracted automatically or manually based on MPEG-4 facial animation to build the face model. Then, according to Facial Animation Parameters of visual phoneme and expression stream, the feature points after image warping are calculated. The next step is to generate the in-between frames by using the image warping algorithm based on scan lines and combining with the correlative time parameters. Finally, with adding the actions such as nodding, shaking heads and winking, the face animation is implemented. Experimental results show that the proposed system can generate smooth and realtime facial expressions under platforms with low computing capacity.

Keywords: MPEG-4 · Image warping · Face animation · Visual phoneme

1 Introduction

As the speedy development of mobile communication technology and the rapid popularization of mobile network, the mobile devices such as Smartphone, PAD are widely used. However, they are also facing increasing challenges from high power consumption. Limited to the actual objective conditions, the mobile devices are often unable to get power supply in time. Therefore, providing the low power software for platforms with limited computing capacity has become one of the main solutions and also become one of the focuses in software development.

Combining with computer graphics, computer animation and virtual reality, the virtual avatar technology is used widely at present. Especially along with the hot showing of science fiction movie, Avatar, this technology is known by more people, and is employed by more animation and movie production companies.

© Springer International Publishing Switzerland 2015
Y.-J. Zhang (Ed.): ICIG 2015, Part II, LNCS 9218, pp. 621–635, 2015.
DOI: 10.1007/978-3-319-21963-9_57

However, one of key problems in virtual avatar is that how to provide realistic and realtime animation in the platforms with limited computing capacity.

Designing a virtual avatar system generating natural and realtime face expressions with low power consumption is one focus of the recent research. In this paper, we design one simple virtual avatar system which is implemented based on single image and can achieve accurate and realtime fusion and synchronization of facial expressions, mouth shapes and voice. Besides, the system adopts one image warping algorithm based scan lines to avoid high power consumption on the mobile devices.

2   Related Work

Facial expressions and speech are two most important communication ways for human, as well as the key parts in virtual avatar system. How to implement the fusion and synchronization of facial expressions, mouth shapes and voice accurately, realistically and in real time is presently one hot research in computer animation and virtual reality.

Nowadays 3D facial animation is studied widely and deeply. The first step is usually to create the 3D face model [1], and then different approaches are employed to control the face motion. The methods for 3D facial animation can divided into two categories: the parameter model based technology and physical model based technology [2]. Parke [3] firstly introduced the parameterized models for facial animation, and with controlling the expression parameters and structural parameters to synthesize different facial expressions and postures, but the reality remained to be improved. Waters [4] presented a muscle model based on the physical properties of muscle, which can create the subtle expressions using muscle vectors and radial functions. The difficulty of this method is to master the anatomy, histology and dynamics of facial muscles. The Facial Animation Parameters (FAP) in MPEG-4 standard [5] defines a complete collection of basic movements which can be used to generate facial expressions. Currently, the MPEG-4 based methods are widely used for 3D facial animation [6–9]. Physics-based facial animation typically use mass-spring or finite element networks to model the elastic properties of skin [10,11]. In paper [12], one physical 3D facial model consisting of cutaneous tissue, subcutaneous fatty tissue, and muscles is embedded in the mass spring system to generate realistic facial animation. The other methods based on physical model [13–15] can enhanced the reality of animation. However, one general shortcoming of 3D facial animation is high computational complexity. In addition, the modeling of 3D faces usually needs special equipment of high construction cost. Another way for facial animation is based on images. Because the textures come directly from the images, images based method can provide facial expressions with high reality. Arad et al. [16] proposed one image morphing algorithm with Radial Basis Function (RBF) to generate facial animation based on single image. The facial animation based on key frames is one of the most widely used methods in computer animation [17]. This method was first put forward by Beier and Neely [18], and in this method corresponding triangular meshes with similar topological structures are constructed for the neighboring key frames. Afterward, more key-frame based methods are proposed to improve the animation effects [19,20]. However, all those approaches with neglecting the fusion of mouth shapes and facial expressions are not suitable for facial animation driven by speech.

In addition, current speech animation systems are mostly concerned with generating the lip animation to match the speech and missing the face expressions, while facial animation mainly focuses on modeling of the face and the facial motion analysis. In paper [21] motion capture-based facial animation extracted information from the expression axis of a speech performance. To map the audio information to the visual information representing the facial movements, paper [22] trained a set of neural networks using a large collected set of audioCvisual training data from real human subjects. Similarly, in paper [23] a novel motion capture mining technique was provided with learning speech coarticulation models and expression spaces from recorded facial motion capture data. To generate one lively and convincing animation, sophisticated facial motions are required in motion capture-based algorithms. Above all, on the one hand, the current researches cannot balance the facial expressions, lip movements and speech. On the other hand, the high computational complexity brought by the animation limits the use of corresponding software or systems in mobile devices. Different from the previous complex spline interpolation, 3D model-based or motion capture-based approaches with sophisticated facial motions, in this paper the proposed virtual avatar system is implemented on single image with simple algorithm and low power consumption. The system employs the image warping based on scan lines to accomplish the facial animation quickly and effectively with less computing resource and memory space. Moreover the system adds some other actions, such as nodding and winking, and it can also be used to generate the facial animation of animals and cartoon characters.

3   Image Warping Based on Scan Lines

Our proposed simple virtual avatar system is designed based on single image, and the key is implementing of the image warping. Different from the prior image warping based on scattered points or fragments, in this paper we use the image warping algorithm proposed in [24]. To make it simple, the main task is to generate the warped target image using the input source image and the known feature points in both source and target images. The detailed process is illustrated as follows:

Firstly, the facial feature points are defined as shown in Fig. 1, and the next section offers specific details on feature points.

Secondly, neighboring feature points are joined by splines as Fig. 2 shows, and the points located in the splines are calculated by liner interpolation. Some other points are added to limit movement range of feature points distributed within the rectangular boundaries as shown in Fig. 2. The addition of those points is helpful for the control of face movement and the construction of splines.

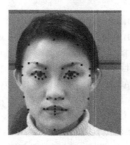

Fig. 1. Facial feature points.

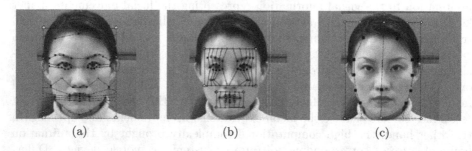

(a)　　　　　　　　　(b)　　　　　　　　　(c)

Fig. 2. Facial splines (a) Horizontal facial splines (b) Vertical facial splines (c) Vertical splines of face contour.

The splines consist of horizontal splines and vertical splines, of which the horizontal splines covering the whole face are used to control the face warping in vertical direction, as Fig. 2(a) shows, vertical splines covering the mouth and eye areas are used for horizontal warping of mouth and eyes, as Fig. 2(b) shows, while the vertical splines of face contour are used to control the shaking of head as shown in Fig. 2(c). The horizontal splines and vertical splines are constructed independently without sharing the same feature points to avoid generating spline grid and can be used in the following image warping separately.

Here, we set the images before and after warping as the source image and target image separately. Then, after the construction of facial splines in both two images, the coordinates of points between splines from the source image to the target are calculated, of which the y coordinates are calculated according the horizontal splines of two images while the x coordinates are calculated according the vertical splines. In this step, the scan lines are used as shown in Fig. 3, where Fig. 3(a) shows the vertical displacement while Fig. 3(b) shows the horizontal displacement.

We take the calculation of vertical displacement of one point C as an example. The solid splines in Fig. 3(a) separately represent the horizontal $spline1$ and $spline2$ in source image while the dotted splines separately represent the horizontal $spline1'$ and $spline2'$ in target image. The vertical line is one vertical scan line which progressively scans the horizontal splines in source and target images. In Fig. 3(a), A is the intersection of scan line and $spline1$ while B is the

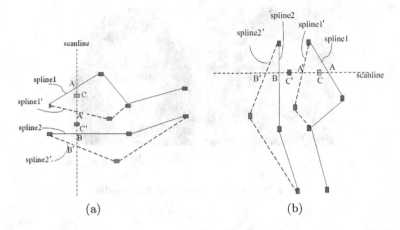

Fig. 3. (a) scan line between horizontal splines (b) scan line between vertical splines.

intersection of scan line and *spline2*. Their corresponding intersections in target image are A' and B'. C is one point located in scan line between A and B in source image, and its corresponding point in target image is C'.

Assuming $A(x, s1)$, $B(x, s2)$, $A'(x, d1)$, $B'(x, d2)$, $C(x, y)$, $C'(x, y')$, the vertical coordinate y' of $C'(x, y')$ is calculated by linear interpolation formulation as (1).

$$y' = d1 + (y - s1) \times \frac{(d2 - d1)}{(s2 - s1)} \tag{1}$$

The vertical displacement from C to C' is $\Delta y = y' - y$. Similarly, the horizontal displacement Δx of C can be achieved by using the scan lines between the vertical splines, as shown in Fig. 3(b).

In this way, we can get the coordinate of $C'(x + \Delta x, y + \Delta y)$ after warping. Finally, when coordinates of all points are achieved, the warping image, namely the target images, is generated based on the feature points.

4   Virtual Avatar System

The proposed virtual avatar system consists of three parts: facial modeling, speech processing and facial expression processing.

4.1   Facial Modeling

The first step of virtual avatar is to build parametric model of the face and then to define and mark the facial feature points on the model. MPEG-4 provides the face mode standard and corresponding face definition parameters (FDP). To build one nice face model, the feature points should be representative, express the face features and be able to uniquely identify the face. In this paper, the feature points we selected from FDPs are shown in Fig. 4, including mouth, eyes, brows, nose and the face contour.

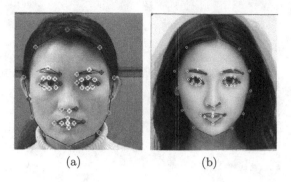

(a)   (b)

Fig. 4. The feature points of face model.

4.2 Speech Processing

In this stage, the input audio files are transformed by speech recognition engine to produce phoneme-timestamp streams, which are further transformed to visual phoneme and timestamp streams, through which the locations of facial feature points are achieved. Based on the feature points, image warping is implemented to generate the facial animation. At last the synchronization of speech and animation is achieved according to the timestamps of phonemes. In this system, we use Microsoft Speech Recognizer as the speech recognition engine to convert the one audio to the phoneme streams with timestamp.

Visual Phoneme. Speech utterance can be segmented into sentences, words, or even phonemes, where phoneme is the smallest unit. The phoneme- timestamp streams reflect the duration of one phoneme. According to MPEG-4, the phonemes with the same lip movements are classified together as one visual phoneme. Each visual phoneme is corresponding to a set of FAPs, where Table 1 shows one sample. MPEG-4 provides more detailed visual phonemes and FAPs.

As Table 1 shows, the visual phoneme has a corresponding set of masks and maximum values for FAPs. In this table, ae, ax, ah, aa and ay belong to one visual phoneme with the same lip movements when speaking. The following number 0 is the label of the visual phoneme. There are 68 FAPs in MPEG-4. The next 68 numbers (0 or 1) are the masks of FAPs where 0 illustrates the FAP does not work while 1 works. The numbers in last line are the coefficients of FAPs with corresponding masks equal to 1, where absolute value is the magnitude of displacement while the sign is the direction of displacement.

After the locations of feature points are calculated based on the visual phonemes, we use the scan-line based image warping algorithm to get the image after warping. The frames between images before and after warping are generated by simple linear interpolation.

The relationship of facial expressions and FAPs is same as the visual phonemes with referencing to MPEG-4 standard. The MPEG-4 Facial Animation Standard is simplified and applied in this 2D facial animation generating.

Table 1. One sample of visual phoneme

#	ae	ax	ah	aa	ay	0									
0	0	1	1	1	1	1	0	0	1	1	0	0	0	0	0
0	0	0	0	0	0	0	0	0	0	0	0	0	0	0	
0	0	0	0	0	0	0	0	0	0	0	0	0	1	0	1
0	0	0	0	1	1	1	1	0	0	1	1	0	0	0	0
0	0	0	0	0	0										
180	60	−350	30	0	30	0	0	−407	30	30	0	0			

Transition of Visual Phonemes. If the shape of mouth recovers to neutral state every time when the process of each visual phoneme is finished, the generated facial expressions will be unrealistic. Therefore, to remedy abnormal expressions, we introduced the transition of visual phonemes based on the linear interpolation method. New FAPs are interpolated based on prior FAPs and current FAPs to generate new expressions to instead the nature state. The experimental results show that the introduction of transition can achieve the reality and realtime requirement. Figure 5(a) shows movement amplitudes without transition while Fig. 5(b) shows amplitudes with transition.

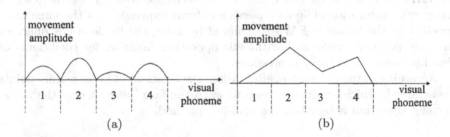

Fig. 5. (a) The movement amplitudes of visual phonemes without transition (b) The movement amplitudes of visual phonemes with transition.

Merging of Visual Phonemes. If the frame rate is 20fps while the lasting time of visual phonemes is too short to produce one frame, some abnormal expressions such as sudden change of mouth will emerge. Therefore, the visual phonemes with short duration should be merged to create more fluent and natural animation in real time as Fig. 6 shows.

4.3   Expression Processing

To make the generated animation more realistic and natural, our designed system takes both lip movements and facial expressions into consideration. In addition, we add some other random face motions, such as nodding, shaking heads and winking to generate more abundant facial animation.

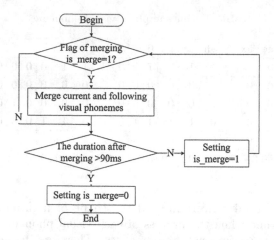

Fig. 6. The merging of visual phonemes.

Facial Expression. The relationship of facial expressions and FAPs is similar to the visual phoneme, so do the transition and merging of parameters. With considering the lip movements and facial expressions, our system completes the fusion of FAPs of visual phonemes and facial expressions. The fusion is to put the FAPs of visual phonemes and FAPs of facial expressions together, which brings synchronization of lip movements and facial expressions at the same time. Specifically, the fusion of FAPs is achieved by using the Boolean OR operator for corresponding masks and arithmetic operation Addition for coefficients of visual phonemes and facial expressions.

According to the parameters after fusion, the locations of facial feature points are achieved, which are further used to warp the face image, where the image warping algorithm is based on the scan-line method.

Winking. In this part, we add the winking to the facial expressions using four FAPs concerning with the eyes: both upper and lower eyelids of eyes, which are also used in FAPs of facial expressions. Therefore, we set the winking as an individual expression. When winking occurs, the other FAPs related to eyes will be disabled. The process of winking in the virtual avatar system is shown in Fig. 7.

Head Movements. The head movements consist of shaking head and nodding, which are set as periodic movements in this paper, and periodic changes of motion amplitudes are shown in Fig. 8.

The nodding is implemented by adding same value to the Y value of all feature points while the shaking head is moving the vertical splines of face contour as shown in Fig. 2(c) where the moving amplitude of the middle spline is larger than the others. Figure 9 shows the process of nodding, and the shaking has similar process.

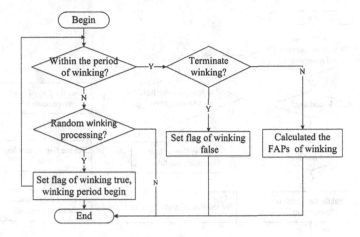

Fig. 7. Process of winking.

Shading of Mouth. Under the nature state, the lips are pressed together. When speaking, the shapes of mouth change with the opening and closing of mouth alternately. When the mouth is opening, the region lies between two lips should be shaded. Figure 10 shows the shading process of mouth. The inner lips can be seen as two curves, which are computed at the first step of shading.

For the convenience of computing, in the system the feature points of mouth are rotated to horizontal direction firstly, and then we use Lagrange interpolation to obtain the inner boundary curves of mouth. To simplify the shading of mouth and ensure the quality of generated animation, we combined the sample image of mouth into the neutral face image so that the inner structure of mouth could be shown when mouth was open. In facial animation, the warping of mouth is based on it center. Within the mosaic and fusion of mouth sample image and face image, the corresponding center points first are matched. Then the mouth sample image is rotate to the same direction as face image and its inner lip curves is also get. According to the corresponding points in the curves, the sample image is scaled and warped to suit change of mouth in face image which can be achieved with simple linear interpolation.

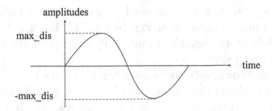

Fig. 8. Periodic changes of amplitudes.

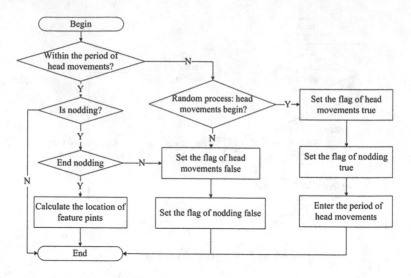

Fig. 9. The process of nodding.

4.4   The Virtual Avatar System

After the facial modeling, speech processing and expression processing, we get the whole realization process as shown in Fig. 11, where the upper dotted box presents the calculation of displacement of feature points while the lower is the corresponding image warping.The additional points are shown as Fig. 2(a)–(c), located on the sides of rectangles.

5   Experiments and Discussion

5.1   Experimental Results

Figures 12, 13, 14, 15 and 16 show the samples of generated animation by the virtual avatar system. The Figs. 12, 13 and 14 are the facial animation generated from three different human face images, from which we can see the facial expressions of delight (as Figs. 12(a) and 13(a)), anger (as Figs. 12(b) and 13(b)) and surprise (as Figs. 12(c) and 13(c)) respectively and corresponding mouth movements. The system can also be used to generate the facial animation of cartoon characters and animals as shown in Figs. 15 and 16. From the figures, we can see the winking as Figs. 15(c) and 16(c) show, and the motions of head as Figs. 16(a) and 16(c) show.

The action of the brows, eyes and mouth can best reflect the facial expression. When the emotions of one person or animal change, the shape information of such organs changes correspondingly. As Fig. 15 shows, the shapes of the brows, eyes and mouth are in harmony with emotion. In terms of animation effects, the generated facial expressions for cartoon characters and animals are better than that for humans. From the Figs. 13 and 14, some distortion occurred when the

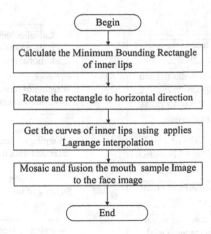

Fig. 10. The shading of mouth.

eyes were closed. On the contrary, the action of wink for cartoon and animals looks more natural.

It is also worth mentioning that the shading of mouth can help to promote reality. Such as Figs. 13, 14(c), 16(b) and 16(c) when the mouth is open widely, the teeth look natural. The results of the experiment clearly demonstrate that the system can generate realistic facial animation with both mouth movements and facial expressions.

5.2 Discussion

Compared with the current facial animation achieved from multiple images, videos 3D models, such as the realtime facial animation based on 3D models in [25, 26], the approach in this paper with only one available image cannot show better animation effect. However, the proposed system enlarges the application fields of animation. On the other hand, it also contains advantages of storage, computation and communication. Different from previous methods, the proposed virtual avatar system is implemented based on single image, and every frame of the facial animation is generated with only using the input image, FAPs and the essential feature points, so that this system needs small computer memory and storage space. Within the communication of different mobile devices, only facial feature points are transferred after the completion of facial modeling to produce the warping images. Furthermore, the key scan-line based algorithm of this system can achieve the warping image with the simplest linear interpolation without complex calculations, which has the advantages of saving computation time and computing resources and avoids higher power consumption. Another advantage of scan-line based algorithm is that the interpolation points can controlled within the feature points, so are the corresponding values. Therefore, the abnormal warping images and the boundary overstepping can be avoided so that the quality of generated animation can be improved further. In a word, the

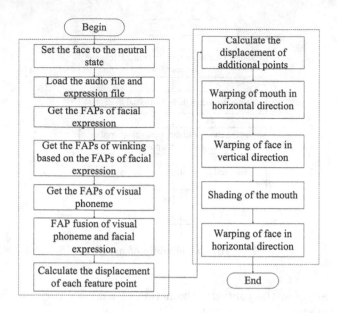

Fig. 11. The whole realization process of the virtual avatar system.

proposed avatar system can provide facial animation of high quality and with effectively saving the computing cost.

However, according to the experimental results, some details of human facial expressions need to be refined. For the human face, the feature points can be extracted by the system automatically. But for cartoon characters and animals, the feature points location is achieved manually. Therefore, the presented avatar system should be improved in the effect of human facial expression animation and the self-adaptive operation.

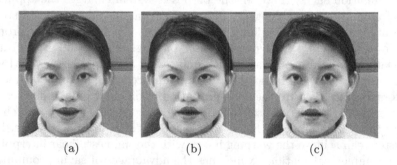

(a)   (b)   (c)

Fig. 12. The first sample of human facial animation.

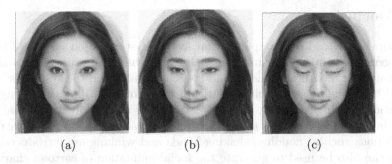

Fig. 13. The second sample of human facial animation.

Fig. 14. The third sample of human facial animation.

Fig. 15. The sample of facial animation for cartoon character.

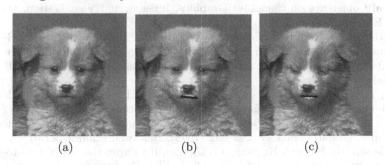

Fig. 16. The sample of animal facial animation.

6   Conclusions

This paper provided one simple virtual avatar system based on single image, which generated the facial animation with fusing the facial expressions and synchronization of mouth movements and speech. In addition, the system is implemented using the image warping algorithm based on scan lines that brings less calculation and high velocity, and we can run our system on the normal computers in real time. To make the animation more abundant and more realistic, some actions such as nodding, shaking heads and winking are introduced. The system can also be used to generate the facial animation of cartoon characters and animals. The experimental results showed that the proposed virtual avatar system is of excellent performance and practical value.

References

1. Lee, Y., Terzopoulos, D., Waters, K.: Realistic modeling for facial animation. In: ACM Proceedings of the 22nd Annual Conference on Computer Graphics and Interactive Techniques, pp. 55–62. ACM Press, New York (1995)
2. Kahler, K., Haber, J., Seidel, H.P.: Geometry-based muscle modeling for facial animation. In: Graphics Interface, pp. 37–46. Morgan Kaufmann Press, Toronto (2001)
3. Parke, F.I., Waters, K., Alley, T.R.: Computer Facial Animation. AK Peters Wellesley, Mass (1996)
4. Waters, K.: A muscle model for animation three-dimensional facial expression. ACM SIGGRAPH Comput. Graph. **21**, 17–24 (1987)
5. Pandzic, I.S., Forchheimer, R.: MPEG-4 Facial Animation: The Standard, Implementation and Applications. Wiley, New York (2002)
6. Duarte, R.L.P., Rhalibi, A.E., Merabti, M.: Coarticulation and speech synchronization in MPEG-4 based facial animation. Kybernetes: Int. J. Syst. Cybern. **43**, 1165–1182 (2014)
7. Parreira, D.R., El, R.P., Carter, C., Merabti, M.: Survey and evaluation of Mpeg-4 based 3D character animation frameworks. In: 2013 5th International Conference on Games and Virtual Worlds for Serious Applications, pp. 1–8. IEEE Press, Dorset (2013)
8. Obaid, M., Mukundan, R., Billinghurst, M., Pelachaud, C.: Expressive MPEG-4 facial animation using quadratic deformation models. In: 2010 Seventh International Conference on Computer Graphics, Imaging and Visualization, pp. 9–14. IEEE Press, Sydney (2010)
9. El Rhalibi, A., Carter, C., Cooper, S., Merabti, M.: Highly realistic MPEG-4 compliant facial animation with charisma. In: 2011 Proceedings of 20th International Conference on Computer Communications and Networks, pp. 1–6. IEEE Press, Lahaina (2011)
10. Lee, Y., Terzopoulos, D., Waters, K.: Constructing Physics-based Facial Models of Individuals. Graphics Interface, Canadian Information Processing Society (1993)
11. Koch, R.M., Gross, M.H., Bosshard, A.A.: Emotion editing using finite elements. Comput. Graph. Forum **17**, 295–302 (1998). Blackwell Publishers Ltd
12. Anderson, R., Stenger, B., Wan, V., Cipolla, R.: Expressive visual text-to-speech using active appearance models. In: 2013 IEEE Conference on Computer Vision and Pattern Recognition (CVPR), pp. 3382–3389, IEEE Press, Portland (2013)

13. Li, D., Sun, C., Hu, F., Zang, D., Wang, L., Zhang, M.: Real-time performance-driven facial animation with 3ds Max and Kinect. In: 2013 3rd International Conference on Consumer Electronics, Communications and Networks, pp. 473–476. IEEE Press, Xianning (2013)

14. Yu, H., Garrod, O., Jack, R., Schyns, P.: Realistic facial animation generation based on facial expression mapping. In: Fifth International Conference on Graphic and Image Processing, pp. 906903-1–906903-5. SPIE Press, Hong Kong (2014)

15. Zhang, Y., Prakash, E.C., Sung, E.: A new physical model with multilayer architecture for facial expression animation using dynamic adaptive mesh. IEEE Trans. Vis. Comput. Graph. **10**, 339–352 (2004)

16. Arad, N., Dyn, N., Reisfeld, D., Yeshurun, Y.: Image warping by radial basis functions: application to facial expressions. Graph. Models Image Process. **56**, 161–172 (1994)

17. Pan, H., Liu, Y., Xu, G.: Review on methods of facial synthesis. Appl. Res. Comput. **25**, 327–331 (2008)

18. Beier, T., Neely, S.: Feature-based image metamorphosis. ACM SIGGRAPH Comput. Graph. **26**, 35–42 (1992)

19. Edge, J.D., Maddock, S.: Image-based talking heads using radial basis functions. In: IEEE Proceedings of Theory and Practice of Computer Graphics, pp. 74–80. IEEE Press, Birminghan (2003)

20. Perng, W.L, Wu, Y., Ouhyoung, M.: Image talk: a real time synthetic talking head using one single image with chinese text-to-speech capability. In: Pacific Graphics' Sixth Pacific Conference on Computer Graphics and Applications, pp. 140–148. IEEE Press, Singapore (1998)

21. Chuang, E., Bregler, C.: Mood swings: expressive speech animation. ACM Trans. Graph. **24**, 331–347 (2005)

22. Hong, P., Wen, Z., Huang, T.S.: Real-time speech-driven face animation with expressions using neural networks. IEEE Trans. Neural Netw. **13**, 916–927 (2002)

23. Deng, Z., Neumann, U., Lewis, J.P., Kim, T.Y., Bulut, M., Narayanan, S.: Expressive facial animation synthesis by learning speech coarticulation and expression spaces. IEEE Trans. Vis. Comput. Graph. **12**, 1523–1534 (2006)

24. Dong, L., Wang, Y., Ni, K., Lu, K.: Facial animation system based on image warping algorithm. In: 2011 IEEE International Conference on Electronics, Communications and Control, pp. 2648–2653. IEEE Press, Ningbo (2011)

25. Weise, T., Bouaziz, S., Li, H., Pauly, M.: Realtime performance-based facial animation. ACM Trans. Graph. **30**, 77–86 (2011)

26. Bouaziz, S., Wang, Y., Pauly, M.: Online modeling for realtime facial animation. ACM Trans. Graph. **32**, 40–49 (2013)

Optimized Laplacian Sparse Coding for Image Classification

Lei Chen[1]([✉]), Sheng Gao[1], Baofeng Yuan[1], Zhe Qi[1], Yafang Liu[1], and Fei Wang[2]

[1] Beijing Key Laboratory of Intelligent Space Robotic Systems Technology and Applications, Beijing Institute of Spacecraft System Engineering, Beijing 100094, P.R. China
chenleibit@gmail.com
[2] Xi'an Jiaotong University, Xi'an 710049, Shaanxi, P.R. China

Abstract. Laplacian sparse coding exhibits good performance for image classification, because of its outstanding ability to preserve the locality and similarity information of the codes. However, there still exists two drawbacks during the Laplacian graph construction: (1) It has expensive computational cost, which significantly limits the applicability of the Laplacian sparse coding to large-scale data sets. (2) Euclidean distance does not necessarily reflect the inherent distribution of the data. To construct a more robust Laplacian graph, we introduce a local landmarks approximation method instead of the traditional k-nearest neighbor algorithm, and design a new form of adjacency matrix. Based on the Nesterov's gradient projection algorithm, we develop an effective numerical solver to optimize the local landmarks approximation problem with guaranteed quadratic convergence. The obtained codes have more discriminating power compared with traditional sparse coding approaches for image classification. Comprehensive experimental results on publicly available datasets demonstrate the effectiveness of our method.

Keywords: Laplacian sparse coding · Laplacian matrix · Image classification · Nesterov's gradient projection

1 Introduction

Image classification is one of the fundamental problems in the field of computer vision and pattern recognition. The bag-of-features (BoF) model [18] has been commonly used to generate feature representations for image classification due to its invariance to scale, translation, and rotation. It consists of four steps: local features extraction, visual words generation, feature coding, and feature pooling. Among these steps, feature coding is the most important one which greatly influences the image classification system in both accuracy and speed. The essence of the feature coding is how to activate the codewords, *i.e.*, which codewords are activated and how large the amplitudes of their responses are [7]. Various coding strategies [6,10,19,20,22–24,27] are proposed to encode local features in literature.

© Springer International Publishing Switzerland 2015
Y.-J. Zhang (Ed.): ICIG 2015, Part II, LNCS 9218, pp. 636–645, 2015.
DOI: 10.1007/978-3-319-21963-9_58

Recently, Gao *et al.* [6] and Zheng *et al.* [27] imposed a graph Laplacian constraint on the standard Lasso formulation to take into account the local manifold structure underlying the input data. They quantize local features more robustly from the perspective of similarity between codes. Since the obtained sparse codes vary smoothly along the geodesics of the data manifold, Laplacian sparse coding (LSC) shows good performance for image classification. Generally, in the Laplacian sparse coding, k-nearest neighbor (KNN) algorithm is used to construct the Laplacian graph. However, the construction cost of the KNN is $\mathcal{O}(n^2 \log k)$, which significantly limits the applicability of the LSC to large-scale data sets. In addition, the edge weight matrix W_{ij} between samples $\mathbf{x}_i$ and $\mathbf{x}_j$ is estimated via hard-assignment [16] expressed as

$$W_{ij} = \begin{cases} 1, & \text{if } \mathbf{x}_i \in N_\varepsilon(\mathbf{x}_j) \text{ or } \mathbf{x}_j \in N_\varepsilon(\mathbf{x}_i) \\ 0, & \text{otherwise}, \end{cases}$$

or via a Gaussian function defined as

$$W_{ij} = \exp\left(\frac{\|\mathbf{x}_i - \mathbf{x}_j\|^2}{\sigma^2} \right).$$

Here $N_\varepsilon(\mathbf{x}_j)$ represents the set of ε nearest neighbors of $\mathbf{x}_j$. In this case, the edge weight matrix W_{ij} may not characterize the underlying distribution of the data and it is difficult to choose an appropriate kernel bandwidth.

In this paper, we extend the original Laplacian sparse coding and present an optimized Laplacian sparse coding for image classification. To construct the Laplacian graph, we introduce a local landmarks approximation (LLA) method instead of the traditional k-nearest neighbor algorithm, and design a new form of adjacency matrix. The local landmarks approximation method is able to provide nonnegative and sparse adjacent matrix W_{ij} and the total time complexity scales linearly with the number of samples.

2   Preliminaries

2.1   Sparse Coding

Let $\mathcal{X} = [\mathbf{x}_1, \mathbf{x}_2, \cdots, \mathbf{x}_n] \in \mathbb{R}^{d \times n}$ be a data matrix with n samples in d dimensions, $\mathcal{B} = [\boldsymbol{b}_1, \boldsymbol{b}_2, \cdots, \boldsymbol{b}_k] \in \mathbb{R}^{d \times k}$ be the dictionary where each column represents a visual word, and $\mathcal{S} = [\boldsymbol{s}_1, \boldsymbol{s}_2, \cdots, \boldsymbol{s}_n] \in \mathbb{R}^{k \times n}$ be the coding matrix. The goal of sparse coding is to learn a dictionary and corresponding sparse representation such that each input local feature $\mathbf{x}_i$ can be well approximated by the dictionary $\mathcal{B}$ while maximally preserving the signal fidelity. The objective of sparse coding can be formulated as

$$\arg\min_{\mathcal{B}, \mathcal{S}} \sum_{i=1}^{n} \|\mathbf{x}_i - \mathcal{B}\boldsymbol{s}_i\|_2^2 + \lambda f(\boldsymbol{s}_i) \tag{1}$$

$$\text{s.t. } \|\boldsymbol{b}_l\|_2 \leq 1,$$

where $f(\cdot)$ measures the sparseness of s_i, and λ is the tradeoff parameter used to balance the sparsity of the codes and the reconstruction error.

A straightforward choice of $f(\cdot)$ is the ℓ_0 norm, i.e., $f(s_i) = \|s_i\|_0$. $\|s_i\|_0$ enforces s_i to have a small number of nonzero elements. However, solving Eq. (1) has been proven to be an NP-hard problem [13]. Recently, a sparsity regularization term, ℓ_1 norm, replaces ℓ_0 norm to approximately solve Eq. (1), i.e., $f(s_i) = \|s_i\|_1$. In this case, although Eq. (1) is not convex in both variables, it is convex in $\mathcal{B}$ only or $\mathcal{S}$ only. Therefore, it can be solved by alternatingly optimizing one variable while fixing the other one. Optimization toolboxes [12] can be used to efficiently solve Eq. (1).

2.2   Laplacian Sparse Coding

The data is more likely to reside on a low-dimensional sub-manifold which has a much smaller intrinsic dimensionality in real applications [1]. The geometric structure of the data is important for discrimination, i.e., close-by features tend to have similar codes and distant ones have different codes. To make the basis vectors consider the intrinsic geometric structure of the input data, Gao et al. [6] and Zheng et al. [27] imposed a graph Laplacian (similarity) constraint on the sparse coding and presented LSC. LSC constructs a KNN graph $\mathcal{G}$ with n vertices where each vertex corresponds to a feature $\mathbf{x}_i$. Let W_{ij} be the weight matrix of $\mathcal{G}$. If $\mathbf{x}_i$ is among the K-neighbors of $\mathbf{x}_j$ or $\mathbf{x}_j$ is among the K-neighbors of $\mathbf{x}_i$, $W_{ij} = 1$, otherwise, $W_{ij} = 0$. Define D is a diagonal matrix whose elements are column (or row) sums of W, i.e., $d_i = \sum_{j=1}^n W_{ij}$ and $D = diag(d_1, d_2, \cdots, d_n)$.

The criterion for preserving the geometric structure in graph $\mathcal{G}$ is given by

$$\min_{\mathcal{S}} \frac{1}{2} \sum_{i,j=1}^n \|s_i - s_j\|^2 W_{ij} = \mathrm{tr}(\mathcal{S}L\mathcal{S}^\top),$$

where $L = D - W$ is the Laplacian matrix. Integrating the criterion into Eq. (1) leads to LSC.

3   The Proposed Method

In this section, we introduce a local landmarks approximation (LLA) method to efficiently construct the Laplacian graph, and design a new form of Laplacian matrix L. Then the new L is incorporated into the original LSC to improve the sparse representations.

3.1   Local Landmarks Approximation

Given $\mathcal{X} = [\mathbf{x}_1, \mathbf{x}_2, \cdots, \mathbf{x}_n] \in \mathbb{R}^{d \times n}$, let $\mathcal{D} = [\mathbf{d}_1, \mathbf{d}_2, \cdots, \mathbf{d}_m] \in \mathbb{R}^{d \times m}$ denote a set of landmarks which is acquired by performing k-means clustering algorithm on $\mathcal{X}$. Considering the geometric structure information of data points, we aim to find a cross-similarity matrix $H \in \mathbb{R}^{n \times m}$ that measures the potential relationships between data points in $\mathcal{X}$ and landmarks in $\mathcal{D}$. We reconstruct $\mathbf{x}_i$ as a combination of its s closest landmarks in the feature space. Similar to locality-constrained linear coding (LLC) [19], a local landmarks approximation method is proposed to optimize the coefficient vector $\boldsymbol{h}_i \in \mathbb{R}^s$:

$$\min_{\boldsymbol{h}_i \in \mathbb{R}^s} g(\boldsymbol{h}_i) = \frac{1}{2}\left\| \mathbf{x}_i - \sum_{j=1}^{s} \boldsymbol{d}_j \boldsymbol{h}_i \right\|^2,$$

$$s.t. \quad \mathbf{1}^\top \boldsymbol{h}_i = 1, \ \boldsymbol{h}_i \geq 0 \tag{2}$$

where s entries of the vector $\boldsymbol{h}_i$ correspond to s coefficients contributed by s nearest landmarks. The constraint $\mathbf{1}^\top \boldsymbol{h}_i = 1$ follows the shift-invariant requirements. It is easy to see that the constraints set $C = \{\boldsymbol{h}_i \in \mathbb{R}^s : \mathbf{1}^\top \boldsymbol{h}_i = 1, \ \boldsymbol{h}_i \geq 0\}$ is a convex set. The main difference between LLC and our method is that we incorporate inequality constraints (*i.e.*, nonnegative constraints) into the object function as we require the similarity measure to be a positive value. Therefore we need to develop a different optimization algorithm to solve Eq. (2).

In this section, we employ Nesterov's gradient projection (NGP) [14] method, a first-order optimization procedure, to solve Eq. (2). A key step of NGP is how to efficiently project a vector $\boldsymbol{h}_i$ onto the corresponding constraint set C. We detail NGP for solving the constrained optimization problem Eq. (2) by adopting the Euclidean projection. Denote

$$\mathcal{Q}_{\beta,\boldsymbol{v}}(\boldsymbol{h}_i) = g(\boldsymbol{v}) + \nabla g(\boldsymbol{v})^\top (\boldsymbol{h}_i - \boldsymbol{v}) + \frac{\beta}{2}\|\boldsymbol{h}_i - \boldsymbol{v}\|_2^2, \tag{3}$$

which is the first-order Taylor expansion of $g(\boldsymbol{h}_i)$ at $\boldsymbol{v}$ with the squared Euclidean distance between $\boldsymbol{h}_i$ and $\boldsymbol{v}$ as a regularization term. Here $\nabla g(\boldsymbol{v})$ is the gradient of $g(\boldsymbol{h}_i)$ at $\boldsymbol{v}$.

We can easily obtain

$$\min_{\boldsymbol{h}_i \in C} \mathcal{Q}_{\beta,\boldsymbol{v}}(\boldsymbol{h}_i) = \Pi_C\left(\boldsymbol{v} - \frac{1}{\beta}\nabla g(\boldsymbol{v})\right), \tag{4}$$

where $\Pi_C(\boldsymbol{v}) = \min_{\boldsymbol{v}' \in C} \|\boldsymbol{v} - \boldsymbol{v}'\|_2^2$ is the Euclidean projection of $\boldsymbol{v}$ onto C. The projection operator $\Pi_C(\cdot)$ has been implemented efficiently in $O(s \log s)$ [3].

From Eq. (4), the solution of Eq. (2) can be obtained by generating a sequence $\{\boldsymbol{h}_i^{(t)}\}$ at $\boldsymbol{v}^{(t)} = \boldsymbol{h}_i^{(t)} + \alpha_t(\boldsymbol{h}_i^{(t)} - \boldsymbol{h}_i^{(t-1)})$, *i.e.*,

$$\boldsymbol{h}_i^{(t+1)} = \Pi_C\left(\boldsymbol{v}^{(t)} - \frac{1}{\beta_t}\nabla g(\boldsymbol{v}^{(t)})\right)$$

$$= \min_{\boldsymbol{h}_i \in C} \mathcal{Q}_{\beta_t,\boldsymbol{v}^{(t)}}(\boldsymbol{h}_i). \tag{5}$$

In NGP, choosing proper parameters β_t and α_t is also significant for the convergence property. Similar to [14], we set $\alpha_t = (\delta_{t-1} - 1)/\delta_t$ with $\delta_t = (1 + \sqrt{1 + 4\delta_{t-1}^2})/2$, $\delta_0 = 0$ and $\delta_1 = 1$. β_t is selected by finding the smallest nonnegative integer j such that $g(\boldsymbol{h}_i) \leq \mathcal{Q}_{\beta_t,\boldsymbol{v}^{(t)}}(\boldsymbol{h}_i)$ with $\beta_t = 2^j \beta_{t-1}$.

After getting the optimal weight vector $\boldsymbol{h}_i$, we set $\boldsymbol{H}_{ij'} = \boldsymbol{h}_i$, where j' is indices corresponding to s nearest landmarks and the cardinality $|j'| = s$. For the rest entries of $\boldsymbol{H}_i$, we set zeros. In contrast to weights defined by kernel functions (e.g., Gaussian kernel), the local landmarks approximation method is able to provide optimized and sparser weights.

The time complexity of seeking m landmarks using k-means clustering is $\mathcal{O}(mn)$ where n is the number of samples. The time complexity of solving the optimal H is $\mathcal{O}(smn)$, where s is the number of nearest landmarks of each data. We use a fixed number $m \ll n$ of landmarks for calculating H, which is independent of the sample size n. Thus, the total time complexity scales linearly with the n.

3.2 The New Laplacian Matrix

Note that the adjacency matrix $W \in \mathbb{R}^{n \times n}$ between all samples encountered in practice usually have low numerical-rank compared with the matrix size. In Sect. 3.1, we have obtained the nonnegative and sparse $H \in \mathbb{R}^{n \times m}$, $m \ll n$. Each row H_i in H is a new representation of raw sample $\mathbf{x}_i$. $\mathbf{x}_i \rightarrow H_i$ is reminiscent of *sparse coding* [19] with the basis $\mathcal{D}$ since $\mathbf{x}_i \approx \widetilde{\mathcal{D}}\boldsymbol{h}_i = \mathcal{D}H_i$, where $\widetilde{\mathcal{D}} \in \mathbb{R}^{d \times s}$ is a sub-matrix composed of s nearest landmarks of $\mathbf{x}_i$. That is to say, samples $\mathbf{x} \in \mathbb{R}^{d \times n}$ can be represented in the new space, no matter what the original features are. Intuitively, we can design the adjacency matrix W to be a low-rank form

$$W = HH^\top, \tag{6}$$

where the inner product is regarded as the metric to measure the adjacent weight between samples. Equation (6) implies that if two samples are correlative (i.e., $W_{ij} > 0$), they share at least one landmark, otherwise $W_{ij} = 0$. W defined in Eq. (6) naturally preserves some good properties (e.g., sparseness and nonnegativeness).

With the design of W, Laplacian graph regularization can be approximated as

$$\mathcal{S}^\top L \mathcal{S} = \mathcal{S}^\top (diag(HH^\top \mathbf{1}) - HH^\top)\mathcal{S}, \tag{7}$$

where $\mathbf{1}$ denote the column vector whose entries are all ones. Nonnegative W guarantees the positive semi-definite (PSD) property of L. Keeping L PSD is important to ensure that the graph regularizer $\mathcal{S}^\top L \mathcal{S}$ is convex.

3.3 Optimized Sparse Coding

Integrating Eq. (7) into Eq. (1) leads to the optimized Laplacian sparse coding,

$$\arg\min_{\mathcal{B}, \mathcal{S}} \|\mathcal{X} - \mathcal{B}\mathcal{S}\|_2^2 + \lambda \sum_{i=1}^{n} \|\boldsymbol{s}_i\|_1 + \gamma \text{tr}(\mathcal{S}L\mathcal{S}^\top)$$

$$s.t. \ \|\boldsymbol{b}_l\|_2 \leq 1, \ \boldsymbol{s}_i \geq 0, \tag{8}$$

where γ is a graph regularization parameter to balance the sparsity and similarity.

Given a dictionary $\mathcal{B}$, sparse codes $\mathcal{S}$ can be solved using the accelerated proximal gradient (APG) algorithm discussed in [2]. Since the original APG method is designed for unconstrained minimization problem, we need to convert the constrained minimization problem Eq. (8) into an unconstrained one via the indicator function $\phi(\boldsymbol{s}_i)$ defined by

$$\phi(\boldsymbol{s}_i) = \begin{cases} 0 & if \ \boldsymbol{s}_i \succeq 0, \\ +\infty & otherwise. \end{cases} \tag{9}$$

With $\phi(\boldsymbol{s}_i)$, Eq. (8) can be optimized as

$$\arg\min_{\mathcal{S}} \|\mathcal{X} - \mathcal{BS}\|_2^2 + \lambda \mathbf{1}^\top \mathcal{S}\mathbf{1} + \gamma \mathrm{tr}\left(\mathcal{SLS}^\top\right) + \phi(\mathcal{S}). \tag{10}$$

The APG method can be applied to Eq. (10) with

$$\begin{aligned} F(\mathcal{S}) &= \arg\min_{\mathcal{S}} \|\mathcal{X} - \mathcal{BS}\|_2^2 + \lambda \mathbf{1}^\top \mathcal{S}\mathbf{1} + \gamma \mathrm{tr}\left(\mathcal{SLS}^\top\right) \\ G(\mathcal{S}) &= \phi(\mathcal{S}), \end{aligned} \tag{11}$$

where $F(\mathcal{S})$ is a differentiable convex function, and $G(\mathcal{S})$ is a non-smooth convex function.

Then, we describe the method of learning the dictionary $\mathcal{B}$, while fixing the coefficient matrix $\mathcal{S}$. The problem becomes an ℓ_2-constrained optimization problem

$$\arg\min_{B,\mathcal{S}} \|\mathcal{X} - \mathcal{BS}\|_2^2 \tag{12}$$
$$s.t. \ \ \|\boldsymbol{b}_l\|_2 \le 1.$$

There are many methods for solving this problem [6,27]. Due to the space limitation, we omit the technical details here.

4 Experimental Results

We test the proposed method on three datasets: UIUC-sport [9], Scene-15 [5,8,15], and Caltech-101 [4].

We adopt the commonly used SIFT descriptor [11] as the low-level feature. The 128 dimensional SIFT feature is densely extracted from images on a grid with a step of 8 pixels under the scale of 16×16. We randomly select $500,000$ features to learn the dictionary size of 1024. After all features are encoded, the Spatial Pyramid Matching with levels of $[1 \times 1, 2 \times 2, 4 \times 4]$ is performed. In training and testing procedure, the one-vs-all linear support vector machine (SVM) is used for its advantages in speed and excellent performance in maximum feature pooling based image classification [22]. In the UIUC-sport dataset and Caltech-101 dataset, we set $\lambda = 0.35$, $\gamma = 0.08$, and in the Scene-15 dataset, we set $\lambda = 0.4$, $\gamma = 0.2$. For each dataset, the training images are randomly selected, and the results reported are the averages of 5 independent experiments.

4.1   UIUC-sport Dataset

The UIUC-sport dataset [9] contains 1579 images of 8 categories including badminton, bocce, croquet, polo, rock climbing, rowing, sailing, and snow boarding. The number of images ranges from 137 to 250 per category. For fair comparisons, we randomly select 70 images from each class as training data and 60 images for test as the same with previous methods. The comparison results are shown in Table 1, where the results of other methods are available from published papers conveniently. From Table 1, the results indicate that our method outperforms other coding methods. By adding the Laplacian term, similar features will be encoded into similar sparse codes. Thus, our method is nearly 6 % above the ScSPM. Moreover, the proposed method outperforms LLC by 5.6 %. It is because that the LLC only uses the geometrical relationship between the feature and visual words but doesn't take into account the geometrical relationship between features.

Table 1. Comparison results on UIUC-sport dataset.

Methods	Classification accuracies (%)
SAC [10]	82.29 ± 1.84
ScSPM [22]	82.74 ± 1.46
LLC [19]	83.09 ± 1.30
HIK+one class SVM [21]	83.54 ± 1.13
LSCSPM [6]	85.18 ± 0.46
LR-LGSC [25]	87.14 ± 1.52
Our Method	88.71 ± 1.02

4.2   Scene-15 Dataset

The Scene-15 dataset contains 4485 images of 15 different scenes, where 8 categories are originally collected by Oliva *et al.* [15], 5 are provided by Li *et al.* [5] and 2 are added by Lazebnik *et al.* [8]. The number of images per category ranges from 200 to 400. This dataset contains not only indoor scenes, such as store, living-room, but also outdoor scenes, such as streets and mountain etc. To keep consistent with the previous work [6,8,20,22], we randomly choose 100 images per category and test on the rest. Table 2 shows the comparison results with previous approaches. The classification accuracies of the previous works are acquired from [6]. It indicates that the proposed method can achieve extremely high performance on scene classification. Our method outperforms the ScSPM by 7.3 % and is nearly 1 % above the LSCSPM. The probable reason is that the local landmarks approximation method is able to provide optimized and sparser weight matrix W_{ij}.

4.3   Caltech-101 Dataset

The Caltech-101 dataset [4] contains 101 object categories, such as cameras, chairs, flowers, vehicles, etc. All the categories are with significant variances in

Table 2. Comparison results on Scene-15 dataset.

Methods	Classification accuracies (%)
SAC [10]	82.70 ± 0.39
SPM [8]	81.40 ± 0.50
ScSPM [22]	84.30 ± 0.50
LLC [19]	81.50 ± 0.87
HIK+one class SVM [21]	84.00 ± 0.46
LSCSPM [6]	89.78 ± 0.40
LR-LGSC [25]	90.58 ± 0.54
Our Method	90.67 ± 0.41

shape and cluttered backgrounds. This dataset has 9144 images in all, and the image number varies from 31 to 800 per category. Moreover, it is individually added to an extra "background" category, *i.e.*, BACKGROUND_Google. For each category, we randomly select 5, 10, 15, ..., 30 images for training and test on the remaining as the same with previous work. The results compared with previous methods are listed in Table 3, which indicates that our method outperforms the state-of-the-art methods. From Table 3, we see that the performance gap between our method and other methods is narrowed when the training images increases.

Table 3. Comparison results on Caltech-101 dataset.

Number of training sample	5	10	15	20	25	30
D-KSVD [26]	49.60	59.50	65.10	68.60	71.10	73.00
ScSPM [22]	–	–	67.00	–	–	73.20
LCSR [17]	–	–	–	–	–	73.23
LLC [19]	51.15	59.77	65.43	67.74	70.16	73.44
SAC [10]	–	–	–	–	–	74.21
Our Method	54.31	64.73	69.56	72.38	73.35	74.88

5 Conclusion

In this work, we have proposed an optimized Laplacian sparse coding which integrates the new graph Laplacian regularizer into the traditional sparse coding. We obtain more discriminative sparse representation for image classification. A nonnegative and sparse adjacency matrix is designed to make the graph regularizer convex. The total time complexity for constructing Laplacian graph scales linearly with the number of samples. Experiments on three public datasets demonstrate our method is competitive compared with the state-of-the-art methods.

Acknowledgment. This work was supported by the Natural Science Foundation of China (No61231018 and No61305112), National High Technology Research and Development Program (2013AA014601).

References

1. Belkin, M., Niyogi, P., Sindhwani, V.: Manifold regularization: a geometric framework for learning from labeled and unlabeled examples. J. Mach. Learn. Res. **7**, 2399–2434 (2006)
2. Bohan, Z., Huchuan, L., Ziyang, X., Dong, W.: Visual tracking via discriminative sparse similarity map. IEEE Trans. Image Process. **23**(4), 1872–1881 (2014)
3. Duchi, J., Shalev-Shwartz, S., Singer, Y., Chandra, T.: Efficient projections onto the 11-ball for learning in high dimensions. In: International Conference on Machine Learning, pp. 272–279. ACM (2008)
4. Fei-Fei, L., Fergus, R., Perona, P.: Learning generative visual models from few training examples: an incremental bayesian approach tested on 101 object categories. Comput. Vis. Image Underst. **106**(1), 59–70 (2007)
5. Fei-Fei, L., Perona, P.: A bayesian hierarchical model for learning natural scene categories. In: IEEE Computer Society Conference on Computer Vision and Pattern Recognition, vol. 2, pp. 524–531. IEEE (2005)
6. Gao, S., Tsang, I., Chia, L.: Laplacian sparse coding, hypergraph laplacian sparse coding, and applications. IEEE Trans. Pattern Anal. Mach. Intell. **35**(7), 92–104 (2013)
7. Huang, Y., Wu, Z., Wang, L., Tan, T.: Feature coding in image classification: a comprehensive study. IEEE Trans. Pattern Anal. Mach. Intell. **36**(3), 493–506 (2014)
8. Lazebnik, S., Schmid, C., Ponce, J.: Beyond bags of features: spatial pyramid matching for recognizing natural scene categories. In: IEEE Computer Society Conference on Computer Vision and Pattern Recognition, vol. 2, pp. 2169–2178. IEEE (2006)
9. Li, L.J., Fei-Fei, L.: What, where and who? classifying events by scene and object recognition. In: IEEE International Conference on Computer Vision, pp. 1–8. IEEE (2007)
10. Liu, L., Wang, L., Liu, X.: In defense of soft-assignment coding. In: IEEE International Conference on Computer Vision, pp. 2486–2493. IEEE (2011)
11. Lowe, D.G.: Distinctive image features from scale-invariant keypoints. Int. J. Comput. Vis. **60**(2), 91–110 (2004)
12. Mairal, J., Bach, F., Ponce, J., Sapiro, G.: Online learning for matrix factorization and sparse coding. J. Mach. Learn. Res. **11**, 19–60 (2010)
13. Natarajan, B.K.: Sparse approximate solutions to linear systems. SIAM J. Comput. **24**(2), 227–234 (1995)
14. Nesterov, Y.: Introductory Lectures on Convex Optimization, vol. 87. Springer Science & Business Media, Boston (2004)
15. Oliva, A., Torralba, A.: Modeling the shape of the scene: a holistic representation of the spatial envelope. Int. J. Comput. Vis. **42**(3), 145–175 (2001)

16. Philbin, J., Chum, O., Isard, M., Sivic, J., Zisserman, A.: Lost in quantization: improving particular object retrieval in large scale image databases. In: IEEE Computer Society Conference on Computer Vision and Pattern Recognition, pp. 1–8. IEEE (2008)
17. Shabou, A., LeBorgne, H.: Locality-constrained and spatially regularized coding for scene categorization. In: IEEE Computer Society Conference on Computer Vision and Pattern Recognition, pp. 3618–3625. IEEE (2012)
18. Sivic, J., Zisserman, A.: Video google: a text retrieval approach to object matching in videos. In: IEEE International Conference on Computer Vision, pp. 1470–1477. IEEE (2003)
19. Wang, J., Yang, J., Yu, K., Lv, F., Huang, T., Gong, Y.: Locality-constrained linear coding for image classification. In: IEEE Computer Society Conference on Computer Vision and Pattern Recognition, pp. 3360–3367. IEEE (2010)
20. Wang, Z., Feng, J., Yan, S., Xi, H.: Linear distance coding for image classification. IEEE Trans. Image Process. **22**(2), 537–548 (2013)
21. Wu, J., Rehg, J.M.: Beyond the euclidean distance: creating effective visual codebooks using the histogram intersection kernel. In: IEEE Computer Society Conference on Computer Vision and Pattern Recognition, pp. 630–637. IEEE (2009)
22. Yang, J., Yu, K., Gong, Y., Huang, T.: Linear spatial pyramid matching using sparse coding for image classification. In: IEEE Computer Society Conference on Computer Vision and Pattern Recognition, pp. 1794–1801. IEEE (2009)
23. Yu, K., Zhang, T., Gong, Y.: Nonlinear learning using local coordinate coding. In: Advances in Neural Information Processing Systems, pp. 2223–2231 (2009)
24. Zhang, C., Liu, J., Tian, Q., Xu, C., Lu, H., Ma, S.: Image classification by nonnegative sparse coding, low-rank and sparse decomposition. In: IEEE Computer Society Conference on Computer Vision and Pattern Recognition, pp. 1673–1680. IEEE (2011)
25. Zhang, L., Ma, C.: Low-rank decomposition and laplacian group sparse coding for image classification. Neurocomputing **135**, 339–347 (2014)
26. Zhang, Q., Li, B.: Discriminative k-svd for dictionary learning in face recognition. In: IEEE Computer Society Conference on Computer Vision and Pattern Recognition, pp. 2691–2698. IEEE (2010)
27. Zheng, M., Bu, J., Chen, C., Wang, C., Zhang, L., Qiu, G., Cai, D.: Graph regularized sparse coding for image representation. IEEE Trans. Image Process. **20**(5), 1327–1336 (2011)

Author Index

Ali, Sajid I-321
An, Ping II-103, II-116
Anzhi, Yue I-278
Arab, Maryam II-147
Atitey, Komlan I-373

Bai, Junlan I-415
Bai, Lian-fa I-240, III-111
Bai, Ti I-462
Bao, Xiuguo I-529
Bao, Yanxia III-552
Bernal, Salvador Garcia I-100

Cai, Bin III-522
Cai, Zhanchuan I-43, I-198
Cang, Yan I-373
Cao, Jianwen II-75
Cao, Ting III-212
Carter, Christopher III-545, III-562
Chan, Ka-Hou III-349
Chan, Wentao III-260
Chang, Chin-Chen I-415
Chang, Shaojie I-462
Chao, Jia II-219
Che, Xiaodong II-240
Chen, Changhong I-307, III-247
Chen, Chongmu III-310
Chen, Lei II-636
Chen, Lu III-111
Chen, Ping I-218
Chen, Qiang I-480
Chen, Shuhan I-30
Chen, Shumiao III-1
Chen, Wufan III-483
Chen, Xi I-462
Chen, Ying III-11
Chen, Yiqiang III-453
Chen, Yuyun III-169
Chen, Zengsi I-252
Cheng, Guojun I-53
Cheng, Hailong III-430
Cheng, Yuanzhi I-629, III-410
Choe, Chunhwa III-402
Choe, Gwangmin III-402

Chunmeng, Huang III-46
Cui, Yingjie II-11
Cui, Ziguan II-226

Da, Feipeng I-541, II-347
Davis, Graham III-583
Deng, Hong I-86
Deng, Huan II-208
Deng, Jiankang II-373
Deng, Lujuan III-483
Deng, Xing I-541
Di, Huijun III-236
Ding, Youdong I-504, II-524
Dong, Jing I-151
Dong, Lanfang II-621
Dong, Zhen I-176, II-185
Dongxu, He I-278
Du, Sheng I-504
Du, Weiqiang II-361
Duan, Huilong I-562, II-438
Du-Yan, Bi III-360

El Abdi, Moad I-110
El Rhalibi, Abdennour III-545, III-562, III-583
Elad, Michael III-333
Ettaïeb, Saïd II-475

Fan, Heng III-20
Fang, Yuchun I-288
Fei, Xuan I-654
Feng, Liu II-156
Feng, Qi III-402
Feng, Qianjin III-483
Feng, Tiejun III-11
Feng, Xiaoyi II-462
Feng, Ye II-446
Fu, Jianbo II-240

Gai, Shaoyan II-347
Gan, Jun-ying I-350
Gan, Peng III-68
Gan, Zongliang I-307, II-226, III-247
Gao, Huiping I-21
Gao, Sheng II-636

Ge, Jing   II-301
Ge, Ning   I-229
Geng, Lei   II-361, III-11, III-68
Geng, Li-Chuan   II-18
Geng, Ze-xun   II-18
Gong, Yan   III-212
Guang-chao, Wang   II-156
Guo, Chengan   I-338
Guo, Chun-Chao   II-275
Guo, Feng   I-64
Guo, Jinlin   I-447
Guo, Shuxuan   I-447
Guo, Yubin   I-405
Guo, Yueting   III-223
Guo, Zijun   I-405

Hamrouni, Kamel   II-475
Han, Bo Chong   III-420
Han, Jing   I-240, III-111
Han, Lizhen   III-599
Han, Sokmin   III-402
Han, Zhenqi   I-110, I-288
He, Jing   II-147
He, Min   I-529
He, Wenjing   III-453
He, Yujie   II-491
He, Yu-Jie   III-393
He, Yuqing   II-453
Hou, Xiang-Dan   III-474
Hou, Xiaodan   II-565
Hou, Yangyang   III-212
Hou, Yu   II-103
Hou, Zhiqiang   I-434, III-491
Hu, Bin   II-275
Hu, Dan   III-491
Hu, Gengran   III-169
Hu, Jing   II-584
Hu, Weiling   I-562, II-438
Hu, Xiao-Jun   II-275
Hu, Xuefeng   I-75, I-516
Hu, Xuelong   I-30, III-137
Hu, Yangyang   I-516
Hu, Yuanyuan   I-307, II-226
Hua, Geng Guo   II-219
Huang, Dongjin   I-504, II-524
Huang, Shiqi   II-164
Huang, Wei   III-1
Huo, Lichao   I-165
Hurst, William   III-583

Idrees, Muhammad   I-321

Jayarathne, Uditha L.   I-664
Jia, Yu   I-43, I-198
Jian, Wang   II-156
Jian, Yang   I-278
Jiang, Bo   III-55
Jiang, Chen   III-125
Jiang, Chuan   III-430
Jiang, Li   II-197
Jiang, Qiuping   I-10
Jiang, Wuhan   II-11
Jiang, Xiaoyue   II-462
Jiang, Zhiguo   III-34
Jianglei, Huo   III-46
Jian-kang, Qiu   I-571
Jin, Fei   II-600
Jin, Lianbao   I-470
Jin, Peiquan   II-173
Jin, Wuwen   III-285
Jing, Junfeng   III-460
Jingbo, Chen   I-278
Juan, Su   I-188

Kaba, Djibril   I-614, III-321
Kang, Wang   I-321
Kapsouras, Ioannis   II-547
Ke, Wei   III-349
Khatibi, Siamak   II-572
Kim, Hun   III-402

Lai, Jian-Huang   II-275
Lai, Junhao   I-43, I-198
Lao, Songyang   I-447
Lei, Hang   I-218
Lei, Lin   I-278
Lei, Xiaoyong   I-165, I-297
Leng, Chengcai   I-470
Li, Bo   I-470
Li, Chenglong   III-55
Li, Chuguang   I-43, I-198
Li, Congli   I-206, III-180
Li, Donglai   I-1
Li, Dongxiao   III-499
Li, Feng   II-361
Li, Hong   III-271
Li, Huifang   III-382, III-444
Li, Jing   III-573
Li, Kun   II-453
Li, Ling-yan   III-125

Li, Min   II-491, III-393
Li, Panpan   II-103
Li, Pengfei   III-460
Li, Rui   III-125
Li, Tao   II-611
Li, Xinghua   III-444
Li, Xulong   I-321
Li, Yang   I-136, III-34
Li, Yongmin   I-614, III-321
Li, Yujie   III-137, III-510
Lian, Luzhen   I-136
Liang, Wei   I-176, II-385
Liang, Xiaoying   I-151
Liang, Xuefeng   II-90
Liao, Qingmin   I-53
Liao, Qiyu   II-500
Li-fang, Wu   I-571
Lin, Wang   III-360
Lin, Yi   II-34
Lin-Yuan, He   III-360
Liu, Bao-Di   I-121
Liu, Bin   I-423
Liu, Changshu   II-453
Liu, Daizhi   II-164
Liu, Feng   I-307, II-226, III-247
Liu, Guichi   II-197
Liu, Hongcheng   I-218
Liu, Jingtai   III-197
Liu, Jiquan   I-562, II-438
Liu, Ju   II-301, II-430, III-573
Liu, Jun   III-223
Liu, Junfa   III-453
Liu, Junquan   I-541
Liu, Kejia   I-423
Liu, Kun   II-584
Liu, Ningzhong   I-21
Liu, Ping   III-11
Liu, Qingshan   II-373
Liu, Renzhang   III-169
Liu, Sha   III-223
Liu, Ting   II-312
Liu, Weiwei   II-538
Liu, Xiabing   II-385
Liu, Xiaofan   I-552, II-292
Liu, Xiaohui   I-614, III-321
Liu, Xiaojun   II-584
Liu, Xijia   I-229
Liu, Xuehui   II-75
Liu, Yafang   II-636
Liu, Yang   II-252, III-68

Liu, Yaqin   III-94
Liu, Yu   II-510
Liu, Yue   II-34, II-127
Liu, Zhigang   II-164
Liu, Zhisheng   I-263, I-589
Long, Dan   I-252
Long, Jiangtao   I-263, I-589
Lu, Chunyuan   I-470
Lu, Fei   I-297
Lu, Huimin   III-137, III-510
Lu, Sheng-tao   I-480
Lu, Wenjun   I-206, III-180
Lu, Xin   II-75
Lu, Zhentai   III-483
Lu, Zhimao   III-297
Luo, Chang-wei   III-125, III-522
Luo, Xiongbiao   I-664
Lv, You   III-321

Ma, Fei   I-562
Ma, Huan   III-483
Ma, Lizhuang   I-504
Ma, Ran   II-103
Ma, Wanli   I-121
Majdisova, Zuzana   II-261
Mandun, Zhang   III-46
Mao, Huiyun   I-494
Mendoza Chipantasi, Darío José   I-603
Meng, Rusong   III-34
Miao, Zhenjiang   III-188
Mou, Xuanqin   I-462

Na, Yuewei   I-579
Nan, Li Ji Jun   II-219
Ni, Kui   II-621
Ni, Yubo   II-284
Nie, Yixiao   III-94
Nikolaidis, Nikos   II-547
Niu, Yu   II-240

Pan, Jing   II-453
Pan, Weishen   I-494
Pan, Yanbin   III-169
Pan, Zhigeng   III-545, III-562, III-583
Pang, Yanwei   II-453
Pautler, Stephen E.   I-664
Pei, Mingtao   II-185, II-312
Pei, Yuru   II-538
Peng, Jinye   II-462
Peters, Terry M.   I-664

Ping, Xijian   II-565
Pitas, Ioannis   II-547

Qi, Lin   II-197
Qi, Zhe   II-636
Qiangqiang, Zhou   II-48
Qiao, Xiaotian   III-499
Qin, Jirui   III-94
Qing-jia, Li   II-156
Qiu, Bo   III-420
Qiu, Guoping   I-100
Qiu, Shirong   III-94
Qu, Lei   III-260
Qu, Xiwen   III-160
Quan-He, Li   III-360

Rao, Yunbo   I-218
Ren, Dongwei   I-86
Ren, Meimei   II-584
Ren, Mingwu   III-285
Ruan, Su   II-475
Rui, Jie   II-600
Runyu, Wei   I-571

Serikawa, Seiichi   III-137, III-510
Shan, Chunyan   II-361
Shang, Shikui   III-169
Shao, Feng   I-10
Shao, Jun   I-218
Shao, Wen-Ze   III-333
Shen, Bin   I-121
Shen, Huanfeng   III-382, III-444
Shen, Ju   I-640
Shen, Yang   III-552
Shen, Yu   II-1
Sheng, Linxue   II-1
Shenruoyang, Na   III-46
Shi, Changfa   III-410
Shi, Xiangbin   I-361
Shi, Yuying   I-64
Shi, Zhe   II-396
Shui, Bin   II-240
Si, Dandan   II-226
Si, Dong   II-147
Si, Jianmin   I-562, II-438
Skala, Vaclav   I-394, II-261
Smolik, Michal   I-394
Song, Hao   I-176
Song, Shaoyue   III-188
Song, Shengli   III-483

Su, Guangda   II-252
Su, Jingjing   III-68
Su, Long   II-361
Sudirman, Sud   III-545, III-562
Sun, Chengjian   II-396
Sun, Guoxia   II-301
Sun, Hongling   II-127
Sun, Jiande   II-430, III-573
Sun, Lei   III-197
Sun, Pan   I-562
Sun, Sheng   II-138
Sun, Weidong   III-534
Sun, Xi   III-260
Sun, Xiaoning   I-206, III-180
Sun, Yankui   II-446
Sun, Yue   III-197
Sun, Yuling   II-361

Tan, Taizhe   II-138
Tan, Yufei   III-11
Tang, Guijin   III-247
Tang, Jin   III-55
Tang, Pengbin   II-524
Tang, Wen   II-75, II-524
Tang, Wenhua   II-430
Tang, Xinjian   I-405
Tao, Linmi   III-236
Tao, XiaoMing   I-229
Tefas, Anastasios   II-547
Tian, Feng   III-599
Tian, Ye   III-297
Tu, Dengbiao   II-252
Tully, David   III-545, III-562, III-583

Velasco Erazo, Nancy del Rocío   I-603

Wan, Shouhong   II-173
Wan, Wenbo   II-301, II-430
Wang, Bin   I-350, I-562, II-438
Wang, Bingshu   I-75
Wang, Chao   II-600
Wang, Chenxing   II-347
Wang, Chenyang   II-611
Wang, Chuang   I-614, III-321
Wang, Da-Han   III-310
Wang, Dong   II-373
Wang, Fan   II-600
Wang, Fei   II-636
Wang, Hanzi   I-579, III-310
Wang, Hao   I-338

Wang, Hongxia II-164
Wang, Huan III-212
Wang, Jian II-284
Wang, Jianfu II-621
Wang, Jianxin II-116
Wang, Jing II-252
Wang, Jingjing II-60, II-500
Wang, Jinjiang III-11
Wang, Jinke I-629, III-410
Wang, Juan I-229
Wang, Kai II-1, II-611
Wang, Kuanquan I-86
Wang, Le II-11
Wang, Lianghao III-499
Wang, Linlin I-361
Wang, Qing I-480, II-417
Wang, Qingyun II-75
Wang, Qiong-Hua II-208
Wang, Taifeng II-417
Wang, Tianjiang III-402
Wang, Weiqiang III-160
Wang, Wulin III-573
Wang, Xinting III-552, III-599
Wang, Yajie I-361
Wang, Yatao II-621
Wang, Yaxing I-614, III-321
Wang, Yin II-524
Wang, Ying I-516
Wang, Yiting II-164
Wang, Yong-tian II-34
Wang, Yumeng II-385
Wang, Yunhong I-263, I-589
Wang, Yunong II-417
Wang, Yu-ping I-480
Wang, Zeng-fu III-125, III-522
Wang, Zidong I-614, III-321
Wei, Chen I-188
Wei, Xiaodong II-127
Wei, Zhen-Le III-148
Wei, Zhihui I-654, II-1, III-1
Weidong, Zhao II-48
Wen, Wei II-572
Wu, Enhua III-271
Wu, Fukun II-510
Wu, Guo-xi II-18
Wu, Jia II-347
Wu, Juerong III-499
Wu, Jun II-361, II-462, III-11, III-68
Wu, Lin I-263, I-589
Wu, Qiang III-573

Wu, Wen III-271, III-349
Wu, Xian II-621
Wu, Xinxiao I-176
Wu, Yanyan I-361
Wu, Yuwei II-185
Wu, Zhize II-173
Wu, Zhongke I-321

Xiang, Hang I-447
Xiang, Jinhai III-20
Xiao, Guobao I-579
Xiao, Liang I-654, II-1, III-1
Xiao, Yu II-361
Xiao, Zhitao II-361, III-11, III-68
Xie, Fengying III-34
Xie, Yanhong II-611
Xie, Zhifeng I-504, II-524
Xing, Yan II-208
Xiong, Naixue II-90
Xiong, Yude I-136
Xiong, Zhao-Long II-208
Xu, Guangyou III-236
Xu, Haoyu I-288
Xu, Jie I-529
Xu, Mingxue II-621
Xu, Ning III-160
Xu, Qiong I-462
Xu, Su III-369
Xu, Wanjun I-434
Xu, Xiaohong I-405
Xu, Xiaozhou III-534
Xu, Ying I-350
Xu, Zhijia II-138
Xue, Cuihong I-136
Xue, Song III-180

Yan, Jingqi I-1
Yang, Bo II-252
Yang, Hongyu II-240
Yang, Hua II-555
Yang, Jianjun I-640
Yang, Jing II-373
Yang, Shiyuan III-137
Yang, Wenming I-53
Yang, Xiaofeng I-121
Yang, Yubo II-252
Yang, Zhenjie II-361, III-68
Yang-yang, Zhang I-188
Ye, Ben I-43, I-198
Ye, Kun III-68

Yin, Ruoxuan   III-247
Yu, Jing   III-534
Yu, Jun   III-125, III-522
Yu, Lingyun   III-522
Yu, Meng   I-278
Yu, Nenghai   I-423, II-60, II-417, II-500
Yu, Renping   I-654
Yu, Wangsheng   I-434
Yu, Xiaohao   III-491
Yu, Yang   I-136
Yu, Yi   I-541
Yuan, Baofeng   II-636
Yuan, Fei   III-68
Yuan, Qiangqiang   III-444
Yuan, Quan   III-382
Yuan, Yuan   I-278
Yue, Lihua   II-173
Yue, Zhen   II-407
Yufei, Chen   II-48
Yu-sheng, Wang   II-156
Yu-xin, Mao   I-571

Zang, Hongbin   III-369
Zeng, Wenchao   II-407
Zeng, Xueying   II-407
Zha, Hongbin   II-538
Zha, Qiwen   II-252
Zhang, Bo   II-600
Zhang, Buyang   II-555
Zhang, Cuicui   II-90
Zhang, Dengfeng   I-176
Zhang, Dongping   I-53
Zhang, Fang   II-361, III-11
Zhang, Hao   II-565
Zhang, Hong   II-600
Zhang, Hongwei   III-460
Zhang, Hongying   III-369
Zhang, Hongzhi   I-86
Zhang, Jianxin   II-323
Zhang, Jie   I-470
Zhang, Jingdan   II-11
Zhang, JinLi   II-491, III-393
Zhang, Kan   II-446
Zhang, Lang   I-434
Zhang, Lei   III-460
Zhang, Ming   III-499
Zhang, Minghui   III-483
Zhang, Ming-Jing   III-474
Zhang, Mingmin   III-599
Zhang, Peng   II-333

Zhang, Pu   I-541
Zhang, Qiang   I-151
Zhang, Qun   II-385
Zhang, Rongguo   II-584
Zhang, Shaojun   III-430
Zhang, Sheng   III-430
Zhang, Shiye   II-185
Zhang, Tao   II-565
Zhang, Wenyao   I-552, II-292
Zhang, Xinpeng   II-361
Zhang, Xu   II-438
Zhang, Yanbo   I-462
Zhang, Yanci   II-240
Zhang, Yang   III-68
Zhang, Yi   I-240, III-111
Zhang, Yongjun   III-223
Zhang, Yu-Jin   I-121
Zhang, Zhange   II-323
Zhang, Zhifeng   III-483
Zhao, Danfeng   I-307
Zhao, Qian   I-64
Zhao, Yong   I-75, I-516, III-223
Zhao, Yue   II-301
Zhao, Zhengkang   I-21
Zhao, Zhuang   I-240
Zhao, Zhuo   III-460
Zheng, Aihua   III-55
Zheng, Changwen   II-510, III-80
Zheng, Chi   I-100
Zheng, Hong   II-333
Zheng, Ling   I-30
Zheng, Ning   I-552, II-292
Zheng, Qian   III-483
Zheng, Quan   III-80
Zheng, Shijiao   II-555
Zheng, Shuai   II-116
Zheng, Yandan   I-288
Zheng, Yin   I-121
Zheng, Zhigang   III-522
Zhicheng, Wang   II-48
Zhou, Baoliang   III-55
Zhou, Dongsheng   I-151
Zhou, Mingquan   I-321
Zhou, Ping   I-30
Zhou, Xingshe   III-491
Zhou, Yingyue   III-369
Zhou, Yujia   III-94
Zhu, Ce   I-415
Zhu, Hai Jing   III-420
Zhu, Haogang   III-321

Zhu, Songhao   II-396
Zhu, Tonglin   I-405
Zhu, Wenqian   I-75
Zhu, Yonggui   I-64
Zhuang, BingBing   II-500

Zong, Yun   II-438
Zou, Weijie   I-405
Zou, Xuemei   II-116
Zuo, Wangmeng   I-86
Zuo, Yifan   II-116

Printed in the United States
By Bookmasters